Austria

Austria

A Phaidon Cultural Guide

with over 500 color illustrations
and 12 pages of maps

PRENTICE-HALL
Englewood Cliffs
New Jersey 07632

Editor: Franz N. Mehling

Contributors: Dr Marianne Mehling, Elisabeth Palicka, Ernst Rebel, Dr Albin Rohrmoser, Dr Jürgen Wertheimer

Photographs: Löbl/Schreyer, Ellbach/Obb

Ground-plans and maps: Huber & Oberländer, Munich

Library of Congress Cataloging in Publication Data

Knaurs Kulturführer in Farbe: Österreich. English.
   Austria: a Phaidon cultural guide.

   Translation of: Knaurs Kulturführer in Farbe:
Österreich.

   Includes index.
     1. Art, Austrian — Guide-books. 2. Art — Austria —
Guide-books. 3. Austria — Description and travel —
1981–   — Guide-books. I. Mehling, Franz N.
II. Mehling, Marianne. III. Babel Translations (Firm)
IV. Title.
N6801.K5713   1985   914.36′04′5   85-11991
ISBN 0-13-053836-1

This book is available at a special discount when ordered in bulk quantities. Contact Prentice-Hall, Inc., General Publishing Division, Special Sales, Englewood Cliffs, N.J. 07632.

This edition published in the United States and Canada 1985 by Prentice-Hall, Inc., Englewood Cliffs, New Jersey 07632

Originally published as *Knaurs Kulturführer in Farbe: Österreich*
© Droemersche Verlagsanstalt Th. Knaur Nachf. Munich/Zurich 1977
Translation © Phaidon Press Limited, Oxford, 1985

ISBN 0-13-053836-1

Translated and edited by Babel Translations, London
Typeset by Electronic Village Limited, Richmond, Surrey
Printed in Spain by H. Fournier, S.A.–Vitoria

Cover illustration: the stairs of the Schloss Mirabell, Salzburg
(photo: A.F. Kersting, London)

Preface

It is not just the beauty and variety of its alpine landscape which has made Austria one of the most popular tourist destinations in Europe. The history of the country is just as fascinating. Austria has long been the intermediary between the culture of the South and that of Germany and the other countries in the North, and its own development has been fertilised by this relationship.

It is the aim of the *Phaidon Cultural Guide to Austria* to make the reader more familiar with the country and its culture and to introduce numerous art treasures in words and pictures. For unlike traditional art guides, the same importance is given to the illustrations as to the text: more than 500 of the churches, castles, palaces, theatres, museums and works of art described here are also shown in colour, including over 50 ground-plans of famous buildings. This enables readers to form in advance an accurate impression of the places and objects of interest they would like to see during a visit to the country.

As with the other guides in the series, the text is arranged in alphabetical order of place names. This gives the book the clarity of a work of reference and avoids the need for lengthy searching. The link between places which are geographically close, but which are separated by the alphabet, is provided by the maps on pages 276–87. This section shows all the places described which are within a short distance from any given destination and which, therefore, it might be possible to include in a tour.

The heading to each entry gives the town and its post-code (Gurk 9342) or postal address (Christkindl=Steyr 4400) in bold type and, below, the region and a reference to the map section, comprising page number and grid reference (p.282 ☐ P 10: page 282, map square P 10). Since each map covers two pages and the system of grid squares runs across both, only the even page numbers are given.

Within each entry the sights generally appear in the following order: sacred buildings, secular buildings, other particularly significant objects of interest, museums, theatres, less significant objects of interest (under the heading **Also worth seeing**) and places of interest in the immediate vicinity (**Environs**). Larger towns and cities are provided with a brief introductory text, which summarizes the history and importance of the place. The individual sights are printed in bold type, followed in some cases by the street name and number where they are to be found.

The appendices consist of a glossary of technical terms, an index of the most important artists whose works are discussed, and a list of towns, castles, houses and churches included in the Environs sections.

The publishers would be grateful for notification of any errors or omissions.

Absam = Hall in Tirol 6060
Tirol   p.284□G 8

Pfarrkirche zum hl.Michael (Parish church of St. Michael): A popular pilgrimage church, it was originally late Gothic but its present rococo decoration dates from 1780. Behind the right side altar there is a fine *fresco* (1470) of the Day of Judgement by the Haller master. The late Gothic *crucifix* by the triumphal arch is dated 1492 whereas the image of St. Michael at the high altar, and also the ceiling paintings, are by Jos.A. Zoller (1780).

Also worth seeing: Opposite the S. front of the church is the late Gothic portal of the *Mesnerhaus*. *Jakob Stainer* (1617–83) once made violins near the church

Abtenau, fresco in the Pfarrkirche St. Blasius

(Stainergasse 7). Also on the Stainergasse is the *Ansitz Krippach,* a town house with a garden which has been owned by the v.Kripp family since 1454. To the N. of Absam is the *Herrensitz Melans;* a double arcade leads to the chapel (documented 1516), whose ceiling has an interesting groin vault.

Abtenau 5441
Salzburg   p.284□L/M 7

Abtenau is the main town of the Lammertal and stands on the 'Salzburg Dolomitenstrasse'. In 1124 Archbishop Konrad I presented it to the church of St. Peter, Salzburg, which today still holds the rights of the Abtenau parish. The town has enjoyed market rights since 1500, but the population still includes a large proportion of farmers. The market square, most of which is untouched, is dominated by the Gothic church with its steep saddle roof and the slender tower of its façade.

Abtenau, St. Florian in the Pfarrkirche

Parish church of St. Blasius: The elongated choir, with its net vault, dates back to the church's consecration in 1501 or 1511. It continues as a heavy, pilastered nave, whose N. aisle is a Gothic chapel which was enlarged in baroque style (*c.* 1660) and which was probably part of the older Gothic core of the church. Two late Gothic figures — St. George and St. Florian—stand on brackets in the nave and used to guard the high altar which was carved by Andreas Lackner and painted by Ulrich Bocksberger (1518). However, the figures from it have now been transferred to the Österreichische Galerie in Vienna and are among the best examples of the Danube school of carving of Salzburg. There is a late Gothic *fresco* (painted tabernacle with angels) on the N. wall of the choir. The *statue of the infant Christ* by the N. pillar of the triumphal arch (early-17C) is probably by Hans Waldburger; and the statues in the gorgeous *baroque high altar* (set up in 1684) and in the two *side altars* (1702&5) are by Simeon Fries.

Admont 8911
Steiermark   p.282□P 7

Benediktinerabtei (Benedictine abbey): The abbey was founded in the 11C by Archbishop Gebhard of Salzburg (1074). The Carinthian countess Hemma (see Gurk) had set aside her large estate in the Ennstal for this purpose. Thus the first monastery in Styria was established in 'valle Ademundi', in the valley of Edmund. Somewhat later a convent was added, and it was consecrated simultaneously with the new church (1121). In the 12&13C this endowment became one of the richest and most powerful in the whole of Austria. It was extensively enlarged and altered during the 17C, eventually comprising five

Admont, library ▷

courtyards. The church was then completely reworked in baroque style in 1615 -26. More recent plans for enlargement drawn up by Gotthard Hayberger (1742) were only effected at a later date and to a limited extent. In 1865, the abbey, except for the library, was almost entirely burnt down. Using the remains of the wall, Wilhelm Bucher rebuilt a basilica in neo-Gothic style, as well as some parts of the abbey itself.

Abbey church of St. Blasius: The church was consecrated in 1869. Only the lion on the portal and the lowest storeys of the towers survive from the original church. The interior has a nave and two aisles, and still contains some of the earlier decoration: the *Immaculata* by M.Altomonte (1726) is surrounded by garlands by J.Th. Stammel. The large crib (1755) and the Corpus Christi in the side altars are also by him. The *high altar* is surrounded by embroidered wall hangings from the abbey workshops, and in front of the altar there is a copy of the well-known *'Admonter Maria'* (1310), the original of which is now in the Joanneum in Graz.

Abbey building: The four courtyards which survived the fire were combined into one during the rebuilding and laid out as a park: with Franz Pernegger's Neptune fountain (1665). The *library,* built by Jos. Hueber (1774) to plans by Hayberger, is today the most interesting part of the abbey. The gorgeous hall of the library is 236 ft. long and rises two storeys. Two side rooms frame an elliptical one with a central dome and ceiling frescos by Altomonte (Religion and the Church protecting Art and Science). Apart from the ceiling frescos, there are 18 sculptures by Stammel; note the depictions of Death, the Last Judgement, Hell and Heaven, and larger-than-life statues of the Prophets Moses and Elijah and the Apostles Peter and Paul. The library of Admont, with its 145,000

works from all fields of knowledge, is one of the world's great baroque libraries. The attached *Naturhistorisches Museum* (natural history museum) has an extensive collection of butterflies, grasshoppers, birds, mammals and minerals. The *Kunsthistorisches Museum* (art history museum), the contents of which are closely associated with the history of the abbey, contains works by J.Stammel, splendid baroque works by the Admont lay brothers, and paintings from Schloss Röthelstein.

Environs: Schloss **Röthelstein,** with its large cellars cut into the rock, is on the Klosterkogel above Admont. It was built in 1655 and extensively damaged in World War 2. But much has survived, such as the (smoke kitchen) and the wallpaper paintings with motifs from the legend of the 'Prodigal Son' (1777). There are about 370 paintings in the Schloss. Some of them are now hanging in the chapter house of the collegiate church, others in the museum. Some miles up the Enns is the *pilgrimage church* of **Frauenberg.** Some remnants of the earlier Gothic church (1410-47) have been incorporated in the present one (1683-7). The interior is decorated by *frescos* of the life of the Virgin Mary (possibly by A.Maderni). The *cross altar* is one of the most important works of J.Th. Stammel. The tabernacle with the Crucifixion relief, and the carved angels at the Holy Sepulchre, are among the finest achievements of the baroque in Styria.

Aflenz 8623
Steiermark   p.280□S 7

Aflenz was first mentioned in the documents in 1025, and from the 12C un-

Wallfahrtskirche Frauenberg (Admont) ▷

Ruined castle of Aggstein in Wachau

til 1848 it was owned by the Benedictine monks of St.Lambrecht. The factory near Mariazell which manufactured cannons and ammunition also belonged to these monks until 1899. The town was given market rights by Emperor Frederick III in 1458.

Parish church of St.Peter: This church dates from around 1500, although most of the walls were built earlier. The nave opens into three niches towards the choir.el. The altars are late baroque. The interior is decorated with 18C paintings by J.A. Mölk. Wooden reliefs and a *crucifix* (*c.* 1200) are to be found on the N. wall of the choir. To the E. of the church is the *ossuary* with a Romanesque substructure, a late Gothic chapel, an octagonal ground plan, a stellar vault (1519), and dome. The *priory building*, with the prelacy which was built

by Domenico Sciassia in *c.* 1660, is also worth looking at.

Environs: The ruins of *Burg Schachenstein* (1471) are 3 km. S.

Aggsbach-Dorf 3642
Lower Austria   p.278□S 4

Former charterhouse of Marienpforte and church of Maria Himmelfahrt: In 1380, Heidenreich v.Maissau, cupbearer and land marshal of Austria, founded a charterhouse in which he installed 12 monks from Mauerbach (near Vienna); note the founder's tomb. The monastery declined during the Reformation, and was dissolved under Emperor Joseph II. The individual buildings and courtyards date

Alpl, house of Rosegger's birth

mainly from the 16&17C. The church, a single-aisled, narrow building built along Carthusian lines was consecrated in 1392. Features include the keystones, the baroque pulpit with the four Evangelists, and the 17C Assumption on the high altar, under which there are still some remains of the original altar by J. Breu of Augsburg (now in the Herzogenburg: winged altar with life of the Virgin Mary and Christ's Passion, 1501; a fine example of the Danube school).

Aggstein = Aggsbach-Dorf 3642
Lower Austria   p.278 □ S 4

Castle ruins: W. Huber from Feldkirch, a painter at the bishop's court in Passau, travelled down the Danube in 1542 as a building inspector. His sketches included one of the 13C Burg Aggstein, which still had a keep. The Duke sent two punitive expeditions against the rebellious lords of the castle and it was restored by Scheck v.Wald in 1429 (see inscription). He was one of the robber knights who plundered ships by stretching ropes across the Danube and demanding booty; although it is possible that the abbots of Melk, with whom there were territorial disputes, were active in spreading such stories. He was known as the 'Schreckenwalder' and was said to force his prisoners to leap from the beautiful castle, 980 ft. above the Danube. The castle fell to the lord of the province in the 15C, was destroyed by the Turks in 1529, and was rebuilt and fortified by Anna v.Polheim in 1606 to provide protection against the Turks and Swedes. It fell into ruin from the 18C onwards. Viktor

Altenburg, fresco in the crypt

v.Scheffel visited this 'wild monument to a wild species of men' in 1860. Four courtyards and a well-preserved fortified main gateway survive. In the second courtyard is the *Burgverlies* dungeon with an oubliette 26 ft. deep. The *kitchen*, with its medieval smoke outlet and drain, is in the middle courtyard. To the E. is the *former chapel*, with its rudimentary Gothic vaulting. The rainwater cistern is 36 ft. deep.

Alpl 8671
Steiermark   p.280□T 7

Waldheimat: The house where the poet Peter Rosegger (1843–1918) was born, and also the school which he founded in the forest. A game enclosure and an observation room.

Altenburg 3591
Lower Austria   p.278□T 3

Benedictine abbey: A letter written by Bishop Reginbert of Passau in 1144 states that the widow of Hildburg, the Count of Bouige, had founded a cell at her Altenburg residence and wished to hand it over to the Benedictines in perpetual memory of her family, although the twelve monks and their abbot found it very difficult to maintain the small abbey in this poor region. Bishop Bernhard of Passau consecrated an altar in 1288; a hospital was built with donations from Hadmar von Sunnberg and the local aristocracy and the abbot received pontificals from the Pope in 1516 (among other things, this gave him the right to ordain priests). The monastery was ruined economically by taxes raised for defence (against the Turks), by peasants' wars, and by the aggressive, Protestant nobles of Horn, Rosenburg, Messern and Greillenstein. In the late 16C, Abbot Hofmann (monument) built defensive walls and a strong tower in which he installed the treasury. In 1619 the abbey was plundered by the 'Horner Stände' led by Puechheim. 25 years later the troops of Tortenson completed its destruction. Benedict, the new abbot, took over a set of ruins, which he had flattened to provide a new basis to build on. The abbey building, abbot's court and abbot's lodgings had been built by 1680. In 1715 Placidus Much was elected abbot. He was a perfect example of a baroque builder (his coat-of-arms is the beehive) and he had the church rebuilt by Munggenast. He added the library, the imperial wing and the marble hall to the existing core of the building, and, given his desire to achieve perfection, one can safely assume that some Gothic remains were destroyed. Lightning struck the tower in 1820 and it was rebuilt, although along simpler lines. The monastery was badly damaged in

Altenburg, library

World War 2, but has been successfully restored over the last few years.

The *abbot's court* is the finest of the five courtyards. The E. front extends for 680 ft. and halfway along its lines are broken by the projecting E. end of the church. One end of the E. front is occupied by the elegant and splendid *library*. The dome frescos are by P.Troger (Pallas Athene and Hercules; the Judgement of Solomon; Divine Wisdom; and the Light of Belief); and, in the side domes, the four faculties. A concert performed here on an August afternoon is a quite delightful pleasure. Immediately below the library, and reached by the same staircase, is the *'crypt'*, so named because of its position: this is an underworld with memento mori scenes, painted altars, and a symbolism of life and death which is repeated in the light and dark of the baroque upper rooms with their

Masonic imagery. The Christianization of the Heathen gods (Hercules Christianus) is somewhat surprising when coupled with Letterer's fountain figure of Leda and the swan on the imperial staircase. The triumphal of the Counter-Reformation is to be met with everywhere: the angel against the dragon, truth against falsehood; imagination, gold and music against Protestant frugality. All the monasteries built around this time have the appearance of princely residences but only in the South German area do they take such a cheerful form. In the *Festsaal* banqueting hall, Apollo is seen in triumph in the centre of the ceiling and the haloed putti of Aurora drive out the night. Finally, in the *imperial wing*, secular thought is combined with belief: quam bene conveniunt.

Stiftskirche (collegiate church) of St.

Lambert: The church of St.Lambert (in 937 Lantpert was the bishop of Freising) was built by J.Munggenast in 1730–3. It is an oval, domed church with six apses and is painted in delicate pastel. The *dome fresco* is by P.Troger. The virtues and God the Father with the Lamb of the Apocalypse are depicted in the sanctuary, and the Woman of the Apocalypse and St. Michael's fight with the dragon are seen as symbols of the church in the main dome. The *high altar* has an Assumption and above this a Holy Trinity.

Altenmarkt im Pongau 5541

Salzburg   p.282☐M 8

This town, which probably occupies the site of the Roman way station of 'Ani', is mentioned in 1074 as having a parish priest. It was then known as 'Rastat' (Radstadt), but this name passed to the present town of Radstadt when it was founded in the late 13C. However, Altenmarkt continued to be the area's religious

Altenmarkt, St.Ämilian

centre. The town has grown considerably as a result of tourism, but its heart consists of a hamlet clustered around a church.

Dekanats-Pfarrkirche hl.Maria: The existing church was built between 1390 and 1400 and consecrated in 1418 but its form—a nave and two aisles (a rarity in the Salzburg area) and a groin vault—is indicative of an older, early Gothic architectural tradition. The aisles were lengthened in 1867–75. The tower of the façade, with its stellar-vaulted main section and a twin-bayed Gothic porch (*war memorial chapel* with a fine *Pietà* of 1394—the original is in the churchyard) was given a baroque belfry and a double onion dome in 1762. Much of the interior has been restored. The most outstanding item is the *Schöne Madonna* of Altenmarkt on the left side altar. The refined, courtly features of this classical image of the Madonna dating from *c.* 1400 rather suggest a work by Prague court artists. The figure is documented as being in Altenmarkt as early as 1394 (the original is at present being restored).

Annakapelle: This chapel is linked to the church by a two-storeyed passage with a Gothic stellar vault. According to letters of indulgence dating from 1395, it was built as an ossuary, and is one of the few surviving examples in Salzburg. An octagonal building whose small choir, with its three-sided apse, considerably enhances its external appearance. The chapel was turned into a *baptistery* by moving the *marble font* from the church.

Environs: From the late Middle Ages until 1866, **Flachau** was the seat of an iron foundry with a hammer mill. The church was built by the builders of the archbishop's court in 1719–22 and displays

St.Ämilian, Virgin of the protecting cloak ▷

the influence of Joh. Lukas von Hildebrandt, while the *marble high altar* with its Immaculata by Joh. Mich. Rottmayr dates from 1722. **Filzmoos**, set in splendid mountain scenery, is visited by pilgrims to the 'Filzmooser Kindl', a 15C Gothic miraculous figure of the clothed infant Christ. There are also the remains of late Gothic frescos in the Gothic parish church of St. Petrus and St. Paulus.

Altenmarkt=Kleinglödnitz 9345
Kärnten   p.282☐O 10

St. Ämilian: This late Gothic parish church (mid-15C), with its high defensive wall, resembles a castle and was used by the population as a refuge from the Turks (1478)—there are arrow slits not only in the *Rundkarner* (ossuary; S. wall) but also in the W. wall of the church. The inside of the church, with a net vault over the nave and a stellar vault in the choir, is of particular interest for its fine decoration. The *frescoed symbols of Evangelists* in the choir, and also the *Virgin Mary sheltering supplicants under her cloak* to the left of the triumphal arch, are probably by Thomas v.Villach (*c*. 1470). The group of figures (Virgin between Peter and Paul) on the right of the triumphal arch was only uncovered in 1954. There are remains of a fresco of the Day of Judgement on the N. wall. The *carved Madonna* at the high altar dates from about 1460, but was reworked in baroque style. Note the small wooden figures of *St.Anthony* and *John the Baptist* on the N. wall of the choir, as well as those of *Rupert* and *Ämilian* and—by the altar —*St.Martin:* all of which date from 1500 – 30. The significance of the medieval *Schalenstein* in the choir is obscure, as is its date.

Environs: *Pfarrkirche St.Jakob der Ältere* (in **Deutsch-Griffen**), with Gothic frescos

(*c*. 1430) and notable decoration. *Gothic ossiary.* 15C *Kirchenburg* castle, and *Pfarrkirche St.Margaret* (both in **Glödnitz**). *Filialkirche St.Johannes d.T.* (*c*. 1330) in **Flattnitz**. Also see Zweinitz.

Althofen=Treibach 9330
Kärnten   p.282☐P 10

An old settlement; in 953, under Emperor Otto I, the fortified residence passed to the Archbishop of Salzburg. There are high Gothic remains (wall, Schloss, keep) and some late Gothic houses in the town, some with Renaissance elements (Riederhaus with sgraffito frieze, late-16C).

Pfarrkirche St.Thomas v.Canterbury (upper Markt): The previous church was mentioned in 1307, and the church of St. Thomas was built *c*. 1400. The nave and choir, each of which has a ribbed vault, are flanked by a small N. tower and a N. chapel. The massive main tower is to the S. The entire building was extensively

Schloss Ambras

renovated in 1908–10. Note the Gothic angel on a bracket in the tympanum of the W. portal (1400), and the three Roman stones that have been incorporated in its flying buttress. Inside there is a rococo pulpit dating from *c.* 1750.

Filialkirche St. Cäcilia: (lower Markt): The choir of what was originally a late Romanesque church was has a 15C stellar vault. The E. wall has an important *fresco* of St. Christopher (1524). There is also a beautiful late Gothic *winged altar* by the workshop of the younger Villach (1510).

Also worth seeing: *Kalvarienbergkapelle* N. of the uppermost part of the Markt (late-17C), and *early Gothic ossuary* in the graveyard with remains of frescos from the second half of the 13C.

Schloss Ambras = Innsbruck 6020
Tirol   p.286 □ F 8

Owned by the counts of Andechs in the

11C, the schloss, which passed to the Habsburgs in the 14C, is impressively situated on rising ground near the village of Amras, S. of Innsbruck.

Schloss Ambras is best known for the large *collections* installed by Archduke Ferdinand II of Austria-Tirol (1564–95) in a specially built museum in the Unterschloss. Weapons and harnesses, the chamber of art and miracles, a library (with the Ambras collection of epics, which contains the only manuscript of the Gudrunlied), coins, medals and a portrait gallery were originally housed in the schloss. Many items have been transferred to Vienna but most of Ferdinand's *weapon collection*, part of his *chamber of art and miracles*, and a historical portrait gallery with Gothic pictures and panel paintings can still be seen at Schloss Ambras.

The schloss was first mentioned in the 10C but was burnt down during fighting in 1133. After being rebuilt it became important in the second half of the 16C as the home of Ferdinand II.

The steep front of the *Hochschloss* (upper

Schloss Ambras, Spanischer Saal

Schloss) overlooks the court of the lower Schloss to the N and the *Unterschloss* (lower Schloss), through which the main gate leads into the court, faces the Hochschloss. The long *Spanischer Saal* (Spanish hall), which was built by G.Luchese in 1570–1 and is the earliest monumental Renaissance hall on German soil runs between the Unterschloss and the Hochschloss. The *coffered ceiling,* and the *inlaid doors* by the Innsbruck woodworker Konrad Gottlied date from 1571 and are very well preserved. Frescos of the Tyrolean princes, and grotesque paintings by Dionys van Halaert, cover the walls. The *park* is also Renaissance.

Ampass = Hall im Tirol 6060
Tirol   p.286☐F 8/9

St. Veit: The former parish church was built in 1521 but the altars and choir stalls were reworked in the 17C. The beautiful *Gothic wooden figure* of St.Anne is on the left side altar.

Pfarrkirche zum hl.Johannes d. Täufer: The present parish church dates from at least as far back as 1256, it was altered in 1574, and rebuilt in 1689 after an earthquake. Gothic elements are still to be found on the flying buttresses, in the tower and in the louvres. There is an early-16C *fresco* of St.Christopher on the S. side of the choir. The substructure and cornice are Renaissance, while the crown of the tower and the façade are baroque. The rococo stucco and the paintings are by J.M. Strickner, 1744.

Also worth seeing: On the way towards Hall (q.v.), there is an interesting late Gothic *way column* on the left.

Anras = Abfaltersbach 9913
Tirol   p.284☐K 10

Alte Pfarrkirche: The old parish church is hidden between the *Bischöfliches Pfleghaus* (1755–7; sgraffito around the windows) and the new parish church and

Anras, Pfleghaus with Alte and Neue Kirche   *Ardagger, Stiftskirche, crypt* ▷

is very reminiscent of the baptistery in the cloister of Brixen cathedral. Like the latter, it was built in *c.* 1250, originally had a flat roof, and now has a two-bayed Gothic net vault. Today the church is used as a sacristy, belfry and war memorial, and has accordingly suffered from inferior building work. Some remains of late Romanesque *ornamental frescos* and a *winged altar* dating from 1513 have survived. The bell tower is 16C.

Neue Pfarrkirche zum hl.Stephan: This imposing building with its transept-like chapels was built by Franz de Paula Penz in 1753–5. There are frescos on the S. side, including a Glory of St.Stephen by Martin Knoller (1754). The typically rococo *high altar* (martyrdom of St. Stephen) is by Anton Zoller (1755). There is a 15C *Virgin* carved in a robust rustic style.

Ardagger = Amstetten 3300
Lower Austria   p.276□R 5

Ardagger Abbey: Agnes de Poitiers, the second wife of the Emperor Henry III (1017 – 56), being in distress over her children, promised an endowment in honour of St.Margaret of Antioch. The church was consecrated in 1063. Archbishop Anno of Cologne (who a year previously had siezed the young Henry IV and had overthrown Queen Agnes), his co-regent Adalbert of Hamburg-Bremen, the Archbishop of Mainz, and the Bishop of Freising, attended the brilliant ceremony in order to demonstrate their power. Relics of St.Lambert of Maastricht, St.Ulrich of Augsburg and Corbinian (who died in 725 and was the first bishop of Freising) were interred in the lower church. There was a school of illumination during the 14C.

◁ *Ardagger, St.Margaret window*

The abbey declined after the Reformation and in 1784 it was dissolved in the imperial reform of the monasteries.

Former Stiftskirche and Pfarrkirche zur hl.Margarete: The oldest part of the church is the *crypt* dating from the first half of the 13C. This has a nave, two aisles and tall columns. The ashlar ornament is to be found in almost all Cistercian monasteries. The *image of the founder* in the *window of St.Margaret* behind the high altar (below, middle) depicts a model of the church. The Gothic vaults were originally much higher, but they collapsed when the church was burnt by the Turks and when the church was rebuilt they were set lower down. There is an incomplete Coronation of the Virgin (*c.* 1690) in the *sacristy*. The fountain house in the cloister was installed as a *chapel of the Magi* in 1410, and here there are interesting tomb covers of the priors. The main item of interest is the *window of St.Margaret* at the E. end. Dated 1240, it shows the story of St.Margaret according to the Golden Legend of Jacobe de Voragine (although he was not installed as Archbishop of Genoa until 1292). Olibrius the prefect desires Margaret the shepherdess and tries to force this baptized woman to adopt paganism. She refuses to accept idolatry, is flogged, branded and thrown in the dungeon. The Lord shows her the enemy in the form of a dragon. She is tempted by the devil in human form; thrown in a barrel and beheaded. Angels bear her soul to Heaven.

Artstetten 3661
Lower Austria   p.278□S 5

Schloss: In 1268 this was the seat of a family known as Ortstetten. The schloss, which has often been plundered, was occupied by the French during the Napoleonic Wars and suffered as a result.

It was restored under Archduke Ludwig in 1869 and then fell to Franz Ferdinand von Habsburg-Este. Since 1914, when he was assassinated, it has been the seat of his family, the Dukes of Hohenberg. The *Gothic church*, now the *Pfarrkirche zum hl.Joh.d.T. (parish church of St. John the Baptist)*, is separate from the schloss. There are some interesting cornerstones dating from 1400, a stone relief with the vernicle of St.Veronica, and pretty processional rods. The focal point is formed by the *tombs of Archduke Franz Ferdinand*, the successor to the throne, and of his wife, née Countess Chotek, murdered in Sarajevo on 28 June 1914. After a dramatic transfer of the bodies, the couple was interred here in accordance with the Archduke's will, because the Countess, not being of equal rank, could not be buried in the Capuchin crypt in Vienna.

Au im Bregenzerwald 6883

Vorarlberg   p.286□B 8

It was here, in 1657, that Michael Beer founded the *Meisterschule des Bregenzerwaldes,* an architechts' guild similar to that of the Wessobrunners. The great monastery architects of the 17&18C came from here. The 'Vorarlberger Münsterschema' scheme and the pilaster hall are characteristic of this guild. 94 per cent of the men in the town were architects! The family Beer, with 16 members from various different generations, was the only participant. Christian Thumb (d. 1726), with four brothers and nephews, and Andreas Moosbrugger (1656–1723), with nine family members. 63 monastery churches and pilgrimage churches, 125 town churches, and 120 partial or new monasteries, were designed by the architects of this school. Works by the Beers: Schloss Sigmaringen, Rottenburg, Kreuzlingen, Landshut, Salem St.Blasien, the town hall in Konstanz, E. façade of St.Gallen, and others; by the Thumbs: Ottobeuren, Schöneberg-Ellwangen, Ebersmünster im Elsass, Neubirnau, St.Gallen and others; and by the Moosbruggers: Maria Einsiedeln, Weingarten, high altar of St. Gallen. However, the famous masters

Aufenstein, Alte Schlosskapelle, frescos

never returned to Au, but lived in honour in Konstanz or Bregenz; although as a result this magnificent school disappeared after a century or so.

Environs: See also Damüls, Bezau, Schwarzenberg and Egg.

Aufenstein = Matrei am Brenner 6143

Tirol   p.284 □ F 9

In the Middle Ages Burg Aufenstein stood on a hill here but it fell into disrepair from about 1430 onwards and all that survives is the **Alte Schlosskapelle** (old Schloss chapel). This chapel, which was once two storeyed and in the 19C was used as a school, was consecrated in 1331. It was not until 1957–60 that it was rediscovered and reconstructed as a double chapel. The *frescos* in the lower chapel date from the first half of the 14C. In the upper one there are fragments of a St. Christopher on the N.wall, and some frescos from the mid 14C. The banquet of Nicodemus on the S. wall is by the same artist as the frescos in the lower chapel.

Chapel of St. Katharina: A late Gothic church was built on the ruins of Burg Aufenstein in 1474, but the present baroque form of its nave dates from 1718. The apse, by the high altar, which is late rococo, contains the *oldest wooden carvings* in the N. Tirol: an early-14C, life-sized Annunciation.

Bad Aussee 8990

Steiermark   p.282 □ N 7

In 1290, Duke Albrecht moved the Prince's salt works from Alt-Aussee (see environs) to Bad Aussee and he subsequently conferred market rights on the latter. The entire Ausseerland owes its development

to the extraordinary abundance of salt; there were 15 salt guilds in 1510, and the population consisted mainly of woodcutters, charcoal burners and salt workers. The old market and its major buildings (erected by the 'Hallinger' families and by the prince's administration) still stand and they include: the 14C *Kammerhof*, which until 1924 was the seat of the saltworks administration; the *Herzheimerhaus* (Hauptstrasse 156) with a coat-of-arms dating from 1507, the *Hoferhaus* with 16C frescos, the 16C *Sgraffito house* (Winkler), and the house where *Anna Plochl*, the wife of Archduke Johann, was born.

St. Paul: The parish church has a 13C Romanesque nave and 15C Gothic additions—a four-bayed side aisle and a sevenstoreyed tower. Chapels on both sides of the tower followed in the 17C. Note the *tabernacle* (1523) and two *Gothic statues* above the S.portal. One of the finest works of art in the Ausseerland is to be found in the *Marienkapelle:* this is a stone Virgin—a 'schöne Marie'—of *c.* 1420 by an unknown artist.

Bad Aussee with Pfarrkirche St. Paul

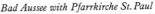

Spitalkirche hl. Geist (hospital church of the Holy Ghost): The Heiliger-Geist-Kapelle belonged to the saltworks hospital, whose main purpose was to care for the salt workers in their old age. The slender Gothic style of the church, with its octagonal tower over the gable, has survived almost unaltered. In the apse there is a *winged altar,* donated by Emperor Frederick III (1449). The main panel is a Holy Trinity. The *fourteen auxiliary Saints,* painted in *c.* 1480, are to be found in the side chapel.

Kalvarienbergkapelle hl. Leonhard: The 'Salzfuhrleut-Kirche' was built in *c.* 1398 and reworked in baroque style in 1732. The present portal, chancel arch, and sacristy, date from *c.* 1400, as do the four panel paintings inside showing scenes from the legend of St. Leonard.

Environs: The prince's salt-boiling plant was originally in **Alt-Aussee** (1147). Guided tours are given from May to October. The *Barbarakapelle,* with the statue of the patroness of miners, is in the mine

Axams, St. Wilgefortis (Mourning)

gallery. The *parish church of St. Ägyd* was built in 1434, with a single aisle and was enlarged by Emperor Franz Joseph I in 1859–61. Six stained-glass windows and the tabernacle date from the Gothic phase of construction (1520).

Axams 6094
Tirol   p.286□F 9

Karl Schönherr (1867–1943), the Austrian playwright, was born in Axams, a town popular for its winter sports. The rococo church, surrounded by beautiful old peasants' houses, is worth looking at.

Pfarrkirche zu den hll. Johannes d. Täufer und Johannes d. Evangelisten: Axams is mentioned in a document in the 10C and, being the main parish, was directly under the protection of the king during Carolingian times. A Romanesque building originally stood on the site of the present church, and was replaced in 1498 by a single-aisled vaulted church of which only the tower survives. The new church dates from 1732 – 4, and was partially rebuilt in 19C style in 1841. Some conspicuous features are the rich *stuccoes* by Anton Gigl of Wessobrunn, the *altarpiece* of the high altar by Joh. Georg Grasmayr (1735), and the *pulpit* by Nikolaus Moll. In the *graveyard* there is the underground *Kapelle zur hl. Wilgefortis,* which was consecrated in 1660. The carved figure of the patroness on the altar is 18C. To the N. of the parish church is the *St.-Michaels-Kapelle,* which dates from the 13C (it was not structurally joined to the main church until later). In 1630 this chapel was vaulted and frescoed. Another item of interest is the *Lindenkapelle* of St. Sebastian, which is designed as an octagon and was built in 1635 as an offering against the plague (stuccoes dating from 1730).

Baden 2500
Lower Austria   p.278□V 5

Baden is on a geological fault with several hot, sulphurous springs having temperatures of 25 to 35 degrees C. In Roman times it was known as Aquae Pannonicae. The town's coat-of-arms dating from 1480 shows two figures in a bathtub on a red-white-red shield. After a relatively uneventful history, Baden had its heyday in the 19C, when Europe discovered the fashion for spas. After an extensive fire in 1812, Baden was rebuilt in the style and manner of Jos. Kornhäusel, as was the *Weilburg* (1820), although this was destroyed in 1945. Baden was the summer residence of Emperor Franz and the imperial family for 30 years. The charming

Baden, spa hotel

villas built by the aristocracy and the upper middle class date from that time onwards. Imperial yellow, white and green are the predominant colours (Engelsbad and Sauerhof dating from 1822).

Dekanatskirche St. Stephan: Romanesque sections (E. towers and lower church) from an earlier church have been incorporated in this late Gothic hall church with its nave and two aisles. The tower, which is in a rather Gothic style and has a dome, was erected in 1697. The altarpiece of the high altar (1745, stoning of St. Stephen) is by P. Troger, and the memorials on the pillars are also of interest.

Also worth seeing: *Pfarrkirche St. Helena:* The *potter's altar* from the Stephanskirche in Vienna was banished here because it depicted the Trinity as three humans (from 1745 onwards, only a dove was permitted). *Hofkirche:* Remains of the medieval Augustinian hermit's church survive here, while the double tombstone is from 1299. Above the *Weilburg*, which was blown up after the war, are the 12C

Baden, Undinen fountain

Rauhenegg ruins. Opposite this is *Rauhenstein*, which resembles a guardian at the entrance to the Hellental. The ruined *Merkenstein* (1494), formerly a prince's schloss, was burnt down by the Turks, as were all the castles in the region.

Museums: *Kaiser-Franz-Joseph-Museum* (Hochstrasse 51) with handicrafts and popular art. *Rollettmuseum* (Weikersdorfer Platz), with prehistoric finds relating to Baden and other exhibits.

Badgastein 5640
Salzburg   p.284□L 9

A number of finds suggest that the Gasteiner Tal was prehistoric communications routes. Its thermal springs were ignored by the Romans, and only began to be used in the Middle Ages. Stagnation occurred after the town had flourished as a Habsburg and Wittelsbach spa during the second half of the 15C and in the 16C. It was not until the mid 19C onwards that Badgastein became famous through such visitors as Emperor Wilhelm I, Bismarck and Moltke, who conducted important negotiations in the town (the Gastein convention between Prussia and Austria in 1865; preliminary negotiations between Prussia and the Vatican in 1879 on a settlement of the struggle between the State and the Roman Catholic Church). Set in a steeply sloping gorge, the buildings of Badgastein contrast strongly with their setting and the waterfall which surges through the middle of the town.

Pfarrkirche zu den hll. Primus und Felizian: First recorded in 1412, it was rebuilt in 1720–36 and replaced in 1866 –76 by a neo-Gothic church. The details and the decoration are by F. von Schmidt; although the *high altar* has a Gothic *Madonna and Child* from the Maria Bühel near Oberndorf. The figure is a masterpiece of Salzburg wood carving from about 1450, and is particularly striking for the rich contrast in the interplay between the loosely billowing garment clothing the solid figure.

Filialkirche St. Nikolaus: First mentioned in 1412. The tower, and also the walls of the square church, probably date from about 1400, while the stellar vault, with its single central column—which emphasizes the tendency towards central planning—probably dates from after the mid 15C, as does the rebuilt choir, also with a stellar vault. Rich frescos were uncovered in 1893 and 1950–2. The *choir frescos* (*c.* 1480) are attributed to the 'Master of Schöder': the S. wall with the legend of St. Nicholas; the N. wall with the rain of manna and the Virgin Mary sheltering supplicants under her cloak; vault spandrels, angels with instruments of torture, and saints. The *frescos in the nave* are dated 1517: N. wall (from the top downwards): Christ and the women, Crucifixion, Christ in Limbo, Resurrection, Ascension. S.

wall: Last Judgement, Tree of Jesse, and, underneath, the founders. A Gothic *marble pulpit,* the oldest in the province according to F. Fuhrmann. Numerous memorials from the 16C to the early 19C.

Also worth seeing: *Badeschloss* (1791), designed by W. Hagenauer, although much of its original character was lost during its rebuilding in 1857. The *museum* was established in 1936 and contains a collection devoted to local history. It is open from 1 May to 30 September or by appointment with the spa administration and it can only be visited with a guide.

Environs: Some 3 km. distant is the former mining town of **Böckstein,** (gold mining on the Radhausberg), with a modest mining village (2nd half of 18C), which has largely survived. The *Pfarr- und Wallfahrtskirche zu U.L. Frau vom guten Rate* is an important example of early Salzburg classicism and was built in 1764 –7 as a centrally planned church (octagonal on the outside, oval on the inside) to designs by W. Hagenauer, the supervisor

Badgastein, St. Nikolaus, pulpit

Badgastein with Raukogel

of court buildings. The early classical high altar is by his brother, J.B. Hagenauer, the court sculptor. The latter's wife Rosa Hagenauer (née Barduzzi) painted the associated altarpiece. The dome fresco is by J.Weiss, 1765.

Baldramsdorf 9805
Kärnten   p.282☐M 10

Pfarrkirche St. Martin: Vaulted by L.Rieder in 1522, it is on the site of a 12C building, which is the cause of the unusual interior arrangement. There is a two-aisled hall structure organized in such a way that the wider N. aisle opens out into a two-bayed choir, whereas the S.aisle ends in an irregular octagonal choir. The net vaulting is uniform. The free-standing late Gothic W. tower was rebuilt in 1885. Inside, there are some interesting decorative elements. In the crown of the vault, above the triumphal arch (N.), is the architect's signature: 'Larentz Rieder Maister der dises Gewölb hat gmacht.' ('Master

Larentz Rieder who made this vault'). In the choir are the remains of some *Renaissance paintings* (Crucifixion with landscape, and others), and also some paintings in late Gothic style (St. Catherine with the keystone of the S. side choir). Apart from the two 18C *baroque altars*, also note two 15C *tombstones with coats-of-arms* and a large *Lenten veil* with 39 scenes from Genesis (1555).

Bartholomäberg =
St. Anton im Montafon 6771
Vorarlberg   p.286☐B 9

Bartholomäberg is the oldest known settlement in Montafon. It has a magnificent site some 1,000 ft. above the valley floor, and is framed by Rätikon and Silvretta.

Pfarrkirche hl. Bartholomäus: This small hall church was built in 1732 on the ruins of a Gothic church which had burnt down. It has an onion dome on the N. tower. The visitor entering through the W.

Badgastein, St.Nikolaus, fresco

portal is surprised by the gorgeous brown and gold of the interior. In addition to the *high altar* (Last Supper, 1740), there are also two rich side altars. The Gothic sacristy entrance has scrolls in hollow mouldings, and a fine wrought-iron door. The Gothic *Knappenaltar* (1525) is somewhat rugged in its details. The outer wings show four pairs of Saints in grisaille in an almost mundane attitude. Antipendium: Christ collapsing beneath the Cross. In the shrine there is a fine St. Anne with the Madonna and Child. The organ (1792) is by a pupil of Silbermann from Strasbourg. The Byzantine-Romanesque *processional cross,* which is decorated with precious stones and enamel inlay, is 12C.

Benesirnitz = Sirnitz 9571

Kärnten   p.282 ☐ O 10

Filialkirche hl. Leonhard: In the 18C this church served as a missionary base for the Counter-Reformation but its first mention is from as far back as 1213 and its various sections were built at different times; the choir being mid-15C, the nave 16C. The pilasters, which project inwards, support an articulated tunnel vault. Apart from an impressive *high altar* (1710?), there are side altars by Benedikt Blass (both dating from 1736) on the left-hand side of the nave. These were originally scenic in conception. That is to say, there was an optical and liturgical interrelation both between the various figures and between the altars. The *Crucifixion* on the triumphal arch dates from 1522.

Berg im Drautal 9771

Kärnten   p.284 ☐ L 10/11

Pfarrkirche Maria Geburt: This late Romanesque church dates from the 13C (first mentioned in 1267) but was rebuilt in the 15C to form a late Gothic fortified church (Carinthia suffered severely during the Turkish invasions). Originally Romanesque, the recessed *W. portal* has small double columns and cubiform capitals. In the

Benesirnitz, St. Leonhard

tympanum there is a 13C painted group of the Virgin Mary with a founder and a martyr. The *wall paintings* in the choir are also Romanesque and the Christ in the apse, flanked by apostles and prophets, was not uncovered until 1960 (all *c.* 1280?). Alterations to the wall and to the vault decorations were made when the church was rebuilt in late Gothic style (nave, fortified tower). The net vault is 15C. The ornamental scrolls (*c.* 1480), which are interesting stylistically, and other naturalistic ornamental forms are typical of the late Gothic. On the baroque *high altar* (*c.* 1700) there is an early 15C stone Madonna and Child in the Soft Style (with a baroque halo). Finally, the *wooden crucifix* on the triumphal arch is late Gothic (*c.* 1500). In the sexpartite rib vault of the NE *ossuary tower* there are numerous *paintings* of the Last Judgement and the Annunciation dating from 1428.

Environs: *St.Athanasius,* a daughter and pilgrimage church with a late Gothic choir and wall paintings (1481), stands outside Berg.

St. Athanasius near Berg

Bernstein 7434
Burgenland   p.280□V 8

Schloss: The schloss is impressively sited on a hill and is a prominent feature far and wide. Bernstein was formerly an important link in the chain of castles in the marches. Rebuilding, after a gunpowder explosion in the 17C transformed it into a splendidly decorated schloss. No trace remains of the keep which stood in the middle of the courtyard and the silhouette is broken only by the baroque NE tower. *Tour:* A route marked by arrows leads around the schloss and through a small museum (prehistoric finds, weapons, alchemist's laboratory, instruments of torture, etc.); and there are also magnificent views. The *Rittersaal* (knights' hall) is an outstanding example of Italian stucco. On the ceiling are seven mythological scenes, and, in between these, putti, Amazons, masks etc., as well as portraits of Dante and Ariosto in small medallions; the deep window recesses are decorated with hunting scenes. The *parapet walk* can be visited. The schloss is used

Schloss Bernstein

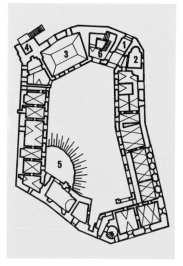

Schloss Bernstein 1 Castle entrance **2** Chapel **3** Rittersaal **4** Tower **5** Rock, site of the old keep **6** Staircase

as a hotel and restaurant and, apart from the restaurant in the Rittersaal, most of the other rooms are reserved for hotel guests. The area around Bernstein is known for its deposits of serpentine and this beautiful green stone is made into jewellery in workshops.

Bichlbach 6621

Tirol   p.286□D 8

Pfarrkirche zum hl. Lorenz: This plain baroque parish church stands in the middle of a beautifully situated mountain village. The church is recorded in a document dating fom 1394 but it was destroyed by Maurice of Saxony in 1552, and rebuilt in 1733–6. All that survives today of the Gothic church is a small N. tower with a helm roof, and a choir. The interesting *frescos* (F.A. Zeiller, 1778 and 1785) depict

the Assumption of St. Lawrence in the nave, and the Feeding of the Five Thousand in the choir. The *Stations of the Cross* are by P.Zeiller, and the *altarpiece* of the high altar (1736; martyrdom of St. Lawrence) is by J.B. Riepp.

Hl. Josef: The church of the carpenters' guild, it stands on a steep rock high above the town. Built by Andreas Hofenegger in 1710 to a plan by J.J. Herkomer, it comprises two square sections (the larger one has a dome, the smaller a tunnel vault), above two octagonal crypts with groin vaults. The decoration of the sanctuary, which is architecturally interesting, dates from the 1st half of the 18C.

Environs: 4 km. from Bichlbach; **Berwang,** a popular ski resort. The *Pfarrkirche zum hl. Jakob* dates from the 1st half of the 15C and was enlarged in 1731. The W. portal, the pointed windows in the netvaulted choir, and the N. tower with its louvres and helm roof, are all Gothic. The pulpit and confessional chairs are from the 1st half of the 18C. The ceiling paintings and altar decorations date from 1944–6. There is an altarpiece (1735) by P.Zeiller on the left choir wall.

Bischofshofen 5500

Salzburg   p.284□M 8

Neolithic finds have shown that the Bischofshofen area was settled at a very early date. After a miraculous apparition, Bishop Rupert built a monk's cell and a small church dedicated to St.Maximilian. A settlement grew up and was known as 'Pongau'—the name of the region. Since the town was the Hofmark of the bishops of Chiemsee, it was eventually given the name of 'Hof' or 'Bischofshof' when a collegiate church was founded in the 12C.

Bischofshofen, Rupertus cross

Pfarrkirche hl. Maximilian: Two earlier churches are known to have stood on this site. One was a church founded by St.Rupert for which there is documentary evidence, and the other was a plain 9C building which was discovered in excavation work and had a transept. The core of the present structure is Romanesque, with a transept that only projects slightly and a massive tower over the crossing, but it was altered in Gothic style and the octagonal dome over the crossing, with its eight-part diamond-shaped star, was given a vault. The walls of the nave have late-15C and 17C *frescos;* there are *late Gothic* sculptures on the two neo-Gothic side altars and in the gallery parapet (St.Rupert and St.Virgil), while the altar (1755) in the S. transept has a good *St.Anne with the Madonna and Child* (*c.* 1520; attributed to Lienhart Astl) and a *predella relief* of Christ

and the twelve Apostles (*c.* 1500). In the NE corner of the transept is the *marble tomb* (the only surviving example in Salzburg) of Bishop Silvester Phlieger of Chiemsee. Dating from 1453, it has a life-sized recumbent effigy and is attributed to Hans Baldauf, the sculptor from Salzburg. The modern entrance door bears the motif of the Rupertuskreuz; the cross itself, along with a diptych by K. Laib, is on loan to the Dommuseum, Salzburg (q.v.).

Kastenhof: This is probably what was once the collegiate church. All that now survives is the massive four-storey tower (mid-13C), which is privately owned.

Filialkirche hl. Maria/Frauenkirche: Standing above the market, this single-aisled church is built of rubble. The choir and lower church date from before 1497 (the date of the fresco on a flying buttress in the choir, depicting the mass of St. Gregory), and the elegant tower is from 1522. Inside there are frescos dating from around 1420. (key obtainable at the parsonage).

Georgskirche: This plain Romanesque chapel (13C) stands on a terrace above the Frauenkirche and is today a *war memorial.* The wall bearing the triumphal arch of this single-aisled church has two zones of *Romanesque frescos* (*c.* 1230), while the semicircular apse has three zones of frescos (Christ and the Evangelists; Crucifixion; Apostles and Saints). The altar bears a *Gothic relief of St.George* (*c.* 1500) on a 19C painted background. The stained-glass windows are by A. Birkle. One widely held theory is that the chapel is a remnant of a vanished castle of the lords of Pongau.

Environs: 1 km. along the Mühlbach road is the **Götschenberg**, a rounded hill with the overgrown ramparts of a medieval keep, which was the valley centre for the Bronze

Age copper mines on the Mitterberg. This site is the starting point for research into Alpine mining and the prehistoric and medieval finds are now in the Salzburger Museum (q.v.). The *Filialkirche zu den hll. Primus und Felizian* on the **Buchberg** (4 km.; approached from the start of the Fritz-talbundesstrasse via the Missionshaus St. Rupert) may have been built on a heathen German cult site. From 1421 until the 19C the most famous Salzburg market was held on the area surrounding the church. Originally Romanesque, the single-aisled church, with its massive N. tower, now ends in a five sided Gothic apse.

Bludenz, St. Laurentius, altar panel

Bleiburg 9150

Kärnten p.282 □ Q 11

Schloss: In the early 17C, the Counts of Thurn-Valsassina converted the early-12C castle into a sturdy three-storeyed Renaissance Schloss. Some parts of the 15C vault paintings have been uncovered in the late Gothic *Schlosskapelle* (rebuilt in 1601). The two altars are 18C. The bronze *family memorial* (1594–5), with its coats-of-arms and allegories, is a fine feature. It was not uncommon for such memorials to be erected as a 'memento mori' while the family was still alive.

Pfarrkirche hll. Petrus und Paulus: The late Gothic two-aisled hall church has four different types of net and stellar vault and the decoration of the ceiling below the W. gallery is especially interesting. *Frescos* (1580) have been uncovered on the N. wall of the choir. The baroque *Marienaltar* is 18C, with some later sections.

Bürgerspitalkapelle hl. Erasmus: The spatial effects and the decoration of this chapel (articulated tunnel vault, three bays, 1766) are late rococo. The painting dates from 1772.

Bludenz 6700

Vorarlberg p.286 □ A 9

The oldest settlement was originally at Montikel (Bronze Age finds). In 940 King Otto I presented Bishop Waldo of Chur with a church 'in loco Plutenes' (palus, meaning marsh in Latin). In 1228 Bludenz fell to the Werdenberg Counts of Montfort. Count Rudolph, the first Werdenberg, built the castle; Albrecht III, the last of the line, abolished serfdom in 1391 and sold the castle to the Habsburgs. When Duke Friedrich IV fled empty-handed to Bludenz on 30 March 1416 from the Council of Constance (he had helped Pope John XXIII to break up the Council and had been banished), the town granted him protection and a retinue. Having had his rights as Duke of Tirol restored to him (1406–39), he confirmed the privileges enjoyed by the town of Bludenz. The Habsburgs ruled through governors, and Bludenz was the offical seat of the governors from 1418–1806. The town suffered three disastrous fires in 1491, 1638 and 1682, and only the church and Schloss remained standing. In 1730 Bludenz became a fief of the Sternbachs, and they built Schloss Gayenhofen in 1746. The Arlbergstrasse was built by Emperor Joseph II. There were uprisings against the Bavarians and French in 1806. In 1918, 80 per cent of the population voted in vain for the town to be united with Switzerland.

Town fortifications: An engraving by Merian dating from 1643 shows a wall surrounding the whole town. Two gates, the lower gate or Mühletor (Türlehaltertor) and the upper gate or Feldkirchertor, as well as the Pulverturm (magazine tower), have survived.

Pfarrkirche St.Laurentius: This large, single-aisled church was completed in 1514. It has a stellar vault in the choir, black marble altars, and two fine paintings dating from 1510 (Visitation and Marriage of the Virgin).

Also worth seeing: The baroque *Schloss Gayenhofen*, built by Franz Andrä von Sternbach *c.* 1746, was converted in 1960 –2 to form the offices of the district Administration. Fine *arcades; Nepomuk fountain* dating from 1730 (a year after John of Nepomuk was canonized); *Spitalkirche zum hl. Geist* (1472, altered in baroque style in 1686) with a medieval ridge turret.

Bludesch=Thüringen 6712
Vorarlberg   p.286□A 9

Pfarrkirche: Built by M. Beer in 1650, it has a marble high altar (1651), a black

stucco pulpit (late-18C), and an organ by J.Bergöntzle, a pupil of Silbermann from Strasbourg.

Nikolauskirche: Excavations carried out in the past few years have proved that this, the oldest church in the Walgau (tower with helm roof and three 14C Gothic louvres), has a Romanesque aisle and remains of Romanesque frescos in the apse. The Montfort founders appear on the high altar with the Madonna. There are important frescos in the nave: Mary and Joseph are seen kneeling before God the Father in Judgement; behind them are angels with trumpets. St.Peter is unlocking the gates of Heaven; opposite is the Descent into Hell. There is a Crucifixion above the chancel arch. Interesting medieval block pews.

Brandhof = Gollrad 8635
Steiermark   p.280□S 7

Jagdschlössl Brandhof am Seeberg: In 1822–8, Ludwig Schnorr of Carolsfeld transformed what had been a farmhouse into this small Schloss for Archduke Johann. There are sculptures by Daniel Böhm in the main hall. The hunting lodge was turned into a memorial for the Archduke. In the chapel there is his christening robe, embroidered by Empress Maria Theresa, and also a wooden Virgin Mary from Schloss Therrberg (*c.* 1450). In the Jagdzimmer (hunting room) there are paintings of the Archduke and his wife, who was a postmaster's daughter from Aussee, by L.Kupelwieser and Ender.

Braunau am Inn 5280
Upper Austria   p.276□L 4

A Roman road running from E. to W.

crossed the Inn near the palace of Ranshofen, which existed as far back as the 8C; and it was here, in *c.* 1260, that the Lower Bavarian Dukes established a bridgehead by founding a walled town. One of the most powerful fortifications of more recent times was built here in the late 17C. The town was Bavarian until it fell to Austria in 1779 along with the Innviertel. While most of the baroque fortifications were razed under Napoleon, the town was able to preserve many of its old buildings despite a disastrous fire in 1874. Its alleyways, squares, towers and churches give a good impression of a Gothic town. At its heart lies the unusually long town square (its proportions are 1:8), which was the focus of the flourishing community of merchants and craftsmen. The fully laden waggons came through the Inntor straight on to this square, which resembles a market street; salt, that much-prized commodity, was the most valuable item of trade; whilst cloth makers were dominant among the guilds. J.P. Palm, the bookseller from Nuremberg, was shot in Braunau on 26 August 1806, on Napoleon's orders, for distributiong the text 'Germany in her deepest humiliation'. Braunau was the birthplace of Adolf Hitler.

Braunau, St. Stephan

Stadtpfarrkirche St.Stephan: Stephan Krumenauer, a pupil of Hans von Burghausen (Hans Stethaimer), is regarded as the main architect of this massive Gothic church with its nave and two aisles. The tall side chapels intensify the broad effect of the nave when seen both from the inside and the outside. The tower, which is 315 ft. tall and was begun by W.Wiesinger in 1492, is the landmark of Braunau and makes a magnificent impression; the elongated baroque onion dome, which was added after the church was struck by lightning in 1759, emphasizes the upward striving effect. Of the three Gothic portals, the W. portal, with its ogee arch, is especially richly decorated. The nave and choir have

the original net vault; note the capitals of the pillars, with heads of saints and angels. The baroque *high altar* by M.Zürn suffered when it was Gothicized. Fortunately, however, the larger-than-life main figures — a Madonna and Child enthroned on clouds, and St. Stephen and St. Lawrence — have survived. The red marble *effigy* of Bishop Mauerkircher of Passau (d. 1485) is a beautiful work by Hans Valkenauer, the famous sculptor from Salzburg. The Gothic *stone pulpit* is an outstanding feature. Interesting for its iconography, it has niches with bas-reliefs of the church fathers, and, between these, statues of Christ and the Evangelists in tabernacles; below, reclining along the base of the pulpit, there are prophets surrounded by strange faces amidst flames (personifications of the constellations?). The Gothic and baroque *processional staffs* of the guilds are also interesting. Outside the church is the renowned *tombstone* of Hans Staininger; the two strands of his curly beard extend far beyond his feet and legend has it that this beard caused him to fall to his death.

Former Bürgerspitalkirche zum Hl. Geist: A beautiful Gothic group of buildings. The hall church originally had two aisles, but the central row of pillars was removed to form a unified area in the baroque style. The decorations date from the late 17C. The *hospital* immediately adjoins the W. wall of the church; the entrance hall of the hospital forming the portico of the church. To the left and right are the former *Kommunestuben*, common rooms, the women being separated from the men. Today part of the town library is housed in these beautiful rooms. The halls on the ground and first floors have rib vaults; Gothic windows and doors, spiral staircase—all in all, this is a splendid example of a medieval hospital.

Also worth seeing: The late Gothic former *St.-Martins-Kirche* was designed as a double church. The upper church is still deconsecrated, but the interesting lower one has been altered to form a war memorial chapel. An *obelisk* marks the site of Palm's execution (see above).

Bezirksmuseum (in the 'Herzogsburg'; Altstadt 10 and 10a): Prehistory, handicrafts, art and culture. The original 16C bell foundry workshop is in the 'altes Haus' (old house), Johann-Fischer-Gasse 8.

Environs: Some 2 km. up the river is **Ranshofen,** which was a ducal court under Tassilo in 788, and then a Carolingian palace. In 898 a chapel was built under Emperor Arnulf. An Augustinian house was established here in 1125 and abolished in 1811. The late Gothic church with its W. tower is now baroque inside and

is outstandingly decorated: the virtuoso *carvings* are of the highest quality: the choir stalls, pews and especially the side altars, where the paintings and retractable image are held only by the abundant acanthus curls, without any architectural structure being used. An immense, ornate *high altar,* good *pulpit*. Some 7 km. S. is **St. Georgen an der Mattig.** This small country church is distinguished by three outstanding altars by the brothers Martin and Mich. Zürn: the church's patron saint with a beggar, a St.George in a dramatic fight with the dragon, and the martyrdom of St.Sebastian. Some 21 km. SW, near the right bank of the river Salzach, is **Hochburg** with the *Pfarrkirche Mariä Himmelfahrt,* which has a nave and two aisles to the W., whereas at the E. end the pier has been removed as in the Spitalskapelle in Braunau; dating from the early 15C, it is the earliest such example. *Franz X. Gruber,* the composer of 'Silent Night', was born here on 25 November 1787, the fifth child of a linen weaver. About 20 km. S. is **Eggelsberg** with the *Pfarrkirche Mariä Himmelfahrt:* a 236 ft. W. tower with an onion dome; followed by a nave and two aisles, with the organ gallery above; the E. end has a single central pier (see above for similar examples); the slender pillars pass without interruption into the ribs of the stellar vault, which is decorated with delicate paintings; the gorgeous altars and pulpit date from the mid 17C; an expressive *crucifix* by Mich. Zürn; a larger-than-life Madonna and Child is attributed to the same artist; chased Gothic portals with old doors, splendid mountings with lily motifs. Travelling first up the Inn and then the Salzach, the route leads to **Ach an der Salzach,** some 20 km. from Braunau. *Pfarrkirche Mariä Heimsuchung:* A central room with a choir was added to the Gothic

Braunau, St. Stephan, tombstone of Hans ▷
Steininger

aisle in 1770; the ceiling frescos are by Joh. N. della Croce; high altar; late Gothic statue of a seated Virgin, and above this is a sculpture of the Trinity (1771). From Ach there is a splendid view of the town of Burghausen on the Bavarian bank of the Salzach.

Bregenz 6900
Vorarlberg   p.286☐A 7

The Celtic town of Brigantion was named Brigantium after the Romans expelled the Celts in the lake war, and it was then a flourishing Roman settlement until its destruction by the Alemanni in 260. St. Columbanus founded a monastery here in 610. The Udalrichings built their castle on the Castrum Brigantium in about the mid 10C. The town was liberated from the Swabian knights' league in the fierce Appenzell uprising against St.Gallen in 1408, and fell to the counts of Montfort. It has been important as a trading centre throughout almost all its history; with periods of particular prosperity after the Arlbergstrasse was built under Emperor Joseph II, and also after it was connected to the railway network in 1872.

Zisterzienserkloster Mehrerau: Mehrerau-Wettingen is half an hour from the centre of the town: Benedictines from Petershausen near Konstanz arrived here in 1097 and settled in the 'Au am See'. A 16C engraving clearly shows the basic Hirsau style plan: the chorus minor is located approximately where the crossing would be. An extensive *crypt,* where the abbots' were buried, was found during recent excavations. Above this there was a Romanesque basilica with a nave, two aisles, and a straight-ended choir. In 1740 F.A. Beer built a single-aisled baroque hall church on its foundations. The stones of the massive Romanesque crossing tower were used for the E. tower. When work on the church and monastery was stopped in 1808 by Napoleon and the Bavarians, these ashlars were used for the foundations of the mole at Lindau. Fine panels depicting the Passion by Adelbert Brouts (in a new version), and two late Gothic statues of the Virgin, are to be found in the *new church* dating from 1854 (rebuilt again in 1962 when it was once more in Cistercian hands). The chapterhouse has a late Gothic triptych (Passion) dating from 1582, and the monastery has a fine portal bearing a coat-of-arms.

Seekapelle St.Georg: The lake formerly came up to the walls of the church, which was founded in 1408 and rebuilt in 1690 –98. It has a beautiful *Renaissance altar* from Schloss Hofen dating from 1610. There are Hohenmeser coats-of-arms on both sides, and the shrine houses a Virgin by the Cross (with something of the appearance of a triptych). Scenes from the Passion occupy small niches on both sides. Relics of dead soldiers from the Appenzell war are to be found in the lower storey of the chapel, consecrated in 1445.

Martinsturm: Standing on Romanesque foundations, the tower probably dates from the 14C. The chapel (1362, with dated frescos) has a recently uncovered niche containing a Christ in a mandorla with the symbols of the four Evangelists, and images of the Monforts, the founders. There are saints on the walls, and below them is the Holy Sorrow, much revered in the Tyrol. The tower and its staircase were built in 1599, while the dome dates from 1701.

Pfarrkirche St. Gallus: This probably stands on the site of the church dedicated to the blessed Aurelia by Gallus and Columbanus. It was first consecrated in 1318,

Bregenz, Martinsturm ▷

and was given a new tower in 1672. It was altered in baroque style in 1738 by A.Beer: the nave was elevated and transept chapels were added. Fine Wessobrunn stucco. The high altar shows Gallus and Peter; Paul and Ulrich. In the *side chapel:* St.Magnus (699–772, apostle of the Allgäu region, a Benedictine from St.Gallen) and Nicholas, the patron saint of boatmen on Lake Constance. The *choir stalls* are from Mehrerau.

Burg Hohenbregenz: This splendidly situated castle was razed by Wrangel and his Swedes in 1647. The *pilgrimage church of St.Gebhard* (1723) on the Gebhardsberg (St.Gebhard, Bishop of Constance in 949, son of Count Ulrich von Bregenz, founded the Benedictine abbey of Petershausen and was buried there, 995) was originally incorporated in the palas of the castle, where Gebhard was born.

Also worth seeing: The houses in the lovely walled, upper town, are all old: the *Deuring-Schlösschen* (1689), the *Altes Rathaus,* a massive half-timbered building, and the *Gesellenspital* with its frescoed coat-

Bregenz, St.Gallus, high altar

of-arms of St. Christopher and St. Peter. The *Kirchlein des Siechenhauses* (church of the hospital for incurables) was founded by Hugo von Montfort in *c.* 1400 and contains a fine Madonna Enthroned.

Vorarlberger Landesmuseum (Kornmarkt 1): Prehistoric finds and from the Roman town of Brigantium. On the 2nd floor there are exhibits relating to Alemannic and Rhaeto-Romanic folk culture; and also art from the Middle Ages until modern times (3rd floor; mainly panel paintings and sculptures).

Theatre: The large *corn exchange* built in 1838 was converted to form the *Theater am Kornmarkt* in 1955. The *Bregenzer Seefestspiele* is held each year in July and August; when famous companies visit the festival and give performances by the lake.

Breiteneich = Horn 3580
Lower Austria   p.278☐T 3

Altes Schloss: This charming little Renaissance Schloss, a square building with a fountain, a dungeon and a hunting room, was built in 1541. Late Gothic forms are found alongside Renaissance galleries (grotesque paintings by an Italian artist). A spiral staircase without a central pillar, a cell vault in the former chapel, arcades along one wing: Breiteneich is a typical house of the Waldviertler minor aristocracy, whose chief riches are the forests. The castles are solidly built and moderately comfortable. The monastery and castle have extensive fish ponds; game, pheasants and partridges are hunted.

Breitenfurt bei Wien 2384
Lower Austria   p.278☐U 5

Pfarrkirche zum hl. Joh. Nepomuk: This pretty example of a baroque schloss church, was built outside the schloss of the imperial chief forestry inspector, Baron von Kirchner. (The schloss itself was torn down under Joseph II in 1796.) The church built by Anton Martinelli was consecrated in 1732. The *dome fresco* shows St.John of Nepomuk being received into Heaven. The altarpiece of the rich *marble high altar* is by D. Gran (St. John of Nepomuk distributing alms).

Breitenwang = Reutte 6600
Tirol   p.286☐D 8

Breitenwang is the valley's oldest settlement and was for long its main town; later being superseded by Reutte. Emperor Lothar II died here in 1137 during his return from Rome and a panel on the W. front of the parish church still commemorates the event.

Pfarrkirche zu den hll. Petrus und Paulus: This church, mentioned in a document in 1094, was enlarged and altered in the 16C. The present church is mainly the result of the most recent rebuilding of 1685–91. The inside of the church consists of a large rectangular area with an articulated tunnel vault and trompe-l'oeil architecture. The *fresco* in the apse is by J.J. Zeiller (Calling of Peter). The *high altar* has a Denial of Christ painted by J.C. Haas in the late 18C.

The square *tower chapel* (the tower is Gothic) adjoins the church to the N., and forms a link between the church and the funerary chapel. The chapel itself has its own small round dome with frescos by J.B. Riepp dating from the 1st half of the 18C.

Totenkapelle (funerary chapel): This architecturally interesting chapel was built in 1724. A narrow portico leads into the rectangular main area. There are two sections of early-18C sculptures by Anton Sturm; on the right and left beside the arch

and under the gallery. The effigies of dead people in medallions and the stucco in the dome are both of interest.

Also worth seeing: *Graveyard* with stone coat-of-arms of the Kleinhanns family (16C) and an 18C wooden memorial to the Zeiller family, as well as a wrought-iron cross on a tomb dating from 1777. The *war memorial chapel* was built in 1526 and originally dedicated to St.Roch and St. Sebastian, but it was transformed by Robert Wurzer into in 1954 and decorated by Max Spielmann. Its late Gothic character was retained (groin vaulting in the nave, three entrance arches in the portico, and articulated choir). The *Kapelle Vierzehn Nothelfer* (chapel of the fourteen auxiliary saints; 1st half of 18C; altarpiece by P.Zeiller, 1718) stands near the town, by the Plansee. The *Bad Kreckelmoos,* which was built in *c.* 1600 and enlarged by J.Ammann in 1719, still has a number of rooms with coffered ceilings and wall cupboards from the Renaissance.

Brixen im Thale 6364
Tirol   p.284☐I 8

Pfarrkirche Mariae Himmelfahrt: Documented from as far back as 788, the parish church, in its present form, was built by the Kitzbühel artist Andrä Hueber in 1789–95. This building, with its three domes and plain façade, has a beautifully arranged interior, where rococo and neoclassical elements compete with one another for supremacy. In 1796, Peter Pflauder stuccoed the bays of the three domes and the semicircular apse containing the altars in neoclassical style. The two side domes were painted by Andreas Nesselthaler in 1795. The rococo frescos in the main dome are the work of the Tyrolean artist J.Schöpf, 1795, who also painted the beautiful Assumption (1796) on the high altar.

Also worth seeing: The area's *isolated farms*, with their distinctive central entrance halls. *Friedhofskapelle* (graveyard chapel) of 1734, with a carved Crucifixion, 1790. *Kapelle hl. Johann d. T.* on the Hohe Salve, dating from the 2nd half of the 16C, rebuilt in 1612, restored in 1643–4, with Gothic relics and a high altar from the 2nd half of the 17C.

Environs: Not far from Brixen im Thale is **Hopfgarten,** which is overlooked by the *Pfarrkirche hll. Jakob und Leonhard,* a beautiful rococo church standing on rising ground. Originally Gothic, it was rebuilt in 1758 by Kassian Singer, an architect from Kitzbühel, and was completed by Andrä Hueber. The *façade,* with unusually arranged windows, is especially impressive. The *ceiling paintings* by J.Weiss (1763) are the main feature inside. From Hopfgarten one can visit the baroque *Elsbethenkapelle* (originally late Gothic) near **Engelsberg,** and also the ruins of *Burg Engelsberg,* which dates back to the Romanesque and was destroyed in the peasants' war in 1526.

Brixlegg 6230

Tirol   p.284□H 8

Pfarrkirche Unserer Lieben Frau: This church was built in the early 16C and most of the structure is late Gothic, while the decoration, including the rococo stucco, is almost all from the 2nd half of the 18C. The *ceiling paintings* were originally the work of Christoph Anton Mayr (1768). The *five rococo altars* are early 18C, but Kaspar Waldmann's Marriage of the Virgin on the high altar is dated as early as 1692.

Also worth seeing: The *Mariahilf-Kapelle,* which was built in the 18C, contains a ceiling painting by Fred Hochschwarzer (1958). The centrally planned *Kreuzkapelle* was built in 1699 and has a late Gothic marble portal, and an altar from the same period. The dome was destroyed in 1945 and rebuilt in 1949. Some remains of the walls of *Burg Mehrnstein* from the early 12C stand on a hill above the town.

Hopfgarten (Brixen)

Environs: Burg Matzen, 12C, with its massive Romanesque keep, stands on the main road to Innsbruck. The castle is privately owned and was rebuilt in 1873. There are two interesting late medieval courtyards. Nearby is **Schloss Neu-Matzen,** where the composer Hugo Wolf spent his summers in the late 19C. The imposing ruins of **Burg Kropfsberg,** which was also built in the 12C as a border castle to protect the Zillertal from the archbishops of Salzburg, are on the same road. Not far away is **Burg Lichtenwerth;** 12C, in good condition and privately owned. It was originally on an island set between the old course of the Inn and a tributary.

Bruck an der Leitha 2460

Lower Austria   p.278☐W 5

Salomon of Hungary ceded this area to his brother-in-law Emperor Henry IV, who donated them to the monastery of Freising. Later, it appears to have come under the sway of the Diepolds of Lower Bavaria. 13C walls survive. The blocks of houses are arranged around the rectangular main square with its four gates. There was a large Jewish community here in the 14C. Bruck was occupied in the first Turkish siege, and in the second one it placed itself under the protection of Emmerich Tökölys, a Hungarian who concluded a pact with the Turks.

Schloss Prugg: Moated in the Middle Ages; the 17C schloss incorporates a 13C tower. J.L. von Hildebrandt made changes from 1707 onwards. The baroque gave way in the early 19C to the Romanesque. However, the chapel in the schloss is still original.

Also worth seeing: The *Pfarrkirche zur Hl. Dreifaltigkeit* (in the main square) was built by Heinrich Hoffmann in 1696–1702. Most of the decoration is 18C. *Augustiner Eremiten-Kloster* (on the corner of Hainburgerstrasse and Johnstrasse; 1663 and 19C) and *Kapuzinerkloster* (Capuchin monastery; Friedrich-Schiller-Gasse), of

Burg Matzen (Brixlegg)

Burg Kropfsberg (Brixlegg)

which the church dating from 1629 survives. There is also a row of *houses* (some with Gothic features) which are worth looking at. *Heimatmuseum* (1 Johnstrasse) with Stone Age tools.

Bruck an der Mur 8600
Steiermark   p.280 □ S 8

This town, which enjoyed the right to store salt, was declared a market in 1230, and in 1263 or 1277 it was elevated to the status of a town. It was initially laid out along typically Styrian lines, with a square enclosed by two tangential streets. Before the town was almost entirely destroyed in a large fire in 1792, it was an important depot for the trade with Venice.

Pfarrkirche Mariae Geburt: The walls and E. tower of the church date from the time of the town's foundation (1272). The two-bayed Gothic choir was incorporated later (consecrated in 1336), followed by the chapel on the N. side of the nave (1465). A net vault was added to the flat ceiling,

and a stone musicians' gallery was also built. The *sacristy door* dating from 1500, which was actually intended for the corn exchange, is an outstanding piece of Austrian Gothic wrought iron. The decoration is now entirely baroque (17–19C). The *altarpiece* (1807) was painted by Matthias Schiffer, an artist from Bruck; there are also two good terracotta medallions of heads (1541) which distinctly suggest the early Renaissance.

Former Minoritenkirche Maria im Walde (Minorite church): This church stands above the river Mürz, to the E. of the main square, and it escaped the fire of 1712. The Minorite monastery was built in 1272 along with the rest of the town. The monastery itself was dissolved in 1782 and was later turned into a *Heimatmuseum*. The nave originally had a flat ceiling and it was not until 1655 that vaults were added and a side chapel built on the N. wall. The *wall frescos* are of particular interest: they are by 14C Viennese court artists and are among the most important Austrian paintings of this period. The high altar (1770),

Bruck, Kornmesshaus

altar of the Cross altar (1710), and pulpit (1710), were only added in the 18C, along with some other items.

Kornmesshaus (Am Hauptplatz): Pankratz Kornmess, an iron merchant had this extraordinary late Gothic house built for himself in 1499–1505. It displays clear Venetian influence, with an arcaded ground floor and a loggia at the front. A typical Styrian wrought-iron *well* (1620) stands in the main square.

Ruprechtskirche: This is a little way outside the town, on the site of the original, early medieval settlement of Bruck. The S. wall of the nave, and the E. tower, survive from the Romanesque church. In 1445 a Gothic choir was added and the nave was widened. Inside, an impressive *fresco* of the Last Judgement (c. 1420) was uncovered in 1937.

Also worth seeing: The 11C *Pöglhof*, once a castle, stands on the N. edge of the town, and was later converted into a farmhouse. The 16C *Filialkirche St.Georg* by the Pöglhof is mainly of interest for its well-preserved vault paintings. The former *Heilig-Geist-Kirche* stands on the road to Graz. The ground plan of the church symbolizes the idea of the Trinity, being in the form of an equilateral triangle, with three independent altars, linked by the central structure.

Environs: Frohnleiten was mentioned as a market as early as 1306 and is a typical example of a medieval street market occupying a single main road. The market was set up across the river Mur in the 13C in order to control the trade. The *Katharinenkapelle* (deconsecrated) stands by the river bank and is on the site of an earlier fortress. The *Pfarrkirche Mariae Himmelfahrt,* consecrated in 1701, was built by Josef Schmerlaib; 60 years later it was badly damaged in a fire, as was the market. The single-aisled interior has three bays. Note the rococo decoration: figures on the high altar by Veit Köninger (1760) and ceiling frescos by Josef A. Mölk (1764). **Burg Rabenstein** stands on a rock above the Mur and, in the 11C, belonged to a

Burg Rabenstein (Bruck)

family of the same name. Its 'upper house' has been in ruins since the 15C; a courtyard, through which the old road along the Mur valley passed, links it to the 'lower house'. The latter was rebuilt by Friedrich von Trauttmannsdorff. Two halls with stucco ceilings and scenes from Ovid's 'Metamorphoses' are the main features.

Brückl 9371
Kärnten   p.282☐Q 10

Pfarrkirche St.Johann d. T.: This late Gothic church was completed in the 1st quarter of the 16C: a single-aisled hall with three bays, an extended choir, and net and stellar vaulting. An important late Gothic crucifix is attached to the N. wall of the choir. The late baroque altar framed by columns (1758) is by J.Pacher from St.Veit. A late classical tombstone with figures in niches (late 3C AD) is to be found by the W. wall of the churchyard. There are also Roman monuments in the *Filialkirche hl.*

Maria Magdalena (in Fresslitzen, W. of Brückl), including the tombstone of Sixtilla (2nd half of the 2C). The *Filialkirche St.Lorenzen* has medieval wall paintings.

Burgau 8291
Steiermark   p.280☐U 9

Schloss Burgau: The moated castle, along with Neudau, was built to protect the passage from the Lafnitzer valley to the plain. In contrast to Neudau, where only a tower and parts of the outworks survive, much of Burgau, which was sold to the local council in 1897, has survived. The inscription on the portal is dated 1588. The castle successfully withstood several sieges and some of its fortifications still exist; the residential schloss, which has an arcaded courtyard and was not built until 1624, is open to visitors. The *Pfarrkirche Mariae Gnadenbrunn* dates from 1624 in its present form, although the choir chapel is 15C.

Bruck, well, Hauptplatz

Bruck, St.Ruprecht, Last Judgement

Christkindl = Steyr 4400
Upper Austria   p.276□P 5

Wallfahrtskirche zum gnadenreichen Christkindl in Baum unterm Himmel: As with many other pilgrimages, this one began with a miraculous healing: in 1695, a sick man placed a small waxen image of the Christ-child, which had been presented to him by the Celestine nuns of Steyr, in the hollow of a tree in here (the district bore the auspicious name of 'Unterm Himmel': under Heaven); there he prayed for healing and his prayer was heard. By 1708 so many sufferers were streaming to the 'Christkindl' that Abbot Anselm of Garsten decided to build a church.

The first architect was G.B. Carlone, and the work was completed by J.Prandtauer. The unusual ground plan is the work of Carlone: four contiguous circles are arranged around the circumference of an inner one to form a cross, each of whose arms ends in a conch. Above this there stands a stately dome on a high drum. Prandtauer gave it a linear alignment by adding the twin towers of the façade; but unfortunately his proportions were later upset when the towers were increased in height.

The heart of the church is the *Christ-child*, which is one of the most charming, but also one of the smallest, miraculous statues in existence. The clay statue of the Virgin Mary in Maria Hollbruck near Sillian is 5 inches tall but this little wax figure is slightly shorter, including the base, and stands in a glass shrine framed with rocaille ornament. The shrine, with a wreath of clouds and angels' heads, rises above the

Christkindl, Wallfahrtskirche

tabernacle, which is in the form of a globe (cf. Mariazell): the Holy Ghost and, as the crowning feature, God the Father, appear above a fantastic cloud formation with a plethora of angels fluttering around it. Together with the miraculous image, these form an *altar of the Trinity*. The dark branches of the 'tree of Christ appear behind the golden clouds, reminding the onlooker of the story behind the miraculous image. There is also some restrained *stucco* from the time of Prandtauer's involvement, in marked contrast to the ebullient decoration which distinguished Carlone's work. The *side altars* also lack conventional altarpieces, and the painting and upper image (see Garsten, below, and Ranshofen, under Braunau) are framed by luxuriant acanthus leaves. *Paintings:* Nativity (Reslfeld), Crucifixion (K.Loth). *Ceiling:* Assumption, by Reslfeld.

Post vom Christkindl (post from the Christ-child): A *special post office* is open from about the beginning of Advent until Epiphany in an impressively decorated room; whence millions of items are despatched all over the world to people who want to receive their Christmas mail from the Christ-child direct.

Environs: Garsten: *Former Klosterkirche Mariä Himmelfahrt:* Collegiate church founded by Otakar I of Steyr in 1082; in 1108 it was under Otakar II. A Benedictine abbey (monks from Göttweig); dissolved in 1787. The present structure (1677–85) is by the Carlone family, with an impressive twin-towered façade; pilastered church with galleries. Frescos by the three Grabenberger brothers; gorgeous stucco, plant ornament and angels; black and gold *high altar* extending up to the vault; *side altars* without any conventional structure, only luxuriantly proliferating acanthus leaves bearing the image and the upper image (Christ-child, Ranshofen); beautifully carved *pews;* the excellent choir stalls are today in the Alter Dom in Linz. The *hangings* contribute greatly to the spatial effect and comprise Dutch tapestries (Alexander the Great) in the choir; wall hangings for pillars, painted by Reslfeld, *c.* 1700 (wars of the Maccabees) and hangings for Advent (Life of the Virgin) and Lent (Passion) by M.J. Schmidt, 1777, on blue cloth in black-and-white, with restrained colouring. Two 14C *tombs:* The beatified Berthold (the first Abbot), and the founder's tomb with Otakar II. The *Losensteinerkapelle,* with the tombs of the Losensteins, contains fine 13–17C monuments.

Garsten, Kripperl (Christkindl)

Damüls 6884
Vorarlberg   p.286□B 8

Damüls, 4,695 ft. above sea level, was settled by the counts of Montfort-Feldkirch with settlers from Wallis in Switzerland.

Pfarrkirche: This church, built in 1484, with an Austrian shield and a Montfort coat-of-arms, is of importance for the *frescos* which were uncovered in 1952 and date from the time of its building. Above the chancel arch there is a Last Judgement, with Christ in a mandorla and the sword of the Apocalypse in his mouth, surrounded by the Apostles. On the right is the choir of Saints, and on the left is the dragon of Hell with the damned. On the right side wall: Adoration of the Magi, and

Damüls, Pfarrkirche

Obeisance. Left side of the nave: 20 frescos depicting scenes from the Entry into Jerusalem to the Descent into Limbo. Note the *Plague Christ* (1640) and *St. Theodul* (a Walser saint; 1350). Wooden coffered ceiling dating from 1693.

Bad Deutsch Altenburg 2405
Lower Austria   p.278☐X 5

The sulphur springs were known to the Romans and it was here that Marcus Aurelius (d. 180 in Vindobona) led his army across the Danube in the Marcomannic war. In 1213, Alban and Joh. Dörr founded the parish church and the ossuary which stand in the middle of the graveyard.

Pfarrkirche Mariae Empfängnis: The pillared basilica (one nave, two aisles), with its early-13C Romanesque nave, its Romanesque chapel (added in the S.), and a fine 14C Gothic choir, has a domed tower. A small outside staircase leads to the oratory via the sacristy (*c.* 1400).

Ossuary: The ossuary (late Romanesque, 1st half of the 13C) is also in the graveyard. It has a fine portal, whose palmettes and crocket capitals show Cistercian influence.

Also worth seeing: The market has some pretty *Biedermeier houses:* the product of the 19C fashion for spas. These houses include *Schloss Ludwigstorff,* which today contains an *Africa museum,* and the *Museum Carnuntium* (42 Badegasse), which is the most important Austrian museum containing Roman provincial finds, with items from the Roman town of Carnuntium (see Petronell).

Dienten am Hochkönig 5652
Salzburg   p.284☐L 8

Pfarrkirche St. Nikolaus: This two-aisled church was vaulted in 1506 and has a single-bayed choir with a five-sided apse. It occupies a site on a hill. The *high altar* dating from 1660 is a further development, progressive for its period, of the usual

Bad Deutsch Altenburg, Pfarrkirche

tripartite triumphal-arch type of altar. The figures in the central niche (St. Rupert, St. Nicholas and St. Erasmus) date from around 1480, while the other figures at the high altar are by S.B. Faistenberger (1660). The figure of St. Nicholas enthroned on the S. nave wall is a typical example of Salzburg wood carving (*c.* 1460).

Diex 9103
Kärnten   p.282□Q 11

Carinthia was plundered by the Turks in 1470–80. The massive hexagonal wall, which surrounds the church and has fortified towers to the E. and W. and a gate in the NE, is a typical example of a fortified church complex into which the population could retreat, frequently taking their herds with them.

Pfarrkirche St. Martin: The church at the centre of the complex was built during the 'Turkish years', but completely rebuilt in the 17C; with the whole church being reorientated along a N.-S. axis. *Late Gothic remains* survive only in the W. portal, in the net vault of the E. choir section (below the S. tower), and in the N. tower. The baroque nave beneath the articulated tunnel vault is two bays long, while the choir has a flattened, round apse. The *altars* are all 18C. Other important works are a *carved Marienaltar* (left altar) dating from *c.* 1500, and a *late Gothic Crucifixion* in a niche of the gate.

Dormitz = Nassereith 6465
Tirol   p.286□E 8

Filialkirche St. Nikolaus: This late Gothic church was altered in baroque style in the mid 18C. The stone portal with its intersecting mouldings, the pointed windows, and the S. tower with its traceried

windows, all give a good idea of the Gothic structure. The *late Romanesque frescos* were detached in 1949 and moved to the Heimatmuseum in Imst. The *rococo stucco* inside dates from 1746. The *ceiling paintings* are the work of J. Jais, 1746. The *altars* date from the 2nd half of the 18C, the *pulpit* from 1746. A *panel painting* of the Mater Dolorosa dates from 1621.

Dornbach = Gmünd 9853
Kärnten   p.282□N 10

Filialkirche St. Leonhard und St. Katharina: Andreas von Weissbriach founded this church in 1461. The church's *wall paintings*, in the Salzburg style, also date from this period. The N. wall depicts the burial of St. Catherine, the S. wall Catherine before Emperor Maximilian, and the E. wall the Annunciation. The eight cells of the vault contain angels making music. However, the most sumptuous item is in the two-tiered *high altar* (1700): this is the central panel of a *winged altar*

Bad Deutsch Altenburg, Museum

of 1463 depicting Mary, Catherine and the infant Christ. This central group is framed by God the Father above and by angels making music along the edges of the panel. The figures and the events depicted are sharply distinguished from the decorative gold ground — a symbol of earthly splendour.

Wasserschloss Dornbach: This Gothic moated castle up the valley from the town was altered in the 16&17C.

Dornbirn 6850

Vorarlberg   p.286☐A 8

The first Alemannic settlement is known to have existed here in *c.* 500. It was under Louis the Pious that a certain Thorro settled on the royal estate of Thorinpuiron in *c.* 825. By *c.* 1000 it was known as Torn-büren; the county fell to the Habsburgs in 1380, and Dornbirn swore the oath of allegiance. In 1655, the peasants prevented Dornbirn from being sold to the counts of Ems and as a token of gratitude Duke Fer-dinand Karl presented them with a coat-of-arms: a shield with a pear tree. Serfdom ended in 1771 when the peasants bought their freedom en masse. There was a revolt against Napoleon and the Bavarians. The first textile factories were founded in 1832 and international trade fairs are now held in this prosperous, flourishing town with its large textile industry.

Stadtpfarrkirche St. Martin (Markt): The church was built in 1839-54, although the free-standing bell tower dates from 1493, with a baroque upper storey of 1767. The grisaille painting is by Kaspar Rick (1849), while the ceiling paintings are the work of Franz Plattner (1876–7).

Rotes Haus (red house; Markt): Next to the parish church, it was built in 1639 by the famous Vorarlberg family of Rhomberg. A typical Rhine valley house, the inspiration for its red paint was the half-timbered brick 'Das rote Hüs' in Strassburg. Today it is used as a hotel.

Museum: The *Vorarlberger Naturschau*

Dornbach, moated schloss

(33 Marktstrasse) is devoted to the mountains, fauna and flora, and the people of the region.

Also worth seeing: Several more fine town houses are to be found near the Marktplatz. The old *Kaplanhaus* (chaplain's house) and 3 Schmelzhüttenstrasse and 9 Riedgasse are also interesting.

Environs: From Dornbirn there are a number of pleasant trips across the Bödele to **Schwarzenberg,** the birthplace of Angelica Kauffmann (1741 – 1807) who painted the 'Coronation of the Virgin', 1801, on the high altar in the Pfarrkirche zur Hl. Dreifaltigkeit (1760, enlarged in 1932); **Bezau,** the main town of the Bregenzerwald with the Pfarrkirche zum hl. Jodok (1771, torn down in 1908 and rebuilt); and **Egg** (Nikolauskirche, 1307).

Drosendorf an der Thaya 2095
Lower Austria   p.278☐T 2

A typical fortified town from around 1200; offering the population a refuge at times of danger. In 1180 the counts of Pernegg founded a settlement with three pastures. It had town gates on both sides and stood on a small plateau above a loop of the river Thaya. The castle in Pernegg (the troops were based in Raisdorf nearby), the monastery in Geras, and the craftsmen's and traders' settlement in Drosendorf, all belonged to the Perneggs. After they died out, the lands passed to the dukes and then Margarethe, the sister of the last of the Babenbergs, brought them to Ottokar of Bohemia as a dowry. He first had to recapture the town, which was already occupied by Austrian troops. However, Rudolf von Habsburg kept the upper hand, ensured that his famiy had control of the county, and added Margrave of Drosendorf to his titles. The scheming Ulrich von Eyczing from Bavaria, chancellor of Albrecht V, appears as one of various vassals (his tombstone is in the Martinskirche in the Stadtplatz) and he began a fishery which survives to the present day. His successor was a Protestant from Litschau. The town was given the power to hold trials in 1559

Dornbirn, Rotes Haus

(the *pillory* dates from 1559). The *Rathaus* is 16C, and behind it is the 16C *Bürgerspital*. The great fire in 1846 destroyed much of the town.

Items worth seeing: The heart of the town is formed by the Marktplatz (market square) with the *Rolandssäule* (column, *c.* 1500) and the *Marktkirche zum hl. Martin*. This church was built in 1461 – 4 and altered in baroque style in the 18C. The *Altstadt-Pfarrkirche* of St.Peter and St.Paul (E. of the town) has been rebuilt several times (16&17C). The most notable feature of the interior is the tabernacle (*c.* 1515). The frescos date from *c.* 1760 and the pulpit from *c.* 1730. Parts of the *walls* and the *Horner Tor* (*c.* 1200) survive. The *Stadtburg* (built in 1180, rebuilt in the 16&17C) is a three-storeyed structure arranged around a rectangular courtyard.

Dürnstein 3601

Lower Austria   p.278☐T 4

Ruined castle: The castle was built in

1140–5, with the hall and chapel leading into the later residence—as the fortress is replaced by something less severe. Richard the Lionheart was held prisoner here from 1192–3, and legend has it that he was discovered by his minstrel Blondel singing a verse of a song which was then completed by the captive king. Richard I, the Plantagenet Duke of Aquitaine and King of England (b. 1157), fought bravely along with the King of France and the Babenberg Duke Leopold V in the Third Crusade in 1191. His fierce temper led him to tear down the Austrian flags and to refuse to share the booty when Acre was captured. Leopold V and the King of France broke off the Crusade. Richard's adventurous return journey took him through Austria on his way to his brother-in-law in Saxony. Shortly before Christmas he was recognized in Vienna, and Leopold seized him and ordered him to be taken with honour to the newly built castle of Hadmar von Kuenstein at Dürnstein. Richard was later taken to Burg Trifels in the Palatinate, where he was released in 1194 after the payment of a ransom of

Dornbirn, St. Martin

150,000 marks in silver. Emperor Henry VI received half of this, and the other half went to the Babenberg Duke, who used the money to fortify Enns, Hainburg, the Vienna Neustadt, and Vienna itself. However, the Pope excommunicated him because he had laid violent hands on a crusader.

The settlement, protected by the 1,770 ft. high rock, grew up around a toll-gate on the bank of the Danube. Only a slender tower, a Gothic window, and some remains of walls, still survive of the former *Pfarrkirche St. Kunigunde* (13C; Kunigunde, the wife of Henry II, founded Bamberg in *c*. 1000). Next to these is the 14C *ossuary*. Behind the church and ossuary is the old *town wall* which, pierced by the *Kremser Tor* (gate), continues as far as the Danube. The *Klarissinnenkloster* was founded in *c*. 1300 and dissolved in 1571. A deeply carved stone portal. The choir is used for exhibitions but is not open at present. Blind arcades and fine tracery. The frescos depict St. Francis (1326), and John and Mary under the Cross (1340). The old convent courtyard is now a restaurant and a ho-

tel. The core of the Rathaus is late Gothic, and recently sgraffiti have been uncovered; arcaded courtyard. Fine town houses. The *Schloss*, standing right on the Danube, with fine terraces, was built by Christoph Wilhelm von Zelking in 1622. It is a massive, three-storeyed, structure arranged around a square courtyard. Today it is a hotel.

Former Augustinian priory and Pfarrkirche Mariae Himmelfahrt: Three and a half centuries passed from the foundation of the priory in 1410 until its dissolution in 1788. It stands on a rock overlooking the Danube and from 1710–40 it was governed by Prior Übelbacher. He ordered the roof and the ridge turret of the convent church of the Poor Clares to be torn down, gave commissions to J. Prandtauer, Munggenast, Matthias Steinl, and the stucco artist Santino Bussi, and generally acted as a great baroque builder. The *S. portal,* now constricted, is by Steinl, 1718 (the divine virtues, flanked by Vigilance and Strength). The wooden door has old cord-like carvings. In the entrance is

Dürnstein with ruined castle

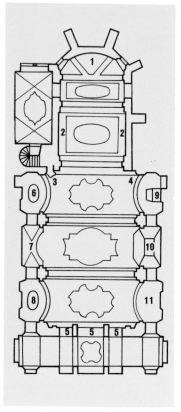

Dürnstein, Stiftskirche 1 High altar **2** Choir stalls **3** Pulpit **4** St. John of Nepomuk **5** Gallery **6** Altar of St. Augustine **7** Altar of St. Monica **8** Altar of St. Jerome **9** Altar of John the Baptist **10** Altar of St. Catherine **11** Altar of Joseph

the form of an altarpiece, the visitor being protected by Christ the Saviour and four Church Fathers.

A Herzogenburg flower basket surmounts the structure. But the whole is overtopped by the elegant *church tower* dating from 1733, which is richly ornamented (putti, obelisks, balustrades) and was designed by M. Steinl and J. Munggenast. The delicate, ornate interior is full of brightness. It is a church to listen to masses by Mozart or Haydn in. Over 100 little angels inhabit the heavens—the divine virtues reappear everywhere. The colouring of the *high altar* is restrained (Assumption). The tabernacle, a large wooden globe, is gilded, and bears bas reliefs of scenes from the Bible; the Equator is a silver strip with the emblems of faith, hope and love; amidst the timbers is the Holy Trinity, with the Holy Ghost in the aureole of a window forming a golden sun. Above the curving side walls, which create the rhythm of the interior, there are stucco reliefs depicting the Annunciation, the Nativity, the Magi and the Resurrection. The choir has a 15C five-sided apse. The two side altars are decorated with paintings by Kremser Schmidt.

An unusual additional baroque structure stands at the S. side of the church on the site of an old *cloister*. Here there is a Christmas altar and a baroque setting for the Holy Sepulchre (Good Friday) by Antonio Galli-Bibiena (from the famous Bolognese family of theatre architects). There is a Mount Calvary in the crypt chapel.

a martial bas relief, and to the left is the court room. In all probability the fine priory courtyard was designed by Prandtauer. Elegant portals lead into the building, with the central feature being the gorgeous church portal, which is almost in

Kellerschlössl: Built by Prandtauer for Prior Übelbacher in 1714. The fresco depicts some revellers. Beautiful stucco by Piazoll. The wine harvests are stored in long corridors (2,600 ft.).

Dürnstein, Chorherrenstift, portal ▷

E

Ebbs 6341
Tirol   p.284□I 7

Pfarrkirche U.L. Frau Geburt: This church is mentioned in documents as early as 788 but it was not until 1748–56 that the present structure was built by Abraham Millauer (Aibling) and his sons Philipp and Leonhard on the site of a Gothic church. It was restored in 1954. The N. tower is the only part of the medieval church still standing. A rectangular single-aisled church with an apse, it appears simple and harmonious from the outside and the gorgeously decorated interior comes as a surprise. It has side niches and a splendid *high altar* (1756) by Jos. Martin Lengauer of Kitzbühel, which incorporates a Gothic statue of the Virgin. The

House front in Walchsee (Ebbs)

twelve Apostles in the niches are also by him. *Ceiling paintings* by J.A. Mölk (1750). Note the beautiful mid-18C *pulpit*, which is combined with a confessional.

Also worth seeing: Beautiful 16C *Inntal courtyards* (e.g. 23&24 Talstrasse). There is an early-16C carved altar in the prettily situated small pilgrimage church of *St. Nikolausberg.*

Environs: Not far from Ebbs is **Erl**, famous for the Passion Plays which have been performed by amateurs since 1633, as in Oberammergau. It was during the plague of 1610 that the townspeople vowed to perform these plays, and this vow has been kept ever since. A new, larger Passion Play theatre was built in 1958. **Walchsee** (some 10 km. to the E.) by the lake has some fine *houses* (see the Gasthof Schopfer-wirt) with a rich rococo façade. The baroque *Pfarrkirche*, restored in the early 20C, was originally Gothic. 10 km. further on is the charming resort of **Kössen,** with its fine *Inntal houses* such as the Gasthof Erzherzog Rainer, and the *Pfarrkirche hll.*

Petrus und Paulus. This 12C church was altered in baroque style by Wolfgang Dinzenhofer and Abraham Millauer in 1722–4; although the ground floor and the tower were untouched. The stuccoes inside are by W.Dinzenhofer; the paintings by S.B. Faistenberger above the organ loft were not uncovered again until the 20C. In the choir there are two late Gothic wooden reliefs.

Eben am Achensee = Maurach 6212
Tirol   p.284 □ G 8

Pfarrkirche zur hl. Notburga: The body of St.Notburga, a pious maid from Rattenberg and the patron saint of maidservants and peasants, rests here, in what was originally a Gothic church. In 1736–8, J.Singer of Schwaz added a new nave to the existing choir and the N. tower. The inside of the church captivates the onlooker with its splendid *stuccoes* and *ceiling paintings* by Christoph Anton Mayr,

Eben, St. Notburga, ceiling fresco

which date from 1754 and were restored in 1899. The *high altar* stands between tall windows and contains the body of St. Notburga in a glass shrine.

Ebenthal 9065
Kärnten   p.282☐P 11

Pfarrkirche Maria Hilf und St. Peter und Paul: This late baroque single-aisled church with its chapels opening through flat arches and its 'Platzlwölbung' vault, was consecrated in 1770. The *vault frescos* were painted by Gregor Lederwasch in 1766 and he is probably also responsible for the *altarpiece* of the high altar (1780). The beautiful *rococo pulpit* dates from 1770.

Schloss Ebenthal: The schloss was built by Christoph Neuhaus in 1567 and was altered in the 18C. The three-storeyed building set in a splendid park houses some fine paintings: the ceiling of the *Grosser Saal* (great hall) has paintings by

J.F. Fromiller. The larger-than-life oil paintings in the *family room* are by the Viennese artist Peter Kobler (1740).

Eberndorf 9141
Carinthia   p.282☐Q 11

Former Stiftskirche Mariae Himmelfahrt: The patriarchs of Aquileia built the Augustinian church and priory in the 1st half of the 12C. At the time of the Turkish invasions (1470–80), the buildings were converted into a late-Gothic fortified church. It was handed over to the Jesuits in 1604. The present appearance is mainly the product of the middle third of the 17C. The long building history means that there are many layers of architecture. An intertwining ribbed vault extending through five bays (1506) rests on round responds projecting in from the walls. The niches of these walls house chapels, above which there is a three-bayed gallery. Opposite the nave is the raised choir, which lies above a massive rib-vaulted *crypt* (1378–91). The

Eberndorf, Stiftskirche, St. Anne with Mary and the child Jesus

visitor descends to the crypt by two side staircases in the nave. Openings through the S. wall connect the nave to a quasi-aisle, the *Ungnadkapelle,* which still contains remains of Romanesque walls. The baroque *Franz Xaver chapel,* with a group of St. Anne, the Madonna and Christ, adjoins this to the E. The focal point of the baroque *high altar* is a carved Gothic *figure of the Virgin* (1470–80). The altar on the E. wall has a late Gothic *figure of Florian* (1520–5). Two oil paintings of Ignatius of Loyola, the founder of the Jesuits, serve as a reminder of the fact that the church was also a fortress used in the Counter-Reformation. The painting in the nave dates from the mid 18C, while that in the Franz Xaver chapel is from the 2nd half of the 17C. The late Gothic *tomb* by Christoph Ungnad (1490), a piece of carving with no equal in Carinthia, is outstanding.

Also worth seeing: The two neighbouring daughter churches of *Unsere liebe Frau am Berg* and *Heiliger Geist* and also the *Friedhofskapelle,* contain some fine baroque decoration.

Eckartsau 2305
Lower Austria   p.278☐W 5

Jagdschloss: From 1192 until their extinction in 1507, the Eckhartsaus were tenants of the abbey of Regensburg. Later owners included the Herbersteins and, in 1720, Count Ferdinand Kinsky. The latter commissioned Emanuel Fischer von Erlach and J.L. von Hildebrandt—the architects of his town palace of Daun Kinsky—to convert the medieval moated castle into a hunting castle.
The alterations involved the rebuilding of the W. wing and the schloss is now arranged around a courtyard. There is a garden front with a central *festsaal.* The ceiling fresco is by D.Gran (1732), and the sculptures and stuccoes are the work of L. Mattielli. The schloss passed to the Habsburgs in 1762. In 1898, Archduke Franz Ferdinand had the E. and S. wings rebuilt and the rest of the schloss renovated; the upper floors of these wings having been torn down in 1820 owing to their dilapidated state. Kaiser Wilhelm II went hunting with the Archduke in 1908. On 11 November 1918, Karl Renner, a Social Democrat, brought the abdication document to Emperor Karl I at Eckartsau for his signature and it was from here that Karl I and his family left for exile in Switzerland on 23 March 1919.

Environs: 8 km. up the Danube from Eckartsau is **Schloss Orth,** a Regensburg fief since the 10C. The Habsburg held it from 1377 onwards, but continually granted it to others. Schloss Orth was the residence of Eleonora Gonzaga, the second wife and widow of Emperor Ferdinand II, and of Caroline, the youngest sister of Napoleon. Three wings, with four massive towers, are grouped around a square main

Schloss Orth (Eckartsau)

courtyard (built in 1550 under Count Salm); additions by Augustin von Auersperg (1679). There is now a *fishing museum* in the schloss.

Eferding 4070
Upper Austria   p.276□O 4

This town, which is unfairly neglected by tourists, is worth visiting for a number of reasons.

History: Settled in the Stone Age and by the Celts; camp of a cohort of Roman cavalry; Bavarian settlement (a genuine Bavarian place-name ending in 'ing'); it was mentioned in the Nibelungenlied (Krimhild spent the night in Eferding on her bridal journey to the Hunnerland). Municipal rights were granted in 1222 (they were granted to Enns in 1212 and to Vienna in 1221); the bishops sold it to the Schaunbergs in 1367, and after the death of the last Schaunberg the Starhembergs succeeded them until the territorial dominion was relinquished in 1848. The schloss is still owned by the Starhembergs. Paracelsus often stayed in Eferding at the house of his friend the preacher J. von Brandt. It was here that Paracelsus wrote 'Origin and Cure of Lithiases'. It was in the 'Goldener Löwe' inn in 1613 that Kepler celebrated his second marriage, to Susanna Reuttinger, the daughter of a middle-class Eferding family.

Stadtpfarrkirche St. Hippolyt: This mid-15C church has a tower with a baroque dome. The double S. portal, with a Madonna and Child on the central pier and St. Hippolytus and St. Agyd at the sides, is a gem of late Gothic stone-carving. The pulpit and altars are mainly early baroque, and the high altar is neo-Gothic. The bakers' altar with its Gothic sections (five reliefs, statues of St. Wolfgang and

Martin) is also worth mentioning. There are many interesting *tombstones*, some with unusual subjects: e.g. Jacob's Ladder (L.Hassler, 1608), Flight into Egypt (U. von Nadlowitz, 1606), Death of Hagar (H. von Praunfalkh, 1607), double relief with the Fall of Man and Christ's Resurrection (G. von Praunfalkh, 1617). In the choir there are some excellent sections from the *tomb* of the last of the Schaunbergs (d. 1559). *Organ gallery* with tracery and double spiral staircase.

Museums: The *Heimatmuseum* and the *Starhembergsche Familiensammlung* are housed in the schloss, and there are exhibits relating to the history of the town and to the princely family, who played such an important role in the history of Austria (e.g. memories of the Turkish siege of Vienna, table from the Starhembergsches Freihaus, at which Mozart composed his 'Magic Flute'.

Also worth seeing: A long square, typical of Upper Austria, forms the centre of the town and is surrounded by many fine houses. *Spitalskirche zur hl. Jungfrau Maria:* Founded in 1325 by Rudolf von Schifer, an official of the Schaunbergs. The façade's tower, with its beautiful stone helm roof, dates from the rebuilding after the fire of 1432, as does the Magdalenen-Kapelle. The latter contains Gothic frescos and many good tombstones; lively Immaculata (1717) on the column outside the church. *Schloss:* Set in a park, the older parts are Gothic, and the S. wing is neoclassical (1784). Some of the excellent decorations (coffered ceilings, doors, stoves) are from other houses, mainly Hartheim. Museums: see above,

Environs: *Fadinger Denkmal* in the 'Wildes Moos' near **Seebach**, about 2 km. NW. The two peasants' leaders S.Fadinger and his brother-in-law C.Zeller were ceremonially buried in Eferding in 1626.

Count Herberstorf, the Bavarian governor, ordered the dead to be exhumed and buried in the 'Wildes Moos'. It has been a monument since 1926. The **Bauernkriegsdenkmal Emlinger Holz** (*c.* 3 km. E. of Bundesstrasse 129) is a monument in the form of an old German meeting place, which was erected in memory of some 3,000 peasants who perished there on 9 November 1626. The **Renaissanceschloss Hartheim** near Alkoven (some 8 km. E of Bundesstrasse 129) has a splendid courtyard with arcades on four sides, the fine furnishings and decorations (ceilings, doors, stove) are now in the Schloss of Eferding or in the Landesmuseum in Linz. **Ruined castle of Schaunberg:** Bundesstrasse 130 N. as far as Pupping (where St.Wolfgang died in 994), and then W., some 10 km. from Eferding. The Schaunbergs were directly subject to the Emperor; they exercised princely power in their small province and held court like dukes. Once immense, it is still impressive as a ruin; there is an observation post on the keep; many splendid architectural details, some with stonemasons' marks

from the guild of builders who erected the Dom of St.Stephan. **Hartkirchen, Pfarrkirche St.Stephan** (Bundesstrasse 130, some 8 km. N.): the whole brilliance of high baroque trompe-l'oeil painting can be seen in this village church. The walls and ceilings are covered with frescos by W.A. Heindl, who painted the scenes, and M. Dollinger, who painted the decorative features. **Aschach an der Donau** (about 2 km. from Hartkirchen, 10 km. from Eferding): A pretty town with charming gabled houses; late Gothic church; 16C castle with later alterations (not open to visitors).

Egg bei Hermagor 9624

Kärnten   p.282 ☐ M 11

Pfarrkirche St. Michael: Late Gothic church N. of the old *Khünegg* Schloss, with parish documents going back to 1244. The three-bayed nave leads into a choir as broad as it is long. Two chapels are attached to the S. wall (15C). The E. one has *late*

Eferding, Stadtpfarrkirche, portal

Memorial to peasants war, Emlinger Holz

Gothic paintings in the quatrefoil panels of the vault, and there are also good *stained-glass windows*: Crucifixion with St.Barbara and the founders, a married couple. The following words appear underneath: 'Gandolf von Kynburg—1490' and 'Dorothea sein hausfrau gep. von Lindt — 1490' (Dorothea his wife). The figures display a lifelike presence which is probably due to the influence of the Italian Renaissance. The *Betstuhlgemälde* (1491) in the Khünbergkapelle, and the figure of St. Martin standing on a bracket above it, are further fine late Gothic pieces. The neoclassical *high altar* is (1837) by Joseph Stauder, and the altarpiece is by Cosroe Dusi from Venice.

Eggenburg 3730

Lower Austria   p.278☐T 3

Finds suggest that there was a large Celtic fortress here and a small Slavonic one in AD 600, which is still referred to as ('Windisches Dorf'). In 1051 it was in the hands of Margrave Adalbert (son of Luitpold I), and the parish belonged to the Babenbergs. The site of the Windisches Dorf was now the church precinct. In 1176 Eggenburg was first termed a 'civitas'. The *Pfarrkirche* and the *Münichhof* (1258) also date from this time. The town archive and officials are housed in the Münichhof, called 'Rathaus'. The *town seal* dates from the same period. It is a line drawing of the church and the ossuary. The *town walls*, most of which still survive, are 13C. On 13 August 1277, after a brief interregnum by Ottokar of Bohemia, Rudolf of Habsburg granted 'his loyal citizens' the same privileges as those enjoyed by the Viennese. A hospital with magnificent prebends was then founded outside the town. In 1322, Frederick the Fair lost the battle of Mühldorf against Bohemia and Bavaria, was captured, and had to pledge

Eggenburg, Weitra and Laa to the Bohemian crown. In 1338 and 1348, swarms of Asian locusts ate the land bare. The story of the desecration of the consecrated bread at Pulkau sparked off persecutions of the Jews. The totally impoverished population, reacting violently to usurious rates of interest, began a reign of terror, which the local lord put a stop to. In 1516, Emperor Maximilian I resettled the Laibach Jews who had fled from the Turks and granted them freedom from taxes for three years. In 1411, the seven-year-old Duke Albrecht V (King of Bohemia and Hungary, German king in 1438) was declared of age in the presence of assembled representatives. Andreas Plank, his teacher and later chancellor, was the parish priest of Eggenburg. This border town was repeatedly raided by Hussites, Bohemian and Moravian robber knights, and Hungarians under Matthias Corvinus, the king with the raven. Matthias was the lord of Eggenburg for four years. Matthias Lang from Augsburg, the later Archbishop of Salzburg and a friend of the Emperor Maximilian, was the parish priest here for four years. Part of the town wall collapsed in a violent earthquake in 1614. During the course of the wars of religion, Eggenburg became Protestant. Torstenson's troops captured the town in 1645; the devastation they caused is still remembered today. Eggenburg returned to Catholicism after fifty years. Only thirteen citizens emigrated. After the end of the plague, the *Pestsäule* (plague column) was erected in 1715—the town had 4,000 inhabitants. The Franciscan monastery was suppressed by imperial command in 1783. A fire destroyed almost the entire town in 1808.

Pfarrkirche St.Stephan: The name of the patron saint indicates a link with Passau. Originally Romanesque, the church, as it then was, appears on the town seal; high Gothic choir, 1330. The nave and two aisles were built in 1485 along

Viennese lines. A small baroque *outside altar* between the choir buttresses dates from 1721. Beside this is a relief of the *Mount of Olives* (1390), with a surround of more recent date. The sturdy Romanesque towers of unequal height — staggered behind the choir — bear the typical Waldviertler tent roofs. Some very early *tomb slabs* with line drawings (there are no actual tombstones at all known to be earlier than 1155). The *ossuary* dating from 1280 and depicted on the town seal has a surprisingly tall lower storey and stood immediately beside the church's choir. The large interior has frescos of the Last Judgement dating from *c*. 1520 in the left-hand aisle. The choir is taller than the nave. There is a net vault borne by bundles of pillars. The *chalice-shaped pulpit* reminds the onlooker of its Viennese model, and bears busts of the doctors of the church — Ambrose, Augustine, Jerome and Gregory the Great. *Tabernacle* (1505), with delicate tracery. Neo-Gothic high altar with a triptych of St. Elisabeth-Helena and Mary Magdalene dating from 1521. Above this is the Coronation of the Virgin; in the predella: Pope Urban and St. Goar, the Rhenish patron of wine growers. The baroque side altars are arranged like those in Vienna.

Gemaltes Haus (painted house; 1 Hauptplatz): Decorated with sgraffiti based on woodcuts by Burgmeier, this outstanding house dates from 1547. On the Hauptplatz front: the story of Lazarus and the Rich Man of the Gospel, who now 'prennen mue in der helen Glut' (must now burn in the bright fire). On Kremser Strasse: the planets with sayings and, above, the story of creation. The following appears in the surrounding scroll: 'Alle Weisheit ist von Gott und is beiy ihm gewesen alsweg Von ewigkeit ...' (All wisdom comes from God and has always been with him from eternity...).

Museum: The geological and palaeontological collection in the *Krahuletz-Museum* displays Neogene finds: marine deposits, sharks' teeth, sea-cow, crocodile, and dolphin skull some 20 million years old. Remains of skeletons of elephants and

Eggenburg, Pfarrkirche, pulpit

Ehrenhausen, mausoleum

rhinoceros, mastodon skull (some 15 million years old); there are also finds from the Ice Age, from the Neolithic (bronze jewellery), and a bridle which is the collection's showpiece and dates from AD 400.

Ehrenhausen 8461
Steiermark   p.280 □ T 11

Castle: A settlement was established below the castle in the 12C, and a keep built at about the same time survives from the medieval castle, which was enlarged by the Eggenbergs, one of the most distinguished and richest families in Styria. After the Eggenbergs died out, the castle changed hands several times.

Mausoleum: Ruprecht von Eggenberg (1546–1611), a general who defeated the Turks, had the mausoleum built for his male descendants. Work continued from 1609, when the architect J.Walter began the project, until 1689, when the interior was started on to a design by Fischer von Erlach.

The originality of the mausoleum derives from the use of mannerist-grotesque architecture and sculpture: for example, the compressed façade, which is extended sideways and is weighed down by heavy cornices and an overwhelming, projecting pediment, breaks all the rules of classical proportion. The gigantic tomb guardians stand on tall pedestals on both sides of the front in marked contrast to the rather modest dimensions of the portal. The pedestals are decorated with land and sea battles. Agitated reliefs fill the spaces between the pediment volutes, and elsewhere. The almost cheerful *baroque interior* contrasts with the dark monumentality of the exterior. The octagonal drum is vaulted by a dome and lantern; both of these were richly stuccoed by the Serenio brothers.

Angels dance round and up, directing the onlooker's gaze up towards the radiant lantern, which appears like some celestial sphere.

The altarpiece by the Eggenberg court painter H.A. Weissenkirchner is the outstanding feature inside. It depicts the Virgin and St.Mark pleading for a Christian victory over the Turks—a subject dear to the founder's heart (cf. the mausoleum in Graz from the same period).

Pfarrkirche zur schmerzhaften Mutter Maria: This baroque church was built in 1752-5 by J.Fuchs, the Viennese trained artist from Marburg. The inclusion of the tower in the overall design of the façade is particularly successful. Inside, the church also impresses by the harmony of its design: a massive and elegantly curving cornice links the four apses and the central dome with one another and unifies the area.

Eisenerz 8790
Steiermark   p.282 □ R 7

In the past, Styria owed much of its wealth to the ore mountain. Once rising to 5,030 ft., the mountain is now much lower as a result of the continuous mining of the spathic iron ore from the pre-Roman period onwards. The operations can be viewed during the summer.

Pfarrkirche St. Oswald: The only fortified church (Taborkirche) in Austria to have survived in its entirety, the present church was begun in 1512 and extensive defences (N. and S. gate etc.) were added at the time of the Turkish invasions. The original Gothic church was burnt down in 1496; only the massive tower was spared. In the spacious interior of the church, Master Kristoff created the W. gallery of artificial stone, richly decorated with hunt

Eisenerz, St. Oswald

scenes (1513–17). The 18C baroque interior decoration was removed in the course of a later renovation. Only the painting of the Virgin with St. Oswald and St. Florian on the high altar survived. The paintings on the wings of the altar, and also the miner's candlestick (1470), can be seen in the Belvedere in Vienna.

Also worth seeing: In addition to the church, note the *Johanneskapelle*, and the former graveyard; numerous old tombstones testify to the town's mining tradition. The *old Rathaus* (1548), and also the *tower* (1580) by the market, are of interest. The bell tolled the change in shifts for the miners. Next to this: *Bergmuseum* (mining museum; 17a Tullstrasse) and *Heimatmuseum* (local museum, 2 Museumstiege).

Environs: Schloss Geyeregg (*c.* 1620) and Schloss Leopoldstein (1680; neo-Gothic alterations, 1890).

Eisenkappel 9135
Kärnten   p.282□Q 12

Pfarrkirche hl. Michael: A document states that this church was originally Romanesque. A large section of the Gothic building was destroyed in 1473 (Turkish invasions); being rebuilt in 1483 as a hall church with a nave and two aisles (stellar vault). The nave of this new building incorporated the powerful tower in the SW corner. The baroque groin-vaulted *Pestkapelle* (plague chapel; fine altar) to the NE was built in 1680.

Filialkirche Maria Dorn: This church

had a similar history. The choir (consecrated in 1386), and parts of the N. tower, which was later renovated, date from before the ravages of the Turks. A square baroque chapel was later added to the W. The church has some good late Gothic *frescos* (*c.* 1480) on its outer S. wall, and also a beautiful *carved Madonna* (1410) on a bracket in the intrados of the triumphal arch.

Eisenstadt 7000
Burgenland　　　　　　　　　　p.278☐W 6

Eisenstadt was not elevated to the status of the provincial capital of the Burgenland until 1925; the small, old town, rich in tradition, has experienced considerable development since then. The present Eisenstadt is subdivided into three clearly distinct parts, which also formed three administrative units up until 1938: the 'Bürgerstadt', which bought its freedom from Prince Esterházy in 1648 and has since been permitted to call itself 'Freistadt' (free town); Eisenstadt-Oberberg which developed around churches and monasteries founded by the princely house; and Eisenstadt-Unterberg, the former ghetto. The heyday of Eisenstadt was the late 18C and early 19C. Joseph Haydn, who was in the services of Esterházy from 1761 onwards, raised the prince's orchestra to an extraordinary standard and here composed many of his works; Fanny Elssler, the celebrated dancer, was the daughter of Haydn's servant; Beethoven, Liszt, and also Lord Hamilton and Admiral Nelson, were among the guests at the princely court. In addition, Joseph Hyrtl and Ignaz Semmelweis, the 'saviour of mothers', came from Eistenstadt families.

Freistadt Eisenstadt, the town: Many of the houses in the three main streets—Hauptstrasse, Haydngasse, Pfarrgasse—have retained their fine baroque appearance; extraordinarily charming is the quiet Haydngasse, where the beautiful tower of the *Franziskanerkirche* is the focus of attention (inside, altars with outstanding reliefs, 1630). The *Rathaus*, with its unusual façade, is in the Hauptstrasse, as is the *Floriani-Brunnen* and a *Dreifaltigkeitssäule* (Trinity column), with numerous saints.

Pfarrkirche St. Martin/Dom (Freistadt): St.Martin's has been a Dom (cathedral) since 1960. There are remains of walls from the 12C but the present church was built to meet the needs of the late 15C and the Turkish threat. Near the town wall, it was extended to form a bulwark and the stately tower with its saddle roof still rises above the wall, which is well preserved here; the tower's massiveness, and also the four turrets with their arrow slits, leave no doubt as to its function.

Eisenkappel, Maria Dorn

Eisenstadt, Bergkirche ▷

It underwent the metamorphosis typical of many churches: baroque in the 18C, altered in neo-Gothic style in the 19C, and finally a restoration in modern times; The latter involving the preservation of old pieces and the addition of contemporary works of art. Late Gothic hall church with a nave and two aisles; tombstones from the Middle Ages (e.g. the knight Hans Sybenhirter) and a captivating Mount of Olives relief in the porch; two fine paintings by Stephan Dorfmeister (apotheosis of the patron saint and an Immaculata, 1777), the pulpit and in particular the superb baroque organ survived the neo-Gothic changes; Fr. Arch. Bolldorf-Reitstätter (see Kobersdorf) was responsible for the dignified alteration of the presbytery; a large sculpture of St.Martin, stalls of the cathedral canons and priest's seat by J. Adlhart; bronze Pietà by A. Hanak.

Schlossbezirk: This has had a separate identity ever since the town became a 'Freistadt' in 1648. Apart from the Schloss itself, the area includes: the *Stall- und Hauptwachgebäude* S. of the forecourt; the

Esterházy-Weinkeller, with a giant barrel holding over 62,200 litres is today one of the features of the neoclassical stables; the park to the N. was laid out as an extensive landscape garden in *c.* 1800, while the *Leopoldinentempel* within was built for the figure of the Princess Leopoldine, which is by Canova.

Schloss: The medieval castle arranged around a courtyard is still apparent in the palace built by Carlo M. Carlone for Prince Paul Esterházy in 1663–73; projecting corner pavilions taking the place of towers. Alfred Schmeller described the impressive façade as showing 'characteristics of barbaric splendour'. The key elements of the ornament are the eighteen busts of Hungarian generals on the mezzanine and, even more important, the magnificent original brackets bearing carved grotesques, almost no two of which are alike, below the roof cornice. The double colonnade before the garden front is by Charles Moreau (*c.* 1800).
Interior: The showpiece is the *Haydn-Saal,* which after being carefully renovated was

Eisenstadt, Schloss, frescos in the Haydn-Saal

restored to its old function as a concert hall; frescos—the myth of Eros and Psyche—decorate the ceiling in brilliant colours, a masterpiece by Carpoforo Tencala (see Trautenfels); there are painted busts of Hungarian heroes and festoons of flowers on the walls. The *Schlosskapelle* with its oratory (so-called 'Haydn room') and a number of fine *Empire halls* are also open. The noble seated figure of the Princess Leopoldine Liechtenstein, an Esterházy by birth, by Canova, is worth mentioning; early-19C Chinese wallpapers; a gorgeous baroque clock, baroque tables and paintings.

Eisenstadt-Oberberg: This mountainside town grew up from the religious endowments of the house of Esterházy; a poorhouse (later a Franciscan monastery, today a cultural centre) dates from 1698, Mount Calvary 1701, church and hospital of the Merciful Brothers 1759.

Mount Calvary: A Mount Calvary is not a rarity in Bavaria and Austria, the stations usually leading to a church on a hill (e.g.

Arzl/Innsbruck, Maria Plain/Salzburg). This is not the case in Eisenstadt: an artificially erected hill with tile-roofed buildings stands amidst houses; a flight of steps leads to the first station, which is at the same time a chapel of mercy; angels and saints in plenty adorn the staircases, parapets and roofs. The Way of the Passion moves through chapels and caves, and also in the open air, to the 'Gipfel' (peak) and the Chapel of the Cross. In order to make Our Lord's Way of the Cross as impressive as possible, 24 stations are depicted here; even if not all of the 260 painted figures are of the highest standard, this 'holy theatre' of baroque Christianity does exude a unique fascination.

Bergkirche Mariä Heimsuchung: Foundation stone laid in 1715, consecrated in 1803. On the outside it is a massive block with truncated W. towers; whereas inside it has a round ground plan and is domed. *Dome fresco* by W.Köpp, 'Ascen-

Eisenstadt, Schloss 1 Towers **2** Staircase **3** Haydn-Saal **4** Wildschwein-Saal **5** Oratory (Haydn room) **6** Chapel

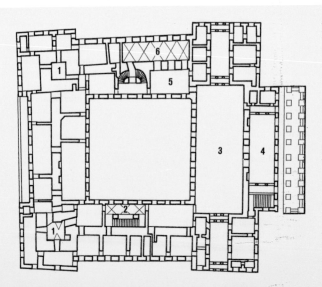

Eisenstadt, Schloss Esterházy

sion of Christ'; round the edges there are groups in an idyllic landscape in the style of the late 18C. Under the N. tower is the *Haydn mausoleum,* founded by Prince Paul Esterházy in 1932 on the bicentenary of Haydn's birth. Haydn died in Vienna in 1809 and was buried there; at the request of Prince Nikolaus Esterházy, his mortal remains were taken to Eisenstadt in 1820, where the absence of his head was noted with dismay. An admirer had stolen it 'out of piety'. In 1895 the real head came to the 'Gesellschaft der Musikfreunde' (society of the friends of music) in Vienna, where the relic was exhibited in a glass case in the society's museum until, in 1954, it was transferred to Eisenstadt in a ceremonial funeral procession.

Eisenstadt-Unterberg: Until 1938 there was an independent Jewish community here which, under the protection of the Esterházy, developed into one of the most important in the country and is linked with names like Samson Wertheimer or Sandor Wolf, an art collector; the rabbinical school was celebrated throughout Austria. The alleyways with their fine old houses form an almost untouched architectural ensemble of great charm. True to the belief of their fathers, the inhabitants adhered to their ancient customs to an unparalleled degree; the iron cross with which the 'shames' locked the alleyway at the time of 'Sabbath rest' is still to be seen hanging by the entrance. The splendid *Wertheimer house* is worth attention. Today it is part of the Burgenland Landesmuseum. Apart from the ghetto, the large *Jewish graveyard* has survived. It is well worth visiting and it lies immediately behind the hospital of the Merciful Brothers.

Museums: *Burgenländisches Landesmuseum* (Museumsgasse Eisenstadt-Unterberg): This museum comprises three houses from the former ghetto—including the Wertheimer house—and an extensive new building; the old courtyards are charming, and their glass roofs mean that they can now be used all year long. The approach is one of an all-encompassing 'Ganzheitsmuseum'; the cultural, artistic and natural history of the province are superbly presented: among other items, there is a magnificent mosaic floor from a Roman villa, and the 'Weinmuseum' (wine museum) where the myth that vines did not come to the province until the time of the Emperor Probus is dispelled. *Haydn museum* (21 Haydn Gasse): Rooms in memory of the composer, who owned the house from 1766–78, and also a Franz Liszt room and a Fanny Elssler room. Information from the Burgenländischer Verkehrsverband, Eisenstadt, Schloss Esterhäzy. Tel: 02682–3384.

Environs: Loretto, about 12 km. N. on the slopes of the Leithagebirge. Archaeological excavations have proved that the district was inhabited in the Neolithic; some significant finds, particularly the so-called Mondidole (moon idols), are today in the Landesmuseum. The parish and pilgrimage church is 17&18C and was originally associated with a Servite monastery. The tree-lined meadow with the baroque group of religious buildings on the one hand, and good farmsteads on the other, forms an unusually compact group. The church is a typical pilastered hall, while both towers of the W. façade are today covered with low spires instead of the baroque lanterns. Inside, the walls are brilliantly stuccoed up to the ceiling. The *Gnadenkapelle* stands in the cloister, and is a faithful copy of the 'casa santa' in the shrine of Loretto, Italy—legend has it that this was the house of the Holy Family in Nazareth; borne by angels to the E. coast

of Italy. It is a typical 'Loretto chapel', a tunnel-vaulted room divided by a wooden screen, with the 'black Madonna' behind it. **Kleinhöflein** (4 km. W.): A parish church with outstanding decorations, late 18C, altars and pulpit. The old organ is in the provincial museum.

Elbigenalp 6652
Tirol   p.286□C 8

Elbigenalp is the birthplace of the painter J.A. Koch and of Anton Falger (1791–1876), who was famous as an engraver, lithographer, painter, carver, collector and chronicler. In the 1st half of the 19C, he founded a school of drawing in Elbigenalp, and today the school of carving is still well regarded. The 'Falger-Museum', the local museum of Elbigenalp, is devoted to the artist.

Pfarrkirche zum hl. Nikolaus: This is the oldest parish in the whole Lechtal and was founded by St.Magnus in Füssen. In

Loretto (Eisenstadt)

1399 there was a chapel here which was later enlarged. The Gothic N. tower and the choir also date from that time. In 1664–74, Georg Falger built the baroque church, and it is this which forms the main part of the present church. A rectangular interior and a ceiling vault, which in 1776 was decorated with frescos and ornaments by P.Zeiller. The *Stations of the Cross* were painted by P.Zeiller, the father of the brothers Joh. Jakob and Franz Anton. The *Gothic font* on the right-hand side of the triumphal arch dates from 1411. The church was extensively restored in 1966–9.

Totenkapelle St.Martin (burial chapel): This two-storeyed chapel in the graveyard is Gothic. Four Gothic frescos with scenes from the life of Mary Magdalene are grouped around the pointed E. window. There is also a delicately painted Dance of Death by Anton Falger.

Also worth seeing: The small *chapel on the Mount of Olives,* built in 1766 and enlarged in 1832, stands high above the town. The hermit and schoolmaster Frater Lukas Liskodin, the teacher of J.A. Koch, formerly lived in it.

Engelhartszell 4090
Upper Austria   p.276☐N 3

Abbey church of Engelszell: 25 km. up the Danube from Passau, on the right bank, Wernhart von Prambach, Bishop of Passau, founded a 'cella anglica' in 1293 and settled it from the Cistercian monastery of Wilhering. A document states that the purpose of the cell was to provide a place of peace in a region particularly afflicted by dispute and quarrels (cf. Rannariedl and Vichtenstein); a hospice for travellers; a place of recreation for the cathedral canons, so that after 'tiring official duties' they could gain new powers in 'healthy air'. It was dissolved in 1786; since 1925 Trappists have been looking after the old abbey.

After a fire in 1699 it was rebuilt; consecrated in 1764. The façade surmounted

Engelhartszell, abbey and church

by a tower was probably modelled on the mother church of Wilhering; it is rectangular outside, and inside there is a long elliptical space with three niches on each side. The middle one is larger and makes the church appear to be centrally planned; the choir is only one bay long, with an oval apse. Grand overall effect produced by the excellent rococo decoration; elegant stucco confined to capitals and niche- and window-frames (all the frames are painted). Excellent frescos in the choir (concert of angels) and ante-choir (Coronation of the Virgin) by B.Altomonte. The nave vault was torn down in the 19C because it was damaged, and the frescos were destroyed in the process; in 1957 a new fresco of the 'Virgin with choirs of angels' was painted by Fritz Fröhlich. *Altars* and *pulpit* with elegant stucco figures, completely in white, by the Wessobrunn artist J.G. Übelherr. The four large angels by Fr. Anton Zauner, who worked with his uncle Jos. Deutschmann in Passau; the *choir stalls* are also from the Deutschmann workshop. The magnificent Chrismann organ is now in the 'Alter Dom' in Linz.

Environs: There are *three castles* near Engelhartszell. **Krempelstein,** or 'Schneiderschlössl'; 10 km. E. of Passau, right bank, built as a tower to collect tolls for the bishops. The great hall and the chapel were added later. In the 16C, Dr. Rupert von Moosheim was imprisoned for five years as a 'heretic'. The legend of the tailor who intended to hurl his dead goat into the Danube, but was himself heaved into the depths by the dead animal, was set here (poem by Gf. Platen). Romanesque inn. **Vichtenstein,** about 7 km. up the river from Engelhartszell. In the 12–14C, there were repeated feuds between the bishops for the possession of Vichtenstein. The castle, which is in good condition, was surrounded by the residential schloss, and no visits are possible. **Rannariedl,** a few km. down the river on the opposite bank.

In the 13C, the castle was the property of the Falkensteins, who made the region unsafe by robbery on the roads and piracy on the Danube. A stately house, no visiting.

Enns 4470
Upper Austria   p.276☐P 5

On the high left bank of the Enns, dominating the nearby confluence with the Danube, is the town of the same name. This important strategic site was probably the reason for a continuity of settlement matched by few if any Austrian towns, and for the town's eminent role in history. A small castle on the site of a prehistoric settlement is known from *c.* AD 50 and the construction of a limes fort for the II Italic legion (about 6,000 men), and also of a civilian settlement, is documented after 180. The name 'Lauriacum', which the Romans had taken over from the Celts, lives on in 'Lorch'. The civilian settlement was given municipal rights in 212. Diocletian's persecution of the Christians in 304

Enns, Stadtturm

resulted in the Roman veteran Florian being martyred by drowning in the Enns. A Christian basilica was built in 360. In the late Roman period, Lauriacum was the site of the Danube flotilla for Noricum. 476: A bishopric, mother church for the first conversion to Christianity of the Baiern who were occupying the region, works by St.Severin. In *c.* 900: 'Anesapurch' (Anisa = Enns river) one of the earliest castles in the area of present-day Austria, a base for campaigns against the eastern peoples. In *c.* 1100, the market was laid out in its present site by the Traungau counts, the 'steirische Otakare', the last of whom gained the dukedom in 1180. In 1186 a hereditary contract was concluded between Duke Leopold V of Babenberg and Duke Otakar von Steyr on the St.George mountain near Enns. In 1192: it was on the basis of the so-called 'St.Georgenberger Handfeste' that Styria and the Traungau were united with Austria. In 1212, municipal rights were conferred by Duke Leopold VI — exactly 1000 years after they were granted by Caracalla.

St.-Laurentius-Basilika (Enns-Lorch): This church is W. of the town centre, in the middle of the graveyard. Until 1553 it was the town parish church. Because of its unique significance as the 'corner-pillar of Baierisch ecclesiastical history' (Zibermayr), St.Laurentius became the seat of a titular Archbishop in 1968 and was granted the title of a 'Päpstliche Basilika' (papal basilica) in 1970. The present structure is a Gothic pillared basilica with a nave and two aisles, and has a W. tower at the end of the S. aisle (was a twin-towered façade planned?). The E. choir is closed at present, and outside there is a blind traceried gable. Inside, the choir is surprising: the floor suddenly stops between the end of the nave on the one hand and the E. end on the other, and the astonished eye sees in the depths what the *archaeologists'* spades have brought to light: three concentric semicircular walls from the earliest sacred sites, a *town temple,* an *early Christian basilica* and a *Carolingian pilgrimage church.* There are some more excavations and Roman consecration stones in the *crypt* below the nave. *Decorations:* Two Gothic tabernacles, remains of Gothic frescos, wooden reliefs (remains of a winged altar), Pietà of *c.* 1420, tombs. The massive organ and the 'Florian door' with eight bronze reliefs relating to the life and death of St. Florian (Peter Dimmel). Outside is the *ossuary, c.* 1507, with a baroque Eccehomo; Pilate in the garments of a Turkish grand vizier.

Pfarrkirche Maria Schnee/Former Minoritenkirche: This late-13C church was altered in the 15C. A hall church with two aisles and four bays. The N. aisle wall opens into three arches leading to the *Wallseer chapel* ('Wallseer', a famous Swabian family which came to Austria along with Rudolf of Habsburg). This chapel is an important piece of architecture. The two-aisled hall structure of the nave passes into a choir with three aisles. An elegant solution: there are four pillars in the choir, with the altar in the square, and an ambulatory around it. The same structure is to be found in the Wallfahrtskirche of Pöllauberg, but the Wallseer chapel is probably earlier. Fine broad decorated gable outside. S. of the church there is an atmospheric *cloister.*

Stadtturm: Standing in the middle of the large main square, the town tower was not built until 1565–8. Although it is both a watchtower and clock tower, it is also status symbol of the self-assured citizens. Enns enjoyed a heyday during the Reformation, and was also the seat of a Protestant 'Landschaftsschule' (countryside school) which was later moved to Linz. A four-storeyed tower built of ashlars with arched friezes, a gallery on the top storey, and a stately Renaissance helm roof.

Museum (19 Hauptplatz, former Rathaus): A local museum; it is of wider interest because of the outstanding Roman finds from Lauriacum.

Also worth seeing: Large parts of the *town fortifications,* with towers and remains of gates, survive. Many good Gothic *houses,* with Renaissance and baroque alterations. In addition to the usual features—projecting storeys, corner towers with round oriels, arcaded courtyards—the broad, rectangular central oriels, and small round turrets at the sides of the attic, are typical of the 'Ensser Haus'. *Old castle* (9 – 13 Wiener Str.): Late Gothic Schloss Ennsegg to the N., 16&17C.

Ernstbrunn 2115

Lower Austria   p.278□V 3

In 1045, Count Rapotto transferred the church and prebend to the bishopric of Passau. The powerful Maissaus were the owners in *c.* 1430, but were accused of high treason and forfeited their property. Then the rich Sinzendorf family purchased it in 1592 and Rudolf von Sinzendorf became the owner. This large complex has four courtyards. In the first one there is an early baroque fountain with the coat-of-arms of the Sinzendorfs. An imposing gatehouse (Sinzendorf coat-of-arms in massive escutcheon between lunettes) leads to the next courtyard. Ponderous Doric columns line the *Steinsaal. The Protestant chapel* is in the round tower. The oldest part of the castle, at the highest point, surrounds a triangular courtyard. 18C *Catholic chapel.* All this is overtopped by a fine *keep* with a double window and an unusual pointed roof with a ball which can be seen far and wide.

Also worth seeing: The *Pfarrkirche zum hl. Martin* was built in *c.* 1700, while most of the decorations are 18C. The plague column (1744) and the Rathaus (17C) are in the large square.

Enns, St. Laurentius, Ecce-homo on the ossuary

Feistritz an der Drau 9710

Kärnten   p.282☐N 11

An ancient settlement; the remains of an early Christian church were discovered inside the *late Roman fort*. The late Gothic *Pfarrkirche hl. Georg*, with its four-storeyed W. tower, has good baroque decoration (late-17C columned altar). Some good *wall paintings* from around 1440 (from the workshop of F. von Villach?) may be seen in the *chapel* (Maria am Bichl). Scenes from the Passion on the S. wall, while the N. wall has stories from Christ's childhood, the Adoration of the Magi, and themes from the life of the Virgin.

Feistritz an der Gail 9613

Kärnten   p.282☐N 11

Pfarrkirche St. Martin: The present church, not the first, was built in the late Gothic style of the 1st half of the 15C. The powerful W. tower is a reminder of the building's former defensive role. The aisle with its three bays has stellar vaults. Some poorly preserved wall paintings (*c.* 1490) may be the work of F. von Villach. The Enthroned Madonna and Child (*c.*

1440), on the neo-Gothic high altar (1885), is also interesting. The decoration of the *Filialkirche St. Magdalena* (daughter church; W. of Feistritz) dating from 1522 is mainly baroque.

Feldbach 8830

Steiermark   p.280☐U 10

This town was first mentioned in 1188, and was declared a market in 1265. The remains of a rectangular fortified area (built at the time of the Turkish invasions), which surrounded the parish church, can still be seen in the triangular Marktplatz. Closely packed houses with large storage cellars were built on the inside of this fortifying wall. A parapet walk ran through all the houses. One of the houses contains the *Heimatmuseum* with handicrafts from E. Styria, and also the *Fischereimuseum* (fishing museum).

Pfarrkirche St. Leonhard (Marktplatz): The nave of the old 14C church is now only a side room. The church was rebuilt by J.Pascher in 1900; and again after being severely damaged in World War 2, and a new tower was built next to it; in addition, a war memorial chapel was added.

The *Franziskanerkloster* (Franciscan monastery; 1642–53) is also in the Marktplatz, and the *Steinerne Metzen* (stone measure for corn) is in the Hauptplatz.

Feldkirch 6800
Vorarlberg p.286□A 9

In *c.* 909 Veldkircha was a Carolingian royal court. Hugo von Montfort founded the town in 1218. Chur held the rights of patronage until 1816 (with some interruptions). Friedrich von Toggenburg (d. 1436) built the *Schattenburg*, which was the official seat of the Austrian governors in the 17C. In 1540, W. Huber, an artist of the Danube school, painted six views of his home town, nestling in the countryside. Since the Middle Ages, the town of Feldkirch has consisted of three parts: the Neustadt (new town) lying below the Schattenburg and containing the Dom; the market quarter with the Johanniterkomturei (commandery of the knights of St. John) and the burial church of Hugo von Montfort; and the suburb on the river Ill. Only three gates still survive of the old town walls—the *Mühletor,* the *Wassertor* and the *Churertor* or *Salztor,* which was rebuilt in *c.* 1600 to form an outwork (next to it is the *Aufbahrungskapelle* (pledged in 1467 during a plague)—and three towers: the *Keckturm,* the *Pulverturm* and the *Katzenturm.*

Dom/Stadtpfarrkirche St. Nikolaus (town parish church): It was first consecrated by the Prince Bishop of Brixen in 1287. In 1478 Hans Sturn built the nave (inscription on pillar). The choir was completed in 1520. A simple front (the church adjoins the former bishop's palace) and a surprisingly beautiful interior. The two-aisled structure with its elegant central columns suffers from the artistic sins of the 19C and the present day. Modern stained-glass windows darken the interior; the Volksaltar by the chancel arch spoils the original intention of uniting the two aisles in the choir in front of the tabernacle. The Marienkapelle and some of the net vaulting in the choir are both 19C. The W.

Feistritz a. d. Drau, wall painting in the Kapelle Maria am Bichl

pillar breaches the gallery (which dates from 1448; the middle parapet is 19C). There is no cross on the triumphal arch. The high altar and Marienaltar date from the 19C. At the altar is a charming S-Madonna from the upper Rhine, with a delicate infant Christ (1430). The *pulpit* is a wrought-iron former tabernacle, which dates from *c.* 1509 and stands on a stone pedestal; it was converted into a pulpit in 1655. (Its original site was along the axis of pillars in the choir.) Above the wooden sounding-board there is rich Gothic tracery with a 'fading' finial. Ten coloured figures collecting manna. The *tombstone* of a Montfort count (1320) is on the Gospel side next to the high altar. There are two *side altars* by the chancel arch: on the right is a painting of the Lamentation by Huber (1521); the vernicle of St.Veronica is in the predella. On the left, the *Annenaltar* depicts the Holy Family in its predella. (The wings of the Annenaltar are on loan to the Bregenzer Landesmuseum.)

The **Schattenburg:** This is the largest and best-preserved castle in Vorarlberg. Oc-cupying a beautiful site on a peak above the town, it dominates the road to Chur. A fine inner courtyard. The palas houses the *Heimatmuseum*; some excellent exhibits.

Also worth seeing: Most of the small *churches* scattered about the town are shut up and not in very good condition. One ex-ample is the St.-Johannes-Kirche, the church of the knights of St.John. First mentioned in 1218, it was in the posses-sion of the order until 1610. Others include the *Frauenkirche* (by the Churer Tor), which was built in 1467–73 and restored in 1953, the *Hl.-Kreuz-Kapelle* (im Kehr), which was founded by Rudolf IV of Mont-fort in 1380 and has some good Gothic figures, and finally the *Peter-und-Pauls-Kirche* (consecrated in 1558; in the graveyard. Among the secular buildings, note the *Rathaus,* which was built in 1493. A fire in 1697 made some major alterations necessary, and the same happened in 1932–7. The main features are the *Ratssaal* (council hall) and the *Ratsstube* with its carved wooden ceilings and decorations dating from *c.* 1700. The *Jesuitengym-*

Schattenburg (Feldkirch)

Feldkirch, St. Nikolaus, altar panel

Roman dancer, St. Jakob d. Ä. See: Tiffen

nasium secondary school was built in 1649–1773. A Jesuit college was founded anew in 1856. This, the famous Stella Matutina, no longer exists today.

Environs: Some smaller towns which have been incorporated into Feldkirch still contain attractive old churches. A particularly captivating example is *St.Michael* in **Tisis** (consecrations in 1442 and 1459). Schloss Amberg in **Levis;** *Satteins,* Tosters and Altenstadt.

Feldkirchen 9560

Kärnten   p.282 □ O 11

This town dates back to Carolingian times but its appearance is now characterized by fine Biedermeier façades, a Renaissance fountain which stands in the Hauptplatz has been reworked in baroque style, and some secular buildings (Bamberger Amthof) have been altered in late Gothic style.

Pfarrkirche Maria Himmelfahrt: This late Romanesque pillared basilica (one nave, two aisles) with its E. choir tower (a parish church in 1285) was altered in the late Gothic style in the 14&15C. Two small chapels by the S. porch are from the previous building. Inside there are good paintings and carvings: the tower vault has some unusually early *frescos* from the 13C (Lamb of God, Majestas Domini, David and Prophet, Angels). The remains of a late-14C fresco (Journey of the Magi) are to be found on the S. wall of the choir. The carved late Gothic *winged altar* in the N. aisle is a splendid product of the Jüngere

Villacher workshop and dates from 1515. The late Gothic *crucifix* on the triumphal arch (1510) is by the St.Veit workshop. The *altars* and the 18C *pulpit* are also worth seeing, as are the *baroque bracketed figures* in the choir and N. wall of the nave. A *Roman fragment of Hercules* (2C AD) is incorporated into the S. wall of the choir. The two-storeyed *circular ossuary* is 13C.

Fernitz 8072
Steiermark   p.280 □ S/T 10

Pfarr- und Wallfahrtskirche Maria Trost: A chapel founded by the lords of Prankh in 1160 was converted into a church by Frederick the Fair in 1314. The remains of the tower N. of the choir also date from this period. The present late Gothic church is from 1506–14. The most striking peculiarity of this hall church, with its nave and two aisles, is the *ambulatory* arranged around a central pillar. The decoration of the pillars becomes better and better towards the choir. Late baroque decorations were added in the 18C, but these were unfortunately altered in neo-Gothic style in the 19C. Among the sculptures, note the *relief of St.Christopher* on the right, front tower pier (early-17C), to the *tympanum relief*, and in particular the *Madonna Enthroned* in the tower porch and the carved *Madonna and Child* (*c.* 1500) at the high altar. The self-portrait of the architect (with a fish in the coat-of-arms) above the organ gallery, and the statues in the main portal (*c.* 1740) by J.Schokotnigg, are also worth mentioning.

Fernstein 6465
Tirol   p.286 □ D 8

Schloss Sigmundsburg: This hunting lodge belonging to the Archduke Sigmund

von Tirol was built in about 1460 and is finely situated on a steep rock on an island in the Fernsee. The four round corner towers stand out from the ruins.

Also worth seeing: The 13C three-storeyed old *Klause* was once used to bar the road. Some rooms vaulted in Gothic style, and some partially restored chambers with coffered ceilings, survive today. On the second floor there is a hall with stuccoes and frescoed medallions (early-18C). Underneath the Klause is a *chapel* dating from 1478 with an altar from the mid 18C. The *Kapelle zu den 14 Nothelfern* in the Fernpass (18C) has an interesting altar from the 2nd half of the 17C with the 14 auxiliary saints.

Fiecht = Schwaz 6130
Tirol   p.284 □ G 8

Stiftskirche St.Josef: The Benedictine abbey is arranged around a courtyard and was built in 1706; it was restored in 1868 after a fire. The church, with its façade facing the courtyard, was installed in the N. wing of the monastery in 1740 – 4 by J.Singer from Schwaz. It has a surprisingly sumptuous interior, with delicate stuccoes by F.X. Feichtmayr, a Wessobrunn artist, and beautiful frescos by M.Günther of Augsburg, which have, however, been restored. A noteworthy feature in the E. choir apse is an Immaculata by Christoforo Benedetti; it dates from 1706 and originally crowned the Annasäule (column) in Innsbruck. The richly decorated pews and confessionals are by Franz Xaver Nissl, 1774–5.

Environs: A little to the N. of Fiecht, on a high rock, is the pilgrimage church of **St.Georgenberg,** which is documented prior to 1000 and was part of a Benedictine monastery. After suffering several fires, the monastery was moved to Fiecht in 1705. However, St. Georgenberg was renovated in *c.* 1735 and 1835. Among the very few items that survive from the Romanesque period are some stone slabs with animal reliefs.

Finkenstein 9584
Kärnten   p.282 □ O 11

Ruined castle: Steeped in history, it stands on a crag (Mallestiger Mittagskogel) 980 ft. above the Faakersee. The bishop of Bamberg was held prisoner in it in 1233, and Emperor Maximilian I is said to have hunted here as a child. In 1508 he presented the residence to the Dietrichsteins, and the castle remained in their possession until 1861, although it has been falling into disrepair since the 18C. Only one of the four fortified gateways still survives today. It bears the coat-of-arms of the Dietrichsteins. Apart from the defences, the castle had a late Gothic chapel, a banqueting hall, and living apartments. The

daughter church of *St. Margaretha* (after 1340), SW of the Faakersee, has some late-15C paintings outside on its S. wall.

Finstermünz = Nauders 6543
Tirol   p.286 □ C/D 10

Zollfeste Sigmundseck (customs-house): It was here, at the former border post, that Archduke Sigmund had a fortress built in 1471. This was enlarged in 1505 and 1513. Today, there remains a tower on the bridge over the river Inn, with late Gothic battlements and machicolations. On the bank, are the tower-like, five-storeyed Klause, which spans the roadway, and a rectangular tower which stands on a rocky projection and has a timber ceiling.

Flaurling 6403
Tirol   p.286 □ E 8

Pfarrkirche zur hl. Margareta: The

Fiecht, St. Josef, pews

parish church stands in the middle of this hillside village. A chapel on the site of the church is mentioned as early as 1326. Alterations and enlargements are known to have been made in 1508, 1574 and 1750. However, in 1836 the church was completely rebuilt and the former W. end was altered to form a choir and apse. Part of the nave of the Gothic church still survives in the present choir, and most of the tower still dates from the Middle Ages.

Risschlösschen: This 15C former hunting lodge of Archduke Sigmund of the Tyrol was used as a parsonage from the 16C onwards. A forecourt and the castle gate are from the old E. main building, and some vaults and passages in the house also survive from the Gothic period. The lower structure, which is the former domestic building, was enlarged in 1501 by Sigmund Ris, the parish priest, who was probably Sigmund's court chaplain. He ordered a *chapel* to be erected between the two buildings. This was decorated anew in baroque style in 1745 and was extensively changed in 1868. It contains a very

fine late Gothic *winged altar,* which depicts the Holy Family and scenes from the life of the Virgin.

Fliess 6521
Tirol   p.286☐D 9

Alte Pfarrkirche Maria Himmelfahrt: This Romanesque church, mentioned in 1300, was rebuilt in 1473 and 1493. The exterior, which is still Gothic, has a fine tower whose core, with its round-arched louvres, dates from the Romanesque, whereas the gable and the helm roof are Gothic. The wall painting of *St. Christopher* dates back to 1520, the *clock face with a coat-of-arms* on the 3rd storey is from 1547 and the *sundial* 1696. The inside of the present church is now baroque. The *font* dates from 1525.

Neue Pfarrkirche zur hl. Barbara: The new parish church was built by N.Schuler in 1794–1804 and is rococo and neoclassical.

Flaurling, winged altar in the chapel of the Risschlösschen

Bideneck ruins: This castle is first documented in the 14C. The new keep, the S. great hall, and probably the barbican to the E., were part of the castle at that time. The living apartments in the W. tower are the result of rebuilding carried out in the 1st half of the 16C. In the S. residence there is a large room with the Bideneck coats-of-arms, and next to this one with a coffered ceiling and Renaissance wood-panelled walls.

Forchtenstein 7212
Burgenland   p.280□V 7

In the Middle Ages, the province was dominated by two powerful dynasties: the Güssings in the S., and the Mattersdorfs in the N. (the name of Mattersdorf was changed to Mattersburg when it was elevated to the status of a town). When their castle was razed in 1294, the 'Mattersdorfs' built a new one on the 'Forchtenstein' and called themselves after it from that time on: their heraldic beast was the Burgenland eagle.

Burg Forchtenstein

Burg Forchtenstein: This castle occupies a commanding site on the slopes of the Rosaliengebirge; a ring of fortifications surrounds the castle, which is dominated by a massive keep. The latter is round, with a keel-like arris on its W., most vulnerable flank. A baroque onion-domed tower, forming what might be desribed as a counterpart to the keep, overlooks the walls in the E. The present structure is mainly 17C. The main gate, which is reached via a bridge crossing the deep moat, is decorated with figures of saints. A stone equestrian monument in the courtyard commemorates the occasion in 1687 when Leopold I elevated Paul Esterházy to the rank of prince. The best part of the Forchtenstein collections is in the *Zeughaus* (arsenal), which has the largest collection of its kind apart from the armouries in Vienna, Graz and Ambras and is a unique monument. Also note the 'Turkish booty' (including a Turkish State tent), gorgeous coaches, a portrait gallery of the Esterházy family, portraits of the princes' hounds; the cistern, 465 ft. deep, was dug by Turkish captives. Guided tours are conducted all

year long. The *Burgfestspiele* are held in summer, with plays by Grillparzer being performed. Information may be obtained from the Burgenländischer Fremden-verkehr-Verband, Eisenstadt (Tel.: 02682 –3384).

Environs: The **Rosalien-Kapelle** is some 6 km. SW of Forchtenstein. The Heuberg, which at 2,448 ft. is the highest point of the Rosalia (short form of Rosaliengebirge, the name of a mountain range), has been crowned by a small church dedicated to St.Rosalia since 1666. This Saint, much revered in Austria, was one of the helpers in times of plague. The early baroque decoration is both uniform and of high quality. The image of Rosalia at the high altar is typical of her: she is shown lying in a grotto, just as she appears on many plague columns. The pulpit in black and gold is especially magnificent. A hand reliquary was stolen by thieves. Some 6 km. NE of Forchtenstein is **Mattersburg.** In the Middle Ages this community, which until 1926 was known as Mattersdorf, was the seat of the family of the same name, one of the most powerful in the province. The stately church was part of a fortified structure of which some remains survive to the present day. The ghetto has disappeared, but a Jewish graveyard remains.

Frankenmarkt 4890
Upper Austria   p.276☐M 6

Pfarrkirche St.Nikolaus: The unique atmosphere inside this church stems from the successful blend of late Gothic and rococo. The double galleries in the W. sweep softly backwards and forwards, obliterating all sharp edges, and bring some harmonious movement into this small, two-aisled hall church. On the ceiling, from which the ribs have been removed, small frescos are surrounded by graceful stucco. This is not simply 'baroque Gothic', but is a happy creation in its own right which we owe to the empathy of an unknown 18C artist. The furnishings are mainly 18C, and the tombstone of Erasmus Kunigswieser dates from 1543.

Frankenburg, memorial to peasants' war

Environs: 3 km. E. of Frankenmarkt is **Vöcklamarkt** with the *Pfarrkirche Mariae Himmelfahrt*, a two-aisled hall structure from the mid 15C, with a baroque interior; the W. gallery on a net vault, with an excellent traceried parapet, survives; the W. tower has a double onion dome. **Schloss Walchen:** 2 km. S. of Vöcklamarkt. This dates from the 2nd half of the 16C, with a baroque Catholic Schlosskapelle; an old Protestant Renaissance chapel was rediscovered as a result of frescos which were revealed. There is an interesting collection of furniture from various periods; folklore exhibits. Visits by prior announcement: Schloss Walchen, 4870 Vöcklamarkt, Tel.: 07682-246. **Frankenburg:** 12 km. N. of Vöcklamarkt. This town owes its dismal fame to the gruesome trial which the Bavarian governor Count

Herberstorff held here on 14 May 1625: he ordered 36 peasants' leaders to play dice for their lives, and 17 of them were hanged. The linden tree which served as a gallows stands on a meadow between two wooded slopes; the evil doings of 1625 are relived in the festival plays ('Frankenburger Würfelspiel'), which are performed annually in peaceful surroundings. Gothic parish church.

Freistadt 4240
Upper Austria   p.276☐P/Q 3

Freistadt im Mühlviertel is one of the places to visit in Austria. Other towns have old quarters, fine groups of buildings, and individual monuments, but Freistadt has, beside all this, an almost intact ring of fortifications, with double walls, towers and gates. Despite its magic, Freistadt has not yet been totally commercialized, and it is still possible to stroll quietly through the old alleys without being pushed along by crowds of people.

Freistadt, Hauptplatz with St.Katharina

The town was founded as a military base and border fort on the ancient salt road to Bohemia and the rectangular main square and the grid of streets betray the fact that the layout of the town was planned. It was granted municipal rights in 1241. Do not fail to take a walk round the *walls.* The two gates with the long slits for the swing beams of the drawbridges are the main items of interest. The *Linzertor* with its steep wedge-shaped roof is the landmark of Freistadt. One fine house follows another, both in the Hauptplatz and in the alleys; there is a wealth of architectural details spanning the centuries (façade towers, gates, oriels, house signs, entrance halls, arcaded courtyards).

Pfarrkirche St.Katharina: The church occupies a key site, at the S. end of the Hauptplatz, and its tall, slender tower is a commanding feature. It owes its present appearance to J.M. Prunner, an artist from Linz, and is distinguished by its tall helm roof with a lantern and by the four elegant wrought-iron balconies. The church is a 13&14C Gothic basilica to which Mathes

*Freistadt, Linzertor with tall roof,
Freistadt's landmark*

*Freistadt, town wall with St. Katharina
in background*

Klayndl added the choir in 1483. The ceiling of the latter has ribs intersecting one another in broad sweeping circles to form star patterns, and is a masterpiece of the 'Schlingrippengewölbe' style of vaulting.

Schloss: This medieval building was later altered and used as a barracks. The sturdy keep, with its wedge-shaped roof, is ringed by a corbelled stone gallery and is an impressive feature. Splendid view.

Museum: This is in the Mühlviertler Heimathaus in the Schloss. Note the collection of Sandler verre églomisé pictures in the Schlosskapelle (14C). The keep is decorated with popular handicrafts.

Also worth seeing: *Liebfrauenkirche*, the former *Spitalkirche*, N. of the Böhmertor; an impressive interplay of light and shade in the choir and nave (mid-15C).

Environs: Some 6 km. E. of Freistadt is **St. Michael ob Oberrauchenödt** (district of Grünbach): an isolated 'Wegkirche' (roadside church) on a rocky crag which forms the watershed between the Feldaist (Black Sea) and the Maltsch (North Sea). Today's two-aisled building dates from the early 16C. A superb winged altar, particulary the three shrine figures (St.Michael, St.Nicholas, St.Stephen), by an unknown artist. The organ dates from 1668, and its bellows still has to be 'milked' (i.e. wound up with a strap). **Sandl** is the centre of the cottage glass painting industry; stained-glass windows with religious motifs were sent from Sandl all over the Austro-Hungarian Empire and even further afield; the best collection of these 'Sandlbilder' is in the Heimathaus in Freistadt. Some 6 km. W. is **Waldburg,** with the *Pfarrkirche Maria Magdalena.* This contains three late Gothic altars. High altar: three shrine figures (Virgin,

Sandl, églomisé painting (Freistadt) ▷

S. Genoveva.

Mary Magdalene and St.Catherine), inner wings carved with the legend of Mary Magdalene, and on the outside a painting of the Passion. The three Saints are of high quality. Carved choir stalls, 1522. Near Waldburg is the *viaduct of the horse-drawn railway* (see Linz), with two lines. Built in 1830, it stands on the footpath to St.Peter. St. Peter contains the former graveyard church of Freistadt, a fine late Gothic building. Next to this is the *Kalvarienberg-Kapelle*, built as a crypt chapel in 1370. **Schloss Waldenfels** near Reichenthal is some 11 km. NW. Arcaded courtyard, tilt-yard, dungeon. To make a visit, telephone 07214–223.

Friedberg 8240
Steiermark   p.280□U 8

The town's foundation was funded in 1194 with part of the enormous ransom paid for the release of Richard the Lionheart. The Babenberg Duke, Leopold V, who had taken Richard prisoner and was obliged to deliver him to the Emperor, Henry VI, received half of the sum. Friedberg is near the once troubled border with Hungary, and as the E. border was fortified the town was made responsible for protecting and controlling the Wechselpassstrasse which was built through it. The town coat-of-arms contains the red, white and red shield of its Babenberg founder.

The town's subsequent development is also of interest: to the W., above the town, two castles stood until the 19C. These survived the troubles of the Counter-Reformation and proved themselves to be true bastions of Protestantism in Styria. Only after the Vorau endowment bought the Schlosses in 1635 was it possible to break down the resistance and from that time on they were allowed to fall into disrepair. Finally, the town, which is situated on the Hochkogel (4,325 ft.), is of

interest for the way in which its medieval planners took the topography of its site into account. There are three parallel streets, two of which flank the Marktplatz, the former trading centre, for which a relatively flat site was selected. On the E. edge, overlooking the town, is the early-15C **Stadtpfarrkirche Jakobus Major**. The exterior is now baroque, but the Gothic interior, a wide, two-aisled hall structure, has survived. Note the late baroque virtuoso colouring of the Apotheosis of St. James (1735) on the *high altar*, painted by Carl Unterhuber.

Environs: 18C pilgrimage church of *Maria Hasel* in **Pinggau**. Good trompe l'oeil wall frescos by the Austrian painter J.C. Hackhofer.

Friedersbach 3533
Lower Austria   p.278□S 3

In 1136, Hartung von Rauheneck (his family castle is near Baden) received a royal gift, cleared the land in the Zwettler district, and built a castle on the Kamp: *Lichtenfels*. From 1200 onwards the Rauhenecks called themselves the Tursen (giants) of Lichtenfels. Today this castle on a hill by the Kampstausee (reservoir) is still in good condition. Romanesque in basic design, it has a rectangular keep, a chapel tower, and a 17C gateway. One hour away by road, the Tursen founded Friedersbach at the fork of two important highways. The Rauhenecks died out in 1335, and the feudal tenure reverted to their lord.

Pfarrkirche St. Laurentius: In 1149, Bishop Konrad von Passau, the brother of Duke Heinrich II, elevated a chapel dedicated to St.Lawrence to the status of a parish church. In 1408, an Öder from Öd enlarged the parish church into a net-vaulted Gothic basilica with a nave and two aisles; the present S. aisle being the old Romanesque chapel. The *stained-glass* windows also date from this period. The 'Annunciation of Friedersbach' is of particular interest for its iconography: the Virgin is chained to God the Father. Late stained-glass windows by 'Herr Kadolt 1497'. A gloria of angels of exquisite quality are seen making music. In the choir there is a Gothic *tabernacle* with a small wrought-iron door. *Mount of Olives:* An early-15C terracotta. In the graveyard there is a fine *ossuary* with battlements, a small semicircular apse and a tall conical roof. This fortified building exudes great charm.

Friesach 9360

Kärnten   p.282□P 10

Between 860 and 1803, Friesach, in the SE of the empire, was a fief of the archbishops of Salzburg. Work on the town fortifications between the castle on the Petersberg on the one hand and the Virgilienberg on the other was begun under Bishop Konrad I in the 1st third of the 12C. There then followed a period of cultural growth and vigorous building activity (foundation of church and monastery) until the town fire of 1289. Fires, sieges and plagues punctuated the eventful history of the town up until the 18C. Three fortified towers, and also large sections of the massive *town wall* and the moat, have survived the turbulence of the centuries.

Petersberg: This is oldest part of the town, and grew up around the lord's seat, which is mentioned as early as *c.* 860; a castle was then built from the late 11C to the mid 12C. It fell into disrepair from the late 18C onwards but the massive, square Romanesque *keep* (after 1100), six storeys tall (the chapel is on the fourth storey), still conveys a feeling of knightly splendour. It was in fact one of the most magnificent examples of its kind in the whole empire. The chapel floor still has some traces of the *paintings of 1210*; remains that give an idea of the artistic heights in which the Bishop's religious and secular claims to power found expression. The N. wall

Friesach, panorama

shows Christ's Entry into Jerusalem, the Last Supper is depicted on the S. wall, and the E. wall has images of Saints. The Virgin Mary on the Throne of Solomon (W. wall) is particularly significant because

Friesach, Stadtpfarrkirche 1 Stained-glass windows (Wise and Foolish Virgins) **2** Scenes from the life of Christ **3** Romanesque font **4** twin towers of W. front **5** Choir stalls **6** Sacristy **7** High altar

(according to Ginhardt) it is the oldest known depiction of the Throne of Solomon in Central European art.

Peterskirche (in the SE): This church, mentioned as early as 927, has a nave with an obliquely square shape and a flat ceiling, a square choir and an apse. There is a late Gothic altarpiece (South German, 1525). The stone Romanesque Madonna (*c.* 1200) from the altar is now elsewhere.

St. -Anna-Kapelle: The late Gothic chapel from *Geiersberg keep* (after 1130) contains some interesting retouched wall paintings from around 1400.

Stadtpfarrkirche St. Barthlmä: This 12C Romanesque pillared basilica, with a nave, two aisles and a twin-towered W. front (it is much altered today) has some good *stained-glass windows*. In the left choir window there is a group of ten panes, the 'Wise and Foolish Virgins' (1280). These panes were transferred here from the Dominican church in the 19C, and they relate a medieval parable: the five wise virgins are waiting for Christ, the heavenly bridegroom, and are holding up their oil lamps. The five foolish virgins, on the other hand, devoting themselves to earthly joys, are letting the lamps go out, and are falling under the spell of the realms of darkness. The right-hand choir window shows scenes from the life of Christ (1330). In addition to the mainly baroque decoration, the numerous *tombstones* and the 12C *Romanesque font* deserve attention.

Dominikanerkirche St. Nikolaus von Myra: This church of the mendicants' order is 245 ft. long and was consecrated in 1264. It lost some of its magnificent effect when groin vaults replaced the flat ceilings which are usual in Dominican churches in *c.* 1600. Nevertheless, the texture of the rubble wall and the severe, restrained plasticity of the structural elements are

Friesach, St. Barthlmä

Friesach, town fountain

somewhat reminiscent of the Florentine monks' churches of the same period. The famous early-14C sandstone *Friesacher Madonna* stands in the S. side choir. The Gothic S-curve of the figure, and the complex play of the folds, are counterbalanced by the firm core of the body. Further notable features are the *wooden crucifix* in the nave (1300), the late Gothic *Johannesaltar* (1510) in the choir, and the splendid red marble tombstone of Balth. Tannhauser (1516).

Heiligblutkirche/Seminarkirche: The church is situated in the so-called 'Sack' W. of the town and is a long single-aisled building with groin vaulting from the period after 1300. The four Romanesque columns of the W. gallery are from an earlier church. The baroque high altar dating (1681) has a carved Gothic *Virgin*

(1420). Next to this are a slightly later St. Bartholomew and St. Catherine.

Deutschordenskirche hl. Blasius The core of this church is also Romanesque. It was rebuilt in the 15C and the early 17C (articulated tunnel vault), and its main item of interest are its carvings. The *high altar* (1515) is from St. Veit (originally it was in the Hl.-Gestade-Kirche, Ossiach). Some other works, such as the 'Frankfurter Altar' (N. wall of choir) were also transferred here from foreign houses of the Teutonic Knights. Among the abundance of fine individual pieces, note two altar wings by F. Pacher (St. Peter, St. Paul, *c.* 1478).

Stadtbrunnen (town fountain): A Renaissance work dating from 1563. The marble basin is decorated with ancient reliefs of myths. The fountain is crowned by a small bronze group of four putti and Poseidon, possibly by Nuremburg bronze founders (*c.* 1520).

Museums: The *Heimatmuseum* in the Fürstenhofgasse contains late Gothic paintings and carvings, and also the *St. Romanus fresco* from the Petersberg. Roman and early medieval finds are among the exhibits in the *Steinsammlung* (stone collection) in the N. Stadtpfarrkirche.

Frondsberg 8191
Steiermark p.280□T 8

Schloss Frondsberg: Gothic elements survive in the W. and N. wings of its medieval castle built by the Feistritzs in the 12C. Franz von Neuhaus altered the castle in Renaissance style in 1577–1600, and from that time on the substance of the schloss has remained almost unscathed although the building has changed hands several times. Consequently it is a unique example of a Styrian Renaissance seat. The triangular arcaded courtyard of the schloss is framed by the two-storeyed building. In addition to the *stellar-vaulted hall* and the *dining hall,* the *Rittersaal* (knights' hall) is of particular interest: inlaid wooden doors, ornamented window frames, a stove with coloured tiles depicting plants, a coffered ceiling, and painted wall coverings.

Fügen 6263
Tirol p.284□H 8

Pfarrkirche Mariae Himmelfahrt: This church, which is probably Carolingian, is first mentioned in documents in 1136. The present structure dates fom the 14&15C. The single-aisled choir with its articulated tunnel vault has some interesting *remains of frescos* on the right of the choir, on the wall of the triumphal arch, and in the W. organ bay (late-14C). Late Gothic half-length reliefs of the twelve Apostles have been incorporated into the modern *high altar.* The *side altars* are also modern; at the left-hand one there is a figure of the Virgin dating from the 1st half of the 15C, and there is a late Gothic Lamentation on the right-hand side altar. The *wooden carvings* on the walls of the aisle, and the *Stations of the Cross* by J.G. Grasmayr, are baroque. In 1769, Mozart played on the *organ,* which came from the ladies' foundation in Hall. Under the sanctuary is a *Gothic crypt,* and to the N. is the late Gothic *Michaelskapelle* with a fine altarpiece of St.Michael (1623), to which Gothic altar wings were added. Note the *wall fresco* of the Magi (1476).

Kapelle am Marienberg: This octagonal building with a neo-Gothic tower and fine interior dates from the 18C.

Wallfahrtskirche zum hl. Pankraz: This beautifully situated late-15C single-aisled church has rich rib and stellar

Fügen, Pfarrkirche

vaulting. There are three late Gothic saints at the left side altar, and at the right altar there is a carved 17C group of St.Barbara by Franz X. Nissl.

Schloss Fügen: This schloss was built by Ferdinand Count Fueger in 1695–1702. The broad *round-arched portal* of red marble is a notable feature, as is the *Schlosskapelle* with an altar dating from 1681.

Fulpmes 6166
Tirol   p.286☐F 9

Fulpmes has long been a centre for wrought iron and an imposing house belonging to the co-operative and decorated with baroque frescos stands in the main square outside the church.

Pfarrkirche zum hl. Vitus: This is documented as early as 1368. The present church is by Franz de Paula Penz (1747). The tall, narrow nave is traversed by a narrow transept. Variety is added by the delicate rococo stucco which covers the entire vault. The *frescos* on the ceiling are by J.G. Bergmüller, as is the façade fresco (1747). On the *high altar* there is a mid-18C painting of the Holy Trinity by J.G. Grasmayr; it includes St.Vitus and others of the 14 Auxiliary Saints.

Fürstenfeld 8280
Steiermark   p.280☐U 9

Fürstenfeld was founded by Leopold VI in *c.* 1215, and the older settlement of Altenmarkt on the left bank of the Feistritz transferred its market privileges to the new town which, with its better site, was intended to secure the border of the Empire. By 1220, the knights of the order of St.

John of Jerusalem had enlarged the church, the commandery, and the *castle.* (This is the oldest establishment of the knights of St.John in Austria.) Traces of the medieval town, with the fan-shaped layout of its streets, are still apparent in the E. quarter, while the NW section displays all the features of a typical Styrian plan: a main square enclosed by parallel streets. A new *ring of fortifications* was built in the 16C to counter the Turkish threat, and the *Schloss- und Mühlenbastei*, the *Ungarn-bastei*, and the *roadside ditch* still survive, as does the *Grazer Tor.* Of the medieval towers, only the *Swartzturm* still stands.

Stadtpfarrkirche Joh. d. Täufer: Originally built by the knights of St.John, it took its present form when it was altered in 1773–9; the buttresses of the choir chapel survive from the earlier Gothic church. The interior was reworked in 1878–9. Both the Pietà (1420) and the statue of the Virgin (1660) were taken from the Ausgustinerkirche. The *high altar* has a work by J.A. Mölk. The schloss of the order of the knights of St. John is the former commandery and, together with the parsonage (built in 1730), it once formed a single complex which was one of the town's main features. It was largely destroyed in 1945 and only partially rebuilt. The former castle was destroyed several times and finally a tobacco factory was established in it.

Augustiner-Eremiten-Kirche und Kloster: The monastery founded by Duke Rudolf VI in 1362 was dissolved in 1811. The church (which has been closed since 1952 because of its dilapidated state) is single-aisled, with a Gothic choir and outside wall. The interior was partly altered in baroque style in 1760. Only a small section of the monastery survives. Next to it is the main square with the *old Rathaus* and the *Mariensäule* (column of the Virgin; 1664).

G

Gaaden 2531
Lower Austria   p.278□V 5

Gaaden was a very popular summer resort
in the Biedermeier period. It was here that
Ferdinand Raimund (to whom there is a
memorial) wrote his 'Spendthrift' in 1883;
and F.G.Waldmüller painted his landscapes
in the countryside around here. The lords
of Gaaden resided in a *castle*, but in 1249

Gaming, Marienthron charterhouse

they divided up their property and built
themselves a new, lower *moated castle*. Both
castles were destroyed by the Hungarians.
A later owner gained possession of Gaaden
after it had been pledged to him by the
monastery at Heiligenkreuz. After 1550,
a Lutheran preacher from Strassburg
served as pastor here. Later, the monastery
at Heiligenkreuz regained control of
Gaaden, whereupon its abbot razed the
moated castle and laid out a fish pond, after
which he built the *upper castle*. In 1683 the
Turks descended on the town, beheading
300 people. In 1792 the pastor converted
the castle into a *parsonage*. The Kalkbauer
family in Gaaden were of some importance. Having become notably rich and
status-conscious, they demanded the privilege of being allowed to attend church worship separately. This finally led to a revolt
of the small farmers.

Gaming 3292
Lower Austria   p.278□R 6

Caroline Pichler wrote in her memoirs in
1809 in the following terms: 'And so we
came to Gaming, a Carthusian monastery,
now destroyed, situated in a narrow,
enclosed, silent and melancholy valley,
which was founded by Albrecht the Lame

or Wise of Austria in the 14C in consequence of a vow which he had taken to free his unfortunate brother Friedrich (the Fair) from his imprisonment in Trausnitz (after the battle of Múhldorf against Ludwig of Bavaria)'. Albrecht II took his vow to found Gaming in 1322.

Monastery The charterhouse of *Marienthron* was founded in 1330 and the church itself consecrated in 1342. It is likely that most of the monastery was by then already built. It comprised 20 monks' cells, making it the biggest Carthusian foundation in the German province of that order. The Reformation and, later, the Turkish invasions brought set-backs. In the 17C the monastery began to prosper once more under its then prior, Hilarion Danichius, and in 1625 the gate-tower was erected. In the 18C, both church and library were altered in baroque style. After Josef II's abolition of the monasteries in 1782, it was allowed to fall into decay. In 1915 it was bought by the abbey at Melk. The church was restored in 1967. The large *library* is especially worth seeing. It is a domed room, with barrel-vaulted wings, which is decorated with some outstanding frescos by Wenzel Lorenz Reiner. To the S. of the monastery's two cloisters is the rectangular *ambitus*, with the monks' cells (built in the 14C) set off it, and the cemetery chapel (built in 1451 – 7), now converted into residential quarters.

Klosterkirche Mariae Himmelfahrt: This is a single-aisled Gothic structure, built 1332–42, which incorporates other elements. It has a richly decorated hexagonal ridge turret. On both sides of the choir stalls are Gothic chapels (originally the sacristy and chapterhouse). The portal (flanked by statues of the founders) is of red marble and dates from 1631. The interior was altered in baroque style (with the ceiling being painted) in 1756. The church was unsatisfactorily restored in 1967.

Gars am Kamp 3571
Lower Austria   p.278□T 3

The area around Gars has been settled since prehistoric times. As early as the Neolithic, a fortified mound stood here, 400 ft. above the cultivated land. When

Gaming, former Kartäuserkloster 1 Monastery church **2** Graveyard chapel **3** Carthusian cells **4** Library courtyard **5** Library **6** Prior's house **7** Gatehouse tower **8** Garden house

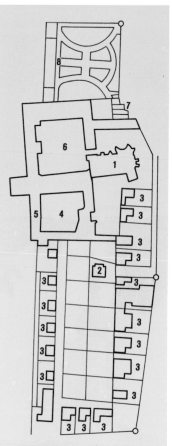

this region was captured by the Babenbergs, the Slavs were driven out and this well-fortified stronghold was destroyed. To replace it, the *castle* was then erected on the hill.

Gars castle: This strongly fortified castle, which was later extended on to three terraces, was considerably altered in the 18C. Margrave Leopold II, who moved his residence from Melk to Gars, was buried, after his death in 1059, in the castle's *Pankratiuskapelle* (consecrated in 1100). His son, Leopold III, was born in Gars, but he too moved his residence, this time to Klosterneuburg, and the castle was enfeoffed to the Kuenrings, Maissaus, and the Protestant Teufels, among others, until in 1622 it finally passed into private hands. 41 lords of the manor are mentioned by the chronicle. 170 years ago, this proud seat of princes fell victim to the new tax on roofs and buildings. Work has been going on in recent years to protect the ruins. The oldest parts comprise the 11C Hochburg, the chapel, hall, and keep. Apart from these, there are some later ad-

Geras, Stiftskirche

ditions, including, to the E., a Renaissance section 300 ft. long which dominates the ruin, the ruin which is this town's landmark.

Pfarrkirche St. Gertrud (Thunau): The parish church of St. Gertrude of Nivelles stands 80 ft. beneath the castle. This late Romanesque basilica, with a nave and two aisles, was begun before 1250 and built in six stages, so that it represents every style from Romanesque to baroque. Its finest features are the *window* of 1330, the Romanesque *stone font*, the *Pietà* of 1420, 16 *frescos*, and 17 *tombs*. The church was renovated in 1975 both inside and out.

Pfarrkirche hll. Simon und Judas Thaddaeus (on the Hauptplatz in Gars): There is a reference to a chapel of St. Simon here as early as 1282. The church which now stands on this site is a simple 17C baroque building.

Geras 2093
Lower Austria   p.278☐T 2

Geras was endowed by the Count of Pernegg as part of a double foundation which established a convent, for canonesses, in Pernegg, and this monastery, for canons, in Geras. It was built about 1153. The foundation was confirmed in 1240 by Frederick II. Later in the 13C, the monastery was destroyed, and then rebuilt. In 1619–20, after it had already been plundered several times, it was at last completely destroyed by Bohemian troops led by Count Schlick.

Monastery: The monastery was rebuilt in 1736–40 by J. Munggenau, who produced a considerable work of art. There are three wings grouped around the *courtyard* (dedicated to the Virgin Mary), which contains a *column*, similarly dedicated, dating from 1653. The main portal has a beautiful vault, which shows an allegorical representation of the three divine virtues. To the left is the lord of the manor's record office, and to the right, behind a magnificent wrought-iron grille, is the *staircase* on which stand putti and vases. Above the porch is the *marble room*, which was the summer refectory, where there is a fresco by P.Troger (the miracle of the loaves and fishes, 1738). The *library* was built in 1803 and contains a fresco by Franz Winterhalder.

Pfarr- and former Stiftskirche Mariae Geburt: This is built on to the wings of the monastery. It has a nave and two aisles, and a tower, which was built in 1667 and has a baroque cupola. Its mannerist *portal* (1665) is flanked by Sts. Norbert (who founded the order) and Augustine. Inside the church, the Romanesque arcades of pillars have been preserved from the original basilica. The church was rebuilt in baroque style following a fire in 1730. The frescos on the ceiling, a series of paintings devoted to the Virgin Mary, are by

Geras, Stiftskirche

Franz Zoller (a pupil of Troger). Note the high altar (1730), which has a 16C statue of the Virgin; and the organ, choir stalls, and pulpit; which date from the middle of the 18C. The confessionals and side altars are 17C.

Gerlamoos 9754 Steinfeld
Kärnten   p.282☐M 10

Filialkirche St.Georg: This church was altered in the 16C but still strongly betrays its Romanesque origins. The flat-roofed nave, the dome above the choir, and notably the strong triumphal arch, all give a Romanesque impression. The church is famous for the *cycle of frescos* on the N. wall of the nave. These were painted in 1470 –80 by Thomas von Villach and depict a series of biblical scenes, arranged one on top of another. At the top is the legend of St.George, and in the middle and at the bottom are scenes giving a religious interpretation of history. Note the *high altar* (c. 1700) and the *two side-altars* (early-18C).

Globasnitz 9142
Kärnten   p.282☐Q 11

Pfarrkirche Mariae Himmelfahrt: Originally a late Romanesque church, it was gradually altered over the years, up till the early 16C. The twisting ribs of the late Gothic vault probably date from around 1510. The nave originally had four bays and was not lengthened until 1946. At the end of the choir the *remains of frescos* were discovered which date from a period ranging from the early 14C until the late 15C. The baroque altars and the figures and painting which decorate them are all mid-18C. It is also worth viewing the *ossuary* and the late Roman ornamented stela which is incorporated in its wall. There are some late Gothic *wall paintings* inside which are dedicated to the Archangels Gabriel and Michael, whose protective mission indicates the defensive nature of this kind of round tower.

Gmünd 9853

Kärnten   p.282□N 10

Gmünd first appeared in the Romanesque period as a fortress. During the 13–15C, this was built up and expanded by the archbishops of Salzburg until it became a well-defended city with a circular wall and bastions (the wall and its gates remain intact). The Turks tried but failed to take the town in 1478.

Altes Schloss: This was destroyed by fire in 1886. The high tower is Romanesque in origin. In the 16&17C, the structure was converted into a schloss incorporating Renaissance features in the W. part. Today, a *museum of local history*, which includes a *gallery*, is housed here.

Neue Schloss and town: The new schloss was built by A.Riebeler in 1651–4 in the SE. part of the town. Its style is modelled on those of Salzburg. A tour of the town throws some light on the various stages of its evolution from a functional architecture to one of ornament—one can even see this change of style in the city gates, whose functional appearance was later beautified with baroque gables and helm roofs! The stately *houses* on the main square are a particularly good example of the drive of the late Gothic and Renaissance periods to decorate and dignify.

Stadtpfarrkirche Maria Himmelfahrt: The late Gothic nave and two aisles (vaulted in 1499) lead up to a beautiful, rib-vaulted choir (1339) of two bays. The N.

Gmünd, ruins of the **Altes Schloss 1** Main entrance **2** S. entrance **3** Rittersaal with stone fireplace and tall windows in the round W. tower **4** Courtyard **5** Courtyard **6** Keep

Gmünd, town gate on the Malta

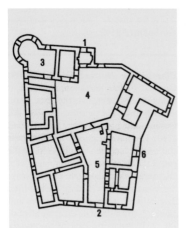

tower and the S. chapel are also Gothic. The *Raitenau chapel* (on the E. side; it contains a statue of Christ executed by Hans Gasser in 1858) and the sacristy are baroque. The baroque *high altar* is outstanding. J.Zanussi's painting of the Assumption (1722) occupies its central part. The life-sized representations of Sts. Peter and Paul at the side of the altar, and the six figures on consoles on the choir walls (mid-18C), are also fine pieces. The two *side altars* and the *pulpit* date are late-18C. The Gothic wall paintings in the *ossuary* (to the NE. of the church) are of some importance.

Gmunden 4810
Upper Austria   p.276☐N 6

Gmunden used to be the property of the Habsburgs and the administrative capital of the 'Kammergut'. For a number of centuries this latter term only referred to the region around the Hallstätter See and the Traunsee, including the two salt mining towns of Hallstatt and Bad Ischl, and

Gmunden, where the 'Salzamt' was located. This area, which was the 'royal jewel of salt production', formed a separate region almost cut off from the outside world, to enter which, even in the 19C, one required a special pass issued by the Salzamt! A knowledge of Austrian history explains how the 'Kammergut' developed on the basis of its own laws and retained its own customs and conventions. The extension of the term 'Salzkammergut' to cover the whole lake district is a result of the advent of tourism.

Pfarrkirche Jungfrau Maria und Erscheinung des Herrn: The second title of the church is unusual in German, for it is dedicated to the 'Erscheinung des Herrn', or 'manifestation (=epiphany) of Our Lord', whereas the more usual term for a church of the Epiphany is 'Dreikonigskirche', signifying its dedication to the three magi (to whom Our Lord was first manifested). The three magi from the East do indeed adorn the high altar (and the feast is on 6 January). The painting of the Adoration of the Magi, one of

Schloss Ort (Gmunden)

T.Schwanthaler's best works, is both magnificent and dramatic. The lively figure of the Christ-child and the expressive face of Kaspar, the black king, are particularly fine. The two side figures, representing Elizabeth and Zacharias, were painted by Michael Zürn the younger.

Rathaus: This is a Renaissance building, later adapted to the Baroque style, on the Seelandeplatz.The tower contains an arcade with chiming bells, which is Gmunden's landmark. (The bells are ceramic rather than metal!)

The town: There are many houses worthy of note which date from the late Gothic and Renaissance periods, some of them with a corner tower, arcaded courtyard, and projecting first floor. The fronts on the Marktplatz, Rathausplatz, and Rinnholzplatz are especially remarkable.

Museum: This is housed in the former 'Kammerhof', which is a commanding building, with a basically Gothic structure but a Renaissance appearance. It contains ceramics, exhibits connected with the salt industry, cribs, and mementoes of Brahms and Hebbel.

Local custom: On the day before the feast of the Epiphany (i.e. on 5 January) the 'three magi' arrive by boat and process solemnly, to musical accompaniment, to 'their' church.

Environs: Schloss Ort (S. edge of the town): The most famous owners of Ort castle and estate were Count Adam von Herberstoff and Archduke Johann Salvator of Tuscany. The latter renounced his rank and title after his break with the royal family and took to designating himself 'Johann von Ort' after the name of his estate. *Lake Schloss*: This is originally a 12C structure, which is situated on a small rocky island in the lake and connected with

the land by a 400 ft. wooden bridge. It now has an extensive exterior, thanks to the restoration which took place after it had been burned down when the peasants stormed it in 1626. It has a triangular arcaded courtyard which is full of atmosphere, where *concerts* are held in summer. *Schloss chapel*: This is Gothic and dates from the reign of Josef II. It contains some excellent early Baroque frescos which have been recently rediscovered, and there is a good late Gothic Madonna. *Land Schloss*: This is more recent, having been built by Count Herberstorff at the same time as his reconstruction of the lake Schloss. It is a square structure which incorporates four corner towers with onion domes. The courtyard contains a beautiful wrought-iron fountain which was made in 1777. 2 km. S., on the lake, is **Altmünster**, which contains the *Pfarrkirche St. Benedikt*. The latter's name and unusual choice of patron saint point to the existence of a Benedictine abbey during the Carolingian period, which, however, did not survive for long. A stone carved in relief indicates a period of Roman settlement. The body of the church is late Gothic. Its furnishings are noteworthy and include a Gothic Coronation of the Virgin, sculptures by Michael Zürn the younger, an altarpiece by J. von Sandrart, and, above all, the *All Saints' Altar*. This is a stone carving strongly reminiscent of the one in Mauer bei Melk; both are outstanding works of art executed during the period of transition from the Middle Ages to the Renaissance. The choir contains the *tomb* and effigy of the much hated Count Herberstorff (see Frankenburg), who was killed by a peasant with an axe at the age of 46. His effigy was sometimes even covered over during the reading of Mass. It was in Altmünster that the *second SOS children's village* in Austria, and also in the world, was established (the first one was in Imst in the Tirol). 16 km. E. of Gmunden is **Scharnstein**, which contains the *Schloss Neu-Scharnstein*. This had fallen completely into decay but has now been restored by its present owner. It is a stately Renaissance Landschloss which boasts many fine details (notably the wooden ceilings!) The museum of criminal law of Upper Austria is also in Scharnstein. To view its special exhibitions ring 07615 550 or 385. **Grünau im Almtal,** which is 7 km. S. of Scharnstein and 23 km. from Gmunden, contains the *Pfarrkirche Jak. d. Ä.* Its magnificent furnishings are explained by its having belonged (indeed it still belongs) to the abbey at Kremsmünster. In fact, the high altarpiece here was until 1712 the main altarpiece of the abbey church at Kremsmünster! The altar itself was made from late Gothic constituent parts by a Bavarian artist called Hans Degler in Weilheim in Upper Bavaria in 1616–18. The altarpiece is early baroque and very impressive. The main group in the upper tier, showing Christ as the Redeemer of the World with Sts. Benedict and Agapitus, was made by Johann Peysser of Nürnberg at the beginning of the 16C. There is some beautiful sculpture dating from 1690 on the 'Christmas altar' by Michael Zürn the younger.

Gneixendorf = Krems 3500
Lower Austria   p.278□T 4

Gutshof Gneixendorf: This lies a little off the road from Krems to Langenlois, surrounded by old buildings. It is itself a lovely building, with simple furnishings which date from the early 19C. It was bought in 1820 from a monastery by Johann van Beethoven, brother of the composer Ludwig, who said of Johann's marriage that it 'proved his immorality and folly' and referred to him variously as 'brother Cain' and 'my dearest brother'. The composer was provided with a reason to accept an invitation from his brother to visit Gneixendorf in 1826 after his ne'er-do-well nephew, Karl, had attempted suicide. His behaviour during his stay there was highly eccentric: he would rush across the fields singing loudly and beating the air; on one occasion he caused a team of oxen to shy away from him. It was here that he completed one of the Late Quartets, opus 130. However, fear of the impending winter made him flee in haste to Vienna, making the journey on a small uncovered cart, sleeping overnight in a cold guesthouse, and finally arriving home with inflammation of the lungs and a high fever. He succumbed to the consequences of this fatal journey on 16 March 1827.

Gobelsburg 3551
Lower Austria   p.278□T 4

Schloss: One branch of the Kuenring family is called Gobelsburg. In the 14&15C, the schloss was owned by the Maissaus. After many disputes with neighbours, their ownership passed to Achaz von Hohefeld, who adapted the castle, originally built in the 16C, to the baroque style. In 1746, the schloss was finally acquired by Zwettl. The *Schloss chapel* has a stucco ceiling and contains a Madonna by Martin Johann Schmidt of Krems. The altarpiece shows St.Bernard and dates from 1746. There is also a *Schloss museum*.

Pfarrkirche Mariae Geburt: The building was originally late Gothic and was altered in baroque style in the 18C. It has a beautiful canopied altar with figures by Schletterer. In the choir there is a way down into the crypt. On the outside of the choir there are two *stone carvings*, one representing the three Magi, the other Adam and Eve in front of an intriguingly stylised tree (this dates from around 1200). *Frescos:* There is a good depiction of the Crucifixion above the S. entrance.

Goldegg, Pongau 5622

Salzburg   p.284□L 8

Until the 16C, the road linking the Pongau and Pinzgau districts passed over the terrace at Goldegg, which covers the foundations of an imperial Roman manor. Goldegg was the seat of the most important family of government officials in the hill country, who were called 'von Pongau'. After they died out, it belonged to the archbishop, and later, in 1527, was let to Christoph Graf von Schernberg (see Radstadt).

Pfarrkirche hl. Georg: Named in a document dating from 1339. The vault is late Gothic and was built in 1516. A historicist restoration was carried out in 1884. The high altar is neoclassical and was executed by W.Hagenauer in 1790 (the painting is by N.Streicher).

Schloss (visitors must be accompanied by the guide): This was the medieval castle of the lords of Goldegg (Pongau). It was demolished in 1322 but rebuilt in the following year. There is a keep in front of the S. and the E. sides. On the second floor of the N. section is the *Rittersaal*, which was decorated with paintings (tempera or fresco painting done on canvas and wood) in 1536, when the castle was owned by Christoph Graf (Graf being his surname) von Schernberg. These wall paintings, which have been preserved almost intact, depict Christian themes as well as some historical scenes (some derived from the woodcuts of Hans Burgkmair), while also conveying the idea of empire. They represent a masterpiece of the humanist imagination. One of the rooms to which visitors are admitted contains *N.Wattek's private collection of folklore.*

Göllersdorf 2013

Lower Austria   p.278□U 4

The margraves of Brandenburg were the feudal lords of Göllersdorf continuously from 1415 until 1779. Their feudal tenants

Goldegg, fresco in the schloss

were the Maissau and Puchheim families. In 1710, Göllersdorf was purchased by the Imperial Vice-chancellor, Freidrich Karl, Count of Schönborn (1674–1746), who was from 1729 the prince-bishop of Bamberg and Würzburg. It was he who initiated the great building projects of the 18C here.

Schloss Schönborn: In 1712, Friedrich Karl, Count of Schönborn, commissioned L. von Hildebrandt to convert and expand the Puchheims' Mühlburg manor-house, which was henceforth to be the 'Schloss Schönborn'. The castle was built in the shape of a horse-shoe, two-storeyed and splendidly gabled, and when, in 1714, the orangery (containing wall decorations) was erected opposite it, the entire commission was completed. Hildebrandt's conception depended on the effects of perspective, so the loss of the carefully laid-out garden in between the schloss and the orangery has been particularly painful. The whole effect of the schloss is nonetheless convincing, thanks to its unique harmony with its natural setting. The side of the castle facing the garden has a peaceful feel; it projects forward in the centre, and the gable catches the eye with the Schönborn coat-of-arms. In the section of the castle which contains the portal there is a very original *canopied chapel of St. Nepomuk* (1733).

Pfarrkirche St. Martin: The original Gothic structure (dating from 1446–58) was altered in baroque style in 1741 by L. von Hildebrandt, who turned it into his finest country church. The massive structure has a cylindrical vault, lavish gable ornamentation, and an octagonal Gothic tower surmounted by a baroque dome. Hildebrandt left two Gothic chapels in place to serve as the transept of his new church, on to which he built a nave. The church was not fully furnished until 1794.

Also worth seeing: The *Loretokirche*, which was built in 1725 as a family tomb

for the Counts Schönborn, was also designed by Hildebrandt. It was he, too, who designed the *Mariensäule* on the Marktplatz (it is a monument to the plague and dates from 1731).

Golling an der Salzach 5440
Salzburg   p.284☐M 7

Pfarrkirche zu den hll. Johannes d.T. und Johannes Ev.: This church has a Gothic nave and aisles altered in baroque style.

Burg: The castle, which is mainly medieval, houses a small *Heimatmuseum*.

Environs: Scheffau, a small settlement at the entrance to the Lammertal which contains the disproportionately large *church of St. Ulrich*, was once the object of an odd pilgrimage which can be seen depicted in the ornamentation of the Gothic door mounting and in the late Gothic stained-glass window (by Saumrossen). The massive early baroque *high altar*, executed in 1629 by the sculptor H.Waldburger, comes from the monastery church in Nonnberg, which received in exchange Scheffau's original late Gothic high altar. However, the figure of St. Ulrich (with a book and a fish), which had formed part of the original altar, and which has been attributed to Lienhart Astl, remained in Scheffau. On the wall of the left-hand aisle there is an expressive *Crucifix* dating from around 1420. There is a fine collection of verres églomisés in the organ loft. **Torren:** The late Gothic *church of St. Nikolaus* occupies a picturesque position on a rock. The triumphal cross, incorporating figures of the Virgin Mary and St.John, is as old as the church itself. The countryside around Golling incorporates a number of **natural landmarks** which deserve a visit, notably the *Lueg Pass*, which was fought over during the Napoleonic Wars and includes the Salzachöfen, the Golling waterfall, known as the *Schwarzbachfall* (or 'waterfall of the black stream'), which has been depicted by many Romantic painters, and the *Lammeröfen*.

Göttweig = Furth bei Göttweig 3511

Lower Austria   p.278☐T 4

Benedictine Abbey: If the last part of J. von Hildebrandt's design (which he produced in 1722) had been carried out, then one of the greatest Baroque castle-monasteries in Europe would now stand here at the E. end of the Wachau.

It was in 1083 (during the investiture struggle) that Bishop Altmann of Passau founded the Augustinian monastery of Göttweig. The Bishop was unshakeable in his support for Pope Gregory VII and the Dowager Empress Agnes. His open call for the deposition of the Emperor Henry IV forced him to flee Passau. The Pope then appointed him as Papal legate to the part of his diocese which fell in the Ostmark. During his time there, he gained important influence over the Margrave Leopold until the latter's defeat in the battle of Mailberg.

In 1094, the monastery was taken over by Benedictine monks from St.Blasien in the Black Forest who brought a period of prosperity during which new foundations were established (at Garsten in 1107 and Seitenstetten in 1116). From about 1200, after the nunnery at Kleinwien had moved here, until 1577, Göttweig comprised both monastery and convent. In 1383 the Abbots won the privilege of wearing pontificals, and in 1401 the abbey was accorded exemption. The 16C saw a great decline in the abbey's fortunes, brought about by the Reformation, the Turkish wars, plague, and fire. There was a lot of building by Italian architects in the 17C (notably the nave of the abbey church, which was built in 1636 to the design of D. Sciassia).

With the election of Gottfried Bessel to the abbacy, which he held from 1714 to 1749,

St. Nikolaus near Torren (Golling)

Göttweig entered a brilliant period of baroque reconstruction, undertaken by J. L. von Hildebrandt in 1719, which spared only the early baroque abbey church, the S. half of the Gothic schloss, including its round towers and former moats, and the Ehrentrudiskapelle (which is on the W. side and dates from the beginning of the 13C). In 1765 the church façade was completed in neoclassical style (by which time it was being supervised by its fourth architect); in 1783, however, work on the S. section came to a complete halt. The *imperial staircase* (Kaiserstiege) stands to the NW of the monastery, with its own three-storeyed building. This is one of the most magnificent staircases possessed by any Austrian monastery, and was completed by F. A. Pilgram in 1739. The ceiling is decorated with a fresco, painted by P. Troger in 1739, which depicts the apotheosis of the Emperor Charles VI (the father of Maria Theresa) as Apollo. On the stone balustrades there are stucco vases by Joh. Schmidt with pictures of the months by Joh. Schmidt and also of the four seasons. The *banqueting hall* contains frescos depicting the wedding at Cana, painted by Joh. Rudolf Byss in 1731, and a veduta of the monastery executed by Joh. Samuel Hötzendorfer in 1735. The *four state apartments* include the so-called *Napoleonzimmer* (Napoleon was here in 1809). The *Cäciliensaal* accommodates part of the *picture gallery*, which includes paintings by Altomonte and Martin Johann Schmidt of Krems. The magnificent but closed *library* in the E. section is decorated with white and gold stucco (dating from 1727). It contains important collections of antiques, coins, written music, and weapons. The *graphological cabinet* holds annual exhibitions. The courtyard has a *pyramidal fountain* which was constructed by J.E. Fischer (the younger) von Erlach. The sculptures are by J.Schmidt.

Pfarr- und Stiftskirche Mariä Himmelfahrt: This was planned by Hildebrandt as a magnificent domed structure with a twin-towered facade, and has remained unaltered. The towers have no lanterns and end in blunt pyramids. A broad flight of steps dating from 1764 leads up to a deep porch with 4 Tuscan columns. This stands like a loggia in front of the pediment of the nave, with its statues, and leads into a narthex with 15&16C Gothic marble tombstones. The *interior* of the church is dominated by gold, brown, and blue colours (painted on marble and imitation stucco in 1861). The Gothic choir, dating from 1402, was reconstructed in 1594, when the present ribbed vault was added. The blue and gold *high altar* and the pulpit were built by Hermann Schmidt from Esschen near Antwerp in 1639 (the painting of the high altar was carried out by Joh. Andreas Wolff of Munich in 1694). The *stained-glass windows* behind the high altar incorporate twelve Gothic pieces of glass (1430–40) which are the work of the same artist who made the votive panels of the Master of St.Lambrecht. On the wall above the *inlaid choir stall*, dating from

Göttweig, Stiftskirche

1766, there are three panels made by an unknown Austrian mannerist at the end of the 16C. There is a splendid *organ front*, which dates from 1703. The *eight sidechapels* contain fine paintings by Michael Christoph Grabenberger (1680), Tobias Bock (1675), and Martin Schmidt. Set beneath the raised sanctuary is *St.Altmann's crypt*, which contains octagonal columns and, in the N. apse, the *tomb* of St. Altmann, decorated in relief by Konrad Osterer in 1540; the S. apse contains *the shrine holding St.Altmann's relics*, which dates from 1688. The *Altmannikrümme* incorporates Arab ivories carved in the last quarter of the 12C. The famous *Drachenleuchter* of Göttweig dates from the same period (around 1180): this was made in Lorraine of cast bronze and is housed in the monastery's treasury, which contains precious paraments.

Götzens 6091
Tirol   p.286□F 9

Pfarrkirche zu den Aposteln Peter und Paul: A church in this place was mentioned as early as 1350. The present parish church, which was built in 1772–5 by Franz Singer of Götzens, must be counted among the most beautiful of all rococo religious buildings. The façade, with its curving pediment and niches for statues, is relatively plain and gives no hint of the magnificent interior. As soon as one enters, one sees a structure, most splendidly furnished, where everything converges on the altar, the whole resembling a stage set. The *stucco decorations*, which cover the whole interior, resembling darting flame, or perhaps luxurious vegetation, are of quite notable beauty. These are not merely decoration, but merge with the architecture which supports them, as in the case of the triumphal arch or the pulpit. The no less powerful, lively, and colourful *dome frescos*,

showing scenes from the lives of the two apostles, were painted by M.Günther in 1775. The most striking of these in its colouring and life-like effect is the one which shows Peter and Paul preaching in the Capitol in Rome, and in the process causing Simon Magus, who could fly by magic, to crash down to earth. The painting on the *high altar* is by A.F. Maulbertsch, and the pictures on the side altars by Andreas Nesselthaler and Toni Kirchebner. The *crucifix*, the large *statues* in the transept, and especially the *altar figures*, are all the work of J.Schnegg, who was in the service of Frederick the Great, and all display a perfect beauty.

Götzis 6840
Vorarlberg   p.286□A 8

Alte Pfarrkirche St.Ulrich: The church was built in 1340 and enlarged around 1509; it has a net vault. There is a large statue of the Madonna with the founders, dating from 1700, by the chancel arch on the Gospel side. There are frescos by the pulpit and the chancel arch. One of them shows a lovely, bucolic figure of God the Father.

Also worth seeing: The 14C ruins of the castle of *Neumontfort*, stand high up to the right of the road to Rankweil. A little way after that can be seen the small *Wallfahrtskirche St. Arbogast im Tale* (Bishop of Strassburg in 550). This was built in 1473 and enlarged in 1710. It has a small wooden section in front, some beautiful altars, and a coffered ceiling dating from the early 18C.

Grades 9362
Kärnten   p.282□P 10

Pfarrkirche St. Andreas: Grades has been a market town since the early 14C.

Götzens, Pfarrkirche

The parish church stands at the E. end of its large, rectangular Marktplatz. The structure is late Gothic, dating from the 15C, but retains some elements of its Romanesque predecessor. A Roman tomb relief has been walled into the W. front. There are remains of some late Roman wall paintings in the flat-roofed nave and on the triumphal arch.

Filialkirche St. Wolfgang: This is one of the most beautiful, and most typically Carinthian, churches. It stands on a small hill W. of the market, a church-fortress surrounded by a massive wall. Its construction began in 1453. Like other similar sites in Carinthia, it was used as a defensive fortress when the Turks attacked the region. A large nave comprising three bays with a groin vault dating from 1523–5 leads into the choir, with its net vault. The *vault*

paintings, dating from the last third of the 15C, are very important. The poetic transition from representational to ornamental forms constitutes a late stage in the development of medieval painting. It is thought that the depiction of plants and tendrils was borrowed from the shapes which had been discovered by the printing of the day. The impressive *side altar* dates from around 1520, although the figure of the church's patron saint, St. Wolfgang, and of Sts. Lawrence and Stephen may come from an earlier altarpiece (perhaps dating from 1474). The paintings and sculptures tend to depict scenes which are connected to each other. The altar is perhaps the work of the younger Villach school. The *pulpit* and *font* are also late Gothic, as are the *keystone carvings* in the area of the singers' gallery in the W. part of the church. The rest of the church furnishings are baroque.

Schloss: This stands high above the Metnitz and contains several fine baroque sculptures by K.Pittner. The castle itself dates from the 15C.

Environs: See also Metnitz, Strassburg, Lieding, and Gurk.

Grafenegg = Haitzendorf 3485
Lower Austria   p.278☐T 4

Schloss: The original moated castle, which was a 16C Renaissance building, was rebuilt under Count Breunner in 1840–73 by the architect of Vienna Cathedral, Leopold Ernst. Even the castles were not spared by the historicism of this period, which tried to beautify a given style until it attained perfection. A statue of Count Breunner stands above the main entrance. The castle was extensively damaged by the occupying forces but has been restored once more in recent years.

Grafenstein 9131
Kärnten   p.282☐P 11

Pfarrkirche St. Stephan: There are documentary references to this settlement as early as pre-Romanesque times. The structure was originally Romanesque, with a single nave, Gothic choir, and baroque side chapels. The stucco covering the barrel vault is rococo and dates from 1756, and the painting on the ceiling of the nave is baroque. The *high altar* dates from the early 18C, while the two *side altars* are post-baroque. The figures depicted in the high altar and the S. chapel are thought to be the work of Christoph Rudolph. In its present form, the *schloss* to the W. of the town dates from the 17C. It suffered in the 2 World Wars, when its frescos were damaged.

Graz 8010-8054
Steiermark   p.280☐S 9

Graz is the provincial capital of Styria and, with its population of 254,000, the second biggest city in Austria. It was founded in the 12C at the point where the old trade route from Bruck to Leibnitz (the Roman Flavia Solva) crosses the river Mur. Its name derives from the Slovenian 'gradec', meaning 'castle', which shows that the area of the present Schlossberg on the left bank of the Mur must actually have been settled earlier. In any case, Graz, which was then held by the Traungaus, was first mentioned in documents in 1128. It won the status of a town in 1189, and in the middle of the 13C acquired a town wall. During the following centuries, historical events conspired to favour the development of its fortunes. The Habsburgs' division of their lands in 1379 led to the establishment of the Leopoldine branch under Duke Leopold III, which chose Graz as its capital. When the Habsburgs later won the emperorship, this naturally brought advantages to Graz (for example, Emperor Frederick III, 1440-93, was a grandson of Leopold III) in the way of the enlargement of the castle, the building of new town gates, the reconstruction of the cathedral, and so on.

In the second half of the 15C, the situation became menacing. In 1478 the Turks stood in front of the gates of Graz for the first time. Although they failed to capture it, the town suffered serious economic damage from their devastation of the surrounding countryside. In terms of its artistic development, though, it actually derived great benefit, eventually, from the Turkish siege. This was because, as a result of these events, the state decided to erect a continuous chain of fortresses along a line running from Vienna via Graz to the

Graz, Hof im Landhaus ▷

Adriatic Sea: this would protect the country's south-eastern frontier and constitute a bulwark against the Muslim threat. Graz was to occupy a key position in this project. Between 1544 and 1625 extensive fortifications and bastions were erected by architects who were primarily Italian. This enabled Italian Renaissance architecture to be 'imported' into Graz uninterruptedly from a relatively early date until the mannerist style of the later Renaissance.

The advance of the Reformation came almost simultaneously with the threat from Turkey. The new Protestant teaching aroused lively interest, particularly in Graz. After the town had become the capital of 'Inner Austria' in 1564, following a second division of their land by the Habsburgs, which strengthened the position of the Catholic court, there were military clashes between the two denominations. The initiatives of the Counter-Reformation included the establishment of various Jesuit schools and the university (1586).

It is only from the second half of the 18C, with the suppression of the Jesuit Order and the conversion of the university into a secondary school, that one can note a decline in Graz's political and cultural importance in favour of Vienna. This was followed, however, in the first half of the nineteenth century, by a new cultural flowering which is closely connected with the name of Archduke Johann. This well-liked prince, who married a commoner and chose to make his private residence in Graz, was responsible for founding the *Joanneum*. Although the 20C has somewhat removed it from the centre of things, the city's creative genius has by no means been exhausted. The 'Forum Stadtpark' and 'Grazer Gruppe' have excited enthusiasm far beyond the boundaries of Austria.

The town: The original centre of the town was the natural fortification provided by the *Schlossberg*, which stands on its own, 400 ft. high. At its base, on the SE side, are the oldest signs of settlement (including the oldest house, the *Reinerhof*, dating from 1164). During the next centuries, the town spread out like a fan, eventually incorporating what had earlier been suburbs

Graz, Hauptplatz with Luegg houses and clock tower in background

(like the Murvorstadt). Today, the city centre is the triangular *Hauptplatz*. From here, the eye is naturally drawn to the *clock tower*, which stands 92 ft. high on the S. slope of the Schlossberg, and is the city's landmark. This tower, which was built in 1561, is one of the few remains of the powerful fortress which was destroyed in 1809, after the 'Peace of Vienna'. One should also note the *bell tower*, built in 1588, which contains the largest bell in Graz, known as 'Liesl'.

Domkirche hl. Ägydius (Hofgasse): This was first mentioned in 1174 and originally built in front of the town walls as a church-fortress. It was a parish church until 1573, and became a cathedral church in 1786. The present building is late Gothic, and was built between 1438 and 1462, supposedly by Hans Niesenberger; only the chapels, sacristy, and ridge turret are baroque additions. The outside is notably simple. Above the W. portal can

Graz, **Dom 1** Barbarakapelle **2** Sacristy **3** Cobenzl Monument **4** Marriage chests **5** Kapelle des hl. Franz Xaver **6** Kapelle der hll. Rochus und Sebastian **7** Kapelle der schmerzhaften Muttergottes **8** Kapelle des hl. Kreuzes

Graz, Domkirche zum hl. Ägydius, view of the interior looking towards the high altar, designed by the Jesuit G. Kraxner

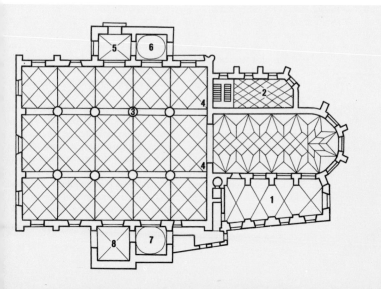

be seen the coat-of-arms of the Emperor Frederick III, who built the church, and his motto, *Aeiou* (i.e. Austria erit in orbe ultima, which means 'Austria will survive until the end of the world'). On the S. façade can be seen what remains of the so-called *Landplagenbild*, dating from 1485, whose bottom level constitutes the earliest picture of Graz, here surrounded by the divine scourges of locusts, war, and plague. The basic concept of the interior consists of a sharp contrast between the relatively wide and spacious nave and the lofty, deep, but narrow choir. The two are connected by an arch which has the effect of a portal; partly because of the use of light, the choir being brighter than the nave, this gives the appearance of a doorway into heaven. As we enter the choir, we see that the ornamentation, too, is enhanced there, as witnessed, for example, by the greater richness of the net vaulting. Conversely, it must be admitted that the nave has been widened in comparison with those in earlier Gothic cathedrals, which had been rather underemphasised, to the point of virtually becoming square. Not much has been preserved of the original Gothic *contents*. What has survived includes the *Crucifixion*, painted in 1457 by K.Laib (on the R. wall); the *original vault painting*, which dates from 1464 and was only rediscovered in 1931; and finally, above what used to be the side entrances, parts of the fresco depicting St. Christopher, which dates from the same period. (The one on the S. side includes a picture of the Emperor Frederick III).

It is, however, the *baroque furnishings*, for which the Jesuits were responsible, that are decisive in producing the overall inside effect. The monumental *high altar* (1730-3) was designed by the Jesuit brother, G.Kraxner. The upward surge of its two storeys underlines the vertical concept of the choir. The altar painting by F. I. Flurer (1733) depicts the 'Miracle of St.Aegydius'. There are also some outstanding sculptures

by J.J. Schoy. The altars in the aisles are also of remarkable quality, especially those on each side of the triumphal arch, i.e. the *Ignatius altar* in the S. aisle, and the *altar of the Blessed Sacrament* in the N. aisle. These altars, which are placed symmetrically, date from between 1766 and 1769 and are of interest above all for their paintings and sculptures. The paintings are by the mannerist G.P. de Pomis, who also built the mausoleum, and the sculptures by V. Königer.

The four *chapels* should also be noted, particularly for their typically Styrian hand-wrought *grilles* (17C). The front pillars also have some well-fashioned *small altars* (the sculptures are by Ph. J. Straub). A noteworthy detail are the two *reliquary chests* next to the altar rails; these were originally the wedding chests of the Duchess Paola Gonzaga of Mantua, who was married and came to Graz in 1477. Each is decorated with three delicate ivory reliefs depicting respectively the triumph of love, innocence, and death, and of fame, time, and eternity (compare Petrarch's 'Trionfi'). Note also the *votive picture* of the Archduke Charles and his family, painted by J. de Monte in 1591, which is in the choir, and the outstanding *tombs and epitaphs* in the aisle (viz. the tomb of Herberstein by the S. wall, dating from 1576; that of Trautmannsdorff by the N. wall, dating from 1631; and of Count Cobenzl, opposite the pulpit, which dates from 1741 and incorporates a painting by G.R. Donner).

Mausoleum: The mausoleum of Emperor Ferdinand II (died 1637) stands to the S. of the cathedral, on the site of the original Katharinenkapelle. Work began on the building in 1614 to the design of G.P. de Pomis, but was taken over in 1633 by Peter Valnegro. The building is one of the most important examples of mannerist art north of the Alps. The façade, in par-

Mausoleum

ticular, reveals the overlaying and distortion of classical elements and proportions which was typical of the period between the Renaissance and baroque styles in architecture. Thus, although the design is to a considerable extent modelled on the Jesuit church 'Il Gesù' in Rome, every individual motif has nonetheless been reinterpreted in a mannerist sense. Thus, the portal in the original model is treated here as a complete façade, the harmonious horizontal of the prototype has become an extended vertical, the rhythmical segmental arches have been turned into a ponderous entablature, and massive statues have taken the place of the more restrained ones in niches. No less unusual is the design and arrangement of the three *domes*, each different in style. These give a suggestion of Venetian motifs, which, however, have also been adapted along asymmetrical and unorthodox lines (particularly in the case of the extremely slender dome above the campanile). The *design* of the interior is that of a Latin cross with a dome over the crossing, with the chapel containing Ferdinand's tomb adjoining the S. arm of the cross. The *stucco decorations* inside the church derive from the design of Fischer von Erlach and date from 1687 – 99. As in the mausoleum in Ehrenhausen, the rich stucco, in which the essential elements are eagles, atlantes, and a lively group of putti, cause one involuntarily to look upwards. *Frescos* by Franz Steinpichler decorate the ceiling of the nave, underneath which is depicted 'the liberation of Vienna' (of 1683). The *stucco* in the crypt is based on the design of Fischer von Erlach, as also is the *high altar* (1695 – 7). The latter was undoubtedly modelled on Bernini's baldacchino altar in St.Peter's in Rome, although in this case it has been converted into a wall altar. The statue of St. Catherine is by Fischer's friend, M.Schokotnigg, who was clearly acquainted with the sculptures of Bernini. In comparison with this splendid interior,

the lower *crypt*, which contains stucco decorations by M.Camin dating from 1641, seems distinctly poor.

Haupt- und Stadtpfarrkirche zum Heiligen Blut (21 Herrengasse): Like the cathedral, this was a foundation of Emperor Frederick III. Only three bays in the southernmost aisle have been preserved of the Corpus Christi Chapel originally erected here in 1440. The present church, dating from 1513–19, is Gothic and was built by the Dominicans, who were clearly inspired by the example of the cathedral (note the width of the interior, comprising a nave and two aisles, and the narrow vertical choir). The church acquired a baroque façade, including four figures in niches by the older and the younger Schokotnigg (see Mausoleum) in 1741–2, and a gable tower in 1780-1. After the church had been designated as a Pfarrkirche (parish church) in 1586, the parish took steps to enrich its furnishings. The most important of these is the *Assunta* by Tintoretto, which was brought to Graz in 1594 and originally placed on the high altar, then moved in 1948 to the restored Altar of St. John of Nepomuk. In fact, the integrity of the original baroque design of 1730 suffered even more ruinously from the introduction of Gothic features in the late 19C than from the effects of war. Magnificent altars by J.J. Schoy and P.J. Straub were removed at that time. *Also worth mentioning:* The tombstone of J.B. Erlacher (died 1649). His widow's later marriage to the sculptor J.B. Fischer produced the famous J.B. Fischer von Erlach. The stained-glass windows date from 1953 and are the work of A.Birkle.

Leechkirche (Zinzendorfgasse 5): This is the oldest surviving building in the city. It was constructed in 1275–93 in Gothic style by the Teutonic Order, on the site of a church called the Kunigundis-Kirche. The towers on the W. side date from before

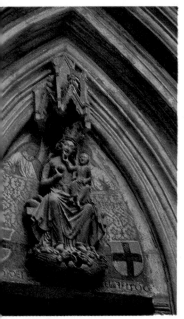

Leechkirche, tympanum

1500. With its high, wide traceried windows and its flying buttresses, this church clearly echoes the style of French Gothic cathedrals. The design of the early Gothic *portal* (dating from the last quarter of the 13C), incorporating a relief of the Madonna in the tympanum, is quite original. The Madonna is one of the most representative examples of early Gothic sculpture in Austria (though the folds in her garments still show the influence of late Romanesque style). The frescos which form the background to the sculpture are late Gothic. The *interior* has a high ceiling, a single aisle, and rib vaults, and, all in all, comes close to achieving the elegance of its French prototypes. The windows in the choir incorporate the oldest *stained glass* in Graz to have survived (they depict the Passion, with figures of the evangelists above). Most of them were made in 1335

–7. The *high altar*, which dates from about 1780, includes a late-15C statue of the Virgin. To the left is the *niche for the sacrament*, protected by a fine grille (1499). 12 *shields* bearing the coats-of-arms of knights of the Order remind us of the church's special character, as do the many *tombstones* (including that of Siegmund, Baron of Egkh, which was placed there in 1606).

Franziskanerkirche und Kloster Mariä Himmelfahrt (Neutorgasse): This was originally founded by the Minorites, and taken over by the Franciscans in 1515. The striking W. tower was built in the years 1636–43 during the course of the fortification of the bridge over the Mur. The church's oblique position, whether because of its incorporation into the city wall or else, according to another theory, owing to the previous existence here of a tributary of the Mur, is remarkable. The present structure is clearly composed of two distinct sections, the *choir*, dating from the middle of the 14C, which is typical for the churches of mendicant orders and has four bays and a ribbed vault, and the late Gothic *nave* and two aisles, which has four bays and a net vault and was built by the Franciscans around 1520. The *baroque furnishings* inside the church have largely fallen victim to its Gothicization during the late 19C. All that has been preserved is the *Antonius Chapel* and its baroque grille dating from 1650. The altar is adorned with an impressive *Pietà* (dating from around 1720). The gaps which were thus left have not been filled by the several modern works of art, such as the pulpit and high altar, that have been placed here. A side door in the right-hand aisle leads into the Gothic cloister, which boasts some fine tombstones (T. Wolfsthaler, 1474; Dr. M. Permeitinger, 1665). Next to it is the *Jakobs-Kapelle*, built in 1320–30. This contains the tombstone of Christoff von Windischgrätz (1549) and a statue of St. Anthony which was sculpted by J.J. Schoy

Maria-Hilf-Kirche

nave with a barrel vault, low aisles with groin vaulting, and a wide sanctuary. The late baroque *high altar* has the picture of the Virgin Mary, *Maria-Hilf*, which was painted by de Pomis in 1611, and which has become the subject of many legends. The precious silver frame (1769) and the figures of angels around the picture were executed by P.J. Straub (who was also responsible for the figures of St. Michael and two other angels which stand atop the pediment of the façade). The tabernacle is by Anton Römer. The side altar on the right of the church includes the painting by A. Jandl of 'St. Michael as patron of the dying' (1770). There is also a chapel on the right-hand side of the church which contains the baroque tombs of the Eggenbergs. The sacristy contains stucco by Androy; there is a funerary tablet in honour of de Pomis on the first pillar on the left.

The *monastery* is built around a picturesque courtyard. The W. wing contains the *Schatzkammerkapelle* with frescos by J.A. Mölk. The *summer refectory* (1691, J. Carlon) contains frescos by A. Maderni and the oil painting of 'The feeding of the five thousand' which was executed by J.B. Raunacher in 1732.

in 1719. The *Monastery* contains some remains of the old church furnishings, including some more works by J.J. Schoy, H.A. Weissenkirchner, and F.J. Klurer.

Maria-Hilf-Kirche and Minorites' Monastery: This church stands out in its setting on the right bank of the Mur, thanks to the generous proportions of the two towers which form part of its façade, and which were built by J. Hueber in 1742–4. The towers flank the central part of the façade, which is older, and was built by the painter and architect G.P. de Pomis in imitation of Palladio's San Giorgio in Venice. The church and monastery, which had been endowed by the Eggenbergs, were constructed under de Pomis' supervision in 1607–11. The *interior* has been altered during the course of several renovations and is less impressive. It has a wide

Klosterkirche und Spital der Barmherzigen Brüder (2 Annenstrasse): The façade of this church, which was built in 1735–40 by J.G. Stengg, is crowned by a fine ridge turret. Inside there is a single aisle; the elegant *galleries* above the chapels are notably striking. The *frescos* in the side chapels are by J. Mayer; the *painting* of the Annunciation which is on the high altar was executed in 1754 by Corrado Giaquinto of Naples, and the accompanying scenes were painted by Schokotnigg in 1752. The side altar on the right side of the church has a *crucifix* made by G. Schweigger of Nuremberg in 1633.

Bürgerspitalkirche zum Hl. Geist (8 Dominikanergasse): This dates back to a

13C foundation. The present church was built in 1461 – 93, in the reign of the Emperor Frederick III, and is one of the most impressive Gothic churches in Graz. The tower and sacristy alone date from the 17C. Note the *Pietà* by J.J. Schoy (*c.* 1730) in a niche on the outside of the church. The interior contains a number of precious works of art, including the painting of *the pentecost* by F.J. Flurer (1734), which is part of the high altar, and various sculptures, notably a late Gothic Madonna and Child, the Vision of St.Bernard (1530), and the excellent Mary Magdalene, thought to be the work of P.J. Straub.

Pfarrkirche St. Andrä: This church, which is mentioned in documents as early as 1270, and the former Dominican monastery are situated close to the Bürgerspitalskirche. The modern church was built by Archangelo Carlone in 1616 –27 and includes late Gothic features such as the nave and two aisles, and the narrow 'Porta coelis' which is copied from the cathedral. The façade was reworked in the late 19C. In the *interior* it is worth noting the painting on the *high altar*, the Martyrdom of St.Andrew, executed by S.Kessler in 1672; the *oil painting* of Mary Magdalene on the W. wall of the sanctuary, which was executed in 1723 by J.C. Hackhofer, an artist from the monastery at Vorau (q.v.); and the *Madonna and Child* and *St.Anne* by H.A. Weissenkirchner, which are in the left aisle. Finally, to the left of the main entrance there is the seated (Gothic) figure of *St.Andrew* (*c.* 1480).

Other churches worth noting: The *St.-Leonhard-Pfarrkirche* is mentioned as early as 1433. Its front and the tower are now baroque; the interior is Gothic, consisting of a single aisle. It contains paintings by J.V. Hauck and J.A. Mölk. *St. Anton von Padua* is a monument to the Counter-Reformation, built in 1601-2 in commemoration of the burning of Prot-

estant books in 1600. It contains good *altarpieces* by G.P. de Pomis (the 'Apotheosis of the Counter-Reformation' and the 'Foundation of the Klarissinnenkloster by the Archduchess Maria'). *St.Paul im Walde:* This is situated in the oldest part of Graz, at the foot of the Schlossberg, and is thought to be one of the earliest churches in the city. It was given its present form by Augustinian hermits in 1619-27. There is an interesting staircase leading up through the house at No. 21, Sporgasse. The interior contains a painting by H.A. Weissenkirchner which dates from 1686. The *Ursulinenkirche* has striking pilasters constructed in 1696-1704 and contains paintings by J.V. Hauck and H.A. Weissenkirchner. The *Welsche Kirche* was built in 1721-5 by the Brotherhood of St.Francis of Paola. It is notable principally for its striking stucco (on the inside of the dome above the choir). Finally, mention must be made of the most impressive monument to the Counter-Reformation in Graz, the *Kalvarienberg*, which is also one of the most striking examples of this kind of architecture in Austria. It was built on the river, in the N. part of the city, during the years following 1606. In front of the main church is a *sacred stairway* with an 'Ecce homo' (from 1723) in the style of the passion plays. Five chapels lead from here to the three crosses (dating from 1606), and there are another four chapels on the way back.

Castle (Hofgasse 13): This was begun in 1438 by the Emperor Frederick III, who used it as his residence. His son Maximilian I expanded the palace in 1494-1500 by adding a new NE section (incorporating a double spiral staircase). This part, together with the early baroque section built by the Archduke Charles II in 1570 (known as the 'Karlsbau'; note the interesting high roof) have been preserved, while the old palace itself was regrettably demolished in the 19C. The *chapel* of the

Archduchess Maria (built in 1596) and the *ceremonial staircase* constructed by D. dell'Allio in 1554 were destroyed at the same time. The *double spiral staircase* was, however, moved and thereby saved (it used to be in the corner of a courtyard). The two stairways, which intertwine as they pass each other in opposite directions, have no central support from the second floor onwards—convincing evidence of the high degree of technical competence which Gothic architecture could deploy around 1500. The *gateway*, with its Gothic pointed arch, also belongs to the older part of the building. The inner courtyard contains a medieval Jewish *tombstone* dating from 1387 (at the base of the Karlbau) and two Roman gravestones; these were placed in the Burg in 1506, on the occasion of a visit here by the Emperor Maximilian I. From the garden of the Burg, one can see the former *chapel*, built in 1447, which has an interesting niche in the double choir.

Landhaus (16 Herrengasse): This represents the most important monumental building built in Styria in the Renaissance. It was occupied by the chancellery and assembly of the Styrian estates from 1494 onwards, and is today the seat of the Styrian provincial government. The relatively modest *Knights' Hall* was expanded in 1557 – 65 by Domenico dell'Allio of Lugano. The *main façade* contains semicircular windows and a loggia which copies the style of Venetian and Lombard models (such as the Palazzo Vendramin-Calergi, Certosa in Pavia). The *arcaded courtyard*, which is bordered on two sides by three-storeyed loggias (those on the S. side dating from 1890), also has an Italian atmosphere. Its classical severity is due not least to the so-called Tuscan order which is employed in all three storeys (compare the bottom storey of the Palazzo Farnese in Rome). This preciseness distinguishes the arcaded courtyard in Graz from similar and roughly contemporary German ones, for example the subtly curving courtyard in the Old Mint in Munich. In front of the baroque *Landstube* on the W. side stands the (originally coloured) bronze *fountain*, which was cast by Auer and Wening in 1589–90. The most

Schloss Eggenberg (Graz)

splendid room inside the Landeshaus is the *Landstube*, which was converted in 1740–1, and is still used for meetings. The two huge baroque stoves are especially interesting, as are the four great doors with allegorical pictures above them, and also the stucco ceiling by J.Formentini, which depicts scenes from Styrian history (including the Turkish and French invaders). Adjoining this room is the *Knights' Hall*, which was used until 1964 as a temporary theatre. This too has a stucco ceiling by Formentini.

Ständisches Zeughaus: Adjoining the Landhaus on the S. side is the Armoury. Given the strategic importance of Graz, its inhabitants must have felt the urgent need for a good supply of weaponry. The Armoury, built in 1643–5 by A.Solar, contains a complete arsenal of every kind of weapon dating from the time of the Turkish wars. The collection comprises some 29,000 pieces, including more than 3,300 helmets and suits of armour, 7,800 small firearms, and many sumptuous hunting and jousting weapons.

Former Jesuitenkollegium (2 Bürgergasse): The Archduke Charles II brought the Jesuits into Styria in 1572 to provide support for his Counter-Reformation policy. A year later, they moved into a section of this severe, barrack-like structure, which was built by Vincenzo de Verda, being finally completed in 1597. However, despite the severity of the exterior of the building, the S. section contains a *ceremonial staircase* which is particularly sumptuous. Its richly stuccoed emblematic motifs constitute, in their own way, a baroque hymn of praise to the Mother of God.

Old University (immediately N. of the College): Today, this building, which dates from 1607–9, houses the provincial archives. Of the original, sumptuous façade, only the Archduke's coat-of-arms is preserved. The interior contains the former assembly hall, which has two aisles and is frescoed by G.P. de Pomis.

Domherrnhof (1 Bürgergasse): This was once a Jesuit seminary for the nobility. It

Schloss Eggenberg, Prunksaal

was built by J.Hueber in 1762–4. The main entrance is sumptuous, and is decorated with sculptures representing the allegorical figures of Religion and Science by V. Königer (1768). The *group of figures* around the fountain, depicting Hercules's fight with the hydra, is by the same hand. To the left of the entrance is the *Hl.-Geist-Kapelle*, which contains frescos dating from about 1770 by J.C. Fibich.

Palais Attems (17 Sackstrasse): This is the most important baroque palace in the city; it dates from 1702–16, and is thought to have been built by A.Stengg. The walls incorporate magnificent pilasters and mouldings, and the roof contains three hips (which are typical of Graz). A wide entrance hall leads into the courtyard; unlike Renaissance courtyards, this contains an inner palace façade. To the left is the huge *staircase* (the stucco is by D.Boscho and dates from 1706). It is worth noting the ceiling frescos here, and in the adjoining room, which depict mythological subjects and are by M. von Görz. The furnishings (stucco, paintings, wainscotting, and marble fireplaces) are all in a uniform style and give an authentic idea of the taste of the aristocracy in the 18C. The palace's loss after 1945 of its Flemish tapestries and of what was once the most extensive picture collection in Austria is to be regretted.

Palais Wildenstein (Paulustorgasse 8): This was built after 1710, perhaps by Stengg. Interesting architecture, with an Italianate colossal order of three quarter columns linking the piano nobile and the floor above. The main decorative theme employed is the griffin's foot, which is borrowed from the Wildstein coat-of-arms.

Palais Saurau-Goess (25 Sporgasse): This is the last palace still in the possesion of its original owners. It was built for P. von Windischgrätz in 1566. The monumental entrance dates from 1630 and incorporates the family coat-of-arms. From a dormer-window beneath the roof of the palace can be seen the half-figure of a Turk with a sword (presumably a mark of ownership), which is the subject of legends dating from the time of the Turkish siege in 1532.

Also worth seeing: The *Palais Lengheimb* and *Palais Welsersheimb* (3&7 Hans-Sachs-Gasse) are baroque buildings dating from the last quarter of the 17C. The *Meerscheinschlössel* (3 Mozartgasse) is a baroque garden palace dating from the beginning of the 18C. The *Krebsenkeller* (12 Sackstrasse) is an early Renaissance house which includes an extended, arcaded courtyard.

Rathaus: This is a 19C building in neo-Renaissance style which only partly fits in with the rest of the Hauptplatz.

Squares: Apart from the *Hauptplatz*, the most impressive squares in Graz are the *Franziskanerplatz*, the *Südtirolerplatz*, with its beautiful baroque façades, the *Jakominiplatz*, *Am Eisernen Tor* (with its 'Turkish column'), and the extraordinarily uniform *Freiheitsplatz* in the N. of the city. From here one can pass via the *Karmeliterplatz* to the *Paulustorgasse*, which contains the only gate to have survived from the Renaissance fortress (1614).

Landesmuseum Joanneum (10 Raubergasse): This was founded in 1811 by the Archduke Johann, whose aim was to provide the whole population of the city with a new cultural centre. The *Lesliehof*, which had been built by D.Sciassia in 1665–74, and a large garden area (the former Botanical Garden), were purchased to house the extensive collections. Graz's Technische Hochschule was established in 1874 by the professors attached to the Joanneum. Today, it incorporates both a scientific museum (covering zoology, mineralogy, botany, geology) and an art gallery (this latter is called the Alte Galerie and is situated at No. 45, Neutorgasse). Outstanding *exhibits* in the Alte Galerie: *Ground floor*: The Admont Madonna (*c.* 1320), the large and small *Pietàs* which also come from the Abbey of Admont and date from around 1400 or 1410, the St. Lambrecht votive panel (around 1440), and the tablets by M.Pacher illustrating the story of Thomas-à-Becket (around 1480). *2nd floor*: Paintings by L. Cranach, P. Brueghel the younger, and Styrian painters of the 17&18C (G.P. de Pomis, H.A. Weissenkirchner, F.J. Flurer); oil sketches by various artists including F.A. Maulbertsch; and, in the domed room, baroque sculptures by J.T. Stammel, V.Königer, and M.Guggenbichler). *1st floor*: Late Gothic ceremonial coach belonging to the Emperor Frederick III (*c.* 1450), and the chalice, 44 inches high, which was wrought by Augsburg goldsmiths around 1570.

Palais Herberstein, now known as the **Neue Galerie** (16 Sackstrasse): This was originally the Eggenbergs' town palace, and was built in 1754 in the rococo style. The façade is without ornament and incorporates two large stone portals. There is an elegant staircase (the putti are by V.Königer, and the ceiling frescos, depicting mythological subjects, are by P.C. Laubmann). The 2nd floor contains a sumptuous rococo suite of rooms (with stucco, sculptures, and stoves). The *Neue Galerie*, which is housed here, includes paintings and sculptures from the 19&20C, notably works by E. Chr. Moser, J. Alt, F.Mallitsch, and W.Thöni.

Theatre Schauspielhaus (11 Hofgasse): The original structure, which was built in 1774-6 by J.Hueber, burned down in 1823, after which a new theatre was built which incorporated the old walls. The

Opera House (11 Hofgasse) is a neo-baroque building dating from 1897-9. It can accommodate eighteen hundred spectators.

Environs: Schloss Eggenberg: This splendid baroque schloss stands on a hill 3 km. W. of Graz. It was built for a family of bourgeois origins (in the trade and credit sector) which nonetheless succeeded in rising to influential positions in the court (see Ehrenhausen). When Hans Ulrich von Eggenberg was appointed, in 1623, to the rank of Reichsfürst, and then, in 1625, to be governor of 'Inner Austria', he decided to build himself a residence suitable for his new-found distinction. The skeleton of the house was finished by 1635, the building work having been overseen by Italian architects following the design of Laurenz van de Sype. Its ground plan is nearly square (262 ft. 5 in. x 213 ft. 3 in.) and incorporates a transverse courtyard and two side courtyards. There are four towers with lanterns at the corners; and there is a central tower with a baroque helm roof at the intersection of the inner courtyards. The three-storeyed outer façade is sadly divided in the middle by the portal (incorporating a balcony and coat-of-arms dating from 1673). Some symbolism has been read into the numbers of some items in the building: for example, there are four towers, 365 windows, 52 windows in the state apartments, and so on. *Inside,* on the ground floor, is the *exhibition of prehistory and early history,* which includes discoveries ranging from the Stone Age until Roman times, one of which is the famous *Strettweg cult wagon* which dates from the 7C BC. The 1st floor houses the *Styrian Hunting Museum*. On the 2nd floor are the state apartments (two sets of twelve), whose furnishings date from two different periods. All the rooms were stuccoed and painted by A. Serenio in the last third of the 17C, which is also when the *state room* was decorated, while the rococo furnishings, such as fireplaces,

Wallfahrtskirche Maria Trost (Graz)

chandeliers, furniture, etc., were installed in the third quarter of the 18C. The *Festsaal*, also known as the *Planetensaal*, is an extraordinary baroque achievement. The walls and ceilings are decorated with paintings by H.A. Weissenkirchner (1684 –5) depicting the signs of the zodiac and the planetary system respectively. In the centre is 'Helios' (standing for the Emperor Leopold I), with the eagle of the house of Eggenberg flying towards it. The adjoining rooms are of interest notably for their rococo furnishings, which include linen wall coverings decorated with various genre scenes by J.B. Raunacher (1757), rooms containing Far Eastern objets d'art such as porcelain, painted silk, and so on. Next to the Schloss are the *deer park* and *lapidarium*, which houses the Roman stone collection belonging to the Joanneum.

Wallfahrtskirche Maria Trost (NE of the old town): Built jointly by Andreas Stengg and his son in 1714–24. The church stands on a hill, and its striking W. front, with its twin towers, can be seen from some distance. The original structure was a small chapel, but it had to be enlarged because of the pilgrims coming to pay homage to the picture of the Madonna (a late Gothic one dating from 1470 which is now part of the high altar). The interior comprises a wide nave with transept, and has a dome over the crossing with a lantern. The walls are painted in perspective, based on the sketches made by Lukas von Schram (1735 – 52), and the sculptures are by J.Schokotnigg and V.Königer. *Also worth seeing* (in the immediate vicinity): **Schloss Gösting,** a fine baroque castle. *Schloss and Kirche St.Martin,* the latter containing the outstanding high altar by J. Thaddaeus Stammel which incorporates life-size effigies of knights. *Cistercian Monastery of* **Stift Rein** (15 km.). The *open-air museum of* **Stübing** is situated 15 km. NW. of Graz. There is also a *Schloss* here, mentioned in 1147, which retains the foundation walls of the original medieval structure. It was partly rebuilt and enlarged in the 19C.

Greifenburg 9761

Kärnten   p.284☐M 10/11

Schloss: This is mentioned in a document of 1166, which says that it was founded (like many such buildings) in the period of the early emperors. What we see today is a baroque structure, comprising two sections, whose E. part incorporates the nucleus of a Gothic castle. The connecting wing has a beautiful baroque *rusticated portal.*

Pfarrkirche St. Katharina: This late Gothic church was built by L.Rieder, having been completed in 1521. The interior comprises a nave and two aisles, with five bays and a baroque articulated tunnel vault, which led up to a choir with net vaulting. The S. portal is late Gothic, and the furnishings of the interior are largely late baroque.

Greifenstein 3422
Lower Austria   p.278□V 4

Castle: This is an instance of a small castle incorporating a keep and palas. It was rebuilt in the 19C by Prince Johann Liechtenstein from some scanty old ruins. The *pages' room* and the *gatehouse* date from the 12C. The setting is stunningly beautiful, with a view up the Danube. There is a restaurant.

Greillenstein = Röhrenbach 3592
Lower Austria   p.278□T 3

Schloss: This was built in the 16&17C by the Counts of Kuefstein (who were originally from Saxony) from the remains of a medieval castle, and is arranged around a courtyard. The Kuefsteins were a Protestant family. In 1619 the Elector Maximilian and the Emperor Ferdinand II concluded the Treaty of Munich, directed against the (Protestant) Bohemian Estates, whose forces stood before the gates of Vienna. In 1620, before the battle of the White Mountain, Maximilian captured Protestant Greillenstein. In front of the façade there stands a massive *tower* which inporates a chapel, round corner towers, an observation platform, and a helm roof. A moat rings the schloss. The *courtyard* (which is arcaded on three sides and is Florentine in inspiration) contains stone balustrades with vases as high as a man which were made by Fischer von Erlach. It is worth noting the attractive *library* and the 16C *court-room*. The Kuefsteins' family *crypt* (1706) is in the neighbouring town of Röhrenbach, and contains the tombstones of members of the family ranging from 1699 to 1746 and *frescos* painted in 1737. In the *park* of the schloss there is a series of grotesque statues of a pilgrim,

Burg Greifenstein

Schloss Greillenstein

a woman selling schnapps, a woman selling kindling, etc., which are carved from Eggenburg sandstone.

Grein 4360
Upper Austria   p.276☐R 5

Grein is a most attractive town, picturesquely situated on the bank of the Danube. The 'Grein whirlpool' ('where death keeps an inn') was one of the passages most feared by boatmen until the reefs were blown up in 1777–91. One prominent victim was the Bishop of Freising, who was drowned here in 972 while visiting the eastern reaches of his diocese.

Schloss Greinburg: The nucleus of the building is late Gothic, but it was largely constructed after 1621. It has a beautiful arcaded courtyard on three storeys, as well as a chapel and a number of individual state rooms. Note the room on the ground floor which has 'cell vaulting' (a form to which contemporary architects are retur-

ning). *Museum:* The Upper Austrian *shipping museum* (which is worth seeing) is housed in the schloss.

The small, intimate *town theatre*, which was built inside the Rathaus in 1790, is particularly interesting. Whereas the few old theatres which still survive virtually all owe their existence to the patronage of princes, this one in Grein results from the historically unique interest of a musical citizenry! The *church* is late Gothic, with baroque furnishings.

Environs: Burg Clam (Klam 4352), *c.* 7 km. NW. This was built in 1149 by Otto von Machland, and since 1454 has belonged to the Counts Clam (nowadays known as the Clam-Martinic family). It is romantically situated above a ravine, and comprises the outer works of the castle, a free-standing keep, and the main castle with its own massive keep covered with a pent-roof. The Burg incorporates an arcaded courtyard full of atmosphere and a Gothic chapel (access is not allowed to the Romanesque chapel). It is worth seeing the *Museum* which contains the art treasures

Grein on the Danube

and family mementoes of the Counts Clam. For visits, telephone 07269/32617.

Baumgartenberg (*c.* 13 km. W.): Former *Zisterzienserstiftskirche Mariä Himmelfahrt*. The monastery was founded in 1141 by Otto von Machland and his wife Jeuta von Peilstein. The first 12 monks came from Morimond, which was one of the order's original four monasteries. The monastery was severely afflicted in 1428 –31 by the Hussite wars, and was finally dissolved in 1784. The architecture is outstanding and harmoniously brings together elements from the style of three distinct periods. The basilica, transept and paradise are Romanesque-Gothic. The splendid choir, based on the model of the Zwettl monastery, is Gothic and was consecrated in 1446 (it forms 9 sides of a 16-sided figure and has an ambulatory). Finally, part of the interior was altered in baroque style, probably by C.A. Carlone, in the second half of the 17C. The layout of the rooms was left unchanged by this process, while the walls and ceilings were decorated with frescos and, above all, the luxurious stucco typical of this period. In fact, the unity of style of the baroque additions partially obscures the contrasts between the first and second periods of construction and turns the nave, transept and choir into a sequence of magnificently decorated areas. *Contents:* The founder's tomb dates from the beginning of the 15C. The pulpit dates from 1670 and is adorned with a fine image of St. Bernhard lying down with the fruit-bearing tree of the Cistercian family growing out of him (like a Tree of Jesse). The choir stall dates from 1690 and is boldly carved with the coat-of-arms of the Lords of Machland (they are the arms of Upper Austria!).

Gries am Brenner 6156

Tirol   p.286☐F 9

Pfarrkirche Mariae Heimsuchung:
First mentioned in 1534. The present church was built in 1825–6 and restored in 1930–1. The flat domes above the square of the nave and aisles and the choir are of interest. The furniture is neoclassical, though the two *panel paintings* depicting the fourteen auxiliary saints come from the 17C Chapel of the Auxiliary Saints, which has been demolished.

Kapelle zum hl. Jakob: This was founded in 1305 and first mentioned in documents in 1426. It still possesses some Romanesque elements, though it was partially rebuilt in 1656. The fine *carved altar* and the four busts of apostles on the mensa date from the end of the 15C. The small *winged altarpiece* in the nave, the *pulpit*, the *gallery*, and the *pews* are all 17C. There are traces of medieval *wall painting*.

Grieskirchen 4710

Upper Austria   p.276☐N 5

Grieskirchen is a friendly town with some noteworthy houses. It was granted its town charter in 1613. At 3 and 4 in the *lower town square* there is a round oriel attached to a doorway which has a fresco of the Virgin. *Kirche hl. Martin* is an early Gothic basilica which was altered in baroque style around 1700. The choir contains some Renaissance tombstones.

Environs: Aistersheim (*c.* 12 km. SW): *Schloss:* During the peasants' war of 1625 – 6, Aistersheim was used as the headquarters, first of one of the peasants' leaders, then of the governor, Graf Herberstorff (see Frankenburg). It is an imposing Renaissance building arranged around an arcaded courtyard, with massive round towers at the corners. The castle's reflection in the water of the moat is wonderfully picturesque. Visits are not permitted. *Haag am Hausruck* (8 km. W.

of Aistersheim): *Schloss Starhembeerg:* This originally belonged to the Bishop of Passau, then became the ancestral castle of the Starhemberg family. The Burgschloss is 16C and contains the *Heimatstuben*, a museum of local culture. **Kallham** (12 km. NW of Grieskirchen) contains the *Pfarrkirche Mariä Himmelfahrt*, a fine baroque church, built in 1713–18 by J.Pawanger, with good baroque furnishings. **Zell an der Pram** (9 km. NW of Kallham): *Schloss:* This was originally a moated castle. Its first phase of rebuilding was at the beginning of the 18C. The S. wing was built on to it in 1760–4 by Fr. Cuvilliés the younger. The interior has been magnificently decorated by artists from the Bavarian Court. The banqueting hall has a gallery incorporating Ionic pillars and a ceiling by Chr. Wink; there is also decorative wall painting by J.D. Stuber; these same artists were responsible for the staircase (trompe-l'oeil architecture). A general restoration is underway. **Peuerbach** (*c.* 20 km. N. of Grieskirchen): *Pfarrkirche hl. Martin* is a hall church with a nave and two aisles and is now partly baroque; it has a long, oval *Kreuzkapelle* built on to the N. aisle, with a dome and lantern but no drum. There are good baroque furnishings. The *former Schloss* (now the district court) has a lavish two-storeyed portal dating from 1574. There are *attractive houses* with interesting gables, oriels, and arcaded courtyards.

Griffen 9112
Kärnten   p.282□Q 11

The ruined *castle* which stands high above the town was built in the first half of the 12C by the Bishops of Bamberg. Change of ownership brought with it alterations in style. The building fell into decay in the 19C.

Stiftskirche Maria Himmelfahrt (Haslach): This large, pillared basilica has a nave and two aisles and is late Romanesque. It was dedicated in 1273 by Premonstratensian monks who had migrated here from Thuringia. The nave ends in a square choir. The following cen-

Schloss Aistersheim, Grieskirchen

turies, particularly the baroque period, brought about important structural alterations. The splendid baroque W. front, with its curving pediment and powerful arrangement of pilasters, dates from the first quarter of the 18C. The *interior* is still Romanesque. The nave and aisles are very clearly separated. The flat end of the choir is typical of the monastic Romanesque; groined vault. The large *high altar* dates from 1776, and contains a beautiful stone Madonna, carved in 1520, in the centre, with Sts. Augustine and Norbert on either side. Note the many *tombstones* and *stones carved with coats-of-arms* which date from the 15–18C, the rococo *ceiling paintings*, and the *stucco* (especially that in the eastern part of the S. aisle, which may be by Kilian Pittner).

The former *monastery buildings* are late Gothic, though much overlaid by baroque. The stucco in the *refectory* (1700, perhaps by Kilian Pittner), and a Romanesque relief in the *cloister*, are important.

Alte Pfarrkirche: Mentioned in documents in 1233. The church was later expanded and altered in the Gothic and baroque styles. The Romanesque *portal* certainly dates from the first phase. The interior comprises a nave and an aisle. In 1963, *wall paintings* were discovered, also dating from the period of the church's foundation, on the walls of the sanctuary. The figures which they depict include those of the Emperor Henry II and his wife Kunigunde. One may also see a fresco of the *Madonna of the Protective Cloak* (1470, E. wall), and 6 painted wooden reliefs, part of the *winged altarpiece* of 1520.

Grins 6591
Tirol   p.286☐C/D 9

In 1948 this village of beautiful walled and gabled medieval houses, with their oriels and flights of steps as well as 18C frescos on their façades, was largely burnt down, but it has since been restored.

Pfarrkirche zum hl. Nikolaus: This church, which was built in 1775 by Franz Weiskopf of Grins, still incorporates in its

Griffen, Stiftskirche

Gröbming, late Gothic winged altar

façade a tower with a pointed window and tent roof from the original chapel which once stood on this site and was first documented in 1439. Inside the church, note the life-like *rococo stucco* and *ceiling paintings* by M.Günther (1779).

Gröbming 8962

Steiermark   p.282□O 8

The town stands on a high plateau above the Emms. It was first mentioned as a settlement, together with its church, in a document of 1170. Until 1830 it belonged to the archbishops of Salzburg.

Pfarrkirche Mariae Himmelfahrt: Built 1491–1500. The interior is wide, and comprises a single aisle of four bays. The nave and the choir, which comprises two bays, are net-vaulted. The fine late Gothic *traceried windows* deserve attention. The *organ gallery*, and the S. and W. portals, date from the same period. The item of most historical interest among the fur-

Gumpoldskirchen, Rathaus

nishings is the *late Gothic winged altarpiece*, which was made in 1520 and was originally a lay altar. The figures of the 12 Apostles take up three rows and are crowned by the enthroned Christ. On the inside of the wings there are 4 richly gilded reliefs of the Passion. Four more scenes from the Passion (Danube School; in the style of Altdorfer) are depicted on the outside. The altar has a precious crown. The original high altar, which was executed in 1635 by Hans Pernegger (who also carved the figure the Virgin and the statues of Sts. Rupert and Wolfgang) was replaced in 1725.

Grossgmain 5084

Salzburg   p.284□L 7

From the 8C onwards, the workers in the Reichenhall salt-works lived in this settlement, now called Grossgmain but originally known by the name of 'Mona'.

Pfarrkirche Mariä Himmelfahrt: First mentioned in 1144 as 'capella S. Mariae Muona'. It was an important place of pilgrimage in the 15–17C, and belonged to the St.Zeno Monastery in Reichenhall until 1803. Around 1500, a new church was built to house the miraculous *Madonna and Child*. The new church originally had a nave and two aisles, but this structure was changed during baroque alterations in 1731. The Madonna, which was cast around 1400, is one of the finest of its kind, as well as being the largest Madonna in Austria to have been cast in the 'Soft Style'. It was incorporated in the *baroque altar* of 1733, which replaced the original altar, dating from 1499, which had been fashioned by the 'Grossgmain Master' (whose style resembles that of Rueland Frueauf the older, and who may have been the teacher of Rueland Frueauf the younger). Of this original late Gothic altar, the carved main group (now at the top of the baroque altar), four panels, and two more panels depicting larger than life figures of the Saviour and a Madonna and Child, have been preserved in the choir of the later church.

Gnadenbrunnen (Kirchplatz): This incorporates a two-sided Madonna (J.Schwaiger, 1693) from whose breasts water spouts (Miracle by St.Bernhard).

Environs: Plaiburg is situated on an isolated hill, to the E. of Grossgmain. This was the ancestral castle of the Counts of Plain, who took sides against the Pope during the investiture struggle under the Emperor Frederick I. All that remains of the castle are the vestiges of the gate-tower and of the curtain walls. It came under the authority of Salzburg after 1260, and until 1594 was the seat of a Pfleggericht.

Gschnitz = Steinach 6150
Tirol   p.286□F 9

Pfarrkirche zu Unserer Lieben Frau im Schnee: This church, which was built in 1755 by F. de Paula Penz, is situated at the end of the small village, which includes some lovely courtyards with painted façades. Penz in fact completely rebuilt the church dating from 1730 which already stood on this site. The interior contains *ceiling frescos* by A.Zoller (1759) which depict the life of the Virgin. The statues which form part of the high altar and the sculptures in the side altars are the work of J.Berger (1763). Note the beautiful *rococo confessionals*, and the *rococo shrine* in the front of the church with three late Gothic statues which have unfortunately been badly restored.

Kapelle zur hl. Magdalena: This is a late Gothic structure built in the 15C next

to a hermitage, and on the site of an earlier chapel which had been mentioned in 1307. The interior of the former pilgrimage church contains net vaulting and wall consoles. In 1960, fragments were discovered here of some old frescos. Those of the Fall, the Flight to Egypt, and Mary Magdalene date from 1200. There are more frescos of the Magdalene on the N. wall, which date from 1460; the frescos on the vault are 16C.

Environs: See Trias, Steinach, and Matrei am Brenner.

Gumpoldskirchen 2352
Lower Austria   p.278□V 5

In 1241 Duke Frederick II granted Gumpoldskirchen to the Teutonic Order. It was destroyed in successive Hungarian and Turkish invasions and now one can hardly recognize the buildings which date from earlier centuries.

Pfarrkirche zum hl. Michael: This dates from the first half of the 15C. The massive, square W. tower becomes octagonal higher up and then ends in a spire. The church has a nave and two aisles, with a *Gothic chapel* (on the right) whose altar, though neo-Gothic, incorporates some old, 14C figures. It is balanced on the other side of the church by a *baroque chapel*. The *Rathaus* is 16C and has wide arcades. A Roman way column stands in front of it.

Environs: Guntramsdorf: The schloss has been demolished after having been damaged in the war. However, a charming garden pavilion survives. In the style of L. von Hildebrandt, it has excellent frescos (grotesquerie and chinoiserie) by J.Drentwett. It is reminiscent of the pavilion at Obersiebenbrunn. To visit, apply to the Gemeindeamt, 2353 Guntramsdorf, telephone 02236/2601.

Guntersdorf 2042
Lower Austria   p.278□ U 3

Pfarrkirche Marie Himmelfahrt: This was built in the middle of the 14C as a basilica with a nave and two aisles. It was vaulted around 1800. The flat ceiling dates from 1960. The choir stands above a crypt to which there is no access. The tower, and a niche with a pointed arch (to the right), are preserved from the original building. Its outstanding feature is the *tabernacle*, which dates from 1505 and has interlacing pinnacles. Note the font (16/17C), the rococo pulpit (1775), the high altar (dating from around 1725), and the relief above the Gothic door which depicts Christ on a ragulé cross.

Schloss: Built by G. von Roggendorf in 1556. This is a Renaissance schloss, comprising two storeys around a courtyard, and surrounded by a fosse. The surface of its massive exterior is broken up by its heavy chimneys. In front of the entrance to the schloss stands the so-called Gypsy Cross

Gurk, Domkirche

(1504), which is a tabernacle pillar with saints at its base. The entrance hall has an interesting net vault.

Gurk 9342
Kärnten   p.282□ P 10

Pfarr- and Domkirche Maria Himmelfahrt: This is one of the most famous and beautiful Romanesque churches in Austria. Its construction was begun under Bishop Roman I, around 1140. The relics of the Countess Hemma, who founded the convent, were transferred to the crypt here, under the choir, after 1170. According to documents, the high altar was dedicated in 1200. The building was essentially finished by around 1220. The transept acquired a net vault around the middle of the 15C, and the choir was given a stellar vault around 1500; a net vault was set above the nave in 1591. The baroque compulsion to adapt older styles to its taste did not spare even this building: in 1678 the helm roofs of the 200 ft. high towers were altered. This pillared basilica, with its nave and two aisles, actually exemplifies, in Romanesque style, a concept of architecture already practised by the Carolingians: thus, the church comprises two poles, one at the W. end, which is guarded by two towers and includes the narthex and bishop's gallery, and the other at the E. end, centering on the choir and including the transept and triple apse. The nave links the two poles, uniting them in a single whole.

The feature which dominates the *exterior* is the massive scale of the walls. Above the window of the main apse (on the E. end) can be seen a carved *lion* and basilisk (1175), which is the only decorative figure on the outside of the building. The lion symbolizes Jesus Christ, as warrior and

Gurk, Dom, baroque high altar ▷

Gurk, Pfarr- u. Domkirche Maria Himmelfahrt 1 Stone relief of lion with basilisk **2** S. portal **3** Tunnel-vaulted porch (with Bischofs-kapelle above) **4** Portal **5** Choir **6** Triumphal arch **7** St. Christopher fresco beside sacristy portal **8** Fall of Saul and the elders **9** High altar by M. Hönel **10** Entrances to the crypt **11** Altar of the Cross **12** Pulpit **13** Carved altar

points, the walls themselves have become malleable.

Inside the *porch* at the W. end, which is square and barrel-vaulted, our eye is held by the magnificent *main portal*, which dates from around 1200. The seven archivolts represent the last phase of the 'abstract' style before carved figures were used in the ornamentation. The tympanum, which is framed by columns, capitals, archivolts, and ornamental features, must once have been frescoed. Just look at the carvings on the wooden doors! On the N. and S. walls of the porch are the famous *wall paintings*, dating from around 1340, which are arranged in four rows and depict scenes from the Old and New Testaments. The wall which encloses the portal has twelve medallions depicting Christ and the Apostles. The decoration of the vault represents a starry sky.

Interior and furnishings: The severe simplicity which is felt in the structure of the interior is in keeping with the Romanesque concept; but the vaults which were added later to the nave and the aisles in fact distort the original impression created by the manipulation of light (by means of the arrangement of the windows) and the regular proportions of height and width, piers and distances. The *transept* is not separated from the nave, but it is slightly set apart from the choir by a triumphal arch. Near the *portal of the sacristy* there is a *fresco of St. Christopher*, whose corpulence seems to threaten to explode the very wall on which it is painted (*c.* 1250). Even these considerable dimensions, though, do not obscure the fact that painting does depend on the styles of other art forms: thus, the saint's corpulence is borrowed from the Gothic statue, while the folds in his garments still derive from Romanesque illuminated manuscripts. The fresco depicting the *Fall of Saul* and the *Elders* on the S. wall of the transept (which date from around 1380) are Gothic, but provincial in comparison.

Saviour. Christ is seen again above the *S. portal* in his persona as the guide to our salvation—'I am the Way'. Both sculptures show a typically Romanesque style. Instead of forming a contrast to the walls, they seem to grow naturally out of them, so that it looks as if, at these particular

Crypt

Carved relief with Hemma

The cathedral church combines elements of architecture, painting, sculpture, and ornamentation and unites them into a single artistic means of expression. Only the most important of these can be considered here.

Bischofskapelle (W. gallery): This is reached by means of the staircase leading up inside the S. tower. It has a groin vault and two bays. The chapel was itself a focus of worship, and as such it counterbalanced the choir in the E. end—originally this chapel and the choir were in each other's range of vision. It is decorated with *frescos* of unique importance, which were painted by Meister Heinrich around 1230. These depict scenes from the Creation of Man (in the E. part of the vault), the heavenly Jerusalem (in the W. part of the vault), prophets, the Symbols of the Evangelists, and the Virgin Mary on the throne of Solomon (E. wall), which is of particular impor-

tance. It is also worth noting the *stained-glass windows* representing the deposition from the cross (which date from the same period).

High altar: This is the masterpiece of the Saxon, Michael Hönel, who created it during the years 1626–32, modelling it on earlier Spanish examples of the type (about 50 ft. high). We may define it as imperial baroque. It comprises a series of tiers, each containing niches and aedicules, and incorporates 72 *carved figures*, some of them larger than life. For all its dramatic quality, the work is based on an ordered framework. On the bottom level, on either side of the two portals, are the four Evangelists. The main, central niche, which rises from top to bottom, represents the Assumption of the Virgin. The middle rows which run off to right and left of it depict the Emperor Henry II and Count

Wilhelm, in front of whom stand the four church fathers. Above them are Thomas à Becket, Pope Leo, St.Florian, and St. George. At the very top, crowning the main central niche, are the figures of the church's patroness, Hemma, and the Empress Kunigunde. The two *side altars* are likewise the work of this master of the baroque. The paintings are by Johann Seitlinger.

Crypt: The stairs in the aisles lead down beneath the choir into the famous crypt of the foundress, Hemma, who by the way, was only canonised in 1938. Exactly 100 columns stand in a space of roughly 4,300 sq. ft. In the half-light, they appear not so much as columns as statues, being of body height. *Hemma's tomb* is in the SE. part. The three heads supporting the sarcophagus show us, once again, the magical symbolism of Romanesque sculptures: it is as if the evil spirits had been summoned forth from the stone, only to be banished once more. The strapwork in the groined vault (18C, perhaps by Kilian Pittner) achieves a surprisingly vital harmony with the older substance of the building.

Other parts of the church which are worth seeing: The large group of lead figures around the *Altar of the Cross* (in the nave) was executed in 1740 by G.R. Donner. The scenic quality of this group of comforters shows how much the baroque style had developed since the period when the high altar was made. The lead reliefs on the *pulpit* are also by Donner. Equally famous is the relief on the Romanesque tympanum (on the N. staircase down to the crypt) which depicts *Samson's victory* over the lion. This is vividly dramatic, with the line of the arms forming a cross with that of the trunk. Finally, from all the plethora of monuments, note the *carved altar* of Prior Galler (1530), which illustrates the transition from the Gothic to the Renaissance style, a splendid *late Gothic statue of the Mother of God* (dating from around 1500), and a *statue of the Redeemer*

(around 1450) in the baroque choir stalls. Finally, there are the *reliefs* depicting scenes from the life of St.Hemma (executed around 1515, perhaps by Lienhard Pampstel).

Stiftsgebäude: The vault of the Trinity Chapel incorporates some interesting painted carved reliefs dating from 1500. There is also a large *lenten veil* (measuring some 30 x 30 ft.) which was made in 1458 by Konrad von Friesach. It depicts 98 scenes from the Old and New Testaments.

Environs: Gnesau (in the Gurk Valley) contains the *parish church of St.Leonhard*, which was originally Romanesque but was later altered in baroque style. The furnishings, which are late baroque throughout, are admittedly not up to the standard of those in Gurk, but even so they show that the architectural and decorative spirit of the baroque permeated the 'hinterland'.

Güssing 7540
Burgenland   p.280☐V 9

Castle: The castle stands on top of a steep, cone-shaped basalt hill, towering over the valley below. During the Middle Ages, it was the seat of the Güssings, a powerful family who owned more than 25 castles, and soon found themselves involved in fighting with their neighbours, the Kings of Hungary and the Archdukes of Austria. The coat-of-arms of the province of Burgenland contains a reminder of this family (see Forchtenstein). It was at Güssing castle, in 1459, that the Emperor Frederick III was elected King of Hungary at the suggestion of the then master of Güssing, the voivode Nik. Ujlaki. In 1522, Prince Franz Batthyany was given the cas-

Gurk, frescos, W. gallery ▷

tle in gratitude for his victory over the Turks, and it has remained in his family ever since. It was another Batthyany who, in the late 16C, brought the famous botanist Carolus Clusius to Güssing and offered him the opportunity of exploring Pannonia.

The visitor climbs up to the Hochburg through its massive fortifications, now partly ruined. A staircase leads from the courtyard of the castle to the *Gothic chapel*, in which particular attention should be paid to the small *chest organ*, which is certainly one of the oldest examples in existence of this type of instrument. The massive *keep* is now crowned by a baroque belfry. There is a *Kunstkammer* which contains some important exhibits, including the figure of a saddler. The *Knights' Hall* has been arranged as an exhibition of the history of the Batthyany family.

Franziskanerkloster: Founded in 1648. The extensive crypt contains some 100 tombs of members of the Batthyany family. Its two side altars are stylistically important examples of 17C neo-Gothic. The *library* contains some precious 13C manuscripts.

Environs: Maria Weinberg (near Gaas-Eberau 7521; *c.* 18 km. E. of Güssing): On a hill some 2 km. to the S. of Gaas can be seen the *Wallfahrtskirche Maria Weinberg*, which may have been built on the site of an earlier castle chapel. The tower of this Gothic church has a baroque helm roof. Some recently discovered windows appear to have been Romanesque. The high Gothic *miraculous image* of the Virgin, represented as a 'vineyard-keeper', stands in the centre of a baroque columned altar. This is an excellent carving in the style of the 'beautiful Madonna'. It is also worth noting the centre column with its baroque Madonna, the Renaissance painting on the triumphal arch, and the Gothic tabernacle (for information about the key, apply to the Katholischer Pfarramt Gaas, tel. 03323/234). **Eberau,** (*c.* 25 km. NE) contains what were once massive fortifications, dating from the 13&14C. Part of the remains of the town rampart can still be recognized. The castle itself has suffered ruinously. No visitors admitted.

Gutenstein 2770

Lower Austria   p.278□U 6

The poet Ferdinand Raimund wrote on 1 May 1827: 'And so I see you in the spring, O my beloved Gutenstein... In mighty Nature's heart reigns noble truth alone ... Here may my bones be laid to rest, and may my tomb be set in Gutenstein'. Raimund shot himself on 6 September 1836 from fear of having contracted rabies from a harmless dog-bite; he was buried in Gutenstein.

Castle: First mentioned in 1220, when it was in the possession of the Babenbergs. It was here that Frederick the Fair died in 1330, after having been imprisoned for three years in the castle of Trausnitz. The castle fell into decay in the 19C.

Also worth seeing: *Pfarrkirche hl. Johannes d.T.:* The choir dates from 1487 and the high altar from 1755. In 1675 Count Hoyos founded a Servite monastery on the Mariahilfberg, for which he built the *pilgrimage church*. This was completed in 1725 and comprises a nave and transept. The miraculous image which the church contains resembles that of the Mother of God in the pilgrimage church in Mariazell. The *foresters' museum* in the Alte Hofmühle houses a collection of wood-working implements.

H

Hadersdorf am Kampf 3493
Lower Austria   p.278☐T 4

Hadersdorf is set on the slopes of the famous Hagenstein vineyard; the parish church of *St. Peter und Paul* was originally Gothic; redesigned in the baroque style in 1768. The *ossuary* dates from 1270. Fine Nepomuk chapel of 1750. 16C *stocks*. The old market-place with Renaissance and baroque façades is also worth seeing.

Hafnerberg = Altenmarkt-Thennenberg 2571
Lower Austria   p.278☐U 5

Wallfahrtskirche zu Unserer Lieben

Hadersdorf, Rathaus (with local collection)

Frau: The pilgrimage dates from 1653. A chapel was built in 1716 and replaced by the present rotunda commissioned by Ildefonso von Managetta, the abbot of Kleinmariazell. Daniel Dietrich was responsible for the work 1729–40, but the interior was not completed for another 20 years. The exterior with gable and onion towers appears restrained, but the interior has very striking late baroque decoration (frescos by J.Ignaz Mildorfer). The finest features are the *high altar* (1744, designed by Balthasar Moll), the *side altars* (statues largely by Christoph Schönlaub), two altar panels (St.Donatus and St.Benedikt, both by J.I.Mildorfer 1752 and 1755), *pulpit* (1745), *organ* (1767) and *St.Francis Xavier memorial* (1761).

Haimburg 9111
Kärnten   p.282☐Q 11

Pfarrkirche Unsere Liebe Frau: This 15C building had a Romanesque predecessor mentioned in 1272. Like many other churches in the area the building was also used for defence purposes (high cemetery wall). The W. tower was rebuilt after the earthquake of 1767, 4 bays, choir almost equally long, net vaulting. In the choir vault *late Gothic painting*, 1473; (Christ the Saviour, martyrdom of St. Barbara). In the church one of the most important Lenten veils in Carinthia (1504).

Ruined castle: On the S. hill is the former seat of the counts of Haimburg, which fell into ruins in the 18C. Last sign of building activity is the stucco, *c.* 1700.

Haiming 6425
Tirol   p.286☐E 8

Pfarrkirche zu den hll.Chrysanth und Daria: The church was first mentioned in 1384 and enlarged in 1511, then further altered in the late 18C and early 20C. Gothic windows and tracery have survived in the tower despite baroque rebuilding. On the N. wall of the church is a late-15C

Hafnerberg, Wallfahrtskirche

fresco. The high nave with pointed arches, flying buttresses and late Gothic portals is essentially early 16C, though the net vaulting was not added until 1907&8. By the S. side altar frescos of St.Anne with the Virgin and Child, 1611. The fine *font* and the four *coats-of-arms* are 16C.

Also worth seeing: The *cemetery chapel,* built 1803, contains a 15C statue of the Madonna which has unfortunately been heavily restored, and baroque statues dating from the second half of the 18C by Hans Reindl. *Schloss St.Petersberg,* mentioned in 1166, came into the possession of the counts of Tirol in 1253 and was acquired by the Emperor in the 19C. The bailey, the chapel and the ruined keep are Romanesque. The *chapel,* with 1811 coffered ceiling, is not open to the public. The *St.Antonius chapel* (in Riedern) has a 17C altar and two 17C statues (St.John and St.Peter, by Barth Steinle, the artist of the high altar in Stams).

Hainburg an der Donau 2410
Lower Austria   p.278☐X 5

This Ostmark border fortress was mentioned in 1043; at the same time a settlement started to develop below the castle (charter 1244). In 1252 the castle was the scene of the unhappy marriage of Ottokar II of Bohemia to Margarethe, heiress of Babenberg, who was 20 years older than the king. The fortified walls and towers date from this time. Turkish invasions in the 16&17C led to the decline of Hainburg, and the town did not recover until the 18C. In the 19C the neoclassical industrial buldings which are the hallmark of the present town were built.

Castle: The ruins of the essentially medieval fortress above the town are visible over long distances. In the courtyard are the remains of the residential buildings, the keep, the palas and the *Pankratius chapel* (12C). The castle has not been occupied since the 16C, but was occasionally used as a fortress until the 18C.

Town fortifications: The fortifications of 1240 extend from the castle to the Danube. Three town gates have survived in good condition: the *Wiener Tor* is considered one of the finest of the period. The side sections are horseshoe-shaped and built of bossed ashlar; they lead to a gate with pointed arch and portcullis. There is rib vaulting in the gatehouse rooms (now open to allow pedestrians to pass). The *Ungartor* is at the E. entrance to the town, and the *Fischertor* (c. 1300) is on the Danube side. The **Haus der Theodora,** a Romanesque house (c. 1230) at the foot of the castle mound, is directly by the town wall.

Also worth seeing: *Pfarrkirche hll. Philipp und Jakob* (c. 1700, earlier building mentioned 1236) with baroque interior; *ossuary* (early 13C) and just beside it the *Lichtsäule* (14C). Various essentially

Hainburg, Wiener Tor

Gothic houses (Ungarstrasse, Wiener Strasse, Hauptplatz). Outstanding is the *Mariensäule* (1749, Martin Vögerl), considered one of the finest rococo columns in Lower Austria. *Heimatmuseum* (local history) by the Wiener Tor.

Halbturn 7131
Burgenland   p.278□X 6

Schloss: Two artists were responsible for the transformation of the former imperial hunting lodge into one of the most wonderful examples of Austrian baroque: the architect J.Lukas von Hildebrandt and the painter Franz Anton Maulbertsch. The building dates from the first decade of the 18C, when the Schloss was on loan from the emperor to the counts of Harrach. Hildebrandt, who had also built two Palais in Vienna and Schloss Mirabell in Salzburg for this important family, was selected to supervise the building after the previous Schloss was destroyed by the Turks in 1683. Shortly after completion the Schloss was returned to the Habsburgs. Maulbertsch painted his masterly ceiling fresco in the Gartensaaal in 1765. The Schloss was plundered and uninhabited during the Second World War and largely burned down in 1949; the central section was almost miraculously spared. Maulbertsch's 250th anniversary in June 1947 was the occasion for general restoration.

Access to the main courtyard is through a splendid iron gate with relief pillars topped with statues; the farm buildings and stables are set around two further courtyards and still look as though they are part of a typical feudal castle; the gardens are lower, and a shadow of their former splendour. The Schloss itself is not connected to the peripheral buildings. It is long, with two corner pavilions and a central section with a curved gable decorated with a large double-headed eagle. The finest interior feature is Maulbertsch's decorated *Gartensaal*. The salient feature of the room is that all the architectural articulation is trompe l'oeil painting; the remaining wall surfaces are painted with delicate garlands of flowers. The overwhelming ceiling fresco is on a theme much loved in the baroque period, 'The Triumph of Light': Apollo drives the chariot of the sun, bathed in a flood of light, surrounded by dawn and stars. Three figures are set around Flora, the youthful flower goddess, one of the artist's most charming creations; she is joined to her beloved, the West wind Zephyr, by a garland of flowers; on the right Diana, who cannot be left out in a hunting lodge, soars towards them; on the left is Mother Earth, with the globe in her right hand; on the lower edge lie the sleeping God of Dreams and Chronos, the god of time. The splendid composition and the fragrant glow of the colours make this one of Maulbertsch's most joyous works. The Schloss is used for exhibitions, and is closed in the winter months.

Environs: Frauenkirchen 6 km. S. of Halbturn. The medieval pilgrimage church was destroyed during the Turkish invasions. The present dignified baroque building with two towers was built in 1687 by Paul Esterhàzy as a thanks offering for his elevation to the rank of prince. (▷ Forchenstein). The pilastered church is the work of Italian artists: the architect was Francesco Martinelli, lavish stucco by Pietro A.Conti, frescos by Luca A.Columba. On the magnificent high altar is a statue of Mary, clothed, according to baroque custom; tradition suggests that the original miraculous image was an oil painting of Maria Lactans (▷ Rattersdorf), which is now on the left side altar. Altars, pulpit, organ and monumental sedilia form a unified and festive baroque entity. The monks' choir in the organ gallery with its painted and carved stalls is particularly noteworthy. Key at the gate of the Franciscan monastery (Tel. 02172-2224). **Calvary,** by the church: Unusual **Jerusalemberg,** an artificial rounded mound with the Way of the Cross and its Stations in a spiral pattern.

Hall in Tirol 6060
Tirol   p.284☐G 8

The name Hall comes from a saltmine which existed from 1232 in this little place, which rapidly grew to be a market town; the mine was owned by Count Albert von Tirol. The town was granted a charter in 1303 and walls were built around it. Hall was an important Inn harbour and had a bridge over the river from 1300. In 1477 the prince's mint was transferred from Merano to Hall (first large silver mint in Europe), and this led to an increase in prosperity for town and castle. The salt mine was finally closed in 1967, after a decline which started in the 18C. Hall is a picturesque town with fine streets and oriels, and medieval fortifications which have largely survived intact.

Burg Hasegg: The old Hasegg castle is reached via the Münzergasse and the *Münzertor* with a fine chased coat-of-arms. The massive *keep* (Münzerturm; rebuilt *c.* 1480) is the emblem of the town. The castle was originally built to protect the extraction plant, shipping and the bridge. It was mentioned in 1306 and must have been built *c.* 1300. In 1567, when Archduke Ferdinand II moved the mint to its present site, town and castle began to flourish. When the last coins were struck in 1809 ('Andreas-Hofer-Zwanziger' and 'Kreuzer') the period of decline began. The mint was reopened in 1975 for the Olympiad. Despite much rebuilding from the early 17C to the late 19C the castle still has a medieval feel. A remarkable feature

Wallfahrtskirche Frauenkirchen (Halbturn) with coloured stucco and frescos

Hall, Ratssaal (1447), beamed ceiling and central column

is the late Gothic **Georgskapelle** in the Burg, built in 1515 by Gregor and Nikolaus Türing the Elder for Maximilian I, who married his second wife, Bianca Maria Sforza, here. There are summer concerts in the late Gothic *Burghof.*

Rathaus (Oberer Stadtplatz): The Rathaus with its steep Gothic roof and battlements with coats-of-arms, the finest in the Tirol, is on the W. side of the square. The building has two sections. In the W. is the so-called *Königshaus*, presented to the town by Duke Leopold IV in 1406 (rebuilt after a fire in 1447); remarkable *Ratssaal* of 1447 with central column and beamed ceiling and the *Bürgermeisterstube*, panelled in 1669. In the E. a wide Renaissance building with stone portal (parts Gothic); balcony from which the city fathers proclaimed the decisions of the council, with town arms.

Stadtpfarrkirche St.Nikolaus (Oberer Stadtplatz): A foundation stone for a chapel was laid in 1281. After rapid extension a tower was added in 1345 (upper part re-

Palm Sunday donkey in St. Nikolaus

newed 1676) and the nave in 1352. In 1430 the church was extended by the addition of the N. aisle (Hans Sewer) and became a Gothic hall church with nave and two aisles. Redesigned in the baroque style 1752, restored in 1913&14 and 1961.

St. Nikolaus is the oldest late Gothic church in the Tirol. The principal exterior features are the massive step gable and light articulation with pilaster strips, painted friezes and blind windows. The *Fiegersche Kapelle* was built in 1490 above the columned vestibule in front of the massive main portal (with Man of Sorrows, Madonna and bust of St.Nikolaus). Special permission is required to visit the chapel. In the interior of the church the extension on the N. side gives the visitor the impression that the church is asymmetrical and that the presbytery is displaced laterally. The Gothic furnishings were stripped out of the church in 1752 and it was redesigned in the baroque style, although the basic Gothic spatial organisation was retained. The stucco and delicate painting in shades of pink conceal the groin vaulting and provide a false perspective. Ceiling painting by J.A.Mölk (1752). An unusual feature at the front end of the left aisle is the *Waldorfkapelle*, 1492–1505; it is closed off with a wrought-iron grille and was brought into being by the knight Florian Waldauf from the Puster valley. He had his collection of relics from all over the world stored here and bestowed privileges and art treasures (late Gothic Madonna, school of Pacher) on the 'little church within the church'. A notable feature of the main church is the *high altar picture* by E.Quellinus, a pupil of Rubens (1657). Remnants of the Gothic furnishings are the little door leading to the gallery, a *Palm Sunday* to the left of the high altar and the *stained glass*. Also worth seeing are the *Renaissance epitaphs* of the Fieger and Gienger families, the *font* (1570), the red marble *stoup* (1506), *Ecce-*

Münzerturm

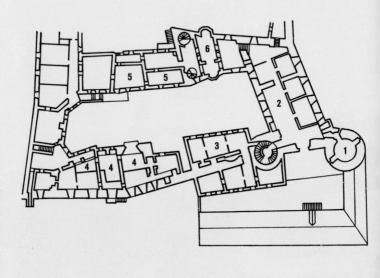

Hall in Tirol, Burg Hasegg, 1st floor 1 Münzerturm **2** Technisches Münzmuseum **3** Library **4** Stadtmuseum **5** Neue Galerie **6** Georgskapelle

homo panel picture (*c*. 1550, and a panel painting of the Mater Dolorosa by Martin Altomonte; late Gothic *monstrance* and *guild poles*. Notable *tombstones* on the N. wall and in the porch.

Kapelle zur heiligen Magdalena (E. of the parish church): the chapel was mentioned in 1330 and has fine frescos (including Last Judgement, 1466) and a fine triptych of 1480 from the former nunnery in the Hall valley. The chapel is now used as a war memorial chapel.

Other churches worth seeing: *Renaissancekirche* of the former *Damenstift* (consecrated 1570, renovated 1691&2) in the Eugengasse with fine marble portal, pretty tower with copper spire. The *Jesuitenkirche* (just next door) was consecrated in 1610. It has a remarkable high altar picture (1609, All Saints) by Matthias Karger of Munich. It is now used as a concert hall. The *Salvatorkirche* (Salvatorgasse) was consecrated in 1406. Notable fresco of Christ in the Mandorla. The *Heilig-Geist-Kirche* or *Spitalskirche* (Münzergasse) was mentioned in 1342. The present building dates from 1727&8 and has three notable rococo altars.

Also worth seeing: The *Stubenhaus* (Oberer Stadtplatz) with beamed ceiling of 1447 is a striking example of an Inn-Salzach house. *Bronze statue of Speckbacher* by Ludwig Penz (1908&9); Schloss *Rainegg* and *Nagglburg*; *Barbarasäule* (1486, Unterer Stadtplatz); **salt-mine buildings**

(Unterer Stadtplatz) with Johann-Nepomuk chapel.

Museums: *Haller Stadtmusuem* (Burg Hasegg): history of the town, salt mining and minting. *Bergbaumuseum* (Oberer Stadtplatz): mining musueum.

Hallein 5400
Salzburg   p.276☐L 7

Third oldest town in the archbishopric of Salzburg (after Salzburg and Laufen); its origin, development and name (Haellinum, the little Hall, in contrast with 'Reichen' (rich)-Hall) all derive from the re-establishment of salt-mining (brine evaporation method) *c.* 1200 on the Dürrnberg. The prosperity which came from the increase in trade and transport (some of the salt was sent down the Salzach on rafts) which inevitably accompanies the production of salt left its mark on the Old Town; there are many fine medieval houses, all of which were rebuilt in the baroque style. Today Hallein is one of the few industrial towns in the Land of Salzburg. Franz Xaver Gruber, the composer of 'Stille Nacht' died here and was buried by the Dekanatskirche.

Dekanatskirche St.Antonius der Einsiedler: The Gothic choir has survived from the medieval building; the late Romanesque tower was replaced by a modern one after the catastrophic town fire of 1943. The spacious nave was designed by court architect W.Hagenauer (1769) in accordance with his neoclassical ideas. The neoclassical high altar picture of the Nativity is by the last Salzburg court painter, A.Nesselthaler.

Keltenmuseum: Housed in the former administrative building of the salt mine since 1971; the Fürstenzimmer is

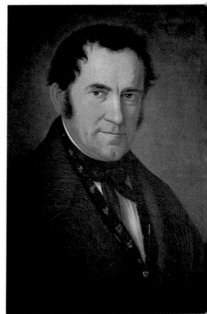

Hallein, F.X. Gruber

decorated with 71 pictures of the historic salt mine by Benedikt Werkstätter. The museum itself is remarkable for its prehistoric finds from the Dürrnberg.

Environs: Dürrnberg (cable-car valley station on the S. edge of the town): After Hallstatt the most important prehistoric site in Austria. It was settled at an early stage because of the rich salt deposits in the Dürrnberg; the salt was mined dry in prehistoric times. Finds from the Neolithic, Bronze and Hallsatt ages through to the La Tène period are to be found in Salzburg (▷ Salzburg Museum Carolino Augusteum, in particular the artistically important 'Schnabelkanne') and Hallein (▷ Keltenmuseum). The *Pfarr- und Wallfahrtskirche hl.Maria* was mentioned in 1347 and replaced by a new building entirely in red marble under Archbishop Wolf Dietrich 1554–1612. Surrounding wall with marble portal like a triumphal arch with obelisks added in 1618 under Archbishop Markus Sittikus (coat-of-arms) by Santino Solair. On the church portal coat-of-arms of Wolf Dietrich. Interior tower with stairs set around four pillars rising to the full height of the tower. Splendid high altar 1749–51 with lavish sculpture, dominated by the miraculous image of Mary Enthroned with Child 1612. The *salt mine* may be visited from May 1 to September 30.

Kuchl: 'Cucullae' featured on the 'Tabula Peutingeriana' (Vienna, Nationalbibliothek), Castorius' Roman map of the world and was mentioned again in Eugipius' 'Vita Severini'. The Salzburg cathedral had extensive property in Kuchl in the Middle Ages, including the *Pfarrkirche hll.Maria und Pankraz.* Powerful late Gothic hall with net vaulting and lavish tracery on the organ gallery. The two tombstones for Wolfgang Panicher are major works of early-18C Salzburg sculpture; one has a Crucifixion relief ascribed to H.Valkenauer (1507).

Oberalm: *Pfarrkirche hl.Stefan* with splendid baroque altar by J.G.Mohr (1707).

Puch: *Pfarrkirche hl.Maria* with remarkable late Gothic sculptures from the shrines of lost triptychs.

Hallstatt 4830

Upper Austria   p.282☐N 7

Until the end of the last century Hallstatt could only be reached by boat or a narrow packhorse road. In the town itself the area between the lake and the mountain has been used to the fullest possible extent. The only connection between the houses by the lake was by boat or by the 'upper route', which led through the attics. And yet this hostile territory was one of the first areas ever settled by man. The oldest finds (for example the so-called 'Schuhleistenkeil') date from *c.* 2500 BC. It was not the earliest period, however, which made the name of this little Austrian town famous throughout the world; enormous numbers of finds from about 3,000 Iron Age graves caused scholars to give the name *'Hallstatt Age'* to the period approximately 800 – 400 BC. The magnificent mountains, including the Dachstein, the huge caves (Rieseneishöhle and Mammuthöhle), the picturesque town with its art treasures, two excellent museums and the salt mine ensure Hallsatt's importance to the tourist industry.

Pfarrkirche Maria Himmelfahrt: The Catholic church is strikingly sited on a rocky spur above the town. The massive tower with its characteristic crown dating from *c.* 1750 was part of the earlier Romanesque building. The church was rebuilt in the early 16C with two aisles, two choirs and a social distinction between the 'people's' and the 'esquires" church. In the S. choir *Marienaltar,* a masterpiece of Gothic carving like the altars in St. Wolfgang, Kefermarkt and Gampern. Signature, on a relief of the Circumcision, '...hart Astl', usually taken to be 'Lienhart'. *Polyptych.* In the *shrine,* above a majestic but tender Madonna, St.Barbara, patroness of miners and St.Katharina, beloved of woodcutters. On the inner panels bas-reliefs from the Life of Mary; high filigree crowning with figures; 'guardians of the shrine' St.Georg and St.Florian (St.Wolfgang, Kefermarkt). *Advent side:* In the centre four bas-reliefs, on the outside four paintings, Life of Mary. *Outside:* Four paintings from the Life of Christ. *Small triptych:* Crucifixion, fine painting *c.* 1450. In the church vault

Ewer from the Hallstatt period

neo-Gothic with attractive slender spire. *Dreifältigkeitssäule* 1774, excellent statues. *Kalvarienbergkirche* with Stations of the Cross, in Lahn, charming buildings. *Custom:* Corpus Christi procession on the lake; with Traunkirchen unique in Austria.

Environs: Salt mine (approximately 1700 ft. above the town; there is a cable railway); thought to be the oldest disused salt mine in the world; it was the site of the grave finds. **'Rudolfsturm',** fortress tower of 1284, Habsburg from that date ('Kammergut' Gmunden); exhibition room in the entrance building; to view telephone 06134-208. **Dachstein caves:** *Rieseneishöhle and Mammuthöhle:* about a quarter of an hour on foot from the middle station on the Dachstein cable railway; to view: telephone 06134-208. **Bad Goisern,** *Heimathaus,* in the park *open air museum,* the last Goisern forge hammer. Meetings of the crossbow society.

chapel of the salt-masters Eyssl von Eysslsberg, ancestors of the surgeon.

Cemetery and St.-Michael-Kapelle: Cemetery created partly by shoring up and partly by piling up material against the mountainside. **Doppelkirche St. Michael:** Upper part church, lower part ossuary. The acute lack of space forced an early change in the method of burial; after about 10 years the bones were placed in the charnel house; approximately 1200 skulls, most with name and date of death, some with a painted garland of flowers.

Museums: *Heimatmuseum* (history of the area, mining, folk art). *Prähistorisches Museum* (original finds, of great importance, e.g. salt carrier made of skins).

Also worth seeing: *Protestant church,*

Hardegg 2082
Lower Austria   p.278□U 2

Raabs-Kollmitzgraben-Eibenstein and Hardegg are the Thaya fortresses on the Bohemian border. In 1483 the Freiherren of Prueschenk took the name Hardegg. In 1495 they were made Reichsgrafen by Maximilian I.

Castle: The castle was first mentioned in 1140 and extended *c.* 1200. It was taken in 1425, presumably by the Hussites, burned down in the 16C and gradually fell into disrepair, until it was rebuilt in the 19C by Prince Khevenhüller-Metsch. First castle gate with late Gothic surround, second with portal with pointed arch, former portcullis. In the *chapel* Renaissance relief, part of the family tomb of the Counts of Prueschenk-Hardegg. *Pfarrkirche St. Veit* (12C, 13C, 15C and baroque redesign in

Burg Hardegg

the 18C); *ossuary* (12C, altered in the late Gothic period.

point is not the displaced gate, but a fine urn in a niche with a coat-of-arms above it.

Harmannsdorf 3713
Lower Austria   p.278□V4

Schloss: Harmannsdorf is on the high plateau of the Manhardsberg, surrounded by a wall with round corner towers and dominated by another tower. Elegant Schloss with deep moat, built around the medieval *Höllenturm* (battlements 19C). The Schloss was built in 1612 and redesigned in the baroque style in 1760—the park, with its many stone statues, dates from this period. Main entrance through gate with grille: the path is lined with numerous stone urns and leads to a flight of steps with stone balustrade. The centre

Hartberg 8230
Steiermark   p.280□U 8

Barrows suggest dense settlement in prehistoric times. In 1125–8 Margrave Leopold I founded the first Traungau Pfalz in Styria here, and the most important market town in E. Styria came into being (charter 1286). The old castle, the church and the market settlement coalesced and were enclosed within a rectangular town wall, parts of which have survived by the W. tower and beside the Schloss.

Stadtpfarr- und Dekanatskirche St. Martin: Originally a basilica with nave and two aisles and two powerful towers (12C); a choir with three bays was added in 1467. The stellar vaulting in the formerly flat-ceilinged nave was added in the 16C. The church was rebuilt in the baroque style in 1745–60; the Gothic vaulting in the choir was removed and J.A.Mölk painted ceiling frescos. The delicately articulated **musicians' gallery** on the N. wall and the *high altar painting* by J.C.Hackhofer are also worth seeing.

Ossuary: S. of the church is the ossuary, built *c.* 1170, a two-storey rotunda with three-sided apse in muschelkalk. The exterior is articulated by multiple rib pillars with crocket capitals and the interior has eight half columns continued in the dome as bands. With the exception of the dome and the walls of the spiral staircase the interior is entirely painted with frescos; unfortunately much of this work has been spoiled by gratuitous overpainting (after 1888). The paintings are divided into two areas, the upper with Christ and the Apostles and the lower with allegories of the Kingdoms of the World after Daniel.

Hartberg, St. Martin with ossuary

In the apse, which was least affected by the restoration, the Tree of Jesse and saints are depicted. The exterior shaped stones were also removed in the course of restoration.

Also worth seeing: In the great hall in the S. section of the *priest's house* (16&17C) are *frescos* by J.A.Mölk illustrating the Bible story. The medieval *Alte Burg* has survived as three storeys, half in ruins. The Rittersaal contains a stone Renaissance fireplace; also a wing with arcades and and an exterior staircase which was originally vaulted. The *Wallfahrtskirche Maria-Lebring* was built in 1472 and altered in 1772; the rib vaults were removed and the ceiling decorated with frescos by J.A.Mölk. Notable statue on the high altar.

Hartenstein = Albrechtsberg an der Grossen Krems 3613

Lower Austria   p.278□S 4

Castle: Fortress on a steep rock in a lonely valley of the Kleine Krems. Built 1178 by Heinrich von Hartenstein, subsequently princely fief of the Maissau, Sinzendorf and Gudenus families. The old buildings consist of keep (walls 13 ft. thick, tapering), palas and round tower at descending levels; 19C building in front of the complex (cold water cure centre). Below the Burg in a steep rock face is the *Gudenushöhle*, a cave discovered in 1883 with tools from the interglacial period and bones of mammoth, rhinoceros, cave bear and cave hyena.

Heidenreichstein 3860

Lower Austria   p.278□R 2

Burg Heidenreichstein: The castle was founded by the Burggrafen of Gars-Eggenburg; it was named after a son of Graf Walter von Gars called Heidenreich.

The castle was mentioned in 1205; it must have been founded before 1180. In 1279 it was taken over by the Landesfürsten, later by the Puchheim family until 1656. The Burg was extended under them. It is now owned by the counts Kinsky. It was never taken and never destroyed and is the *finest moated Burg in Lower Austria;* it is bounded by the Hausteich, the Romau brook and two artificial moats. The square keep with walls almost 10 ft. thick dates from the 13C. It is 131 ft. high and the entrance is at a height of 50 ft. Two gatehouses, one behind the other, with drawbridges and intact bridge cellars. Fine courtyard with arches, well and 2 staircase towers. **Castle chapel** in the E. tower with Gothic acanthus painting. The residential buildings in the courtyard date from the 15C.

Heiligenblut 9844
Kärnten   p.284 □ L 9

Pfarrkirche St. Vinzenz: At a height of over 4,500 ft., at the foot of the Grossglockner, is one of the most important churches in the area, both in terms of the building and the furnishings. In the late 14C gold-mining shareholders and miners replaced the even older Capella S.Vincentii (1301) with a Gothic building. The work took more than a century, under arduous conditions, the choir was completed *c.* 1430 and the nave *c.* 1490. The spire and saddleback roof are very steep; there is a late 15C *Christopher fresco* on the outer N. wall. The *interior* maintains an emphasis on the vertical. Choir and nave are net vaulted.

The church's most precious treasure is the late Gothic double **polyptych** (1520), which in both form and content is within the S.Tyrolean tradition of carving and painting of M.Pacher. The two principal artists involved, Wolfgang Asslinger and M.Reichlich, were known associates of Pacher. The work is nearly 35 ft. high, and thus one of the largest of its kind. The Coronation of Mary is under a tracery baldachin in the central shrine. In the retable statues of the auxiliary saints, in the

Burg Heidenreichstein

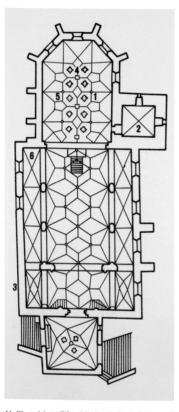

Heiligenblut, Pfarrkirche 1 Choir **2** Tower **3** St. Christopher fresco (outside N. wall) **4** Late Gothic altar **5** Tabernacle **6** Altar of St. Veronica

Heiligenblut, St. Vinzenz

in the N. aisle was also endowed in 1491. It may be the work of Lukas Tausmann. In the stellar-vaulted lower church are *late Gothic carved wooden figures* in the style of the high altar; they may originally have been part of it. The Madonna Enthroned with Child dates from *c.* 1400. The church also has fine baroque tombs.

crowning above the shrine Christ and martyrs. The altar also contains 12 panel paintings at the front and back; the panels can be opened and shut to show different faces. In its combination of architecture, sculpture, painting and ornament the late Gothic polyptych combines all the medieval modes of expression and blends then into a whole.

In the same spirit is the tall *tabernacle* (1494) in the choir: the last Epiphany of the Gothic period. The **Veronika-Altar**

Heiligenbrunn = Strem 7522
Burgenland   p.280 □ V 9

Kellerviertel. Alfred Schmeller, the great expert on Burgenland, has called the Heiligenbrunn Kellerviertel 'a cultural monument of the first order' and anyone who has visited it will agree with this opinion. In other places buildings brought from far and wide are rebuilt in open-air museums for documentary purposes; in Heiligenbrunn a district has survived which developed organically in the 18C, and which still fulfils its original function. The name 'Keller' ('cellar') can be misleading; we are not dealing with undergound rooms, but with small buildings stretching far along the slope below the vineyards. The charming surroundings with many fine old trees (chestnut, oak, lime and also fruit trees) caused the whole district to be placed under protection as an area of outstanding natural beauty as well as an ancient monument.

The 'Keller' are unsophisticated timber buildings with whitened loam-smeared walls. Many still have thatched roofs, a protection against excessive heat and cold. Most of the little houses have two rooms, the actual wine-pressing room and the 'Stüberl'. Wine has been grown in the area since the 12C. The spicy wine, called 'Uhudler' is a homemade drink for consumption when the day's work is done. The area is always open, the local community will give information on visits to the pressing rooms. Tel. 03324-281.

Heiligenkreuz bei Baden 2532
Lower Austria   p.278☐U 5

Margrave Leopold III, the Holy, (1095–1136) was married for the second time to Agnes, the daughter of Emperor Heinrich IV. His son Otto was the 5th of 18 children. When he was 14 his father sent him to one of the famous cathedral schools in Paris. Two years later, on his journey home, he and 15 young noblemen entered the Cistercian monastery of Morimond, the 4th daughter foundation of the Cistercians of Cîteaux. For six years the young man disappeared into the anonymity of monastery life. He was consecrated abbot and a year later became bishop of Freising

(1138). In the Heiligenkreuz foundation document it is stated that the Margrave 'has followed the instructions of his beloved son Otto' and wishes to found a Cistercian monastery. The date of foundation is September 11, 1133. Twelve monks from Morimond and their abbot Gottschalk began a timber building. After a short time the monastery had 300 monks. In 1138 Heiligenkreuz settled Zwettl, to the NE, and in 1142 Baumgartenberg, to the E, among other places, and after 1150 the stone building was started. The W. walk of the cloister has survived. On 31.1.1187 the building was consecrated and Leopold V's great cross reliquary was presented. (He died in Graz and was not allowed to be buried in the chapterhouse until his son and twelve nobles swore to pay back the rest of the ransom money for Richard the Lionheart). Ludwig IX, the Holy, King of France, presented a piece of the Crown of Thorns to Frederick II two years before his death; on June 12, 1246 the last Babenberg died and was buried in Heiligenkreuz, as were 12 other members of his House.

Cistercian monastery: The buildings in the Sattelbach valley are surrounded by a wall. The baroque tower with onion dome (1674) contravenes the Cistercian rule. 16C *fountain* in front of the tavern. There is a hornwork above the *gate arch* on the courtyard side. The *inner monastery courtyard* has fine arches on two levels in the section opposite the church (guest wing completed in 1665 with picture gallery and G.Giuliani's remarkable clay models). The *Dreifaltigkeitssäule* and the *Josephsbrunnen* were built in 1739 to models by G.Giuliani.

After the Gothic buildings were completed, monastery and church went into a decline in the 15&16C; they were revitalised by the 'Swabian abbots' and flourished in the 17&18C. (Emperor Leopold I favoured the monastery). Early baroque monastery building 1637–65. Arcaded court 1670. Rebuilt by abbot Schirmer after damage by the Turks: he employed J.M.Rottmayr of Rosenbrunn, M.Altomonte and G.Giuliani. Much was spoiled by neo-Gothic additions in the last century.

Stiftskirche Maria Himmelfahrt: One of the most important churches in the German-speaking world. It has a nave and two aisles, and from its plan appears narrow. On the asymmetrical W. façade tripartite Cistercian windows; two portals with almost fully rounded columns; Tree of Life in the tympanum. Overwhelming sense of space in the interior with its massive pillars (the Cistercian building regulations forbid columns). The three-aisled hall choir with square bays was completed in 1295. The bays in the nave are also square and are halved in the aisles. The E. choir is extremely light, with a tripartite window.

The present high altar (1887) is neo-Gothic. The very fine choir stalls (1707) are by G.Giuliani. Left of the sanctuary the *Kreuzkapelle*, which was partly demolished when the tower was built. *Ossuary* beneath the church.

Monastery buildings: *Cloister:* S. of the church, built 1220–1240. The 300 pillars are in red marble. The oldest part is the W. wing with Romanesque gate. Notable tracery windows and grave slabs. 28 of the gravestones date from the 13C. (In the case of the Babenbergs it is probable that they were all buried at the same time; some were moved here from earlier graves.) Washing of the Feet (1705) by Giuliani, **Annakapelle. Chapterhouse:** square hall, four octagonal pillars (the Hohenstaufen octagon), in the floor high tomb slab of Frederick the Warlike, who was killed in 1246 in a battle with the Hungarians on the Leitha, which meant the end of Babenberg supremacy. Adjacent *funerary chapel:* the impressive insignia of mourn-

Heiligenkreuz, Zisterzienserkloster **1** Stiftskirche **2** Former ossuary **3** Bernhardikapelle **4** Totenkapelle **5** Cloister **6** Fountain house **7** Abbot's house **8** Sacristy **9** Library **10** Chapterhouse **11** Mönchsoffizin **12** Quadratur **13** Tower

Heiligenkreuz, Stiftskirche ▷

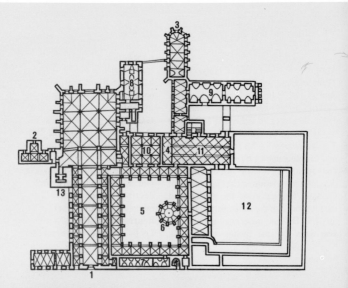

Heiligenkreuz, chapterhouse with tomb cover of Frederick the Valiant

Heiligenkreuz, 13C fountain house, with original grisaille windows

ing, black catafalque, gilded and silvered, watch candles, skeleton with robe and chandelier 7 ft. high, all by Giuliani. Monks' office: hall with three aisles and round pillars; above it is the spartan *dormitory* with three aisles. The *Bernhardikapelle* has a modern interior. The nine-sided well house in the centre of the S. section has fine tracery blind base courses, original grisaille medallions and pictures of the founder, and dates from the 13C. The whole complex is Gothic, but the windows are Romanesque in style. In the late 13C the Habsburgs were still strangers in the land, and the memory of the Babenbergs was cultivated. The first Babenberg family tree is in this well house. The Margrave has made sure that his crown is the same as the Duke's. Shield and covered sword. Otto von Freising in Cistercian habit (not bishop's vestments). 10 stained glass panels survived the Turkish invasion. Lead cross in the *sacristy* by G.R.Donner, a pupil of Giuliani. The *Way of the Cross* on a hill in front of the monastery is by Giuliani and his pupils (1731).

Heiligenkreuz-Gutenbrunn = Reidling 3454

Lower Austria   p.278☐T 4

Pfarrkirche Mariae Himmelfahrt: Added to the Schloss in 1755 – 8 by J.Ohmeyer for suffragan bishop Franz Anton Marxer on the site of a 1733 pilgrimage chapel. Notable features: high altar (1757) by Ferdinand Hohenberg von Hetzendorf; stucco by J.J.Resler, outstanding altar pictures and frescos by F.A.Maulbertsch (1758). Rococo organ case.

Schloss: Built 1738 by J.J.Tepser, extended by F.A.Marxer in 1745; façade with 15 axes with two octagonal towers: staircase tower, stucco and *Marienkapelle* with frescos by P.Troger. Worthwhile *Niederösterreichisches Barockmuseum.*

Heimfels = Sillian 9920
Tirol   p.284☐J 10

Kirche zum hl.Petrus: Single-aisled church with tunnel vaulting, originally Gothic, redesigned in the baroque period; on the left of the choir is an early 16C fresco. The late Gothic (*c.* 1520) *triptych* on the main altar has paintings and reliefs of the life of St. Peter. An early Gothic statue of Peter in the nave dates from *c.* 1450. Very fine enamelled gold *monstrance*, 1591, by Heinrich Eglof of Konstanz.

Schloss Heimfels: It is a short climb from the Petruskirche to the massive medieval fortress, beautifully sited but half in ruins; in the 13C it was the seat of the estate officials of Heunfels. The high palas and solid keep date from this period. A *chapel* was built in the palas in the 14C. Frescos *c.* 1460. The courtyards and residential building date from *c.* 1500, and give an idea of life in the fortress at that time.

Environs: Sillian. The baroque *Pfarrkirche zu Unserer Lieben Frau Himmelfahrt* of 1760 is based on a Gothic building, first mentioned in 1212. Fine features of the interior are the frescos (1760) by J.A.Mölk and the Madonna statue (1460) on the high altar. In the priest's house fine beamed ceiling (1420) and a room in the Empire style. Frescos (1755) on the second floor.

Hellmonsödt 4202
Upper Austria   p.276☐P 4

Pfarrkirche hl.Alexius: Late Gothic building, fine high altar of 1758, painting by B.Altomonte. In the N. Starhemberg vault chapel, opening into the choir through a broad Gothic arch. Outstanding 15–17C tombs.

Environs: Freilichtmuseum Pelmberg, about 5 km. to the SE. 'Mit-

Schloss Heimfels

termayer' farm museum. Typical Mühlviertel farmhouse, first mentioned 1325, but probably older; instructive agricultural museum in a farm which worked until 1953 (to view: Tel. 07215-488).

Wildberg im Haselgraben: 5 km. from Hellmonsödt, in the S. *Schloss and castle ruin;* of strategic importance on the direct route northwards from Linz to Budweis and Prague; massive round keep, walled walk with consoles and trefoil arches (14C), the battlements are now roofed in. The Bohemian King Wenceslas was kept prisoner here in 1394.

Schloss Herberstein = St. Johann bei Herberstein 8222
Steiermark   p.280☐T/U 9

Schloss Herberstein: The Schloss was built *c.* 1230 for the counts of Stubenberg and is in a zoo which has existed since the 17C. The oldest parts (around 1300) are in the W.; the N. two-storey residential quarters and the keep are in good condition. The S. defensive building was rebuilt in the 15C to connect keep and residence. The present design is 16C. Of interest in the interior are the single-aisled *Katharinenkapelle* (14C frescos have been revealed), the *Georgskapelle* and the *Rittersaal*. The *Schlossmuseum* has a fine collection of domestic utensils, including the *Herberstein font* (Augsburg, 16C).

Hermagor 9620
Kärnten   p.282☐M 11

Pfarrkirche hl.Hermagoras und Fortunatus: A three-aisled late Gothic hall with four bays and S. chapel, rebuilt after

the Turkish invasion incorporating older sections (choir). Decorative historicist features in the W. added in 1904. Interesting *keystone painting* in the nave. In the Middle Ages the keystone was a symbol of Christ holding the church together, and this function is stressed by the painting of 1485. The late-14C *wall paintings* revealed in the choir show Apostles. The style suggests an Italian artist. In the S. *Wolkensteinkapelle* is a fine carved and painted *triptych* of *c.* 1500. The main and side altars are essentially late baroque. The fine figures on the main altar are by J.Paterer, 1749.

Herzogenburg 3130
Lower Austria   p.278☐T 4

Augustiner-Chorherrenstift and Stiftskirche hll.Georg und Stephan: a church at the mouth of the Traisen originally dedicated to St. George was moved to Herzogenburg in 1112. In 1148 Bishop Konrad of Passau, the brother of

Herzogenburg, Stiftskirche

Heinrich II, founded an Augustinian canonry at the request of Walter von Traisen. The church was consecrated in 1286 and building of the cloister started at once. The building was not completed until the 16C. After a period of decline prior Wilhelm von Schmerling redesigned monastery and church in the baroque style and had most of the older parts of the building pulled down. The plans were by Prandtauer and after his death Munggenast took over. Fischer von Erlach worked on the inner courtyard 1716–20.

Parts of the *refectory* (with Nativity frescos), parts of the *cloister* and the lower part of the *tower* have survived from the 15C. In 1743 the old tower was blown up and a cylindrical crown built on the massive base; the spire was replaced with a ducal coronet. The entrance portal of the church is 15C. The church has one aisle and the central dome is supported by pairs of pillars set on the diagonal (shallow dome without lantern); it is decorated with a Community of Saints by B.Altomonte. The choir narows in two stages and has a semicircular apse. *High altar* by Munggenast, *altar picture* by D.Gran, 1746, the high baroque painter: Madonna Enthroned with Child. On the left and right the church patrons Georg and Stephan. Inner *Stiftshof:* Fischer's plan was partially executed. Over the central section, the façade of the Festsaal, gable with St. George. Interior *ceiling fresco* by Altomonte (foundation of the monastery by the bishops of Passau; in the staircase tower the transfer of the monks). Lavish *collection of paintings* in the Bildersaal, including J.Breu's Aggsbach altar (▷ Aggsbach).

Gothic church with baroque alterations contains only the core of its predecessor. The articulated tunnel vaulting of the nave with four bays dates from the 17C. Interesting features are the *altars* (*c.* 1470–1770) and the *marble tombstone* of Balthasar von Pibrach zu Biberstein (d. 1556) in the S. exterior wall.

Schloss Biberstein: This dignified Gothic castle dates from shortly before 1400. The higgledy-piggledy medieval rooms were lent the dignity of a four-sided Renaissance courtyard in 1570–80.

Hochfeistritz 9372
Kärnten   p.282□Q 10

Wallfahrtskirche Unsere Liebe Frau: Textbook example of a Carinthian fortress church. Walls and church date from the second half of the 15C, the period of the Turkish invasions. The church tower in the W. façade, the three-aisled hall with four bays and the slightly narrower choir with two bays form a compact and unified whole. Choir and nave have *stellar vaulting*. The ribs, profiles and keystones are carved with particular care; the portals are very fine. The *frescos on the S. wall* (1480) and a carved wooden *Madonna and Child* of 1410 in the Soft Style, above the sacristy, are fine features from the pre-baroque period. The outer parts of the baroque *high altar* (1670, Gurk altar workshop) are by B. Setlinger. *Madonna* with St.Katharina and St.Barbara, magnificent late Gothic carved figures *c.* 1480–90.

Himmelberg 9562
Kärnten   p.282□O 10

Pfarrkirche hl.Martin: An 11C building on the site is mentioned, but the present

---

Hochosterwitz = Launsdorf 9314
Kärnten   p.282□P 10

Burg: It is possible that this fortress stands on the site of a Roman citadel. Earliest

Burg Hochosterwitz

mention is *c.* 860. The present building on the rock is a Renaissance alteration of Romanesque and Gothic predecessors. In the period between 1570 and 1580 the warrior and court official Georg Khevenhüller took over the building and had it altered to its present form. 14 gatehouses connected by walls wind like a serpent around the Burg itself. Each of these gates has a name, a symbol, and a coat-of-arms or inscription relating to this. It is almost as though the sacred concept of the Stations of the Cross were being taken over in secular form. At the same time it is symbolic of a triumphal passage. The joint function of fortress and representative building also chimes with the building's date between the Middle Ages and the modern period. On the Fähnrichstor are the arms of the master of the castle in 1575. In the Hochburg is a fine *Burg courtyard* with arcades; in its NW corner is an old well. The wall paintings in the *chapel* are Renaissance (1570). The church has a *bronze altar* in the same style and also a late baroque altar of 1729. The *collections* include armour, medallions and other historic objects.

Bad Hofgastein 5630

Salzburg   p.284☐L 9

Principal town of the Gasteinertal; it was originally called 'Hof' and along with the 'provincia Castuna' (Gasteinertal) of the dukes of Bavaria was sold in 1297 to the lords of Goldegg and came under the direct rule of the archbishop in 1327. The town flourished through gold mining (*c.* 1400 to *c.* 1560), particularly under the

Weitmoser family. In 1828–30 connection to the thermal springs in Badgastein.

Pfarrkirche hl.Maria: Late Gothic hall church with nave and two aisles and W. tower dating from 1602. The nave has stellar vaulting and the choir and polygonal apse net vaulting. The splendid high altar of 1738 was designed by the painter I.A.Eisl of Neumarkt and has baroque figures by Paul Mödlhammer and a fine Gothic Madonna Enthroned as its central figure (*c.* 1500). Numerous 15–17C tombstones including (outside) those of the most important mine-owning families. In the town numerous mine-owners' houses with coats-of-arms have survived.

Environs: The *Weitmoserschlössl* (on the SW edge of the town) is a typical 16C Salzburg house (1554) with round corner towers.

Hohenems 6845
Vorarlberg   p.286☐A8

Hofgastein, Weitmoserschlössl

In 1170 Alt-Ems was extended as an imperial castle on the orders of the Emperor Barbarossa; in 1191 Emperor Heinrich VI brought the blinded Norman Prince Wilhelm here to secure the Sicilian throne for his son Frederick II. The Ems family were Reichsministerialien in charge of the castle. Wolf Dietrich of Ems married Clara de Medici, the sister of the Medici Pope Pius IV, elected in 1560. She was the mother of three talented sons: Jakob Hannibal, Mark Sittich and Gabriel von Ems. In 1560 Emperor Ferdinand raised the Ems family to the rank of imperial count. Jakob Hannibal became Feldobrist in the service of King Philipp II and supreme commander of the papal troops. Mark Sittich became a cardinal in 1561 and Bishop of Konstanz: he built the palace at the foot of the mountain below the old Burg

'Altems'. His architect was Martino Longo of Milan (1563). He became short of money and gave the palace to his brother Hannibal, who married Hortensia Borromea in 1565. Five years later her half-brother Carlo Borromeo (St. Borromeo), Cardinal Archbishop of Milan and state secretary to the Pope, was a guest in the half-finished palace. Hortensia died at the age of 28. Hannibal built the parish church and sent the principal parts of the altar from Flanders. His brother, the cardinal, died in Rome in 1594. Torquato Tasso wrote his last sonnet on the occasion of his death. The Schloss was completed by Kaspar von Ems. In 1617 he built a chapel to his uncle, canonised in 1610, and also in 1617 introduced a Jewish community which existed until the Second World War. After Kaspar's death the title of count went to other families. Kaspar's large marble tomb (1635) is in the church. In 1759 the male line of the counts of Ems died out, and the title passed to the Habsburgs and the possessions via the heiress Rebecca to the House of Harrach. In 1755 and 1779 two manuscripts of the Nibelungenlied were discovered in the palace library: the Hohenems manuscripts G and A.

Schloss Hohenems: A simple rectangular Renaissance building with projecting sections on two axes, and portal. Fine courtyard with a blind façade on the mountain side: arches, open windows, frieze with armour, hunting arrows and musical instruments. Fountain and coats-of-arms on the central axis. The *Schubertiade* initiated by the baritone Hermann Prey takes place here in June. The fine rooms have fireplaces and coffered ceilings with rosettes. Fine rosary picture by Moritz Frosch of Fedkrich, 1569: angels hold a garland of roses around the Cross with Mary and John.

Pfarrkirche zum hl.Karl Borromäus: Built 1796 – 8 over an older building (former burial place of the Ems). Single room with shallow tunnel vault. On the high altar the large red marble tabernacle with copper doors is an unfortunate solecism. The central figures (originally coloured) were sent from Flanders in 1575 by Hannibal von Ems, who commissioned local artists (Esaias Gruber) to provide a framework; this resulted in a fine combination of Flemish and German work. In the central shrine Coronation of Mary by the Holy Trinity; in the arched spaces below Count Hannibal and Hortensia Borromea. In the predella Adoration of the Magi. Tombs of Mark Sittich and Kaspar von Ems.

Also worth seeing: Extensive ruins show how large Burg Altems used to be. On a ridge nearby is Burg Neu-Ems, called Burg Glopper. It was built in 1343 by knight

Ulrich I of Ems with the permission of Emperor Ludwig the Bavarian. It was destroyed in the Appenzell Wars of 1407 and rebuilt in 1408.

Hollabrunn 2020
Lower Austria   p.278□U 3

Principal town of the wine-growing area on the border of the Bohemian Mark and the Ostmark. Originally in the possession of the Cham-Voburgs. The town frequently changed hands, and so did the monastery. The church was rebuilt by the Sonnenberg family, and bears their arms on the keystones. In the 17C Gundacker von Dietrichstein built a *Capuchin monastery* (now used as an administrative building) and replaced the church roof, which had been destroyed by fire.

Pfarrkirche St.Ulrich: Nave with three bays, articulated tunnel vault. 13C choir. Tombstones, above all that of Georg Gilleis, 1593.

Also worth seeing: *Wegsäule,* 1649, to commemorate the Peace of Westphalia. *Städtisches Museum* (13 Hölzlgasse) with primeval finds and works of art from the region.

Hollenburg = Maria Rain 9161
Kärnten   p.282□P 11

The building was first mentioned as 'Hollenburch' in 1142. In 1514 Emperor Maximilian I sold it to the humanist Sigismund von Dietrichstein. In the 16&17C the lords of the castle undertook alterations in stages; stylistically the building is somewhere between medieval purpose-

Hohenems, Renaissance altar ▷

Hollenburg, arcaded courtyard

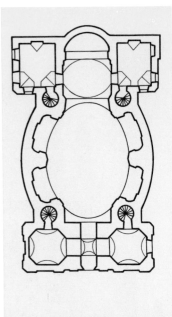

Hollenegg, Pfarrkirche zum hl. Ägydius:
Four niches open off the elliptical main area; the
entrance is opposite the elliptical choir, which is
set at right angles

building (undecorated façade, irregular arrangement of windows, 14&15C) and modern representational architecture: rib vaults in the SW hall (1516), twin Renaissance windows in the S. building and above all the fine inner courtyard with two-storey Renaissance arcades in the E. (1558). In the wall of the courtyard are two *Roman grave slabs* (2C AD) and a large *coat-of-arms* of Sigmund Georg von Dietrichstein (1593). The *Burg chapel* contains a late-14C fresco cycle. Fine view from the Südost-Söller.

Hollenegg = Deutschlandsberg 8530
Steiermark   p.280 ☐ S 10

Schloss Hollenegg: Seat of the family of the same name which died out in the 16C

(mentioned since 1163). The building no longer has the character of a medieval fortress. A diagonal wing divides the rectangular Schloss into two courtyards. The residential buildings are set around the N. courtyard and a wall passage runs round the S. court. Friedrich of Hollenegg had the NW and SE corners fortified with two cannon towers by Francesco Marmoro in the 16C. The *tower* in the NE corner is considerably older; it is connected to the 14C ring wall. A fine staircase tower with arcades (1577) leads to the E. residential section. His style is akin to that of the dell'Allio school (castle and Landhaus in Graz); this shows particularly in the arches of the three-storey E. wing. The interior was largely decorated in the late 18C for the counts of Khuenberg: frescos by

Schloss Hollenegg

P.C.Laubmann (1750, restored 1885) in the great hall of the N. section. In other rooms rococo stucco ceilings, stoves, inlaid doors and French tapestries. The furnishings were completed from Schloss buildings in Riegersburg and Limberg. The 15C late Gothic *triptych* from the Schloss chapel in Riegersburg is notable.

Pfarrkirche hl.Ägydius: The church is in the arcaded S. courtyard and is presumably by Johann Fuchs (consecrated 1778). Elliptical nave with four niches, elliptical choir bay. Side altar panels by Laubmann, 1753. On the W. side arches hatchments with carved reliefs.

Filialkirche hl.Patrizius: Also by the architect of the Hollenegg church and like it elliptical. The sanctuary behind the tabernacle is made to look larger by trompe l'oeil painting (frescos by Laubmann).

Environs: the ruined **Deutschlandsberg** was mentioned in 1153. Seat of the lords of Lonsperch, in ruins since 1860. Extended by an outwork with protruding round tower. Renaissance arches over the cistern in the courtyard. The *Pfarrkirche* was built in its present form by Jakob Schmerlaib in 1688-1701. Nave with side chapels with galleries below them. High altar painting by Carolus Laubmann.

Horn 3580
Lower Austria   p.278□T 3

After the migration of the peoples the 'first Bavarian settlement' began between the Lech and the March. Battles were fought with Moravian princes. The Hungarians penetrated as far as the Lech, where they

Ruined castle of Deutschlandsberg (Hollenegg)

were defeated in 955. The population had left the country, which was resettled by the Bavarians. They took the names of their towns, villages and families with them, and remained under the patronage of their bishops until 1803. Count Gerold and his wife Christine, Bavarians, signed over a church on their lands to Egilbert, Bishop of Passau *c.* 1050. This church, dedicated to St. Stephen, is the present *Friedhofskirche zum hl. Stephan* above the Taffa valley. The original wooden church was replaced by a Gothic building. The Gerolds were succeeded by the Poigens. The first *castle* dates from this period; its tower has survived. The town came into the hands of the Maissau family, who commissioned the interior of the Spital *c.* 1400. At this time the Horn basin was more densely populated than it is today, but the population was decimated by plague and the Hussites.

Robber knights forced the payment of large sums of protection money. In 1539 Hans von Puchheim (Emperor Maximilian had given him Horn in fief) built a new *castle*. The Puchheims were Protestants and the whole population took this faith in 1539. In 1593 a Protestant church was built on the site of the old *Georgskapelle* in the Marktplatz. Horn played an important role in the Habsburg fraternal feud: Matthias sought allies against his brother, but refused to acknowledge the privileges of the Protestants. On October 3 1608 166 noblemen formed the Horner Bund. Wallenstein was in Horn in 1625. In 1645 Torstenson forced the Brüderschaft to pay an enormous sum for a letter of protection, the *Salva Guardia*. By 1652 the town was Catholic again. The Piaristenkirche was consecrated in 1662, and the Order took over the grammar school, founded in 1657.

In 1679 the daughter of the last count of Sprintzenstein (Sprinz=sparrow hawk) inherited Horn and brought it to her husband Count Hoyos. In 1890 the *Georgskirche* was rebuilt and a spire added on the pattern of the Tein church in Prague. This very attractive town was heavily modernised after the war. Once charming Marktplatz with fountain and false façades.

Churches: *Alte Pfarrkirche hl.Stephan:* Outside the town in the cemetery. Gothic choir. High altar 1674. Rare 17C wooden grave panels. Stone pulpit 1500. The *Schulkirche der Piaristen* (zum hl.Antonius von Padua), now state school, was rebuilt after a fire in the 19C. The St.Antony is by Schmidt of Krems. The *Stadtpfarrkirche hl.Georg* was built in 1593, interior 17&18C. The *Altöttinger Kapelle* (1655) is a copy of the chapel of Altötting in Bavaria.

Also worth seeing: *Schloss:* the plain building with attractive Venetian chimneys and a baroque portal façade is occupied by the counts. Terrace on the garden side. Adjacent is the *former Land court* with two tiers of arches. In the Bürgerspital with chapel is the extremely well designed *Höbarth-Museum.* Important primeval collection and coin finds: an earthern pot from Allensteig with 3,000 10C silver

Horn, town wall with tower

coins (Krems and Fischau Pfennigs), finds from the Old and Middle Stone Ages. Count Ferdinand Kurz of Senfftenau, imperial vice-chancellor, built an estate in the manner of the Fuggerei in the impoverished land; parts of it have survived.

Igls 6080
Tirol   p.286□F 9

Pfarrkirche St. Aegidius: This church was mentioned in 1286, rebuilt in the 15C and redesigned in the baroque style in 1700; it still has a late Gothic tower, but the dome dates from 1883. In the *Totenkapelle* is a late Gothic fresco. Ceiling paintings by J.M.Schmutzer, 1777.

Also worth seeing: The *Hohenburg* was probably originally Romanesque. It fell into disrepair and was rebuilt in 1877. The nearby *Wallfahrtskapellle Heiligwasser* was built in 1662 and has 1720 stucco and a carved Madonna on the altar dating from the first half of the 15C.

Environs: Worthwhile excursions to Götzens, Aldrans, Ampass and, of course, ·Innsbruck.

Illmitz, evening by the Neusiedlersee

Illmitz 7142

Burgenland   p.278□W 6

Illmitz is in the so-called Seewinkel (lake corner); when the borders were drawn in 1921, leaving Ödensee in Hungary, an area came into being in the SE of the Neusiedlersee with Hungary to its S. and E., and the lake in the W.; it is thus only accessible from the N. Geographically the area is part of the eastern Puss valley area; it has a number of small and very small salt lakes, locally known as 'Lacken'; the most important are nature conservation areas.

Village buildings: In **Illmitz** two characteristic village buildings have survived; a *barn* with a reed roof and the *Floriani-Hof;* the latter, in the Streckhof, has a curved baroque gable and reed roof and is one of the finest of its kind. Unfortunately such buildings are a rarity.

Environs: Apetlon (3 km. S. of Illmitz): From Apetlon, a typical Breitanger village, one soon reaches the nature conservation area of the 'Lange Lacke'. Wooden wells and also a primitive reed hut of the kind built by shepherds, give the visitor from the West an impression of a completely different culture.

Imbach = Senftenberg 2541

Lower Austria   p.278□T 4

Pfarrkirche Mariae Geburt: In 1269 Albero von Feldsberg and his wife Gisela presented their castle of Imbach to the Dominican Order, founded by St.Dominic in 1215. In 1285 the church was built from the stone of the castle; it is the first church with two aisles in Austria. It combines elements of the mother church in Toulouse (tall, slender lines) with Lilienfeld building experience. The monastery flourished in

the 15C. Pilgrimage to the 'Ähren-madonna'. The monastery never recovered from a disastrous fire in 1759. Dissolved in 1782 by Emperor Joseph II.

The church (originally a church of All Saints) has a square W. tower with stone spire and brick corner turrets. In the centre of the two-aisled hall church are high octagonal pillars without capitals. Narrow ribs with keystones. Lavish, low choir separated from the plainer nave by a Gothic arch. Nuns' choir in the W. The finest features of the furnishings are the statue of the Madonna (*c.* 1300) on the baroque *high altar,* the sacrament niche with rose grille (1400) and a relief in lime wood dating from the 16C (Bohemian work; the Good Shepherd with 4 Apostles) and a pilgrimage picture, Madonna im Ährenkleid; tempera on wood). *Katharinenkapelle:* the funerary chapel of the Wallsee von Drosendorf family built on to the N. wall has fragments of paintwork. Blind arches with figure consoles (angel, wild man, woman in veil etc). To the left of this fine, light chapel is access to the *Heiliggrabkapelle,* a copy of the

Pfarrkirche in Senftenberg, 1512

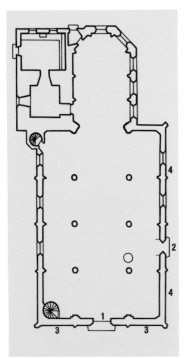

Imst, Pfarrkirche, Maria Himmelfahrt 1 W. door with rose-window above **2** S. door with angel and coat-of-arms **3** and **4** W. and S. wall with remains of frescos

Church of the Holy Sepulchre in Jerusalem.

Imst 6460

Tirol   p.286□D 9

Imst stands on a picturesque site on a mountain slope; it was mentioned in 763 as 'oppidum humiste' and is divided by the terrain into an upper and a lower town. There are fine houses in the Hauptstrasse, which winds through the town from NE to S. The most important are the *Alte Berggerichtshaus* (1 Floriangasse), the *Hotel Post*

(formerly Ansitz Sprengenstein; No. 231), the *priest's house* with a baroque door and staircase, the 18C *Spital der Barmherzigen Schwestern* and the old *Rathaus,* which at the time of writing houses the Heimatmuseum (local history). Imst also has a number of fine old fountains.

Pfarrkirche Maria Himmelfahrt: The church was first mentioned in 1305, extended in 1350, altered in the second half of the 15C, redesigned in the baroque style in 1780, made Gothic again in 1822 and restored in 1970. The massive, towering building in the Oberstadt still looks Gothic from the outside. The façade has step gables with towers and blind niches. There is a rose window over the large and lavishly articulated West door. The smaller, pointed-arched S. door has a statue of an angel with inscription and coat-of-arms. The N. tower was restored to its old design in 1900. The W. and S. walls, formerly painted with frescos to a height of over 13 ft., now have only a few badly damaged fragments. A massive *c.* 1495 *St.Christopher* has been rediscovered and restored. The interior of the hall church with nave and two aisles has late Gothic pillars without capitals, which flow into the net vaulting; the furnishings are largely neo-Gothic.

St.-Michaels-Kapelle (in the cemetery): This little rotunda, a late Gothic, twostorey chapel on a square plan, dates from the late 18C. In the lower church groin vaulting. The upper church has round tracery windows, a fine portal and rib vaulting springing from a central column. In the altar niche is a Gothic wall fresco of Michael and Daniel dating from 1490, in good condition. In 1970 a late Gothic grave cross was mounted above the altar.

Johanneskirche: This church is 14C, but was redesigned in the baroque period; the choir with pilaster strips shows its Gothic origins most clearly. In 1960 an almost square coarse crystalline slab with a christogram dating from the second half of the 5C was discovered under the church. At the same time *frescos* dating from the second half of the 14C were discovered in the apse and restored by F.Walliser.

Stationskapellen, Heilig-Grab-Kapelle and Pestkapelle: 7 pentagonal chapels of the Stations of the Cross were built in the second half of the 17C on the Kalvarienberg; they lead via the Laurentiuskirche and the Heilig-Grab-Kapelle, which is also 17C, to the Pestkapelle (plague chapel), a building unique in the Tyrol; it is built of stone and wood and has a stone sacristy articulated with triangular pilaster strips; the nave now has a wooden tunnel vault, but was originally an open vestibule.

Also worth seeing: The *Kapelle Unser Herr im Elend* in *Brennbichel* is a baroque rotunda, 1685; altar with carved figures contemporary with the church. *Kapelle Maria Schnee* in *Gungelgrün:* this rococo building dates from 1734 and has delicate rococo stucco and ceiling frescos by Johannes Balthasar Riepp. 17C Madonna and gilded carved figures on the high altar. Completely restored in 1975. A particularly striking modern building is Ekkehard Hörmann's *old people's home* of 1976.

Environs: The *Pfarrkirche zu den Heiligen Drei Königen* in **Nasserieth** dates from the early 15C; it was altered in 1698 and rebuilt in 1846&7. The font, 1507, is late Gothic and the N. tower baroque. The *Pfarrkirche zum heiligen Ulrich* in **Tarrenz** was altered in the late 15C. The nave was extended in 1730 and the Kreuzkapelle added; the Kapelle zum heiligen Franz Xaver followed in 1811. The Gothic style was reimposed in 1883. The lower part of the N. tower with pointed louvres is Gothic, the baroque crown dates from

Imst, panorama

1680. The nave has one aisle and late Gothic net vaulting. In the choir 15C pilaster strips, bases and remains of cornice paintings. On the S. façade late Gothic wall frescos of St.Christopher, half walled in when the Franz Xaver Kapelle was built in the baroque. The *St.-Veit-Kapelle* of 1604 in the cemetery still has late Gothic arches in the choir. Altar and choir stalls early 17C, the large crucifix dates from 1709. The *Kapelle zum heiligen Johann Nepomuk* in **Obertarrenz** contains a fine altar from the second half of the 18C.

Innsbruck 6020
Tirol   p.286□F 8

Innsbruck, the capital of the Tirol, stands at the crossroads of important routes between Germany and Italy and was important in the Middle Ages for this reason.

History: the oldest finds date from the Bronze Age and were found in the present areas of Hungerburg and Hötting. The earliest settlers were probably Illyrians, followed by Rhaetians. At the time of the birth of Christ the military base of Veldidena was expanded by the Romans. Insbruck itself was founded in 1180 by the counts of Andechs beside a bridge over the Inn. They added a new settlement S. of the Inn to their possessions on the N. bank, which included Hötting and a former market. The name 'Innsprucke' was first officially mentioned in 1187. In 1239 the last count of Andechs granted a charter to the town. The outline of the medieval walled town still shows in the Marktgraben, Burggraben, Rennweg and Herrengasse. Then as now the town revolved around the Herzog-Friedrich-Strasse with its old trading houses and the Goldenes Dachl.

Innsbruck had around 5000 inhabitants in the mid 16C and grew in three directions after the accession of the Habsburgs in the 14C. In the S. the 'Neustadt' or 'Vorstadt' came into being and extended as far as Wilten. In the N. and E. court and monasteries established themselves in the 14–17C and built increasingly splendid castles and churches. In the SW, on the 'Innrain', whole streets were built from the 16C; the 18C St.-Johannes-Kirche was the crowning glory of this development. In the 19C industrialization and the arrival of the railway and improvement of other means of transport led to expansion throughout the valley, and as a result of this places like Pradl, Wilten, Mühlau, Amras, Arzl, Vill and Igls became part of the town. The Olympic Games in 1964 and 1976 led to the modernisation of the town by the building of high-rise buildings, stadia, ring roads and the Olympic centre on the edge of the town.

Dom/former Stadtpfarrkirche St. Jakob (Domplatz): The Domplatz is just beyond the Goldenes Dachl. The massive façade of the church soars in baroque curves; it is in unclad stone and the two towers have large round arches and high oval windows. The niche statues and equestrian staue of St.Jakob on the gable, planned in the baroque, were not added until 1941–60 by Hans Andre.

According to the market charter the Dom, the most important baroque building in the N. Tirol, had a predecessor even in the 12C; this was a Gothic church, much enlarged and altered in the 14–16C and redesigned in the baroque *c.* 1710. In the late 17C the church was so badly damaged by an earthquake that it had to be pulled down.

The present building includes the former nave walls; it was designed by J.J.Herkomer, started in 1717 and largely complete by 1722. The church was badly damaged by bombing in 1944, repaired 1946–50. Innsbruck became a cathedral town in 1964 and St.Jakob was chosen as the cathedral church.

The *interior* is cruciform with transept apses; nave and crossing are vaulted identically, the choir has a high circular dome which is a powerful source of light. Contrary to custom there are no side chapels, and the line of the walls of the single-aisled building is only broken by uniform shallow altars, massive coloured marble pilasters and confessionals; this produces an effect of remarkable unity.

The *interior decoration* is largely by the Asam brothers. Egid Quirin Asam was responsible for the lavish *rococo stucco,* Cosmas Damian painted the beautifully composed trompe l'oeil *ceiling frescos* on the life of St.James in 1722&3. The post-war arch fresco over the high altar is the work of Hans Andre. Fine rococo pulpit by N. Moll (1724). In the left transept is the tomb

Innsbruck, Maria-Theresien-Strasse

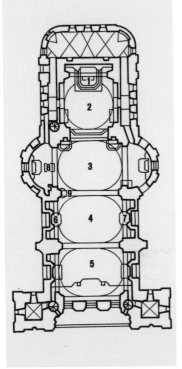

Innsbruck, Dom When Innsbruck became a diocese in 1964, the former Stadtpfarrkirche St. Jakob was elevated to the status of cathedral. **1** High altar with miraculous image by Lukas Cranach the elder. On festival days, the altar is decorated with a silver frontal donated by Karl Philipp of the Palatinate in 1712. The antependium, tabernacle and angels in glory are gorgeously decorated on these occasions. **2** Dome fresco: St. James fighting the Saracens **3** The Saint trying to induce the people to adore the Virgin Mary **4** St. James pleading for suffering mankind **5** The Saint pleading for church, empire, province and town **6** Relics of St. Benignus **7** Relics of St. Vitalis **8** Monument to Archduke Maximilian II, where Archduke Eugen, a Grand Master of the Teutonic Order, has been interred since 1955. On the cover of the monument, the figure of the Archduke is seen kneeling at the feet of St. George **9** Pulpit

Innsbruck, Hofkirche 1 Monument to Emperor Maximilian I (1451-1519) **2** Ferdinand V, the Catholic, King of Aragon (1452-1516), father of John the Mad **3** Johanna the Mad (1479-1555), married to Philip the Fair, son of Emperor Maximilian I **4** Philip the Good, Duke of Burgundy (1396-1467), grandfather of Mary of Burgundy **5** Charles the Bold, Duke of Burgundy (1433-77), father of Mary of Burgundy **6** Zimburgis of Masovia (d. 1429), wife of Duke Ernst the Iron, grandmother of Emperor Maximilian I **7** Margaret of Burgundy (1480-1530), daughter of Emperor Maximilian I, stadholder in the Netherlands **8** Maria Blanka Sforza (d. 1511), daughter of Lodovico Sforza, known as il Moro, and second wife of Emperor Maximilian I **9** Sigmund the Rich, Duke of

of Maximilian II, German Master of the Teutonic Order, cast in bronze in 1620 by H. Reinhart from a model by Caspar Gras. On the high altar is the magnificent silver-mounted miracle picture 'Maria hilf' by Lukas Cranach the Elder, brought here in 1650.

Dreiheiligenkirche (Dreiheiligenstrasse): Dedicated to Saints Sebastian, Rochus and Pirmin. In the plague year 1611 a town official swore an oath, and as a result of this a Renaissance church was built in 1612; it was redesigned in the baroque in the mid 18C. The rococo stucco and ceiling frescos by J.M. Stricker date from this period. The rococo altars and pulpit are by J.G. and

B. Gratl of Amras. On the high altar 3 plague saints by Melchior Stölzl, 1613.

Hofkirche (Universitätsstrasse/Rennweg): Set diagonally to the Hofburg is the inconspicuous Hofkirche with its plain Renaissance façade. Emperor Maximilian I planned an eternal and in its way unique monument to himself; the execution of the project started under his direction, but was not completed until after his death. He wanted a cortege of people who were important to him to watch in perpetuity over his tomb. He had most of the figures made in Innsbruck and wanted to set them up in the Georgskapelle in Wiener Neustadt, where he was later buried, but this proved

Austria, Count of Tirol (1427-96), son of Frederick the Poor and cousin of Maximilian I **10** Arthur, legendary Celtic king from the 6C **11** Ferdinand of Portugal, ancestor of Eleonora of Portugal, the mother of Maximilian I **12** Ernst the Iron, Duke of Austria, Count of Habsburg and Tirol (1377-1424), grandfather of Maximilian I **13** Theodoric, King of the Eastern Goths (454-526) **14** Albrecht II, the Wise, the Lame, Duke of Austria (1298-1358), grandfather of Ernst the Iron **15** Emperor Rudolf of Habsburg (1218-91), son of Count Albrecht of Habsburg **16** Philip the Fair, King of Castille (1478-1506), son of Maximilian I and married to Johanna the Mad **17** Clovis I, King of the Franks (466-511) **18** Kunigunde, Duchess of Austria (1465-1520), sister of Maximilian I **19** Elisabeth of Görz (d. 1313), wife of Albrecht I **20** Mary of Burgundy (1457-82), heiress of Charles the Bold, first wife of Maximilian I **21** Elisabeth of Hungary (d. 1443), wife of Albrecht II **22** Godfrey of Bouillon (1061-1100) **23** Albrecht I, German King, Duke of Austria (c. 1250-1308), son of Rudolf of Habsburg **24** Frederick IV the Poor, Duke of Austria, Count of Tirol (1382-1439), father of Sigmund the Rich **25** Leopold III the Pious, Duke of Austria (1351-86), son of Albrecht II **26** Count Albrecht of Habsburg, father of Rudolf of Habsburg **27** Leopold III the Saint, Margrave of Austria (d. 1136) **28** Emperor Frederick III (1415-93), father of Maximilian I **29** Albrecht II of Austria, German King, King in Hungary and Bohemia (1397-1439) **30** St.Francis **31** St.Theresa, both by B. Moll **32** Altar by Michael Umhauser. Altarpiece of the Assumption by Kaspar Waldmann (?) **33** Altar by M.Umhauser. Altarpiece: St.Anthony (c. 1600) **34** Choir stalls: 1562-5, by Hans Waldmann **35** Fürstenchor **36** Choir organ: 1555-60 by Jörg Ebert, one of the five most famous organs in the world **37** Monument to Andreas Hofer **38** Silver chapel, older section **39** Silver chapel, newer section **40** Silver altar **41** Renaissance organ **42** Monument to Archduke Ferdinand II **43** Monument to Philippine Weiser

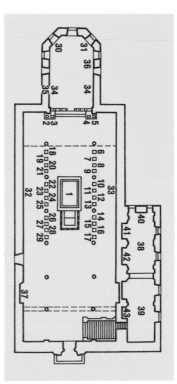

technically impossible. More than 30 years after his death his grandson Ferdinand I, the brother of Charles V, built the Hofkirche as a worthy setting for this colossal monument. Building, to plans by Andrea Crivelli of Trento, began in 1553 under Nikolaus Türing the Younger of Innsbruck, whose grandfather had built the Goldenes Dachl. When he died in 1558 Marx della Bolla undertook direction of the work until 1563. Shortly before 1700 and again in 1731 the interior was redesigned in the baroque style by G.Gumpp (e.g. ceiling stucco). Despite the pointed windows and the slender buttresses this is the first building in the N. Tirol which can be called Renaissance.

The church is a high hall with nave and two aisles and a choir with a single aisle. In the choir and on the entrance side of the nave are transverse galleries.

The visitor is struck first of all by the *Kaisergrab*, the most magnificent imperial tomb in the German-speaking world. The cenotaph of Maximilian I was started by Bernhard Abel and completed by A.Colin in 1584; design by Florian Abel (1561). The grille around the sarcophagus is by Jörg Schmiedhammer. The largest bronze figures surrounding the cenotaph were cast in various workshops, most of them in Innsbruck, between 1509 and 1550. The finest of the statues were cast in the lifetime of Maximilian. The three most important

(Nos. 10, 13 and 26) were designed by Dürer and cast in the workshop of Peter Vischer (Nos. 10 and 13) in Nuremberg, and by Godl in Innsbruck (No. 26) on the basis of a statue by Hans Leinberger to Dürer's design. The following figures were made in Innsbruck under Gilg Sesselschreiber: 3, 4, 5, 11, 12, 15, 16, 19, 20, 28, 29. When Sesselschreiber was dismissed by Maximilian in 1518 for working too slowly he was replaced by the former founder Stefan Godl.

The Hofkirche also contains the *tomb of Andreas Hofer* with a statue by J.Schaller (see plan; Hofer's body was brought here from Mantua in 1823). The high altar was designed by Nicolaus Pacassi, built 1755 – 8 and decorated with J.C.Auerbach's Crucifixion. The two lead statues on the right and left of the altar by Balthasar Moll are of interest (see plan), also the 16C *choir organ,* the *princes' choir,* a *Renaissance gallery* with fine wood inlay by Hans Waldner (1567) and the 23 statues of the 'Holy Kindred' of the House of Habsburg (cast by Godl to a design by Jörg Kölderer) on the balustrade of the W. gallery.

From the Hofkirche the visitor can reach the so-called *Silberne Kapelle* (silver chapel), which is also joined to the Hofburg and was built by Archduke Ferdinand II of the Tirol (1564–95) for himself and his wife Philippine Welser. The two marble tombs are by A.Colin (tomb of Philippine 1581, Ferdinand's more splendid monument 1588 – 96). The Gothic vaulting of this bipartite chapel, the *altar* with silvered Madonna and silver reliefs by Anton Ort dating from the 2nd half of the 16C and the small 16C *organ* are also worth seeing.

Alte Pfarrkirche St.Ingenuin und Albuin (Hötting; Steinbruchstrasse/ Schulgasse): This beautifully-sited 15C church was redesigned in the baroque style in the mid 18C. The choir and the E. part of the nave are late Gothic. The rococo

stucco is 18C. The ceiling pictures are by J.M.Strickner, 1752. On the triumphal arch two figures, St.Joachim and St.Anne, dating from 1700. The Gothic tower has a baroque copper crown.

Jesuitenkirche zur Heiligsten Dreifaltigkeit/Universitätskirche (Universitätsstrasse): After the collapse of a Jesuit church started in 1619 a new building was built 1627 – 46 under the direction of Father Karl Fontane by Hans Schor and C.Gump the Younger. The church was badly damaged in 1943 and was rebuilt, completion 1953. The heavy, dark façade prepares us for the austerity and gloom of the interior. The dominant colours are black, white and gold, which tone with the reddish-brown of the marble. The church is cruciform, with a nave with two bays, choir, gigantic crossing dome, wide side chapels, two-storey galleries on three sides and a vestibule, also with two bays and divided by a *wrought-iron grille* (1667) with golden roses; the vestibule also contains an expressive 18C crucifix. The black *pulpit* endowed by Archduchess Claudia in the first half of the 17C is in harmony with the dark confessionals and the altars; their furnishings are largely baroque.

Johanneskirche/St.Johann Nepomuk am Innrain (at the and of the Innrainallee): This relatively small but beautiful church was started in 1729 and is attributed to A.Gumpp. The harmonious façade has two towers. The sides are richly articulated with blind doors, niches, gables and scrolls. The open vestibule was built in 1750. It contains two statues by J.Jenewein Lechleitner of *c.* 1730 and a fresco by J.Schöpf, 1794. The interior is rococo with pink marbled pillars, gilded capitals, pale yellow beams, yellow

Hofkirche, monument to Maximilian I

and green walls and vaulting, and gold-framed altars with lavish decoration. The large ceiling fresco by J.Schöpf dates from 1794 and shows the martyrdom of St. Johann Nepomuk; it has neoclassical traits. The wooden statue of the saint on the high altar (1730), the four statues in the choir niches, the Crucifixion on the left side altar and the guardian angel in the nave were all created by J.J.Lechleitner in 1730.

Pfarrkirche Mariahilf (Mariahilf-strasse/Kindergartenweg): Outside the town, in the N., on the other side of the Inn, a church was built in 1647 – 9 by C.Gumpp as the result of an oath sworn by the Tyrolean Landstände. The harmonious baroque building with a round dome has a square vestibule, choir and 4 semicircular side chapels. The stucco dates from 1650, the vault frescos from 1689 (Kaspar Waldmann) the wrought iron grille in the vestibule from 1731, pulpit and altar are neoclassical. The church was badly damaged by bombs and restored in 1953&4.

Mentelberger Pfarrkirche zur Schmerzhaften Muttergottes (until 1948 chapel of Schloss Mentelberg): A building dating from 1622 was followed in the mid 18C by a domed church designed by J.M.Umhaus. The rococo stucco and the ceiling pictures by M.Günther (1770) are of particular interest. The miraculous image (Pietà) dates from *c.* 1500. In the vestibule is the carved wooden '7 sleepers' dating from the second half of the 17C.

Servitenkirche and Servitenkloster (Maria-Theresien-Strasse): The church was endowed by Anna Katharina, the wife of Archduke Fedinand of Tirol. After the first building of 1620 had been destroyed by fire Giovanni Speraindio Colleto built a new church and the adjacent Servitenkloster; severe war damage (1944) was made good in 1946&7. The high altar picture (Mar-riage of the Virgin) was painted in 1628 by Martin Theophilus Pollak. The *Peregrini chapel* with lavishly stuccoed articulated tunnel vault and the restored *Kunstkammer,* including pictures by Tyrolean painters, are also of interest.

Spitalskirche Heilig Geist (Maria-Theresien-Strasse): A baroque church with a very fine tower with dome and lantern was built on the site of a Gothic hospital church in 1701 to a design by J.M.Gumpp the Elder. In the interior lavish stucco; late Gothic crucifix on the high altar.

Pfarr- und Wallfahrtskirche Unserer Lieben Frau unter den vier Säulen/Basilika Wilten: Wilten, the Roman Veldidena, begins at the S. end of Maria-Theresien-Strasse; it has two splendid baroque churches, the Stiftskirche St. Laurentius and the basilica, built by Franz de Paula Penz in 1751–6 on the site of a church mentioned in 1140.
The elaborately articulated façade with two towers is set in an open square and appears bright and airy because of its light yellow colouring. The interior is one of the most harmonious rococo compositions to be found anywhere. The 14C *miraculous image* on the altar came from the Gothic church; it is crowned by delicate rocaille architecture on pilasters which seems to make the whole sanctuary soar. This is complemented by the apparently weightless *ceiling frescos* by M.Günther (1754) and the vigorous *rococo stucco* by F.X.Feuchtmayer of Wessobrunn. The angels with candles to the left and right of the altar were probably the work of A.Faistenberger. The harmonious blend of gold, pink and yellow adds to the rococo balance of the interior, in which nothing strikes a jarring note.

Stiftskirche St.Laurentius and Stift in Wilten: After the destruction of Wilten and its Roman citadel the village of Wilten

Wilten, Stiftskirche, portal

Wilten, basilica

came into being on this site *c.* 900, and a Romanesque church was built in honour of St.Laurentius. The church and a collegiate foundation attached to it were mentioned in 1120. After fires, frequent rebuilding and the decline of the Premonstratensian monastery founded in 1138 the foundation became important again at the end of the 16C and reached its economic and cultural heyday after 1650. The foundation was temporarily dissolved from 1807–16; it was badly damaged by bombing in 1944, and successfully restored after 1945.

Stiftskirche St.Laurentius: Legend tells of two warring giants, Haymo and Tyrsus; Haymo is said to have endowed the church in expiation for a crime against his fellow. In 1644 attempts were made to find the grave of the ostensible founder Haymo, but

in the course of these excavations the tower collapsed into the church. This gave rise to the building of a new church, built from 1651 to plans by court architect C.Gumpp the Younger. The fine N. façade tower with crown and lantern was completed in 1667; its complement in the S. was never built. The church was made more elaborate 35 years later. A pilastered vestibule with pediment and gallery was added in 1716 by G.A.Gumpp (statues by N.Moll); this and the reddish-yellow colouring of the whole building and the two larger-than-life figures to the left and right of the portal make an imposing, bizarrely baroque impression which is not altogether unattractive.

The massive tunnel-vaulted nave with side chapels, low galleries and slightly narrower choir is relatively light because of the stucco, 1702&3 by Bernado Pasquale.

Kaspar Waldmann's *ceiling frescos* are divided into small panels (1702–7). The interior moves towards Paul Huber's *high altar* of 1665 with trompe l'oeil columns. The altar picture shows Mary as the Madonna of the Rosary and is by Egid Schor (1671). The baroque side altars were decorated in the rococo period; *Anna-Altar* by Nikolaus Moll, 1719; *late Gothic crucifix* on the cross altar. In the vestibule is a larger-than-life sculpture of the legendary founder Haymo, protected by an 18C *wrought-iron grille* by Adam Neyer.

Kloster: The *abbey* and the *monastery buildings* are adjacent to the church in the S.; they are built in a rectangle around the cloister. From 1669 the disparate medieval buildings were rebuilt as a splendid baroque whole. In the abbey the surrounds of the *arches* in the gatehouse are still Gothic. Over the entrance is a *bronze statue* of the giant Haymo by Kaspar Gras. The vestibule is two storeys high; the upper part is decorated with early-18C stucco by Bernardo Pasquale and a *ceiling painting* by Egid Schor dating from 1696; the wall frescos, oil paintings and statues are notable. The *Gartensaal* has trompe l'oeil paintings giving views of neatly trimmed gardens. The Altmutter-Saal, decorated in the 19C with wall paintings of oriental landscapes by Franz Altmutter, has a coffered ceiling; decorative wall paintings of hunting scenes *c.*1712 by K.Waldmann in the Jagdzimmer. The spacious *Norberti-Saal,* the original ballroom and reception room, has ceiling frescos of the life of St. Norbert, the founder of the Premonstratensian Order.

On the ground floor of the monastery building is the *chapterhouse,* a Gothic hall with rib vaulting in which frescos of the Pacher school have been revealed. The Sigmundaltar of 1491 from St.Sigmund in the Sellraintal is also here. The originally Gothic *refectory* was redesigned in the baroque style in 1708 and became Gothic again

in 1958. The *library* was built in the first half of the 18C and rebuilt in the 19C. In the courtyard *gravestones* and *slabs* from the 14–18C.

The *Stiftsmuseum,* which formerly housed a collection of musical instruments and a physics section, is still worth seeing today despite war damage, especially the Ludovica room, restored in 1961.

Hofburg: The Hofburg was built in the NE corner of the Old Town from 1453 as the castle of the princes of Tirol. The most active builders were Archduke Sigismund the Rich and Emperor Maximilian I. Before Maria Theresa started radical alterations in 1755 the Schloss was as it is seen in Dürer's two water colours of 1495, painted on his first Italian journey. The pictures are now in the Albertina in Vienna. There is still late Gothic vaulting in the cellars of the W. wing and the NE corner section of the main façade. Empress Maria Theresa had the Hofburg rebuilt in the baroque style by J.M.Gumpp the Younger. First came a new S. façade with rocaille, and the staircase on the Hofgasse side. After the Seven Years War the E. and N. sections of the building were altered by K.J.von Walter to fit in with Gumpp's design; the façades in the N. small courtyard were also altered. Alteration of the main building on the Rennweg was undertaken in 1766 by K.J. von Walter, who redesigned the façade and interior. The state rooms on the second floor of the Hofburg were decorated in 1773. F.A. Maulbrecht's large ceiling fresco was not completed until 1776. Damage caused in the Second World War was made good. Two medieval side towers were skilfully transformed into protruding domed corner towers in the long, almost neoclassical façade on the Rennweg; it is articulated by two slight projections and Corinthian

Virgin Mary suckling the infant Christ, Cranach, Kapuzinerkirche

pilasters. Interesting *rooms,* particularly in the E. wing. The *Riesensaal,* which is two storeys high, was called the *'Familiensaal'* in the reign of Maria Theresa, as it housed oil portraits of the Empress's family. It has gold and white rococo decoration and very fine ceiling frescos (F.A. Maulbertsch and his pupil J.J.Winterhalder: Triumph of the House of Habsburg and Lorraine). Other rooms in the *NE section* still have the original rococo decoration from the second half of the 18C. Notable are the *Fürsten-zimmer* with Louis XVI furniture, the *Ordenszimmer* with fine wall frescos and the *Gartensaal* with painted copies of Flemish tapestries. In a corridor on the first floor of the W. section is the 16C *coat-of-arms relief* of Maximilian I. On the second floor of the S. wing is the *death chamber of Emperor Franz I,* which Maria Theresa had made into a memorial chapel by Pacassi.

Old Town: In the Hofgasse is the late Gothic *Burgriesenhaus* (No. 12), built by Duke Sigmund of Tirol for his house giant Nikolaus Haidl; then the *Deutschorden-shaus* (No. 3), built in the 16C, presumably by Gregor Türing, for the Teutonic Order and restored in 1954. As well as the old painted façade it has late Gothic tracery and 2 oriels with stone reliefs with coats-of-arms and inscriptions. The Hofgasse ends in the very fine medieval Marktplatz, of which the finest feature is the famous *Goldenes Dachl.*

Goldenes Dachl: This magnificent oriel was added to the so-called 'Neuer Hof', two houses converted at very little expense into a princely residence by Duke Friedrich IV. From the 15C it was used only as a chancellery, and was radically altered in 1822. A room with groin vaulting and pilasters in the N. wing of the Neuer Hof has been used for the solemnization of marriage since 1940.

The *oriel* with the golden roof was built by

Maximilian I in the late 15C as a spectator gallery for the court at public games in the market-place. It was built by Nikolaus Türing of Memmingen.

The oriel protrudes like a balcony from the first and second storeys and is supported by two slender pillars on the ground floor, thus forming a small open arcade. Under the first-storey windows is a balustrade with 6 relief coats-of-arms. The frescos to the left and right of the windows show two mercenaries waving flags. The oriel in the second storey is supported on corbels and has very fine relief figures on its balustrade (copies; originals in the Ferdinandeum). The central relief shows Maximilian I with his two wives. Four richly profiled posts are topped with ogee crockets. The roof with copper shingles gilded in the firing protects the spectators' stand behind the posts; its rear wall is decorated with frescos. Diagonally opposite the Goldenes Dachl is the *Helblinghaus,* (10 Herzog-Friedrich-Strasse) with a very fine rococo façade. The house on the corner was originally late Gothic but was stuccoed in all four upper storeys shortly after 1725, presumably by A.Gigl, and is considered to be one of the finest buildings of its kind. Also in the Herzog-Friedrich-Strasse, (No. 6, towards the Inn) is an old inn, the *Goldene Adler,* in which famous visitors including Goethe have stayed (various Gothic features: façade painting from the first half of the 16C and a fresco dating from *c.* 1510 revealed in the stair well in 1955). Opposite the 'Adler' is the *Alte Regierungsgebäude* (No. 3). J.M.Gumpp the Elder provided several 16&17C houses with a communal baroque façade with balcony after 1725. In the rear section of the building is a 16C late Gothic hall (Türing school). Above that is the so-called *Claudia-Saal;* heavy wooden coffered ceiling and late Renaissance portal added under Claudia de Medici. On the second floor remains of a former chapel with net vaulting (delicately painted 1511 –17).

Hofburg with Hofkirche

On the same side of the road (No. 1) is the Weinhaus, the so-called *Otto-Burg*, at the point by the Inntor at which the Herzog-Friedrich-Strasse used to begin; it is a tower-like four-storey building with 4 oriels one above the other and late Gothic vaulting in the interior. If we now return to the Goldenes Dachl and follow the street in the other direction from the Helblinghaus onwards we arrive in the pedestrian precinct, the narrow, medieval section of the street, containing a large number of interesting buildings. Opposite the Helblinghaus is the *Alte Rathaus* (No. 21) with the *Stadtturm*, one of the most striking Innsbruck landmarks, altered in the Renaissance style in 1560. The gargoyles were added in 1586.

Opposite the Rathaus is the *Katzunghaus* (No. 16) with fine early-16C reliefs on the oriels (some copies, some originals). The *Trautsonhaus* (No. 22) was altered in 1541 by G.Türing for Hans von Trautson. The pointed arcades with groin vaulting, the oriels, the sandstone reliefs on the balustrades and the blind tracery are all recognisably late Gothic. The coats-of-arms and the sculpture on the lowest storey of the oriel and the façade painting show incipient early Renaissance style. The *Kohleggerhaus* (No. 35) is particularly striking for the late 15C frescos in the arcade vaulting.

At the level of the Marktgraben and the Burggraben the street becomes the Maria-Theresien-Strasse, but shortly before this, diagonally opposite the Kohleggerhaus, is the Schlossergasse, in which is the *Karlsburg* with the *Kolbenturm*, an old seat of the nobility on the E. side of which are remains of façade painting from the second half of the 16C. At No. 21 Schlossergasse

Andreas Hofer, 1809, arsenal Altes Zeughaus

is the house of *town architect G.Türing* with a late Gothic portal. From the Schlossergasse one reaches the Kiebachgasse and the *Gumpphaus,* (No. 16), owned by the Gumpp family from 1653 (baroque stucco), and the originally late Gothic former *Theresianische Normalschule* (No. 10); façade late rococo with neoclassical overtones. If we now turn from the Seilergasse along the opposite side of the Herzog-Friedrich-Strasse into the Riesengasse, we reach the pillared portal of the *Damenstift* (1 Stiftgasse), which in the early 15C was the *'outer Burg'* of the Hofburg and was chosen in 1771–3 to be the home of the noblewomen's foundation endowed by Maria Theresa. K.J. von Walter was responsible for the alterations (designed by Pacassi), which made the building uniform with the section of the Hofburg adjacent in the N. by the addition

of an extended façade. Inside on the ground floor there is still a section of the medieval town wall and in the great hall of the Stift cellar the former W. wall of the old building with late Gothic windows and wall frescos dating from 1505.

At 3 Burggraben is the *Hauptwache,* once the court stables; late Gothic vaulted and pillared hall on the ground floor.

Maria-Theresien-Strasse: In the centre of the street is the Madonna statue (Immaculata, copy; original in the Stiftskirche in Fiecht) on the Annasäule (1706, Christoforo Benedetti); diagonally opposite the Spitalskirche is the premier residence in the street, the *Palais Lodron* (No. 7), which has a fine stucco façade dating from 1749. The *Palais Troyer-Spaur* (No. 39) was built in 1681–3 by J.M.Gumpp; it is a two-storey building with central oriel and balcony. Diagonally opposite is the *Palais Trapp-Wolkenstein*; J.M.Gumpp the Elder provided two older buildings with a uniform façade in the late 17C; (under the balcony fine relief of Mary and the combined coats-of-arms of the Trapp and Spaur families; rococo stucco ceiling on the second floor; baroque chapel with Mary altar.) One of the finest secular buildings in the Tyrol is the **Alte Landhaus** with courtyard (No. 43), built 1725 – 8 by G.A.Gumpp, coloured decorative façade of the central section with central windows emphasised by columns and stucco by Alessandro Callegari 1728. Inside, simple tripartite vestibule with coffered stucco ceiling, monumental staircase, statues by Franz Egg 1898&9 on the ground floor, and by N.Moll 1728 on the first and second floors; wrought-iron banisters. *Landtagssaal:* high pilasters, magnificent fireplaces and semicircular niches with figures on the walls; putti and statues presumably by N.Moll, rococo stucco by J.Singer; ceiling and wall fresco by C.D.Asam. *Landhauskapelle:* rectangular all with semicircular altar niches by A.Gumpp, stucco by A.Gigl, A.Gratl and J. inger, altar picture by J.G.Grasmair, 1731.

Adjacent to the Landhaus is the *Fugger-Taxis-Palais* (No. 45), built from 1679 by J.M.Gumpp the Elder for Count Hans Otto Fugger von Kirchberg-Weissenborn; it passed to the counts of Welsberg in 1702 and to the counts of Thurn und Taxis in 1784. It now houses the government offices of the Land Tirol. On the main floor of the building, which has a lavish stucco façade, is the *Paris-Saal* with rococo wall decoration restored in 1953. The fine ceiling painting (Judgement of Paris) is by Martin Knoller, 1785. *Palais Sarntheim* (No. 57) built between 1681 and 1686 for Count Sarntheim; the stucco ceilings in 2 rooms on the second floor and the architectural proportions survive from that building. At the S. end of Maria-Theresien-

Stadtturm

Strasse is the triumphal arch built on the occasion of the marriage of Leopold (later Leopold II) the son of Maria Theresa, in 1765. The arch is based on Roman models and has white marble statues and reliefs (B.Moll 1774).

Domplatz: If we now return to the Goldenes Dachl and go to the Dom, we find the 15C *Prechthaus* at No. 4 Pfarrgasse, at No. 5 the late Gothic *Ettlhaus* with Renaissance chapel and in the Domplatz at No. 3 the 15C *Kräuterhaus,* the old *Kaiserspital*.

Universitätsstrasse: The *Neue Stift* was built in the middle years of the 16C; it now houses the *Museum für Tiroler Volkskunst und Kunstgewerbe* (folk and applied art). The *Jesuitenkloster, Jesuitenkirche* and *Alte Universität* (Nos. 4 and 6) were built at the

Helblinghaus

Goldenes Dachl

Altes Landhaus

same time. The theological faculty with the Kaiser-Leopold-Saal (No. 8) was commissioned by Archduke Maximilian I and built 1603–6 by Abraham Jäger as the first Innsbruck grammar school; it was altered by G.A.Gumpp in 1722. The *Servitenkloster* was built opposite in the early 17C; the *Klosterkaserne* now stands on this site. Nearby (at the Kaiserjäger-Kapuzinergasse junction) is the 16C *Kapuzinerkloster*. In its *church*, altered in the neoclassical style, the high altar picture (1606) is by Cosimo Piazza and the Madonna and Child in the side chapel by Lukas Cranach. Returning to the Universitätsstrasse we turn into the Sillgasse to find the *Palais Pfeiffersberg*, built between 1712 and 1723, presumably by G.A.Gumpp; it is now used as a Jesuit college. Further down the Universitätsstrasse at No. 22 is the *Palais Tannenberg-*

Enzenberg, a unified building with an impressive central portal built by J.A.Gumpp the Elder between 1712 and 1723; it contains an early rococo room with paintings by C.A.Meyer (c. 1740). In the continuation of the street is the *Palais Ferrari,* at No. 4 Weinhartstrasse, built in the late 17C by J.A.Gumpp; it has a remarkable façade.

Also worth seeing: *Albersheim,* house of the nobility since 1561 (39 Innrain); *Rainfels,* 16C house (17 Innstrasse); *Schlandersbergeck,* 15C hunting lodge (19 Stiftgasse); *Dogana,* late 16C riding school, now the vestibule of the *Kongresshaus,* built 1970–3 to replace the toll house (Rennweg); *Altes Zeughaus, c.* 1500, (Zeughausgasse); *Leopardischlösschen,* 16C Pradl (13 Egerdachstrasse); *Windegg,* 16C house (23 Adamgasse); *4 Angerzellgasse,* hunting lodge, first half of the 16C; *Liebenegg,* 16C Schlösschen (2 Liebeneggstrasse); *Augenwiedstein,* house with baroque portal (4 Haymonsgasse); *Landgerichtsgebäude* in Wilten with Gothic, Renaissance and baroque features (1 Klostergasse).

In the suburb of *Mühlau: Ehrentreitz,* the priest's house, former 16C hunting lodge (2 Schlossfeld) and the late Gothic *Sternbachschlössl* (Grabenstein-Rizol huntinglodge), 16C. The chapel and the wings with stucco and frescos by K.Waldmann are 18C additions (1/2 Sternbachplatz).

In the suburb of Hötting: Ettnau or Malfartischlössl, 16C, heavily restored (25 Höttingergasse); *Lichtenthurn hunting lodge,* late Gothic with 18C S. wing and chapel (15 Schneeburggasse); and near Hötting *Schloss Buchsenhausen,* 16C (7 Weiherburggasse) with late 17C chapel with an altar picture by M.Knoller; *Weiherburg,* late Gothic hunting lodge, 15C, with late Gothic St. Anna chapel (37–9 Weiherburggasse).

Fountains and Hofgarten: Opposite the Hofburg in the Rennweg is the Leopoldsbrunnen, designed by C.Gumpp for Archduke Leopold V. Kaspar Gras made the models for the bronze figures in 1622, but they were not placed in position until 1893. The equestrian staute is of the Archduke. *Hofgarten,* laid out in the 15C,

Peasants' room, 16C, Volkskundemuseum

redesigned in the English style in 1858. Some baroque buildings in the W. The *Musikpavillon* is Biedermeier.

Museums: *Tiroler Volkskundemuseum* (2 Universitätsstrasse): a museum with a fine collection of folk art directly by the Hofkirche in the Neue Stift, built 1553–61 for Emperor Ferdinand I by Andrea Crivelli and N.Türing the Younger. The façade, presumably by G.A.Gumpp, dates from 1719. *Tiroler Landesmuseum Ferdinandeum* (15 Museumstrasse): this 19C musuem has fine collections of art history, prehistory and natural history, mainly from the Tyrol; there is also a picture gallery including works by Cranach, Rembrandt and Terborch.

Theatres: between the Leopoldsbrunnen and the Hofgarten, in Rennweg opposite the Hofburg, is the *Tiroler Landestheater,* built 1844–6 with neoclassical façade by Giuseppe Segusini on the site of the Komödientheater built by Archduke Ferdinand Karl in 1653–5; it has been owned by the town since 1886. Opera, operetta and straight plays are performed here; the interior has been much altered, most recently in 1961–7. Adjacent are the *Kammerspiele* of the Tiroler Landestheater, built 1956–9.

Irrsdorf = Strasswalchen 5204
Salzburg   p.276□M 6

Site of two Roman graves with lavish burial offerings. A Roman relief survives in the church, mentioned since *c.* 1000.

Filialkirche hl.Maria: This pilgrimage church was largely rebuilt *c.* 1408; the interior dates from the 15C, the early 16C and the late 17C. The Gothic tower has corbels with heads (including a so-called three-faced head). The portal under the tower (dated 1408), with a half-figure of the Madonna and Child on the gable, has two carved *oak doors,* important works in the Soft Style dating from *c.* 1400. It represents the meeting of Mary and Elizabeth (Christ and John on the bellies of the two pregnant women) and is continued in the ogee arch, suggesting a Mariological cycle. At the bottom is one of the founders at prayer, with his coat-of-arms. On the N. wall is the fine *marble tombstone* of a kneeling priest (1410). The 3 *carved altars* inside the single-aisled church with stellar-vaulted choir, the *pulpit* and the *oratories* have lavish sculpture by M.Guggenbicher (1482–91). On the *high altar* is the shrine figure from the late Gothic triptych, a Madonna and Child, attributed to the Master I.P. and dated *c.* 1520–5; the panel reliefs are attributed to the same artist and are in the Salzburg Carolino Augusteum Museum. On the S. wall (above the landing) above a base with inlaid Roman grave relief is the massive *calcareous sandstone figure* of a standing Madonna and Child dating from the early 15C. On the balustrade of the organ gallery is an *Annunciation* dating from *c.* 1460. The adjacent small *Leonhardskapelle* has a carved altar by M.Guggenbichler (1714).

Environs: Strasswalchen with the *Pfarrkirche hl. Martin,* a late Gothic hall church with nave and two aisles (first half of the 15C), and baroque extensions. The high altar is an early work of M.Guggenbichler (1675). See also Mondsee and Zell am Moos.

Irschen 9773
Kärnten   p.284□L 10

Pfarrkirche St. Dionys Areopagita: This two-aisled Romano-Gothic hall (first mentioned 1190) is supported by two round pillars which, unusually, are not

Bad Ischl, Kaiservilla

placed centrally, and has stellar vaulting dating from the late 14C. The rib-vaulted choir has blind arches, in contrast with the half apse. Windows and buttresses Gothic. In 1940 *high Gothic frescos* were revealed on the N. wall of the choir (saints, Coronation of the Virgin, cardinal virtues as figures, with lions at their feet). In the apse is a splendid late Gothic *triptych* (*c.* 1515 –20.

Bad Ischl 4820

Upper Austria   p.276□N 7

Ischl was the preferred spa and summer resort of Franz Joseph (1854–1914), as Baden had been for Franz I. The little town, previously almost unknown, became the summer centre of the monarchy, with con-

siderable cosmopolitan flair. Ischl's connection with the ruling family goes back a little further, however. The childless Archduchess Sophie had been sent to Ischl by her doctor for a salt cure, and this proved a success: Franz Joseph was followed by three more sons (including Maximilian, later Emperor of Mexico), jokingly known as the 'salt princes'.

Museums: *Kaiservilla:* Wedding present of the Empress Mother to Franz Joseph and Elisabeth; Biedermeier country house, enlarged as a summer residence by the addition of wings; fine garden, fountains by V.Tilgner.

Heimatmuseum with exhibits on folklore, mining and the salt industry, and ethnogaphy. *Lehár-Villa:* memorabilia of the operetta composer. *Haenal-Pancera-Familienmuseum:* domestic culture (7

Traunkirchen (Ischl), Fischer pulpit

all part of an ancient mystical custom.
Traunkirchen: *Pfarrkirche Mariä Krön-ing.* Schloss-like church on a unique site above the Traunsee. A Benedictine monastery founded *c.* 1020 did not survive the storms of the 16C; Jesuit residence from 1622-1773. Rebuilt after a fire, consecrated 1652. The exterior is dominated by the high hipped roof and the towers with mansard-like square roofs (W. tower 1718, octagonal E. tower above the choir). Charming ridge turret with double onion on the *Michaelskapelle* in the SE. Interior rather austere, befitting the Jesuit style of the period. Splendid *ship pulpit* illustrating the Miracle of the Fishes (1753). From the earlier church memorial stone for a mass endowed by the knight Hans Herzheimer in 1494 (similar to the one in the Münster of Frauenchiemsee, Bavaria, 1510). *Johannesbergkapelle:* on a steep hill, presumably on the site of an earlier place of worship; Roman head in the wall, famous bell dating from 1639. *Custom:* Corpus Christi procession on the lake, the only one in Austria apart from Hallstatt.

rooms, including Renaissance, Louis XV, Empire), paintings (including Rembrandt, Caravaggio, Defregger), autographs (including Schumann, Brahms, Bruckner, Johann Strauss, Richard Strauss, Queen Victoria and the writer and pacifist Bertha von Suttner). **Operetta festival** in the summer.

Environs: Wildenstein ruin (in the S.), fell into ruins after a fire in 1715, exhibition room. *Locomotives from the Salzkammergut local railway* by the road to Strobl. **Ebensee,** salt town (since 1607) at the S. end of the Traunsee. The *Glöcklerlauf* on the evening before Epiphany is worth mentioning: young men dressed in white carry illuminated stars on their heads and wear cow bells on their belts; the rhythmic running, the ringing of the bells and the flickering of the lights in the 'Kappen' are

---

Jenbach 6200

Tirol   p.284☐G 8

Pfarrkiche St. Wolfgang: The church was built 1487-1500 by Gilg Mitterhofer of Schwaz; the exterior still looks late Gothic; tower 1650. The church was restored in 1829. The two late Gothic *side portals* and the tripartite pointed-arched *windows* are worth seeing. The interior is baroque, with a single aisle and slightly narrower choir; Gothic features remaining are the articulated tunnel vaulting and a *late Gothic Madonna* on the side altar.

Judenburg 8750

Steiermark   p.282☐Q 9

Important prehistoric finds were made in

Traunkirchen (Bad Ischl), panorama

Strettweg near Judenburg, including the so-called *Strettweg cult chariot* (Landesmuseum Schloss Eggenberg, Graz), a princely cinerary urn and grave goods. At the SE end of the town is the 'Alte Burg', the oldest area of medieval settlement. In the 10C the Burg was the family seat of the Eppensteiners and seat of the Gau counts. First mentioned *c.* 1074 as 'Iudinberg' and in 1103 as 'mercatum Judenbergense', charter 1224. The town was built in the 13C with a system of parallel streets around a triangular marketplace; the town wall was built at the same time. The medieval Jewish colony lived on the NW edge of the town until the expulsion of the Jews in 1406. Judenburg became the most important trade and cultural centre in the Steiermark at an early date because of its site at the junction of important trade routes.

Stadtpfarrkirche St. Nikolaus: First mentioned in 1148. The free-standing Stadtturm was built 1448–1520. In 1840, after a fire, an upper storey and the spire were added. The church itself was built *c.*1500, only the choir has survived from this building. In 1673 D.Sciassia, the architect of the Lambrecht Stift, made the church into a baroque pilastered church with galleries with chapels under them. The exterior and nave were redesigned in the neo-Renaissance style in 1885–1902. In the interior gilded pillar statues of the 12 Apostles by B.Brandstätter (*c.* 1750), from the Judenburg studio. On the altar of the Frauenkapelle N. of the choir Mary with Child in sandstone (*c.* 1420, possibly by Hans von Judenburg). The carved wooden *Mary with Child* on the side altar (*c.* 1500) is notable. *Rococo pulpit* dating from 1781.

Jenbach, late Gothic Madonna

Judenburg, St. Nikolaus

Magdalenenkirche, former Spitalskirche: Mentioned *c.* 1270, building *c.* 1330. The tower was rebuilt after a fire in 1805 and is too low. On the S. exterior wall fresco of St. Christopher (*c.* 1500). The finely restored *windows* (1380 – 1420) are particularly worth seeing: in the choir and on the S. wall scenes from the Life of Mary, Apostles, and scenes from the Old Testament. With the windows in the E. nave these date from the late 14C and are, like the W. windows (1420), from a Judenburg studio. *Wall paintings* on the N. choir wall: Crucifixion, and Death of Mary, busts of the Apostles and the suffragan bishop (14C). A fresco of St.Augustine with other saints and a scroll was transferred from the former Jesuit or Augustinerkirche. *Baroque furnishings:* 17C altars, high altar with Mary Magdalene (1743); crucifix and Man of Sorrows on the pillars *c.* 1740. Immaculata on the right side altar by Balthasar Brandstätter (1730).

Also worth seeing: The former *Neue Burg* was built in the 16C; it has three sections; the splendid muschelkalk staircase and the arcades are 18C additions. *No. 4 Martinsplatz* is made up of two knights' houses; altered in the 17C.

Environs: Schlösschen Thorhof on the mountainside was built in the 17C by Sixtus Prilss; Renaissance country house with wall paintings on the first floor (fables, grotesques). The **Liechtenstein ruin** (on a rocky crest E. of the town; the castle could only be reached by means of ladders) was mentioned in 1140. In ruins since the 16C; below the ruins is *Schloss Liechtenstein*, built *c.* 1650 by the Seckau Domstift. *Schloss Weyer*, built in the late

16C by Christoph Praunfalkh; three storeys with arcades, two towers on the façade side. NE of Judenburg *Gabelkofen*. Renaissance castle in particularly good condition, formerly moated. A curtain wall with four round corner towers and a gatehouse surround the residence, which formerly had 4 corner oriels. Tower S. of the entrance with baroque onion dome; arcades and steps in the courtyard. *Fohnsdorf* was a market with five fortress towers un-

til 1289; coal-mining town since the 18C. The *Pfarrkirche hl.Rupert* is the oldest parish church in the area; nave and E. tower Romanesque, net vaulting, late Gothic choir. Renaisssance triptych (*c.* 1525). The *ossuary* became a war memorial in 1952. *St.Peter ob Judenburg:* late Gothic nave with net vaulting, 2 aisles, choir and tower added in the baroque. High altar picture by J.Lederwasch, pulpit (1774) by J.Nischlwitzer. Gothic crucifix (1520).

K

Kaja = Hardegg 2082
Lower Austria   p.278□U 2

Ruined castle: The core of this romantically sited castle dates from the 12&13C, when it was known as Chiowe. Kaja was a princely fief. Count Burkhart, the chancellor of Emperor Charles IV, died in Kaja. The castle was damaged by fire and Moravian robber-knights, and fell into

disrepair from the 17C onwards; it has not been inhabited since. Slight restoration in the 19C. The basic construction is still clearly discernible. The keep and the chapel survive in good condition.

Environs: Karlslust (near Niederfladnitz): The river Thaya forms the border with Moravia between Hardegg, Kaya and Karlslust. In the late 18C, Count Auersperg commissioned the Viennese architect Polenfürst to build the very pretty Karlslust hunting lodge, a three-winged complex with original decorations in a beautiful setting in a meadow in the forest. It is owned by Count Waldstein.

Kaltenbrunn = Prutz 6522
Tirol   p.286□D

Pfarrkirche Maria Himmelfahrt: This surprisingly large pilgrimage church stands in a very isolated setting on a steep wooded slope, mentioned as a place of pilgrimage in 1285. Only the choir dating from 1502 survives from the Gothic reconstruction begun under Archduke Sigmund. The nave dates from 1533. The interior was redesigned in baroque style by Franz Laukas in 1730, with beautiful stucco and windows. The ova

Katzelsdorf, St. Michael

Gnadenkapelle in the middle of the main area, with its painting of the Virgin Mary dating from 1400, is by Gallus Gratl (1714). The large wooden crucifix in the choir is the work of Andreas Thamasch (1697).

Kapfenberg 8605
Steiermark   p.280☐S 8

Mentioned in 1197 as the castle of the Stubenberg family, with a settlement nearby. In the 13C it developed into a typical market town with parallel streets laid out around a market square.

Pfarrkirche hl.Oswald: This late Gothic building was erected in 1490. In 1752-5 it was altered; the side aisles were extended to the E. and the musicians' gallery (with its delicately stuccoed parapet) was raised by a further storey. The choir with its double niche and rib vault remained Gothic. The building was furnished in uniform style in 1770-80. The high altar has a painting by J.V. Hauck (1738), the statues on the side altars are probably by V. Königer, and the marble relief of 'Christ in Limbo' dates from 1584.

Filialkirche hl.Martin: First mentioned in 1183; nave with three bays and stellar vaulting (late 15C); the choir is 14C. Much altered in 1915.

Environs: Wallfahrtskirche Frauenberg/Maria Rehkogel (above Kapfenberg): In 1489-96, an artist from Braunau converted a chapel with a miraculous image (Our Lady of Sorrows, 1354) into a single-aisled church with a W. tower. The portal and the nave with net vaulting survive from that time. The musicians' gallery and the oratories were built in 1682 -8. Additional chapels and the choir with three bays were added in 1769. The wall paintings are by J.Gebler (1773). In the

middle of the church is a 17C statue of the Virgin Mary. Some late works by V. Königer: the high altar dating from 1773, the Nepomuk group, and the Peter and Magdalene altar of 1779.

Karres = Imst 6460
Tirol   p.286☐D 9

Pfarrkirche St.Stephan: Built in the 1st half of the 14C and expanded in the 16C, this church with low nave, tall gabled roof and broad, pointed-arched portal is typical of the late Gothic period in the N. Tirol. The S. tower with pointed windows and slender spire dates from 1506. The inside was redesigned in baroque style by J.Jais *c.* 1736, when side altars, stucco and ceiling paintings were added. *Totenkapelle*, 1st half of 18C.

Katzelsdorf = Leitha 2801
Lower Austria   p.278☐V 6

Former Schloss: Johann Sigismund von Weisspriach founded a Franciscan monastery in 1462. (He is buried in the church together with his wife.) During the Reformation, the monastery came into the possession of the barons of Teufel, who set up a Protestant school in the monastery (they built the Schloss tower in 1643). Queen Caroline of Naples, the sister of Napoleon, owned the Schloss in 1822. In 1845 it was acquired by the Duchess of Angoulême, the unfortunate daughter of Marie Antoinette and Louis XVI. The counts of Chambord inherited it from her. Schloss and domain finally came to Don Jaime of Bourbon, who sold it in 1940. The former Schloss is now a farm (Renaissance gate and fine arcaded courtyard).

Pfarrkirche hl.Radegundis: Single-aisled Gothic church with rib vault, built in 1462 and restored in 1750. Corbel figures in the choir. The main altar has a 14C statue of the Virgin Mary. There are two early baroque *chapels* on the N. side, and on the S. side is the *Annenkapelle, c.* 1360.

Environs: ▷ Wiener Neustadt and ▷ Forchtenstein are worth visiting.

Kauns = Prutz 6522
Tirol   p.286☐D 9

Berneck ruin: Near to Kauns, high above a narrow valley, we find the interesting ruins of this castle, which in the 13&14C was the family Schloss of the lords of Berneck. From then until the 18C it changed hands repeatedly, one of the owners being Maximilian I. The W. keep, the E. block of the residential building, and part of the exterior wall are from the original building. The remaining buildings, including the *Burgkapelle,* are late Gothic and date from the 15&16C. The coat-of-arms (of the Mulinen and Baumkirchs) on the entrance wall dates from the 17C.

Also worth seeing: The *Pfarrkirche St. Jakob* in the village of Kaun on the mountain slope dates from the Middle Ages, but was completely rebuilt in *c.* 1900; only the N. tower retains Romanesque features. The 17C *Schranz-Kapelle* has a large 16C carved crucifix.

Kefermarkt 4292
Upper Austria   p.276☐Q 4

In the late 15C, Christoph von Zelking, lord of Schloss Weinberg (see Environs) built a church dedicated to St.Wolfgang, a saint whom he revered very greatly; it later became the parish church. He then

endowed an altar, and provided for its completion in his will. This is all we know of the origins of this altar, one of the most famous works of late Gothic carving.

Pfarrkirche St.Wolfgang: This church with W. tower, nave, two aisles and five bays was built in 1470–76 on a commanding height. Kefermarkt and St.Wolfgang im Salzkammergut attract admirers of medieval art in their hordes, but the Kefermarkt altar was not as fortunate as Pacher's work: it was altered in the baroque period and some sections were removed (predella, exterior panels, rear side of the interior panels); but this 'modernization' may have preserved it from complete destruction. In the 19C it was so riddled with woodworm that it seemed likely to be completely destroyed. Credit for ordering restoration work (1852–55) is due to Adalbert Stifter who, as local schoolmaster, was also responsible for cultural matters.

The shrine of the *high altar* stands on the neo-Gothic predella; the three main figures are set in niches under baldachins and stand on imaginatively designed pedestals. The side panels are in bas-relief; the two 'guardians of the shrine', St.George and St.Florian, are now on the choir walls; delicate crowning with strong upward movement, eleven towers containing saints. Despite the grand scale of the work the characterisation of the three principal figures is the most striking feature of this altar. 'Peter is hard and grim, Wolfgang is mild, and Christopher is of inspired sentimentality, almost diseased.' (W. Pinder). Peter and Christopher are people of passion, and have nothing in common with the balance and harmony of Pacher's figures, though both artists delight with their loving treatment of detail, in this case the the hems and fastenings of the garments, the mitre, the bishop's crosier and the pedestals.

Panels: Annunciation, Nativity, Adoration of the Magi, Death of the Virgin Mary.

Genre treatment of the scenes. The architecture and landscape depicted are stylistically significant. In the 'Annunciation', the Virgin Mary is kneeling in an open hall with both Gothic and Renaissance elements, a mixture typical of the period. An open window reveals a landscape of the kind painted a little later by the 'Danube school'. More powerful still is the 'romantic scene' which forms the background to the Nativity. Apart from the altar, the ribs of the vault, the galleries (especially the balcony-like upper gallery) and the Zelkingen tombstones deserve attention.

Environs: Schloss Weinberg (N. of the town and above it): A stately Renaissance building with a massive façade tower. The dominant feature is the ring of two-storeyed buildings with round towers at the corners (accommodation for the garrison; the outer windows were pierced later). This Schloss suffered severe war damage and cannot be visited; the archives (now in the Landesarchiv) and the rococo pharmacy (now in the Landesmuseum) were salvaged. **Prandegg ruins** (about 15 km. to the E.): beautifully maintained building, accessible through a long vaulted passage, splendid view from the keep. **Wartberg ob der Aist** (15 km. to the S. of Kefermarkt): *Pfarrkirche Mariä Himmelfahrt:* Net-vaulted late Gothic hall with a nave and two aisles; an extension aisle at right angles to the choir has been added. Gothic tabernacle and stone pulpit (new figures). Next to this is the *St.-Michaels-Kapelle;* two storeys, and, underneath, crypt chapel of the Starhemberg family. *Wenzelskirche:* Elevated site on a granite peak at the edge of the town; it was secularized for a long time, and is now the Freistadt district memorial for the dead of two World Wars. Steep, high saddleback roof; rich S. gate; fine two-aisled hall with net vaulting; fragments of frescos depicting King Wenzel, *c.* 1390 in the choir. **Schloss Riedegg** is above Gallneukirchen, some 17 km. to the SW of Kefermarkt. A new building was erected in the early 17C on the site of the old castle. The building is well looked after. An interesting horsemen's staircase leads from the cour-

Kefermarkt, carved altar in St. Wolfgang

tyard to the first storey. The chapel with stucco is late 17C. Beautifully organised *Afrika-Museum* of the Marianhill mission (Tel.: 07235–224).

Kematen im Tirol 6175
Tirol   p.286□F 8

Pfarrkirche St. Viktor: This 14C late Gothic building has been much extended and rebuilt. The baroque tower with triple dome and fragments of late Gothic wall frescos in the nave (1st half of 15C) are of interest.

Also worth seeing: *Crucifixion* dating from 1700 in the graveyard; in the village two old *granaries* with carved gables, 1705. The *Ferklehen residence* dates back to the Middle Ages. It was rebuilt in the 16C, and most of it was destroyed by a fire in 1703. The rococo chapel is worth seeing. The early-16C *Burghof residence* has been much restored. The *Oberer Lotterhof* dates from the 16&17C.

Schloss Weinberg (Kefermarkt)

Environs: In **Afling,** a small village above the Inn valley, is the pretty *rococo chapel of Maria Schnee* dating from 1778. Its interior had to be restored in 1930&1 after being damaged by lightning.

Keutschnach 9074
Carinthia   p.282□P 11

Schloss: This four-storeyed cubic baroque building with a hipped roof was owned by the counts of Orsini-Rosenberg from 1659 to 1926, before that by the lords of Keutschach.

Pfarrkirche St. Georg und St. Bartholomäus: This pillared basilica with nave and two aisles, the core of which is Romanesque, was first mentioned in 1242; Romanesque E. tower with adjacent polygonal rib-vaulted choir; flat ceiling of the nave replaced by a groin vault in the 18C. The *stucco* in the choir is particularly beautiful, and may be the work of K.Pittner. The *high altar* and *side altars* are baro-

Kematen, Pfarrkirche St. Viktor

que, 1730&31. The early Romanesque sgraffito saints on the S. outer wall are important.

Kindberg 8650
Steiermark   p.280☐S 7

A settlement grew up in the 12C below a castle, and became a market town in 1232. An ironworks built in the 19C aided industrial development.

Schloss Oberkindberg: A three-winged complex built before 1680, with four corner towers and a wide central projection. In 1773&4, J.Hueber built the courtyard façade and two oval stairwells, and also redesigned the interior. The chapel in the NW tower was given a new altar (1785); it has a painting of St. Jerome by H.A. Weissenkirchner (*c.* 1680), and also parts of a Gothic triptych dating from 1500. Rococo stucco ceilings and wall paintings.

Pfarrkirche St.Peter und Paul: Mentioned as early as 1232. The Gothic church was redesigned by J. Hueber in 1773 using the old masonry. Notable interior features are a 15C statue of the Virgin Mary, and the altarpiece by Carolus Laubmann (1775).

Also worth seeing: *Kalvarienbergkirche* (17C); *Filialkirche hl.Georg* (mentioned in 1232), redesigned in baroque style in the 17C.

Kirchberg am Wechsel 2880
Lower Austria   p.280☐U 7

A convent of Augustinian canonesses was founded here in 1271. It was insignificant for a long period, until nearby St.Corona became a pilgrimage church. Emperor Joseph's dissolution of the monasteries in 1782 stopped development until the middle of last century.

Pfarrkirche hl.Jacob d.Ältere: Begun in 1743, tower 1829, nave approximately oval. The high altar is a splendid work of the high baroque, side altars rococo.

St. Wolfgang: Legend has it that this church outside the town was founded by St. Wolfgang. The *chapel* built in 1339 forms the N. aisle of the church built 100 years later. The central supports have been missing since the vaulting collapsed in the 18C. In the N. aisle, the portal (St. Wolfgang and three knights in the typanum) and the net vaulting survive. The *pulpit* came from the Capella speziosa in Klosterneuburg, and the 'Mariahilf' *high altar* from the Rosalienkapelle of the Freihaus in Vienna. On the reredos 15C frescos (St.Christopher) by Jörg Brunner. Paintings by Kremser Schmidt (1794) and J. Spillenberger (1672) on the side walls.

Environs: St. Corona am Wechsel:

Kirchberg a. W., St.Wolfgang

Frauenstein (Kirchdorf), Madonna

Wallfahrtskirche St.Corona: A simple 17C baroque building. The high altar dates from 1710. A document of 1724 says: 'Gesundbrunnen, vulgokayserlicher Brunnen' (mineral spring, known as the Emperor's spring).

Kirchdorf an der Krems 4560
Upper Austria   p.276☐O 6

Pfarrkirche hl.Gregor: Parish church since the 10C. The church was built in the 15C and has been altered many times, most recently in 1962. It is a happy combination of the Gothic and modern styles. Modern timber ceiling with St.Andrew's cross designs, and glowing abstract stained-glass windows; a late Gothic crucifix and an altar of the Virgin Mary (shrine and predella carved, wings Danube school); splen-

did tombs, late-16C stone etchings; the tower has a fine neo-baroque onion dome.

Environs: Burg Altpernstein: Impressive setting on a rock above the road from Kirchdorf to Micheldorf. An imposing, well-preserved early-16C fortress. Access via a bridge over a deep rocky gorge. The chapel is early baroque. Splendid view of the Totes Gebirge from the restaurant. **Micheldorf** (3 km. S.): Georgenberg with St.-Georgs-Kirche (Kalvarienberg); excavations in the 1950s proved continuity of settlement and worship over 2000 years: a Gallo-Roman peripteral temple, a late classical refuge castle, an early Christian choir with apse, a Carolingian church, and the present Gothic building redesigned in the baroque style. **Frauenstein** (some 10 km. S. of Kirchdorf): Pilgrimage church on rising ground to the E. of the Steyr valley; it has a superb Virgin of Mercy endowed by Emperor Maximilian, who is the first supplicant kneeling on the 'men's side'; Gregor Erhart, 1515. **Klaus an der Steyr** (11 km. to the S. of Kirchdorf): Mountain church above the Schloss, with an excellent baroque altar (Baptism of Christ statue in a colonnaded round temple with massive crown). Concerts. *Schloss:* Beside the ruins 16C new building, altered in the baroque style. The public is only admitted when events are being held. Information may be obtained from the Kulturring, 4564 Klaus an der Steyr, Tel.: 07585-155. **Inzersdorf** (some 5 km. to the N. of Kirchdorf): The modern church contains an excellent wooden statue of the Virgin Mary in the Soft Style dating from the early 15C.

Kirchenthal=St.Martin bei Lofer 5092
Salzburg   p.284☐K 7

Wallfahrtskirche hl.Maria: This building, designed by J.B. Fischer von

Erlach and erected between 1693 and 1701, is one of the plainest designs by this great Austrian baroque architect, and is successfully integrated into the stony world of the Lofer mountains. The three-storey façade was suggested by the Dom in Salzburg and is faintly reminiscent of the pilgrimage church of Maria Plain near Salzburg. The shape of the crowns occurs again in the St. Johann Spitalskirche (see Salzburg). The ground plan is cruciform, with shortened transepts. The neo-baroque high altar has a miraculous image and an early-15C Madonna Enthroned. There are two elegant side altars of red marble dating from *c.* 1700, and the altarpiece of the left-hand one is a painting, by J. Zanussi, of Joachim and Anne, the parents of the Virgin Mary (1719).

Environs: St. Martin bei Lofer: The *Pfarrkirche hl. Martin* is a basically Gothic building partially redesigned in the baroque style. The altarpiece of the S. side altar is by J. Zanussi (1721). **Lofer:** The *Pfarrkirche hll. Maria und Leonhard* contains remains of early-15C Gothic frescos.

Kitzbühel 6370

Tirol   p.284☐J 8

Kitzbühel, like Innsbruck, has a long history, which results from its location on the trade route between Germany and Italy. The first finds are as old as *c.* 1300 BC. There was a castle *c.* 1100 AD, the settlement called 'Chizbühel' was in existence in *c.* 1165, and in 1271 Kitzbühel was granted a charter. The town developed rapidly from the 15C onwards, owing to the rich mines; tourism gave additional impetus in the 19C. It is not surprising that Kitzbühel, which has been spared the ravages of war throughout its history, still looks prosperous and picturesque today, with its colourfully painted houses and churches.

Pfarrkirche St. Andreas: The present church was built by Stefan Krumenauer in 1435 on the site of a small Romanesque church dating from 1180. It was redesigned in the baroque style in 1785, rebuilt in 1896 and recently restored. The church's

Kitzbühel with St. Andreas and Liebfrauenkirche

inconspicuous exterior shows a small choir, a hip-roof, a low, slender N. tower with a baroque dome, and a pointed-arched, contoured main portal. The inside of this church (nave and two aisles) has late Gothic pillars, stucco, and ceiling paintings by J.Gold, who unfortunately replaced the old paintings in 1897; A.Hueber's *stucco* and M. Kirchner's paintings, 1786, survive only in the apse. The 15C *frescos* in the choir, which also contains a tracery window, were only revealed very recently. The massive, solemn *high altar*, in black and gold, is a very fine piece of work by the sculptor S.B. Faistenberger (1663); the altarpiece by J.Spillenberger dates from the same period. The side altars are baroque and rococo. The choir stalls with twining plant decorations are by Franz Offer, a pupil of I.Günther, 1762. The galleries in the choir and on the W. wall are decorated with paintings and date from the 17C. Oil paintings by S.B. Faistenberger are to be found in the organ gallery and in the right aisle (the Faistenberger family of artists lived in Kitzbühel from 1620 onwards). The *memorial* on the N. nave wall is to the Kupferschmied family; it is by the sculptor Hans Frosch, 1520, and is one of the largest tombs in the Tyrol. The *Rosa-Kapelle* adjoins the choir in the S., has a large tracery window and an articulated tunnel vault, rococo stucco, a fine ceiling painting of St.Rose by S.B. Faistenberger, 1751, and a statue of the Virgin Mary (*c.* 1460).

Liebfrauenkirche: This church on the N. edge of the graveyard is a unique combination of massive square tower and small two-storey chapel. The substructure of the tower was originally a fortress and probably dates from the 14C, while the upper section was built by W.Egartner in 1566. The chapel is mentioned as early as 1373 and its upper storey was redesigned in baroque style in 1735. The high altar by G. Faistenberger dates from 1702 and contains a copy, by L.Cranach (1670), of the Mariahilf painting in the Dom in Innsbruck. The fine frescos dating from 1739 are by S.B. Faistenberger. The door grille dates from 1739, and the very fine rose grille in front of the high altar is by Meister Witting of Kitzbühel, 1778. The *Ölbergkapelle* in the graveyard contains late Gothic frescos.

Stadtkirche St.Katharina: This church in the middle of the Old Town dates from the 14C, and is now a war memorial. Gothic rib vaulting, a 15C carved Virgin Mary on the S. wall and the 16C late Gothic triptych have survived inside.

Other churches: The *Spitalkirche zum Hl.Geist*, built in the 19C on the site of a Gothic church, is a sober building, but its altar has a painting of the Holy Trinity by S.B. Faistenberger. A 16C life-size carved group is to be found in the nave. In the Vorstadt is the *Kapuzinerkirche;* built in 1702, with 18C altars and pulpit.

Also worth seeing: The 15C *Jochbergtor* is the only town gate to have survived. The corner tower with 16C staircase tower still survives from the *Pfleghof,* a castle of the dukes of Bavaria (originally 12C). The *Kapsburg* in the S. of the town is a 17C aristocrat's house. *Schloss Lebenberg* (originally 16C) on the hill is now a hotel. The following houses, with late Gothic, Renaissance and baroque features, are also of interest: *Nos. 14, 15, 22, 24* and, in the Hinterstadt, *Nos. 28* and *32;* there is a small 17C courtyard between the latter pair and adjacent to that the famous 16C *Goldener Greif inn.*

Heimatmuseum: This museum has an interesting collection of Tyrolean folk art

Klagenfurt, Wappensaal in the Landhaus

Landhaus

and is housed in the old *Getreidekasten* (granary), which has original beams.

Klagenfurt 9020
Carinthia   p.282☐P 11

Klagenfurt, the capital of Carinthia, stands on the E. bank of the Wörthersee. The name comes from the Bavarian 'Klag' or 'Klaga', women who laid out the dead and wept at night by a ford (Furt); the town was built by Hermann von Spanheim in 1170 -90 on marshy terrain on an important ford over the river Glan. It is mentioned in the late 12C. Between 1246 and 1252, Berhnard von Spanheim (1202 – 56) transferred it to the dry but stony ground below the Kreuzbergl; then as now the Alter Platz was the focal point. A devastating fire almost entirely destroyed Klagenfurt

in 1544; the town was rebuilt and considerably expanded as the local parliament wanted a permanent site, the peasants were in revolt, and the Turks posed a threat. Also the town was fortified, making Klagenfurt the most significant fortress in the Alpine provinces. The Lendkanal also dates from this period; it fed the town moats and became an important waterway from the lake to the town. The principal buildings also date from this pre-baroque phase and were expanded and in some cases redesigned in the baroque period. The city walls were blown up by French troops in 1809, clearing the way for the building of the modern town.

Dom und Pfarrkirche St. Peter und Paul (Lidmanskygasse): The town became the property of the Carinthian parliament as the result of an imperial bequest in 1518.

Lindwurmbrunnen

Celtic vase, Landesmuseum

This new-found political independence was strengthened by the ideas of the Reformation and, after 1578, led to the building of the Dom. It is a Protestant church designed to emphasise the importance of preaching, a rare example of Austrian Reformation architecture. After a building period of 13 years, it was dedicated to the Trinity. The architect was probably Christoph Windisch, and in 1604 it was handed over to the Jesuits (and dedicated to St.Peter and St.Paul). The Franz-Xaver-Kapelle chapel on the S. side was added in 1660, and the presbytery followed in 1665. The church was given new interior decorations in 1727 after a fire, and in 1787 the Bishops of Gurk moved their residence from Strasbourg to Klagenfurt. Since then, St.Peter und Paul has been a Catholic cathedral. The *spatial impression* made by the pilastered hall, the earliest example of its kind in Austria, is characterized by three surrounding gallery arcades and by the extensive articulated tunnel vault. The late Gothic spatial layout is here seen in its transition to the early baroque style. The rich stucco on the walls and vault ensures architectural unity. The stucco ornament in the galleries is by K. Pittner (1725), while the ceiling paintings (retouched several times) were originally by J.F. Fromiller. The *high altar* was built in 1752, and the paintings by the Viennese artist D.Gran are particularly fine. The interiors of the *side chapels*, (1725–1727) are also worth seeing: the two E. chapels on the N. and S. sides are decorated with 11 different types of marble, evidence of the baroque craftsman's understanding of his material and its decorative qualities.

Stadtpfarrkirche St.Egyd (Pfarrgasse):

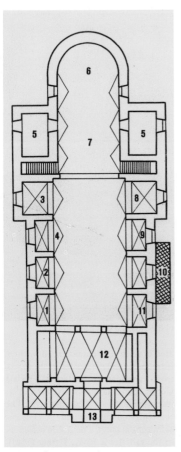

Klagenfurt, Dom 1 Rosalia **2** N. entrance **3** and **4** Side altars of Mary and St. Anne **5** Sacristy **6** High altar **7** Presbytery **8** Ignatius **9** Josefsaltar **10** Franz-Xaver-Kapelle **11** Barbara **12** Gallery **13** W. entrance

The onion tower 301 ft. high (1733) is the tallest building in the town. The present church was built in 1692–97 on the foundations of an earlier building dating from the 13C. An inscription on the lowest vault of the tower reminds us that the old building was destroyed by an earthquake in 1690. A striking interior feature is the *painting in the choir,* some of J.F. Fromiller's finest work. This late baroque allegory deals with the warlike beginnings of the Christian religion: St.Egyd is seen driving sickness, war and distress out of the town. The *altarpiece* by A. Cusetti (1761) and the *ceiling paintings* by J. Mölk (1761) are also of interest.

Former Stiftskirche Unsere Liebe Frau (at the S. edge of Klagenfurt): This is one of the most significant monasteries in Carinthia. Founded in 1142 by Count Bernhard v. Spanheim, the buildings were used by the Cistercian monks as a residence, a workplace and a place of prayer; they were later extended to look like a fortress. The monks had immigrated from Lorraine, from where they imported late Romanesque Burgundian monastery architecture. The pilastered basilica with tunnel-vaulted nave, two aisles and straight choir was consecrated in 1202. The late-15C spire was added at the time of fortification against the Turks. The deliberately austere, functional interior design expresses the puritanical Cistercian spirit. The three *stained-glass windows* in the choir, *c.* 1400, are perhaps the finest feature. They depict Annunciation scenes (left window) and the twelve Apostles (right window). The composition of the figures, and the closeness of the lines to the objects depicted, are the last word in a particular phase in the development of stained glass in Europe. The solemn effect created by the *baroque high altar* (1622) in front of the windows harmonizes with the stained glass. Also worth seeing are the plain Romanesque *portal* (S. aisle, facing towards the cloister), and some 13C *tombstones* to be found at the entrance to the *Taufkapelle* and in the cloister. The great *Festsaal,* with decorations by K.Pittner, is in the *former collegiate building.*

Stiftskirche Viktring, choir window

St. Peter a. Bichl, Carolingian guilloche works

St. Peter am Bichl (to the NE of Klagenfurt): This Romanesque church with a flat ceiling is first mentioned in 1399, but is in fact considerably older. Two late-9C *Carolingian tracery stones* are of great interest from the art-historical point of view. They probably originate from the nearby Königspfalz of Karnburg. The two stones have a double symbolic content: in their function as a component of the W. wall (at the entrance to the church) they drive away the 'powers of darkness', while their twining ornamentation evokes order in a menacing world.

Other churches: The *Heiligengeistkirche* is the third-oldest church in the town, first mentioned in 1355; it contains a fine altar panel by Lorenz Glaber (1635) and a rococo pulpit. There is a charming late baro-

que high altar in the *Marienkirche* (1613–24; 1636). The *Kreuzbergkirche* (1737) has frescos by J.F. Fromiller, the most famous Carinthian fresco painter, who also painted the St. Sebastian in the *Bürgerspitalkirche* (1663&4).

Landhaus (Alter Platz): This is the most significant secular building in Klagenfurt and was built in 1574 on the site of the old ducal castle, burned down in 1535. The local parliament commissioned this building, as they did the Dom. H. Freymann, J.A. Verda, and finally Ulrich Vogelsang, designed the building in the German Renaissance style, which can now be seen only in the courtyard. The building is given a proud southern character by its *arcades;* the important rustication on the ground floor reminds us of the original defensive purpose of such buildings. This design, functional yet formal, becomes more forceful and takes on baroque character in two massive towers with double onion domes. The rendering of the façade in 1740 altered the appearance of the exterior. The large *Wappensaal* shows how the rulers of Carinthia saw themselves vis-à-vis their Habsburg overlords. J.F. Fromiller's ceiling painting (1739–40) commemorates the homage paid by Carinthia to Charles VI (1728), while the 665 painted ecclesiastical and secular coats-of-arms on the walls and window jambs point to the ancient political privileges enjoyed by Carinthia. The fresco on the S. wall shows Maximilian's imperial bequest of 1518. On the N. wall is a depiction of the Duke's installation in the Fürstenstein near Karnburg. In the small Wappensaal, Fromiller (1740) painted 298 coats-of-arms and also the allegory 'Truth as the daughter of Time'. The Landhaus still houses the Carinthian parliament, and musical and theatrical performances are held in the courtyard.

Also worth seeing: The *Alter Platz* is the

Schloss Velden (Klagenfurt)

historical heart of the city. Many of the old buildings have names like 'Zur blauen Kugel' (The Blue Ball), 'Zum goldenen Anker' (The Golden Anchor), or *'Zur goldenen Gans'* (The Golden Goose; No. 31). The latter dates back to the 15C and was the first Rathaus. The staircase is an especially noteworthy feature of the present *Rathaus* (Neuer Platz), which was built 1580–82 and rebuilt from 1650 onwards. The building was the palace of the counts of Rosenberg until 1918, and then passed into the possession of the town. The *Lindwurmbrunnen* (dragon fountain; Neuer Platz) is the emblem of the town (since 1287 it has been included in the city seal). U. Vogelsang, the stonemason, carved the monster from a single block of stone (1590–93). Michael Hönel, who was also responsible for the Gurk altar figures, created the club-swinging giant in 1632&3.

It is said that there was a popular festival at the unveiling of the monument. Legend has it that the dragon is associated with the adventurous early days of Klagenfurt, which was built in a battle against swamp and marsh.

Museums and art collections: *Landesmuseum* (Museumsgasse 2; founded in 1844). Exhibits from all periods, including prehistoric and Roman; also architecture, stained glass, bronzes, triptychs, statues, reliefs, panel paintings, applied art and utensils of all kinds from the Middle Ages to the 19C. The *Diözesanmuseum* (Mariannengasse 2; founded in 1917) contains one of the most significant collections of liturgical objects in Austria, also varied exhibits from the general history of art. Of especial importance is the *'Magdalenenscheibe'* (1170), perhaps the oldest stained glass in Austria. *Kärntner Landesgalerie* (Burggasse 8; founded in 1933 and reopened in 1965) with modern Carinthian paintings and sculpture.

Environs: At the W. end of the Wörthersee, by the lakeside resort of the same name, is the former Renaissance Schloss of **Velden,** built by B.Khevenmüller in 1590. It was altered in the 17C and is now used as a hotel. In the N. of the town is **Schloss Mageregg,** a stately 19C building used for representative purposes; it contrasts with the Renaissance and baroque buildings of Klagenfurt. Originally built by Wolf Mager von Fuchsstatt in 1590, it was redesigned by Domenico Venchiarutti in 1841. The park is a game reserve. *Zollfeld* (and the Kärntner Herzogsstuhl) and *Karnburg* (and the Kärntner Fürstenstein) are two places of interest dealt with in detail under ▷ Maria Saal.

Kleinmariazell, frescos by Bergl

Bad Kleinkirchheim 9546
Carinthia   p.282☐N 10

Wallfahrtskirche St. Katharina im Bade: This late Gothic, net-vaulted church (1492) was built above a tunnel-vaulted grotto. The result is an interesting piece of symbolism: grotto and water signify this world; the windows and vaults symbolize light and the world beyond. This architectural device is repeated in the grotesque ornament on the W. choir gallery. The grotesque figure, half representational and half abstract, also symbolizes the transition between heaven and earth. A similar, if accidental, role is played by the *triptych:* late Gothic sections (shrine figures dating from before 1500?), and Renaissance sections (rear side, 1573) are built on historical and stylistic contrasts.

Pfarrkirche St.Ulrich: This plain baroque church has remains of Gothic-

Romanesque architecture. The tunnel vaulting and pilaster articulation date from 1743. The high altar, side altars, and pulpit decorations are 18C. There is a monumental painting 'Lechfeldschlacht' (battle of Lechfeld) by Jonas Ranter (1928).

Kleinmariazell = Altenmarkt-Thenneberg 2571
Lower Austria   p.278☐U 5

Former Benediktinerstift: Founded by Rapoto and Heinrich von Schwarzenburg-Nöstrach in 1136 as a monastery in a cleared section of the Wienerwald; confirmed by Margrave Leopold III immediately after Heiligenkreuz. (In the picture of the Babenberg family tree, Leopold III is shown with the monasteries of Heiligenkreuz, Klosterneuberg and Kleinmariazell.) It was settled by Benedictine monks from Niederaltaich (Bavaria). Consecrated by Otto von Lonsdorf, Bishop of Passau, in 1256. It was the favourite monastery of Duke Friedrich II. He was the last of the Babenbergs, and the monastery was always loyally devoted to him. It fell into decline in the Reformation. The Turks destroyed the church, which was rebuilt in 1606–1616 by Abbot Perckhofer of the Schottenkloster in Vienna. It was redesigned in baroque style under Abbot Pach of Kremsmünster *c.* 1750. The old church and the Romanesque ossuary were pulled down in 1782. Excavations carried out in the last few years have revealed a tunnel-vaulted 13C cellar, part of the cloister (with a simple groin vault and windows without tracery), and the S. portal (rectangular with acanthus and animal ornamentation; related to the style of the Viennese stonemasons' lodge).

Kirche Mariae Himmelfahrt: The core of the building is a 12C Romanesque basilica, with alternate columns and pillars, square choir, and transept. The thick walls on the W. side suggest a tower which was never completed (the present tower with baroque dome dates from 1765). Portal with porch and inscription on the empty tympanum. The N. portal originally led out of the church (now into a baroque baptismal chapel): late Romanesque disc bases and early Gothic crocket capitals. First-class stonemasonry in the ornaments on the portal (stylistically related to the ossuary in Mödling). *Inside:* The Romanesque church was rebuilt in late baroque style. The transept and nave are of equal width. Above the crossing is a shallow dome with frescos by J.W. Bergl (1764). Scenes full of movement and vitality from the life of the Virgin Mary cover the entire ceiling: heavy draperies with tassels and cords, double columns in elaborate perspective. On the side walls childhood of Christ in a grisaille frame. *High altar:* St. Florian and St. Leopold portrayed in a theatrical style similar to that of the Gutenbrunn altar. Above the tabernacle Madonna and Child, and above them God the Father with an Archangel.

Kleinwetzdorf, Heldenberg

Kleinwetzdorf = Glaubendorf 3704
Lower Austria   p.278☐U 3

Heldenberg (on the Horner Bundesstrasse): In 1833, Joseph Pargfrieder,
a military supplier, purchased Schloss
Wetzdorf, rebuilt it in the classical
style, and presented it to Field Marshal
Radetsky on condition that the Field Marshal be buried with Pargfrieder in the
mausoleum which he had built for the purpose. Field Marshal Count Wimpffen also
gave in to Pargfrieder's hero-worship.
Wimpffen was the first to die, in 1854, and
is buried in the crypt along with his friend
Radetzky (d. 1858) and Pargfrieder (d.
1863). The latter is in the lowest crypt, in
a seated position wearing knights' armour.
'...three heroes in blissful peace — two
fought the battles—the third bought the
shoes!' The so-called *Heldenberg* was built
around the mausoleum. This is a memorial
grove with 200 cast-iron soldiers, military
leaders, and archdukes (statues by Adam
Ramelmayr). A colonnaded hall of fame is
the focal point of this strangely charming
grove of heroes.

Klosterneuburg 3400
Lower Austria   p.278☐V 4

Margrave Leopold III endowed a secular
college beside his residence, and commissioned the abbey building (1114–36). Legend suggests that the Margrave was a
member of the retinue of Emperor Henry
IV, but when Henry V, who was fighting
against his father, offered the Margrave the
hand of his sister Agnes, Leopold crossed
over to the son's camp. This treachery induced him to build an expiatory monastery. When he was standing with his wife
one day on the balcony of his castle, the
wind blew away her veil, which was found
undamaged on an elderberry bush nine

years later. The Virgin Mary appeared to
the Margrave in a dream and demanded
that he build a monastery on this site. In
the old church there was an 'elderberry column' in the place where the veil was discovered, and the seven-armed candlestick
dating from 1114, the oldest item in the abbey, is called *'Holunderstrauch'* (elderberry
bush) because there is a piece of elderberry
wood in its shaft. Influenced by his great
son Otto von Freising, the Margrave
presented the secular college to the
Augustinians, thus establishing a double
foundation (the convent died out in 1568).
Leopold died in 1136, and Margravine
Agnes in 1143. Leopold was interred in the
chapterhouse of the monastery. The *Verdun Altar* was built under Provost Wernher
in 1181. The richly endowed monastery
gained great power: the Margraves resided
in Vienna, Leopold VI moved his court to
Klosterneuburg. The latter was responsible for the Cappella speziosa of 1222, the
first work of Burgundian Gothic in Austria
(pulled down in 1799). When the
Babenberg line died out in 1268, the
Habsburgs were unwelcome successors:
the loss of the freedom of the Empire made
the Viennese rebellious. In 1308 Albrecht
II retired resentfully to Klosterneuburg, to
which he had granted a charter 1298. In
1317, the energetic Stephan von Sierndorf
became provost. It was under him that the
cloister was completed. Its rich stained glass
is linked thematically with the Verdun
altar. Sierndorf turned Leopold's burial
site into a *cult chapel*. A miracle book was
established. Leopold was canonized on 6
January 1485 under Pope Innocent VIII.
This was the beginning of a new period of
success for the monastery. In 1616, Archduke Maximilian, the German Master
of the Teutonic Order, endowed the
Austrian ducal crown worn by St.Leopold;

*Klosterneuburg, riding out to the hunt
(Leopold III), by Rueland Frueauf the
younger (1470-1545)*

the basic shape is that of the Austrian imperial crown. St. Leopold became the patron saint of Austria in 1663 under Emperor Leopold I. After a happy conclusion to the Turkish wars, Emperor Charles VI commissioned the younger Fischer von Erlach to build an Austrian Escorial—an imperial monastery Schloss — in Klosterneuburg. Construction work was begun by Donato Felice d'Allio: only two wings had been completed when the Emperor died. In 1755, under Franz Stephan of Lorraine, the architect was dismissed. In 1836 J. Kornhäusel closed one of the four courtyards and altered the Leopoldskapelle.

Stiftskirche Unsere Liebe Frau: The original building dating from 1136 is a basilica with a nave, two aisles, and a square choir with one large and two small apses. The baroque decoration was added over

Klosterneuburg, Stiftskirche Unsere Liebe Frau, with the two towers enlarged in neo-Gothic style

Klosterneuburg, Stift 1 Stiftskeller **2** Former Gothic chapel **3** Dead man's lantern, 1381 **4** Stiftskirche **5** Former chapterhouse, Leopold chapel **6** Cloister **7** Leopoldihof with fountain dating from 1592 **8** Gothic gate **9** Pfisterstiege **10** Prior's house **11** Kaiserzimmer **12** Marmorsaal, 1st stage **13** Library, 1st storey **14** Former Chorfrauenkirche

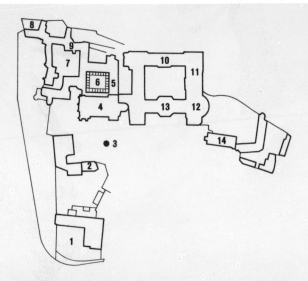

this Romanesque core, although the fabric had been much damaged by fire, particularly in 1330. In 1634–45, new vaults were built, the windows were enlarged, the W. gallery was inserted, and the side aisles were subdivided into chapels. The fine brown marble and stucco on the walls was completed in 1723. 150 years later a disastrous restoration was begun under the Viennese Joseph von Schmidt: he raised the towers in neo-Gothic style, removed the statues dating from 1394 from the smaller S. tower, and replaced the roofs of the N. and S. towers. The church façade has been restored to its original purity of design. The *interior* is overwhelming in its refinement and splendour: it was redesigned in baroque style under the supervision of G.B. Carlone. The massive nave has three tunnel-vaulted chapels on either side. The nave vaults are supported on massive pilasters set in front of the former pillars. The capitals have angels' heads and garlands of fruit. The stucco is very rich and somewhat ponderous (mainly Italian work). Romanesque rib vaulting survives in the N. transept. The

choir is by d'Allio, the abbey architect: the pulpit on the right-hand side before the crossing is supported by an angel; Salvator mundi by M. Steinl above the sounding-board. Opposite this is an altar with St. Leopold. Raised crossing. The marble high altar is by M. Steinl (the original altarpiece by Schmidt was replaced in 1833 by a somewhat dry 'Birth of the Virgin Mary' by L. Kuppelwieser). The ceiling fresco in the choir dome dating from 1729–30 is J.M. Rottmayr's last work. The *choir stalls* are outstandingly well carved (M. Steinl, 1723; the imperial oratory was also designed by Steinl). The festival organ was built in 1636, using the pipes of two earlier organs.

The central point of the abbey church is the *Verdun Altar* in Leopold's burial chapel, the former chapterhouse, rebuilt under Emperor Leopold in 1677. The present altar (overall height of decorated screen is 3 ft. 7 in.; width 8 ft. 8 in.; side panels 3 ft. 11 in.; gilded copper with champlevé) came into the possession of the monastery in 1181 and was on the ambo of the Romanesque church. After a serious

Verdun Altar

fire in 1330, the plates were re-assembled by Viennese goldsmiths, who added six more panels. This is the maturest work of Nikolaus von Verdun. The almost detached figures, the small columns, ornaments and the delicacy of the drawing make it even finer than the shrine of the Magi in Cologne.

Cloister: The oldest walk runs alongside the church. Small, delicate columns in the Cistercian tradition. In the N. walk is the former *well house* containing the 'elderberry bush'. In one corner of the cloister is the *Freisinger Kapelle*, endowed as a burial place by Berthold von Wehingen, Provost of St. Stephan and Bishop of Freising, together with his brother. Berthold's tombstone slab dating from 1410 is of red marble. The whole cloister has been much restored. The abbey collection of stone monuments is now in the *former refectory,* including the *Klosterneuburg Madonna* of 1300. The visitor passes through a late Gothic passage into the *Augustinussaal,* with fine stucco. Above this is the *gotischer Albrechtssaal*

Knittelfeld, tombstone

commissioned by Albrecht II in 1438, the year of his kingship, for the Kirche zu den neun Chören der Engel in Vienna.

The baroque abbey: Four courtyards were envisaged in the plans drawn up by Fischer von Erlach, but none of these was completed at the time of building. The high point and symbol of the entire complex is the imperial crown resting on a tasselled cushion above the massive dome (the ducal crown is in the N. corner above a smaller dome). The abbey, with *staircase, Kaiserzimmer, Festsaal* and *library,* can only be visited with a guide. The frescos by D.Gran in the Kaisersaal date from 1749 and are interesting and informative. The *Stiftsmuseum* is also worth seeing.

Knittelfeld 8720

Steiermark   p.282□R 9

In 1224 Leopold VI established a typical Steiermark H-shaped settlement on a stone road at the end of the Ingeringtal; a round tower in the NE corner and fragments of a 14–16C curtain wall have survived. The Stadtpfarrkirche, Rathaus, and Spitalkirche were destroyed in 1945. Knittelfeld was rebuilt as an industrial town.

Pfarrkirche hl. Johannes: The hall with nave and two aisles and the tower were destroyed, and only the choir with two bays (1435) and the adjoining sacristy with rib vault (1454) survived. Reconstruction work was carried out to plans by Prof. F.Zotter of Graz; the choir was included as a side chapel. A late Gothic carved 'Christ on the Mount of Olives' (1510), the crucifix, and some Gothic and baroque figures survive of the old furnishings. The red marble arms of Peter and Anna Murer (1476) from the Salzburg Eybenstock workshop are notable. The churchyard wall, with a late Gothic portal, survives.

Pfarrkirche St.Johann d.T. im Felde:
This was probably an earlier parish
church; Romanesque building in sandstone ashlar. Square choir with semicircular apse; net vault inserted in the 16C. 16C
crucifix and high altar, remaining decorations 18C.

Environs: SW of the town is **Schloss
Spielberg,** rebuilt in *c.* 1570 in the style
of the dell' Allio school (it was an
aristocratic seat as early as 1141); the old
decorations survive in good condition.

Kobersdorf 7332
Burgenland   p.280□V 7

Schloss: This 'magnificent, picturesque
moated Schloss' (Schmeller), severely
damaged in the war, would have been
doomed if Bolldorf-Reitstätter, the lady architect, had not bought it and made
sacrifices to restore and rescue the building.
A moat still surrounds the building on all
sides; the exterior is dominated by massive
round towers, fine Renaissance windows,
and a barbican protecting the main portal.
Inside, an atmospheric arcaded courtyard
welcomes the visitor. The church,
distingushed by its rich 17C stucco work,
stands in a former tilting yard; restoration
revealed a Gothic portal. *Theatrical performances and concerts* are held in the
Schlosshof.

Environs: Stoob: Some 7 km. to the S.
is a 13C mountain church known as a centre for Hafner (= 'Plutzermacher': makers
of earthenware bottles).

Köflach 8580
Steiermark   p.282□R 9

Market rights granted in 1170. Coal

deposits were discovered in the 18C, and
coalmining influenced the development of
the town.

Pfarrkirche St.Magdalena: Mentioned
in 1245, owned by the abbey of Lambrecht
until 1786. D.Sciassia, the abbey architect,
altered the church from 1643 – 49.
Cruciform ground plan, two bays and a
square crossing. The original rib vault was
later replaced by a dome. Interior frescos
and high altar painting by J.A. von Mölk,
the latter spoiled by later retouching. The
two-storey *circular ossuary* in the Romanesque style was redesigned as a *war
memorial* in 1926.

Kollmitz = Raabs an der Thaya 3820
Lower Austria   p.278□T 2

Castle: Fine site on a loop of the Thaya
between the castles of Raabs and Eibens-
tein. The loop is closed at its narrowest
point by the 'Böhmische Mauer', 525 ft.
long. The medieval castle was altered in

Königswiesen, intertwining rib vault

St. Thomas a. B. (Königswiesen)

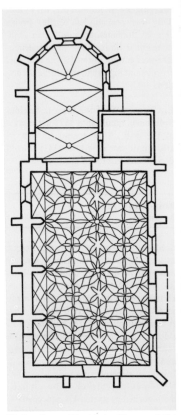

Königswiesen, Pfarrkirche Diagram of the vault of 1520

the 16&17C, and in the 17C it became Protestant. Hans Adam von Hofkirchen murdered his neighbour Niklas von Puchheim, who was also a Protestant, at Raabs; the castle was then occupied by imperial troops (1620). The castle was inhabited until 1800, but was then intentionally allowed to fall into disrepair in order to save taxes. The two tall round towers, and the walls—with fragments of frescos—running down to the Thaya, are of great charm.

Königswiesen 4280
Upper Austria   p.276□R 4

Pfarrkirche Mariä Himmelfahrt: One of the outstanding late Gothic churches in Austria. Hall with two aisles and a gallery;

extremely ornate rib vaulting with tremendous movement in its curves. Neo-Gothic furnishings mar the effect of this unique church.

Environs: Pabneukirchen: 15 km. towards Grein is the *Pfarrkirche* hll.Simon und Judas Thaddäus: late Gothic hall with a nave and two aisles; noteworthy organ gallery: the horizontal supports built of voussoirs, the decorations are partly late Gothic tracery and partly Renaissance rosettes, and in the middle is a particularly elegant projecting balcony. **St. Thomas am Blasenstein** (5 km. to the W. of Pabneukirchen): This Romano-Gothic church stands on a granite peak and is visible for miles. Hall with raised nave and two aisles; fine architectural details, especially in the N. choir; 18C furnishings; corpse of a mid-18C priest, mummified by unknown causes, in a glass coffin in the crypt underneath the S. aisle (key obtainable from priest's house). **Ruttenstein:** This is an extensive ruin, some 7 km. to the SW of Königswiesen, on a wooded peak above the valley of the Grosse Naarn. It has outworks and a castle with a tower-like palas. Fine windows.

Korneuburg 2100

Lower Austria   p.278□V 4

Korneuburg, at the foot of the Bisamberg, was originally a single parish with Klosterneuburg. The walled settlement with four gates was granted its charter in the 13C.

Augustinerkirche: This church (monastery founded in 1338 and dissolved in 1808) stands at the far end of the town. It was built in 1745–48. The original rococo high altar is a noteworthy feature: four weighty columns (two painted columns in the background frame a Last Supper scene by F.A. Maulbertsch, 1770) support an open heavenly globe in which God, holding the earth in his hands, is enthroned.

Also worth seeing: *Pfarrkirche St.Ägyd* (15C, suffered to some extent from 19C restoration work). *Raaber Kreuz,* erected in 1598 by imperial decree. Rudolf II wished to commemorate the great victory over the Turks when Raab (in Hungary) was conquered by Count Palffy and Prince Schwarzenberg.

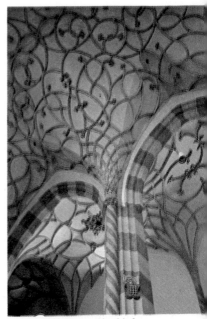

Kötschach-Mauthen, Pfarrkirche

Environs: Burg Kreuzenstein: Built in 1140 and largely destroyed by the Swedes in 1645. Rebuilt under Count Hans von Wilczek in 1897 in the fashionable historicist architectural style as a museum for his late Gothic collection (which suffered at the hands of the Russians). The gate has a round tower and a wall passage. Bridge over a deep moat. Inside, castle courtyard, well and the *Kaschauer Gang,* an arcade from the church in Kaschau. The family vault is beside the chapel. The castle, visible for miles, has a very attractive silhouette.

Kötschach-Mauthen 9640

Kärnten   p.284□L 11

The market community of Kötschach-

Mauthen is located on the N.-S. alpine route between the Gailberg and the Plöckenpass. The Roman staging post of *Loncium* was in Mauthen, on a Roman road over the Plöckenpass. Remains of a late Roman fortified tower survive on the Maria Schnee church hill.

Pfarrkirche Unsere Liebe Frau (Kötschach): The unequal proportions of nave and S. aisle prove that this late Gothic hall church with nave and two aisles is based on an earlier building destroyed by the Turks. B.Firtaler was the architect of the new building (1518-27) and created the admirable vault decorations in artificial stone. The net vault, a development of the high Gothic rib vault, which had a structural function, is transformed into a fantasy of loops and curves symbolic in design and colouring and unique in the German-speaking world. A late Gothic fresco by N.Kentner (1499) of the life of the Virgin Mary was revealed in the NE of the long polygonal choir. M. Strickner was responsible for the late baroque ceiling paintings (1750) on the same theme, also in the choir. The neoclassical high altar by Franz Stauder (1833) has a portrait of the Virgin Mary which may date from the Gothic period. The pulpit of 1769, the altar of Our Lady of Sorrows with expressive carved Pietà in the N. aisle, also known as Knappenschiff (squire's aisle), and the two choir altars are all rococo works by the monks Bruno M. and Gabriel M. from the nearby Servite monastery. When the church was rebuilt in 1976, two smaller late Gothic frescos (Virgin Mary as a virgin of the temple, and a coat-of-arms) were revealed on the S. wall of the choir.

Pfarrkirche St.Markus (Mauthen): The core of this church is Romanesque. After being destroyed by the Turks in 1478 it was rebuilt in the late Gothic style (narrower load-bearing walls, net vault). The church was reoriented in the baroque period

(1742): the E. choir was moved to the W. and a portal leading into the former E. choir tower was built on the site of the choir. The interior is mainly rococo. The exterior frescos dating from 1514 are of great interest, though weatherworn. Bold perspective foreshortenings, for example in the 'Death of the Virgin Mary', show that the artist was trained in N. Italy.

Also worth seeing: *Schloss Weildegg* (Waldegg) in Würmlach, built by Hieronymus Weilandt in the 16C, is a three-storey square building with four circular corner towers. Round-arched windows with small columns above the E. and W. entrance gates. Attic storey with firing slits, machicolation on the E. side. *Schloss Mandorf* (1520&1): Massive rectangular three-storey building; main façade facing S., with eight bays; late Gothic portals and window jambs; net vault in the hall. *Filialkirche hl.Johann Nepomuk* (in the Einsiedel Wald): Built in 1720 and restored in 1962. Small nave with choir and adjacent sacristy to the E. Six wayside shrines by the path leading up to the church.

Krems an der Donau 3500
Lower Austria   p.278☐T 4

In the Life of St.Severin (the Apostle of Norikum and founder of Mautern monastery near Krems, where he died in 482), it is stated that Krems was the centre of the Rugier empire. An imperial document of 995 refers to an 'orientalis urbs' called 'Chremisa'. The Babenbergs had a ducal court (Curia ducis) here in 1120. The Krems Pfennig, the oldest Austrian coin, was minted in 1130-90, bearing the image of St.Leopold. The first St.-Veits-Kirche was completed in 1153, and the town continued to expand. The Dominican mon-

Krems, Piaristenkirche

Krems, former Dominikanerkirche; the cloister has been uncovered

Krems, Gozzo's former Stadtburg, built in 1260-70

astery became part of the town *c.* 1300. Rivalry with Vienna, originally a smaller town, persisted until the 13C; Krems still ranks higher than Vienna on an Arab map of the world of 1150. The two towns of Krems and Stein have always been complementary: Stein lived from salt and wine, Krems from the iron trade, and only in the 19C were the two towns separate for 90 years; a curious fact is that the small town of 'Und', with a Capuchin church, lies between Krems and Stein. Krems and Stein had a common mayor, and Frederick III granted them a common coat-of-arms consisting of a golden double eagle on a black ground. Gozzo, the town judge (d. 1291), had a castle built for himself in the town in 1275. The Piarist church was begun by the Viennese stonemasons' lodge in 1470. Krems was the centre of the Danube school, and Jörg Breu lived here. The St. -Veits-Kirche church was altered by Italian artists, and is one of the earliest baroque churches in Austria. In the 2nd half of the 16C the town was Protestant—the Counter-Reformation was complete in 1624. A grammar school was founded by Jesuits in 1616, and its pupils' theatre became famous. Kremser Schmidt, the artist, died here in 1801. Although the town was bombed and looted in the war, some 400 pre-1800 buildings survived. Krems was energetically rebuilt, and is considered the most beautiful town in Lower Austria.

Pfarrkirche St. Veit (Pfarrplatz): Completed by Cypriano Biasino in 1630 (earlier building 12C). On the W. façade niches with baroque Saints (Leopold and Vitus); step gable with small obelisks. The central window in the façade portal is flanked by onion half domes. Outer chapel with sculpture of St. Anne and the Virgin Mary dating from 1320. The Gothic tower was raised and the baroque dome added in

Krems, Steiner Tor

1798. Surprisingly spacious *interior:* nave with four side chapels on each side, vaults supported by fluted pilasters, vault frescos by M.J. Schmidt. Narrow choir with high altar by J. Matthias Götz and altar painting by J.G. Schmidt depicting the martyrdom of St.Vitus (1734). The *pulpit* and the *choir stalls* are also by Götz. The *Kreuzaltar* on the right of the transept is the work of M.Steinl. The *Marienaltar* dates from 1757, with a small Bohemian statue of the Virgin Mary dating from 1420. Figures by Schletterer on the *Nepomukaltar.*

Piaristenkirche: This Gothic church was built in several stages on the foundations of an older church of 'Unsere Liebe Frau'. The choir dates from 1475, the baldachin portal from 1477 and the nave from 1515. The influence of the Viennese stonemasons' lodge may be detected. Access to the church, which stands on a high mound, via a steep, partly roofed stairway. Tall nave with saddle roof, narrow choir and a W. tower scarcely higher than the gable, with small spire and four turrets. Late Gothic ribs and corbels. On the W.

side tombstone of Rabi Nachlifa dating from 1429. *Inside:* hall church with nave and two aisles, net vaulting in the nave, stellar vaulting in the polygonal choir. The fine high altar dates from 1756 and has an altarpiece by M.J. Schmidt, who was also responsible for most of the side altars.

Former Dominican church: The monastery and church were founded in 1236. The choir dates from the 14C, and the monastery died out in the 15C: the Landesfürst used the church as a powder magazine. After an explosion, it was rebuilt in 1566 and once again taken over by the Dominicans. In 1785 it was dissolved and secularised. Since 1891 it has been a *museum.* It is a basilica with a nave, two aisles, and an early Gothic choir (frescos). Massive pillars with crocket capitals. In *c.* 1280, the rich judge Gozzo endowed frescos (Last Supper, Crucifixion, Coronation of the Virgin Mary) for the E. wall of the N. aisle. On the N. wall is a painted double tomb dating from 1320. Excellent *town museum.* The E. walk of the cloister adjacent to the church was revealed

Krems, Mocking of Christ, Pfarrkirche Stein

recently. The *Weinbaumuseum* (viticulture) with fine equipment in the courtyard.

Bürgerspitalkirche 'hll.Philipp und Jakob (Obere Landstrasse 15): On the portal Frederick III's motto AEIOU (Austria Erit In Orbe Ultima), dated 1470. The church is built into the row of houses. The windows have rich tracery. The high altar by Matthias Schwanthaler dates from 1680. Gothic tabernacle.

Also worth seeing: *Alte Post* (Obere Landstrasse 32): the 16C inn, in an arcaded courtyard, housed the formerly hereditary post office. *Biasinohaus* (Schmidgasse 3): house of the church architect (d. 1636). *Gattermannhof* ((Untere Landstrasse 52): built by Hans Rattenberger in 1553, provincial merchant's palace. *Göglhaus* (in the 'Täglicher Markt' as distinct from the 'Hoher Markt'): in 1155 this was owned by the Eggenburg family, who built the chapel *c.* 1500. It was not until 1817 that the house was acquired by a Gögl. There are late Gothic oriels and net vaults in the chapel, and arcades with columns in the courtyard. The *Lagerhaus* (Untere Landstrasse 4): the Maria Immaculata in a round-arched niche dates from 1740; this was the residence of Lager, a master baker and the grandfather of Franz Liszt. *Mesnerhaus* (Körnermarkt 8): medieval house redesigned in the baroque style in 1745. Relief sculpture of St. Nepomuk. *Mohrenapotheke* (pharmacy; Obere Landstrasse 2): built by Wolfgang Kappler, doctor and pharmacist, in 1532 (portrait in the museum). Ceiling fresco: allegory of pharmacy by M.J. Schmidt, 1780. *Haus zum Pelikan* (Untere Landstrasse 4): rococo façade with rich decorations. The pelican, the central motif, dates from 1750. *Pfarrhof* (priest's house; partly built into the Passauer Hof): baroque portal. Rococo stucco, strapwork and paintings by J.G. Schmidt in library, chapel and the entrance. *Powder magazine* dating from 1744. *Rathaus:* Donated to the town by Ulrich von Dachsberg in 1453. In the entrance hall fine Renaissance columns dating from 1549. Groin vault in the Ratsstube (council chamber). Fine Renaissance oriel dating from 1548 on the street corner (underneath

Stift Kremsmünster

is a small stone sculpture of Samson and the lion). *Schwanthalerhaus* (Obere Landstrasse 22): home of M.Schwanthaler; his carved wooden 'Türkenmadonna' dates from 1685. *Grosses Sgraffıtohaus* (Margarethenstrasse 5): Old Testament scenes and portraits of Ludwig of Hungary and Christian of Denmark (*c.* 1550). *Kleines Sgraffıtohaus* (Untere Landstrasse 1), late Gothic house with similar motifs and scenes from the history of the town. *Steiner Tor:* 1480, baroque upper section 1754; Gothic round towers with inscribed tablet: AEIOU 1480. One of the four town gates, and a Krems landmark. House of the *Vier Jahreszeiten* (Four Seasons; Körnermarkt 4): charming rococo façade.

Gozzo-Burg (Hoher Markt): Gozzo, the town judge, built a castle in the town in 1275. From the 13–15C it was owned by the Habsburgs, then privately owned and divided into three; keep, chapel, palas and hall survive.

Kremsmünster 4550

Upper Austria   p.276☐O 5

Kremsmünster is one of the oldest and largest monasteries in Austria, and also one of the most significant from the artistic and historical point of view. The Benedictine abbey was founded in 777 by the Bavarian Duke Tassilo. Legend has it that the building stands on the site where Tassilo's son Gunther was killed by a furious boar while out hunting. History knows nothing of this; the border abbey was probably intended as an outpost of Christendom against the Avars. The *abbey* is an architectural monument which has grown over the centuries. The complex (a walled area of 256,200 sq.ft., six courtyards, extensive gardens) stands on a terrace 165 ft. above the Kremstal. The buildings date mainly from the 17&18C. Prandtauer again had to complete a work begun by Carlo An-

Kremsmünster, Stift 1 Eichentor **2** Outer Stiftshof **3** Schmiedhof (Stiftsschrank) **4** Meierhof **5** Fish pond **6** Brückentor **7** Prälatenhof **8** Church **9** Konviktshof **10** Konventgarten **11** Observatory **12** 'Mosque' **13** Klerikatstrakt **14** Konventtrakt **15** Abteitrakt (exhibition rooms)

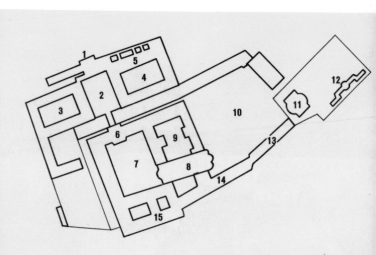

onio Carlone (see St. Florian and Christkindl).

Stiftskirche Göttlicher Heiland und Hl.Agapitus: The present building is a Romanesque-early Gothic basilica with nave, two aisles, six bays, transept and choir with three apses. Church redesigned in the baroque style from 1680 by A.Carlone. The layout of the medieval buildings meant that the church could not be placed centrally, in the manner favoured by baroque artists. In order to draw attention to the church on its corner site, a splendid façade with balcony was built and two stately towers with onion domes and lanterns were added at the sides. The balcony gives the façade something of the character of a Schloss. The most recent restoration emphasised the medieval appearance of the other walls, especially the three lofty apses at the E. end. The *interior* is very high and light. The excellent stucco forms panels in the vaulting, decorated with frescos of the four Grabenberg brothers. The pillars are undecorated below the capitals; during church festivals

they are draped with sumptuous Flemish tapestries (dating from 1551). The organ gallery has a vigorously curving parapet, and the organ dates from the mid 19C. To the left and right of the entrance are the *tower belfries*, revealed during rebuilding as fine rooms from the original church, contrasting effectively with the baroque sections. To the S. is the *Gunthergrab*, a stone slab with statue dating from *c.* 1300, an outstanding work depicting the legend of the foundation of the abbey. The *altars* are uniform in design: a lavishly framed picture under a red damask baldachin, supported by a pair of angels. The angle of the painting is an unusual feature: the picture is inclined towards the onlooker. The marble angels are by various artists; the kneeling angels on the Candida and Agapitus altars (in the side choirs) are masterpieces of high baroque, and betray Bernini's hand in the training of the artist, Michael Zürn the Younger. The *high altar* picture of the Transfiguration is an effective work by the Munich artist J.A. Wolf; first-rate tabernacle, probably designed by Prandtauer. The early Gothic

Stiftskirche, tomb of Gunther, depicting the story of the foundation, c. 1300

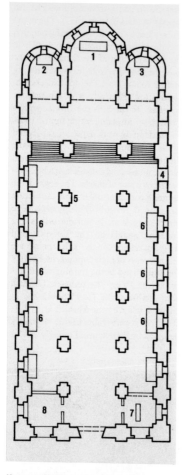

Kremsmünster, church 1 High altar, 'Transfiguration of Christ' **2** St.-Candida-Altar, kneeling Angels of Wrath **3** St.-Agapitus-Altar, kneeling Angels of Wrath **4** Entrance to Marienkapelle **5** Pulpit **6** Altars with standing Angels of Wrath **7** Tomb of Gunther **8** Ground floor of N. tower

blind arcades in the apse are a noteworthy feature behind the high altar. The *Frauenkapelle* is at right angles to the easternmost bay in the S.; it is a baroque

chapel built by C.A. Carlone in 1677, with a 'Rosenkranzkönigin' .

Monastery: *Eichentor*, pavilion with accentuated central projection and mansard roof. St. Agapitus of Präneste (= Palestrina), the church's youthful patron Saint, is seen in a niche between lions. S. of the gate is the *Fischkalter*. These working fish ponds, originally built by Carlone and later extended by two ponds by Prandtauer, are a unique achievement: the five ponds with decorative fountains are set in arcades, and the perspectives and reflections which they conjure up are an architectural experience of a kind which is rare north of the Alps. The *outer court* with domestic buildings (the abbey alehouse is on the right) ends in a moat which reminds us of the former fortifications. *Brückentor:* The core is 14C, and the façade dates from the 17&18C. Three statues: the founding Duke is seen at the top in the middle, and the imperial promoters Charlemagne and Henry II are seen on the right and left somewhat lower down. *Prälatenhof:* This is the heart of the complex, and the most important buildings are grouped around it: church, guest rooms and Abteitrakt (art collections). *Sternwarte* (observatory): This, the 'first high-rise building in Europe', stands alone in the garden. Called the 'Mathematical Tower', it was built 1748 – 58. *Mosque:* A charming garden house dating from 1640, with an Oriental look (in the Hofgarten behind the Sternwarte).

Art collections in the Abteitrakt: *Zimelienraum.* Tassilo chalice, gilded copper vessel, medallions in niello technique (Christ and symbols of the Evangelists, Saints underneath); these items date from between 764 and 769. The Tassilo candlesticks are intended to hold the Agilolfing sceptre. *Disc cross*, 1170 – 80,

Kremsmünster, Fischkalter

Codex Millenarius. *Five galleries,* with exhibits from the Middle Ages to the Biedermeier period. *Kunstkammer* with exhibits in Maria Theresa glass cases. *Rüstkammer* (armoury), a unique monastic arsenal. *Bibliothek* (library), a room 215 ft. long, divided into departments. Frescos in lavish stucco; some 400 old manuscripts, 1400 more recent manuscripts, 630 early printed books. The *collection of old musical instruments* is in the library. The *Kaisersaal* is also in the Abteitrakt. It takes its name from 15 portraits of emperors painted by M.Altomonte; ceiling fresco depicting the 'Triumph of Light' by Melchior Steidl.

Scientific collections in the Sternwarte: From its inception the building had a double function as observatory and 'universal museum'. The idea was that everything worth knowing from the fields of geology, mineralogy, palaeontology, botany, zoology, physics and astronomy should be presented. Above all this, on the top floor, is a *chapel.* The *Anthropological Cabinet* is more recent, dating from *c.* 1900. Today it is divided into collections relating to folklore, ethnography, and cultural history. The museum has been restored, and is unique in conception.

Also worth seeing: *Kalvarienbergkirche:* Steep stairs with 'stations of the Cross' lead to this charmingly sited little church on a hill opposite the abbey. Cruciform building, probably by J.M. Prunner of Linz. Excellent frescos by W.A. Heindl.

Krenstetten=Aschbach 3361 Markt
Lower Austria   p.276☐Q 5

Pfarrkirche Mariae Himmelfahrt: This pilgrimage church is under the abbey of Seitenstetten; hall church with nave and two aisles, redesigned in the baroque style after a fire in 1797. The choir dates from *c.* 1500. Striking net vaulting which lends great charm to this bright church. 16C stained-glass windows. Neo-Gothic altars with old statues.

Krieglach 8670
Steiermark   p.280☐T 7

Pfarrkirche hl.Jakobus: Except for the 14C choir, the present church dates from 1512. In the 18C, the nave was extended by the addition of two elliptical side chapels, and the minstrels' gallery was also enlarged; the interior is rococo. There is a Last Judgement fresco dating from 1420 in the sacristy.

Peter-Rosegger-Museum (Roseggerstrasse 223): This was set up in 1949 in memory of the poet (1843–1918), who lived here. Five rooms: his study and the room in which he died are still in their original condition. Memorabilia, documents and works.

Kronburg=Zams 6511
Tirol   p.286☐D 9

Ruined castle: This is based on an early Schloss rebuilt by Johann von Starkenberg in 1380. It was owned by the Fiegers for three hundred years, but fell into disrepair from 1802 onwards. The four-storey keep still has some old vaults. Remains of two-storey wooden galleries in the courtyard, and late Gothic hall on the ground floor of the palas.

Krumau am Kamp 3543
Lower Austria   p.278☐S 3

Castle: One of the earliest castles in Austria, with keep, palas and chapel (a good example of the development of the palas from a simple hall); built *c.* 1160 by the Babenbergs. In 1261, the castle became the dower house of Queen Margarethe, the widow of Henry of Hohenstaufen and the rejected wife of Ottokar. She died here in 1267 and was buried in Lilienfeld. The castle was inhabited until 1781. In 1815 it was acquired by a Viennese banker, who rebuilt the roof.

Kufstein 6330
Tirol   p.284☐I 7

Finds discovered in the Tischof cave (Kaisertal) suggest that Stone Age huntsmen lived here 30,000 years ago, but it is only from the Bronze Age that the narrow part of the valley between the Inn and the mountains can be proved to have been permanently settled. Kufstein was first mentioned in 788, and in 1393 the Bavarian Duke Stefan III granted its charter. In 1504, Maximilian I conquered it for the Tyrol and Austria, and in 1703 it was burned down in an invasion carried out by the Electorate of Bavaria and lost many of its medieval buildings. In the 19&20C the town gained new importance as a result of its excellent commmunications. It became an Alpine centre at the foot of the Kaisergebirge, and also attracted industry.

Festung Kufstein; Built on a rocky outcrop, this 12C fortress stands imposingly over the town. Largely destroyed when Maximilian conquered Kufstein, it was rebuilt 1505–22, when it was strengthened and enlarged. The *Bürgerturm,* the *Schlossrondell* and in particular the imposing *Kaiserturm* are among the features dating from this period. In 1546, the *Tiefer Brunnen* was sunk to the level of the Inn, and in the 18C the *Caroli-Bastion, Eugen-Schanze,* and *Josefsburg* were built. Today the fortress contains the world-famous *Heldenorgel* (heroes' organ; Bürgerturm) and, in the Obere Schlosskaserne, (barracks), an interesting *Heimatmuseum* (natural history, folklore etc.).

Pfarrkirche St.Vitus: A late Gothic hall

Festung Kufstein

church, built *c.* 1400 on the site of an earlier church, redesigned in baroque style in 1660, extended and decorated in late classical style in 1840 – 44; neo-Gothic decoration 1959.

Also worth seeing: *Dreifaltigkeitskirche,* with a crypt chapel, next to St. Vitus, *c.* 1500; splendid rococo altar, 1765. The 17C *Kleinholzkirche* in the Zell district. 13C *ruined castle* with chapel on the Thierberg.

Kundl 6250

Tirol   p.284☐H 8

Wallfahrtskirche St. Leonhard auf der Wiese: The church is said to have been founded by Emperor Henry II in 1012 and consecrated by Pope Benedict VIII in 1020. The present building was erected by Christian Nickinger and Jörg Steyrer in 1480–1512. The nave is not articulated, whereas the narrow choir is strongly articulated. There is a 17C baroque statue of St. Leonard in the open chapel by the graveyard wall. The tall spire springs from the SW corner of the nave and is articulated by cornices. On the S. side is a baroque fresco of St. Christopher. *Inside* the rich articulation is immediately striking. The gallery (in the W.) is supported by a pillar; the choir and nave are separated by a wrought-iron grille. The nave has four bays and notable stellar vaulting with square keystones. The bases of the choir arch are richly sculpted (on the left a bear and an angel with a scroll, and on the right a lion and a dragon); similarly decorated pilasters (with the bust of a bearded man) are to be found in the choir itself. The late Gothic *painting* of the ceiling (St. Wolfgang and St. Leonard, *c.* 1512) in the choir is also very fine. On the N. wall is a Crucifixion fresco showing the founder (late 16C). The impressive rustic *furnishings* of the church

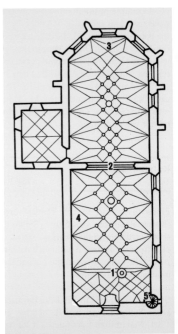

Kundl, Wallfahrtskirche St. Leonhard 1 Red marble W. gallery with wrought-iron grille from 1695 underneath **2** Chancel arch with freestanding St. Leonard (1481) underneath **3** High altar with statues of St. Leonard, Wolfgang, Henry II, Virgin Mary and St. Michael **4** N. wall with late-16C Crucifixion fresco **5** Tower

date from the 17C. The main items are the high altar (with Leonard, Wolfgang, Henry II, Virgin Mary and Michael), the side altars, pulpit, choir stalls, doors, and ends (with lions) of the pews. The freestanding *stone figure of St. Leonard* at the entrance to the choir is an impressive and original feature.

Also worth seeing: *Pfarrkirche Mariae Himmelfahrt,* mentioned as early as 788, present church 1735&6. Stucco by A. Gigl, frescos, organ, and fine high altar. Only fragments of the walls of the *Kundlburg* survive.

Laa an der Thaya 2136
Lower Austria p.278☐V 3

This town was fortified by the Landesfürst *c.* 1190. Being a border town, it was repeatedly involved in wars: Ottokar, Matthias Corvinus, the Hussites and the Thirty Years' War; occupied by the Prussians in 1866. Great names among its clerics include Aeneas Silvius, the later Pope Pius II.

Pfarrkirche St.Veit: This church dating from 1260 remains essentially unchanged. It is a pillared basilica with nave, two aisles, five bays, and a transept; pointed arches on square pillars. The choir has a semicircular apse with a superb high altar by Ignaz Lengelacher of Nikolsburg (1745). Also a 13C crucifix and a Pietà (*c.* 1400).

Castle: This was originally a dam for filling the town's ditches. It was later converted, and has a 13C keep and late Gothic courtyard. The castle houses the only Austrian *beer museum.*

Laas Kötschach 9640
Carinthia p.284☐L 11

Filialkirche hl.Andreas: B.Firtaler, architect of the church in Kötschach, was also responsible for this medium-sized late Gothic building (1510 – 1535); note the unorthodox design of the buttresses. A hall with four bays leads into a slightly lower and narrower choir with three bays. Remains of a *St.Christopher fresco* dating from 1520 are to be found on the outer S. wall. The most striking feature of the interior is the magnificent *decorative rib vaulting:* the artificial stone grows across the ceiling

Laa, St. Veit, high altar

like a crystal or a plant. The keystones in the vault are usually emblems of Christ, but here they bear the coats-of-arms of secular rulers. The sacristy wall, next to the portal and to the right of it, has unfortunately been whitewashed, but has a fresco depicting the architect (1535). Copies of two late Gothic shrine guardians (1500, originals in the Landesmuseum in Innsbruck) stand on corbels on either side of the baroque high altar of 1680 (central picture by Christoph Brandstätter, 1834). St. George and St. Florian represent the dual task of knighthood: defending the faith and protecting the population. Late Gothic wood carvings dating from 1500 in the choir (Christ the Redeemer and St. Andrew) and on the S. wall (crucifix). Opposite the sacristy is a large painting of the founder (1537).

Ladis = Ried im Oberinntal 6531
Tirol   p.286 □ D 9

Laudeck ruin: This 13C castle is

beautifully sited above the picturesque town. The enormous rectangular keep with Romanesque windows, the small palas and the barbican in the W. are original.

Also worth seeing: The town has some attractive houses with *façade painting* and late Gothic details (e.g. houses Nos. 3, 6, 22 and 23). The *Pfarrkirche St.Martin* was rebuilt in the classical style in 1831.

Lambach 4650
Upper Austria   p.276 □ O 5

Benediktinerstift: In *c.* 1040, Arnold II and his wife Regilindis, a member of the family of the counts of Welds-Lambach, established a canonical foundation in their family castle; under their son, Bishop Adalbero of Würzburg, it became a Benedictine abbey in 1056. Bishop Adalbero, who was later canonized, and his friend Bishop Altmann of Passau, consecrated the building in 1089. The Benedictine foundation of Melk was

Laas, intertwining rib decoration

Ladis with ruins of Laudeck

founded from Lambach in the same year. Most of the present church is a mid-17C reconstruction, and expansion of the monastery continued into the 1st third of the 18C. Long buildings, S. façade 785 ft. in length. The monastery stands on rising ground above the river Traun, and, in accordance with its early date, does not have the church at its centre.

Stiftskirche Mariä Himmelfahrt: Early baroque, 1652–56, probably the work of P.Luchese. Only the westwork was taken over from the old building; the Romanesque towers were raised in 1639. Single-aisled church with shallow chapel niches; the ceiling with tunnel vault, excellent frescos by M. Steidl in the stucco. Monumental high altar with a painting of the Assumption by Sandrart; the same artist also painted a Madonna of the Rosary (including the monastery); the splendid organ is by C.Egedacher, 1657. Despite the high quality of the baroque decorations, the unique significance of Lambach lies in the Romanesque frescos. Wall paintings were first discovered in the belfry of the

towers in 1868, but most of the frescos were behind walls built in the baroque period; they were uncovered and restored from 1957 onwards, and opened to the public in 1967. The room is a domed W. gallery, originally joined to the nave by three arches. Dome and walls are covered with frescos, some in a very good state of preservation, depicting the story of Christ's childhood and youth. This cycle is significant both artistically and iconographically (it is work of the highest calibre, in the late Ottonian-Byzantine style).

Monastery: Built around three courtyards. Outstanding features: *entrance tower* with a magnificent portal, 1693, J. Auer. *Treasury:* Romanesque Adalbo chalice, paraments. *Library:* ceiling painting by M. Steidl. *Summer refectory:* exquisite room, with a painting by Wolfgang A. Heindl. *Abbey theatre:* opened in 1770 with a performance for Marie Antoinette, who stayed in Lambach on her bridal journey to France.

Environs: Stadl-Paura: Pfarr- und

Stift Lambach, Romanesque frescos

Wallfahrtskirche zur Allerheiligsten Dreifaltigkeit: It stands on the right bank of the Traun, about 1 km. upstream. In 1713, during a plague, M. Pagl, abbot of Lambach, vowed to build a Trinity church; the resulting building is one of the most unorthodox churches in the province, and also one of the best. The architect was J.M. Prunner of Linz and it was consecrated in 1725. The *number three*, the symbol of the Trinity, recurs in the ground plan, the vertical section, and the decorations. The ground plan (see diagram) is an equilateral triangle with three corner towers and three identical façades; three portals lead into the interior. *Inside*: Circular domed rotunda; tripartite lantern reflecting the exterior design. Opposite the doors are three semicircular apses with arched openings into the towers behind them. Three important altars, dedicated to the Trinity, and uniform in design: 1. Each altar has a spherical tabernacle under a baldachin with figures representing the three divine virtues (Jos. M. Götz). 2. Magnificently painted trompe l'oeil architecture framing the round arches. 3. Altar paintings on the outer walls of the towers, each lit by concealed side windows. The design and the indirect lighting create a theatrical effect of great charm. Dome: Trinity, C. Carlone, trompe l'oeil architecture by Fr. Messenta who was probably also heavily involved in the design of decorations. Three valuable *organs* above the entrances, by Johann I. Egedacher, 1723. Opposite the church is the *priest's house*, formerly an orphanage for the children of parents shipwrecked on the river Traun. The Pfarrhaus has a *Schiffleutmuseum* (sailors' museum) with interesting exhibits on navigation on the Traun and the importance of the salt trade to the town's economy. **Fischlham** (about 7 km. E.): Splendid pulpit in the form of a ship in the *Pfarrkirche* (1759). *Schloss Bernau in Fischlham:* An attractive ensemble surrounded by water, with pagoda-like roofs. **Steinerkirchen:** *Pfarrkirche* a late Gothic church in a commanding position, massive W. tower, excellent high altar from the former Minorite church in Wels. Frescos dating from 1518 have been un-

Stift Lambach, entrance tower

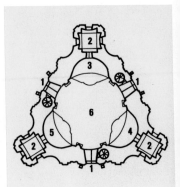

Lambach, Stadl-Paura, Pfarr- und Wallfahrtskirche 1 Three entrances, surmounted by three organs **2** Three towers **3** Gott-Vater-Altar **4** Heilig-Geist-Altar **5** Gott-Sohn-Altar **6** Dome fresco, Trinity

covered in the choir. Early-16C hatchments. **Schloss Almegg:** Originally a medieval castle. Reconstruction work in the 16C, 17C and 19C. An atmospheric courtyard with arcades and fountains; in the interior early baroque leather wallpaper and a fine fireplace. Open to the public by prior arrangement: Freiherr von Handel, Schloss Almegg, A 4654 Bad Wimsbach.

Landeck 6500
Tirol   p.286□D 9

The town 'bei Landecke' is mentioned as early as 1254. The three settlements called Angedair, Perfuchs and Perjen joined in 1430 to form a parish community, and in 1900 they became the district of Landeck, which was not granted a charter until as late as 1923.

Pfarrkirche zu Unserer Lieben Frau Himmelfahrt: This basilica built in the late 15C on the site of an older church mentioned in 1270 is, along with the hall churches of Seefeld and Schwaz, one of the most significant Gothic ecclesiastical buildings in the N. Tirol. The basilica was completed in 1521. The tower burned down in 1777, and the step gable and spire (like the spire in Imst) were added in 1861. The nave of this three-aisled church is almost twice as tall as the side aisles, and almost twice as wide as those aisles taken together. The pilaster strips and tracery windows on the outside of the building date from the 15C. The richly carved W. Portal, with its tympanum relief of the Madonna and Child with two angels, dates from 1506. The beautifully articulated N. portal has a red marble tympanum relief with a coat-of-arms and a Tirolean eagle. *Inside*, the nave with four bays has stellar vaulting, and the side aisles have unorthodox rib vaulting; low choir with

Schloss Landeck

delicate net vaulting. Attractively carved Gothic doorways lead to the sacristy and the tower. The high altar and side altars are neo-Gothic. The large *triptych* on the S. wall of the nave is originally late Gothic, with some more recent additions. The Epiphany in the shrine dates from the early 16C. The covering stone and tomb slab of the late 15C *monument* of the knight Oswald von Schronfenstein are let into the S. wall, underneath the gallery. Two excellently carved *hatchments* dating from 1497 and 1588, also by the S. wall. The *font* by the W. portal, decorated with coats-of-arms, dates from 1506.

Pestheiligenkirchlein auf dem Burschl: This little church was built in 1656 after a vow to Sebastian, Pirmin and Roch, the Saints of the plague. Its nave contains a fine Renaissance coffered ceiling and three notable 17C altars.

Schloss Landeck: The enormous keep, built *c.* 1200, together with the palas and curtain walls, is impressively sited on a rocky height. This building, extended in the 15C and largely destroyed in the 18C, was partly restored in 1949. A large hall with a late Gothic net vault, and the *chapel* with frescos from the 1st half of the 16C, are notable features. Since 1973 the Schloss has been a *Heimatmuseum* (local history).

Environs: *Pfarrkirche Maria Hilf* (late 17C and 1932) in **St. Anton am Arlberg:** Late Gothic triptych dating from the early 16C. The 17C *Pfarrkirche St. Rochus* in **Schnann** has notable 18C ceiling frescos. **Stanz** is the birthplace of J. Prandtauer, who built the Melk abbey. The *Pfarrkirche zu den hll. Petrus and Paulus* survives in good condition and is one of the oldest churches in the area (15C). Also 18C *Kapelle zu den hll. Lorenz und Sebastian*, and **Burg Schronfenstein** (on a high cliff; difficult to reach, but with a splendid

view); only the keep is medieval; privately owned. **Pians:** *Kapelle zur hl. Margaretha,* 14C, with rib vault and fine frescos from the 1st half of the 15C at the entrance to the choir, on the triumphal arch in the choir and in the vault.

Landsee = St. Martin 7341
Burgenland   p.280□V 7

Burg Landsee: This castle, first mentioned in 1158, was one of the most powerful in the province. Only minimal repairs were carried out after a gunpowder explosion in 1707, and the building finally began to fall into ruins after a fire in 1772. The ruins are some of the most interesting and worthwhile in the whole of Austria. The core of the complex is the huge keep, whose walls are 33 ft. thick in the W. A narrow courtyard adjoins this residential tower. Four rings of walls with moats in between, and six gates, protect the main castle. Many architectural details, such as rib vaulting, fireplaces, and fragments of stucco etc., still survive.

Landeck, Pfarrkirche, St. Oswald with founders

Längenfeld 6444

Tirol   p.286☐E 9

Pfarrkirche hl.Katharina: This church mentioned as early as 1303 was altered in 1518 and extended in 1690. The high tower (245 ft.) is Gothic, but was painted in 1820. The tower was restored in 1970, the façade of the nave in 1974. The richly carved W. portal, framed with stucco in 1690, also dates from the late Gothic period. Items from the old church are the 7th buttress of the nave on the S. side, with the coat-of-arms of a guild, and the *graveyard turret* next to it. The former S. portal functions as a tombstone. The *interior* was redesigned in the baroque style in 1690. A tall altar (1697) by Kassian Götsch on the S. side is in the Tyrolean Renaissance style, as is the pulpit by the same artist. The *font* and cover date from the 15C.

Filialkirche Hl.Dreifaltigkeit (am Kropfbühel): This church built in 1661, with tracery windows and an octagonal dome, is typical of the Tyrolean late Gothic style. The high altar is by K. Götsch, 1670, while the side altars with their fine carvings date from the 2nd half of the 18C.

Langenlois 3550

Lower Austria   p.278☐T 4

This town was first mentioned in 1082. It acquired market rights in 1310, and a charter in 1925. It was the victim of fires, severe hailstorms, and the plague on several occasions. A hospice with an Elisabethkirche was founded in 1420. Emperor Maximilian I granted a coat-of-arms in 1518. Numerous documents in the *Stadtmuseum.*

Pfarrkirche hl.Lorenz: This church first mentioned in 1277 has a late Romanesque nave (extended *c.* 1400 by the addition of side aisles), and was redesigned in the baroque period. In 1754 a tower was built which been much altered since (originally a fortified tower in the town wall). The

Pians (Landeck), Margarethen-Kapelle with 15C frescos

church was restored in 1959. Tracery work and windows have been revealed in the choir, and also early Gothic frieze on the ceiling. The late Gothic high altar (1500) depicts five female Saints. The altarpieces are by M.J. Schmidt. On the outside of the choir is a late Gothic Ecce-homo dating from 1415. Tombstones with coats-of-arms.

Also worth seeing: *Rathaus* with the initials of Emperor Charles VI in the gable and arcaded courtyard. Fine *Stadtplatz:* The road crosses a baroque bridge over the Loisbach, and then widens into the square, which is surrounded by 17C houses. In the middle is a plague column dating from 1713.

Launsdorf 9314
Carinthia   p.282□P 10

Pfarrkirche Maria Himmelfahrt: The Romanesque church with its E. tower was first mentioned in 1303; groin vaulting and extensions added in the Gothic and late

Gothic periods. The W. porch has an interesting and elaborate *coffered ceiling*, (1520). There is a medieval *demon stone* on the outer wall of the choir. The most interesting interior features, apart from late Gothic frescos and two baroque side altars, are the three late Gothic carved fgures on the high altar: Madonna and Child between St.Catharine and St.Barbara.

Lavamünd 9473
Carinthia   p.282□R 11

Pfarrkirche Mariae Himmelfahrt: This was first mentioned in 1193, and the present building dates from the 14&15C. This hall, with nave, two aisles, and three bays, has a fortified tower in the W. and a narrower polygonal choir. The nave has net vaulting, while the choir and aisles are rib-vaulted. The pulpit and altars are baroque, the Madonna statue on the high altar is essentially late Gothic.

Marktkirche Johannes der Täufer (in

Langenlois, Stadtplatz with Pestsäule

the W. of the Markt): A severely symmetrical late baroque complex dating from the 2nd half of the 18C. Late baroque decorations.

Lavant = Lienz 9900
Tirol   p.284 □ K/L 10

This village has attracted attention as a result of excavations made from 1948 onwards. An early Christian church was discovered inside a walled refuge castle. The bishop of Agcuntum resided here for a time. The oldest building probably dates from the 4C AD. It was later altered several times and finally destroyed by falling rock in the early 6C; a small emergency church was set up in the W. part of the ruin and was used until a new place of worship (St. Ulrich) was built.

Pfarrkirche zum hl.Ulrich: This church first mentioned in 1020 was rebuilt *c.* 1500 in the late Gothic period and redesigned in baroque style by Thomas Mayr in 1770.

Launsdorf, Pfarrkirche Maria Himmelfahrt, late Gothic carved Madonna and Child Enthroned, c. 1440

Lavant, early Christian basilica

The church has a baroque façade, a Gothic W. portal and a slender Gothic spire. The interior, with dome frescos dating from 1771 and sombre altars, makes a uniform and harmonious impression (the high altar dates from 1668).

Kirche zu den hll.Petrus und Paulus: This church, built in the 2nd half of the 15C on a site used for early Christian worship, is thought to have been largely built with the stones of the ruined castle of Trettenstein (Schloss Lavant, which stood on the same site *c.* 1200). Fragments of *Roman relief stones* were discovered in 1956 in the exterior walls of the church. Inside there is a late Gothic wooden ceiling (1516) with curved wooden ribs attached with gilded nails. The ribs in the choir appear to hang down. Three fine renovated triptychs, all dating from 1450–1530, were placed here in 1873. Some Roman marble fragments with inscriptions and figures were used in the construction of the high altar.

Laxenburg 2361
Lower Austria   p.278□V 5

The hunting lodge of Laxenburg was originally called Lachsendorf. In 1388 the settlement around the lodge was granted market rights. Maximilian I had the park planted in Flanders style in 1500. In 1655 Laxenburg was in the possession of Eleonore of Gonzaga. It was rebuilt in 1683 after being destroyed by the Turks. The *Blauer Hof* and the *Grünes Haus* were expanded under Maria Theresa. Joseph II had the park laid out in the *English* style. In 1798 – 1801, Franz II built the *Franzensburg* on the island, using parts of older buildings from Klosterneuburg and elsewhere. The ponds and canals are fed by the water from Triesting and Schwechat. The buildings were wrecked by the army of occupation, and only recently rebuilt.

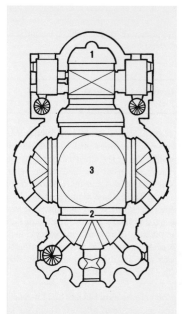

Laxenburg, Pfarrkirche 1 Sanctuary **2** Gallery **3** Fresco by Adam Obermiller, 1713

Altes Schloss: The former moated castle, with remains of Gothic walls (despite rebuilding which continued into the 18C). The *Blauer Hof* opposite the parish church was lived in by Maria Theresa (much restored). To the left of it are the remains of the old Ballhaus *(Passespielhaus)*. Adjoining this are the *dining hall* and *theatre wing*. The *Grünes Haus* was presented by the Empress to her favourite daughter, Marie Christine of Sachsen-Teschen.

Franzensburg: The Franzensburg (1801) is reached by a bridge. The romantic view of the Middle Ages which prevailed before the March revolution of 1848 led to the building of a garden pavilion in the form of a medieval Gothic castle with tilting yard, towers and battlements. The visitor passes through the Knappenhof with tower

Laxenburg, Franzensburg

into the castle proper, with round tower. The different parts of the building came from all over Austria and from many different periods, and can no longer be identified. The most notable rooms are: Habsburger Saal; 1822–36), Spinnstube (spinning room), Lothringer Saal, Ungarischer Krönungssaal (Hungarian coronation room) with a ceiling from Eger, Speisesaal (dining hall), and chapel, consecrated in 1801; the columns and capitals are from Klosterneuburg and date from *c.* 1220).

Pfarrkirche zur Kreuzerhöhung: Built as the court church by M. Steinl in 1693 –99 by order of Emperor Leopold I. Typical early baroque architecture and ground plan. Façade with powerful curves and W. tower above the portal. Baroque interior.

Lech am Arlberg 6764
Vorarlberg   p.286 ☐ B 9

Pfarrkirche St. Nikolaus: Lech, at an altitude of 4745 ft., is a Walser foundation on the uppermost reaches of the river Lech. The nave and tower of this parish church date from the late 14C. The choir was added later. The very delicate stucco and altars date from 1790. 17C cross on the choir arch.

Leibfing = Pettnau 6020
Tirol   p.286 ☐ F 8

Pfarrkirche hl.Georg: This church on a hill above the village was mentioned in 1090. The present building dates from

1496, was redesigned in baroque style in 1682 and 1720, and restored in 1909&10. In 1962 frescos were discovered on the façade of the church, which has a particularly beautiful Gothic tower with a baroque dome. The wall paintings dating from 1350 were left on the exterior wall, while those from 1450 were transferred to the choir.

Environs: Oberpettnau: The *Kapelle zu den hll.Christof und Barbara* (chapel of St. Christopher and St. Barbara; 15&17C; ceiling painting and high altar picture by J.A. Zoller, 1774), and the *Gasthof Öttl* (late Gothic, with a façade painted in baroque style) and the 18C *Ansitz Sternbach* in **Unterpettnau.**

Leibnitz 8430
Steiermark   p.280□T 10

There was a Celtic settlement on the Frauenberg 2000 years ago. In 70 AD, the Romans under Emperor Vespasian founded 'Flavia Solva' here, but after flourishing in the 3C, it fell into decline as a result of the barbarian invasions of 405&6. The area was under the archbishop of Salzburg from 860 AD onwards. The fortified town of Leibnitz itself was not built until the 13C, and was partly destroyed in the Hungarian war of 1479. The town lost most of its older buildings in a fire in 1829.

Stadtpfarrkirche St.Jakob: Mentioned in 1170. A choir with three bays and polygonal apse was added to the Romanesque building in the 15C; the nave was vaulted at the same time. The decorations are 17&18C. The painting of 'The Calling of St.James' is by Joseph Wonsiedler (1845).

Environs: Schloss Seggau (on the Seggauberg): Owned since 860 by the archbishop of Salzburg, to whom the S. section of the castle belonged. In the 13C the bishops of Seckau built a further section to the N. After damage in the Hungarian war in 1479, both sections were rebuilt, the southern by Archbishop

Schloss Seggau (Leibnitz), Roman stone monuments

Leonhard of Keutschach, the northern by Bishop Scheidt. In 1595, Martin Brenner combined all three sections, including the later *Schloss Polheim;* from that time they belonged to the Bishops of Seckau, who rebuilt the curtain wall. A collection of *Roman stone monuments* from a tower pulled down in the S. section is to be found at the side of the courtyard and in the inner passage of the former court section. **Frauenberg** (S. hill): Remains of an temple (of Isis?) from the 1C AD were excavated here in 1951&2. The lower vault of a building below the old school house it is used as a *museum* in which figures, vessels, and parts of the temple of 'Flavia Solva' can be seen. The *Wallfahrtskirche Frauenberg* was altered on five occasions; it started as a small chapel in the 12C. The last alteration was to the late baroque style in 1766. Three elliptical spaces with flat domes painted in a variety of ways. The masonry buttresses on the S. side have survived, as have two windows of the tower from the 3rd stage of construction (1520). Frescos were uncovered in 1977.

Leoben, Hacklhaus (c. 1680)

Leoben 8700
Steiermark   p.280 □ R 8

First mentioned in 982, this town was at an important junction on the trade route to Italy. Iron ore was mined near here in the first few centuries AD. A castle was built on the Massenberg in the Carolingian period. The original settlement, with the Pfarrkirche St.Jakob, extended to the foot of the castle walls and acquired market rights in 1173. Later, *c.* 1262, the Bohemian king Ottokar moved the town to a strategically more favourable location in a loop of the river Mur; the formal layout of the market town, which can still be discerned, and the prince's castle, later a Jesuit monastery, date from this period. Parts of the town wall with defensive towers, and also the toll-house of 1615, one of the five town gates, have survived.

Pfarrkirche Franz Xaver: Built in 1660–5 by the Jesuits. Simple, two-towered façade. The baroque domes were removed in 1855. The nave is spacious, with four bays and a groin vault supported by pilasters. Round-arched side chapels separated by galleries. The choir has two bays. The 17C interior is in the 'gnarled' style, usually in black and gold. The *pulpit* is richly decorated with columns and pilasters; the size of the *high altar,* which takes up the entire choir wall is impressive. On the S. wall is a Romanesque *crucifix* dating from *c.* 1225.

Former Pfarrkirche hl.Jakob: The orginal Romanesque building dates from the period before the resiting of the town.

The nave was rebuilt in 1506–09, and 100 years later the rib vault was replaced by an articulated tunnel vault. The W. tower was rebuilt by Joh. Mayer, and the square Romanesque tower was pulled down at the same time. The interior of the Gothic choir was redesigned in baroque style in 1771. The chapel with a single bay on the S. side (c. 1400), was redesigned to form a sacristy with oratories above. Here we find the altar picture by J.C. Hackhofer (1716; St. Nepomuk). The high altar (which has a painting with a view of Leoben, now in the choir) was removed in the 19C and replaced by the present seated figure of St. James (c. 1520) in a skilfully carved frame.

Kirche Maria am Waasen: Parish church since 1222. Nave with four bays and a net vault (1482), and a steep 14C choir with two bays. The tower was added during restoration work around 1900. The *stained-glass* side windows (c. 1420) are the chief item of interest. The *pulpit* dating from 1731 was transferred from the former Göss parish church.

Museum der Stadt Leoben (in the 'alte Burg'): a rich collection relating to the town's artistic and cultural history.

Environs: Göss: *Benediktinerinnenstift:* oldest abbey in the Steiermark, founded c. 1000 by Count Palatine Aribo. In 1020 it was an imperial abbey under the spiritual direction of Princess Abbess Kunigunde I. The abbey was dissolved in 1782, and thereafter became an episcopal residence of the diocese of Leoben. *Former abbey church,* parish church since 1782. Originally an early Romanesque basilica with a nave and two aisles, altered and rebuilt in the 14&16C. The crypt with its simple rib vaulting on three pillars dates from the 11C; choir with two bays and 14C frescos of scenes from the life of the Virgin Mary. The nave is a most important example of Styrian late Gothic. The S. gate has notably skilful tracery and fluting. *Inside:* Musicians' gallery (1715) with stucco balustrade. Altars installed after the dissolution of the monastery, side altar pictures are by Kremser Schmidt. The sacristy has ceiling paintings (1642) of scenes from the life of the Virgin Mary. Copy of the *Göss cross* (wood; 12C original in the diocesan museum in Graz). The well-known *Gösser Ornat*, vestments embroidered by the nuns of Göss under Kunigunde (about 1250), are today in the Österreichisches Museum für Angewandte Kunst in Vienna. To the S. of the choir is the two-storey *Bischofskapelle.* The wall and vault paintings have kept their colours especially well. The walled former *monastery building* is also worth seeing; it was completed in 1566.
Trofaiach: The *Pfarrkiche hl.Rupert,* mentioned by name in 1195 and built c. 1462 above the Romanesque remains of an early church. The nave has a stellar vault, and the hall was raised in 1703&4. The W. tower is Gothic, Romanesque remains inside. The altars date from the first half of the 18C. *Dreifaltigkeitskirche:* Built c. 1524 on remains of older walls.

Bad Leonfelden 4190

Pfarrkirche hl. Batholomäus: Gothic, altered in the 19C. On the outside, in the S., is an impressive Mount of Olives built of granite (c. 1500). Also *Filialkirche Maria Schutz am Bründl:* Consecrated in 1761, extended 1778–93. Good decorations: high altar, pulpit and organ date from the late 18C; the choir stalls are Empire. *Former Spitalskirche,* secularised since 1787 and now a *Heimathaus* (local museum), exhibits on rural life and hand weaving.

Environs: Schenkenfelden (about 12 km. E.): *Pfarrkirche,* a two-aisled hall

Above the richly fluted S. portal is a builder's inscription dating from 1525. *Kalvarienberganlage:* The main church is on the steep Tierberg in the N. of the town; an octagonal building with an enormous onion dome with lantern; inside there are two particularly noteworthy alabaster sculptures in glass cases, a Pietà and a Christ at the scourging pillar on a richly designed socket. Four chapels of the Stations of the Cross, chapel of the Holy Sepulchre, chapel with Pietà picture, and behind the church is the Jakobsbründl with a fine wrought-iron grille. J.M. Prunner (1712) was the architect of this charming complex. **Waxenberg** (some 15 km. SW): *Ruined castle,* destroyed in the peasants' war, rebuilt, reduced to ashes by lightning in 1756; the keep (98 ft. tall) is isolated on a rocky outcrop. **Piberstein** (about 15 km. W.): Half in ruins, but lived in; a stately building on a granite block, with curtain wall and corner towers; the chapel dating from 1730 has no connection with the old castle. **Helfenberg** (17 km. W.): Schloss dating from 1607 above the town on the site of an old castle. The courtyard has stone fountains decorated with coats-of-arms, and in the garden there are six stone dwarves (18C). The Schloss can be visited: inquiries at the Gutsverwaltung (estate office). **Hirschbach im Mühlkreis** (about 16 km. E.): *Pfarrkirche,* hall church dating from *c.* 1500, choir especially noteworthy; after two narrow, dark bays, it widens into a bright apse with many windows; the fluted responds are continued as ribs in the vaulting. The vault panels are decorated by tracery work placed in front of them, an unusual feature.

Lermoos, Pfarrkirche zur hl. Katharina, with Sonnenspitze in background

Lichtenwörth-Nadelburg, Nadelburg factory village (1753), wall with gate

Lermoos 6631
Tirol   p.286□E 8

Pfarrkirche zur hl.Katharina: On the site of the present baroque church there originally stood a late Gothic church which was destroyed by the mercenaries of Moritz of Saxony and then pulled down. The new building was erected by Franz Kleinhans in 1751–54. Splendid rococo interior with an almost oval main area and a square domed area, behind which the high altar is placed in a round apse. The tall windows make the room very bright. Giuseppe Gru decorated the ceiling and the dome with trompe l'oeil paintings (1784). Two important *rococo sculptures* of St.George and St. Nepomuk in the side niches. The *pulpit*, decorated entirely in gold, makes a delicate impression. The 14 Stations of the Cross panels, the large Cross and the sculpture of Our Lady of Sorrows on the Cross altar are from the late Gothic church. *Crypt* with nave, two aisles, six Tuscan columns, and square groin vaults.

Lichtenwörth-Nadelburg 2493

Lower Austria   p.278□V 6

Nadelburg: This town was completely impoverished by a Turkish siege and Kuruz invasions. The Bishop of Wiener Neustadt was unable to help the town any longer, and so he sold 'Winkelmühle und Hofgarten' in 1753 to the royal and imperial Münz-und-Bergwerkwesen-Direktions-Hofkollegium (mint and mining college) which, under Maria Theresa, established a factory for manufacturing medals and brass needles. Specialist workers were obtained from Aachen and Nuremberg, and a settlement of 50 houses and a church, surrounded by a wall with three gates, was built. In 1815, the entire complex passed from the state into private hands and, considerably expanded, existed until the beginning of the Second World War.

Also worth seeing: *Filialkirche hl. Theresia:* At the request of the Empress,

N.Pacassi, who worked on the Palace of Schönbrunn, built a late baroque domed church in honour of St.Theresa (1756–59) with an impressive interior, decorated in white. The *Pfarrkirche hl.Jakob* (in Lichtenwörth) was built in the early 15C (polygonal choir with a rib vault), was in ruins in 1869, and was rebuilt in 1908 (tower, nave, exterior).

Lieding-Strassburg 9341

Kärnten   p.282□P 10

Pfarrkirche hl.Margaretha: Nave and the W. portal (both *c.* 1200) survive from the Romanesque building. The typanum in a rounded arch (Christ as lion releasing St.Margaret from the dragon's mouth) is supported by two pairs of recessed columns. The single-aisled nave with four bays leads to a choir which is equally wide but up five steps (1330–40). Underneath it is a groin-vaulted crypt. The fine Gothic *choir windows* date from 1340. The late Gothic baldachin altar (1770), and also the pulpit and side altars, are by Georg Hittinger.

Lienz 9900

Tirol   p.284□K 10

This town, mentioned in the 11C, was granted a charter in 1242 and became a Görz customs post in *c.* 1250. The counts of Görz built their residence *c.* 1280 (Schloss Bruck). The town flourished from this time until the death of the last count of Görz (*c.* 1500). Excavations (between Lienz and Dölsach) revealed the Roman town of *Aguntum,* which enjoyed the status of a town in AD 50 and fell into disrepair in *c.* 600 after war damage. Exhibits from

Schloss Bruck (Lienz), 15C fresco

Lienz, tombstone for Count Leonhard

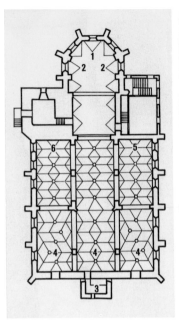

Lienz, Stadtpfarrkirche St. Andreas 1 Baroque high altar, 1756 **2** Choir stalls, 2nd half of 17C **3** Porch with Romanesque lions **4** 15C organ gallery with organ case of 1618 and Gothic sculptures **5** Right side altar with wooden crucifix, 1500 **6** Left side altar

this period can mainly be found in the *Freilichtmuseum Aguntum* (Aguntum open-air museum).

Stadtpfarrkirche St. Andreas: The present Gothic church, with a nave, two aisles, seven bays, and a stellar vault, was built in the 15C and consecrated in 1457. A 5C early Christian complex, a 10C building, and a Romanesque church consecrated in 1204 (some surviving sections) preceded this building. Severe damage resulting from lightning (1737) was repaired in 1760 (choir, and a baroque renovation was carried out at the same time), and in 1909 (tower). The church was restored in 1967&8. Some Romanesque remains survive in the W. section of the church (including the *portal lions*). The side aisles are so designed that they form individual chapel-like rooms. The presby-

tery was given late baroque decorations in 1760. The *ceiling fresco* (1761) is by J.A. Mölk, the sculpture at the high altar is by Franz Engele (1756), and the altarpiece is by J.A. Zoller (1761). Some noteworthy features are: the wooden crucifix dating from 1500; the associated group of Saints by Paterer (1775) at the side altar; St.Anne with Mary and the child Jesus (1515); and the four sculptures on the organ parapet (15C). The *organ front* is dated 1618. The two significant *red marble tombstones* are by Christoph Geiger (they are dedicated to Leonhard, the last Count of Görz; and there is a double tombstone to Michael von

Wolkenstein, d. 1523, and his wife). In the fine octagonal *crypt,* under the choir, a Crucifixion group (1510) and an early-15C stone Pietà are notable. The *Totenkapelle* (burial chapel) in the war memorial in the graveyard was built by Clemens Holzmeister in 1924, and the wall paintings are by Albin Egger-Lienz.

Franziskanerkirche (Franciscan church): The church was formerly part of the Carmelite monastery endowed by Countess Euphemia of Görz in 1349 and taken over by Franciscans after its dissolution in 1785. The church probably dates from this period, but was redesigned in 1444 after a fire and restored in 1947&8. The Gothic Pietà (*c.* 1400) on the rear side altar on the left is noteworthy, as are the wall paintings (from 1400 to *c.* 1500).

Further churches worth seeing: The *Dominikanerinnenkirche* dates from 1243, but was altered on various occasions; the present building is essentially late Gothic. Late Gothic wooden Wolfgang figure (1510). Work on late Gothic *Filialkirche hl.*

Michael (am Rindermarkt) began in the late 15C, it was vaulted in 1530, and the N. tower with its onion dome was built in 1713. Ornate net vaulting inside. The high altar (St.Michael) dates from 1683, the side altars from 16C, and there are noteworthy tombstones. *Spitalkirche hl.Josef* (rococo), badly damaged in 1945, rebuilt in 1957. *Antoniuskapelle* in the town square, originally 16C.

Schloss Bruck: In 1280, the counts of Görz built this residential Schloss on the rocky peak at the entrance to the Isel valley. After the death of the last Görz, Bruck passed to Maximilian I who sold it to the barons of Wolkenstein-Rodenegg. After changing hands several times it passed into private ownership in 1827, and finally the town purchased it and expanded it into a *museum.* The keep, the gatehouse and chapel, and the palas are among the oldest sections of the complex. Other parts (barbican with gatehouse, round tower) date from the 16C. The two-storey *Burgkapelle zur Hl. Dreifaltigkeit* (in the gatehouse) was originally Romanesque, but was converted

Schloss Bruck (Lienz), painting by Egger-Lienz

in the 15C (groin vault). Noteworthy *frescos* on the vault and walls. Remains of Romanesque painting (1270) in the reveal of the windows on the S. side. The Holy Trinity in the round apse is a work in the Soft Style by Nikolaus Kentner (1452). Most of the paintings on the N., E. and S. walls are by Simon von Taisten (*c.* 1490), and include a Virgin of Mercy with founders. In the upper storey is the so-called *Görzer Altärchen* by S. von Taisten, and in the lower storey is an altar whose style is closely related to the Pacher school.

Also worth seeing: Remains of the *town fortifications* can still be seen by the Isel. Few secular buildings survive; they include the *Liebburg* (16C) now used as a local government building, and the *Tammerburg,* (16C; panelling and groin vault).

Museums: The *Freilichtmuseum 'Klösterle-Schmiede'* (open-air museum) has existed since 1966, and includes a blacksmith's forge dating from *c.* 1500, with Gothic timbering. *Bezirks-Heimatmuseum* (in Schloss Bruck), with numerous interesting exhibits relating to Tyrolean culture, art (including originals by the painter Albin Egger-Lienz) and history; Celtic and Roman finds from excavations in the vicinity.

Lilienfeld 3180

Lower Austria   p.278☐T 5

'Mit schwerem Herzen scheide ich von hinnen, Du Feld der Lilien, die da sä'n und spinnen' (It is with a heavy heart that I depart hence, O thou field of lilies sowing and spinning). These are the words of the 28-year-old Grillparzer who, after his mother's death, was the guest of Abbot Ladislaus Pyrker.

Historical background: In 1132,

Leopold III's son entered the monastery of Morimond; his father subsequently founded several Cistercian monasteries, including the monastery of Marienthal, on land belonging to a lord of Lilienfeld. It was built in accordance with the established architectural rules of the Cistercians (frugal wall decorations; only a ridge turret; monasteries on cleared land in valleys, with small farms). It was here, at the end of June 1217, that the Crusading armies of Leopold VI united with Ulrich of Passau and the local aristocracy. Two years later, Leopold brought to the monastery a particle of the Cross which is still exhibited annually. In 1230 the Duke died in Monte Cassino; his remains were brought back to Lilienfeld. Ottokar of Bohemia confirmed the monastery's privileges, and in they were accepted by Rudolf von Habsburg in 1277. In 1350, the Concordantia caritatis, a Bible for the poor, appeared here. In 1462 Pius II conferred pontifical rights upon the abbot. It was in 1478 that abbey and church were first opened to the people on high feast days. Lilienfeld was a meeting place for refugee clergymen in the Reformation. The abbot's power was so great that he was successful in his protest to the Pope against the appointment of Richelieu to be the abbot-general of the order (1637). Abbot Cornelius Strauch was the imperial war commissar, and his successor Kolweiss (1650–95) was appointed by the Emperor to be a member of the Reformation Commission for the re-Catholicization of Lower Austria. In 1671 Kolweiss became rector of Vienna university. The *Kaisertrakt* (imperial section) was completed under him. 7000 Turks arrived in Lilienfeld in 1683 but were beaten back. The *library* was built in 1700, and the *baroque redesign* of the church began in 1717. The black marble came from the nearby district of Türnitz. The abbey was dissolved in 1789. Art

Lilienfeld, Stiftskirche, W. portal ▸

treasures were destroyed in indescribable acts of vandalism. The dissolution was revoked by Emperor Leopold a year later. The abbey was severely damaged by fire in 1810. Ladislaus Pyrker, a highly cultured Hungarian, a friend of Grillparzer and a patron of Schubert, was elected abbot in 1812. Great damage in the post-war period. Excavations performed in the last few years confirm that there were five phases of construction.

Stiftskirche Mariae Himmelfahrt: The design shows the influence of Burgundy. The nave was completed in 1263; it is a cruciform pillared basilica with a double ambulatory. The small chapels were added in the 14C. The prescribed ridge turret above the crossing was replaced by a large W. tower in the 18C. There are late Romanesque ornaments in the choir (notably a stylized lily). The high altar is of black Türnitz marble (altarpiece of the Assumption by D. Gran, 1745, Trinity above). The choir pillars on very high plinths offer some fine perspectives. *High tomb* of Leopold the Glorious, and the *tombs* of Queen Margarethe and Duchess Zimburgi of Massovien (the latter was Emperor Frederick's mother, who died here while on a pilgrimage to Mariazell). To the left of the crossing pillars is the *pulpit,* and to the right is the *choir organ* of black marble with white alabaster reliefs (St. Bernhard and David). 10 *side altars* with paintings by M.Altomonte, J.G. Schmidt (*c.* 1740), and Schnorr von Carolsfeld (1836). *Gothic baptism chapel* dating from 1300. *Gothic W. portal,* with 32 small columns and an empty tympanum.

Zisterzienserstift: The *cloister* shows Burgundian influence. Built in the mid 13C. The reading walk is the oldest section. Rib vaulting with corbels. The small columns of the clustered pillars have crocket capitals and plain bases. The *well*

house was rebuilt in the 19C. A *monks' portal* leads into the church. The visitor passes through the doubly articulated portal with columns into the *chapterhouse,* which is set lower: it is a square room with Gothic vaulting and piers. Double pews. The *library* has a painted and richly stuccoed ceiling dating from 1700. Part of the Gothic *monks' dormitory* still survives above the chapterhouse. The *Pforte, Cellarium maius* (storage cellar) is the only one in Austria to have survived from the Middle Ages; above it is the lay brothers' dormitory. Lilienfeld has the largest medieval monastery complex in Austria. Permanent exhibition: *1000 years of the Babenbergs in Austria.*

Lind im Drautal 9753

Carinthia   p.282☐M 10

Pfarrkirche hl.Bartholomäus: The 15C nave and 14C choir are Gothic; the W. façade and tower have been redesigned in the baroque style. According to Ginhart, the tombstone of a knight on the outer choir wall may be the *oldest tombstone with figure* in Carinthia (*c.* 1350). Late Gothic Virgin of Mercy on the altar, 1480. The other furnishings are baroque.

Kapelle Maria Hilf: Built in 1347, it stands high on a mountain slope. Gothic and late Gothic *wall paintings* have been discovered inside.

Linz an der Donau

Upper Austria   p.276☐P 4

In the heart of the modern city the core of the old town has survived to an extent which is almost unequalled. Linz, like

Linz, Hauptplatz with Trinity column

Hofgasse seen from Hauptplatz

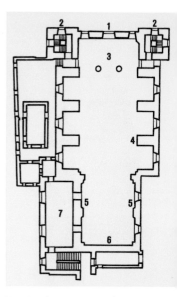

Linz, Jesuitenkirche 1 Main portal **2** Towers **3** Bruckner organ **4** Pulpit **5** Choir stalls (Garsten) **6** High altar **7** Sacristy

many other Austrian towns, owes its origin to good communications: merchandise (salt) came by boat from the Alpine area down the Traun to the Danube, and then went eastwards along the river or overland through the Haselgraben to Bohemia. Finds prove that there were settlements here in the Paleolithic period. After the Bavarian conquest the Roman town of Lentia became an important Bavarian outpost. Parts of the walls of the Martinskirche date from the Agilolfing period. We first find the name mentioned as 'Linze' in 799, when the Martinskirche and 'Castrum' are mentioned. Development was hindered by the defeat at Pressburg in 907, when many of the Bavarian aristocracy were killed in the battle against the Avars. Linz began to flourish after Leopold VI, a Babenberg, bought the town from a Passau ministerial officer *c.* 1210; it has been Austrian ever

since. Linz was soon granted a charter. The town's confident view of itself shows in the layout of the gigantic main square, praised by Adolph von Menzel as one of the finest squares in the German-speaking world. From the 16C onwards Linz was incontestably the main town of the 'duchy on the Enns'; the Habsburgs were in Vienna, however, and Vienna was and remained the seat of government. The town was repeatedly involved in wars: in 1626 it was besieged by the rebellious peasants, and in 1742 wrested from the Bavarians by Maria Theresa's General Khevenhüller; the cannonade which brought the city down made its mark in military history. Linz was repeatedly occupied in the French wars (and the town was almost destroyed in the 'battle of Ebelsberg' in 1809). Fires in the town also caused much damage. Despite adversity, Linz grew into a modern city

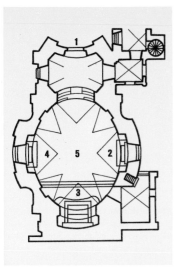

Linz, Deutschordenskirche 1 Façade: tower, 'Virtues', Harrach coat-of-arms **2** Death of St. Joseph **3** High altar, Crucifixion **4** St. John of Nepomuk **5** Ceiling relief: God the Father with angels

Linz with Landhausturm

eminent in the fields of business, culture and science. It was here that *Johannes Kepler* completed 'Harmonices mundi' (Kepler-Haus, Rathausgasse 5), his chief work. In 1783, *Mozart* composed his 'Linz symphony' in the house Altstadt 17 (Starhemberger Haus). *Adalbert Stifter* (who died in the house Untere Donaulände 6) and *Anton Bruckner* worked here for years. Marianna Jung, the 'schöne Linzerin' (married name: von Willemer), went down in literary history as Goethe's Suleika (Pfarrplatz 4). The *Linz-Budweis horse-drawn railway*, built in 1832, deserves mention as the first railway on the Continent. The electric *Pöstlingsbergbahn* funicular railway, opened in 1898, aroused the admiration of engineers as being the steepest adhesion railway in Europe. Since 1962 the University of Social and Economic Sciences has been here.

The city: The 'Landstrasse' follows the age-old route which runs northwards from the Alps through the foreland. The imposing main square (720 x 197 ft.), built in 1260, the future heart of the city, stands beside the Danube on this route. Its appearance changed in 1940, when the two bridge buildings were added; a bridge replaced the old ferry in 1497. The Schloss and Martinskirche are on the easternmost spur of the Freinberg, known as the Römerberg, and the oldest part of the town is on the slope below this. In 1830–32 fortifications were built, a chain of powerful towers, of which almost a dozen have survived. 'New Linz', which, with the surrounding region provides accommodation for about half a million people, is a typical modern city.

Alter Dom/Jesuitenkirche (Domgasse):

It was not until 1785, during the reform of the church by the Empress Josephine, that the province on the Enns was given a bishop of its own. The Jesuit church was selected to be the Dom (cathedral), which was made more splendid by outstanding decorations taken from monasteries which had been dissolved. The building, by P.F. Carlone, (1669–78) is typical of the order: three longitudinal chapels with galleries, in the nave. The two towers with their characteristic domes — which replaced onions in 1805—are a characteristic feature of the Linz skyline. The interior is dominated by the magnificent furnishings in the Austro-Italian baroque style: stucco, altars, pulpit. Pews from Garsten, 1633, and magnificent pew-ends with human and animal masks and grotesque dwarfs; the organ from Engelszell is by Krismann, the famous organ builder; Bruckner worked as Dom organist from 1856–68.

Former Deutschordenskirche (church of the Teutonic order; Harrach-Strasse): This church by J.L. von Hildebrandt is important artistically and has an immensely

Deutschordenskirche

charming façade. In the concave curve of the central section are a splendid portal and window, and above them a gable with the ostrich-feather coat-of-arms of the Harrach family. The squat façade tower, with its peculiar mushroom-shaped dome, is unmistakable. Sandstone figures embody the virtues of the knights of the Order. The *interior* is elliptical, with a dome over the crossing, and is decorated to the precise plans drawn up by Hildebrandt. The ceiling has no central painting, but an infinitely delicate relief, showing God the Father amid putti; very delicate foliage and strapwork.

Martinskirche (Römerstrasse): Probably the oldest church in Austria to have survived in its original form. Careful restoration work separated the original sections from later accretions. The building materials included ancient spoils, and ten Roman tombstones have been discovered. *Periods of construction:* 1. Open pillared building, early 8C, Agilolfing period. 2. The arches were walled, with 2–3 niches in each, Carolingian, late 8C. 3. Insertion of Gothic windows and portals. 4. The Carolingian E. wall was pierced, a triumphal arch built, and a late Gothic choir added. Gothic Madonna fresco on the triumphal arch. A famous *Volto Santo* picture, a secco painting dating from *c.* 1440, on the N. wall. A painted copy of the Lucca crucifix.

Minoriten- or Landhauskirche Klosterstrasse): The old church was rebuilt in the mid 18C by J.M. Krinner; the articulation of the façade is unusual: there are two storeys of windows, and between them is a third mezzanine-like storey with transverse oval lunettes. An enchanting rococo interior: side niches with altars placed diagonally; vigorously curving beams. The decorations are also captivating. The

Martinskirche

21 Hauptplatz: 'Wild men' holding a sign with an elephant

Landhaus: N. entrance with fine window in Renaissance portal

stucco and design of the altars are by J.K. Modler, while the paintings are by M.J. Schmidt and B. Altomonte.

Pöstlingberg-Kirche zu den Sieben Schmerzen Mariens (above the left bank of the Danube): A double-towered pilgrimage church which is visible for miles as the landmark of Linz. The origin of the pilgrimage was a wooden Pietà set up after the miraculous healing of Prince Gundomer of Starhemberg. The church was built by Johann M. Krinner in 1738–47. The stucco is in the manner of J.K. Modler. In the middle of the massive high altar is the miraculous image, surrounded by clouds.

Stadtpfarrkirche Mariä Himmelfahrt (Pfarrplatz): Sections dating from the 15–18C, W. tower with lantern and gallery. In the choir, Gothic stone coat-of-arms of Emperor Frederick III; the urn containing his heart is interred here. The *Johann-Nepomuk-Kapelle* in the W. of the S. aisle is significant; it was endowed by J.M. Pruner, the city architect, as his burial church. Lavish and harmonious baroque, with frescos by B.Altomonte. An outer chapel attached to the choir is dedicated to the same much-revered Saint and was originally part of the Deutschordenskirche. The architecturally attractive shallow niche was designed by L. von Hildebrandt, and the figure of the Saint is by G.R. Donner; this is a small but excellent work by the two great masters of Austrian baroque.

Other religious buildings of interest: *Barmherzige Brüder* (Herrenstrasse): Noteworthy façade with concave curve and colossal Corinthian order; early-18C elongated oval rotunda by J.M. Pruner. *Elisabethinenkirche* (Bethlehemstrasse): mid-18C, a building with a round dome and façade tower; pendentive dome with splendidly colourful frescos by B.Altomonte. *Kalvarienbergkirche* (on the

N. slope of the Freinberg facing the Danube): octagonal building with ridge turret; good distant view from the N. bank of the Danube. *Kapuzinerkirche* (Kapuzinerstrasse): The tomb of Montecuccoli, the conqueror of the Turks, is of historical interest (see Mogersdorf); baroque monastery library in the Stadtmuseum. *Karmeliterkirche* (Landstrasse): The façade has no tower, but strong vertical movement; probably by J.M. Pruner, it is articulated with fluted Ionic pilasters, high gable with lateral scrolls, tympanum. *Maria-Thal-Kapelle* (Zaubertal): Picturesque building on tall piers above the valley; chapel of the former hermitage, late 17C, rebuilt in the mid 18C; oval with dome, fresco by W.A. Heindl and a statue of the Virgin Mary dating from *c.* 1340 and reworked in baroque style. *Neuer Dom* (Baumbachstrasse): Built from 1862–1924, this huge building is in the style of the French Gothic cathedrals. Its area is about the same as that of the Stephansdom, though the tower, at 440 ft., is lower than the 'Steffel' (see Vienna). *Ursulinenkirche* (Landstrasse): The double towers with unorthodox crowns are landmarks; impressive façade wall, colossal order, articulation by three-quarter columns and pillars. Tympanum with mid-18C Immaculata with angels.

Landhaus (between Promenade and Klosterstrasse): After the tug-of-war to determine the permanent administrative seat had been decided in favour of Linz, it was necessary to build a Landhaus. This 16C building was badly damaged by the town fire of 1800. The following survived: 1. N. entrance with Renaissance portal and window, putti holding coats-of-arms between them. 2. An extremely effective arcaded courtyard. 3. Tower, with gallery and lantern dome related to the Stadtpfarrkirche, but distinguished by bold upward-curving gables above the clock faces and graceful decorations at the corners of the

roof. In the courtyard *bronze fountain,* an excellent work by Peter Guet, 1582.

Schloss (on the Römerberg, the E. rocky projection of the Freinberg): Frederick III, who resided in Linz from 1485 until his death in 1493, built a massive castle; Archduke Matthias and Rudolf II ordered most of the medieval building to be pulled down and replaced by an immense block with no particular decorations. The fire of 1800 and continual use for purposes other than that intended (barracks, prison, refugee camp) made the building look shabby and neglected. After excellent restoration, the building found a suitably dignified function when the *Schlossmuseum* (see Museums) was established here. In the W., the *Friedrichstor* dating from 1481 still survives, and on the machicolation is a richly decorated stone with the coat-of-arms, monogram and motto of Friedrich III.

Rathaus (Hauptplatz): The octagonal corner tower with astronomical clock survives

Former portal of Schloss Hartheim, at present in Oberösterreich Landesmuseum

from the building of 1513&14. Baroque alteration, effective façade with colossal pilaster order.

Bischofshof (Herrenstrasse): Built in the early 18C to plans by J. Prandtauer for the abbey of Kremsmünster. Three façades; rusticated ground floor; Tuscan double pilasters connect the first storey to the second; the vertical line is also accentuated by the rich window decorations. In the stairwell is an outstandingly good grille by Valentin Hofmann, who trained his nephew J.G. Oegg, who built the gates of the Würzburg Residenz.

Also worth seeing: *Dreifaltigkeitssäule* in the Hauptplatz. *Other secular buildings:* As mentioned above, Linz has many fine old buildings. A considerable number of the houses in the square bounded by the Schloss, Promenade, Graben and Danube are essentially medieval. Numerous 17&18C ecclesiastical and secular houses are grouped around the Promenadestrasse, Herrenstrasse and Landstrasse. Characteristic of the streets of Linz are oriels several storeys high set on shell-like bases, which look like towers at some corners; some examples: Hauptplatz 4: two round oriels and an arcaded courtyard; Hauptplatz 10: Gothic detail, dragons holding coats-of-arms. Hauptplatz 18: early baroque façade, narrow, elongated courtyard with arcades. Hauptplatz 21: baroque 'wild men' holding a sign with an elephant which is remarkable from the point of view of natural history. Hauptplatz 34: former Gasthof 'Stadt Frankfurt', where Montecuccoli died; Beethoven stayed here on numerous occasions. Hofberg 10: 'Altes Apothekerhaus', effectively sited, with 17&18C façade. Altstadt 10: Tradition has it that Frederick III died here on 19 August 1493; the present building has round oriels decorated with onions and dates from the late 16C and early 17C. Altstadt 17: 'Mozart-Haus'.

Landstrasse 12: Palais Weissenwolf, Atlas portal in the Viennese baroque style. Landstrasse 16, Schlägler Stiftshof, glazed arcade. Landstrasse 22, Florianer Stiftshof: Splendid round oriels, arcade. Landstrasse 32, Palais Mannstorff palace: a high baroque two-winged building to plans by J.M. Pruner.

Museums: *Oberösterreichisches Landesmuseum* in the Schloss: Collections on cultural history; archaeological department, applied arts, paintings, department of folklore and military history, museum of new wine and railways. This is one of the most extensive Austrian provincial museums. *Landesmuseum* (Museumstrasse 14): Permanent exhibition 'Der Boden von Linz' (the territory of Linz), with a library. *Nordico* = *Stadtmuseum* (Bethlehemstrasse 7): The name is reminiscent of 'Nordische Stift', where young men from Nordic countries were educated in the Catholic faith. The building is late 17C. There are excellently presented exhibits relating to the city's history from primeval times until the present day; baroque library of the Capuchins. *Neue Galerie* (Hauptplatz 8): Largely devoted to modern art.

Landestheater (Promenade): Neoclassical building, interior altered in the 20C. Next to it is the *Kammerspiele*, an independent building dating from 1955/56.

Environs: Pulgarn (10 km. eastward along the left bank of the Danube) *Schlosskapelle Selige Jungfrau:* In 1303 monastery was founded as a hospital of the Holy Ghost, Jesuits were here from 1600 onwards, and from 1837 it belonged to the abbey of St. Florian. The church was rebuilt *c.* 1512, single aisle, fine spatial effect. Tabernacle, and gallery with small projecting organ loft. Altar put together from carvings of varying provenance and quality. **Traun** (about 12 km. SW, on the left bank of the river Traun): *Schloss:* Apart from a brief interruption, this Schloss has been in the possession of the Counts of Abensberg-Traun since 1111. Present building dating from the 2nd half of the 16C, with four corner turrets; façade *c.* 1725. *Heimatmuseum,* mainly devoted to *fishing in the river Traun.* **Pucking:** *Filialkirche St.Leonhard:* This pilgrimage church some 22 km. to the SW is approached by the autobahn underpass. The discovery of wall paintings in 1946&7 made this small church into an object of interest of the first order. 'St.Leonhard is the first example in Austria north of the Alps of a church completely painted in the Gothic style which has been restored'. These are the words of Dr. Juraschek, provincial conservator. There is a painted area of some 3230 sq.ft. showing Christ and Apostles, Madonna, bishops, St.Michael, and some 200 different ornaments: sun, moon and about 3000 stars. Painted demons' heads support the vault. Baroque high altar, and good Gothic statue of St. Leonard.

Litschau 3874

The earliest castle buildings date from the 12C. In the 13C it was in the possession of the Kueringers, and in the 16C of Wenzel Marakschy von Noskau. He was Colonel-General of the imperial troops and became infamous for his cruelty during the peasants' revolts. In 1722 the Counts of Seilern, who are still the owners today, built a poorhouse. Some remnants of the old town wall still survive in the town. The Manessische Liederhandschrift (song manuscript) mentions a 'Litschner' (person from Litschau).

Burg: The *keep* with battlements dates from the 13C. The *Neues Schloss* next to it is a simple, shingle-roofed building with

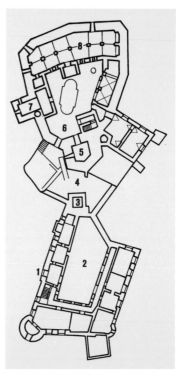

Lockenhaus, Burg 1 Entrance hall **2** Unterer Burghof **3** Kleiner Turm **4** Mittlerer Hof **5** Grosser Turm **6** Grosser Hof **7** Chapel tower **8** Rittersaal **9** Cult chamber (underground)

the year 1783 inscribed above the gate arch.

Pfarrkirche hl. Michael: Gothic hall church with Romanesque remains, *c.* 1450. It has a rib vault and tracery windows. Gothic seat niche with a trefoil; frescos of angels behind. In the choir, very fine Apostle frescos, post 1400.

Lockenhaus 7442

Burg Lockenhaus: This powerful complex consists of the 17C Unterburg and the Romanesque-Gothic Hochburg, first mentioned in 1242. Three outstanding rooms: the *Kapellenturm* (chapel tower) with remains of Romanesque frescos, the *Rittersaal*, a splendid two-aisled hall with rib vault, and finally the so-called *Kultraum*. The latter, an underground room with a tunnel vault, has an apse at each of its two narrow ends; it derives its only light from a circular opening in the middle of the ceiling. This design, unique in Austria, gave rise to conjecture that the Knights Templar may formerly have been the lords of this castle; almost all the documents were destroyed when the Order was cruelly persecuted by Philip IV of France.

Pfarrkirche zum hl.Niklaus: Rebuilt in the 17C, this originally belonged to an Augustinian hermitage monastery. Underneath the church is the extensive Nadasdy vault; excellent sarcophagi, especially that of Franz Nadasdy, who was executed in Vienna in 1671 for high treason (Vienna, Altes Rathaus).

Luberegg = Emmersdorf an der Donau 3644
Lower Austria   p.278 □ S 5

Schloss Luberegg: In 1780, to enable closer supervision of his estate workers, Josef Edler of Fürnberg built a wooden country house here, which he called Luberegg. Emperor Franz I acquired it in 1795 and built the small Schloss and its side buildings in the neoclassical style (he usually spent the summer here). The round towers, faced in wood, were built for

the supervision of stacked timber. Bands often played on the tower platform while the court was in residence. The interior is especially charming, and demonstrates the simple elegance of the imperial house in contrast with the pomp of the court of Napoleon.

Ludesch 6713
Vorarlberg   p.286 □ A 9

Alte Pfarrkirche St.Martin (old parish church): The *Pfarrkirche zum hl.Sebastian* in the valley was built under Governor Rudolph von der Halden in 1637 as a token of gratitude for the end of the plague. The road leads past it to the hill site of the *Alte St.-Martins-Pfarrkirche*. The freestanding tower with an ossuary on the lower floor is a typical feature of this ancient building. The 12C tower is joined to the W. entrance of the church by an open porch. The nave and Gothic choir are of particular interest for the *frescos* on both sides (*c.* 1500). On the Gospel side is Christ's Passion, and on the Epistle side is the life of the Virgin Mary. Each of these stories is told in 24 paintings. Apostles and the Trinity in the vault paintings. The *high altar,* dating from the same period, is the largest shrine altar in the Vorarlberg (half relief of St.Martin in the predella; in the shrine, under a lavish baldachin, Madonna and Child with Saints). The *plague altar* dating from 1635 is of interest: a wrought iron altar which formerly stood in the choir arch is now a kind of gate in front of the presbytery. The Mysteries of the Rosary surround a statue of the Virgin Mary. Two 15C *shrine altars* with Virgin Mary motif (dated 1487).

Buildings, monuments, archaeological finds and ancient customs show that Celtic, Roman and Christian culture have influenced life on this mountain in Lower Carinthia. For example the 'Vierbergelauf' (four-mountain run), held after Easter every year, is based on a heathen ritual of invocation. A Roman podium temple and some secular buildings dating from the 1C BC and from the imperial period have been found below the mountain peak. The *Freilichtmuseum* (open from May to October) exhibits numerous finds (sculptures, ceramics, utensils, etc.) documenting the history of a *Celto-Roman mountain town*.

Filialkirche St. Helena und Magdalena: The main Celto-Roman shrine was here on the mountain peak; the 'four-mountain run' also begins here. The oldest parts of the present church are in the *Magdalenenkapelle*, which in 1462 was incorporated in the new late Gothic hall as a kind of S. aisle. The main and side choirs have net vaulting; the nave has a stellar vault. The mysterious stone with three heads in the nave is another link with the age-old traditions of this site. It is certainly

a heathen sacrificial stone from the pre-Christian period. However, the finest feature of the church is the *late Gothic triptych*. The carved figures in the shrine and the painted figures on the predella tell the story of Helena, the empress mother, who encouraged the development of Christendom by endowing churches and, so legend has it, found Christ's cross on Golgotha. The splendid ensemble is dated 1502. The two *side altars* are baroque (1700). The

Magdalensberg, empress's mother Helena

statues of saints and four carved reliefs on the *Magdalenenaltar* (S. choir) are late Gothic.

Mailberg 2024
Lower Austria   p.278☐V 3

Schloss: In 1137, the town of Zogelsdorf and the forest of Mourberg were given to the Knights of the Order of St. John by Chadolt; the gift was confirmed by Emperor Frederick I in 1156; town and forest are still owned by the Order of Malta (rechristened after Emperor Charles V gave the island of Malta in fief in 1530). This is the oldest commandery anywhere (not just in Austria). According to the inscription in the courtyard, Knight Commander Karl Tettauer of Tettau rebuilt the entire Schloss, using his paternal inheritance (1594–1608). After a major fire, Schloss and church were rebuilt in the baroque style by Anton Count Colloredo, the Knight Commander at the time. Late Gothic wood carvings (late 15C, Danube school) and the Gothic triptych are on display in a *chapel* in the Schloss. The Schloss also contains a *Maltesermuseum* (museum of the Maltese knights) with an exhibition which presents a different topic every other year.

Malta 9864
Kärnten   p.282☐M/N 10

Pfarrkirche Maria Hilf: Late Gothic church. The choir was built in the 1st half of the 14C, the nave from 1463 onwards. The vault contains interesting late-15C paintings. The paintings on the N. choir wall are older (14C), and include the depiction of the *birth pangs of the Virgin Mary*. The *baroque high altar* dates from 1740. 'Christ on the Mount of Olives', the pain-

ting on the left *triumphal-arch altar* (1671), is by L. Willroider (1864). The altarpiece in the baroque *S. chapel* is a 'Marriage of St. Catherine' in the Venetian manner (1622). The corbel statues in the aisle (*c.* 1720), and a *late Gothic Madonna and Child* in the sacristy, are also worth seeing.

Mannersdorf am Leithagebirge 2452
Lower Austria   p.278☐W 6

Kapelle hl. Donatus: Maria Theresa was very fond of this town (the young Empress saw it as a sign of heavenly favour that one of her horses was killed by lightning here, while she remained unhurt). She built the chapel in 1747 out of gratitude. Pillared arcades support an octagonal baldachin with a half-hipped roof.

Also worth seeing: *Pfarrkirche hl. Martin,* early baroque building dating from 1638, baroque interior. *Schloss:* An earlier building (*c.* 1600) was altered in the 18C. The portal is set off the central axis; in the central pilaster baroque niche with St. Florian. There are arcades in the courtyard. Fine staircase and ceiling fresco in the Festsaal. In the 'Wüste' (desert) are the picturesque ruins of a *Carmelite monastery.* The young Empress liked to perform her devotions in this groin-vaulted chapel of St. Anne. *Scharfeneck ruins:* Gothic ruin at the edge of the Leithagebirge. The round towers and keep have original sections.

Marchegg 2293
Lower Austria   p.278☐X 4

Schloss Marchegg: Founded by King Ottokar II of Bohemia in 1268 as the easternmost town in Austria at the confluence of the Weidenbach and the March.

Most of the town wall, with two gates, survives. Count Niklas Salm, who defended Vienna in the 1st Turkish siege, owned the Schloss from 1529. In 1733 the medieval Schloss was redesigned in the baroque style, after several earlier alterations. The chapel dates from the 17C. The provincial government has made the decrepit Schloss into a *Jagdmuseum* (hunting museum).

Pfarrkirche hl.Margarete: The parish dates from 1268. Building began in 1278 (the choir has three bays and elegantly articulated walls; tall, narrow windows; keystones with figures stones and seat niche with a central figure). Nave 1790, and W. tower 1853 – 6, incorporating Roman stones.

Maria Dreieichen=Stockern 3744
Lower Austria   p.278☐T 3

Pfarr- und Wallfahrtskirche zur Schmerzhaften Muttergottes: The Manhardsberg separates the vineyards and

Marchegg, hooded falcon in Jagdmuseum

Marchegg with delicate rococo gate, a hunting museum since 1959

the forest. The pilgrimage church is on a hill deep in the forest. A wealthy citizen placed a waxen Pietà on the Molder Berg among three oaks, trees which enjoy particular regard in the land of pine forests. The land was laid waste by Swedes and the plague, and the waxen image was burned and replaced by a wooden Pietà. Legends, spontaneous cures, and in particular the long route to Mariazell, made Dreieichen a centre of pilgrimage, and Count Hoyos, the richest landowner in the region, built a hermit's cell for a Capuchin monk from Scheibbs, who took over the guardianship of the shrine. 40,000 pilgrims came here in 1740. Building of the large pilgrimage church began in 1744 under the supervision of the great Placidus Much (abbot of Altenburg). The artists he commissioned included J.Munggenast (after whose death Wissgrill, a builder's foreman from Horn took over the work) and P.Troger. The towers date from the early 19C. Fine, light interior. Dome fresco by P.Troger (Holy Trinity, Church Fathers and saints). Troger inverts Gutenbrunn motifs laterally. Behind the solemn high altar are fragments of the three oaks and the miraculous image a painted statue with a quality of heartfel rural piety.

Environs: Stockern: Stockern, a forme 16C *moated castle*, is in the immediate vicinity of Dreieichen. It belonged to Bert von Suttner (née Countess Kinsky), whe in 1898 wrote the novel 'Die Waffe nieder' (Lay down your arms) and, as a friend of Alfred Nobel, contributed to the establishment of the Nobel prize, which she won in 1905 (peace).

Maria Elend, Rosental 9182
Kärnten   p.282□O

Pfarr- und Wallfahrtskirche: Lat Gothic hall church with a nave and two aisles (originally 1478), with an older choir and baroque articulated tunnel vault with five bays. The late Gothic rib vaulting in the choir was replaced by strapwork stucc after 1730. Still more significant than th splendid *high altar* dating from 1730 is th

Maria Dreieichen, Wallfahrtskirche zur Schmerzhaften Muttergottes

late Gothic triptych in the apse of the S. aisle (*c.* 1515): the shrine contains a carved scene with the Virgin Mary, on the panels reliefs of the 14 auxiliary Saints, and on the outside painted scenes from the Life of Christ. The altar was built by the Villach altar workshop.

Environs: Baroque *Gnadenkapelle* (1750) to the S. of Maria Elend, and *St.Jakob* with a *parish church* which is basically late Gothic but has been redesigned in the baroque style.

Maria Feicht=Glanegg 9555
Kärnten   p.282☐P 11

Wallfahrtskirche hl.Maria: This church dating from the 1st quarter of the 16C, with its precisely positioned buttresses, tracery windows, stellar vaulting, and polygonal apse is still in the Gothic architectural tradition. The interior has a *Roman tombstone* (S. portal, on the right) and a *baroque high altar* dating from 1681.

Maria Gail am Faakersee=Villach 9500
Kärnten   p.282☐O 11

Pfarrkirche: Sections of the nave and of the massive choir tower are all that survive of a church on this site mentioned in the early Romanesque period. The present pilastered hall with three bays was reconsecrated after the Turkish assaults of 1486. The net-vaulted choir, which extends eastwards beyond the narrower space under the tower, dates from 1415. Gothic stone reliefs from the 2nd half of the 14C (including the legend of St.George) are impressive features of the W. portico. Inside, the church has numerous frescos from the period around 1300. The *late Gothic trip-*

tych (1520) from the Friesach workshop is a significant feature, depicting the Coronation of the Virgin Mary by God the Father and God the Son. Reliefs and paintings show scenes from the history of the Virgin Mary and from the story of the life and sufferings of Christ. The altarpiece does not have an architectural crowning section; the predella figures are kept elsewhere; the figures of St.George and St.Florian, the guardians of the shrine, are by the gallery, separate from the altar. The three late Gothic statues on the right *side altar* are in the same style, but from another altar. The *high altar* and *pulpit* are 18C.

Maria Laach am Jauerling 3643
Lower Austria   p.278☐S 4

Wallfahrtskirche: Early foundation. In 1432 the parish came under the abbey of Vilshofen in Lower Bavaria. The church, which is the burial place of the Kuefstein family, was Protestant for over 70 years during the Reformation, in the 17C it was

Maria Gail, late Gothic winged altar

Maria Laach, miraculous image

baldachin is an angel with brocade cloths. Christ the Saviour is seen above the delicate crowning. Panels with relief images: Annunciation, Visitation, Nativity, Magi. In the outer row in oil on wood: Mount of Olives, Judas-kiss, Scourging, Ecce Homo; underneath this: Crowning with Thorns, Procession to Calvary, Crucifixion, Resurrection. In the closed position: Circumcision, Presentation in the Temple, Coronation of the Virgin Mary, Death of the Virgin Mary. A fine wooden sculpture: Madonna and Child dating from 1440 (the church was a pilgrimage site for expectant mothers). *High tomb of the Protestant Baron Georg von Kuefstein* (d. 1603), the adviser of Emperor Ferdinand I and Maximilian II. A fine Renaissance tomb in coloured marble by A.Colin. The knight kneels on a pedestal with his helmet off; metal sabre. At the front is a round shield with a coat-of-arms. A Latin inscription names his four sons as donors of the tomb, 1607. *Wall tomb of Anna Kirchberg*, the wife of Hans Georg of Kuefstein: 1615.

the *Wallfahrtskirche zu Unserer Lieben Frau sechs Finger.* In 1634 Emperor Ferdinand II appointed Hans von Kuefstein, who had become Catholic again, to the rank of imperial Count. The Protestant church was recatholicized. The Count brought the miraculous image with him from the Rhineland (in the left aisle; 1440). The first report of a miraculous healing dates from 1719. The pillared basilica has a nave, two aisles, and a net vault. The oldest section is the 14C choir. The tower dates from 1512. The *tabernacle* has a Gothic door. The *chalice pulpit* is 15C. *Miraculous image:* The Virgin Mary, holds the end of a delicate cord in a mannered gesture, while an angel hands a rose to the Christ Child. *High Gothic polyptych c.* 1500. The Queen of Heaven, with crown and sceptre, is seen in the central shrine; the naked Christ Child is holding a napkin. Under the

---

Maria Langegg = Aggsbach Dorf 3642
Lower Austria   p.278☐S 4

Pfarr- und Servitenkirche Mariae Geburt: A chapel was built in 1605 as a token of gratitude for a healing, and was presented to the Servites in 1645. The Patres had to flee from the Swedes, but returned with the miraculous image and built a monastery in several stages. The church was consecrated in 1773. Fine tower façade with three entrances. Flat dome with fine frescos by J.R. von Mölk (the magnificent high altar is also by him). On the pulpit, reliefs of the history of the Servite order, and on the sounding-board Hope and Charity, overlooked by Faith. A famous *baroque organ* survives intact. *Mon-*

astery: Four sections around a square courtyard. Baroque *picture gallery,* and *treasury.*

Maria Lanzendorf 2326
Lower Austria   p.278□V 5

Wallfahrtskirche: A place of worship, held by legend to have been founded by soldiers of Marcus Aurelius, was rebuilt in 1145. A priest's house is mentioned in 1349, and pilgrimages are referred to in 1418. The miraculous image was lost in a fire in 1683. Three years after the building was handed over to the Franciscans in 1699, work began on a new church intended to enclose the Gnadenkapelle; the church was consecrated in 1703, and enlarged in 1728. Emperor Leopold I presented nine Turkish flags in gratitude for the victory in Peterwardein (Prince Eugen). At this time Maria Lanzendorf was one of the most famous pilgrimage sites in Lower Austria. The *ceiling fresco* (a late work by J.M. Rottmayr) in the choir dome was unfortunately destroyed by war. The high altarpiece is also by Rottmayer. W. façade: the gable between the baroque towers is by M. Steinl. The *Gnadenkapelle* has rib vaulting, stucco, and wall facing of red marble. The *miraculous image* is a Pietà dating from 1683. To the right of the church are a *Kalvarienberg* (Mount Calvary) dating from 1699 and a *Scala sancta.*

Maria Luggau 9655
Kärnten   p.284□K 11

Pfarrkirche Maria Schnee: Late Gothic, built by B.Firtaler after 1520. The exterior still has the hallmarks of the period; (W. tower, buttresses). The tower vault shows Firtaler's decorative talent: intertwining stucco rib ornaments as a varia-

tion on the brittle geometry of the net vault. In the single-aisled interior the *baroque decorations* are heightened by the vault *paintings* and *stucco* (1730/40). The *high altar* (1749) by Paul Huber of Innsbruck houses the late Gothic miraculous image (1513) which is clad in brocade, as tradition demands. The image still draws a large number of pilgrims.

Environs: St.Lorenzen im Lesachtal: The *Pfarrkirche St.Lorenzen,* dated 1474, is a late Gothic building with significant wall paintings and three fine carved Saint figures dating from 1500. The gable paintings on the farmhouses are also worth seeing.

Mariapfarr 5571
Salzburg   p.282□N 9

This is the original parish of the Lungau district, with the 'ecclesia ad Lungouve' mentioned in 923 (this might possibly also refer to the daughter church in Althofen near Mariapfarr). From 1153 on it was incorporated into the Dom chapter. Petrus Grillinger, one of the most artistic late medieval Salzburg clergymen, was the parish priest here (1419 – 47). He bequeathed the *Grillinger bible* (today in the Staatsbibliothek — State library — in Munich) and the *Grillinger-Altärchen* altar, which today can only be seen in Corpus Christi processions.

Pfarrkirche hl.Maria: The original Romanesque building was altered in the Gothic period. There is a massive tower above the original choir of the Romanesque church. Its spire dates from the period after the fire of 1854. The choir dates from 1360; c. 1446, the church was expanded into a Gothic basilica with a nave and two aisles. The *Georgskapelle* in the extension of the S. aisle was added c. 1421.

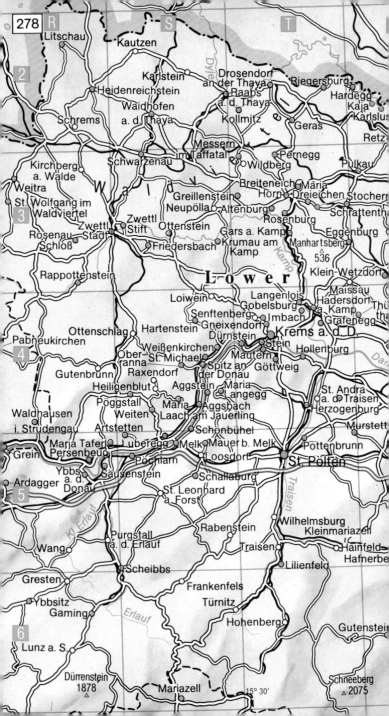

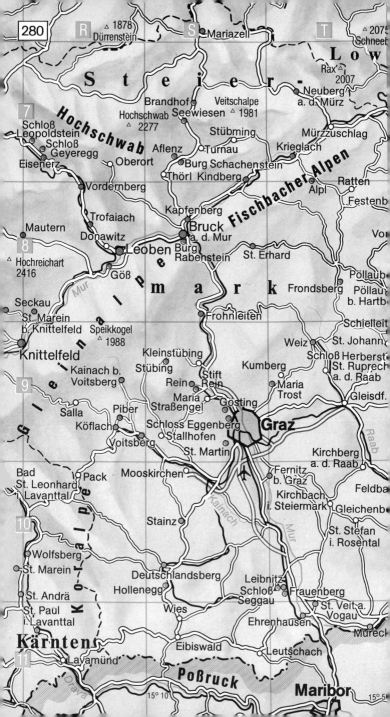

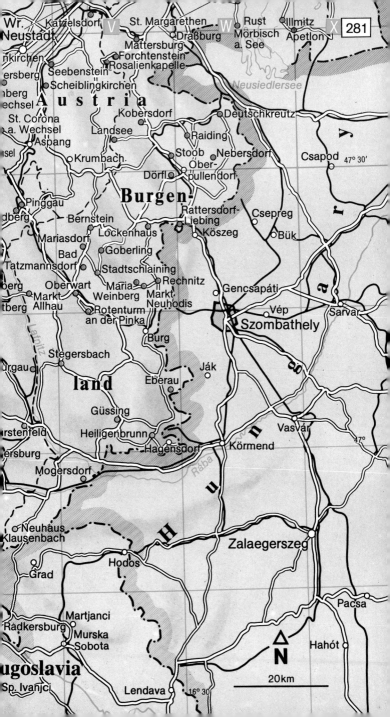

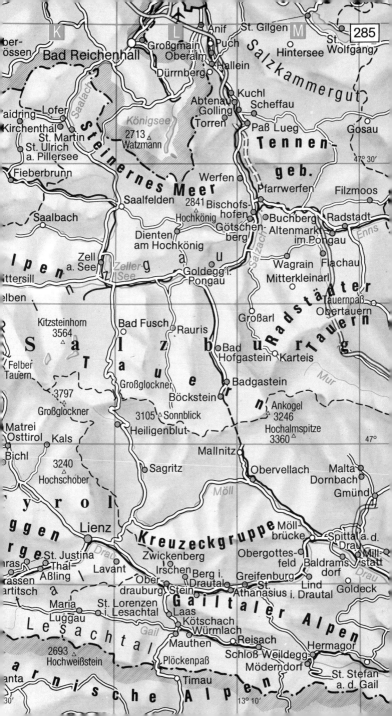

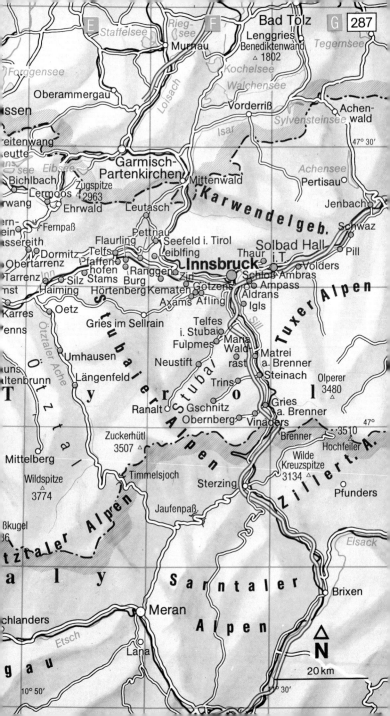

The restoration of 1946 brought to light important fragments of medieval *frescos:* scenes from the Life of Christ in the square choir tower (*c.* 1220) and in the choir (*c.* 1360); scenes from the life of the Saint, and an iconographically interesting Passion (*c.* 1430), are to be found in the Georgskapelle. The most significant medieval items include: the *crucifix* dating from *c.* 1430, which survives in its original setting (in the Georgskapelle, where we also find the much-restored *hatchment* and the *tombstone* of Konrad Thaunhauser dating from 1483); the *panels* of the lost Gothic high altar (*c.* 1500) which are used on the present neo-Gothic high altar; and the *Standing Madonna and Child* (*c.* 1400). Gothic *triumphal arch cross*. The *baroque crucifix* in the crypt is vividly realistic.

Maria Rain 9161
Kärnten   p.282☐P 11

Wallfahrtskirche Maria Rain: This church located in beautiful mountain scen-ery opposite the Karawanken massif was built in the mid 15C. The double-towered late Gothic building now has a baroque W. façade and additional buildings in the E. (trefoil choir dating from 1729). The decorations, which are also baroque, include paintings by J.Fromiller (*c.* 1740) and H.L. Göritzer (1694) on the high altar. The late Gothic figure of the Virgin Mary there dates from the 2nd half of the 15C.

Maria Saal 9063
Kärnten   p.282☐P 11

Propstei- und Wallfahrtskirche: This church on a rocky hill above the Zollfeld, surrounded by fortifying walls, ossuary and residential buildings, is one of the most splendid fortified churches in Carinthia, and also the oldest church in the province.
A church was consecrated here in pre-Carolingian times (751–52); it was followed by Maria Saal as the seat of the bishop and prior until 1072, and as a pilgrimage

Maria Saal, Wallfahrtskirche

Early-16C Keutschacher memorial stone

church in subsequent centuries. The present late Gothic design dates from the 1st half of the 15C. The buildings were walled at the time of the Turkish and Hungarian wars in the 2nd half of the 15C, and thus survived the Hungarian siege in 1480. The *exterior* of the building, which has a nave, two aisles and three choirs, has *Roman stones* in its double-towered W. façade and on the outer S. wall. These stones were finds from the nearby Zollfeld. A feature of particular interest here is the stone relief of a *Roman carriage* dating from the 3C or 4C AD. In the tympanum of the S. portal is a *late Romanesque relief* of Christ the Saviour, probably early 15C. The early-16C red marble *Keutschacher Epitaph* on the outside S. wall is also significant; the work of H. Valkenauer, a Salzburg artist, it shows the Coronation of the Virgin Mary on a wreath of clouds. On the S. wall are

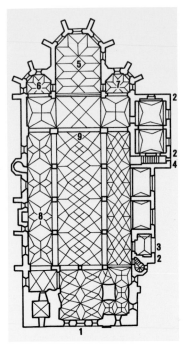

Maria Saal, Propstei- und Wallfahrtskirche
1 W. façade 2 Roman stones on S. wall 3 S. portal 4 Keutschacher memorial stone 5 High altar 6 Arndorfer Altar 7 St. -Georgs-Altar 8 Modestusaltar (Sachsenkapelle) 9 Triumphal arch with Last Judgement fresco

Roman wagon, outer wall of Wallfahrtskirche in Maria Saal

other fine late Gothic tombs. Light is impressively handled in the *interior* of this hall church with stellar and net vaulting: the baroque *high altar* (1714) is brightly lit, and draws the eye from the darkness of the nave. In the middle is the famous late Gothic *miraculous image* of the Virgin, 1425): her ecstatic expression transcends the paint and stone used in the figure's making. To the left of it is the *Magi fresco* dating from 1435; probably painted by a Northern Italian artist, it was uncovered in 1884. In the transept vault are *fresco figures* dating from the same period: Madonna and Child, accompanied by eight female Saints; Church Fathers, and symbols of the Evangelists. The two *side choir altars* are important. In the N. choir is the *Arndorf Altar*, a late Gothic triptych (1520) from the Villach workshop showing scenes from the life of the Virgin Mary. The carved figures of St. George and St. Florian originally stood guard over the shrine of the Virgin Mary; they are now set on brackets at the entrance to the choir. The somewhat later and more austere *St. George altar* the S. side choir depicts the

fight with the dragon. The church's long history shows in the *Modestus-Altar* in the *Sachsenkapelle,* endowed by Barbara Sachs in 1451. The simple Carolingian table on six columns certainly came from the first church. Originally there were walls between the six columns (removed in 1953); the sacrificial table was at the same time a sarcophagus. Today the relics of the saint are in a Roman child's sarcophagus underneath the altar table, but the original function of an altar, as a place of burial and of sacrifice, is still evident. The church has some baroque furnishings, for example the *pulpit* and the *organ,* both dating from the 1st half of the 18C, but the general impression is late Gothic, not least because of the many panels of *vault paintings* in the nave (1490). Religious elements (Christ's family tree), secular subjects (self-portrait of the artist), figures and ornaments are woven into a visual poem of great artistic merit. A Last Judgement in the same style is to be seen on the *front wall of the triumphal arch.* A three-dimensional figure of Christ in the circular medallion lends added force to the surrounding painting.

Magi fresco in the Wallfahrtskirche

Ossuary and Totenleuchte: The late Gothic Totenleuchte (graveyard turret or 'lantern of the dead') dating from 1497 is outside, opposite the S. portal. It contains a light intended to burn for ever to protect the dead (in the former cemetery) from evil spirits. Behind it is the *ossuary,* a Romanesque octagon in which the bones of the dead were kept. The building was also used as a fortress tower in times of war.

Also worth seeing: The *plague cross* on the E. edge of the town has late Gothic frescos dating from 1523. Pilgrimage processions began here. *Freilichtmuseum* Open-air collection of farm buildings showing developments particular to Carinthian rural architecture.

Environs: Zollfeld: The site of the Roman town of *Virunum* is about 5 km. N. of the hill on which the church of Maria Saal stands. Excavations since the late 18C have shown that it was the provincial capital of Carinthia between the 1C and 5C AD. A broad range of finds from the site can be seen in the Landesmuseum in Klagenfurt. In the middle of the Zollfeld, not far from the main road, is the *Kärntner Herzogsstuhl* (Carinthian ducal throne). This strange monster, built of Roman stones, is wreathed in legend. It was used by the lords of the province of Carinthia as a symbol of their power from the 8&9C onwards. Judgement was pronounced, and homage was paid to the princes here until 1651. The Herzogsstuhl was complemented by the *Fürstenstein* (prince's stone) NW of the church of *St. Peter und Paul* (parts Carolingian; W. tower 15C; Annakapelle 14&15C) near **Karnburg.** Here, on a rocky plateau, where the foundations of a Carolingian palace have been discovered, the Carinthian princes had to be installed before they sat in judgement in the Zollfeld. Today the stone is in the Landesmuseum in Klagenfurt.

Mariastein = Kirchbichl 6322
Tirol   p.284 □ H 7

Castle: This castle, originally called

Ossuary with dead man's lantern

'Stein', was built by the lords of Freundsberg *c.* 1350 on a towering rock above the Inn. The tall five-cornered *residence tower*, lower storeys 14C, is of interest. It contains the dungeon, with 15C Gothic rib vaulting. In the upper storey is the *Kleiner Rittersaal*, with a coffered ceiling dating from the 2nd half of the 16C; it is now a *museum*. In the uppermost storey are two chapels one above the other (the lower has a ceiling dating from 1550 and a rococo altar, and the upper chapel has the carved miraculous image of the Madonna Enthroned with Child dating from 1470). Since this *Gnadenkapelle* was built in 1587, the castle has been the goal of the Maria Stein pilgrimage.

Environs: Wörgl (7 km. S. of Mariastein): The most notable feature is the *Pfarrkirche hl.Lorenz*, rebuilt to a baroque design *c.* 1740 (stucco 1740, ceiling paintings, high altar 1913 with baroque figures, late Gothic wooden statue of the Madonna and Child, and prayer stools dating from *c.* 1740). The *Werberg ruins*, sparse remains of a 13C castle which fell into ruins in the 14C, are also of note.

Burg Mariastein

*Tyrolean Archduke's crown
(Schlossmuseum, Mariastein)*

Maria Taferl 3672
Lower Austria   p.278□R 5

Here, as in Dreieichen, the miraculous tree was an oak, first with a picture mounted in it, and then a cross. When the tree withered, a Pietà was placed in its crown, and the leaves began to turn green again. Originally the Easter Monday service was held by the stone table outside the church. Miracles began to be reported. The first miracle book dates from 1600, when the foundation stone of the present church was laid. The church was completed by J. Prandtauer. A. Beduzzi painted the ceil-

1 *Carinthian ducal throne, Zollfeld*

Maria Taferl, table slab outside the church

ing frescos in 1714–18. The miraculous image and the oak tree were destroyed by fire in 1755 (the copy is now protected by a metal casing). The whole site was modernized in 1959.

Wallfahrtskirche zur Schmerzhaften Muttergottes: Superbly sited 1440 ft. above the valley of the Danube. Broad double-towered façade with small clock gable and central marble portal. Massive single-aisled church with transept. The frescos in the nave show scenes from the life of St. Joseph, and those in the main dome and the transept scenes from the life of the Virgin Mary, by A. Beduzzi. Subtle perspectives, well-balanced furnishings, and trompe-l'oeil architecture. The legend of the building's foundation is depicted under the organ gallery. There is a majestic *high altar* by Götz, the Krems

artist (1736), with built-in Gnadenaltar and ambulatory for the pilgrims. Fine stucco and magnificent baldachin drapings. Side altars with altarpieces by Johann Georg Schmidt from Vienna and, in the transept, by M.J. Schmidt, ('Kremser' Schmidt). There is a richly gilded *pulpit* by M. Tempe modelled on the pulpit in the Dom in Passau (1727). The organ front dates from 1759.

Mariathal = Kramsach 6233
Tirol   p.284 □ H 8

Pfarrkirche hl.Dominikus: This 17C former monastery church looks severe and undecorated from the outside. The main items of interest inside are the splendid black-and-gold *high altar* and the *side altars*

Maria Wörth on the Wörther See

dating from the 17C (the reliquary coffin of St. Privata (*c.* 1730) is on the left side altar), and also the beautiful late-17C *pulpit, choir stalls, pews* and *confessionals.* The marble memorial stone to the founding family is in front of the choir. Adjoining the church in the S. is the *Gnadenkapelle,* a fine 18C chapel of the Virgin Mary with a rococo altar, rich stucco and a wrought-iron grille dating from 1739.

Maria Wörth 9082
Kärnten   p.282☐O/P 11

Pfarrkirche St. Primus und Felician: This essentially late Gothic building on a rocky peninsula at the S. end of the Wörther See was a base for the conversion of Carinthia to Christianity under the bishops of Freising in the 12C. Two Gothic choirs with stellar and net vaulting; square nave with two aisles. The main choir is elevated above an originally Romanesque hall crypt with a groin vault. The marble portal (S. entrance), and the *ossuary* to the E. of the church (1278), survive from the Romanesque period. The Romanesque building was gradually altered in subsequent centuries.

The powerful *baroque high altar* (1658) symbolizes the counter-reforming vigour of the Jesuits who took over the church in 1598. In the centre is an exceptionally beautiful late Gothic carved Virgin Mary dating from 1420. At the side are Primus and Felician, the patron saints of the church. In the W. of the *baptismal chapel* are two late Gothic altar panels depicting the Church Fathers Hieronymus and

Gregor (1470), from a triptych. Late Gothic copy (1469) of a medieval Italian painting of the Virgin Mary to the left of the high altar. Notable *hatchment* by Ulrich Peuschner of Leonstein (1530) on the wall of the S. side choir.

Rosenkranz- oder Winterkirche: This small Romanesque building to the W. of the Pfarrkirche has some significant 11C *Romanesque frescos*. The paintings are closely related to contemporary book illuminations. The *carved Virgin Mary* (1420) by the baroque high altar is in the Soft Style. The carved Lamentation is also late Gothic (post 1500).

Environs: Reifnitz: *Ruined castle* and *Filialkirchen St.Margaret and St.Anne:* Remains of a Romanesque and late Gothic building, and small late Gothic churches with baroque decorations. Charming views of the countryside.

Mariazell 8630

Steiermark   p.280☐S 6

This is the largest and most important Austrian place of pilgrimage, mentioned in 1266. Legend has it that it was founded by the monks of St.Lambrecht in 1157. Mariazell acquired market rights in 1342, and a charter in 1948.

Pfarr- und Wallfahrtskirche Mariae Geburt: The original Romanesque building (*c.* 1200) was converted in 1380 -96 into a Gothic hall church with a nave and two aisles. The Gothic W. tower was built in the late 14C, and there was another period of considerable building activity in the 17C, when the church was rebuilt to baroque designs under D.Sciassia (1644- 1683, reconsecration 1704). The nave was extended by chapels with galleries; the Gothic choir was replaced by a transept

and a new sanctuary with an elliptical dome; finally, two baroque side towers were added and the Gothic central tower retained, thus forming the present characteristic three-towered façade. The interior is dominated by the imposing *high altar* by Fischer von Erlach (1692–1704) with a larger-than-life Crucifixion (in silver, to designs by L. Mattielli, 1714). Another excellent silver piece is the *altar tabernacle* by J. Drentwett, 1727. In front of this, beneath the dome, is a late Gothic *Madonna* on a column (16C).

However, the religious centre of the pilgrimage is the *Gnadenkapelle* at the centre of the church (the end of the original nave). The chapel was built in 1653 and contains the 13C *late Romanesque miraculous image.* The Gnadenaltar of 1727 was based on a design by Josef E. Fischer (the son of Fischer von Erlach) executed in silver by artists from Augsburg; silver grille by Johann Wagner of Vienna (1756); above the beams is a group of figures (St.Joseph, St.Joachim, St.Anne) by Mattielli. In the side chapels we find altarpieces by J.A. von Mölk (1777) and Tobias Bock (St.Stephen before the Virgin Mary, 1665). Fine *stucco:* in the nave, the side chapels and the galleries by Mattia Camin, in the sacristies by Alessandro Serenio, and by Bertoletti to the W. of the more recent building and in the dome. Valuable votive gifts in the *Schatzkammer,* including: the *Schatzkammerbild* (*c.* 1380, a gift from Ludwig I of Hungary); wooden figure of a Madonna and Child and ivory relief of the Virgin Mary (both 14C); late Gothic chasuble; Pazifikale donated by Emperor Leopold I. Also a crystal candlestick, and rich vessels belonging to Emperor Charles VI. Portrait medallions of the imperial family on the antependium.

Also worth seeing: The *Geistliches Haus,* built by the abbey of Lambrecht 1693–

Mariazell ▷

Mariazell, Wallfahrtskirche

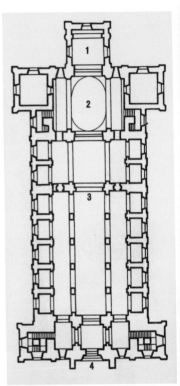

1709; the *Gnadenkapelle hl.Lambert* and
the *refectory* with stuccoed groin vault and
ceiling paintings. Also paintings in the
Prälatur, including 'Adoration of the Magi'
by M.J. Schmidt (1786).

Environs: Seewiesen: 14C *Pfarrkirche
hl.Leonhard*, set in charming countryside,
parish church since 1756; single-aisled
Gothic building with a 14C carved wooden
St.Anne with the Virgin and Child. The
altarpiece is by H.A. Weissenkirchner
(1688), the statues by Andreas Marx
(1697). ·

Matrei am Brenner 6143

Tirol   p.286☐F 9

Matrei and Steinach are in the broad

Mariazell, Wallfahrtskirche 1 High altar by
Fischer von Erlach **2** 16C late Gothic Virgin Mary
on column **3** Gnadenkapelle with Gnadenaltar
(1653) and 13C late Romanesque miraculous
image **4** W. façade with three towers

Wipptal, which is spanned by the gigantic *Europabrücke* (2,850 ft. long, 590 ft.
high, 650 ft. wide), completed in 1963 and
the highest bridge in Europe. Matrei is
near the autobahn exit; its favourable position on the safest pass across the Alps to
Italy made it important in Celtic times, and
as the Roman Matreium. It still looks like
a picturesque little medieval town, although it was badly damaged by fire in
1916 and by bombing in 1945. The
Gasthaus Krone (No. 54), with its late
Renaissance arcade, and the former late

Europabrücke near Matrei on the Brenner

Gothic *Gasthaus zur Uhr* (No. 60), are notable.

Pfarrkirche Maria Himmelfahrt: This church was first mentioned in 1311. The tower with tracery windows and parts of the narrow high-gabled nave survive from the late Gothic period. Pointed-arched portal in the façade. *Late Gothic frescos* dating from *c.* 1500 were revealed on both sides of the portal in 1925. In 1754&5 the church—particularly the choir, windows and interior decoration—was redesigned to plans by the painter J.A. Mölk. The beautiful ceiling frescos in the wide, bright interior, baroque almost throughout, are also by Mölk. The three altars are rococo. By the high altar is a Man of Sorrows dating from 1350.

Kapelle zum hl. Johannes: This late Gothic chapel, mentioned in 1284, has survived in its original form (war damage repaired in 1961); it is thought to be the work of the Türing family of stonemasons, from Innsbruck; the elaborate and delicate exterior is evidence of this. Inside rich rib ornament, with blossoms, fruit, heads, figures and animals. The late Gothic gallery on round, twisted, red-marble pillars and arches, is decorated with very fine tracery and heraldic reliefs.

Also worth seeing: Spitalskirche zum Hl. Geist (16&17C, with neo-Romanesque furnishings); *Schloss Matrei* (13C; completely destroyed in the war and only partially rebuilt); *Latschburg,* 18C nobleman's seat; the 13C *Ansitz Arnholz* (only the 16C round tower survives).

Environs: Wallfahrtskirche **Maria**

300 Matrei in Osttirol

Waldrast (first chapel for the miraculous image 1429; Jesuit monastery with church 1624; dissolved in 1785; rebuilt in neoclassical style in 1850; only the choir still late Gothic).

Matrei in Osttirol 9971
Tirol   p.284☐K 9

This town was inhabited in prehistoric times and values links with its earlier culture; it maintains traditional customs such as the 'Klaubaufgehen', in which figures wearing wild disguises with skins, bells and masks storm through the neighbourhood on St. Nicholas' eve.

Pfarrkirche St. Alban: The parish existed in the Carolingian period, the church was first mentioned in 1170. The Gothic tower was part of a new building erected after a fire in the first half of the 14C; in 1770–80 the church was enlarged to a design by W. Hagenauer, who incorporated the tower into the nave. The interior has surprising architectural unity, with a shallow dome above the former crossing and a fine organ gallery. F.A. Zeiller painted the ceiling frescos and Franz Grassmayr created the stucco in 1783. Most of the sculptures are by Virgil Rainer and Johann Paterer. The altars date from *c.* 1800, pulpit 1784. There are *tombstones* dating from 1600 in the graveyard.

Kirche St. Nikolaus: This church is a little off the beaten track. It dates from the Romanesque period, although it was not mentioned until 1346. The façade has 14C frescos, and on the tower is a large St. Christopher dating from 1530. The interior of the nave was redesigned in Gothic style in 1470. The most interesting feature is the *tower:* it was adapted to form two choirs, one above the other, with groin vaulting; they open on to the net-vaulted nave. In the lower storey are frescos depicting the story of Adam and Eve among other topics (late 13C). The frescos in the upper storey tell an imaginative story of the four elements, saints, Apostles and the new Jerusalem, possibly the work of an artist from Padua, *c.* 1270. The three wooden figures, all from the 1st half of the 15C, are also notable: St. Nicholas in the upper choir, St. Alban in the gallery, and Madonna and Child in the lower choir.

Matrei in E. Tyrol, Filialkirche St. Nikolaus 1 Gothic gallery **2** Gallery-like structure with round opening into the lower chapel and two side staircases to the upper storey **3** Ambo **4** Choir tower

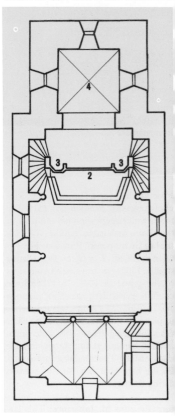

Also worth seeing: *Kapelle zum hl.Florian* ('Bachkapelle', originally 17C). *Gerichtsgebäude* (court house; originally 1530 or 17C). *Widum* (an 18C building). *Priests's house* (18C). *Wayside shrines* (15&17C, in the town and on the bridge). *Schloss Weissenstein* (originally 12C, rebuilt in the 19C). Also a *Heimatmuseum* (local history) in the Gemeindehaus (community centre).

Environs: Bichl: An old *Roman tomb stele* dating from BC 200, set up at house No. 5. *Kienburg ruins* from the 12&16C. **Kals:** Old *wooden houses,* 15C *priest's house,* and 15C *wayside shrine. Pfarrkirche zum hl.Rupert* (15C; frescos 1500). 14C *Kirche zum hl.Georg.*

Mattighofen 5230
Upper Austria   p.276☐L 5

Agilolfing palace in the 7C, and after that a Carolingian court. In 1007 Henry II presented the town to the bishopric of

Bamberg, which he had founded; in 1437 Hanns Kuchler endowed the parish church with an institution for secular canons, later granted the title of priory. In the 16C the town came under the counts of Ortenburg, and then became a Bavarian border province; since 1779 it has belonged to Austria.

Pfarrkirche Mariä Himmelfahrt/former Propsteikirche: Now an early neoclassical basilica with nave, two aisles, shallow dome over the crossing and transepts ending in conches. Choir and W. tower essentially Gothic. Rich *frescos* by J.N. Della Croce on the ceilings, 1780. Good furnishing dating from the same era; the statues of St. Peter and Paul in the choir are by T. Schwanthaler, 1676, from the old altar. 15C marble tablet of the founder, Johann Kuchler. Former *cloister* with Renaissance paintwork, mid 16C.

Environs: Pischelsdorf am Engelbach (about 8 km. to the NW): *Pfarrkirche Mariä Himmelfahrt,* 1392 – 1419. Historically interesting building. Hall with

Matrei i. O., frescos in St. Nikolaus

Schloss Weissenstein near Matrei i. O.

a nave and two aisles, which are continued to form the ambulatory. **Lochen** (about 15 km. S.): *Pfarrkirche Mariae Himmelfahrt.* The church's chief attraction is its rich decoration, with works by M.Guggenbichler; the high altar is among his best work. Pulpit, crucifix, Our Lady of Sorrows, Good Shepherd, and Man of Sorrows by the same artist. **Gebertsham** (about 3 km. S. of Lochen): *Filialkirche hl.Kreuz:* This small late Gothic church stands beside a farm on a rise above the NE shore of the Mattsee, immediately by the border of the province of Salzburg. There is a splendid view across the Voralpensee. Inside the church, which is inconspicuous from the outside, is a very fine *triptych*. This notable work is attributed to Gordian Gugg of Laufen, and was probably built between 1515 and 1520.

Mattsee 5163
Salzburg   p.276☐L 6

This is a market town which developed from the settlement attached to a monastery; archaeological finds in the surrounding hills have shown that it has been inhabited since prehistoric and Roman times. Tradition has it that the monastery in the centre of the Trumersee area was founded by the Bavarian Duke Tassilo III (first mentioned in 783&4), and that after this, when it was a royal abbey ('Mathaseo'), it came into the possession of the bishopric of Passau in 907 along with Altötting. The Benedictine abbey became a priory in the 10C. In 1390 and 1398 Salzburg purchased Mattsee, but the church was not subject to the See until 1807).

Kollegiatskirche St. Michael: Clearly Romano-Gothic, though the interior was redesigned in baroque style *c.* 1700; the church forms the S. side of the priory. The Gothic choir adjoins the basilican nave and transept. The furnishings were renewed in the course of the baroque redesign. The high altarpiece by J.Zanussi depicts the patron Saint of the church worshipping the Trinity. This altar also has figures by the

Mattsee, Kollegiatskirche St.Michael

woodcarver Paul Mödlhammer. On the choir walls life-size figures of St.Sebastian and St.Peter attributed to Michael Zürn the younger. The figures by the side altars are close to the style of M.Guggenbichler.

Propsteigebäude: A plain building with two stucco ceilings dating from 1700 and an ornate tiled stove, *c.* 1800. A *Stiftsmuseum* is being established at the time of writing; it will display applied art, and oil paintings by J.M. Rottmayr from the priory collection.

Pfarrkirche St.Lorenz: Rebuilt in 1777 – 79 to plans by W. Hagenauer. Neoclassical marble altars dating from 1779. The Mesnerhaus is the house where the composer Anton Diabelli (1781–1858) was born.

Schloss: Only the S. section survives.

Mauer bei Melk = Loosdorf 3382
Lower Austria   p.278□S 5

Pfarrkirche Mariae Namen: 'Ad muri' is the old Roman name, referring to the frontier rampart which protected Noricum against attacks from the N. The blessed Gotthalm died in Mauer. He was the servant of St.Koloman (murdered as a 'Bohemian spy' in Stockerau in 1012). Miracles occurred at Gotthalm's burial, and the small daughter church quickly gained a great reputation. In the 15C, the lords of Albrechtsberg chose the church as a burial place. The S. aisle is the oldest section, dating from the 13C. The Gothic *tabernacle* dates from 1506. The main altar 'hl. Maria am Grünen Anger' (Virgin Mary by the green meadow) has many figures of saints. The *carved altar of lime wood,* built *c.* 1509, was originally intended to be the high altar of a large pilgrimage church. Here it seems slightly out of place by the

N. wall of the church. St.Peter and St. Magdalene are depicted kneeling at the feet of the Virgin Mary enthroned in clouds with saints and supplicants packed behind them. Angels bearing the crown of the Virgin Mary hover above her. On the left is God the Father, and on the right is the Holy Ghost. The side panels have bas reliefs of scenes from the life of the Virgin Mary. The altar is the most important work of Gothic carving in Lower Austria. The heads resemble portraits and the figures relate to each other pictorially: the Virgin Mary presents the Christ Child, and the jubilation of the angels directs the eye to the God the Father in Majesty. This altar is related to the altar in Kefermarkt, and was probably constructed in Passau.

Mauerbach 3001
Lower Austria   p.278□U/V 5

Frederick the Fair founded the first Carthusian monastery in Lower Austria in Mauerbach in 1313. The monastery was for a long time called Allerheiligental. The baroque monastery was built by Abbot Georg Fasel (1616 – 31). Dissolved by Joseph II.

Kartäuserkloster: This has two courtyards: the Priorenhof with the Kaisertrakt, and the Klosterhof. The church and *library* are on the S. side, and the *cells,* which are built at right angles and have small gardens, are in the other three wings. The cells are not interconnected. On the courtyard side there is a passage from which the food was passed through an angled opening and placed in front of a small door.

Former Klosterkirche: Single-aisled Gothic church with monks' choir and a laymen's area. The high altarpiece depicts the Assumption. Frederick the Fair (and his wife Isabelle of Aragon?) is buried in the groin-vaulted *crypt*. A tablet (1557) is the only tombstone. The monastery has been disused ever since an *old people's home* which used it was abolished.

Mautern 8774
Steiermark   p.282□Q/R 8

Market rights were conferred upon this town in 1634. A Franciscan monastery was founded in 1669.

Klosterkirche hl.Barbara: This church, probably built by D.Sciassia, was consecrated in 1676. It is a rotunda with two bays and a cruciform extension, furnished in the 'gnarled' style. The Cross altar dates from 1676, the Lamentation altar from 1677. The wooden sculptures in the choir are by J.T. Stammel.

Pfarrkirche hl.Nikolaus: Mentioned in 1187. A single-aisled building from the late Gothic period (1442–62). Revaulted in the baroque style in the 17C; the net vault in the choir has survived. Notable furnishings: the high altar with its rococo tabernacle (1786). The Cross altar, with tabernacle relief and crowning group by Stammel (1740) and altarpiece by J.Lederwasch.

Schloss Ehrnau (a little way upstream): It dates originally from the 13C, was rebuilt by the abbey of Admont in the 15C; present design 17C. It is a plain rectangular building with short wings and arcaded courtyard. Now a welfare home.

Ruine Kammerstein: mentioned in 1150, fell into decline from the 18C onwards. The surviving buildings include the keep (W.), two towers in the citadel, parts of the residential building in the E., and the curtain wall of the outworks.

Mautern an der Donau 3512
Lower Austria   p.278□T 4

Site of the Roman military camp of Faviani. Imprints on bricks are evidence of the presence of the XIV legion. The town (Mutaren) is mentioned in the Nibelungenlied in connection with Kriemhild's bridal journey. Göttweig was incorporated from 1348. The fortified walls correspond to the Roman complex. In 1481 the town was occupied by the troops of Matthias Corvinus, the Hungarian king. The French destroyed the wooden bridge built in 1463; it was rebuilt, then burned down in 1866 by the Austrians as they fled from the Prussians. An iron bridge was then built (badly damaged in the last war).

Pfarrkirche St.Stephan: An early-15C Gothic hall church with a nave and two aisles. The entire building is massive: the saddle roof, the S. tower with its baroque onion dome, the buttresses and the late Gothic S. portal. The high altar dates from *c.* 1700 (altarpiece, school of Kremser Schmidt); paintings of the Way of the Cross by Kremser Schmidt. The *Totenkapelle* (burial chapel) contains the memorial to his father (1761) and a Renaissance tomb dating from 1598. On the N. wall is a condemned criminals' altar dating from 1635.

Also worth seeing: *Nikolaihof.* Originally owned by Passau. Farm buildings with Agapitkapelle (mentioned in a synodal report in 985). The chapel was secularised long ago, and has been subdivided. *Margarethenkapelle:* Built on the remains of a Roman wall (ashlar and mixed mortar; in front of it is a Roman tower moat). Late Romanesque nave with square choir. Frescos on the nave wall (1260). The

Mauer near Melk, carved altar

chapel houses a *museum* of Roman finds. *Schloss:* Owned by the bishopric of Passau. It was built in 1551 under Prince Bishop Wolfgang Count Salm using parts of older buildings. In the square courtyard, window with Renaissance frame. In the SE corner Gothic spiral staircase with twisted hand-rail. The *Schlosskapelle* dates from 1620. *Janaburg,* built by Sebaldus Janer in 1576. Round-arched colonnaded portal with keystone. Statues in shallow niches. In the courtyard Renaissance fountain with coat-of-arms.

Mauterndorf, Lungau 5570

Salzburg   p.282☐N 9

Mauterndorf owes its importance to the N.-S. route over the Alps (Radtstädter Tauern), which existed even in Roman times. It was the centre of the 'predium in Lungowe' which King Heinrich II presented to Archbishop Hartwik, and after the latter's death it passed to the chapter of the Dom in Salzburg, to whom it belonged until the

Mautern a. d. Donau, schloss

secularization of 1803. The customs post referred to in the royal deed of gift was the first such post in the eastern Alpine area. The right to hold markets was conferred upon the town by Frederick II in 1217. The prosperity resulting from trade and from mining in Lungau found its expression in a number of splendid town houses with stepped gables, unusual in the province of Salzburg, which have survived in good condition.

Burg Mauterndorf: Built by the Dom chapter after Pope Innocent IV, in 1253, gave permission to build castles which served to protect the owner's territory. It was extended under Archbishop Leonhard of Keutschach in 1339 (chapel) and *c.* 1500 (residential rooms). The magnificent site and harmoniously grouped, well-proportioned, lucidly designed buildings make this one of the finest medieval castles. Items worth seeing inside the castle are the Keutschach rooms with tendril ornament and the *chapel* dedicated to St.Henry (II). The *frescos* on the triumphal arch wall (mid 14C) depict personified virtues, medallions with Saints, and the throne of Solomon with a Coronation of the Virgin Mary. The *triptych* dating from 1452 has three shrine figures which are among the best and most modern achievements of Salzburg sculpture in the mid 15C. On the left wing of the altar coats-of-arms and the founder, later Archbishop Burkhard von Weissbriach.

Friedhofskirche St. Gertraud (graveyard church): This is a simple Romanesque country church with a semi-circular apse. The tympanum in the present tower chapel has survived from the original Romanesque entrance; it is decorated with a fresco of the 'Lamb of God' and with painting resembling a chessboard. The flat wooden ceiling is Gothic; the richly ornamented gallery parapet dates from 1513. The painted memorial stones are stylistically linked with the fine Renaissance altars. The *graveyard* is a rare example of a walled 'graveyard for innocent children' (key obtainable from the priest's house).

Also worth seeing: *Pfarrkirche hl. Bartholomäus* with late Gothic reliefs from the altar of the Barbarakapelle in Tamsweg on the side altars.

Environs: Schloss Moosham (road to St. Michael): Splendidly sited above the Murtal, it must have been in existence as early as *c.* 1202. It is very large, and consists of an 'old' and a 'new', or an 'upper' and a 'lower' Schloss. It was owned by the Archbishops from 1285 onwards, and until 1788 it served as a local court of law. Hans Count Wilczek purchased the almost ruined Schloss in 1886 and restored it sympathetically. The upper Schloss was extended in 1516 – 22. The *Kapellentrakt* dating from this period was redesigned in baroque style and decorated with a fresco by G.Lederwasch (1780). The choir has a Gothic stained-glass window dating from

c. 1440. There is a *fine collection* of folklore from the Lungau area (guided tours).

Mauthen 9642
Kärnten   p.284□L 11

Pfarrkirche St.Markus: This church is basically Romanesque. After being destroyed by the Turks in 1478 it was rebuilt in the late Gothic style (net vaulting). The church was reoriented in the baroque period (1742): the E. choir was moved to the W., and a portal was pierced in the former choir tower in the E. The interior is rococo. The *exterior frescos* dating from 1514 are of great interest, though weatherworn. Bold foreshortening of perspective, for example in the 'Death of the Virgin Mary', shows that the artist was trained in N. Italy.

Mayerling = Alland 2534
Lower Austria   p.278□U 5

Schloss: Archduke Rudolf, the Crown

Burg Mauterndorf

Prince, purchased the simple baroque house from the abbey of Heiligenkreuz in 1886. He had it converted into a hunting lodge. His suicide here with Baroness Mary Vetsera in 1889 has never been explained. The young woman is buried in the cemetery at Heiligenkreuz, the Crown Prince in the Capuchin vault. Emperor Franz Joseph presented the Schloss to Carmelite nuns from Baumgarten, and at the Empress's request the Crown Prince's room became a funerary chapel.

Melk, Stift 1 Platform **2** Marmorsaal **3** Library **4** Stiftskirche **5** Sacristy **6** Abbot's house **7** Stairwell **8** Abbot's courtyard fountain **9** Gatehouse between the bastions **10** Kaiserzimmer **11** Fortified tower

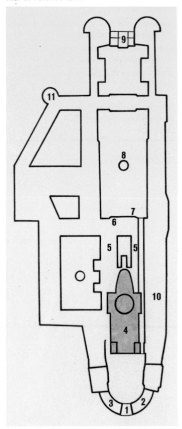

Melk 3390
Lower Austria   p.278 □ S 5

The architectural splendour of Melk, the perfect interplay of landscape and building, can only be fully appreciated from the Danube. Melk was a Hungarian border fortress c. 900, and in 976 was conquered by Leopold I, supported by Emperor Otto after the battle of the Lechfeld in 955. Leopold settled Benedictine monks from Lambach here. The relics of St. Koloman were brought here from Stockerau on 13 October 1113, and the monastery was formally established under the seal of Bishop Ulrich of Passau. It was richly endowed by Leopold III. When the Babenbergs changed their place of residence (Leopold II moved his palace to Klosterneuburg in 1106), Melk was neglected in favour of Klosterneuburg and Heiligenkreuz. Even the most valuable gift, the particle of the Cross presented by Margrave Albrecht, was stolen and reappeared in the Schottenkloster in Vienna. The Margrave was astonished at the protest lodged by Melk. 15 Babenbergs are buried in the Hauskloster in Melk; they have been moved around on several occasions. The town acquired market rights in 1227. There was a disastrous fire in 1297, and the town was rebuilt in 1306. The Melk reform took place in 1418 (Order reformed to tighten discipline). The monastery was Protestant for a short period during the Reformation. There were repeated serious fires: the monastery burned down in 1683, and was completely rebuilt under Abbot Berthold Dietmayr (1700 – 26). Prandtauer started to build in 1702 but was

Stift Melk ▷

unable to complete the work; he was succeeded by J. Munggenast. Parts of the new monastery were destroyed in a fire in 1735, and the towers were rebuilt by Munggenast.

Benediktinerstift: The abbey buildings run from E. to W. and are set on a granite rock 185 ft. high; the façade on the Danube side is asymmetrical, and the S. side, 10,050 ft. is completely unarticulated and functional. In the gatehouse there are two statues by L. Mattielli of St.Koloman and his successor, St.Leopold (to the right is the *Schimmelturm,* a Gothic fortified tower). The forecourt and second portal have statues of St.Peter and St.Paul, the patron Saints of the abbey. There are galleries in the passage, and in the vault a ceiling painting of St. Benedict. *Prälatenhof:* This is dominated by the tall drum dome of the church; the lantern repeats the silhouette of the dome. In the middle of the courtyard is a 17C *fountain* with two basins. On the left is the access to the stairwell, which has a splendid staircase with putti and sculptures by L.Mat-

tielli. The Kaisergang has a *picture gallery* and gives access to the *Kaiserzimmer,* now a *museum.* In the *Prälatenkapelle,* an intimate, friendly room with frescos by Bergl, we find the former high altar with panel paintings by J. Breu (1502: Christ before Pilate; St. Florian and St. Paul; Flight into Egypt; Man of Sorrows; Jesus among the Doctors; Crown of Thorns; Christ at the pillar; Crucifixion). The library in the N. and the Marmorsaal in the S. enclose the Kolomani courtyard in front of the church, and are connected by an articulated gallery which opens up the view of the dome between the towers to the visitor approaching along the Danube from the W. There are 70,000 books and 2000 manuscripts and early printed works in the brown and gold *library.* Frescos by P.Troger (Hercules christianus, Divine Virtue and Wisdom). Opposite this is the *Marmorsaal,* where tall pilasters with atlantes support the cornice. The room has windows on three sides; the ceiling frescos harmonize with this brightness: the apotheosis of Hercules as the conqueror of evil soars above high baroque architectural painting.

Stift Melk, library

Stift Melk, spiral staircase

Stiftskirche hll.Peter und Paul: The central portal dates from 1732. A curving W. façade: the figure of the Saviour, flanked by humble angels, is seen above the central section which curves forwards (the Saviour's position on the Cross is taken from Michelangelo). The two towers have delicate baroque domes. The balance of the colours in the unique *interior* is a work of genius. The *ceiling frescos* are by J.M. Rottmayr (Ecclesia triumphans and Holy Trinity). The dome is 210 ft. high. Hovering angels make music in the open vault of heaven. The apotheosis of St.Benedict is depicted in the tunnel vault. The side chapels have paintings by Troger and Rottmayr. The altar of St.Koloman is in the left transept, and that of St.Benedict is in the right. Subtle lighting effects: light is concentrated in the dome and high altar areas. The low *chapels* are connected: curving galleries by A. Galli-Bibiena, the theatrical architect, above the arches. The *pulpit,* which almost looks too small, is by the crossing pillar on the gospel side. The incomparable *marble altar* is by A. Beduzzi: exquisite deployment of columns, empty space, crowns, baldachin and medallion. The decoration of the *sacristies* is of the same standard as that of the church. The church's three greatest treasures are: the *Melker Kreuz,* a processional Cross donated by Rudolf, the founder, for the fragment of the True Cross, dates from 1362 and has a base attached some 50 years later. Gilded silver overlaid with precious stones, pearls and a Roman cameo. The front can be lifted off, exposing the fragment of the Cross underneath. This is the work of a Viennese goldsmith. The second treasure is the *Tragaltärchen Swanhilds* (portable altar of Swanhild); Swanhild was the first wife of Margrave Ernst, who resided in Melk. Swanhild came from the Rhineland originally and probably brought this ivory altar with her; it is the oldest item which definitely belonged to the Babenbergs. The third precious item is a female *head*

reliquary with a crown, dating from the 13C. This is a somewhat heavy-handed work. The *picture gallery* and the rich *monastery treasure* are important.

Messern im Taffatal 3761
Lower Austria   p.278☐T 3

Burg Wildberg: A settlement in a cleared area at the edge of the Wild forest. The oldest section of the castle (12C) is by the steep valley. This section was redesigned in the Gothic style in the 14C and was altered again in the 16C. The original castle was built by the Counts Poigen-Rebgau-Hohenburg, who from 1130 onwards called themselves the Counts of Wildberg. The Poigen-Wildberg family died out in 1210 and the castle was given in fief to the Vohburgs. The Babenbergs took over their coat-of-arms from the Wildbergs, the *Bindenschild,* first officially worn in 1230. The Maissaus owned the castle exclusively in 1382. The fief then fell to the Puchheims, and the building thereby became a centre of Protestantism. There is a famous printing press, which produced the valuable 'Wildberger Drucke' prints. After the Counter-Reformation, the castle came into the possession of the Altenburgs. It has been restored in the last few years. The castle is set high in a loop of the river Taffa. Access from the mountain side over a moat. Massive complex with many different sections. Long forecourt behind the portal. The battlements date from 1600. Baroque pavilion beside the 2nd gate. The inner castle courtyard is behind the 3rd gate. In the N. corner is an open kitchen building with pillars in the lower storey and small arches above. Opposite this is the imposing *Herrenhaus* with its Renaissance façade. Inside remains of fine decorations, old ceilings and vaults. On a stone door frame is the *Bindenschild:* yellow, red, yellow, the authentic Austrian coat-of-arms.

Metnitz, Metnitztal 9363
Kärnten   p.282□P 10

Pfarrkirche St.Leonhard: This Gothic
hall with a nave and two aisles has an
unusual interior. Groin vaults on eight
smooth round pillars. It has not yet been
possible to date the church (1330?), as the
design is unique in Carinthia. The narrower polygonal apse dates from the 14C.
The church has very interesting fresco
cycles from three periods of Gothic painting. The *choir frescos* (*c.* 1330) include:
Christ in Judgement (vault), the Coronation of the Virgin Mary, Saints, animals
and landscapes. The *paintings in the Annakapelle* are some 100 years later (1420),
but the *frescos of the Dance of Death* on the
N. wall of the hall are the most important
of all (1500). They were originally on the
outside of the ossuary, where their subject
matter was appropriate, and were recently
transferred into the church. Their subject
is death, and they combine a fearful vision
and a grisly sense of satisfaction and justice. Of the *late baroque decorations,* the
main items worth mentioning are the 13
carved Apostles in the nave by Balthasar
Prandtstätter (mid 18C). The *Gothic
ossuary* outside the church combines fortified tower, burial chamber and chapel;
now a war memorial chapel.

Michaelbeuern 5152
Salzburg   p.276□L 5

The medieval layout of this monastery is
still discernible. The first known document of King Otto II, dating from 977,
mentions the monastery of St.Michael in
'Biwern'.

Benediktinerabtei: Apart from St.Peter,
this is the only Benedictine abbey in the
Land of Salzburg, and also the only medieval monastery of any kind in the province
outside the city of Salzburg itself. The date
of its foundation is obscure, but it was first
mentioned in 977. Poverty, and a historical
situation different from that obtaining in
abbeys elsewhere in Austria, meant that

Burg Wildberg near Messern

baroque architectural enthusiasm passed this abbey by. In the 17&18C, Michaelbeuern provided a number of professors for the university of Salzburg, which was run by a Benedictine congregation. They included P.Odilo von Gutrath, the geographer (d. 1731), and P.Michael, the historian (d. 1854). The university was abolished in 1810 and continued as a secondary school.

Stiftskirche St.Michael: This building, consecrated in 1072 and rebuilt after the fire of 1364, was redesigned in baroque style in the 17C. An attempt to restore the Romanesque design in 1938 ended with the church being partly rebuilt. Some parts of the original Romanesque pillared basilica have survived, such as the tower, the 13C colonnaded portal (with a new tympanum), the beginnings of a westwork and parts of the transition to the former monks' choir. The finest item of the furnishings is the *high altar;* sculptures by M.Guggenbichler of Mondsee. The altarpieces (1691&2) are by J.M. Rottmayr of Laufen, who was brought up in the monastery as a choirboy.

Monastery buildings: The monastery courtyard is reached via the gatehouse. The buildings are irregular in layout, and date from various periods. The plan dating from 1768 to rebuild the entire monastery did not progress beyond its opening stages (model in the library). This meant that the 16 – 18C monastery buildings have survived, as have some Romanesque sections (the former *refectory*). The *monastery library* makes a very modest impression beside the *Abtsaal,* stuccoed *c.* 1720. An especially precious item in the library is the so-called *Waltherbibel,* a leading work of Romanesque book illumination in the Salzburg province. A rich and interesting *collection of folklore* is housed in a section of the monastery; the monastery art treasures include noteworthy late medieval sculpture (some from Dorfbeuern; guided tours).

Environs: Dorfbeuern: The *Pfarrkirche hl.Nikolaus und hl.Johannes der Täufer* is under the monastery of Michaelbeuern. It is a late Gothic building with splendid net vaults in their original polychrome. The rich main portal has iron mountings.

Michelstetten = Asparn an der Zaya 2151

Lower Austria   p.278□V 3

Pfarrkirche St.Veit: This medieval fortified church (the parish was founded in 1128) is a Romanesque ashlar construction. The E. tower above the square choir has an entrance at a high level, and also machicolations and arrow slits. There was a pilgrims' hospice in the two storeys above the church. The nave was revaulted in 1720. An early Gothic triumphal arch leads from the nave, which has been redesigned in baroque style, into the choir of 1290, with its beautiful frescos depicting Christ Enthroned surrounded by the symbols of the Evangelists and by the Apostles. Female figures with three-dimensional emblems on the window walls.

Also worth seeing: *Schloss:* The Gothic castle was altered into a Renaissance moated Schloss in the 16C, and was destroyed by fire in 1883. The sturdy outer wall makes an unfriendly impression. Inside is a pretty, many-cornered courtyard with galleries, a hall and a kitchen. On the *Halterberg* there is a medieval *Fluchtburg* (refuge castle) with tall ramparts. The primeval rampart called *Alte Stadt* on the Steinmandl has finds which date from the Stone Age, Bronze Age, Iron Age and early Middle Ages.

Millstatt 9872
Kärnten   p.282☐N 10

An old and famous Benedictine abbey, founded in the 2nd half of the 11C, stands on the N. shore of the Millstätter See in the middle of this town. Fragments from the Carolingian period prove that the area was inhabited at an earlier date than this. The abbey was a significant centre of medieval monastic culture before falling into decline and being dissolved by the Pope (1469).

Former abbey: This complex to the S. of the church dates from the late 15&16C; the proud Order of the Knights of St. George resided here at that time and gave the buildings a dignified appearance (fortified towers and a surrounding wall were built because of the threat from the Turks). The splendid *cloister* (S. side of church), on the other hand, dates back to the early 12C. The Romanesque columns and capitals are quite magnificent: human, animal and plant elements mingle to form the demons on the capitals, where the opposing elements of Christianity seem to confront each other at the point where thrust and abutment also meet. The *Carolingian guilloche stones* in the passage from the Kirchplatz to the Stiftshof are some 300 years older still. Their magic ornaments are rooted in pagan invocation, like the tangled demons on the Romanesque capitals.

Pfarrkirche and former Stiftskirche: This 11C Romanesque pillared basilica originally had a flat roof; the massive W. building with its portico and double-towered façade was added under Abbot Heinrich II *c.* 1170. The appearance of the church's exterior and interior was altered under the knights of St.George in the late Gothic period (vault, choir, chapels), and by the Jesuits in the baroque period (redesign of chapel, altars). The objects of greatest interest: carved *ornaments* on the transoms and the edges of the pillars still survive from the former *early Romanesque* tripartite arch on the W. front. The fine *Romanesque portal* with attached columns is in the porch. This entrance, friendly and

Millstatt with Pfarrkirche

Millstatt, Romanesque portal

at the same time menacing, was built by Master Rudger *c.* 1170. Christ blessing is seen in the tympanum; Abbot Heinrich II, kneeling beside Him, delivers the Church into His hands. The power of the knights of St. George is symbolically represented inside the basilican nave. The *keystones of the vault* bear the coats-of-arms of the international princely houses, showing the supraregional connections of the Order. The *Siebenhirten-Kapelle* (N. aisle) and the *Geumannkapelle* (S. aisle) contain the tombstones of the grand masters of the Order (both post 1500). The *Geumanngrab* is of interest for its coloured frame and the link between the figure and the flat area. The artist was probably H.Valkenauer from Salzburg. Another painted work is the *tomb relief* of Duke *Domitian* (1449) in the SE chapel, redecorated by Jesuits in 1716. The right side chapel has a large and captivating *Last Judgement fresco*, which was on the W. façade until 1963 but had to be transferred into the church because of damage by the weather. Painted by U. Görtschacher *c.* 1515, this fresco impresses by its modern, almost Renaissance, style.

The lords of Millstatt had a proud tradition in religious conflicts, symbolized in the late Gothic frescos (1490) on the *churchyard gate*. Duke Domitian and Jesus Christ are depicted as a unity, which includes Siebenhirter, the grand master of the Order at that time (his coat-of-arms is below St.George). Thus heavenly and earthly rank are symbolically combined.

Mistelbach an der Zaya 2130
Lower Austria   p.278☐W 3

Pfarrkirche St. Martin: Two flights of steps with Way of the Cross and Mount of Olives groups lead to this church on a green hill. After 1750, pilgrims came to worship in a chapel called 'Maria in den Gruften', pulled down in 1787. The hall church, which dates mainly from the late 15C, has nave, two aisles, Gothic paradise, polygonal apse and a tower in the S. (the tower was redesigned in baroque style in 1755). On the roof cornice on the W. side there is a toad gargoyle. Inside, the *high altar*

Millstatt, cloister

Millstatt, Geumanngrab

Mödling, ossuary portal

dates from 1728 and there are numerous tombstones, of which the oldest dates from 1362.

Ossuary: Dedicated to St. Catherine. Romanesque round ossuary with apse; redesigned in baroque style. The portal has small crocket capitals and a semicircular tympanum (a small, frightened, human head between stylized dragons). The surfaces are filled with acanthus leaves.

Also worth seeing: *Priest's house:* Former Barnabite priory (Salvatorian since 1923). Square baroque building, erected 1691–1700 and altered in 1750. Baroque ridge-turret above the charmingly decorated *chapel*. Ceiling fresco (1760) by F.A. Maulbertsch in the *library*. The excellent *Städtisches Heimatmuseum* (local history) is housed in the *Schlössel* of 1727.

Mittersill 5730
Salzburg   p.284□I 8

From 1180 the counts to whom the Bavarian Dukes had given the Oberpinzgau took the name of the castle of Mittersill; this indicates the probable age of the castle. The town of Mittersill is a later foundation dating from the 13C; in 1228 the Pinzgau came under the rule of Salzburg.

Schloss: Set on a high ridge on the pass road to Kitzbühel. When the Pinzgau was taken over by Salzburg, this Schloss became the seat of an administrator. The medieval building was destroyed in the peasants' wars in 1525/26 and was rebuilt in its present form in 1532 at the peasants' expense, with the characteristic turrets on the W. side. The *chapel*, dated 1533, possesses an interesting late Gothic *triptych* c. 1450, attributed to the 'master of the Aussee altar'. The castle has been in private hands since 1880.

Dekanatskirche hl.Leonhard: This church mentioned in 1357 was destroyed by fire and then rebuilt 1747–49 to designs by Johann Kleber, the court building administrator. The (poorly) framed stone figure of *St. Leonard* dating from c. 1420 –25 is the chief item of note apart from the decorative *rococo pulpit* by the sculptor Petrus Schmid (1763).

Annakirche: A small church (1751) with great architectural movement designed under Tyrolean-Swabian influence with frescos (1753) by Christoph Anton Mayr who came from Schwaz, as did J.Singer, the architect of the church.

Environs: Felben: This has a medieval residential tower dating from the 12&13C, a typical example of a very simple medieval defensive building. The *Filialkirche* *hl.Nikolaus* is late-15C. The baroque high altar (1631) is particularly unusual; it is furnished with early-15C wooden statuettes of the 14 auxiliary Saints. The pulpit and high altar date from *c.* 1631.

Möderndorf = Hermagor 9620
Kärnten   p.282☐M 11

Filialkirche hl.Martin: Late Gothic building (mentioned in 1483) with net-vaulted choir and nave with a flat ceiling. On the outside S. wall is a *St. Christopher fresco*, probably by U.Görtschacher (1525). The painted architecture of the frame is of interest. Inside, fine late-Gothic *carving:* a wall-mounted Madonna and Child and two triptychs from the 1st quarter of the 16C. The painted Saint figures on the panels confirm that painting had precedence over carving at that time. Baroque high altar with columns dating from *c.* 1680.

Mödling 2340
Lower Austria   p.278☐V 5

The town of Mödling dates back to a 6C Slav settlement. The picturesque limestone rocks and go. ges made the town extremely popular with the Romantics. A village mentioned in 907 around a church on a high site with ossuary and graveyard was significantly extended in the 11C and acquired market rights in 1252. Some 200 years later, in 1529, the Turks destroyed the town; it soon recovered, and was granted a charter in 1875.

Pfarrkirche St.Othmar: This building started in the high Middle Ages but not completed until 1523 was destroyed by the Turks in 1529, only six years after completion. It remained a ruin until it was restored in the 17C. The interior is a wide hall. The walls and pillars are Gothic, while the white plaster vaulting is late Renaissance. In the choir is a Gothic *tabernacle* (post 1500). Under the *upper church* is a *lower church* partly built in the rock with a single-aisled chapel-like area and irregularly-shaped adjacent areas forming a kind of ambulatory.

Ossuary: This late-12C ashlar rotunda was raised by the addition of an extra storey with a belfry and onion dome at the time when the church was restored, and has since served as the church tower. The ossuary itself is underground. The *portal* has a four-tiered archivolt and a round-arched *door* with three steps. The *relief* above (a horseman pursuing a stag) is said to represent Theoderich. The *painting* in the baroque-vaulted interior dates from the 19C and shows scenes from the life of St. Pantaleon. 13C *frescos* (in poor condition) have been revealed in the apse and among the adjacent wall pictures.

Also worth seeing: *Spitalskirche zum hl.Agyd* (under construction in 1443); the *Missionshaus St. Gabriel,* a neo-Romanesque bare brick building (1889–1914), now ethnographic museum. *Rathaus* (Schranneplatz, a Renaissance building with a baroque onion dome. Houses: The so-called *Herzogshof* (Herzoggasse 4; 2nd half of 15C). The *Beethovenhaus* (Hauptstrasse 79). The *Thonetschlössl* (Klostergasse 2), and the *Dreifaltigkeitssäule* (Dreifaltigkeitsplatz), 1714.

Environs: Burg Liechtenstein (near Mödling): This Romanesque castle is mentioned from the 12C and was romantically restored in its original style from 1873 onwards. Together with the 16C Schloss opposite, extended by J.Engel in neoclassical style in 1820–22, the castle is at the centre of a large *romantic park* containing several mock ruins: the *Schwarzer Turm* (1810), the *Pfefferbüchsel* (pepper pot; 1818), an observation tower, and the *amphitheatre*, all interesting examples of romantic neoclassicism. Another neoclassical imitation is the *Husarentempel* on the Kleiner Anninger. **Bad Vöslau** (in the direction of Wiener Neustadt) with its *Pfarrkirche hl.Jakob der Ältere;* (1860–70), and the *Schloss,* formerly a 17C moated castle, redesigned in neoclassical style in 1733.

Möllbrücke 9813

Kärnten   p.282 □ M 10

Filialkirche St.Leonhard: This 15C hall church, with two bays, stellar vaulting in the nave and rib vaulting in the choir, has a noteworthy *late Gothic triptych.* Most of the work is carved, but some of the side panels are painted. They give a clear impression of the close and 'realistic' relationship between man and art in the late Middle Ages. In a world of wars, epidemics and natural danger the tangible presentation of auxiliary and patron saints was close to the concerns of all believers. Prayers for a successful harvest were offered to the almost life-sized statue of St. Leonard in the middle shrine; St.Florian, the guardian of the shrine, is an auxiliary saint in the event of outbreaks of fire; and St.George did not slay only the dragon, but also the enemies of the Empire and of Christianity. Bishops and emperors are guarantors of orderliness, and the female Saints present the cause of mildness and mercy. Martyrs evoke the purpose of human suffering and man's ability to bear it. The Leonhardsaltar (altarpiece, shrine panels and crowning) shows the individual styles of two different artists. The painted, fixed outer wings and their rear sides are stylistically ahead of the carving. Unfortunately, both artists are anonymous. Further features worth mentioning are the late

Gothic *prayer stool,* and above this the bracket statue of *St. Leonard* (1420). The *pulpit* and *side altars* are baroque.

Mondsee 5310

Upper Austria   p.276 □ M 6

Numerous lake-dwelling finds from the end of the Neolithic period (*c.* 2500–1800 BC) gave the East Alpine lake culture the name 'Mondsee-Kultur'. Roman tombstones (church portico) are evidence of Roman settlements. In 748 a monastery was founded by the Bavarian Duke Odilo II, the father of Tassilo (see Kremsmünster). The ancient Benedictine abbey was dissolved in 1791.

Former Stiftskirche zum hl.Michael: The present building consecrated in 1487 is a hall church with a nave and two aisles. The ante-choir has side chapels and the main choir is reached by 14 steps (the crypt has been filled in). To the N. of the choir is the sacristy (the former Marienkapelle), which also has an apse; this gives an impression of two choirs from the outside. After 1730 a façade, not directly connected to the main body of the building, was erected in front of the church. Twin-towered façade with a concave central section, façade narrower than the church; of the two central entrances, the right-hand one is precisely on the central axis of the church. The view from a distance is dominated by the massive mansard-style roof, and by the towers. The interior appears Gothic; there are excellent baroque decorations, especially the five *altars* by the artist M.Guggenbichler, who was associated with the abbey. Particular attention should be drawn to the *Corpus Christi altar* with the famous 'Kindln': these are putti carrying grapes. The *sacristy door* is Gothic with an ogee arch, and above it

Mondsee, former Stiftskirche St. Michael ▷

Mondsee, detail of high altar

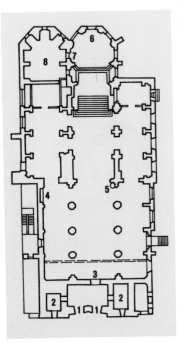

Mondsee, former Stiftskirche 1 Double portal of façade **2** Towers **3** Entrance to nave **4** Corpus-Christi-Altar **5** Pulpit **6** High altar **7** Sacristy door **8** Sacristy

under baldachins are seven Gothic wooden statues; outstandingly good *wrought-iron door*, with masterly openwork lock and ring handle (1487).

Museums: *Heimatmuseum* in the former monastery library. Primeval ceramics (Mondsee culture), works by Guggenbichler, national costume, handicrafts and transport. Dugout canoes. *Mondseer-Rauchhaus:* Open-air museum, original isolated farmstead with household effects, outhouses such as granary, 'Dörrhäusl (drying house) for fruit, mill, etc.

Moosburg in Kärnten 9062
Kärnten   p.282□P 11

Schloss: The early-16 Schloss stands in the E. of the area where the old Carol-

ingian palace (9C) formerly stood. The Ernau family acquired it in 1514. It has been altered several times. The mannerist metalwork ornaments with their figures of secular and ecclesiastical rulers are also worth seeing in the 16C section of the building.

Pfarrkirche St.Michael: This originally Romanesque church, later altered in Gothic style, was re-oriented in the baroque period (1755–69); the choir was moved to the W., the portal to the E. On the outside, three *Roman stones* (3C AD) let into the wall, and a Carolingian tracery stone (W. graveyard wall), are worth seeing, as are the *coat-of-arms tombstones* of the rulers of Moosburg. The church decorations are baroque, and the altarpiece is probably by J.F. Fromiller, an artist from Klagenfurt.

Murau 8850
Steiermark   p.282□P 9

A settlement whose original centre was the present Schillerplatz was built here as early as the 13C at the intersection of various trade routes (salt route). The charter was granted in 1298; in the 14C Otto III of Liechtenstein walled the town, including the old castle of Grünfels. Of the former seven town gates, two remain; the medieval character of the town has survived well. Three 15C late Gothic columns should be mentioned: the Lichtsäule outside the parish church, the Armesündersäule on the road to Ranten, and the Martersäule on the W. slope of the Schlossberg.

Pfarrkirche hl.Matthäus: This church was built on the Schlossberg by Otto von Liechtenstein, and the space for the priest's house was created by retaining walls. Construction work on this yellow tufa church was begun in 1295; the choir, with its rib vault and sculpted keystones, was consecrated in 1296. The nave of the early Gothic basilica is supported on octagonal pillars, and like the side aisles it has groin vaulting. There is an octagonal tower above the crossing. The minstrels' gallery with spiral staircase dates from the late 15C. Extensive *fresco cycles*, mainly from the 14C, survive inside. In the S. transept the remains of a painted *triptych* dating from *c.* 1500. The *tomb* of the Liechtensteins, with a painted tabernacle, is in the N. transept (15C). Another very noteworthy feature is the *Gothic Crucifixion* (*c.* 1500), which was taken from the former high altar and used in the baroque building. The *Rosenkranzaltar* in the N. transept is from a Judenburg workshop (1740), while the altar in the S. transept is by C.Paumgartner (1645).

The eleven statues of the Apostles on the pillars (1777) are by Joh. Reiter. The *memorial stones* are also of interest.

Friedhofkirche hl.Anna: This was built in the late 14C, and has a ridge-turret instead of the S. tower pulled down in the 18C. The aisle has three bays with a net vault, minstrels' gallery on pillars, and Gothic tracery windows. Frescos in the N. wall: six Passion scenes (15C), St.George and founders (*c.* 1500); the choir has a Coronation of the Virgin Mary, eleven saints (*c.* 1400), and St.Anne with the Virgin and Child (post 1400); bracketed figures on the choir arch. *Late Gothic triptych* with carved relief (*c.* 1515) below the stone baldachin decorated with frescos in the NE corner of the aisle. The high altar dating from 1727 has a St.Anne with the Virgin and Child (*c.* 1500). Four 15C stained-glass windows in the choir. The organ is late-17C.

Filialkirche hl.Leonhard: Late Gothic hall church (tufa) in good condition, built by Otto von Liechtenstein in 1445, and

Murau with parish church of St. Matthäus

still surrounded by a defensive wall. Impressive portals lead into the interior, with three-bay nave, net vaulting, windows with rich tracery, corbels with carved heads. A spiral staircase with a wooden gallery above leads to the three-storeyed minstrels' gallery (elegant tracery balustrade). The high altar has statues of saints (*c.* 1520).

Filialkirche hl.Ägydius: This, the oldest church in the town, is Romanesque, with nave, two aisles and a square choir. In the 13C, the S. aisle was added and the N. aisle extended. The fine ceiling, with late Gothic stencilled patterns, was added in 1530. There are frescos in the S. aisle (life of Virgin Mary and Saints, 14C) and on the N. choir wall (Annunciation, Passion, St. Aegidius, 15C).

Also worth seeing: The *Schloss* has been in the possession of the Liechtensteins since the 13C. It was rebuilt by the architect Valentin Kaut (1628 – 41). Rectangular arcaded courtyard; no towers. The chapel with Gothic windows is in the central part of the E. section; there is good stucco both here and on the 2nd storey. *Burg Grünfels:* A tower built *c.* 1300 survives, also remains of the original town fortifications. The castle was converted into a residential building in the 17C. *Spitalskirche Hl.Elisabeth:* The sacristy, the remains of a tower, and five windows, survive from the 14C building. The vault and Renaissance portal were stuccoed in the course of reconstruction work in the 17C. The building was secularised in 1928. *Kapuzinerkloster and Kirche* with paintings by J. and G.Lederwasch.

Mureck 8480
Steiermark   p.280☐T 11

Pfarrkirche hl.Bartholomäus: Mentioned in 1187, present design 18C. The articulated main façade has projecting cor-

nices. Pilaster building with narrower choir. The paintings at the high altar are by J.V. Hauck (1713). The *Patriziuskapelle* and the 17C *Rathaus* are also worth seeing.

Murstetten = Perschling 3142
Lower Austria   p.278☐T/U 5

Goldburg castle: In 1526, the Swabian knight Wolfgang Althan married Anna von Heitzing, who brought him Murstetten as her dowry. The Althans altered the Goldburg in 1580 and called themselves 'von der Goldburg zu Murstetten'. After the Goldburg had been destroyed by the Turks, Gundacker von Althan built a high baroque Schloss with an enormous park and fountains. Maria Theresa and her son were the guests of Gundacker at fairy-tale parties. In 1809 the French bombarded the Schloss and set it on fire. Today it is in ruins and looks wild and picturesque.

Pfarrkirche Verklärung Christi: In the choir there are still late Romanesque fragments including the vaulting of the crypt. The nave dates from 1616. It is a post-Gothic building with a groin vault and a tracery window. The tombs of the Althan family (1578) by A. Colin of Mecheln are of interest.

Muthmannsdorf 2723
Lower Austria   p.278☐U 6

Pfarrkirche St.Peter und Paul: Outside the town, in the middle of the graveyard in the 'Neue Welt'. The oldest section is the E. tower dating from 1200, with fine frescos in the groin vault (Lamb of God and twelve Apostles). 13C chapel in the N., choir in the E: rib vaulting on small half columns with carved keystones; simple 18C nave. On the Epistle side Gothic Madonna dating from 1420 on the baroque altar.

Nauders 6543
Tirol   p.286□D10

Pfarrkirche zum hl.Valentin: the present choir and tower are part of the early-16C church built on the site of an 11C building. The façade and the neo-Romanesque interior both date from the baroque. The two fine, late Gothic carved

altars on the left and right hand sides of the end of the nave were probably part of the 16C furnishings.

Schloss Naudersberg: built in the 13C on a hill with a panoramic view; keep and palas are from the original building. It was extended in the 15&16C with outworks, round towers, barbicans and the castle chapel.

Nauders, Schloss Naudersberg

Also worth seeing: *Kapelle zum hl.Leonhard*, a Romanesque church mentioned in 1391; flat ceiling with a painted lozenge pattern and *frescos* exposed in 1951. There is a *graveyard chapel* on two floors, with a 17C Crucifixion.

Neuberg a.d. Mürz 8692
Steiermark   p.280☐T7

The Cistercian abbey was founded by Duke Otto the Cheerful in 1327; dissolved in 1786. The distinctive medieval appearance of the buildings has remained unchanged.

Former Stiftskirche Mariae Himmelfahrt: this building was begun in 1327 but not consecrated until 1481; it has a massive late-15C hipped roof. The extremely bright interior with nave and two aisles has 8 pairs of pillars and rib vaulting. The long nave and the symmetrical articulation of the altars are striking features. The large Gothic tracery windows and the rose window in the W. façade are unusual aspects of the church. The paintwork in the vaulting was restored with reference to the surviving original sections. *Furnishings:* the eye is caught by the gilded *high altar*, 66 ft. high, by H.J.Huldi (Ulm), H.G.Mader (Überlingen) and T.H.Stainmüller (Olmütz), dating from 1611&12. Painting and surround by G.Terzano. The high altar is flanked by two complementary altars (by the third pair of pillars, dating from 1668 and incorporating parts of late Gothic triptychs. In the left aisle *Georgsaltar* (1622); in the right *Marienaltar* with a Gothic stone statue known as the *Neuberg Madonna* and dating from 1350. Next to it is a late baroque carved altar with a 15C Gothic image of the seated Virgin. The two-storey, rib-vaulted *Loreto Chapel* and its spiral staircase are 15C in origin; it contains another 15C Madonna statue and a Crucifixion from the same period. There are altars with carved decorations dating from 1720 and 1750 by the second pair of pillars, and the *pulpit* and its support date from 1670. The *sacristy* is 14C, with rib vaulting.

Nauders, Romanesque frescos in St.Leonhard

Monastery buildings: these have survived in their medieval form, and include a picturesque yet plain *cloister;* pointed arched windows with reconstructed tracery. The lion, pelican, unicorn etc. on the corbels in the E. walk are Christian or Evangelists' symbols. 15C hexagonal *well house* in the S. walk; opposite is the *refectory,* with tympanum (*c.* 1420. The *chapterhouse* is on the E. side, and has four columns, and delicate capitals, corbels and keystones. The *Joseph chapel* (1404), and the *St. Bernhard chapel* in the garden behind the church are also interesting.

Filialkirche Mariae Himmelfahrt: this former parish church has been a graveyard chapel since the abolition of the monastery. It is a late Gothic building with painted vaulting of 1522.

Neuhaus am Klausenbach 8385
Burgenland   p.280☐U10

The distinctive features of this village are the two adjacent churches on the mountainside; Catholic late 17C and Protestant *c.* 1800, with very similar baroque towers. On the top of the hill are the remains of a former Batthyany castle (observation point). Some 2km to the N. is the Schlösschen Tabor, on a small hill; it is a 15C building redesigned in baroque style in the 17C. It is an attractive building with a handsome arcaded courtyard, and a fine panoramic view.

Environs: Mogersdorf (about 22 km. NE of Neuhaus): the victory of the imperial general Montecuccoli over the Turks at the battle of Mogersdorf-St. Gotthard (now Szentgotthard, Hungary) had the same significance as that of Arch-Duke Karl over Napoleon at Aspern in 1809. Rainer Maria Rilke used this battle of 1664 as the background to his 'Life and Death of Cornet Christoph Rilke'. In 1964, the year of the tricentenary, the neo-Gothic church ruins on the Schlösslberg were turned into a memorial; by the chapel is a large stone cross visible from a great distance; there is also a stone table with a

Neuberg a. d. Mürz, former Stiftskirche Mariae Himmelfahrt

Neuberg a. d. Mürz, former Stiftskirche, nave with gilded high altar

Hungarian drinking vessels in Schloss Kittsee (Neusiedl am See)

map of the area showing how the troops were positioned in 1664. An old barn has recently been made into a restaurant.

Neusiedl am See 7100
Burgenland   p.278□X6

This town, which gave the lake its name, is situated on the narrow north bank; it is dominated by a massive medieval tower known as the 'Tabor', which affords a fine panoramic view; the church contains an unusual and very fine mid-18C *ship pulpit*.

Seemuseum: this is a branch of the Burgenland Landesmuseum dealing with the particular features of the Neusiedl area (see below).

Neusiedler See: this shallow, salt-water steppe lake is unique among Europe's inland seas and is set in particularly interesting countryside. Wind and weather have a great influence on its level, and extreme drought can drain it completely (the last time this happened was in 1865–71). These fluctuations make it difficult to give precise measurements: about 35 km long, with a width ranging from 4–14 km and an average depth of 110 cm, (maximum 170 cm). The national boundary runs through it, and around a quarter of its area is in Hungary (area around 320 sq. km. at the time of writing). It is surrounded by reeds, which give it a distinctive appearance; on the E. side especially the open water can only be reached via long causeways, and Podersdorf is the only village set directly on the water. The reeds, known as 'Rohr', play an important part in the building industry, and fishing is also important: a good year will bring in up to 400,000 kg. There are about 30 types of fish in all, predominantly carp, perch and pike. The lake's most important contribution to industry, however, is as a regulator

Schloss Kittsee (Neusiedl am See)

of climate, which affects the local harvest of high quality wine. There are many kinds of flora and fauna, and the bird sanctuary is among the most celebrated in Europe: over 280 species of birds live in the reed belt, including over 150 breeding birds. The most interesting are herons, spoonbills and great bustards (see Rust, research station).

Environs: Kittsee (about 25 km NE of Neusiedl): *Schloss:* the 'Neue Schloss' was built by an unknown architect of the Viennese school in the first half of the 18C; its gallery supported by sturdy atlantes probably dates from the same period, but was brought to Kittsee in 1900 from a Pressburg palace and built on. Its geographical location as Austria's most easterly palace makes it ideally suited to being an *ethnographic museum* of E. and SE

Europe. The museum has only been there a few years, but it has many rooms filled with interesting exhibits on folklore and folk art.

Neustift im Stubaital 6167
Tirol   p.286 □ F9

Pfarrkirche zum hl.Georg: this building, huge in proportion to the small village, was built from 1768–74 on the site of a 16C chapel. It is some 160 ft. long and 100 ft. wide, and was designed by Franz de Paula Penz. The exterior looks rather like a monastery, and the nave has a fine 'Descent of the Holy Ghost' ceiling painting and a painting of St. Joseph by J.A.Zoller (1772) on the W. wall. Joseph Keller's ceiling frescos in the choir date

Neustift im Stubaital, Pfarrkirche St. Georg

from the same period, and so do Franz Haller's frescos on the spandrels in the nave. By the organ are two paintings by F.Altmutter. The high altar and side altars were designed as a uniform whole by the architect J.Santer from Bruneck.

Niederleis 2116
Lower Austria   p.278☐V3

Schloss: formerly a moated castle; the bridge was built by Giovanni Giuliani in 1735, while the Schloss was under the abbey of Heiligenkreuz. It has a massive gate tower with a mansard roof and lanterns. It has belonged to the counts of Wallis for over 100 years and they established an interesting *museum*, with sculptures from ancient to neoclassical times and tapestries, furniture, faience, dried flowers etc.

Niederweiden = Engelhartstetten 2292
Lower Austria   p.278☐X5

Schloss Engelhartstetten: Rüdiger Graf Starhemberg, who defended Vienna in the second Turkish siege, commissioned this hunting lodge from J.B.Fischer of Erlach in 1694. It was bought by Prince Eugen in 1727 and by Maria Theresa in 1755; she added an extra storey. Magnificent main building with a double staircase leading to the oval state room. The wings protrude to form a courtyard. This elegant Schloss has been restored after many years in a state of disrepair.

Oberau = Wildschönau-Oberau
6311
Tirol   p.284 ☐ H8

Obergottesfeld = Sachsenburg
9751
Kärnten   p.282 ☐ M10

Pfarrkirche hl.Margareta: this extensive rococo building was erected in 1751 –2 to a design by Hans Holzmeister on the site of a church built in 1394 and destroyed by fire in 1719. The exterior is attractively painted and the fine tower has three domes on top of each other. There is a carved wooden Margaret statue over the marble portal in the W. façade. The interior walls are stuccoed and the ceiling is decorated with frescos by J.A.Mölk dating from 1751. The five rococo altars have carved wood figures by J.Gregor Fritz, and the pictures of the Stations of the Cross are by Christof Anton Mayr and date from 1762. The rest of the rococo decorations in delicate colours also contribute to the vibrant atmosphere of this church.

Also worth seeing: *Chapel of St.Antonius* (octagonal rotunda with unusual Giotto-style frescos of 1707). The high altar is very fine and was made, also in 1707, by Franz Lanner; the angel figures are by J.Michael Mayr. A number of houses in the village have popular *wall paintings,* see the Schellhornhof and the 'Kasten'.

Filialkirche St.Ruprecht: this is a small flat-ceilinged Romanesque building (mentioned 1166) with a semicircular apse. There is an ancient-looking late Gothic depiction of Christ in the vaulting which actually dates from *c.* 1420; also symbols of the Evangelists, plant ornaments and, in the nave, a picture of Mary and the 12 Apostles. Valuable *late Gothic triptych* dating from around 1520, a product of the Villach school. The contents of the shrine have now been replaced by a figure of St. Rupert. The Mary scenes in the fine panel reliefs and the predella suggest that it was originally a Mary altar.

Oberhautzenthal = Sierndorf 2011
Lower Austria   p.278 ☐ U4

Pfarrkirche Mariae Himmelfahrt/former pilgrimage church: this is a late Gothic hall church with two aisles, redesigned in the baroque style in 1710. The NE tower dates from 1519 and has a lower storey containing the treasury and sacristy; baroque crown 1710. There is a pointed arched doorway on the W. side with multiple ribs and tracery, influenced by the Viennese school. The high altar dates from 1740 and is flanked by St. Leopold and St.Joseph; there is a miraculous image of the Madonna with Christ Child over the tabernacle (1450). There is a confessional built into the high altar. On the epistle side is a Gothic niche containing a Pietà and St.Nepomuk. There are gravestones and a lid of Heinrich von Hardegg's tomb dating from 1577, Johann Stahl with a metal sword and hatchment. The *parish garden* contains figures from Schönborn park which date from 1717.

Obermauern=Virgen 9972
Tirol   p.284 □ J9

Wallfahrtskirche zu Unserer Lieben Frau Maria Schnee: this is the daughter church of the parish of Virgen and probably existed in early Christian times; the present building dates from 1456, and was

Obermauern, Maria-Schnee

the goal of countless pilgrimages, particularly in the 17–19C. The nave is steep, with a high Gothic tower in the N.; the lower section of the tower is probably Romanesque and has some window tracery and an unusual rose window in the W. over the pointed-arched portal. The *exterior* has some old *frescos*, including some primitive work (1400) on the vestibule, Madonna with angels on the N. side, and a large St.Christopher (1468) over the side portal. The S. side of the tower has Romanesque stone reliefs, and the sundial dates from 1601. The *interior* is surprisingly beautiful; the nave has three bays and net vaulting and is entirely covered with frescos. The miraculous image, a Madonna (1430), is housed in a late Gothic shrine of 1510 and stands on the *high altar,* which dates from 1680. The wooden sculptures of St.Barbara and St.Elisabeth are probably from the previous high altar, and those of St.Peter and St.Paul date back to *c.* 1430, *pulpit* 1500. The main attraction of the interior, however, is the large number of fine old *frescos* by Simon von Taisten. The two nave arches are decorated with a cycle depicting Christ's Passion, and the choir has scenes from the life of Mary (1488). There is a St.Sebastian of 1484 over the right side altar, to the left of which is a painted tabernacle. Painted keystones in the vaulting.

Obernberg am Brenner=Gries am Brenner 6156
Tirol   p.286 □ F9

Pfarrkirche zum hl.Nikolaus: built in 1761 and attractively situated on a hill a little way outside the village. It has a beautiful tower with dome and lantern. On the exterior is a *Celtic stoup.* The choir has an impressively painted trompe l'oeil ceiling; rococo altars and pulpit.

Obermauern, frescos by S. v. Taisten

Environs: St.Jacob bei Vinaders: visible from the church zu den hll.Sigmund und Christoph, which belongs to the village of Luegg and has interesting Romanesque and baroque elements, is the small church of St.Jakobus major und minor bei Vinaders, situated on a hill. Choir and tower have early Gothic elements, interior with two triptychs (1490 and 1600) and furnished in baroque style with a fine pulpit.

Oberndorf 5110
Salzburg   p.276☐L6

Under the 1816 Munich border agreement between Bavaria and Austria the suburbs of the old Salzburg town of Laufen on the right bank of the Salzach fell to Austria. Most of the landing stages for the salt and the Laufen boatmens' houses were on the Oberndorf side. It was in the church at Oberndorf that, in 1818, 'Silent Night, Holy Night' was heard for the first time; the words were written by Joseph Mohr and the music by the teacher Franz

Obernberg am Brenner, St.Nikolaus

Gruber. Because of the permanent danger of flooding the site of village and church was changed 1900 – 6. The new parish church of St.Nikolaus has neoclassical furnishings. A 'Silent Night Memorial Chapel' was built on the site of the old St.Nicholas Church in 1937.

Mariabichl/Maria Bühel, Wallfahrtskirche hl.Maria: this is an attractive baroque pilgrimage church situated on the top of an old Salzach terrace. It was begun in 1663 and completed in 1722; it has an ornate double onion tower, the top of which was rebuilt after a storm in 1960. The church can be reached on foot up a long flight of stairs; at the bottom is a Johann-Nepomuk statue by J.A.Pfaffinger (1720) and at the top a huge Calvary group (1721). The church, which has a single aisle and transept with dome, was built in 1721 – 22. J.M.Rottmayr painted the pictures on the side altars in the transept and A.Beduzzi, the imperial court architect, designed the high altar. The four larger-than-life saints on the walls of the nave were carved by J.A.Pfaffinger.

Oberranna = Mühldorf 3622
Lower Austria   p.278☐S4

Castle Ranna (N. of Spitz an der Donau): this Ottonian castle is situated on a wooded hill; Pilgrim of Grie (later known as Ranna), gave his castle while seriously ill to Count Leopold III, who presented it to his sister Gerbirg (d.1142). When Pilgrim recovered he wanted to revoke the gift, and in 1122 possession was established in Gars. The keep, church and crypt were built by the Gries, and in 1388 the castle came into the hands of the Neideggs, who fortified it in the 16C with curtain walls and ditches. The four wings and arcaded court (heavily restored) date from this period. The *Burgkapelle hl.Georg* dates from the

Pilgrim period and is in the Ottonian style; two transepts and two crossing towers (the E. crossing tower has three Romanesque storeys and a saddle roof, with a broad semicircular apse on the E. side and the short transepts to the right and left). The W. transept was built shortly afterwards, with a *crypt* under a gallery: it consists of a square hall with two bays supported on four columns with cushion capitals, one with a hunting scene: frieze depicting two heads and two arms with horn and cudgel. The arches have hewn voussoirs.

Obersiebenbrunn 2283

Lower Austria   p.278☐W4

Schloss: owned by the Sibenbrunn family in 1169; it changed hands a number of times before coming to the Grabners, an important Protestant family. Emperor Karl VI acquired the Schloss in 1725, and gave it along with other properties to Prince Eugen, who had it altered and a splendid garden added. The Schloss has four wings

and a portal tower; at the centre of the overgrown park is the *garden pavilion* by L.von Hildebrandt (1729), an oval building with unusual shingle roof: in the interior charming grotesques painted by Jonas Drentwett, of the celebrated Augsburg family of goldsmiths. It was renovated in 1962. The basic theme is the seasons of the year: the joys of country life are depicted with gods, signs of the zodiac and pictures of the months, accompanied by four abduction scenes—Paris and Helen, Nessos and Deianira, Diana and Endymion, Pluto and Proserpina.

Obervellach 9821

Kärnten   p.282☐M10

This town was known in the 16C for its copper and gold mines; despite a gradual decline in the mining industry, copper continued to be produced until 1830. Some of the houses in the Markt reflect, with their arcades and Renaissance portals, its former economic importance.

Obervellach, triptych, 1520, in St.Martin

Pfarrkirche St.Martin: L.Rieder built the late Gothic nave with its net vaulting c. 1500; the choir is by Andreas Bühler and dates from a generation earlier. There is a late Gothic chapel of 1509 on the N. side of the hall, and a baroque chapel on the S. The crypt under the choir suggests earlier buildings. The N. chapel houses the celebrated triptych by Jan van Scorel, which dates from 1520. Although painted early in the Dutch painter's career, it is considered one of the finest examples of international Renaissance style. The middle section depicts the Holy Kindred, the left St.Christopher and the right St.Apollonia, and in the centre of the reverse side the coats-of-arms of the founders, Christoph Frangipani and Apollonia Lang, are visible. (The angels on the side panels take their names from the founders, and their faces may also be modelled on them.) Right and left on the reverse side are the Scourging of Christ and the Bearing of the Cross. The story of this remarkable altar and the reasons behind its iconography have not yet been clearly established. The late Gothic frescos in the nave (from around 1420) and the choir (around 1509) depict, among other things, the Madonna, the Apostles and the auxiliary saints. The wood-carving in the church is also of note: the cross altar in the S. chapel has a Christ on the Cross from 1515, and three crowning figures which are the remains of a late Gothic altar of 1520, formerly on the N. wall of the nave, and the choir has a remarkable relief of the Mount of Olives. The 17&18C baroque redecoration is only evident in paintings and the two carved statues of St.Peter and St.Paul over the offertory portals of the high altar. The late Gothic wrought-iron lock on the S. portal is a remarkable example of the medieval attitude to this craft.

Schloss Trabuschgen (N. of the village): This is a three-storey building established during the late Gothic period and converted into a baroque Schloss between the 15C and the 18C; it is now a hotel. The ceilings and panels of the interior were painted by J.F.Fromiller.

Oberwart 7400
Burgenland   p.280□V

Place names ending in 'wart' refer to the old border guard settlements; the citizens of these towns had certain obligations, and also certain privileges. One section of the extensive town has old farms with beautiful arcades, and the picturesque Calvinist church, priest's house and outbuildings make an attractive ensemble around a garden. The Rathaus is neoclassical. A striking feature is the Catholic parish centre with its huge flight of steps leading up to the old baroque parish church. To the right is the new church, and to the left the social centre, a huge and imposing building in concrete.

Environs: Stegersbach (28 km. to the S. of Oberwart, down the main road): Its old name was 'Stegraifebach' (Stegraif = stirrup), referring to the 'border watch' and the town's significance in the old system of guarding the border. The Neue Pfarrkirche St.U MAgydius (1974) is based on the idea of a 'spiral to God'; the spiral design symbolises the stairway to heaven. It is an impressive and highly unusual construction, and was erected by the 'Team 3 P' Anton, Egon and Eva Presoly. The Batthyanysches Schloss is a two-storey building with fine arcades, now a Landschaftsmuseum for S. Burgenland (geology, fauna, flora, history and local customs). **Markt Allhau** (about 12 km. W.): This Protestant parish church is a late-18C classical building with an interesting high altar which incorporates the pulpit and the organ and dates from 1795. **Rotenturm an der Pinka** (c. 4 km. downstream of

Oberwart): This is the site of an old moated castle; the new castle was built in 1860–62, a romantic building using Moorish design and including a magnificent staircase.

Oberwölz 8832
Steiermark   p.282□P 9

This area has yielded finds from the Hallstatt period from 1000–800 BC. In 1007 it was given to the diocese of Freising by Emperor Heinrich II; in 1256 it was mentioned as being a market and in 1305 a town; and in 1317 a city wall was built and it became the fortress of the Freisinger Kammergut. The medieval fortifications have survived to a lrge extent: three of the five gates are still standing, as well as two towers.

Stadtpfarrkirche St.Martin: This is a pillared Romanesque basilica with a nave and two aisles; it has a mighty E. tower, and was consecrated in 1280. The choir is late Gothic, and there is an early Gothic chapel in the S. aisle and a 15C Gothic vestibule. The frescos were painted by J.A.von Mölk in 1777 to replace the Gothic net vault. The south exterior wall has a 'Last Judgement' of 1500. There is a baroque high altar, and an 18C rosary- and Joseph altar of the Judenburg school.

Filialkirche hl.Sigismund: This was first mentioned as a hospital chapel in 1360, and some parts of the choir originate from this period. Long choir, hall with two aisles, and a three-aisled gallery with ashlar balustrade. There is a spiral staircase leading up to the organ gallery, with six Station of the Cross pictures by Johann Lederwasch.

Rothenfels Castle: This was the seat of the Freising administrator until 1805; despite much renovation, its character has been well preserved.

Environs: Zeiring. *Oberzeiring:* This

Burg Rothenfels, Oberwölz

became a market in 1284, and the parish church of St.Nikolaus was built in 1365. An interesting cycle of frescos dating from 1340 – 50 was found in the 12C former graveyard chapel (which was once a squires' chapel). **Unterzeiring:** To the N. of *Schloss Hanfelden* (which in its current form dates from 1508) is the priory, which dates from 1074 and was a gift to the abbey of Admont. Inside it is the St.Agatha Chapel, which was built in 1424. **St. Oswald:** Late Gothic hall church with two aisles and 15C stellar vaulting. To the E. of Oberwölz is *Baierdorf*, which has a defensive tower in good condition.

Oetz 6433
Tirol   p.286☐E 9

This village was known in the 12C, and contains some attractive houses with fine façade painting, such as the Gasthof Stern, with frescos dating from 1573 and 1615.

Pfarrkirche hl.Georg und hl.Nikolaus:

This is a very beautiful church on a steep cliff with an *Unterkirche*, the *Michaelskappelle*, which is situated under the present choir and was originally built in the 14C. (Under restoration at the time of writing.) It includes Gothic ribs and articulated tunnel vaulting. The *Engelaltar* by Ignaz Waibl is interesting, and dates from 1683. The *Oberkirche* was built in 1660 and has three Gothic portals; it was renovated in baroque style in 1745. The fine rococo stucco is interesting, and so is the Gothic altar opposite the pulpit. The baroque St. Kassian and St. Nikolaus are by the sculptor Hans Reindl, who also made the side-altar statues. The *sacristy* contains a fine baroque crucifix, and the tower houses a *memorial chapel* and *ossuary*.

Environs: Umhausen: The *Pfarrkirche hl.Vitus* was built in 1482 in one of the earliest sections of the Oetz valley to be settled. It was renovated in 1682 and 1771, but still has a fine late Gothic portal and the mainly neo-Gothic interior furnishings include one of the finest crucifixes in the Tyrol, which dates from 1580.

Oberwölz, left: Spitalskirche with Hintereggertor, right: Baierdorf, fortified tower

Ossiach 9570
Kärnten   p.282☐O 11

The history of the Benedictine monastery in Ossiach began in pre-Romanesque times and was at its most eventful in the 15&16C (Turkish invasion 1484, visit of Emperor Charles V in 1552); after the long baroque period of monastery politics it was abolished by imperial decree in 1783.

Pfarr- and former Stiftskirche Maria Himmelfahrt: This pillared basilica is Romanesque in origin, dating from 1028, but was altered in the late 15C and reconsecrated in 1500, before being further renovated in the late baroque style in 1737–44. The N. exterior wall bears the epitaph of the Polish king Boleslaus II, which is said to have been brought to the monastery at Ossiach by the Archbishop of Krakow, who after the king's death spent his last years here as a silent penitent. The choir has three apses and is situated behind the crossing tower; it dates from the Romanesque period. The *interior* is decorated with baroque stucco and allegorical paintings by J.F.Fromiller, whose work can be seen on the vaulting and on the walls, and dates from 1750. The architecture of the church is continued artificially in the painting on the ceiling over the choir (God the Father in a wreath of angels). There are three Corinthian columns (the fourth is Gothic), which are the oldest part of the church; they originally stood in the crypt, but the restoration work of 1974 saw them moved to form supports for the steps up to the organ gallery. The *late Gothic triptych* dating from around 1510 is also interesting; it is located in the NW chapel, and is from the wood-carving school of St.Veit. The three-dimensional carvings include a Madonna and Child between St. Margaret and St. Katharine, and the 12 Apostles in relief on the inner wings, with polychrome scenes of Christ and Mary on the outside.

Abbey building: This is a two- and three-storey monastery complex to the SW of the church; it was built 1622–28, extended 1741–49 and thoroughly restored in 1960.

Oetz, Gasthof zum Stern

The wall and ceiling paintings are by J.F. Fromiller.

Ottenstein = Rastenfeld 3532
Lower Austria   p.278 □ S 3

Castle: In 1178 Hugo von Ottenstein was the lord of this castle, in 1266 Hadmar II Asinus (the ass of Ottenstein, a nickname referring to pious humility). In 1360 one Albero von Ottenstein was the master of the kitchen to Duke Rudolf IV. The castle changed hands on a number of occasions and was frequently destroyed and rebuilt; in the 16C it became the property of the Stodoligks, who built the 'Stöckl', the second gate, in 1530. The Lambergs occupied the castle and kept it for the next 400 years, extending it and starting an art collection (which formed the basis of the

Viennese Akademie der Bildende Künste). Behind the outbuildings, which include a gatehouse, are a moat and the 'Stöckl' with a round tower (embrasure and coats-of-arms of the Lambergs). There is a stone bridge over the castle moat leading to the second gatehouse; irregular courtyard with fountains. The *keep* has a staircase dating from 1200, and the *castle chapel* is a square building with groined vaulting and an apse dating from 1177. There are unusually arranged frescos on the walls: Christ in the Mandorla in the apse, with six-winged cherubim on each side; in the centre of the vault the Lamb, Ezekiel and Isaiah. On the panels Resurrection, the women at the tomb, Christ in Purgatory and the entry into Jerusalem. In the spandrels are Intelligence, Moderation, Strength and Justice. The four rivers of paradise in greenish-blue.

Ossiach, Pfarrkirche

Ossiach, fresco in the Pfarrkirche

Paternion 9711
Kärnten   p.282□N 11

Pfarrkirche hl. Paternianus: Although the church has a Gothic core (the former choir was incorporated as an E. side chapel), it should still be regarded as a baroque reconstruction, with work being completed in 1676. The nave has three bays, and there are side chapels and flat cell vaulting. The interior decorations are mainly late baroque (according to the parish chronicle, they were altered in baroque style in 1765). Note the late Gothic console figure of St.Paternianus which has been reworked in baroque style and stands to the right of the high altar.

Schloss: This building dates from the late Gothic period, was in the possession of the Dietrichstein and Ortenburg families, and today belongs to the Foscari Widmann Rezzonico family. The W. section, with its chapel, dates back to the oldest phase of construction.

Perchtoldsdorf 2380
Lower Austria   p.278□V 5

Perchtoldsdorf was founded by the

Babenbergs. The town became famous because of the 'massacre of Perchtoldsdorf' during the Turkish siege of 1683. The Turks promised the 'accursed Giaurs' a safe passage. They surrendered their weapons and collected 100 ducats for the mediator. The soldiers then drew their sabres and cut them down.

Pfarrkirche hl. Augustinus: A Gothic hall church. A Viennese-style choir with two aisles and a five-sided apse replaced the three apses in 1340. The middle apse is above a lower church. The short nave is a hall structure with three bays and a stellar vault. The free-standing *tower*, 148 ft. tall, dates from the 1st half of the 15C and is built as a defensive tower with a well and a chapel with stellar vaults.

Also worth seeing: *Castle:* An old ducal castle (*c.* 1340) with an ossuary and the *Martinskapelle* (1514). Only vestiges still survive of the old core of the building. The *Rathaus* with a Gothic oriel (late-15C) and arcaded courtyard.

Perg 4320
Upper Austria   p.276□Q 4/5

The lords of Perg, who were related to the

Machländs (see Baumgartenberg), were one of the province's famous families. They died out with Friedrich von Perg, who fell in 1191 in Antioch during the Third Crusade. From the 14C onwards it was the main town of the millstone industry and it declined in the late 19C owing to the manufacture of artificial stones. The market dates from 1269, a town since 1969. Pretty houses, especially 1 Herrenstrasse, the 'Seifensiederhaus', with stucco and window frames. A pillory dating from 1683.

Pfarrkirche hl. Jakobus d. Ä.: The choir is from 1416, and the nave is a hall structure (one nave, two aisles) dating from *c.* 1500. There are richly carved capitals and keystones with foliage in the choir, and on the S. wall is a fine session niche.

Kalvarienberg-Kapelle: This centrally planned building standing on rising ground has a dome and an elliptical ground plan. The sacristy is semicircular. A good Crucifixion, 1729, originally in the open air.

Environs: Altenburg bei Windhaag (6 km. NE): *Filialkirche St.Bartholomäus.* A church surrounded by a wall and standing in an attractive hilly location on the site of a 12C castle. In 1512, Lasla Prager from Pragthal (see Mauthausen) ordered the St. -Anna-Kapelle, with the crypt underneath it, to be added to this Romanesque-Gothic building; intending to use it as the family's burial site. The frescos in the small crypt are excellent examples of the 'Danube school' and, with their astonishingly good state of preservation, are of great artistic importance. Last Judgement and patron saints of the founders. The key is obtainable from the house next door. There is no lighting. **Schloss Schwertberg** (about 6 km. NW): This developed from an old moated castle. Its present form is the result of early-17C alterations by A.Canevale. No visits possible. **Mauthausen** (on the left bank of the Danube, opposite the mouth of the Enns): First mentioned in 1208 as 'Muthusen', i.e. the houses at the toll post which the Babenbergs had built for the river Enns. *Pfarrkirche St.Nikolaus.* A two-aisled Gothic hall church with an extra aisle in the W. bay. The high altar dating from 1708 has a set of alternating pictures by M.J. Schmidt for the different church feasts. *Karner hl. Barbara:* This late-13C ossuary has the remains of wall paintings from the time of its building. Alleyways with flying buttresses, pretty façades. Note the 'Lebzelter-Haus' on the Donaulände. *Schloss Pragstein,* originally on a rocky island. Built by Lasla Prager in 1491 (see Altenburg near Perg) in order to dominate the crossing; a block-like building, tapering to a keel-like point facing upstream, forming a breakwater. A pillory with flat ornaments dating from 1583. *Heimatmuseum im Schloss Pragstein:* Primeval history, local history, lighting, shipping.

Pernegg = Hötzelsdorf 3753
Lower Austria   p.278□T 3

Former Prämonstratenserstift: The remains of the castle of the counts of Pernegg, whose last descendant died in the 13C when of unsound mind, stand on a keel-shaped rock parallel to the Mödringer Graben rift valley. In 1153, a Countess of Pernegg founded a Premonstratensian convent which continued until 1858. The church and convent were taken over by Geras and used as an external benefice. From the 19C onwards this was a summer boarding-school, in 1939 it was a National Labour Service camp, and today it is a charitable holiday home.

Perchtoldsdorf, fortified tower

Former Stiftskirche/Pfarrkirche hl. Andreas: This church built in 1586 is one of the finest churches in the Waldviertel. It has a splendid site on a wooded hilltop in the middle of the graveyard, and is surrounded by a defensive wall with round towers; a massive diagonally set W. tower dating from 1635. In the NE is a *round ossuary* with an early Gothic waterspout and a small choir. A baroque N. portal dating from 1735, and to the left of it is a statue of St. Andrew with a metal cross. The *interior* is a wonderful mixture of late Gothic, Renaissance and baroque. Large traceried windows lend the nave the brightness of baroque. Ambulatory galleries between projecting pilasters, including baroque altar niches with rich garlands of fruit (the wonderful harmony is unfortunately disturbed by architectural 'uncoverings'). A double nuns' choir to the W., and below this is a small chapel in a tower. In the stellar vault there are four angels with a harp, an organ, trombone and trumpet between Church Fathers with scrolls and symbols of the Evangelists. A splendid large Christ on the Cross, 1580,

Pernegg, stellar vault

is seen at the modern high altar. *Pfarrhof* The attractive parsonage has suffered much from secularization. *Prälatenkapelle* with frescos and rich stucco. Man of Sorrows with original paint (1515); beautiful white Pietà (1600).

Persenbeug 3680
Lower Austria   p.278☐R 5

The German settlement of Persinpingun is mentioned as early as 863. Ybbs, on the opposite bank of the Danube, and Persenbeug are jointly mentioned in 1096. In 1617 major rebuilding was carried out under Count Eusebius of Hoyos. Emperor Franz II purchased the schloss in 1800. Today it is owned by the Salvator family. Emperor Karl was born here in 1887.

Schloss: A large statue of St. John of Nepomuk stands in a rotunda. The schloss has a steep Danube front, with living apartments. The road follows the old moat and passes through a gate tower with a tunnel-vaulted passage into an elongated forecourt, from which another gate (1620) opens into the inner courtyard with its fine fountain. There is a baroque wrought-iron gate at the entrance to the *Schlosskapelle;* a single-aisled chapel dating from 1620 whose choir projects beyond the schloss façade. A fine Renaissance pulpit; the lower church has a Pietà dating from 1621. There is a massive keep on a rock above the Danube.

Also worth seeing: The town contains original *Biedermeier houses* and the Kleines and Grosses Schiffsmeisterhäuser (small and large shipmasters' houses). *Pfarrkirche hll. Florian und Maximilian:* A heavy building with a W. tower. The high altar is of polychrome marble; large net-vaulted choir. Three late Gothic sculptures (St. Catherine, 1430, and Ecce Homo from about the same period; Virgin Mary dating from 1530).

Petronell 2404
Lower Austria   p.278☐X 5

Carnuntum: The Romans under the Emperor Augustus occupied Noricum and the Danube became a fortified border. In AD 14, Carnuntum on the Bernsteinstrasse became their largest garrison, with a civilian town and an amphitheatre, surrounded by a 490 ft. wide strip which was clear of buildings. There were fine houses with heating, channels, water pipe, frescos and glass. Marcus Aurelius (121–180) had his headquarters in Carnuntum during the wars with the Marcomanni, and it was here that he wrote his 'Reflections'. His son Commodus built the second amphitheatre in *c.* 200. It has seats for 13,000 (the arena is 500 ft. x 225 ft.). Gladiator fights were held to organ music: the dead and the corpses of the animals were thrown into the Danube from a death chamber. In *c.* 350, a triumphal arch (the *heroes' gate*) was erected for Emperor Constantine at the edge of the civilian town. The valuable finds are displayed in the *museums* of Petronell and Bad Deutsch Altenburg (*Freilichtmuseum* [open-air museum] in Carnuntum). The Quadi (a West Germanic tribe who migrated to Spain with the Vandals) were conquered by the Romans in *c.* 350. In 433, Huns occupied the area. The Vohburg-Cham had estates here in *c.* 1000. They were faithful vassals of Emperor Henry III. In 1085, his widow, Agnes of Poitiers (when on the way to Hungary to the wedding of her daughter Judith) gave them Carnuntum in fee. In 1189, during the Crusade, Barbarossa had to wait here for the Hungarian king to grant permission for his passage. The country had become so empty of people after the Turkish wars that Croats were settled here. In 1574, there were 32 Croatian families here as against 28 German ones. In about 1700 the Kuruzi invaded (these were Hungarians hostile to the Habsburgs and incited by Rákóczi); as cruel as the Turks, they were called 'K(u)ruzitürken' (Kuruzi Turks).

Petronell, Heidentor

Pfarrkirche hl. Petronilla: This single-aisled church has a straight, square choir (round-arched frieze) and a Romanesque triumphal arch. The choir has groin vaulting. The S. chapel is 14C.

Rundkapelle hl. Johannes der Täufer: The ground plan of this church built in 1200 consists of two intersecting circles and it is a unique combination of two Romanesque chapels. The ashlar walls are articulated by 18 three-quarter columns. The windows were enlarged in the baroque period. A boy-like Christ being baptized by John appears in the tympanum of the recessed portal. Kranichberg tomb cover; burial place of the Abensberg Traun family.

Schloss: 1637 (date on the tower clock). Similar to Hungarian examples; fine inner courtyard with a fountain. In the central section, a double staircase leads up to the main floor. The tower with its canopy above the portal occupies the central bay. Frescos by Tencala (cf. Palais Lobkowitz in Vienna) in the Rittersaal (knights' hall).

Piber = Köflach 8580
Steiermark   p.282 □ R 9

Pfarrkirche hl. Andreas: This is one of the oldest parishes in the region and the parish church dates back to the early 13C. The original flat roof was replaced by net vaults in the 16C. Semicircular apse; octagonal crypt; the present sacristy was originally a 14C chapel. There is a tower with a baroque onion dome; the decorations are 18C. On the outside are the remains of fortifications (tavern) from the time of the Turkish invasions.

Schloss: A square building with three-storeyed arcades in the style of D. Sciassia. Today it is a Lipizzaner stud (Spanish Riding School, Vienna).

Pill = Schwaz 6130
Tirol   p.284 □ G 8

Pfarrkirche St. Anna: This church built

Pill with St. Anna

in 1516 was altered in baroque style in the 18C, decorated in neo-Gothic manner in the 19C, and restored in 1931 and 1972. It contains a late Gothic choir, vaulted frescos dating from 1750 by Christof Anton May from Schwaz, a Gothic St.Anne with the Madonna and Child (1520), and a painted wooden memorial from 1587.

Hl.-Kreuz-Kirche: This pilgrimage church is beautifully situated E. of Pill. At the main altar is the miraculous image, a baroque crucifix which is said to have originally been thrown into the river Inn by Bavarian soldiers, and was rescued at this spot. This decidedly beautiful, small, centrally-planned church dating from the late rococo was built by Joh. Michael Umhauser in 1764–6 to plans by Franz de Paula Penz. There are frescos by Chr. A. Mayr dating from 1767.

Plessnitz = Kremsbrücke 9862
Kärnten   p.282☐N 10

Filialkirche hl. Johannes d. T.: This

Pöchlarn on the Danube

small church is documented as existing in 1465. The groin-vaulted choir is separated from the flat-roofed nave by a pointed triumphal arch. Late Gothic stencil painting (1513) in the W. gallery. The high altar includes fragments of a late Gothic winged altar. The pulpit and side altar are late baroque (1730).

Pöchlarn 3380
Lower Austria   p.278☐S 5

Once the Roman border fort of Arelape, it was here that Rüdiger von Bechelaren hospitably received the Burgundians passing through to Etzel's court. Giselher, the brother of King Gunther, became betrothed to Rüdiger's daughter. Pöchlarn was completely burned down on 29 March 1766. Only some towers and the remains of the town wall survived the conflagration.

Pfarrkirche Maria Himmelfahrt: Built in *c.* 1400, and rebuilt in baroque style after 1766. There are Roman tombstones in the

church wall. The late Gothic choir has a fine altarpiece on the high altar by J.M. Schmidt of Krems. The former *ossuary* (1429) is S. of the church.

Also worth seeing: *Schloss:* At one time a moated castle, in 1576, David von Höch, Bishop of Regensburg, rebuilt it. Oskar Kokoschka was born in a house on the Donaulände on 1 March 1886.

Pöggstall 3650

Lower Austria   p.278☐S 4

In 1135, the daughter of the warden of the Dom in Regensburg presented 'Pechtal' to the Kremsmünster monastery. Work on building the castle was begun by the Maissaus in the 13C, and continued by the Rogendorfs in 1521. The 'Messerer Gericht', a settlement around the ironworks which processed pig iron from Steyr, was built in 1629. The town adopted Protestantism, but reverted to Catholicism in 1659.

Pfarrkirche hl. Anna (in the Schloss): This is the former Schlosskapelle dating from 1480. A late Gothic hall church with two aisles; delicate net vaulting. A late Gothic high altar with a double wing dating from 1480 (in the middle shrine: St. Anne with the Madonna and Child; above them is a Crucifixion dating from 1500; panels with Saints and scenes from the Passion). Choir stalls with pointed arches bearing the date 1492. The windows are from 1415. Side altar: Madonna and Child, 1500 (founders holding the horns of the moon). The rich late Gothic galleries contain coats-of-arms of the Rogendorfs. Memorial stone and tombs.

Schloss Rogendorf: On the S. side there are barbicans (outworks which defend the drawbridge gate, 165 ft. in diameter) which were designed to cope with firearms. At the side is a long vaulted vehicle entrance leading into the polygonal main courtyard where there are two storeys of broad arcades on pillars. On the left a Renaissance portal precedes the stairwell with its Gothic spiral staircase. Keep with torture

Pöllau, former Stiftskirche St. Veit

chamber. A magnificent fortified structure.

St. Anna im Feld: Outside the town, in the graveyard. A hall church with a nave and two aisles dating from 1400. There are frescos in the choir. A Gothic tower visible from afar. The building has been restored in recent years after suffering a fire in 1810 and falling into disrepair. Tombstones of the Rogendorfs.

Pöllau bei Hartberg 8225
Steiermark   p.280□T/U 8

Former Stiftskirche St. Veit: This was built in 1701–12 to a design by J. Carlone from Graz. The church is a splendidly successful example of the Styrian high baroque, which was influenced by Roman models. The imitation of St. Peter's becomes especially clear in the ground plan (with the semicircular apses of the transepts and choir) and in the dome (high drum with eight windows), and also in the tunnel vaulting of the nave. The severe ar-

Pöllauberg, Wallfahrtskirche

ticulation is relieved by galleried side chapels. The colourful *vault* and *dome frescos* by M. von Görz also betray Roman inspiration, especially in so far as their trompe l'oeil features are concerned: four Church Fathers and two Augustinian Saints, and also the twelve Apostles, are seen amidst the false architecture; the Virgin and St. Augustine in the exedra; Ascension of St. Vitus; in the tunnel vault we see the Adoration of the Cross, of the Lamb and of the Immaculata; in the dome there is a jubilant choir of angels. The original trompe l'oeil painting of the altars is now partly covered by altarpieces. Note the altarpiece by J.C. Hackhofer (1722) in the left transept (statues by M. Schokotnigg, 1722); the 2nd side chapel on the left has an altarpiece by J.A. von Mölk (1778); 'Crucifixion' by Altomonte (1725, in the 3rd side chapel). Altarpieces by M. Görz: 2nd and 3rd side chapels on the right. The St. Vitus at the high altar is attributed to J.A. Mölk.

Stiftsgebäude: Only the moat and parts of the outer walls still survive from the old moated castle. The W. section of the 1st courtyard is a remnant from the Middle Ages. The N. section with its two octagonal towers was built in the 17C; the central section being added somewhat later. After the old Veitskirche had been torn down, a sacristy was erected on this site and decorated with ceiling frescos by M. Görz. The *library* (today a community hall) has a fresco by A. Maderni (1699).

Pöllauberg = 8225 Pöllau bei Hartberg
Steiermark   p.280□U 8

Wallfahrtskirche: Built on a steep mountain in the 14C, this is one of the most unorthodoxly arranged of the Styrian Gothic churches. There are two aisles (three bays, groin vault), while the choir, supported by three pillars, expands into three aisles, as does the W. narthex Another unusual feature is the lavish decoration (rich tracery on several storeys) of the façade portal. The *interior decorations* are equally interesting: elegant engaged shafts (with filigreed brackets and traceried pinacles). The apse of the choir is particularly richly decorated with blind arcades and an arched baldacchino; Symbols of the Evangelists on the capitals. The massive *high altar* (by the Schokotnigg brothers, 1710–30) and the richly stuccoed *organ loft* (organ, 1684) are fine baroque items. There is a statue of the Virgin on the central pillar (1616), and there is also a Gothic statue of the Virgin, a 15C miraculous image.

Pörtschach am Wörther See 9210
Kärnten   p.282□O 11

Schloss Leonstein: The core of this two-storeyed building dates back to the 16C. The small Renaissance-style inner courtyard is worth seeing. Nearby are the *castle ruins,* the former seat of the Leonsteins, which was mentioned in a document of 1166 and was already in ruins in the 17C. *Pfarrkirche hl. Johannes d. T.:* This modern church is of the post-baroque period and was given its present form in the early 20C.

Pottenbrunn 3140
Lower Austria   p.278□T 5

Schloss: An old 16C moated castle with an originally Romanesque keep to which a gallery with stone balustrades and arcades was added in the Renaissance. A similar gallery was also added to the double-gabled main building at that time. The Schloss was severely damaged in 1945. It was rebuilt and set up as a *tin-figure museum* exhibiting interesting battle scenes (35,000 figures).

Pottendorf 2486
Lower Austria   p.278□V 6

A man named Poto was the brother of the Bavarian Count Palatine Aribo, who fought the Hungarians in *c.* 1050. In 1606, the Counts of Zinzendorf built this moated Schloss on the site of an earlier building. L. von Hildebrandt built the church in 1714 under Count Gundacker von Starhemberg. The Pottendorf spinning mills have been here since 1784.

Pfarrkirche hl. Jakob: The façade has three storeys: the portal pavilion, above this is the gable structure, and the crowning feature is the church tower with its baroque dome (rebuilt in late baroque style in 1769). At the high altar is a painting by Peter Strudel of St. James being borne by angels; the oratory has a late baroque Madonna with a sleeping infant Christ.

Schloss: A rectangular courtyard and three medieval towers. The chapel was damaged in the war and is now a ruin. Frescos (1400); tombstones of the Pottendorfs.

Prutz 6522
Tirol   p.286□D 9

Pfarrkirche Mariae Himmelfahrt: The only features surviving from the original 11C church are on the tower. The present church was built in 1521 and was later altered in baroque style. It was restored in 1877, when it was given some neo-Gothic decorations. The pulpit and high altar are baroque. The late Gothic *Antoniuskapelle* was added to the N. in 1676.

Totenkapelle: There is a double chapel in the graveyard. The small rococo church of St. Philomena has frescos dating from 1350 on the entrance front and inside there are 18C stuccoes. The actual Totenkapelle (burial chapel) adjoins the church to the N. and contains a Pietà dating from 1500 and a wooden memorial (1586).

Also worth seeing: The 14C *Oberer Turm* (upper tower; in the town), the 17C *Unterer Turm*, and the *Gasthof Gemse* (hotel).

Pulkau 3741

Lower Austria   p.278☐U 3

In 1158, Duke Heinrich II presented Pulkau to the Scottish monastery in Vienna as an endowment. A miracle of the Host has come down to us, dating from 1338. Some Jews from the town obtained a Host in which the rabbi pierced a hole. Blood flowed from the damaged section, and the frightened Jews threw the Host into the well in the rabbi's house. The water turned red; the Jews tried to feed the Host to some pigs, which collapsed to their knees and screamed. This story came to the ears of Pope Benedict XII in Avignon via the Duke. Jews were burned to death in a wave of anti-semitic hysteria which flared up everywhere. In 1396 Pope Boniface IX granted permission to build a church which was never completed.

Pfarrkirche hl. Michael: This church stands on the hill in the middle of the graveyard. The basic structure of the E. tower is early Romanesque, and is similar to that of Oberranna. The hall of the church is of protracted length, and beautifully articulated: Gothic arcades on a Romanesque wall. The capitals have leaf and animal ornament. There is a frescoed niche for the sacrament (St. Catherine, *c.* 1320); baroque alterations, 1674.

Ossuary: Dedicated to St. Bartholomew (1260). A two-storeyed round building with a cylindrical substructure, stone spire. Water-spouts at the base of the pointed gables and figures (the lazy mason) at the top. Inside there is an eight part vault. A four-part apse with a triumphal arch.

Heiligblutkirche: The focal point of the church (building permission was granted in 1396 by Pope Boniface IX) is the well (filled up with earth in 1786) of the rabbi's house. The church is a torso: a transept adjoins the three bays of the choir. Above the transept is a late Gothic gallery. The large *winged altar* by J. Breu is a masterpiece of the Danube school. Christ with St. Sebastian and St. Bartholomew (the patron saints of well and vine-growers) is seen in the shrine beneath tabernacles. On the wings of the predella: Christ's Entry into Jerusalem, the Deposition; Last Supper

Pulkau, Romanesque ossuary

and Entombment. Inside: Desecration of the Host (in the Last Supper there is a self-portrait of Breu, with three companions).

Purbach am Neusiedlersee 7083
Burgenland   p.278☐W 6

The market is encircled by a wall which survives almost in its entirety. Entrance is gained through three gates, some with a barbican. The farm buildings face outwards and are incorporated in the fortifications, forming the 'defensive frontage of barns' that is a feature of Purbach. The high altar of the baroque *Pfarrkirche* has an image of St.Nicholas, the patron Saint. Attractive houses, including the *Nikolauszeche*. The Purbach landmark is the *Purbacher Türke*, the stone bust of a Turk on a chimney. Legend has it that this Turk, after consuming wine in abundance, failed to make his retreat, became a Christian, and stayed in Purbach until his death.

Environs: Breitenbrunn (5 km. N., on the lake): The stately fortified tower has a pointed helm roof with four small columns. It houses an *Ortsmuseum* (local museum). *Pfarrkirche*, with excellent rococo decorations. The key is at the Pfarramt (rectory). Typical alleyways between houses with cellars. **Donnerskirchen** (5 km. S., on the lake): The market place extends from the lake towards the slopes of the Leithagebirge. The baroque *Pfarrkirche St.Martin* occupies a dominating site above the town. Roman finds, today in the Landesmuseum, suggest that there was an early Christian church which must be one of the oldest in Austria. There is a particularly interesting *wayside shrine with a mercy seat* in the group of trees beside the fire station. Its image of God the Father displays conspicuously eastern features.

Pürgg 8981
Steiermark   p.282☐O 7

Pfarrkirche hl. Georg: Romanesque basilica with massive W. tower (consecrated in 1130?). Inside, the nave has a net vault, while the two aisles have groin vaulting. Romanesque tower and doorway with 13C mountings. *Frescos* (*c.* 1300) of the legend of St.Catherine and scenes from the Passion have been uncovered in the bell tower. Late Gothic gallery with a stone bust (imitation relief) of the chancellor Konrad Zeidler (1442). At the altar in the gallery are a Lamentation and two painted 16C wings. The figures are 15C. The high altar is 14C. The right-hand window in the choir has stained glass from the same period. Numerous red marble tombstones (15&16C).

St.-Johannes-Kapelle (to the S., outside the town): This is especially worth seeing for its excellent and very early *frescos*, which were painted before 1200 at about the time of the Crusades. A hall with six windows, and a square choir. The frescos depict the following scenes: At the bottom of the N. wall: 'Feeding of the Five Thousand'; on the S. wall: 'Nativity', 'Joseph's Dream'. The Wise and Foolish Virgins are depicted on the upper strip. A figure of the devil, and the fable of the cat and the mice, are seen below the former wooden gallery. Lay and clerical founders are depicted on the wall of the triumphal arch, with Cain and Abel above them. In the choir: the Lamb of God, surrounded by symbols of the Evangelists. Personifications of the four worlds are seen in the spandrels. A 13C Romanesque *crucifix* on the altar.

Pürgg, parish church ▷

Raabs an der Thaya 3820

Lower Austria

p.278☐S 2

Schloss Raabs: The Counts of Raabs came from Nuremberg and founded the early castle of Castrum Rakoucz on a steep crag. This became the centre of a county as forests were felled at the confluence of the German and Moravian Thaya rivers. The male side of the family died out in 1192. One daughter married Friedrich von Zollern and became the ancestor of the Brandenburgs. The younger daughter married a Count of Hirschberg in the Upper Palatinate. The imperial county fell to the Habsburgs in the 13C, and Duke Rudolf IV styled himself Count of Raabs, among other titles. After much feuding and damage in battle, the castle passed to the barons of Bartenstein in 1760. It fell into disrepair and frequently changed owners. In recent years it has been in Swiss hands (there is a restaurant).

The outer castle is entered from the W. A stone bridge leads over a deep moat into an early tower with a gatehouse. The pentagonal Gothic keep forms part of the 17C residential section. In the second courtyard there is an arcade and also the oldest section of the castle, with a flat-roofed chapel.

Pfarrkirche Mariae Himmelfahrt (in Oberndorf): Originally a Romanesque basilica with a nave, two aisles, and no vaulting (the parish was founded in 1189). The choir dates from *c*. 1300. Greatly expanded in the 15C. Note the early neoclassical decoration (1774). Madonna (1480) and tombstones, including that of Jörg von Puchheim (1458).

Radkersburg 8490

Steiermark

p.280☐U 11

This was built in the 12C as a settlement associated with the castle situated on the E. spurs of the Windische Büheln. The castle which formerly belonged to the Oberradker lords passed to the Eggenberg family in 1623, and today it is in Yugoslavia.

Stadtpfarrkirche St.Johann d. T.: The present church, with its late Gothic main portal, dates back to the 15C. The W. tower has arrow slits and was fortified. Inside, the 16C altarpiece is by Alois Bogner. There is an impressive late Gothic crucifix in the right aisle. The other decorations date from the late 18C and 19C. Tombstones.

Schloss Raabs a. d. Thaya ▷

Also worth seeing: *Filialkirche Mariahilf:* Rebuilt in 1643, using a medieval chapel. A massive square tower with pilasters and onion dome. The centre of the town is the *Hauptplatz* (main square) with the *Rathaus* (late Gothic octagonal clock tower, rebuilt in 1806), the *Pestsäule* (plague column; 1680) and No. 9, the family house of the Princes of Eggenberg, 2nd half of the 16C. Palace, and town houses.

Radstadt 5550

Salzburg   p.282☐M 8

Between 1270 and 1286 (see Altenmarkt), the old town of Radstadt was moved from the Ennsniederung valley to a ridge above the Ennstal. The purpose of this was to secure the border with the Austrian Steiermark. The status of a town was conferred on the new Radstadt in 1289, and it was the only town of the historic Salzburg mountain territory to receive this status. It was first besieged in 1296 in a war between the archbishops of Salzburg and Duke Albrecht I. This war revolved around the claims to the lands of the newly founded town, which belonged to Admont monastery. Radstadt successfully withstood this two-month siege, and also another siege by rebellious peasants from 14 April to 2 July 1526. The great judgment upon the rebellious peasants was held outside the town on 11 July 1526. Radstadt has remained a small town despite its good communications. The town's most famous son is Paul Hofhaimer (1459–1530), a composer and organ virtuoso who was the court organist of Emperor Maximilian I.

The Town: The regular rows of houses are a survival of the ordered late-13C layout, even though the houses have been rebuilt several times following fires. Most of the medieval town wall has also survived, forming a rectangle whose long sides curve outwards. The three conspicuous round towers which survive at the corners date from around 1530. The Oberes Tor, or Salzburger Tor, a gate on the narrow W. side, was torn down in the 19C, while its counterpart, the Steyrer Tor on the E. side, is still standing and, following enlargement, is now a house.

Stadtpfarrkirche Mariä Himmelfahrt: The town church is situated away from the narrow rectangular Stadtplatz and immediately beside the N. flank of the town wall; such a position was in keeping with late-13C town planning. The basilican structure, with its nave and two aisles, dates from the early 14C, while the elongated Gothic choir is early 15C. The church lost much of its character as a result of the historicizing rebuilding of the town after the fire of 1857. The N. tower, contemporary with the nave, has strong Romanesque features. The *Schustersäule* (cobbler's column), a late Gothic lantern tower built of tufa and dating from 1513, is in the *graveyard*.

Environs: *Schloss Tantalier,* W. of Radstadt; is one of the typical country houses which arose in the Salzburg region in the 16C with the enlargement of manor houses. The Salzberg manor house was enlarged in 1569, when extra floors and corner towers were added. **Obertauern:** A small church standing a little way below the head of the Tauern mountain pass which was used by the Romans, as is indicated by the way station called 'In Alpe' on the Tabula Peutingeriana and by numerous Roman milestones still surviving along the road. Parts of the present road follow the course of the ancient road. The old church was built in 1619 to a plan by Santino Solari, the architect of the Dom in Salzburg. The altarpiece, which is by Arsenio Mascagni (*c.* 1620), depicts 'Peter in Chains'; the church is dedicated to St. Peter. The church has been enlarged in modern style.

Radkersburg, Pfarrkirche

Raiding, house where Liszt was born

Raiding = Lackendorf 7321
Burgenland   p.280□W 7

On 22 October 1811, a son was born in the Esterházysches Wirtschaftsgebäude to the manager of the prince's sheep farm. The son was later to become world-famous: he was Franz Liszt. Prince Paul Esterházy presented the building to the community as a gift in 1971, and today it contains a memorial. There is another Liszt memorial room in the Landesmuseum.

Environs: Deutschkreutz (*c.* 12 km. E.): This once important schloss was badly damaged during after the last war. It cannot be visited. **Nebersdorf** (*c.* 7 km. S.): The schloss contains a hall with a fresco of 'Gods on Olympus' by S.Dorffmeister, 1773.

Ranggen = Kematen im Tirol 6175
Tirol   p.286□F 8

Excavations carried out behind the 'Burschelhof' at the N. end of the village have revealed finds from the La Tène period, including the remains of a prehistoric house which can today be seen on the hill. This is one of the oldest human settlements in the Tyrol.

Pfarrkirche hl. Magnus: The present hall-like church was built by Franz Singer from Götzens in 1775 on the site of a church mentioned in 1359. The façade frescos are by Jos. Kremer from Zirl (18C), while the impressive ceiling frescos inside are by F.A. Zeiller, 1778. The high altar is the work of J.A. Zoller, 1782, and the statues were carved by Joh. Schnegg in

1778. Near the entrance is a memorial (1500).

Rankweil 6830
Vorarlberg   p.286□A 8

Pfarrkirche St.Peter: This is the oldest church in Rankweil. Mentioned in a document dating from 850. Consecrated in 1238, altered in baroque style in 1625. The tower dates from 1731. This is small church of simple design. On the gospel side is a raguly cross dating from 1400, showing the legend of the abbess of the convent of the Poor Clares at Valduna. The abbess, ready to die the martyr's death, advances with the Cross towards the attacking soldiers — and now Christ raises his hand against the enemy.

Pfarrkirche Maria Heimsuchung: The Montfort retainers' castle stood 165 ft. above the bottom of the valley. It burned down in the 14C. and a *church* arose on its site in 1377. The castle courtyard became

Rankweil, Maria Heimsuchung

the graveyard, the keep acquired a new function as the church tower, the residence was turned into the nave, and the castle chapel was converted into the rather small choir. The old parapet still surround the entire complex. The nave was vaulted anew in 1678. The Gnadenkapelle, and also the round tower with its spiral staircase, are by Michael Beer of the Bregenzerwald architectural school. Ascending a granite staircase, the visitor reaches the castle gate with its gatehouse, and upon entering it is captivated by the winding layout of the buildings: the quiet graveyard, the dark wood of the parapet, the wooden saints in the wall niches (St.Barbara, St. Catherine, St.Christopher and St.Francis). The steep stairs lead up into the church through some passages. Inside the pilgrimage church, which is 600 years old and has been radically restored three times, one is struck by a bleak estrangement. All the old altars were sold or destroyed in the late 19C, and more recently concrete galleries were built and the church was most thoroughly modernized. The Madonna at the Gnadenaltar is a delicate carving from 1470. The *silver cross* beside the Gnadenkapelle is Romanesque (1233), enclosed in a silver case dating from 1728, the work of an artist from Augsburg. There is another wooden cross dating from the mid-12C. A Mount of Olives grotto (17C) and an interesting tombstone relief (1629).

Rappottenstein am Kleinen Kamp 3911
Lower Austria   p.278□R 3

Castle: Rapoto von Kuenring built the Höhenburg on a Hohenstaufen model in c. 1160. In 1259 it was called castrum, a fortified castle. It was never captured. In 1645, Colonel Harrant defended it against the Swedes, after he had had the keep fortified with 'Spanish Reutters' and the drawbridges repaired. The Abensberg-Traun family purchased the castle in 1664, and it is still in their possession today. With its authentic core—only the extensions and fortifications were rebuilt—it is one of the best-preserved castles in Austria.

The outer walls of the upper castle hewn from the rock are entirely plain and form an irregular polygon with a tower at the front, protected by the large outworks and five courtyards. The entrance is on the SE side through a projecting gate flanked by round towers. The brewery is in the 1st courtyard, the domestic buildings are in the 3rd, and in the 5th is the *keep* (with the St.-Pankraz-Kapelle dating from 1378), through which the visitor enters the narrow arcaded courtyard (1601) of the upper castle. Inside there are Renaissance frescos and, in the archive room, a beautiful stellar vault.

Rattenberg, Inn 6240

Tirol   p.284□H 8

Rattenberg's heyday as a centre of the mountains ended in the 17C. Little has been changed architecturally since those times, and the result is that this is one of the most compact old towns in Austria. Rattenberg, which was a border village between Bavaria and the Tyrol on the river Inn, grew up at the foot of its castle. It became a town in 1393, and attained prosperity in the 15C along with the emergence of the mining industry. The broad multi-storeyed houses still have some fine old oriels, marble portals, patios and pretty inn signs. Note in particular the *old Rathaus* (today it is the court building; Bienerstrasse), the *former Stadthaus* (today the Gasthof Traube hotel; Klostergasse), and the *Gasthof Stern* hotel (Sepp-Maier-Platz) with its beautiful strapwork stuccoed ceiling dating from 1735.

Schloss Rattenberg: The now ruined castle was originally built by the Bavarians in the 11C as a border fortress with the Tyrol and possession of it alternated between the Bavarians and Tyroleans. From the 16C onwards it was also used as a prison. Today the substructure of the keep survives from the Romanesque castle. Some remains of the main castle, and the upper section of the keep, have survived from rebuilding work in 1300 and 1340. It was under Maximilian I that Michael Zeller enlarged the castle into a large fortress with outer curtain walls, a watchtower and round towers which are still identifiable today in the remains of the walls. The upper castle was also built at that time. It stands on a slab of rock, and has five towers and a gun turret (ruined).

Pfarrkirche St. Vigil: This peculiar late Gothic hall church, with its two aisles and two choirs, was built from 1443 onwards. The N. half of the church served the citizenry, while the S. half was used by the miners and their relatives. The choirs and the S. side of the nave are decorated on the outside with red marble slabs. There are

Rappottenstein, Burg

splendidly embellished entrance portals in the N. and S. The interior, where the vault is still Gothic (with baroque stucco on the ceiling of the nave), was redecorated in 1733 in a baroque style of rare beauty. The two-storeyed sacristy attached to the N. side also has a Gothic vault. The two aisles of the church are separated by three round marble pillars. In 1733, A. Gigl added some splendid stuccoes rivalling in beauty the ceiling frescos by M. Günther dating from 1737 (Günther also painted the fresco above the oratory in the sacristy). The frescos in the two choirs are by S.B. Faistenberger, 1729. The two high altars, with their paintings by J.Zanussi from the 1st half of the 18C, should also be noted. The beautiful wooden sculptures on the S. altar are by J.M. Guggenbichler from Mondsee. The other rococo altars, and the pulpit by A.Gigl dating from 1733, are also fine.

Servitenkirche St.Augustin: The monastery church dating from 1384 was rebuilt in 1707–9 by Diego Francesco Carlone in Lombard high baroque style, renovated in 1893–5 and restored in 1950. The *tower*, which is separate from the church, stands above the Hoferkapelle in the cloister, and has a baroque dome and a lantern. Most of the baroque decorations surviving in the church are in the choir, where there are stuccoes by Paolo d'Allio and wall and ceiling frescos by Joh. Jos. Waldmann dating from 1711, at the high altar dating from 1766, and in the pulpit, which is also by d'Allio. The beautiful effigy (1396) of Hans Kumersprucker, the founder of the monastery, and his wife, is a notable feature of the nave.

Servitenkloster: The most interesting features of the monastery, built around 1400, are its beautiful cloister and net vault; the *Wolfgang-* or *Hoferkapelle* (15C, net vaulting and an early-16C Virgin with a crescent moon), and the *Ecce-homo-Kapelle* from the early 18C with stucco by Paolo d'Allio and frescos by Joh. Jos. Waldmann.

Spital and Spitalskirche: The hospital, rebuilt in *c.* 1500, has a pointed marble

Rattenberg, panorama with St. Vigil, Servitenkirche and ruined castle

portal and was originally founded in 1381 by Hans Kumersprucker. The church attached to it in 1500 has stuccoed capitals and vault frescos dating from 1720.

Environs: Alpbach with the *Pfarrkirche St.Oswald.* This church was mentioned in 1369, rebuilt in *c.* 1500 and altered in baroque style in 1724. There are frescos by Christof Anton Mayr (1751) in the nave, and statues by Franz Xaver Nissl dating from *c.* 1770 on the wall of the choir. **Brandenberg** with the 17C *Pfarrkirche hl. Georg.* **Kramsach** was settled in prehistoric times. It contains the ruined remains of *Burg Neidegg*, which collapsed in the Middle Ages; it is a town of old stonemasons' workshops (with a late Gothic wayside shrine).

Rattersdorf-Liebing 7443
Burgenland   p.280☐V/W 8

The small border community of Rattersdorf, where there is a crossing to Güns, has a distinguished *Wallfahrtskirche* (pilgrimage church): a fortified wall surrounds the group of buildings which developed from the 13C to the 17C. The lower storey of the tower is the oldest section, and is today a chapel entered from the outside. The *N. church* was rebuilt by Paul Esterházy in 1696 after being destroyed by the Turks; the *S. church* is connected to the N. one by arches and consists of the Gnadenkirche built in the 14C and the side aisle added in 1502. A charming Maria lactans in a splendid Louis XVI frame adorns the altar (*c.* 1660, copy of an ex voto image; the old miraculous image is lost). The altar is surrounded by an unusual and extremely impressive wall resembling a screen and adorned with 34 oil paintings of saints and some flower pieces, *c.* 1760. The artist is the Augustinian lay brother Jonas, whose self-portrait is behind the altar. *Also worth*

mentioning: A Gothic Madonna in a baroque frame. Late-17C font: a 'wild heathen' supports the font which is decorated with the baptism of Christ.

Environs: Dörfl im Burgenland (*c.* 12 km. N.): An old smithy on the main road, with original decorations.

Rauris 5661
Salzburg   p.284☐L 9

This town had its own provincial court of justice from the mid 14C onwards. Rauris received a considerable impetus when gold-mining in the Tauern mountains (Kolm-Saigurn) was at a peak in the 15&16C. Some handsome houses belonging to shareholders in mining companies date from this period, and gave this town a character resembling that of a market, although the town was not officially acknowledged as such until 1884. It has become well-known recently through some cultural events which attempt to bring con-

Reichersberg, Stiftskirche St.Michael

temporary art to a rural population (the Rauris day of literature is held in the spring, the Rauris painters' days in autumn).

Pfarrkirche hl. Jakobus d. Ä. und Martin: The tower and choir are late Gothic (*c.* 1510–16), and the nave was rebuilt in 1774–80. Two figures by Sebastian Loscher from the former high altar dating from 1522 have survived on the right front side altar. There is a Lamentation by the same carver in the *Michaelskapelle* built in 1497. There is a *serpentine lantern* dating from 1499 in the *graveyard*.

Reichersberg 4981
Upper Austria   p.276□M 4

Augustiner-Chorherrenstift: The priory, visible from afar, stands on the high terrace on the right bank of the Inn. In 1084, Wernher and Dietburg (the latter was the sister of Archbishop Gebhard of Salzburg), the two last nobles of Reichersberg, summoned Augustinian canons from Saxony to their castle. The community of the order of St. Augustine has withstood all the adversities of time. Today, the priory has taken on new roles besides its religious one: concerts held in the church and banqueting hall make it a cultural centre for the area, and together with the Volksbildungswerk (adult education institution) it has become a centre of adult education. Almost everything was levelled to the ground in a fire in 1624, and the present church and priory date from the early 17C.

Stiftskirche St. Michael: A single-aisled church, consecrated in 1644 and decorated in the 18C. The frescos by the Munich court painter Chr. Wink (particularly the apparition of St. Michael on Mt. Garganus and the foundation of the order by St. Augustine) produce an overwhelming effect. *Inside* note the chapel altars by Joh. B. Modler, mature rococo. Outstanding pulpit with symbols of the Evangelists, possibly by Jos. M. Götz. A red marble

Ried (Reichersberg), Rathaus

founder's tombstone of high quality, *c.* 1470. An effective painting of the 'Liberation of St. Peter' by J.H. Schönfeld in a splendid frame by Th. Schwanthaler. The *sacristy* has an excellent stuccoed ceiling, with bas-reliefs of figures, by F.J.I. Holzinger.

Stiftsgebäude: The gatehouse leads into the 405 ft. long *outer courtyard.* Its first third is lined by single-storeyed domestic buildings; powerful round corner oriels, crowned by onion domes, mark the beginning of the wings of the actual monastery, which house the banqueting halls. The N. wing is especially festive in appearance, with its two-storeyed arcades. The courtyard resembles a garden, and the middle of it is adorned by an excellent fountain by Th. Schwanthaler displaying St. Michael battling with Lucifer. In the S. section there is a large *banqueting hall* (Augustinus-Saal), on which J. Abert painted frescos of Divine Providence and the four elements in 1695. In the N. section is the *Prälaten-Oratorium,* an intimate oratory with a window towards the church and, in the dome, a fresco of 'Heavenly Jerusalem' by Wink. *Bayerischer Saal,* with frescos by Joh. N. Schöpf depicting ancient myths. An inner courtyard, and an early cloister where there are the following buildings: *Summer refectory* with octagonal hallway built by C.A. Carlone and stuccoed in outstanding style by his brother Giovanni Battista (1695). *Library* containing scenes from the history of the priory by Joh. N. Schöpf. *Stiftsmuseum:* Gothic and baroque sculptures (Schwanthaler); stained-glass windows; documents; tombstones from the 13–18C.

Environs: Ried im Innkreis: This is the main town of the fertile Inn region, and has been part of Austria since 1779. It was elevated to the status of a town in 1857, and in 1867 the first agricultural exhibition was held here and developed into an agricultural fair of international status. It is of importance to the art lover because it is the home of the Schwanthalers, the family of sculptors which, over the centuries, repeatedly produced creative artists and had its workshop here from 1632–1838. *Pfarrkirche hl. Peter und Paul:* Apart from the choir and tower, this was rebuilt after 1720. Note the shoemakers' Martin-Altar, built by Mart. and Mich. Zürn in 1656; the captivating Mount of Olives, a late work by Th. Schwanthaler, *c.* 1700. *Innviertler Volkskundehaus:* Furniture, national costume, guilds, weapons, history of the town, extensive collection of archery targets; baroque sculptures by the Schwanthaler and Zürn families; cribs; 60,000 devotional images; 300 verres églomisés; death crowns; rare amulets of widely varying kinds. **Aurolzmünster** (about 13 km. SE): This once famous building erected by artists of the Munich court to plans by J.K. Zuccali is highly important architecturally, but it is in a desolate condition and its future is uncertain. **Obernberg am Inn** (some 4 km. up river): A friendly market, houses with good façades. *Pfarrkirche* of the 'Hl. Abendmahl des Herrn' (Last Sup-

Obernberg, Apothekerhaus

per): early-16C wooden relief of the Holy Family, attributed to the artist of the Altötting doors, a pupil of Leinberger. On the way to the market stands the *Ufer Filialkirche zum hl. Nikolaus,* where there is an altarpiece of St. Nicholas, depicting a procession of ships outside the town of Ufer. The castle was mentioned in 1199, and the present building dates from the mid-16C. Houses Nos. 37, 38 (pharmacist's house), and 57 in the Hauptplatz have especially fine façades, probably by Joh. B. Moderl. Two town gates, and in the Gurtentor there is a *Heimathaus* (museum of local history).

Rein 8103

Steiermark   p.280☐S 9

Cistercian abbey: This is the oldest abbey of this order in Austria, and was founded by Margrave Leopold I in 1129. It was altered several times from 1720 to 1782, when the N. half of the abbey and the outer courtyard were built. Most of this work was carried out by J.G. Stengg from Graz.

Rein, Cistercian abbey

Stiftskirche Mariae Himmelfahrt: The present pilastered church dates back to a Romanesque basilica which had a nave and two aisles and was altered into a single-aisled structure in the 18C. The vault is increased in height by trompe l'oeil architecture; frescos by J.A. v. Mölk (1766), choir frescos by Jos. G. Mayr. The altarpiece on the high altar is by Kremser Schmidt (1779); there are also expressive statues. The altarpieces in the 1st, 2nd and 4th chapels on the left are by Jos. Amonte, 18C; those in the 4th chapel on the right are by J.V. Hauck (1731). There is an interesting funerary chapel of Ernst the Iron Duke (d. 1424), with a red marble slab decorated with figures. The plague chapel dating from 1681 has been converted into a baptistery.

Stiftsgebäude The *Kreuz- und Dreifaltigkeitskapelle* is in the S. wing. Built in the early 16C, it was originally a monks' chapel for the sick, dedicated to St. Stephen the martyr. There is a groin vault and traceried windows; carved capitals and brackets. 15C stained-glass windows in museums.

Wallfahrtskirche Strassengel: Another Cistercian foundation. This monument to the Austrian high Gothic, standing on a narrow crag, has an outstanding tower. Both the ground plan and the overall design are inspired by the contemporary Stephansdom in Vienna. The exterior captivates by its clarity and simplicity: a massive roof, and surrounding buttresses; the W. portal (with a relief of the 'Annunciation' in the tympanum, *c.* 1400; the S. front depicts the 'Lamentation'; but the most striking feature is the elegant E. tower, crowned by a pointed helm roof. The *St.-Anna-Kapelle* and the *sacristy* were added in 1754. The *inside* is a Gothic hall church with a nave, two aisles and a choir with a slender apse. The only Gothic items still surviving are the fine *stained-glass win-*

dows in the choir and S. rose-window, the miraculous image of the Virgin in a robe of ears of corn (15C), and a ragulé cross from the mid 13C. *Baroque decoration:* Side altars with painting by Kremser Schmidt (1781), and the high altar was designed by Fischer von Erlach.

Reith im Alpbachtal 6235
Tirol   p.284□H 8

Pfarrkirche hl. Petrus: In this church which is the last work of the architect A. Hueber, built in 1801 – 03, only the substructure of the tower and an octagonal font of red marble still survive from the old Gothic structure. After the simple exterior, the splendid interior, where neoclassicism breaks through in the final stages of the late baroque, is a considerable surprise. In the main area, where there are a nave and two aisles, the three flat domes and the dome over the choir were *frescoed* by Jos. Schöpf, 1804. There is no stucco in the church, whose interior is decorated in a harmonious series of shades. The three altars and the pulpit are by Anton Bichler, 1805-6. The altarpieces are also by Jos. Schöpf.

Reith bei Kitzbühel = Kitzbühel 6370
Tirol   p.284□I 8

Pfarrkirche hll. Ägydius und Sylvester: Only the N. tower with its octagonal spire survives from the originally Gothic church; the present one having been built by Abraham Millauer in 1729 –31. The ceiling paintings inside are by S.B. Faistenberger, 1729. The high altar dates from the end of the 17C, while the side altars and the pulpit are from 1700. The carved group of the Holy Family is by Joh. Blieml, 1783.

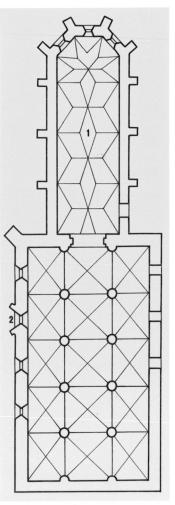

Retz, Dominikanerkirche 1 Long choir with three bays and stellar vault **2** N. portal with 13C tympanum

Retz 2070
Lower Austria   p.278□U 2

Count Berchthold von Rabenswalde-

Schwarzburg, feudal lord of the county of Hardegg from 1278–1312, moved the administration seat to Retz, a town in the interior of the county. In 1305 he founded the 'second' town and presented it with his coat-of-arms, the lion rampant. The Hussites destroyed the town in 1425, and it was rebuilt under the Meidburgs and Eyczing. The new *Schloss* was built in 1491 as the first one, the *Althof*, was gradually falling down (despite this, the imperial Counts of Gatterburg, who owned the Schloss from 1709 onwards, styled themselves the barons of Althof zu Retz). The town was occupied by the Swedes in 1645, and when they withdrew only 28 houses were still standing.

Pfarrkirche St.Stephan: Rebuilt in 1706 on Romanesque foundations. The nave had to be re-roofed after the fire of 1731, and another storey was added to the tower. The high altar by L. Kuppelwieser, 1852, depicts the stoning of St.Stephen, and the side altars have St. Augustine and St. Monica by Altomonte. There are large figures in the *burial chapel* dating from

1750, and the tombstones are from 1439.

Dominikanerkirche: 1295. One of the first hall churches in Austria to have a nave and two aisles. After the Hussites devastated the church in 1491, a new choir with a stellar vault was built. An early Gothic N. portal: in the tympanum there is a Virgin Mary on the lion's throne, with founders. Early Gothic windows in the upper zone. The relics of Placidus the martyr are at the left side altar. They were transferred hither from Rome in 1696. The marble tombstone of the Eyczings. *Monastery:* A 14C book of the dead.

Also worth seeing: *Rathaus:* This stands in the middle of the especially beautiful and extensive Hauptplatz. The Marienkapelle was built in *c.* 1300 and altered in 1510; its nave has a flat roof. This is adjoined by the massive *town tower,* which is essentially Gothic, with a Renaissance helm roof and a gallery dating from 1615. Above the N. gateway is the *Verderberhaus:* castle-like, with battlements, it was built by Firenz von Görz,

Reutte, Rathaus

a merchant, in 1583. Opposite this is the *Sgraffitohaus,* built in 1576 by Augustin Resch, the town judge: there are cycles of paintings depicting the Old Testament, Greek legends, and the ages of man. The 13C *town wall* survives in good condition, with a parapet walk and the Nalber-Tor and Znaimer-Tor gates. The four round corner towers were added in the 16C. *Trinity column* (1744), *statue of the Virgin Mary* (1714), *plague column* (1680; all in the Hauptplatz). The *windmill:* the first windmill (wooden) was erected in 1772. A year later, a new one was built on a stone foundation with a revolving roof. The whole town is riddled with *wine-cellars* down to a depth of 65 ft. Some of these passages date from the 13C.

Reutte 6600
Tirol   p.286□D 8

The Hauptstrasse (main street) of Reutte has a number of stately, broad-fronted houses with painted façades, well-formed gables and buttresses, grilles and pretty inn signs. They include the houses at: 1 Untersteig (this is the house where the Zeiller family of painters lived in the 17&18C; most of the façade frescos are attributable to them). 7 Obermarkt (Ehrenheim residence), and next to it is the Gemeindeamt (communal administrative office), with a curving gable. 1 Obermarkt (Strahlenburg, with a coat-of-arms dating from 1704). 25 Untermarkt (Sternhaus residence). There are also the Goldene Krone (with a pretty coach fresco from 1777) and Schwarzer Adler (a fine window frontage, with a portal and a gable fresco) inns.

Kirche St. Anna: After a fire in 1846, the old church, originally built in 1490, was erected anew. There is a St.Anne with the Madonna and Child dating from *c.* 1515 at the high altar. The two larger-than-life figures of St. Magnus and St. Afra are early-18C.

Environs: All that survives of the **Ehrenberg ruins** are the remains of some

Schloss Riegersburg

walls from the extensive 13–18C fortifications. **Tannheim,** with the *Pfarrkirche hl. Nikolaus.* This broad building with its large W. tower was built by Andreas Hafenegger in 1722–5 on the site of a medieval church. The sumptuous altars date from *c.* 1725, and the statues are by Anton Sturm. P.Zeiller was responsible for the altarpieces of the two side altars. The ceiling painting is by Jos. Keller, 1804. There is also the 17C *Kapelle Maria Hilf.*

Riegersburg 2092
Lower Austria   p.278□T 2

Schloss: In 1731, Franz Anton Pilgram, acting by order of Imperial Count Sigismund Khevenhüller, the governor of Lower Austria, converted a moated castle into a baroque schloss; further alterations were made in the 19C. The schloss, completely destroyed in 1945, was rebuilt in the 1960s by the granddaughter of Count Khevenhüller Metsch, the adjutant of Emperor Maximilian of Mexico. It was redecorated from the resources of the Austrian Museum of Applied Art. The schloss, prettily situated by a pond, has a gorgeous front: two corner pavilions with ponderous domes flank a central section of five bays. The pediment bears the coat-of-arms of the Khevenhüllers and is crowned by a figure of Atlas. The urns, putti and the figures on the roof are by Joseph Kracker. Four different shapes of window.

Riegersburg 8333
Steiermark   p.280□U 9/10

Riegersburg fortress: Built on a basalt rock to protect the N. flank of the E. border of Styria. Its ownership was disputed until 1945. In the 13C the building consisted of two castles, the older *Kronegg* to the N. and the *Lichtenegg* which was built later, probably as a counterpart to the Kronegg. In 1571 the upper fortress was expanded and the lower one torn down. Bastions and gates were added in the 17C, making the castle completely impregnable.

Feste Riegersburg

Behind the outer fosse is an outwork with the Wenzelstor; the round arch is flanked by statues of Mars and Bellona. The first courtyard of the upper schloss has an arcade. In the inner castle courtyard there is a well (90 ft.) with a wrought-iron crown (1640). The best of the rooms inside the castle are the *Rittersaal* (the main room, with paintings), the *Fürstenzimmer,* and the *Weisser Saal.* The *chapel* dating from 1430 is Gothic; it has two baroque altars.

Hauptpfarrkirche hl. Martin: This church was built in the 15C from basalt ashlars hewn from the castle rock. Its nave has four bays and a groin vault; it was enlarged in the 17C, when two chapels were added. 18C decorations: altarpiece of high altar by Anton Jandl; altarpiece of St.Wenzel by L.Kupelwieser in the S. side chapel. Good memorials.

Environs: Gleichenberg: *Schloss Kornberg,* a former medieval fortress (13C), extensively rebuilt in the 17C; destroyed in World War 2. Some parts of the medieval arcaded courtyard and of the W. section have survived. Next to these there is a 13C curtain wall, 13 ft. thick.

Riezlern 6991
Vorarlberg   p.286□C 8

Kleinwalsertal: A 13C Walser settlement. The great Mt.Widderstein (8,320 ft.) forms the S. end of the valley. In 1451, Duke Siegmund of the Tyrol conquered the Tannberg, making the valley Austrian and putting an end to democratic autonomy. The territory fell to Bavaria at the peace of Pressburg in 1806, and after the Congress of Vienna of 1816 it returned to Austria. A treaty of accession to the customs union came into force in 1891 and still applies today: the valley belongs to Germany economically and to Austria territorially. The Kleinwalsertal includes Riezlern (seat of the Rathaus and Walsermuseum), Hirschegg and Mittelberg. The valley is politically a single community. In **Mittelberg** the Pfarrkirche hl. Jodok of 1463 (rediscovered frescos) is worth seeing.

Rohrau, house where Joseph Haydn was born

In **Hirschegg:** War memorial and Leidtobelbrücke. In **Riezlern:** A neo-Romanesque church (the paint work is by Prof. Martin von Feuerstein), and also the Unterwestegg chapel with its late Gothic winged altar.

Rohrau 2471
Lower Austria   p.278☐X 5

Schloss and picture gallery: From 1524 onwards this was owned by the imperial Counts of Harrach, who played an important part in Austria's history. Ferdinand Bonaventura founded the picture gallery in 1668. Emperor Leopold I sent him to Madrid as an ambassador to persuade Charles II, the last Spanish Habsburg, to draw up a will and testament in favour of the Austrian line. Bonaventura's son was a viceroy in Naples, while his son attended the governor in Brussels. In this way, paintings from all over Europe were brought to the gallery on the Freyung, which was moved to Rohrau in 1960 (200 paintings,

Schloss Rosenau, freemasons' lodge

including some by Ruysdael, Valckenburg, Jordaens, van Dyck, Rubens, Breughel, and a fine portrait of Bonaventura by Rigaud). The former moated schloss dates from the 16C. Extensive alterations were made in the 18C. The domestic buildings are in front of the schloss. A classical portal.

House of Josef Haydn's birth (No. 60): The room where the birth took place; mementoes.

Rosenau Schloss 3924
Lower Austria   p.278☐R 3

Schloss: A sturdy Renaissance schloss was built by von Greiss in 1590, and 150 years later Leopold Count von Schallenberg had it altered in baroque style. The architect was—probably—Munggenast, who worked in Zwettl and Altenburg during this period. Another doubtful point is that of whether P.Troger and D.Gran painted the frescos. It is, however, certain that Rinkolin, the Italian trompe-l'oeil artist, painted the staircase in 1744. Schallenberg was a freemason and installed a lodge on the first floor. In 1868 the schloss came into the possession of Ritter von Schönerer, whose son was a member of the chamber of deputies, a member of the German National People's Party, an anti-semite, a converted Protestant, and the head of the movement advocating separation from Rome. The schloss has been restored over the last few years, and an excellent *museum of freemasonry* was set up in the process. In front of the façade of the schloss (built around a courtyard) there is a two-storeyed pavilion overlooked by a massive clock tower. The mysterious symbolism of freemasonry begins with the two flights of stairs (the friendly guide — the open or closed windows, etc.). In the first room are ceiling paintings with the allegory of the four seasons, and in the second room are a Diana and Actaeon and an Athene and Apollo. Cabinets and authentically decorated lodge rooms with charming Empire furnishings.

Pfarrkirche hl. Dreifaltigkeit/Former Schlosskapelle: Dome fresco dating from 1740: Joachim and Anna; St. Leopold; angels waving the Austrian flag. This fresco by D.Gran was covered by whitewash for a long time.

Rosenburg 3573
Lower Austria   p.278☐T 3

Castle: The founders of the castle called themselves Rosenberg in *c.* 1200. The ownership passed from them into the hands of Duke Albrecht and it was not until 1569 that it was first called 'Rosenburg'. At the time of the Reformation, the castle was a focus of Protestantism under the Grabner and Jörger. 13 towers of this extensive castle appear on an etching dating

from 1659. From 1678 onwards it was owned by the Counts Hoyos-Sprinzenstein. Count Johann Ernst rebuilt it in 'historicizing' style after a devastating fire in 1809. The visitor passes through the first gate and enters the arcaded *Turnierhof* (tilt yard), built in 1640. It was here that the ladies watched the tournaments. The octagonal *gate-tower* built in 1583, with its double gallery and conical roof, leads into the 1st *Schlosshof*, built in the Protestant period. On the right is the castellan's house, and on the left a two-storeyed arcade. A double flight of stairs leads into the state rooms, and another similar staircase built into the former upper moat takes us to a fish pond. Another gate leads us into the inner *Burghof*. This ends in the castle's oldest section which drops steeply to the river Kamp and is overlooked by the Gothic *keep*. The late Gothic chapel has two round traceried windows and a small portal. Above the river Kamp are two particularly beautiful Renaissance balconies with delicate arcades. The interior is finely furnished, and there are old weapons and early paintings.

Burg Rosenburg with tiltyard

Rottenmann 8786
Steiermark   p.282□P 7

'Rotenmannum' was first documented in 927, but the area was probably already settled under the Romans. There was a market here in 1230, and in 1279 it became a walled town; parts of the wall survive. An important medieval centre for the distribution of ore and salt. An Augustinian priory was established here in the 15C.

Pfarrkirche St. Nikolaus (a collegiate church until 1785): A late Gothic hall church with a nave and two aisles from the period 1440–78. From 1488 onwards it was converted into a collegiate church, whose liturgy made it necessary to expand the choir and reduce the nave: the hall was shortened by one bay, while the choir with its three aisles was extended and given a seven-sided apse (Christoph Marl was the architect). The middle of the three octagonal pillars supporting the choir vault was unfortunately removed in the 18C. Some of the items inside date back to the original church: the *font* and *pulpit* date from 1515, while a large Gothic *crucifix* dates from around 1510. Beside the sacristy door there is a *praying stool* for Emperor Frederick III and his wife, donated by their son Emperor Maximilian in 1514. There are *remains of frescos* in the choir vault (1509). The *high altar* and *side altars* are 18C; the high altar has an altarpiece by Ph.C. Laubmann (1760), and the side altars paintings by Kremser Schmidt (1777). Splendid 17C *choir stalls*.

Also worth seeing: The old *priory*, the oldest sections of which (the S. section) are from the 15C. It was extensively altered in about 1700. The *Spitalskirche* (1446–51) is to the NW, a little way outside the town. It is a single-aisled structure with niches for the sick. *High altar* and *Floriani-Altar* from the 1st half of the 18C.

Environs: St. Georgen (c. 1 km. E. of the town): The *Filialkirche St. Georgen*, mentioned as early as 1042, is the oldest parish church in the area. In 1414, this originally Romanesque building (windows on the N. wall) was enlarged, and in 1480 its groin vault was added. The church's showpiece is its *winged altar* (c. 1525) from the circle of artists around Lienhart Astl. The paintings on the wings depict St. Ursula, St. Barbara. St. Catherine, and St. Anne with the Madonna and Child when the wings are closed, and the Massacre of the Innocents and the Flight into Egypt when they are open. **Burg Strechau** (built on a steep, rocky ridge 3 km. outside the town): Like various castles in Styria (see Friedberg), this fortress was a bastion of Protestantism in the 16C. However, its present appearance is mainly the result of alterations carried out in the 17C after it had passed to Admont Abbey: the extensive three-storeyed *arcaded courtyard* of the upper castle, with Tuscan columns (see Landhaus, Graz), was built in 1629–32. In the N. wing there is a Protestant *chapel* (1579) with contemporary frescos. The altar of 1637 and the crucifix by J.Th. Stammel are in the chapel which the abbey built later. The *Rittersaal* with its stuccoed ceiling, and various rooms with original decorations. **Stainach-Irdning:** A market town; a parish mentioned in 1140 and held in the 15C by the later Pope Pius II. The church has an early Gothic nave and tower; alterations were made in the 18C. The altarpiece on the high altar is by Ph. C. Laubmann. The *Falkenburg*, built as a hunting lodge in the 18C, was converted into a Capuchin monastery. *Schloss Donnersbach:* A medieval fortress dating from the 16C, with the *Pfarrkirche hl. Ägydius.* **Stainach:** *Schloss:* This is the seat of the Traungau family, and was later divided into Upper, Middle and Lower Stainach. Only the latter survives—now a country house. **Niederhofen:** *Pfarrkirche hl. Ruprecht:* A hall church with two aisles dating from the 15C. Traceried windows; ornate rib vault supported by round pillars. A late Gothic W. tower. Some especially fine 15C tempera paintings in the choir chapel. Remains of a winged altar by Lienhart Astl on the right side altar.

Rust am Neusiedlersee 7071
Burgenland   p.278☐W 6

Rust is one of the best-known towns in the province, and not without reason: the local wine ('Ruster'), a fine lakeside resort, and the storks nesting there, are the reasons for its popularity as a centre of tourism. However, its artistic importance should not be forgotten; apart from the highly significant Fischer-Kirche, the small town of Rust has also retained much of its historical appearance. In addition, there is the scientific institute of the Wilhelminenberg research society (Wien XVI, Professor König). The fauna and flora of the lake are studied here (see Neusiedl).

Filialkirche St. Pankratius und Ägydius, Fischer-Kirche: This picturesque group of buildings is surrounded by a defensive wall. Parts of the wall of the oldest church, which dates from the 12C, have survived. The *Marienkapelle* was added to this little church in the late 13C. A larger choir, the 'Pankrazi-Chor', was added in the N. after 1400, and finally, in the early 16C, the Romanesque nave was replaced by a transverse one which combines the Marienkapelle and the Pankrazi-Chor into a single church. The tower was not rebuilt after falling down. The attractive nearby tower belongs to the Protestant church. Fine decorations: there are some very good *frescos* by the windows of the Marienkapelle (late-13C). The frescos covering the Pankrazi-Chor are 15C, while those in the transept are 16C. The decorations on the keystones betray the basis of this little town's economy: two crossed fishes on one keystone, vine-grower's knife and vineyard hoe on the other. The finest altar is the *Dreiheiligen-Altar:* St.Florian, St.Ursula, St.Catherine, late Gothic, in an early baroque shrine. The positive organ dates from 1705; a relief of the Virgin of

Rust, panorama

the 'Angelic Salutation' dating from *c.*
1700; a Gothic statue of the Virgin; a stone
pulpit, decorated with delicate flower paintings dating from *c.* 1800, etc. (Key obtainable from the Katholisches Pfarramt
(Catholic parish office), Tel. 02685–295).

The Town: The historical appearance of
whole terraces of houses has survived almost intact. Particular attention should be
paid to: the Rathaus, Rathausplatz 2 ('Zum
Auge Gottes'), Hauptstrasse 3.

Environs: Mörbisch am See (*c.* 5 km.
S., by the lake): The name of Mörbisch has
become famous over the last 20 years
through the *Seefestspiele* (lake festivals), at
which classical operettas are performed.
Information: Burgenländischer
Landesfremdenverkehrsverband (provincial tourist association), Eisenstadt, Schloss
Esterházy, Tel. 02682–3384. The court
alleyways are a typical feature of the town,
with their old winegrowers' cottages which
are distinguished by their flights of steps

and their porches with arches. **St.
Margarethen im Burgenland** (4 km. W.
of Rust): The name of St.Margarethen is
associated primarily with the famous
quarry which has been exploited since
Roman times and has supplied materials
for many important Viennese buildings,
ranging from the Stephansdom to the ring
roads. The limestone quarry, with its steep
sides up to 130 ft. in height, has been the
annual venue of the 'symposium of European sculptors' since 1959. The sculptures
they carve remain in situ and thus form a
kind of *open-air museum*. The *stage for the
Passion play* is set against the magnificent
back-drop of the quarry; performances are
not held every year. Information obtainable
from: Gemeinde (municipality) St.
Margarethen, Tel.: 02680–202. **Oslip** (*c.*
5 km. N. of St.Margarethen): Two notable
early mills, Cselleymühle and Stor-
chenmühle.

In addition to Eisenstadt (q.v.), the area
around the Neusiedlersee contains a
number of places worth visiting.

Rust, Fischerkirche 1 Marienkapelle **2**
Pankratius-Chor **3** Drei-Heiligen-Altar **4** Stone
pulpit **5** Transept and nave

St.Margarethen, open-air museum

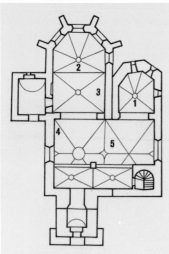

Saak = Nötsch im Gailtal 9611
Kärnten   p.282☐N 11

Pfarrkirche St. Kanzian: The impression created by this late Gothic church is determined by the 17&18C baroque decorations. The high altar dates from *c.* 1740, and by the left side altar is an early-16C Virgin and Child.

Schloss Wasserleonburg: This Schloss was first mentioned in the 13C. The Habsburg fief passed to the bourgeoisie in 1522; after this it was in aristocratic hands again until the early 19C. Architecture from all periods.

Sagritz = Döllach im Mölltal 9843
Kärnten   p.284☐L 10

Pfarrkirche St. Georg: Only the W. tower of the church is still late Gothic; the nave and polygonal apse are late baroque (1769–79), on old foundation walls. Paintings *c.* 1600 in the hall of the tower. Paintings in the choir by C.Brandstätter the Younger (1840). The altar and statues are 18C; the tombs with coats-of-arms on the N. wall of the nave are Renaissance. To the W. of the church opposite is the late Gothic *Antoniuskapelle* (early-16C). The fresco fragments on the outside and in the vaults are worth seeing (16C).

Salzburg 5010, 5020
Salzburg   p.276☐L 6

Salzburg, the chief city of the Land of the same name, has 128,845 inhabitants, making it the fourth largest city in Austria. It is the seat of the Land government and of an archbishop, and has a university and a college of music and performing arts. Salzburg, the 'city of Mozart', has become world-famous for its Easter and summer festivals.

History: The Salzburg basin is an old area of settlement. Prehistoric finds on the *Rainberg*, one of the city's three mountains, indicate that it was continuously peopled up until the Neolithic period (5000–2000 BC). The Roman province of Noricum and the Roman settlement of *Juvavum* were both established at about the same time (15 BC). Emperor Claudius (AD 41–54) raised the settlement to the rank of a municipium. After town life collapsed and Juvavum was destroyed by barbarian invasions, the Bavarians captured the territory and the former city was presented *c.* 700 to the Rheno-Franconian Bishop Hruodbert (Rupert), a political refugee at the court of the Bavarian duke Theodo. Rupert founded the monastery of *St.Peter.* It stands at the foot of the steep Mönchsberg, and initially was also a bishopric. Government of the city was deputed to a Vogt, and later to a city judge (first named in 1120). When the Salzburg bishops were raised to the rank of archbishop, Salzburg became the seat of the metropolitan of the old Bavarian dioceses, and after the victory over the Avars Salzburg became the centre of missionary work in the Alpine and Danube areas as far as W. Hungary. In 1077, the passionate defence of the Papal interests during the contest for investiture induced Archbishop Gebhard to build the *fortress*. A new outbreak of the dispute between Emperor and Pope led to the destruction and plunder of the city and its churches by the army of Frederick Barbarossa. In the course of the city's reconstruction, the massive Romanesque Dom was erected on the site of the first Dom, founded by Bishop Virgil (745-85). The core of the *'Fürstenstadt'* (princes' city) developed together with the medieval *residence,* built in 1110 and itself later rebuilt. Until the mid 12C, the gradually evolving *Bürgerstadt* (citizens' city) was outside the curtain wall, which enclosed only St.Peter and the Dom district. At this period, Salzburg once again reached the size it had been as a Roman city. The oldest market square, dating from around 1000, is thought to be the *Waagplatz* (market rights first acquired in 996). The oldest medieval bridge led over the Salzach at a point opposite the Waagplatz.

The first and decisive changes in the compact medieval city were made by Archbishop Wolf Dietrich of Raitenau (1587-1612). His rigorous town-planning measures, influenced by Italian ideas, laid the foundations for Salzburg's develop-ment into one of the finest baroque residence cities in Europe. The Dom fire of 1598 provided an opportunity for extensive alterations. The *Neubau* and the *Residenz* replaced the medieval court. The building of the *Hofmarstall* (court stables) allowed the construction of a new road linking the Dom district and the Bürgerspital, downstream on the Salzach. The building of *Schloss Altenau,* later Schloss Mirabell, moved the town on the right bank of the Salzach further down the river. Many of the ambitious plans of Wolf Dietrich, the first prince of Salzburg baroque, who died in 1617, were realized by his successors. Most of this work was done under his cousin and immediate successor Archbishop Markus Sittikus, Count of Hohenems (1612-29). The construction of the Dom was completed in 1628 under Archbishop Paris Count Lodron (1619-53). The Archbishop managed to prevent the Thirty Years' War from affecting the archbishopric. However, the war still made it necessary to provide the town with massive fortifications. In 1622 the Archbishop founded a Benedictine university. It was only from the time of Wolf Dietrich onwards that such Orders as the Franciscans, Capuchins and Ursulines were given permission to settle here. The absence of significant aristocratic families and their palaces is another characteristic feature of Salzburg, except where they were recruited from the relatives of the clerical rulers. The archbishops Johann Ernst Count Thun (1687-1709) and Franz Anton Fürst Harrach (1709-27) completed the work begun by Wolf Dietrich. It was under Hieronymus Count Colloredo (1772-1803), last of the Salzburg archbishops and also the secular ruler, that the town developed into an important centre of Catholic enlightenment in the southern German-speaking area. The French occupied Salzburg in 1800, and in 1803 the abbey was secularized. For a short period (1803-5), Salzburg became the seat of a newly

Salzburg by night

formed yet short-lived electorate ruled by Ferdinand of Tuscany. The town finally became Austrian in 1816 when, in a decision reached in Vienna, the much-reduced former archbishopric was awarded to the Enns territory and the town was reduced to the rank of main town of an administrative district.

The insignificance into which Salzburg sank at this period was made up for by the Romantics and Nazarenes, and somewhat later by the Biedermeier painters and realist writers. In 1850, Salzburg once again became the capital of its own crown territory. It was connected to the international railway network in 1860. The new town grew up on the right bank of the river Salzach, which has been canalised since the mid 19C.

Towards the end of the Second World War, even the Old Town suffered bomb damage, most of which has been repaired in keeping with the earlier architecture.

I. LEFT BANK OF THE SALZACH

Dom hl.Rupert und hl.Virgil: History: Excavation in 1956–8 and 1966&67 finally clarified the design of the earlier buildings (see Domgrabungsmuseum, Neue Domkrypta). 1. Dom built by Bishop Virgil (767 – 74). Archbishop Konrad I (1106–47) added two massive W. towers. It was under him that the Augustinian rule was introduced for the Dom chapter (1122), and this made it necessary to build a Dom monastery. The Dom and its monastery were destroyed when the city was sacked by the followers of Emperor Frederick Barbarossa in 1167. Work on the construction of a late Romanesque Dom was begun under Cardinal Archbishop Konrad III in 1181. The monastery was rebuilt. The Dom was consecrated between 1198 and 1201. A false impression of a nave and four aisles was given by using the southernmost aisle as a walk of the cloister; the transept has conches towards the E. and to the sides. A suitable W. portal was added in the Gothic period. Archbishop Wolf Dietrich (1586 – 1612) planned to modernise the old building, but this was made unnecessary by the Dom fire of 15 December 1598. The first rebuilding project dates from 1601. A second plan has survived: dating from 1606, it was drawn up by Vincenzo Scamozzi from Vicenza, a pupil of Palladio. Archbishop Markus Sittikus (1617 – 19) appointed Santino Solari, a Northern Italian artist, and he producd the plan which was finally executed between 1614 and 1628 (when the Dom was consecrated). Instead of the

domed Venetian basilica planned by Scamozzi, a church was built using the concepts of Roman early baroque architecture. It became the model for baroque church architecture north of the Alps. The façade was not completed until 1652 – 5 when the towers were extended. The air raid on Salzburg on 16 October 1944 brought down the dome (rebuilding work was completed in 1959).

Dom: Exterior and surroundings: With the exception of the richly articulated double-towered façade of light-coloured Untersberg marble, the nagelfluh building is plainly and lucidly designed. The surrounding squares enhance the massive impression it makes from the side, with its clearly visible, dominant nave and the trefoil E. section with octagonal dome. The *Residenzplatz*, with the *Neubau* (q.v.), the *Michaelskirche* and the *Residenz* (q.v.), is at the N. flank of the Dom. In the centre of the square is the *Residenzbrunnen*, one of the most splendid baroque fountains N. of the Alps. It was built by Giovanni Antonio Dario between 1656 and 1661 by order of

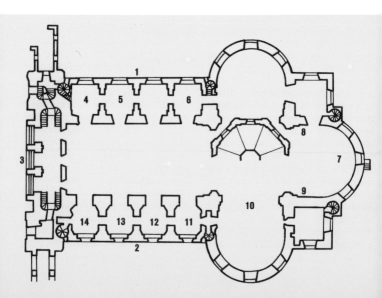

Archbishop Guidobald Count Thun. The statues are attributed to an artist called Tomaso (di Garona?), who contributed to the statuary on the Dom façade.

At the S. flank of the Dom is the *Kapitelplatz* (2), occupying the area of the medieval Dom monastery. The canonical courtyards in the area between the Kapitelplatz/Kaigasse and the Mozartplatz were built from the time of Wolf Dietrich onwards. Two of them, combined in 1864 by a façade, form the new *Erzbischöfliche Residenz*. Together with the S. flank of another chapterhouse (the Kapitelgasse runs between the two), they make up the E. side of the square. There are canonical buildings on its S. side, and in the W. is a section (1658) of the Stiftskirche St.Peter. The square is dominated by the *Kapitelschwemme* drinking-trough, which in its present form was built under Archbishop Leopold Anton Firmian in 1732. In the niche is Neptune standing on a sea horse. This is a signed work by the sculptor Josef Anton Pfaffinger.

The *Domplatz* (39) is like an atrium in front of the Dom façade. It is surrounded in the N. and W. by the Residenz sections built from 1595 to 1605, and in the S. by a section of the monastery of St.Peter built in 1658 to make the square more regular. The square contains the *Mariensäule* built by the brothers Wolfgang and Johann Baptist Hagenauer in 1766–71 for Archbishop Sigismund Count Schrattenbach. This column is of importance stylistically, because of its early neoclassical features. The lead figures (Angel, Devil, Wisdom and Church) and lead reliefs (founders and archbishopric of Salzburg) are on the theme of the Immaculata.

Dom: Façade and interior: The emphatic plainness of the buildings framing the sides of the square allows the *Dom façade* to emerge as the dominant feature. The towers are set forward of the central façade with three arches opening into the portico. The columns of the three-storey middle section and of the four-storey towers follow the scheme Doric, Ionic, Corinthian. The decorations on the statues are schematically arranged. Three portals

Dom

Portal by Ewald Mataré

with bronze doors dating from 1957 and 1958 lead from the portico, which has staircases at the sides (the right-hand staircase leads to the Dommuseum, q.v.). The doors are dedicated to the three divine virtues. From left to right: Faith (Toni Schneider-Manzell), Charity (Giacomo Monzù), and Hope (Ewald Mataré). The inside of the Dom is of clear design and overwhelming dimensions. The abundance of light flooding into the crossing with drum dome leads the onlooker eastards through the twilight of the nave, which receives only indirect light; it has tunnel vaulting and is articulated by a colossal order of composite double pilasters, continued in the vault. There is a row of arches in front of the side chapels, and above these arches are galleries behind which the oratories are placed; all this is framed by the colossal pilasters. On the model of Il Gesù in Rome, the chapels adjoining the nave are connected, and thus resemble aisles.

Dom, decorations: The festive appearance of the interior is heightened by J.Bassarino's lavish stucco, *c.* 1630. The wall and ceiling paintings in their stucco frames in the nave (Christological cycle), in the presbytery (where the Christological cycle is continued), in the S. transept (Mariological cycle), in the N. transept (life of St.Francis) and in the dome (Evangelists and Old Testament; restored when the dome was reconstructed) are by Donato Mascagni and his fellow-artists Ignazio Solari and Francesco da Siena. Some important furnishings: the bronze *font* (4) dating from 1321 is by a Master Heinrich and rests on 12C bronze lions. The bronze cover is modern, by T.Schneider-Manzell. In the same chapel is the *altarpiece* showing the baptism of Christ, by Franz de Neve (1674), and in the subsequent chapels are the altarpiece of *St.Anne* (5) by Joachim Sandrart and the altarpiece of the *Crucifixion* by Karl Skreta. The *high altarpiece,* depicting the Resurrection, is by

Donato Mascagni (7), and the painting of Christ in Limbo (9) is also by him. Opposite this is the Entombment (8) by Ignazio Solari. A staircase (10) in the S. transept leads into the archbishops' *crypt.* This was redesigned after the war, and part of it is in the same area as the late Romanesque crypt under the crossing. The crypt altar has a monumental *crucifix* from Seekirchen. The altarpieces in the S. chapels are as follows: the Descent of the Holy Spirit (11) is by Karl Skreta; the altarpieces in the subsequent chapels (12, 13, 14) are by Heinrich Schönfeld. The core of the large organ is the instrument built by the Salzburg court organ builder Joseph Christoph Eggedacher in 1702&3 (it is the second largest church organ in Austria).

Former fürsterzbischöfliche Residenz: Work on the new palace was begun on the site of the medieval bishop's court (the latter was pulled down under Wolf Dietrich), was continued under Markus Sittikus, but was only completed under Paris Lodron, who built two storeys. Another storey was added under Archbishop Guidobald Count Thun. Archbishop Franz Anton was responsible for rebuilding the façade of the Residenz, and also for the redesign and decoration of the *state rooms* begun under Archbishop Johann Ernst Graf Thun and carried out under the supervision of L.von Hildebrandt. The Residenz lost most of its original decorations as a consequence of the secularisation of the abbey. The Residenzgalerie (q.v.) has been on the third storey since 1955. To the visitor, the main building, with its entrance on the Residenzplatz, is the most interesting item of the complex, which is laid out around three courtyards. A gently rising staircase with a tunnel vault leads from the arcaded W. section of the main courtyard, where there is a Hercules figure in a stalactite

Residenzbrunnen with Dom

niche, and continues to the 'belle Etage' where the state and work rooms formerly used by the clerical rulers of the province (Prunkräume) are to be found; there are guided tours. The massive *Carabinierisaal* (the living quarters of the bodyguard, and the archbishops' theatre and banqueting hall) was increased in height in 1665, and decorated in 1689 under Archbishop Johann Ernst Count Thun. The mythological ceiling frescos were painted by the young J.M. Rottmayr who had just returned from Venice. The central theme not only of the ceiling paintings by (J.M. Rottmayr and M.Altomonte) in the other public and private rooms, but also of the rich stucco by Alberto Camesina, adapted to the themes of the paintings, is the story of Alexander the Great, a theme related to the patron of the work. The *Audienzsaal* contains tapestry from Brussels (siege of Rome by Porsena, Rape of the Sabine women, Etruscan battle) with the coat-of-arms of Archbishop Wolf Dietrich. The ceiling paintings which have Alexander as their theme are by J.M. Rottmayr (1711), stucco by A. Camesina. The dome fresco

and altarpiece in the *chapel* are by J.M. Rottmayr. In the *Schöne Galerie*, built in 1710 to a design by J.L. von Hildebrandt, there is a niche for the 'Jüngling vom Magdalensburg'; this was found in Carinthia in 1502 and later transported to Salzburg; since 1806, the original has been in the Kunsthistorisches Museum in Vienna); ceiling fresco is by J.M. Rottmayr (1711). The *Weisser* or *Markus-Sittikus-Saal* has classical stucco by Peter P. Pflauder (1776), on allegorical themes. In the *Kaisersaal* there are portraits of the Habsburg Emperors up until Charles VI (18C).

'Neubau' and Glockenspiel (Residenzplatz): The Neubau has a number of splendid rooms; it was begun by Archbishop Wolf Dietrich in 1588 as a palace for himself and his guests and took over—temporarily at least — the function of the Residenz while the medieval episcopal court was being altered. The building with tower originally had only one inside courtyard, but was extended several times. Its original proportions were lost as a result

'Göttermahl', by J.M. Rottmayr

of the S. extension of the façade on the Residenzplatz. This extension housed the *Hofbibliothek* (court library; today the main post office). It was especially the Prunkräume which suffered as a result of the building's being put to a use for which it was not intended. Archbishop Johann Ernst Count Thun ordered the tower to be increased in height, and also had a chime of 35 bells installed there in 1702. The bells had been commissioned by the Archbishop from the Antwerp bell-founder Melchior de Hace and had originally been intended for the town of Breda in N. Brabant. The Glockenspiel chimes daily at 7 a.m., 11 a.m. and 6 p.m.

Franziskanerkirche (Hofstallgasse/ Sigmund-Haffner-Gasse): The nave of the building, begun in 1208 and consecrated in 1223, has survived, while the choir fell victim to a plan for rebuilding the entire church drawn up *c.* 1408. The architect was Master Hans von Burghausen, *c.* 1350 – 1432. By about 1445&6, work on the choir had progressed as far as the beginning of the vault.

Stephan Krumenauer (d. 1461) completed the choir. The tower was not completed until the late 15C. The present roof of the tower dates from the Gothic redesign of 1866&7. The church served temporarily as a cathedral while the Dom was being rebuilt, and in 1643 it was transferred to the Franciscan Order. The W. façade was redesigned *c.* 1700. The severe design of the basilican nave clashes abruptly with the hall choir with its fine net vault.

Inside the building, the buttresses are the starting point for the baroque ring of chapels, which are like a text book on the development of ornament in the 17C. The *Engelskapelle* (2) was consecrated by Archbishop Wolf Dietrich in *c.* 1600, while the *Karl-Borromäus-Kapelle* (3) was consecrated by Archbishop Markus Sittikus in 1614. Ottavio Mosto's stucco in the *Franziskuskapelle* (4), consecrated by Archbishop Johann Ernst Count Thun in about 1690, is the peak of high baroque ornament. Altarpiece and frescos showing scenes from the life of the Saint by J.M. Rottmayr, 1693. The most significant item of the furnishings is the high altar (1)

Gobelinsaal, Residenz

Hof, 4 Mozartplatz

Detail of Residenzbrunnen

designed by J.B. Fischer von Erlach in 1708. It replaced the altar by Michael Pacher, which was destroyed. Pacher's Madonna Enthroned (the Child is late 19C) is a miraculous image forming the focal point of the baroque new altar. The latter is designed with the confidence of a great artist to fit in with its Gothic surroundings. The figures of St. George and St. Florian at the sides are set up in the manner of Gothic shrine guardians. They and the Trinity on the altar are the work of Simon Fries. Remains of late Gothic frescos (5) dating from 1456 (pillar in front of and to the right of the altar), 1446 and 1447 (triumphal arch). The stairs up to the pulpit (6) have Romanesque architectural elements; also from the Romanesque period (*c.* 1220) is the *portal* in the portico of the S. entrance (7), with warriors on the door lintel, and Christ in the drum.

District of the Kloster St.Peter: Design and history: After the Roman Juvavum fell into decline, at the beginning of the history not only of the city but also of the later archbishopric of Salzburg, St. Rupert founded the Benedictine abbey in the shadow of the Mönchsberg. Abbot and bishop continued to be one person until 987, giving considerable political and cultural importance to the monastery of the abbot bishops Virgin and Arno. When a separate bishop's residence (Residenz) was founded under Archbishop Konrad I in 1100, the result was that the old residence, which had subsequently been converted into a monastery, remained in Benedictine hands. The monastery building, which had originally stood between the Mönchsberg and the church, was pulled down at the same time. The W. wing of the cloister, with well house dating from the late

Franziskanerkirche

Salzburg, Franziskanerkirche 1 High altar of 1709 with Virgin Mary by Pacher **2** Engelskapelle, founded c. 1600 **3** Borromäuskapelle, founded c. 1614 **4** Franziskuskapelle, founded c. 1690 **5** Gothic frescos **6** Pulpit with Romanesque sculpture, c. 1220 **7** Romanesque portal, c. 1270

12C, goes back to the time when the old bishop's residence was converted into a monastery building. The *Marienkapelle* (former St.-Veits-Kapelle) is the earliest work of Gothic religious architecture in the city. The outer courtyard of the Benedictine abbey became the present irregular square under Abbot Edmund Sinhuber (1674–1702). Abbot Beda Seeauer (1753 –83) was responsible for the spacious proportions of the abbey and its Romanesque church, and also ensured the unity of the

façade of the outer courtyard. The foundation of the *Collegium Benedictum* (1925), including the construction of a central house of study for German-speaking Benedictines led by Abbot Petrus Klotz (1926), led to the monastery's being enlarged by a further building in the W. (this was designed by P. Behrens, the outside frescos are by A. Faistauer, and in the entrance hall is an expressive crucifix by J. Adlhart). The monastery, which was elevated to the status of an archbishopric in 1927, is the only monastery in the Germaan-speaking world to have a continuous tradition going back to its foundation, which was before 700 (temporary dissolution from 1942–5). Its work in the fields of art and science have meant that it has at all times been one of the focal points of cultural life in the Salzburg area. Its school of writing and book illustration attained supraregional importance several times in the course of the Middle Ages; Johann von Staupitz, the humanist and friend of Martin Luther, determined the history of the monastery for a short period; the St. Peter monastery had as decisive a share in the foundation of the Salzburg university (q.v.) as it did in the efforts to have it rebuilt. On 26 October 1783, W.A. Mozart gave his E minor mass (K. 427) its first performance in the Stiftskirche.

Stiftskirche St. Peter: The character of this high Romanesque basilica, rebuilt between 1130 and 1143 after the fire of 1127, has been maintained despite two radical alterations (in 1605–25 and 1753–85, the Romanesque E. section was pulled down, the crossing dome was added and later raised, the W. tower was extended, the nave was raised and vaulted, and the interior furnishings were largely replaced). Outside there is a striking contrast between the severe blocks of the basilican nave and the baroque crossing dome, and also between the simple tower (though this was later raised) and the lavish late baroque dome.

St. Peter

Inside the church, the late baroque, almost rococo, decorations mask the essentially Romanesque substance of the building. From the outer courtyard (with the fountain originally designed as a fish pond by Bartolomäus von Opstal in 1673), the visitor enters the Stiftskirche through the *W. portal* which was built in 1757 to harmonise with the late Romanesque portico. The *portico* dates from the 1st half of the 13C. It has heavy rib vaulting and blind niches which were originally open arches. The *Roman tombstones* do not originate from Salzburg. They were not set up here until 1957. The monumental *late Romanesque portal* dating from 1230–40 and built alternately of red and white marble has a tympanum with figures. At the sides are symbols of Paradise (trees and birds). A carved *rococo door* by Lorenz Härmbler. Beyond the tower is the *rococo grille* which dates from 1768 and is the work of Philipp Hinterseer, the court master locksmith. The nave, whose original flat ceiling was raised in 1620, and was removed and replaced by a vault in 1620, has aisle arches. Despite the rococo stucco the capitals are clearly Romanesque. Remains of what must originally have been rich decorations, with Romanesque frescos (e.g. the column shaft). The rococo work dates from the second baroque redesign. The delicate stucco is by Benedikt Zöpf, while the frescos and the uppermost row of paintings on the two upper walls of the nave are the work of F.X. König (from 1757 onwards). The large-scale painting of the Procession to Calvary on the right (S.) wall of the nave is by Kaspar Memberger, 1591, and opposite is the Raising of the Cross by Ignazio Solari. *Furnishings:* In the N. transept is the miraculous image of *Maria Säul,* a late and ornate 'Schöne Madonna' dating from *c.* 1425. Opposite this, in the S. transept, is the *wall tombstone slab* of St. Vitalis, a leading work of Salzburg red marble sculpture, *c.* 1450. All the altarpieces in the church, with two exceptions, are by

Kremser Schmidt, and he also painted a total of some 30 pictures for the abbey. The *high altarpiece,* showing St.Peter, St.Paul and St. Benedict interceding with the Virgin Mary, is also his work. In the right aisle is the *rock tomb of St.Rupertus,* with a bas-relief slab dating from 1444. The *table tomb* of the imperial colonel Hans Werner von Raitenau (d. 1593), who was the father of Archbishop Wolf Dietrich, is in the 5th of the series of late Gothic chapels adjoining the right aisle. These chapels also contain a *Biedermeier memorial stone* to the composer Michael Haydn (d. 1806, brother of Joseph) dating from 1823 and to Mozart's sister 'Nannerl' (Marianne von Bertold zu Sonnenburg).

Petersfriedhof: An ancient graveyard in a picturesque location between the Stiftskirche and the Mönchsberg and the Mönchsberg and the abbey on the E. side. Innumerable Romantics have made it famous through their drawings and paintings. Arcades were built around the graveyard in 1626. and have gradually been decorated with memorial stones and wrought-iron. The *Katharinen-* or *Mariazellerkapelle* can be seen from the graveyard. It is attached to the S. transept of the Stiftskirche and its exterior is still in its original Romanesque form. It was founded by the Babenberg Duke Leopold VI. Peter Pflauder stuccoed the interior in 1792, using mirrors. Opposite, by the Mönchsberg wall, is the *Kreuzkapelle,* which was built in 1170 and appointed by Dom Provost Anton Count Lodron (d. 1615) to be his tomb (the Lodron memorial stone is by Konrad Asper). Behind this is the so-called *Gebetshöhle* (prayer cave) of St.Rupert, with a well-preserved Romanesque altar table; Gothic frescos in the narrow passage up to the Ägidiuskapelle. From the *Communegruft* (the burial place of Michael Haydn, of Mozart's sister 'Nannerl', and of Andreas Nesselthaler, the last Salzburg court painter), the way leads up

Salzburg, Festung Hohensalzburg 1 Upper storey **2** Upper and lower B.-v.-Rohr bastion **3** Rubble **4** Arsenal **5** Hoist cable and hoist building **6** St. -Georgs-Kirche **7** Bürgermeistertor **8** Keutschnach arch **9** Lodron arch **10** Cistern **11** Inner bastion **12** Keutschnach monuments **13** Fortress railway **14** Petersfriedhof

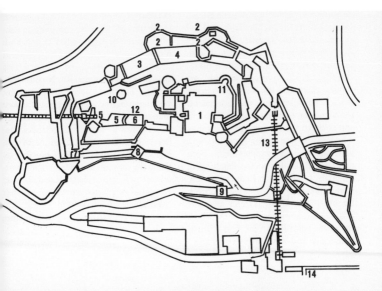

to the so-called *Katakomben* (catacombs; there are guided tours) which, according to tradition, are of early Christian origin. In the middle of the graveyard is the *Margarethenkapelle,* built on the site of the Amanduskapelle, pulled down in 1485.

Festung Hohensalzburg (with a funicular railway): *History:* It is probable that Archbishop Gebhard, who was loyal to the Pope, built a wooden castle in 1077 during the period of the investiture dispute in order to defend himself against the Emperor. Archbishop Konrad I added a stone residence tower to this castle. The outer wall, which surrounded the entire mountain plateau on which the castle stands, was built in the course of the 12&13C. The castle was subjected to an almost uninterrupted series of extensions and conversions from 1465 to 1527. Building activities reached their peak under Archbishop Leonhard von Keutschach (1493–1519). Before him, Cardinal Burkhart von Weisspriach (1461–6) commissioned the four large round towers (1465). The curtain wall was extended under Archbishop Bernhard von Rohr, and the bastion sections (2) named after him were also built at this time. Johann III von Gran (1482–9), the Archbishop's rival and successor, had the so-called *Hoher Stock* (1)—the Romanesque residence—raised, and fire towers added. The refuse tip (3) and the arsenal (4) were also built. Archbishop Leonhard von Keutschach found himself compelled to take measures against the menacing growth of citizens' power, and extended and re-equipped the fortress. The hoisting gear dating from 1502 (5), which is still in use, and has merely been modernized, facilitated the handling of materials. Leonhard von Keutschnach also made some artistic additions to the fortress: he built the Georgskirche and the Prunkräume in the Hoher Stock. When the city was fortified in the Thirty Years' War, the fortress was also modernized. Ar-

chbishop Paris Lodron (1619–53) had the roofs of all the buildings made flat, added the extensive outworks in the W., and built the N. defenses (9) and the associated connecting walls. The expansion of Hohensalzburg into a fortress was concluded when the massive *Kuenburg-Bastei* was built (work completed in 1681). Most recently it was used as a barracks (from 1816 until the Second World War.

Tour of the Festung: Three barriers (7–9) secure the access to the outer ring of buildings including the Grosser Burghof, with the cistern (10) built by Cardinal M.Lang in 1536. The red marble monument to Leonhard von Keutschach, which dates from 1515 and is attributed to H.Valkenauer, is on the side of the St.-Georgs-Kirche (6) facing the courtyard. Above the church entrance is a relief of St.Christopher and the Crucifixion, 1502. Inside the church are 13 late Gothic reliefs showing Christ and the twelve Apostles. The finest feature of the Burg is the *Hoher Stock* (guided tours). The fourth storey, and also the simple third storey with the Burgmuseum (q.v.), is taken up by the *Fürstenzimmer,* which are among the finest Gothic secular rooms in Europe. The *'Salzburger Stier',* a barrel organ installed at the time of Leonhard von Keutschach, can be heard daily at 7 a.m., 11 a.m. and 6 p.m.

Benediktinerinnenstift Nonnberg: *History:* This is the oldest surviving convent in the German-speaking world; it was founded by St. Rupertus (*c.* 700), who made it over to his niece Erentrudis, the first abbess. Donations provided by the house of Agilolfing made it possible to found the convent, and the liberal support offered by Emperor Henry II and his wife Kunigunde enabled the convent and church to be rebuilt. The church was consecrated in 1009. After the devastating fire

Kachelofen of 1501, Festung

of 1423, the convent church was rebuilt on the ground plan of the previous building (1464–1507). Until 1848 it was a home for aristocratic gentlewomen.

Stiftskirche zu Unserer Lieben Frau Himmelfahrt und St.Erentraud: A late Gothic basilica with nave, two aisles, transept and three apses. The baroque dome dates from 1711. The net-vaulted portico with its portal is on the S. side of the church. There are fine 14C *Gothic tombstones* on the wall to the left of the entrance. The *portal* built in 1497–9 has baldachin niches with copies of statues of saints. These figures originally had coloured frames, and probably came from a contemporary shrine altar; the originals are in the Stiftsmuseum. The stone door jamb is decorated with a miniature but high-quality Annunciation. The *Romanesque tympanum* and door lintel with tendril ornaments both date from the early 13C and were adopted from the previous building. A striking feature of the *interior* is the transept, which is considerably higher than the rest of the church and was created when

Romanesque fresco, Nonnberg

the *crypt* was installed (rich net vault above 18 free-standing columns; in the middle is the rock tomb of St.Erentrudis; not open to the public). The arches of the nave wall have galleries with grilles which serve as prayer chambers for the nuns. In the W., below the nuns' choir, is the *paradise*, with a rear wall from the earlier building; the blind niches in this wall contain the most important surviving Romanesque *frescos* in Salzburg (*c.* 1150). The middle window of the main apse was donated by Mayor Clanner in 1480 and is a work by Peter Hemmel von Andlau, the leading German stained-glass artist of the late Gothic period, who lived in Strasbourg. In front of this is the *high altar* dating from 1515. Drawings by Albrecht Dürer were the model for the paintings. The altar is from Scheffau (q.v.). The *Stiftsmuseum*, only accessible by special permission, has important sculptures and artefacts. It is in the *monastery building*, which is of little significance architecturally. Above the monastery gate is the *Johanneskapelle* with a triptych from the Romanesque Dom dating from 1498, which clearly shows the influence of Veit Stoss. There is a high-quality branch crucifix from the early 15C on the rear wall of the chapel.

Erhardskirche (at the foot of the Nonnberg in the suburb of Nonntal): Built by Caspar Zugalli in 1685–9. This building, with side towers and portico in front of the steep dome, has a rich façade. There is notable stucco by Francesco Brenno inside. The *high altarpiece* shows St.Ottilie being baptized by St.Erhard and is by J.M. Rottmayr (signed, and dated 1692).

Kajetanerkirche: This is also by C. Zugalli, and was built for the Theatines in 1685–1700. The towerless façade accords with the rules of the Order, having a transverse oval dome with interior fresco by P. Troger (1727). The *high altarpiece* (1727; martyrdom of St.Maximilian), and

he painting of St.Cajetan in glory dating
om 1735 at the right side altar, are also
y P. Troger. The left side altarpiece show-
ng the Holy Family is by J.M. Rottmayr
708).

estival district: The *Hofmarstall* (court
ables) was built under Archbishop Wolf
ietrich in 1606&7 for 130 horses. It was
nsiderably extended in 1672. It consisted
f a summer and a winter riding school.
he *winter riding school*, dating from 1662,
as ceiling paintings by J.M. Rottmayr and
hristian Lederwasch. The *summer riding
hool* (Felsenreitschule) exploits the natu-
l surroundings with three galleries hewn
ut of the rock of the Mönchsberg. Johann
. Fischer von Erlach built the N. façade
f the stables in 1693&4. This façade was
onstructed jointly with the
ferdeschwemmme (horse pond) which is
igned with it and has a sculpture by
lichael Bernhard Mandl, depicting a
orse-breaker. The Pferdeschwemme dates
i its present form from a restoration of
732 in which the sculpture was turned
arough 90 degrees and the pedestal and

the frame of the basin were rebuilt, along
with the frescoed rear wall. When the
festival association was founded and plans
were drawn up for a building in which to
hold the festivals, the Hofmarstall became
the *Festspielgebäude* (festival building).
After the winter riding school had been
twice rebuilt, by E. Hütter in 1924 and by
Clemens Holzmeister in 1926, the *Kleines
Festspielhaus* was built. The original foyer
has survived, with the frescos by Anton
Faistauer: removed because they were considered to be decadent but replaced after
the war. The Kleines Festspielhaus dates
in its present form from 1962&3 when the
auditorium with its 1327 seats was built.
Works of contemporary art are on display
in the central foyer. The *Grosses
Festspielhaus* was completed in 1960 to
plans by Clemens Holzmeister. An
auditorium with 2371 seats, built into the
mountain, was constructed, retaining most
of the Hofmarstall façade. The stage is
equipped to the highest modern standards.
The *Felsenreitschule* was first used for a
festival performance in 1926. It was given
its present shape from 1968 to 1970, the

estspielhaus, wall paintings by Wolfgang Hutter

architect being Clemens Holzmeister (there are guided tours).

Between the Hofmarstall and the Pferdeschwemme a view is obtained of the *Sigmunds- or Neutor* named after Archbishop Sigismund von Schrattenbach, who built it. This gate was constructed in 1764 by tunnelling through the Mönchsberg. It was designed by the brothers Wolfgang and Johann Baptist Hagenauer. The *former Bürgerspital* has a picturesque arcaded courtyard built from 1556–62 (destroyed in the war and rebuilt in 1955) and the *Bürgerspitalskirche St.Blasius* erected in 1327 and altered in 1550. There is a wooden tabernacle with reliefs dating from 1465, and on the right is a side altarpiece of the Magi by P. Troger (1746). The socalled 'Gotischer Saal', which resembles a gallery, was added at a later date; it is sometimes used as an exhibition room. The *former Ursulinenkirche* was built from 1699–1705 to plans by Johann B. Fischer von Erlach. The building exploits its wedge-shaped site and is a fine feature of the view with its façade projecting between side towers. The way leads past th Klausentor built in 1612 into the subur of *Mülln* with the picturesquely locate *Pfarrkirche* consecrated in 1453. Amon its lavish furnishings are a Madonna datin from 1450 and side altarpieces by J.M Rottmayr (c. 1691). The nearb Landeskrankenhaus (provincial hospita contains the *St.-Johannesspital-Kirche* bui in 1699–1704 to plans by Johann B. Fische von Erlach, with excellent altarpieces b M.Rottmayr (1709).

University district: The secondar school founded by Archbishop Markus A tikus in 1617 was raised to the status of university under Archbishop Paris Cour Lodron in 1622. The university wa dissolved in 1810 but revived in 1962. Th *university building* was begun in 1618 f the secondary school, and completed i 1631. It was then expanded in 1655. Th long, plain building was given a simple a caded courtyard when the transverse se tion was added in 1631. That sectio includes the Aula academica, which has a altarpiece and a series of individual pai

Kollegienkirche

Horse trough

ings by Adrian Bloemart (1636/7), and was redesigned in classical style by W.Hagenauer in 1778. **Universitäts-** or **Kollegienkirche:** Archbishop Johann Ernst Count Thun provided 15,000 guilders in 1694 and appointed J.B. Fischer von Erlach to design the building. Construction work to Fischer's plans was begun in 1696 and the church was consecrated in 1707, but the frescos which were to have been executed by J.M. Rottmayr were not painted. The boldly proportioned nave and transept are arranged around a dominant central dome. The massive corner pillars contain two-storeyed cylindrical chapels. Two colossal order columns form a caesura between the nave and the choir, where the stucco gloriola surrounding the Immaculata joins with the light from the apse window in a struggle between appearance and reality. Apart from the magnificent stucco by Diego Francesco Carlone and Paolo d'Allio on the altar wall, and the altar built by Josef Anton Pfaffinger in 1740, mention should also be made of the two altarpieces in the transept which were painted by J.M. Rott-

mayr in 1721&2. In the side chapels are niche figures whose style is undoubtedly close to that of Meinrad Guggenbichler and Josef Anton Pfaffinger.

Getreidegasse: A series of picturesque 16C courtyards leads from the Universitätsplatz to the Getreidegasse, the most important of the old streets in the Bürgerstadt. On 27 January 1756, Wolfgang Amadeus Mozart was born in No. 9 Getreidegasse, the old *Hagenauerhaus,* (see Museums). The Getreidegasse has numerous five- or six-storeyed houses with typical Salzburg façades.

II. THE CITY TO THE RIGHT OF THE SALZACH

Dreifaltigkeitskirche with priest's house (Marktplatz): Founded by Archbishop Johann Ernst Count Thun in 1694. J.B. Fischer von Erlach was the architect. He adopted Francisco Borromini's design for the Sant'Agnese church in

Alte Hofapotheke (rococo), in the Alter Markt

Rome. The two palace-like wings are connected by the concave façade with towers, which contrasts with the convex dome behind. The sculptures (Faith, Charity, Hope and the Church) above the façade are by Michael Bernhard Mandl. The interior is a slender elongated oval with a tunnel-vaulted transept. The dome with its frescos by J.M. Rottmayr (1700) shows the Virgin Mary being crowned by the Trinity.

The Dreifaltigkeitsgasse leads past the *Primogeniturpalast,* previously known as Borromäum. It was built by Archbishop Paris Lodron for his family in 1631.

Schloss Mirabell: In 1606, Archbishop Wolf Dietrich had the *Schlösschen Altenau* built for his mistress Salome Alt. The name was changed to Mirabell under Markus Sittikus. As a result of the fortifications carried out by Lodron, Schloss Mirabell became part of the city. Various additions were made to the Schloss over the years. J.L. von Hildebrandt converted these additions into a uniform complex in 1721–7 by order of Archbishop Franz Anton Harrach. The Schloss in its present state dates back to the massive rebuilding works performed by Peter Nobile after the city fire of 1818. The W. section, most of which had survived, was included in these works. The baroque design of the façade can still be seen in the inside courtyard and at the sides of the garden. There are vehicle entrances with the old baroque stucco, and in the NE corner is the staircase by Hildebrandt with sculptures by G.R. Donner (the Apollo on the first landing is dated 1727 in Donner's own hand) and his assistants. Hildebrandt found a brilliant solution to the problem of installing a baroque state staircase in the shaft-like area at his disposal. The stairs lead to the *Marmorsaal* (today concerts and wedding ceremonies are held here).

Mirabellgarten: J.B. Fischer von Erlach designed this garden in 1690, and it was altered by Franz Anton Danreiter in 1730. The best of the sculptures here are the groups of figures by Ottavio Mosto (depicting the four elements) around the fountain. The Pegasus embossed in copper by Kaspar Gras from Innsbruck, 1661, was originally intended for the Kapitelschwemme. In the NW corner is the *Vogelhaus* built *c.* 1700 (this aviary is today used as an exhibition hall by the Salzburg city department of culture). The *Zwerglgarten,* with marble dwarfs dating from 1715, is on a terrace which originated with the fortifications. To the W. of the Mirabellgarten is the open-air *Heckentheater,* built between 1704 and 1718.

Sebastianskirche (Linzergasse): Built from 1749 to 1753 by converting a previous Gothic church into a hall church. The ceiling frescos by P.Troger were among the items destroyed in the city fire of 1818. The portal, with its rich sculptures, dates from 1754 and is a work by Josef Anton Pfaffinger to a design by Franz Anton Danreiter. The lavish wrought-iron by Philipp Hinterseer dates from 1752.

On the steps down to the *Sebastiansfriedhof* we find the tomb of Theophrastus Bombastus von Hohenheim (Paracelsus), who died in Salzburg. The graveyard itself is in the style of a Campo Santo and was laid out under Archbishop Wolf Dietrich between 1595 and 1600 after the Dom graveyard had been closed down. In the arcades are some rich *memorial stones* from the period up to the 19C. In the centre of the graveyard is the *Gabrielskapelle,* built in 1597–1603 as a mausoleum for Wolf Dietrich to plans by Elia Castello. The inside of this simple cylindrical building with dome was tiled over all by Hans Kapp the potter. The *tombs of Constanze Mozart* and of *Mozart's father Leopold* are in the graveyard.

Schloss Mirabell, staircase

Maria Plain

Capuchin monastery with Kreuzwegkapellen (reached from Linzergasse, house No. 14): The monastery and church were built by Archbishop Wolf Dietrich from 1599 to 1602 for the Capuchins who were called to Salzburg in 1594. The carved *oak doors* of the Romanesque Dom, which date from around 1450, are the best of the furnishings. A splendid view of the city and its environs can be obtained from the *Hettwär-Bastei* bastion situated below the monastery.

III. IMPORTANT BUILDINGS ON THE PERIPHERY OF SALZBURG

Schloss Leopoldskron (in the area of the city SW of the Festungsberg by the Leopoldskroner Weiher): A late baroque Schloss built by order of Archbishop Leopold Anton Baron von Firmian for his nephew Laktanz Firmian. The cool classical appearance of this picturesquely situated Schloss is the result of conversion work carried out later. It was acquired by Max Reinhardt in 1918. (The interior is not open to the public.)

Schloss Klesheim (to the W., outside the city boundary): This Schloss was built in 1700–09 for Archbishop Johann Ernst Count Thun to plans by J.B. Fischer. The design is based on 16C N. Italian architectural ideas, and in its original form, with an opening in the central section, did not suit the climate of the site. This meant that some changes had to be made, with the result that the Schloss was not completed until 1732. The drive, vestibule and staircase are on a lavish scale. This was the house where Hitler's guests stayed, and today the guests of the Salzburg provincial government are accommodated here. The *Hoyos-Schlösschen* built to plans by Fischer von Erlach is in the park to the N. of the Schloss.

Wallfahrtskirche Maria Plain (on the Plainberg N. of the city and to the right of the Salzach): Archbishop Guidobald Thun ordered an octangular chapel to be built in honour of a miraculous image of the Madonna and Child originating from Lower Bavaria. In 1671, Archbishop Max Gandolf Kuenburg laid the foundation stone for the Wallfahrtskirche, which was built by Giovanni Antonio Dario and consecrated in 1674. Before completion it was presented to the Benedictine university of Salzburg. In 1779, the 28th anniversary of the coronation of the miraculous image was celebrated by a performance of the *coronation mass* composed by Wolfgang Amadeus Mozart for the occasion. Since 1810, St. Peter has been the patron Saint of this church, which in 1952 became a Papal basilica minor. The way to it leads from the Elisabethstrasse, and along the route there

Schloss Klesheim

are 15 wayside shrines dating from 1705 (Mysteries of the Rosary). In the four Kalvarienbergkapellen are sculptures by Thomas Schwanthaler and his workshop, and there is a Pietà by Franz Schwanthaler in the Schmerzenskapelle. The Wallfahrtskirche itself has a double-towered façade. Pairs of chapels adjoin the tunnel-vaulted nave. There are sculptures of St.Maximilian and St.Vitalis by Jakob Gerold at the high altar. The side altars have sculptures by T. Schwanthaler who, together with W. Weissenkircher, also built the sculptured decorations on the altars in the side chapels. The wall paintings which adjoin the right side altar and the chapel altars are by Kremser Schmidt (1765).

Schloss Hellbrunn (at the S. edge of the city): This is the most important late Mannerist Lustschloss N. of the Alps. Many of its original features have survived. The villas of Frascati and Tivoli near Rome and the Venetian terra ferma villas were models for the building. The Schloss and gardens were built 1613–15 and expanded in the 18C by the addition of an Englischer Garten; the design is attributed to S. Solari, the architect of the Dom, but he was to a large extent putting into effect the ideas of Archbishop Markus Sittikus von Hohenems, 1612–19, the building's owner. In typical Mannerist style, gardens and Schloss have no overall pattern. The Schloss has two storeys and is built on a rectangular plan. In front of its main façade is a courtyard formed by the domestic buildings. The garden façade has tower-like projections at its corners, and a central projection. Few of the original decorations have survived, apart fom the magnificent wall paintings in the Festsaal

Mozart family, Mozarthaus   *Schlosspark, Hellbrunn* ▷

and in the octagonal music room. These paintings are by D. Mascagni, who was also worked in the Dom. The excellent restoration work by A.Süss on the paintings has not yet been completed. A full-length portrait of Archbishop Markus Sittikus (1618), also by Mascagni, is to be found in the dining hall, where a stove built for Archbishop Wolf Dietrich in 1608 by Friedrich Strobl was later installed. The *Lustgarten* with its trick fountains (guided tours) is one of Salzburg's most visited attractions. The statues in the Lustgarten are attributed to S.Solari, H.Waldburger, and the young B.Permoser. Archbishop Andreas Jakob Count Dietrichstein (1747–53) added the mechanical theatre with its 256 wooden figures to the five fountains. The *Monatsschlösschen* (Schloss Waldems; it is said that Markus Sittikus had it built in one month in order to win a wager; today

it is the Volkskundemuseum, q.v.) is on the Hellbrunnerberg. On the way to this Schloss is the *Steintheater,* commissioned by Markus Sittikus on the site of a quarry. It is probably the first open-air theatre N. of the Alps. It is thought that the first performance of an opera N. of the Alps was held on its stage. The first mention of a *Tiergarten* in Hellbrunn was in 1424; the original deer park is now a notable *zoo.*

Schloss Anif: This moated Schloss was mentioned in the 16C. After being converted in 1683, it was used by the Prince Bishops of Chiemsee as a summer residence until 1814. In 1838–48 it was rebuilt by Alois Count Arco-Steppberg in the style of the period. The building's fragile elegance, and the way in which it merges with the magnificent landscape, make this Schloss one of the most outstan-

ding works of the first Romantic period. The Schloss is privately owned.

Museums: Salzburger Museum Carolino Augusteum: Founded as a municipal institution in 1834, it took on the function of a Landesmuseum from the very start. The main building (1 Museumsplatz) has a collection of primeval and early history, Roman provincial archaeology, collections relating to the history of art and culture, historical musical instruments, a collection of graphic art, coins and medals, the municipal archive, and a library. The following are still at the planning stage: toy collection, and collection of musical and theatrical history, in the Bürgerspital; an *open-air museum* near Grossgmain. Branches of the museum: *Burgmuseum* in the Festung Hohensalzburg with a collection relating to the history of the province; the most significant public weapon collection in Salzburg. *Volkskundemuseum* Hellbrunn (folklore museum; in the Monatsschlösschen). *Domgrabungsmuseum* (museum of excavations from the Dom; the entrance is in the Residenzplatz, by the Dom arches), showing the Roman and medieval predecessors of the Dom building (open from May to October). **Mozart-Museum** (in the house where Mozart was born, 9 Getreidegasse): This was set up by the International Mozarteum Foundation in 1880 as a Mozart memorial site, with numerous mementoes. The department relating to Mozart in the theatre was added in 1931. **Haus der Natur** (5 Museumsplatz): This was begun in 1908 as a bird museum, from which the extensive nature museum known as 'Haus der Natur' was developed in 1924. Today it is housed in the former Ursulinenkloster. **Salzburger Residenzgalerie** (former archiepiscopal residence): This started as a provincial collection in 1923; most of it is housed in the former archiepiscopal picture gallery. After being reopened in 1952,

it was considerably expanded as a result of generous loans (the Czernin collection and the Schönborn-Buchheim collection). The gallery confines itself to paintings dating from the end of the Gothic period onwards. The chief areas of interest are French and Flemish baroque painting. There are important works of Austrian painting from the 18&19C. There are plans to expand the collection of modern art, especially the contemporary graphic arts in the Rupertinum (Sigmund-Haffner-Gasse). **Salzburger Barockmuseum** (Mirabellgarten): Dating from 1973, this is based on a private collection and is housed in the orangery of the Mirabellgarten. There is a special collection of important Italian 'pensieri' and 'bozzetti' (ideas and sketches). **Dommuseum** (housed in the southern Dom oratories and Dom arches. Access is gained from the Dom portico. Open from May to October.): Opened in 1974. 1. *Kunst- und Wunderkammer;* a successful reconstruction of the Dom art collection, set up by Archbishop Guidobald Count Thun in 1662 and brought to an end in 1805 (the most important items were taken to Vienna at that time). The reconstruction is mainly based on the original, much of which survives. 2. The *Dommuseum proper* with significant works of ecclesiastical applied art, but also of painting and sculpture, from the late Middle Ages onwards. The **Trakl-Gedächtnisstätte** memorial to the poet in the Traklhaus (1a Waagplatz) is also worth visiting.

Theatres: *Salzburger Landestheater* (22 Schwarzstrasse): Built by F.Fellner and H.Helmer in 1892&3 on the site of the former Ballhaus. There are 742 seats. *Kammerspiele of the Salzburger Landestheater* (24 Schwarzstrasse): This is used mainly for contemporary theatre. 137 seats. *Salzburger Marionettentheater* (pup-

Schloss Anif

pet theatre; 24 Schwarzstrasse): 340 seats (Easter to late September). The *Kleines Festspielhaus* is used for theatrical performances from time to time when the Festspiele are not being performed. During the Festspiele in summer, *outdoor theatrical performances* are also held in various squares in Salzburg.

St. Andrä im Lavanttal 9433
Kärnten   p.282☐Q 10

Pfarrkirche St. Andrä: The architectural history of this parish church is as eventful as the history of the little town and bishopric dating back to the 12C. A 9C Carolingian parish church can only be assumed to have existed; parts of the wall (the W. tower) are from the Romanesque period, while the choir and the rib vault are Gothic and late Gothic respectively. The church is a pillared basilica, with nave and two aisles. It was altered in the baroque period and in the 19C by the addition of a chapel and a portico, and also by a new

St. Andrä, Maria Loreto

roof. There are 15&16C *fresco fragments* in the baptism chapel to the N. of the W. tower and in the Annakapelle to the N. of the choir; a late Gothic Virgin Mary relief (1480) was moved into the portico (1524). Inside the church are numerous *memorial stones* from the 15C to the 18C (including the tombstone of Bishop Liechtenberger, d. 1446, by H. Eybenstock?). The high altar is neo-Gothic, and the side altars have late baroque carvings and paintings.

Wallfahrtskirche Maria Loreto: Built by Bishop Count von Stadion in 1683–7. It is a baroque cruciform building, with a choir in the N., tall towers in the S., and a shallow articulated tunnel vault in the nave. There are baroque statues and paintings on the altar and in the chapels.

St. Cäcilia = St. Georgen ob Murau 8861
Steiermark   p.282☐O 9

St. Cäcilia: A daughter church of St. Georgen, mentioned in 1300. This isolated single-aisled hall church has 14&15C frescos. Last Judgement and Magi on the N. wall of the choir, 16C Lamentation by the pulpit.

St. Erhard 8615
Steiermark   p.280☐S 8

Pfarrkirche St. Erhard: The foundation walls of a 12C Romanesque hall were used for this church. It was rebuilt in the high Gothic style in the 14C, with three bays in the nave and two in the choir. The rib vault was added later. The Marien- und St.-Leonhard-Kapelle in the N., on the S. side of the choir, were added in the 17C, along with the new sacristy (the old sacristy, divided off by a wrought-iron grille, became the sanctuary). The dominant exterior feature is the baroque S. tower. The W. façade has portal completed in 14C; tympanum with Bishop Erhard blessing *c.* 1400. Only a few alterations were made to the Gothic church in the baroque period. *Inside:* In the choir, 20 valuable stained-glass windows from the Herzogswerkstatt workshop in Vienna (*c.* 1400). The high altarpiece (1646) and the figure on the column in the presbytery (18C) depict St. Erhard. The organ is by Andreas Schwarz (1722). The pulpit dates from 1700.

St. Florian bei Linz 4490
Upper Austria   p.276□P 5

Augustiner-Chorherrenstift: The tomb of a man who died for his beliefs is at the heart of St. Florian, one of the most important monasteries in Austria. Valeria, a pious Christian lady, laid him to rest here; a shrine was soon built above his grave. The first monastery was founded *c.* 800, and in 1071 it became an Augustinian abbey. In the Middle Ages the abbey became an intellectual and economic centre. The schools of writing and painting were very famous: A. Altdorfer made the *Sebastiansaltar*, one of his most splendid works, for the abbey in 1518. The foundation stone of the present buildings was laid on the day of the feast of the Assumption in 1686; three great architects, C.A. Carlone, J. Prandtauer and G. Hayberger, built a most splendid monastery here. St. Florian acquired additional significance through A. Bruckner's work as organist (1845–55). The abbey maintains its own theological school, and has 32 parishes in its care. One particular function of the foundation is the encouragement of music. The importance of the St. Florian boys' choir school extends beyond the province. Organ recitals and other musical events maintain the tradition of the 'Bruckner abbey'.

St. Florian, Stift 1 Stiftskirche 2 Sommerrefektorium 3 Library 4 Marmorsaal 5 Adlerbrunnen 6 Staircase 7 Marienkapelle 8 Hauptportal 9 Meierhof

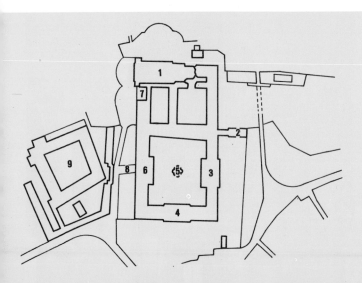

Stiftskirche Mariä Himmelfahrt: This church, a leading work by C.A. Carlone, is at the N. end of the W. building, which has 34 sets of windows. The façade has two towers with unusual domes; the interior is extremely impressive. The vestibule between the towers leads to a high single-aisled nave with four chapels on each side and galleries above. There is a crossing, and a choir with a rounded apse. The church is articulated by enormous half-columns on tall bases with a rich cornice. Very fine ceiling painting; colourful frescos by Gumpp and Steidl in the pendentive domes in the individual bays. *Furnishings:* Massive high altar; carved choir stalls and musicians' galleries with side organs; black marble pulpit; superb wrought ironwork. The *Bruckner-Orgel,* the large organ built by Franz Xaver Krismann from 1770–4, is one of the best-sounding and largest instruments of its period. *Marienkapelle:* S. of the vestibule, with fine baroque decorations. *Herrensakristei:* ceiling by J.A. Gumpp and M.Steidl; the lavabo is the work of Leonhard Sattler. *Prälatensakristei:* A soaring space with light stucco by F.J.I.

Holzinger (1737), and a fresco by Altomonte; inlaid cupboards with delicate carving by Sattler. Splendid paraments. The plain sarcophagus of Anton Bruckner, 'God's musician' (1824–96), is under the great organ. Tombs of various priors; the oldest sections of the building, and also the tomb of Christin Valeria, are in the *crypt.* The relics of St.Florian have been lost.

Stift: When C.A. Carlone died in 1708, he had completed the church, but the monastery buildings had only just been begun. Prandtauer was asked to continue the work, as he had been at Kremsmünster and Christkindl. The library was added 1744 –50 by G. Hayberger. The *W. building* houses the main portal and the stairs: the long side measures 670 ft. Carlone broke the monotony by inserting the lavish projecting portal. It is almost three storeys high, and has balconies on the 1st and 2nd storeys. The statues are by L.Sattler: massive atlantes on the ground floor, on the 1st floor 'Virtues' and pilaster herms supporting the upper balcony, and on the 2nd storey urns. The *Bläserturm* tower rises

St.Florian, Stiftskirche, Bruckner organ

above the portal. Beyond the entrance is the large Stiftshof with the *Adler-Brunnen* in its centre, and behind this the E. building containing the library. The *staircase,* is almost a house in itself, and unique in its design. It was conceived by Carlone and completed by Prandtauer in splendid style as a worthy entrance to the imperial apartments. The combination of rising arches continued horizontally on the second floor and the enormous two-storey arch with attached columns in the central axis (a Palladio motif), was made possible by Prandtauer's idea of the concave Kaisergang on the 2nd floor. *Marmorsaal:* Built by Prandtauer from 1718 – 24, it resembles a pavilion and dominates the façade of the S. building. This façade is the secular counterpart of the church in the N. It is dominated by massive Corinthian columns on tall plinths and the virtuoso ceiling fresco. The hall is a demonstration of imperial power and celebrates the triumph of Christianity over the Turks (ceiling fresco). On the narrow sides are large portraits of Charles VI and Prince Eugen. The inspired artist was Altomonte, and the design was by his father Martin. *Library:* In the E. building, it was built by G. Hayberger (Steyr) in 1744–50. In contrast to the Marmorsaal, where the spatial impression is created by the architecture, the effect in the library derives primarily from the interior decorations. The walls of books are surrounded by a curving gallery and show the intimate interpretation of space of the rococo period. The ceiling fresco is by B. Altomonte. *Kaiserzimmer:* A series of 13 magnificent princely apartments, included in the guided tour. Adjacent is the *Bruckner-Zimmer,* containing the composer's modest furniture (deathbed, piano, armchair), some of it from his flat in Vienna (Belvedere, see Vienna). *Abbey collections:* Apart from the splendid showrooms, the abbey also has a valuable collection of paintings and other works of art. The best of these are the paintings by

St. Florian, stained-glass window

St. Florian, portal by Prandtauer uniting all three storeys; sculptures by L. Sattler

the Danube school, especially those by A.Altdorfer and W.Huber. *Sommerrefektorium:* An Italianate hall built in 1726–30 to plans by Prandtauer, and a feature of the E. view of the buildings; not open to the public. *Gartenpavillon:* In the Hofgarten, built by Carlone in 1681; a graceful building with a flight of steps and a loggia. Mansard-style roof. *Meierhof:* Opposite the main entrance; square, with massive roof and storerooms underneath.

Environs: Schloss Tillysburg (some 6 km. E.): Acquired by a nephew of the famous general in 1629; an interesting imitation, on a smaller scale, of the staircase by Prandtauer at St.Florian was built in the E. wing of the Schloss in the 18C. **Jagdmuseum Schloss Hohenbrunn** (hunting museum; some 2 km. SW): The former abbey hunting lodge. A baroque building by Prandtauer with charmings arcades in the upper storey.

St. Georgen am Längsee 9313
Kärnten   p.282☐P 10

Former Benedictine convent: This, the oldest monastic foundation surviving in Carinthia, was founded in 1002–08. The convent's eventful history over the following centuries included raids by the Hungarians (1259), pillage by the Turks (1473), and fire (1527). Adjacent to the church in the W. are Gothic buildings in the N. (with a Renaissance loggia dating from 1446), and baroque sections. Carlone built the two-storey sections in 1654–8. There are late Gothic statues in the chapel of the E. section, and also in the corridors.

Pfarrkirche and former Klosterkirche: Romanesque sculptures on the columns were revealed in a recent renovation. It is not clear from the present single-aisled Gothic building, later much altered in the baroque style, that it was built on the plan of the Romanesque basilica which had a nave and two aisles. The oldest feature is the portal (1259) in the N. wall. Inside there are six groin-vaulted bays. The *baroque altar decorations* are early 18C. Numerous *Roman stones* from the 3C AD are built into the arcades in the monastery and the N. wall of the church.

St. Georgen am Weinberge = Mittertrixen 9102
Kärnten   p.282☐Q 11

Pfarrkirche: Late Gothic choir and nave with three bays and a net vault, built in the early 16C. The baroque Annenkapelle, which has a tunnel and groin vault is S. of the choir. There is a late Gothic alabaster relief in the crypt. The wooden statues of St.Florian and St.George at the chapel altar date from the same period (early 15C). High altar *c.* 1750.

Schloss Frankenstein: Today this is a two-storeyed baroque building with an inner courtyard in the NW and the Josefskapelle in the NE tower. The Schloss is in private hands.

St. Georgen ob Murau 8861
Steiermark   p.282☐O 9

St. Georg: Consecrated in 1188, present building 1477. It is a late Gothic hall church with nave, two aisles and stellar vaulting. Underneath the gallery is a 13C Romanesque animal head, formerly a gargoyle. 14C stained-glass windows in the S. of the nave. There are two triptychs dating from 1455. To the S. of the church

St. Florian, painting by Altdorfer ▷

is a two-storeyed *round ossuary* with a round apse; the statues are by Johann Nischlwitzer. *Roman stones* in the S. outer wall and E. wall of the priest's house.

St. Gilgen 5340
Salzburg   p.276□M 6

The area around the Aber- or Wolfgangsee was presented to Salzburg by the house of Agilolfing in the 1st half of the 8C. It is not certain that the foundation of St.Gilgen can be traced back to a monk's cell by the Abersee in the 8C; the town is not named until 1376. The Alt-Hüttenstein fortress was built as a consequence of disputes over ownership with the Mondsee monastery (q.v.). The court (now the district court) in St.Gilgen may have been set up as a result of the protection provided by this fortress. When the existing court building was erected in 1719&20, Nikolaus Pertl, the grandfather of W.A. Mozart, was then employed by the court. Mozart's mother Anna Maria was born in the new court

St. Johann in Pongau

building in 1720, and Mozart's sister Nannerl (Marianne) lived there from 1784–1801. She was the wife of Johann B. Berchtold von Sonnenburg, who was also a court employee.

Pfarrkirche St. Ägyd: Except for the late Gothic portico and the Romanesque-style 14C tower with double onion dome dating from 1727, the church first mentioned in 1376 is dominated by the building dating from 1767. The three altars in the transitional stage between rococo and neoclassicism, with their paintings by Peter A. Lorenzoni (1768), also belong to this phase of expansion. The early-18C Madonna and Child in the choir is from the workshop of M.Guggenbichler.

Environs: The *Jagdschloss Fuschl,* which formerly belonged to the Prince Archbishop, can be seen from the road to Salzburg. No documents exist to prove its age. The first information is provided by invoices dating from the 16C for repair works. The massive, tower-like building has been privately owned since 1865 and is now a hotel. See St.Wolfgang.

St. Johann im Pongau 5600
Salzburg   p.282□M 8

This is the administrative centre of the Pongau district. It may have been mentioned as early as 924 as one of the 'loca' in the Pongau region. There was a market here in the 13C, when the town contained one of the branches of the regional court of Pongau.

Dekanatspfarrkirche hl. Johannes der Täufer: The church was rebuilt from 1855–61 after the fire which destroyed the market town in 1855. Georg Schneider, an architect from Munich, designed the neo-Gothic basilica with nave, two aisles, and choir with polygonal apse, while the twin towers in the W. (1873–6) were the work of Josef Wessiken from Salzburg. The church's dominant site above the Salzach valley, and also its majestic interior, make the building a leading work of historicist ecclesiastical architecture in Salzburg (it is known as the 'Pongauer Dom'). The neo-Gothic altars have some late Gothic figures. *Annakapelle* NW of the church: This two-storeyed building was formerly the *ossuary*. On the altar of the groin-vaulted lower storey is a carving of St. Heinrich II and St.Kunigunde enthroned (south German, *c.* 1530).

Environs: The Kleinarler Ach and the Grossarler Ach join the Salzach at St. Johann. The main town of the Grossarl valley is the market town of **Grossarl** with the *Pfarrkirche hl. Ulrich*, a single-aisled hall dating from 1768&9 with uniform rococo decorations. On the way towards Grossarl we find the *Alte Wacht*, a wooden gatehouse dating back to the Middle Ages. The main town of the Kleinarl valley is **Wagrain,** a market town where Josef

Mohr (d. 1848), who wrote 'Silent Night', is buried.

St. Johann im Tirol 6380
Tirol   p.284☐J 7

This beautiful village with its old baroque houses has an 18C priest's house dating originally from the Gothic period (on the 1st floor are frescos dating from 1480).

Pfarrkirche Mariae Himmelfahrt: This church was built by Abraham Millauer in 1724–8 as the 'first large baroque church in the Unterland', on the site of an earlier Gothic building. The beautifully articulated façade which projects between two towers has a colonnaded portal with a gable relief by Georg Doppler the stonemason (*c.* 1725). Inside the building fine stucco by Gabriel Zipf dating from 1726, and ceiling frescos by S.B. Faistenberger (1727). The altars are by Georg Doppler, with paintings by J.Zanussi, 1740. The pulpit is by August and Anton Gigl, 1730. There is a fine

Wagrain, Mohr tomb

Fieberbrunn, seal of confession

Virgin Mary dating from 1440 on the right side altar in the nave.

Antoniuskapelle (in the graveyard): A round building whose vault, with its dome and lantern, was installed in 1669–74. In the dome is an imposing fresco by Joseph Schöpf (1803). The church has been restored several times after lightning and war damage.

Spitalkirche in der Weitau: This hospital founded in 1262 also includes a church, which was redesigned in baroque style in *c.* 1744. The following items are Gothic: the remains of frescos above the vault, the stained-glass window in the choir (the only stained-glass window in the N. Tirol to have survived in its entirety), the marble memorial stones (the best of these dates from 1493), and two bells in the turret dating from 1262. The wall frescos are by J.A. Mölk (1745), and the ceiling frescos in the nave are by Simon Benedikt Faistenberger (1744).

Environs: Fieberbrunn with the

Johann-Nepomuk-Kapelle. This small church built in 1760&1 has very fine frescos by M. Günther dating from 1762. **St. Ulrich am Pillersee,** with the beautifully located *Kapelle hl. Adolar.* The Wallfahrtskirchlein (pilgrimage church) mentioned as early as 1013 was rebuilt in the early 15C. In 1957, some very well preserved *Gothic frescos* were uncovered in the choir, on the walls and in the vault. There is a Gothic *Pietà* on the main altar.

St. Justina = Mittewald an der Drau 9912

Tirol   p.284☐K 10

Pfarrkirche hl.Justina: This small church built in *c.* 1500 and rebuilt in baroque style in *c.* 1630 is very attractively sited on rising ground. On the tower is a large St. Christopher fresco dating from 1513. Inside is the Justina-Altar with a figure in a niche of St. Justina from the 1st half of the 15C.

St. Lambrecht 8813

Steiermark   p.282☐P 9

Benediktinerabtei: This abbey was founded by Count Marquard of Carinthia (d. 1076) and his son Duke Heinrich II. The Benedictine foundation held an important position in the 12C. Its development was helped by the fact that Mariazell, the best-known pilgrimage site in Austria, has always been part of the foundation and administered by it. The flourishing cultural life of the abbey was only brought to an end when it was dissolved by Emperor Joseph II in 1786.

Stiftskirche: After the collapse of the original Romanesque basilica, consecrated in 1160, the present hall church, with its nave and two aisles, was built in the 14C. The entire choir was redesigned in the 17C

St. Lambrecht

after the choir screen had been pulled down in 1639. The two-towered W. façade with the marble *main portal* by D. Sciassia was added in 1645. At about the same time Melchior Mayr painted his *frescos* on the vaults (fragments survive). The *furnishings* of the church were renovated in the period that followed: the high altar is by Valentin Khautt, and the ebony tabernacle with its silver mountings is by Leopold Vogtner (1719). The 17C Benediktiner- and Emmeranaltar was designed by Christoph Paumgartner. The decorations on the pulpit, and the splendid, richly carved choir stalls behind the organ in the priests' choir, are also from Paumgartner's workshop. The original *Gothic decorations* include the St.Agnes in the S. aisle and the 14C wooden crucifix in the portico. There is also a Virgin Mary figure (1642) in the portico. The 17C sacristy is very fine (stucco and vestments).

Ossuary: This dates from the 12C. It is mentioned in the 13C as a parish church dedicated to the twelve Apostles (notice that the number of windows is also twelve).

The ossuary is in the lower storey, and the chapel is on the floor above.

Peterskirche: This was built as a parish church in 1424. The Aflenz high altar from the Villach workshop dates from 1515, with reliefs. There is a wooden Virgin Mary statue on the right side altar (1430); the paintings on the wings are 15C. The paintings on the left side altar (*c.* 1435) showing the Crucifixion and Saints are most impressive.

Abbey buildings: This spacious 17C complex by D.Sciassia is much influenced by the Roman Renaissance. The rooms are lavishly decorated. The corridors are paved in marble, and there is delicate ceiling stucco by Matthäus Camin. The *Kaisersaal,* the *Konklavesaal* (decorated in baroque style in the 18C, with portraits of Emperor Francis II and Maria Theresa), and the *Refektorium,* are all of interest.

Museum: The collections consists of works of art formerly in the abbey and gives a very impressive indication of how

St. Lambrecht

art flourished in this region in the 14&15C. The four halls include: Roman sculptures and inscriptions; haloed Virgin Mary; St. Lambrecht votive tablet (1430); Mount of Olives by Hans von Tübingen; several 15C altar wings; stained-glass windows from the same period; 15&16C sculptures.

Schloss: This was built as a fortified structure in 1390–1420 and was later taken over by the abbey. After the abbey was dissolved the Schloss fell into disrepair. Surviving features are the *keep* and the (rebuilt) *chapel* with its carved triptych (1520) from a Carinthian workshop. In the shrine is a Coronation of the Virgin Mary.

Environs: Neumarkt: A market was founded here in the 13C along with Forchtenstein castle, which is the former seat of the administrator appointed by the prince of the province. The keep and the main residential tract have been rebuilt. The wall surrounding the market also still stands. *Pfarrkirche hl.Katharina:* This is a late Gothic hall church which has belonged to the abbey of Lambrecht since 1252. The fine 18C high altar is by B.Prandstätter. There are 15C frescos in the *ossuary* in the graveyard. *St.Marein:* A hamlet S. of Neumarkt with a parish church is mentioned in 1190. There are two late Roman tombstone reliefs in the Romanesque tower above the choir. To the N. of Neumarkt is **Mariahof:** This fortified church mentioned in the 11C contains a *Kapelle hl.Niklaus* and the *Pfarrkirche hl.Maria.* The latter was described as 'ecclesia Grazluppa' in 1066. The new building dates from 1511; the design is late Gothic.

Bad St. Leonhard im Lavanttal 9462
Kärnten　　　　　　　　　　　　p.282☐Q 10

Stadtpfarrkirche St. Leonhard: This large 14C basilica, with a nave and two aisles, stands on a slightly elevated site at the E. end of the town. There is no doubt that it is one of the most splendid Gothic churches in Carinthia. The special qualities of the building can be seen even from the outside: powerful W. tower and ornate buttresses (see especially the S. buttresses above the sacristy); some of these buttresses have pinnacles. This Gothic delight in articulation shows particularly in the ornaments and decorative architecture of the S. portal. The vegetable and crystal decoration is also found in the Gothic carved altar. *Interior* with rib vault, tall nave and relatively low aisles. The three choirs are placed asymmetrically. The church is lavishly furnished. The *stained-glass window cycles* dating from the 2nd half of the 14C are a special feature. The oldest windows, in the choir, depict the Saints, the Virgin Mary and Christ. The windows in the S. and N. aisles include scenes from the life of Christ and the Virgin Mary, the Annunciation, Christ in Judgement, and Apostle and angel figures. Heinrich and Kunigunde Chroph, the founders, are seen in the W. window. The ornamental panes are 19C. The carving of the *late Gothic triptychs* in the right side choir (1511-13) and on the SW pillar (1510 – 15) is a development of the Gothic enthusiasm for articulation which dominates the exterior. Lorenz Schweiger was involved in the making of both altars. A Madonna Enthroned with Child, dating from the 1st half of the 14C, is to be seen on the triumphal arch on a baroque bracket. The massive early baroque *high altar* in the main choir (1638) is the work of K. Alger and J. Seitlinger, and apart from the central Assumption it also has excellent baroque carved figures. St.Leonard interceding for the prisoners is seen in the tondo above. The St. Leonard's chain around the church dates from 1910. Its symbolical significance is: faith makes men free and releases them from all their chains. The four other altars are also 17C baroque; the rococo pulpit dates fom 1779. Late Gothic and Renaissance *tombstones with coats-of-arms* are let into walls inside and outside the church.

Also worth seeing: The *Gomarn ruined castle* to the SW of the town is 15C (the tower is older). The *Filialkirche St. Kunigunde* and the former *Spitalkirche* are also of note.

St. Martin im Gnadenwald = Hall 6060
Tirol   p.284☐G 8

Kirche zum hl. Martin: A new church was built after the 15C hermitage and the associated church, which was older still, had been destroyed by fire in the late 17C. It was redesigned in baroque style in 1724. Inside the church are a late-17C stuccoed ceiling and frescos dating from 1743 by Michael Ignaz Milldorfer, who also painted the pictures in the side altars. In the monastery courtyard are three late Gothic coats-of-arms from the early 16C.

Kapelle beim Wiesenhof: This chapel has a ceiling fresco dating from 1740 and a carved altar group from the same period.

St. Michael = Weissenkirchen in der Wachau 3610
Lower Austria   p.278☐S 4

Filialkirche St. Michael: In the 10C this was the principal church in the Wachau region. The late Gothic building with early Romanesque parts dates from 1500. It is a hall with nave, two aisles, choir, and a low square battlemented W. tower. On the ridge of the choir roof are the 'Seven Hares', in clay; the figures actually depict

a hunt. Late Gothic stone portals, marble steps made from early tombstones. In 1631 the inside of the church was redesigned in baroque style by Cypriano Biasino. The spiral staircase and the eight Danube school Apostles on the balustrade of the gallery survive from the old furnishings. Beside the church is the *Gothic ossuary* with its small ridge turret above the W. gable. Underneath it is a fresco of St. Christopher. Inside we find an altar built of skulls and mummified remains dating from 1150–1300. The church, surrounded by fortified walls and towers, is one of the most charming in the Danube valley.

St. Michael im Lungau 5582
Salzburg   p.282☐N 9

When the parish rights passed from the town of St. Martin to St. Michael between 1179 and 1225, this meant that one town had gained in status at the expense of another, doubtless because of the rerouting

St. Michael i.d.W., daughter church, late Gothic, with early Romanesque remains

of the mountain pass road built over the Lassnitzhöhe in Roman times. The new road built in the high Middle Ages ran over the Katschberg and therefore favoured St. Michael (today, the Tauernautobahn plays a similar role by helping St.Michael more than the other towns in the Lungau region). The Roman tombstone in the N. entrance hall does not mean that the town was founded in Roman times. The fact that St. Michael is the patron saint makes it more probable that the Carolingians founded the church. St.Michael has had a market since 1416 and a court since 1790 (since 1854 there has been a district court here).

Pfarrkirche St.Michael: In 1225, Pope Innocent III confirmed that the Salzburg Dom chapter had the rights to this parish. The church was first mentioned in 1147. The present choir probably dates from that time; the plain Gothic vault was clearly added at a later date. A massive triumphal arch separates the choir from the spacious nave with its late Gothic net vault. A stellar-vaulted aisle adjoins the nave in the

N., it was presumably added for the church's consecration in 1513. The *fresco fragments* are historically important: fragments of Romanesque frescos from the 1st half of the 13C on the S. wall of the choir. There are three areas, above one another; from top to bottom: fragments of a Fall into Hell, the imperial couple Henry II and Kunigunde enthroned, and Emperor Charles; the latter figure is not clear, but a fragmentary inscription has survived. Next to this, in the reveals of the window cut off by the sacristy building, St.Leonard and St.Ulrich. The scene from the legend of St.Dorothy dates from the late 14C. On the S. wall of the nave is a fresco of St. Dorothy and St. Agnes with the Christ-child dating from *c.* 1430. The popular-baroque *wall painting* depicting the Seven Deadly Sins is rich in narrative content. The two *side altars* have good sculptures (1731) by Paul Mödlhammer, who was also responsible for the figures on the triumphal arch wall; they were formerly on the baroque high altar, which no longer exists. There is a tondo-shaped *Roman tombstone* with three interesting

St.Martin im Gnadenwald, Kirche zum hl. Martin, baroque alteration of 1724

portrait busts in the N. portico. In the *graveyard* is the octagonal two storeyed 14C *ossuary,* with a beautiful dome and octagonal lantern.

Environs: Filialkirche hl.Ägidius: This church stands on the mountainside outside the town, probably on the site of the 'Castrum ad sanctum Michaelem' which was mentioned in 1244 but has disappeared without trace. The Romanesque core of the tower suggests that the church may have developed from the chapel of the castle. **St.Martin,** with the *Filialkirche* of the same name. The town's Roman origin is indicated by the Roman wall remains which have been excavated, and also by the fragment of a tomb stele let into the wall (it shows a portrait of a woman with a 'Noric bonnet', and a man in a toga with a writing implement; 2C AD), and by the Actaeon relief which is now in the Salzburg Museum. There are two late-14C *fresco strips* on the N. outer wall of the nave. Inside the church there is a small Gothic *triptych* with a good late-15C carving of St. Martin.

St. Pantaleon 4303
Lower Austria   p.276 □ Q 5

Pfarrkirche St.Pantaleon: In AD 190, a large Roman legionary camp by the limes was struck and moved to Enns. In the 9C the area was settled by Bavarians who erected an earthwork against the Avars; this can still be seen. The *crypt,* one of the oldest surviving buildings in Austria, is from the church built in the 11C. The originally Romanesque church had a very rare double choir. The crypt underneath the W. choir is a small hall with four columns and eight corner pillars. The ceiling ribs are supported on primitive capitals decorated with guilloche, plants and animals. A semicircular apse is continued in the upper storey, where it forms the second sanctuary (on the outside there is an unusual frieze with rectangular panels). The Gothic W. tower, with its baroque dome, has Romanesque foundation walls. The late Gothic nave, almost square in shape, dates from the 15C. The unusual arrangement of the pillars makes the E.

St. Paul im Lavanttal, frescos by Thomas von Willach with founders

section, with its umbrella-like vault, look as though it is supported by a single pillar. Beyond this, two displaced pillars split the area into three. The E. choir is higher than the nave. The neo-Gothic high altar, with a beautiful figure of St. Pantaleon, dates from about 1450 (St. Pantaleon is one of the 14 Auxiliary Saints, and also the patron saint of doctors).

Moated Schloss: In 1631 this was referred to as 'Veste zum Haus pei St. Pantaleon'. It was rebuilt in the 18C, and most of it was pulled down in the 19C.

Environs: St. Pantaleon is a base for excursions to Enns (q.v.), Mauthausen (q.v.), St. Florian (q.v.) and Linz (q.v.).

St. Paul im Lavanttal 9470
Kärnten   p.282□R 11

This is one of three famous Benedictine monasteries in Carinthia, the others being Ossiach and Millstatt. It was founded by

St. Paul im Lavanttal, portal

Count Engelbert I in 1091 on the site of the old Sponheim castle. The Pope and the Emperor granted privileges to the abbots who ran the estates and monastery. The history of the monastery was dominated not merely by work and prayer, but also by wars, fire and secular arbitrariness. Threats from Turks and Hungarians had to be overcome in the last quarter of the 15C, and the wasteful mismanagement of Abbot Ulrich von Pfinzing in the first third of the 16C. The monastery experienced its second heyday under Abbot Hieronymus Marchstaller in the baroque period (1616 –38), before gradually being deprived of its old functions after the dissolution of 1782.

Stifts- und Pfarrkirche St. Paul: This large pillared basilica has a nave, two aisles, and a twin-towered W. façade. The abbey surrounds it on three sides. (Abbot Marchstaller intended to integrate church, courtyards and wings on the model of the Escorial.) The present church was built in the late 12C and early 13C on the site of an older church of St. Paul. The choir in the E., with its apses, still shows late Romanesque feeling for articulation. The figures and ornaments on the S. and W. portals are also late Romanesque. The Adoration of the Magi (S. portal) and the Majestas Domini (W. portal) derive their expressiveness from the contrast between the massiveness of the stone and the filigree work on the surface. The inside of the church was vaulted in 1367 and 1498, thus losing one of the chief features of monastic architecture. Only the ground plan, with the Chorus major to the E. of the crossing and the Chorus minor to the W. of the crossing, shows the Hirsau style which the first monks brought with them when the church was founded in 1091. The magnificent late Romanesque capitals on the dividing arches contrast to a certain extent with the ascetic simplicity of the style. The capitals dating from *c.* 1200 are a high point of Romanesque decoration. The luxuriance of the design asserts itself against the selfless Benedictine decree: form may only be used in the service of prayer. The *paintings* in the vault of the nave (keystone, quatrefoil figures) are also important in the history of art: Michael and Friedrich Pacher from S. Tyrol designed the 'heaven' of the church *c.* 1470. The secular subject matter treated as respectfully as the religious themes: a flower is just as lovingly and realistically painted as is the figure of the Saint. The *frescos* on the N. and E. transept walls were revealed in 1931. These are late Gothic masterpieces by Thomas von Villach (1493), who painted a self-portrait among the frescos on the E. wall. The fresco of the founders mingles historical events with religious mythology. It shows Engelbert and Hadwiga von Sponheim, the founders of the abbey, being recommended for entry into Heaven by St. Benedict (founder of the Order) and by St. Catharine (a martyr); angels, the coat-of-arms of the province, Apostles and secular lords are also represented. To the N., opposite the rococo pulpit, we find a *late Gothic altar* with four panel paintings (Holy Trinity, St. Erhard, St. Barbara, St. Catherine, St. John the Baptist, St. Andrew and St. Dorothy). These fine panels probably date from about 1460. The statues and pictures on the altars of the main and side chapels are 18C baroque works and items from the 19C Nazarene school.

Abbey buildings: The two-storey buildings have arcaded courtyards. Most of the buildings were completed in 1683. In the W. arcade is a Romanesque statue dating from *c.* 1260 (it was originally in the choir screen). There is an outstanding *collection* in the W. wing, with paintings dating from the 15C–18C by Pieter Aertsen, P.P. Rubens, H. Bock, Johann Zick and many others. Splendid manuscripts, implements, small sculptures, glasses, porcelain and a coin collection.

St. Paul, Stift 1 W. twin-towered façade **2** S. portal **3** Romanesque apse in E. **4** Chorus major **5** Chorus minor **6** Nave vault **7** Fresco of founder **8** Courtyard of former cloister **9** Rabensteiner Kapelle

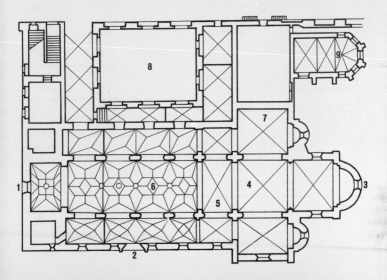

St. Peter in der Au 3352
Lower Austria   p.276☐Q 5

The Schloss was a princely possession from the 14C, and feudal lords succeeded one another rapidly. It was conquered in the peasants' war in 1597, and Count Seemann of Mangern was taken prisoner. There were severe reprisals. Karl Zeller, the composer of the 'Vogelhändler', was born here in 1842.

Wehrkirche St. Peter und Paul: Consecrated in 1050. The late Gothic hall church dating from the 2nd half of the 15C shows clearly discernible remains of a fortified church some 200 years older. A concealed wall passage runs between the flying buttresses. There is a well under the W. choir, and the entire building is surrounded by a fortified wall with arrow slits. High altarpiece by Kremser Schmidt in the 14C choir.

Schloss: The keep and the roofed passage connecting the Schloss with the church were both part of the Gothic moated Schloss. The Renaissance tombstone of Wilhelm von Seemann is in the gatehouse hall with its late Gothic pillars. The large arcaded courtyard with double arches on the 1st floor dates from the 16C.

St. Peter im Holz = Lendorf 9811
Kärnten   p.282☐M 10

This settlement on the plateau of the Holzerberg was Celtic until 15 BC, and then Roman. In the mid 1C AD it became the main town of the province under Emperor Claudius. Fortifications, a forum, baths etc. were discovered by excavation. The population was largely Christianized by the 4C; Teurnia was probably already a bishopric in the late 4C.

The town and the early Christian culture were completely destroyed after the collapse of the Roman Empire and the barbarian invasions in the 5&6C. Christianity was not revived until the time of Bishop Modestus of Salzburg.

Early Christian Friedhofskirche: Excavation work was carried out in 1910. The ground plan of the church and the finds discovered there provide valuable insights into early Christian divine service. The unique floor mosaic in the S. chapel survives in good condition and its twelve panels show symbols of Jesus Christ and his triumph over the world's evil (early 5C). At the excavation site there is a *museum* (open from June to September), with finds from *Teurnia* and various other excavation sites in the region.

Pfarrkirche: An early Romanesque building preceded the present church dating from the 14&15C. It has noteworthy *frescos*. On the outside of the church are pictures of St. Christopher, Virgin and Child, and Saints (between 1430 and 1470). The frescos on the N. inside wall include cycles of the Passion, the legend of St. Dorothy, and the Last Judgement (1370–80). Baroque altar decoration, late Gothic Pietà *c.* 1420.

St. Pölten 3100
Lower Austria   p.278☐T 5

Founded in the Roman period, *Aelium Cetium* became the site of the first monastery in Lower Austria, that of St. Hippolytus, from whom the town's present name derives. The monastery was probably founded under the Carolingians. In 1058, St. Pölten became the first place in the province to acquire market rights, and was granted a charter in 1247. The rectangular Rathausplatz was laid out at the same period, and so was the town wall with its towers and four gates. The latter features were pulled down to make way for roads as the town expanded. The town flourished in the baroque period, when it attracted architects such as Prandtauer, Munggenast and Wissgrill, and painters such as D.Gran and B.Altomonte. The town centre is still recognisably of that period.

Dom Mariae Himmelfahrt: In the 12C, the church of the old St.Hippolytus monastery stood on the site of the present Dom. It was a basilica with a nave and two aisles but no transept; surviving sections are the sturdy, undecorated two-towered W. façade (up to about the level of the roof), the N. nave wall, and the Rosenkranzkapelle. After a devastating fire in 1267, the church was turned into an early Gothic basilica by lengthening the choir, incorporating the Rosenkranzkapelle and moving the S. wall 3 ft. outwards. In the 18C it was redesigned in baroque style, mainly on the inside, to plans by J.Prandtauer. Impressive features are paintings and frescos by Gran and Gedon, the main altarpiece by Tobias Pock

(1658), the Kreuzaltar in the N. aisle by Jakob Schletterer, the Frauenaltar in the S. aisle (1742–4) with its baroque Pietà, and also the tombs of Johann Martin Fischer and Bishop Kerens.

Bischofshof: Roman remains, and also some sections of the medieval monastery, have been excavated in this early baroque monastery (1636–53). It continues the line of the church to the N., has two storeys and is arranged around five courtyards. There is a splendid *staircase* dating from 1727, and also the former *library* with frescos by P.Troger. The present *Bischofstor* is largely the work of J.Munggenast, who rebuilt the original.

Institut der Englischen Fräulein (Linzer Strasse): It is still not clear who designed this baroque building begun in 1715 and enlarged in 1767 – 9. (Prandtauer?). Whoever the artist may be, the façade, with two upper storeys linked by fluted colossal pilasters, is very beautiful. The *painting* on the dome of the choir and in the nave is by Altomonte, while the

St. Pölten, Institut der Englischen Fräulein

Virgin Mary by the right side altar is by L.Cranach the Elder.

Franziskaner-Pfarrkirche   zur Hl.Dreifaltigkeit: This church (1757–68), together with the adjoining monastery, dominates the N. side of the Rathausplatz. The slight concave curve in the central axis of the towerless gabled façade gives this late baroque church considerable animation. The interior is also late baroque, and has four side altarpieces by M.J. Schmidt.

Karmeliterinnenkirche (Prandtauerstrasse 2): This church (1712) looks particularly good from the Rathausplatz. One could hardly imagine a better site for the towerless façade with its concave curve, tall flat pilasters and luxuriant ornamentation around the gable.

Rathaus: This completes the S. side of the Rathausplatz; it consists of two older houses (late 16C), and unites various styles. The Renaissance portal, the niches with seats in the entrance, and the tower (1575), are late Gothic, but the tower dome and the articulation of the walls belong to the baroque period. Inside, the building is decorated with splendid stucco ceilings and sculptures by Christoph Kirschner (*c.* 1722).

Historisches Museum (Karmeliterhof/ Prandtauerstrasse): After a break of nearly 40 years, this was reopened in 1976 in the historic monastery building.

Also worth seeing: *Dreifaltigkeitssäule* (Trinity column; 1767 – 82) on the Rathausplatz, by Andreas Gruber. *Bischöfliches Seminar* (episcopal seminary; Wiener Strasse). *Baroque façades* in the Altstadt: Wiener Strasse Nos. 1, 2, 4 (Renaissance arcades in the courtyard), 14 (Renaissance vault inside), 16 (the façade is attributed to Prandtauer), 21 (1563), 22,

27, 34, 37 (attributed to Prandtauer), 36 (Gothic niches), and 1 Klostergasse, the house where Prandtauer lived.

St. Stefan an der Gail 9623
Kärnten   p.282□N 11

Pfarrkirche: This late Gothic hall church, with a polygonal choir and gabled tower was extended by the addition of chapels in the baroque period. On the vault inside are late Gothic quatrefoil paintings and early baroque vegetable decorations; there is a baroque Last Judgement on the triumphal arch. The high altar and the left side altar in the nave (both 18C?) contain late Gothic figures and reliefs (the torments of St.Stephen and St.Laurence dating from *c.* 1480, the Madonna statue from *c.* 1500). There are also tombstones with coats-of-arms in the S. chapel. The *wayside shrine* in a niche, S. of the church, has high-quality wall paintings from the 1st quarter of the 16C.

Aichelburg ruins and Schloss Greiffenstein: These are houses of the Aichelburg family. The Schloss, built in 1556, was restored in 1965.

St. Veit am Vogau 8423
Steiermark   p.280□T 11

Wallfahrtskirche: This hamlet with its church belonged to the Bishop of Seckau from 1218 onwards and surrounds the parish church (mentioned in a document dating from 1163). It was rebuilt from 1748 onwards by J. Hueber, the architect from Graz, and in the process the church which had previously faced E. was turned northwards. The round attached shafts and the masonry show that the W. tower of the old building was included in the new

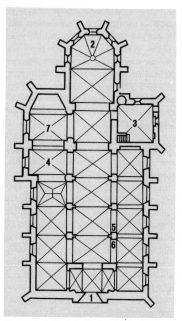

St. Veit a. d. Glan, Stadtpfarrkirche 1 Romanesque W. portal **2** High altar **3** Sacristy **4** Bernhardskapelle **5** Tombstone relief of a standing woman **6** Hl. Martin **7** Kreuzaltar

St. Gandolf (St. Veit a. d. Glan)

building. The interior is wide, with pilasters, four bays and varying depth. The decorations from the rococo period are mainly by V. Königer, who created the statues on the high altar (1756), the Kreuzaltar and in the presbytery. The high altarpiece is by F.de Palco (1752); the organ dates from 1711. The oil paintings above the side doors are the work of A.Jandl, and the ceiling frescos are by F.Barasuttis (1914).

St. Veit an der Glan 9300
Kärnten   p.282□P 10

The former capital of Carinthia developed in the 12&13C at the intersection of important trade routes, and was the seat of the dukes of Carinthia from 1174 onwards. It was mentioned as a town in 1224, and maintained its superiority over Klagenfurt until 1518, as it held the storage rights to Hüttenberg iron. This economic success lasted until the 18C and was accompanied by a level of culture demonstrated by the general dignity of the architecture and the beauty of numerous individual buildings. From the early 13C onwards the town was surrounded by a high wall, much of which still survives. The heart of the town is the *Oberer Platz,* a 'hall in the open air' unequalled in Carinthia.

Stadtpfarrkirche Hl.Dreifaltigkeit:
This late Romanesque church with a tower over the choir has a nave and two aisles. It dates back to the town's heyday under Duke Bernhard von Spanheim, but it looks

late Gothic (much rebuilt and restored). The old flat roof was replaced by groin vaulting in 1449, and the austere three-apse design was removed by the adition of the sacristy and the Bernhardskapelle (both 15C). The Romanesque W. portal is also much altered. The Lamb of God and the symbols of the Evangelists survive in pure late Gothic style in the tympanum relief. The pillared arches on the *inside* are Romanesque, and so are the capitals (Florianialtar). Interesting stonework also in the keystones of the vaults and by the SW pillar (tombstone relief of a woman, standing in a Renaissance niche, 1520; next to her is St.Martin, 1511). The Kreuzaltar (1745) by J.Pacher, and also the high altar (1752), are the best of the baroque furnishings. The Romanesque *ossuary* to the S. of the church has a Carolingian stone in its outside wall; this is the earliest historical evidence in St. Veit, and suggests a 9C church. There is a good late Gothic *crucifix* inside.

Klosterkirche Unsere Liebe Frau: The single-aisled and rib-vaulted Gothic hall church (former Klarissinnenkirche) is to the W. of the Old Town, and was founded by Konrad von Aufenstein and his wife (1323). The church's most precious treasure was the *Gothic tomb monument* of Konrad von Kraig, the Landeshauptmann (d. 1392). This valuable relief is now in the entrance hall of the priest's house. The *S. chapels* are baroque; the high altar is by J.Pacher, 1734.

Rathaus: Tall Gothic gables and the baroque symmetry of the wide façade are unified by pilaster articulation through three storeys (M.J. Pittner, 1755). The pure Gothic metal tablet over the portal dates from 1468 and contains a quotation from the Sachsenspiegel, a crown, imperial coats-of-arms, Carinthian coats-of-arms and Saint figures. These pictorial themes are then repeated in baroque form over the entire façade, on a monumental scale and with allegorical force. The impressive *courtyard* with its three-storey arcades (sgraffito painting) is mid-16C. At periodic intervals the *Rathausgalerie* presents exhibitions of modern art.

St. Veit a.d. Glan, Rathaus, arcaded courtyard

Also worth seeing: As well as its showpieces the town has various more down-to-earth buildings. In the *Oberer Platz* are the *Pestsäule* (plague column; 1715), the *Schlüsselbrunnen* with the late Gothic 'Bartele' dating from 1470, and the *Florianibrunnen* (baroque, later than 1676). There is a late Gothic stone figure of *St. Vitus* outside house No. 14. There are *Roman stones* in the walls of many churches and secular building. Some of these scattered finds have been assembled in 9 Burggasse, where the *Stadtmuseum* and the *Lapidarium* are housed. *Münzkabinett* (coin collection; Oktoberplatz 5).

Environs: Schloss Frauenstein: A late Gothic aristocratic seat dating back to a Romanesque stronghold NW of the town; picturesque arcades; inside *Allerheiligenkapelle*. The **ruined castle of Freiberg**, not far away, is the remains of an old ducal castle. The two other ruins, *the Hoch- und Niederkraig (Kraiger Schlösser* were seats of the Kraig ducal officials until the 17C. Mention should also be made of the Schlösser of **Weyer** (E. of

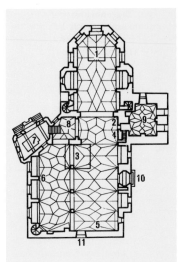

St. Wolfgang im Salzkammergut, St. Wolfgang 1 Pacher-Altar, where carving, painting and architectural structure combine to form a harmonious whole **2** Sacristy door **3** Double altar, Schwanthaler **4** Pulpit **5** Organ **6** Man of Sorrows, Guggenbichler **7** Wolfgangskapelle **8** Rosenkranzaltar **9** Tower **10** S. gate **11** W. gate of Christ's countenance

Schloss Frauenstein (St. Veit a.d. Glan)

the town), **Taggenbrunn** (eastwards) and **Hunnenbrunn** (towards Friesach). **St. Gandolf** with its high *Pfarrkirche* (mentioned in 1136, probably built in the 14C), is some 15 km. away in the direction of Feldkirchen and is of interest for its 15C wall paintings (including a Flight into Egypt).

St. Wolfgang im Salzkammergut 5360

Upper Austria   p.276☐M 7

Pfarrkirche St. Wolfgang: This church, which in the late Middle Ages was one of the greatest places of pilgrimage, surpassed only by Rome, Aachen and Einsiedeln, is splendidly sited by the shore of the lake. The reason why it is so frequently visited is the great popularity of its patron Saint. The enormous crowds of tourists who now travel to the town usually have other motives: the 'Weisses Rössl' (White Horse Inn) of operetta fame and Michael Pacher's magnificent altar.

It was for a long time considered to be a legend which had it that the church was founded by the Saint whose name it bears, but the most recent research suggests that this might be possible. The present two-aisled hall is mainly late Gothic; the S. aisle is continued as a choir with three bays. A powerful tower with a beautiful bell-shaped dome is the main exterior feature. The unique quality of the Pacher altar makes the works by T.Schwanthaler and M.Guggenbichler, highly esteemed in other places, pale by comparison.

Pacher-Altar: Contract signed in 1471. Carving, painting and architectural design are combined into a complete art work of very high quality, which has survived undamaged in its original place. The altar is a polyptych. *Weekday position:* When the wings are closed, the slender structure with its filigree turrets looks like a Gothic monstrance. The overall architectural design (the altar is more than 36 ft. high), and the delicate crowning with Saint figures are most impressive. The closed wings depict events from the life of the patron Saint of the church in four scenes.

St. Wolfgang im Salzkammergut

St. George and St. Florian are the shrine guardians. The predella shows the four Church Fathers. The *Sundays position* is quite different, with painting dominant. There are two sets of four scenes from the life of Christ. The perspective is admirable and suggests that the artist was acquainted with the Northern Italian artists Bellini and Mantegna. He also had a virtuoso knowledge of the anatomy of the human body, particularly impressive when the figures are on the move. In five of these eight scenes, artistically vaulted spaces extend deep in to the picture; the three remaining scenes have a romantic landscape in the background; the Temptation of Christ has a picture of Bruneck, Pacher's home town (by the devil's horns). The predella remains unchanged. *Feast day position:* The greatest splendour was only revealed at holy times: the shrine with its carvings shimmering with gold and the pictures from the life of the Virgin Mary. The main scene, the Coronation of the Virgin Mary, is depicted with incomparable mastery, and casts a spell over every onlooker: the Virgin Mary has

already been crowned, and the empty throne is waiting for her; the 'handmaid of the Lord' is kneeling humbly before her divine Son in order to receive his blessing: her gaze is directed towards the ground, as she passes on to suffering mankind the grace which she receives. The two large figures at the sides depict significant men of the Church: on the right is St. Benedict, the founder of the Order, St. Wolfgang is on the left. There is also fascinating detail: 14 cherubs sing, make music and hold the curtain; we almost feel the fabric of the garments; there is an almost incredible concern with the details of the gold work: crowns, crosiers, mitres, garment borders and fastenings; St. Wolfgang holds a small church: it is a Gothic building in miniature, including the little bell in the tower. *Predella:* A three-dimensional Adoration of the Magi. *Frame:* The patriarchs and prophets, with Adam at their head (around the shrine), appear in the open tendril work, also the Queen of Sheba with maidservants and the Kings of Tharsis (around the predella). These excellent carvings are missed by many

St. Wolfgang i.S., Pacheraltar

St. Wolfgang i.S., Pacheraltar

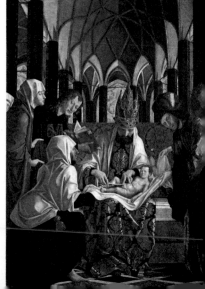

visitors because they are so small. The cycle of pictures on the *inmost* wings proves that Pacher was also among the best painters of his time; the six paintings from the life of the Virgin Mary show great mastery. The gold background instead of natural sky was only rarely used in this period, and gives the paintings an air of solemnity. There is a striking 'Presentation in the Temple': there is a column dividing not only the room but also the figure of the High Priest; the action only take place in the right half, while the left is reserved for the peaceful picture of the inside of the temple. The *rear side* has paintings of saints by various artists.

The main question asked by art historians is 'To what extent did this artistic genius do the work himself?' This has not been resolved. The figures of the main shrine, and the guardians of the shrine, are regarded as indisputably his own work, and so usually are the small figures in the frame. The same applies to the inmost wings. The legend of Wolfgang is attributed to Michael's brother Friedrich Pacher. The bitterest controversy is over the involvement of Michael or Friedrich in the eight paintings of the life of Christ.

Schwanthaler's double altar: A masterpiece of baroque sculpture, which has the misfortune of being placed beside Pacher's unique creation. The Holy Family is on the left, and on the right is the church's patron Saint, with St. Benedict and St. Scholastica at the sides. Former miraculous image of St. Wolfgang seated, probably of Tyrolean origin, in the left tabernacle.

Meinrad Guggenbichler's works: Three altars, the pulpit and a 'Man of Sorrows'. The 'Rosenkranzaltar' with a wreath of delightful cherubs is outstanding, but the most captivating work is the 'Man of Sorrows'.

Also worth seeing: *Wolfgangskapelle,*

allegedly containing the cell of the Saint with the 'Bussfelsen' (rock of penance) in a red marble housing. Early baroque ceiling frescos, organ dating from 1626, notable sacristy portal. *Outside:* Early Gothic sculptures on portals: Countenance of Christ, Lamb of God, St. Wolfgang. Excellent *pilgrimage fountain,* 1515, of bellmetal. Curtain wall, with basket-arched openings allowing enchanting views of the lake.

**St. Wolfgang im
Waldviertel=Weitra 3970**
Lower Austria   p.278☐R 3

Pfarrkirche St. Wolfgang: A hall church with a nave and two aisles (dating from 1407) with an almost square ground plan and a long choir with a polygonal apse. Plain portal dating from 1408, above it tracery windows. The roof was rebuilt (flat) after a fire in 1877. Niches admitting light in the S. pillars of the main choir. There is a fine baroque high altar dating from 1694 in brown-blue and gold with late Gothic figures of St. Erasmus, St. Nicholas and St. Wolfgang.

Säusenstein 3374
Lower Austria   p.278☐R 5

This is the separate parish of the Domvogts of Regensburg. Eberhard von Wallsee founded a monastery in 1334. The Cistercians took it over giving it the name of Gottestal (vallis dei). The abbey was expanded in 1703–60 and dissolved in 1789. The church burned down in 1801, and St. Donatus on the mountain became the parish church. Little survives of the abbey, later called Schloss.

St. Wolfgang i.S., Pacheraltar ▷

Theresienkapelle: Torso of the collegiate church with a small bell tower and rib vaulting in the choir polygon. Tombstone dating from 1383.

Pfarrkirche St.Donatus: Built in 1760. W. façade with central portal. St.John and St. Paul in shallow niches dating from 1777. Tall central tower. Splendid delicately coloured hall. Vault frescos by J.W. Bergl, 1767. There is a flat N.-S. oval dome in the second bay: round dance in concentric circles with many figures, from Revelations. In the front bay is the Martyrdom of St.Donatus (Bishop of Arezzo, d. 350, with lightning flashes). In the narrower choir is a subtle trompe l'oeil dome. High altarpiece by P.Troger (1746). Richly decorated Renaissance pulpit.

Schallaburg = Loosdorf / Melk 3382
Lower Austria   p.278☐S 5

Schallaburg: There was a Count of Scallach *c.* 1110. Otto von Ottenstein

Schallaburg

named himself Count von Schala in 1242. The *Festes Haus* and the *curtain wall* were built under his rule. The Losensteins inherited the castle in 1431, and in 1576 they added to the citadel an *outworks* (with an oblique-angled *arcaded courtyard*) and in the E. a *tiltyard* and the garden. The Losensteins were Protestants. In 1614 the Schloss was so heavily in debt that it had to be sold to the rich Stubenberg family who were also Protestant, and came from Styria. Tombs of all the owners. The Russians destroyed the Schloss in 1945, and it fell further and further into disrepair before being well restored under State ownership in the last decade. The surrounding wall and moat survive only in the S. and E. The visitor passes through an outer gate with arched battlements, crosses the castle moat to the 1st portal (1583) and, going along a narrow path from the moat and through a 2nd portal, enters the famous *Terrakottahof* (built by Jakob Bernecker in 1573). Wide arches support the double arcades of the upper storey with their fine red sculptures. The owner was a humanist and a Protestant. In the S., a portal leads into the smaller *castle courtyard* and to the oldest building which contains the *keep* and the *chapel* dating from 1662 (underneath there is a filled-in 12C *crypt*.) Here we find the *high tomb* of Wilhelm von Losenstein (1587). The knight is in full armour, with is a lion at his feet. He is holding the Bible in his right hand, and in his left is the sword.

Schärding 4780
Upper Austria   p.276☐M 4

The route which ran from Lower Bavaria along the Rott and met Inn at Schärding continued up the Pramtal. This intersection of routes was clearly a site for settlement, particularly since a steep rock above the Inn offered an ideal site for a castle. First mentioned in 804, the town was granted a charter in 1316. From 1248 to 1779, with one brief interruption, it belonged to the Wittelsbachs, who extended it into a stately fortress. Only the barbican, the moat and the outer castle gate (today a *museum*) survive of the powerful *Burg;* parts of the wall, towers and four gates survive from the town fortifications; the *Wassertor* at the end of the Unterer Stadtplatz is the most picturesque feature, and leads directly to the Inn; the diagonal stone balcony on the inside of the gate was used as a pillory. The finest feature is the splendidly balanced *Stadtplatz,* which has survived in excellent condition. The long square is divided by a building into Oberer und Unterer Stadtplatz; the particularly impressive N. side of the Oberer Platz is called *Silberzeile.* The massive *Stadtpfarrkirche* with its stately tower rises in the background above this idyll. The earlier building was pulled down after damage in the War of the Spanish Succession, and the new building (1720–6) is a bright baroque pilaster church with galleries; stucco figures of four knightly saints on the crossing pillars, probably by F.J.I. Holzinger.

Heimatmuseum (in the former Äusseres Burftor): Full local collection.

Environs: Suben (8 km. upstream): *Former Augustinian priory.* Founded *c.* 1050 by Tuta, a Formbach countess (Formbach is now Vornbach, on the left bank of the Inn). In the 12C it was helped by a lavish endowment and became an Augustinian priory, dissolved in 1784. The former priory building is today a penal institution. *St.Lambert:* Only the W. tower survives of the Romanesque church. The new building of 1766–70 is by Simon Frey from Pullach near Munich. The mansard roof dates from 1792. Complicated ground plan, essentially a combination of rotunda and longitudinally planned church. Splendid decorations. Frescos by J.J. Zeiller; the best item is the painting, never restored, of 'Christ driving the merchants out of the Temple' under the gallery. Economical but high-quality stucco by Johann B. Modler. Groups of figures on the beams (Gospels, Church Fathers, Archangels), probably by J.Deutschmann, to whom the magnificent pulpit, high altar, transept altars, the organ

Schallaburg

Schärding, Silberzeile

Suben (Schärding), St. Michael

side (fine view), today half in ruins. *Mariensäule:* Marble, Virgin Mary on a column, surrounded by four armoured putti fighting monsters. This work was built in 1644 under Ferdinand III 'Am Hof' in Vienna, in imitation of the Mariensäule in Munich. When Leopold I had the sculpture replaced by an identical sculpture in bronze, the stone group was brought to Wernstein.

Scheibbs 3270
Lower Austria   p.278 □ S 5

The oldest part of the town is the high Kirchplatz, with the castle built by Otto von Seibes dating from *c.* 1150. In the 14C it was used by the Carthusian monastery of Gaming. The town was fortified in *c.* 1350, and expanded in the 15C. Walls, towers and two town gates still survive between the old graveyard and the Schloss. The town lives from the iron trade. Some hammer forges still exist along the Erlauf upstream as far as Gaming.

Pfarrkirche St. Magdalena: A late Gothic hall church from the late 15C, with a nave and two aisles. It was redesigned in baroque style in 1726. On the N. side is the tower, with its Gothic substructure and baroque dome. There is a NW portal (with a large Mount of Olives on the right, dating from 1632). A splendid interior: red round columns, with rather surprising golden baroque capitals, support the complicated net vault, which is picked out in red. The high altar dates from 1706. There are fine brown and golden oratories on both sides. Chapel with 19C mosaic on the S. wall. Gothic Madonna and fine old tombstones.

Also worth seeing: *Castle:* Square with a plain exterior. Especially fine courtyard with arcades, fountains, window grilles and a wrought-iron gate on the stairs. *Pfarrhof,*

front and two statues (guardian angel and Michael) are attributed. Tombstone of the foundress with a church model, Soft Style, *c.* 1470. **Zwickledt** (about 6 km. N.): A modest 'Schlössl', today a memorial to the artist Alfred Kubin (1877–1959), who lived and worked there for many years. **Wernstein am Inn** (about 6 km. N.): *Pfarrkirche St. Georg:* A noteworthy synthesis of Gothic building with modern additions. Samhaber, the former parish priest, left his collection of drawings by his friend Kubin (see Zwickledt) to Upper Austria, and so the Land paid for most of the new building. The originally Gothic design was revealed; two tunnel-vaulted rooms were added beside the presbytery. Gothic statue of St. George, baroque Way of the Cross, modern windows. *Castle:* Mentioned as early as the 12C, opposite the castle of Neuburg am Inn on the Bavarian

Rathaus and *town houses* with beautiful 15&16C courtyards.

Scheiblingkirchen = Warth 2831
Lower Austria   p.280☐U 7

Pfarrkirche hll.Magdalena und Rupert: The round church of Scheiblingkirchen was consecrated by the Archbishop of Salzburg in 1147 at the same time as the neighbouring church of Thernberg (the oldest rib-vaulted church in Austria). Cylindrical building with a semicircular apse. A cornice rests on capitals with leaf and animal ornaments: a cat-like demon with a crooked back, tail and large claws. Rebuilt in the 17&19C.

Schielleiten = Stubenberg 8223
Steiermark   p.280☐T 9

Ruined castle of Alt-Schielleiten: Built by the Stubenberg family in the 13C; rebuilt in the early 17C by the feudal lords Rinschad. A rectangular complex with an arcaded courtyard and four corner towers.

Schloss Schielleiten: Founded in 1732 by the Counts Wurmbrand-Stuppach. It has been a federal school of sport since 1935. A central pavilion with side wings; inside there is an elliptically vaulted central hall in the Viennese high baroque manner.

Schladming 8970
Steiermark   p.282☐N 8

First mentioned in 1180 (Slaebnich). The mining settlement of Schladming was founded in 1304, after the opening of a silver mine. First mentioned as a town in 1322. The famous 'Schladminger

Schlägl, Stiftskirche, Portal

Bergbrief' (mining regulations) dates from 1408. It was the centre of the Ennstal insurrection of peasants and miners in 1525, and was burned down the same year by way of punishment, losing all its privileges. It was rebuilt in 1526, and the right to hold markets was granted in 1530. Charter renewed in 1925.

Pfarrkirche hl.Achaz: Late Gothic hall church with a nave and two aisles, rebuilt in 1522-32, except for the Romanesque W. tower. Apart from the pulpit and the Pietà on the Kreuzaltar (both 16C), the furnishings are 18C.

Evangelische Kirche: Built in 1852-62, it is a hall church with a nave and two aisles and is the largest Protestant church in the Steiermark, with altarpieces from a Renaissance altar dating from 1570.

Reissingerbehausung: In 1618 house of judge Reissinger, with a Renaissance room; later used by a mining company. Now *Stadtmuseum.*

Schlägl=Aigen im Mühlkreis 4160
Upper Austria   p.276□O 3

Prämonstratenserstift: In the early 13C, Kalhoch von Falkenstein, an official of the bishop of Passau, founded a monastery in a clearing in the upper valley of the Grosse Mühl.The first attempt (*c.* 1204, with Cistercians from Langheim in Franconia) failed. A second attempt, in 1218 with Premonstratensian monks from Mühlhausen (Milewsk) in Bohemia, was successful. The abbey was badly affected by the Hussite and Peasant Wars. Church and abbey were redesigned in the baroque style in the 17C. The monastery escaped Joseph's wave of dissolutions and flourished in the 19C: many paintings were purchased, and a neo-baroque library was built by Abbot A. Fähtz.

Stiftskirche Mariä Himmelfahrt: First built in the 13C, altered in the mid 15C and redesigned in baroque style in 1626–30. The most striking feature of the church is the extraordinary height of nave and choir arch in comparison with the overall size of the building, and the continuing impression of climbing. Steps lead from the monastery courtyard to the church portal (1654, Virgin Mary, angels, coat-of-arms); in the portico there are six more steps leading to the inner Gothic portal. The church is a basilica with a nave and two aisles, the S. aisle being narrower. In the E. bay of the nave, a kind of ante-choir, is a staggered arrangement of steps (2 + 7 + 5 steps) leading to the long, main choir with three bays and two more steps. The bright, direct light in the choir contrasts with the twilight of the nave, which has no windows, and heightens the effect of the sanctuary. The general impression is Romanesque-Gothic; the baroque alteration simply redesigned the building without altering its proportions. Some of the stucco still has Renaissance ornament such as string-of-pearls and egg-and-dart moulding. Splendid organ dating from 1634; pulpit, 1647, by J.Worath who was responsible for many of the furnishings; fine choir screen and choir stalls; the neo-baroque choir organs date from 1954. *Crypts:* Romanesque crypt, the oldest part of the building, is square with a central pillar with a robust capital; in the corners are three stone corbels (heads, ornament), the 4th has been destroyed; to the E. of this Gothic crypt with a groin vault. In the cloister tombstones from the 13C–18C.

Abbey: The picture gallery, the Porträtsaal and the library are open to the public. *Picture gallery:* Built in 1898, it is a rectangular room, divided into two aisles by five granite columns. Ceiling with ten domes decoratively painted in the rococo style. Lit by large windows on both sides. There is an excellent collection, some of it not acquired until the 19C. Gothic paintings, Danube school, and Austrian, Italian and Dutch artists from the 17–18C. The showpiece here is the 'Madonna auf der Rasenbank' 1505, by the 'Meister von Frankfurt'. *Porträtsaal:* A collection of portraits, started in the early 19C. *Library:* An interesting example of a neo-baroque monastery library, with wall cases and a gallery. Rich collection of manuscripts and incunabula.

Environs: Haslach an der Mühl: (10 km. to the SE): Centre of the weaving industry. *Pfarrkirche St.Nikolaus:* The nave dates from *c.* 1500, net vault with twisted ribs; free-standing tower, crown early-20C. Furnishings neo-Gothic. *Museum:*

Schlierbach, library

Heimathaus (local history) in the gatehouse tower. *Webereimuseum:* In the old school building, comprehensive specialist museum of weaving, very modern in design; highly recommended; to visit, telephone 07289–593. **Burg Pürnstein** (about 22 km. S, above the left bank of the Grosse Mühl): A massive half-ruined castle. Curtain wall with round towers, open on the inside. Palas roof in the Hauptburg open to visitors. Burgkapelle, kitchen, *Burgmuseum.*

Schlierbach 4553

Upper Austria   p.276☐O 6

Zisterzienserabtei: This was initially founded by Eberhard von Wallsee in 1355 as a Cistercian convent on the site of a castle. After being dissolved in 1556, it was refounded in 1620, this time as a monastery. After various difficulties, the abbey gained new impetus in the 20C. Within its walls today are a secondary school, a school of agriculture, a cheese dairy ('Schlierbacher'), and a stained-glass workshop. The two towers are striking from a distance, but they are not twin towers despite being of almost identical design. One tower belongs to the church, and the other, the 'Abteiturm', is over the main portal.

Stiftskirche Mariä Himmelfahrt und hl.Jakobus der Ältere: A rare feature of the church is that the N. side of the nave forms the wall of the second courtyard. It was rebuilt in 1660–79 by the Carlone family. Pilaster church with chapels and galleries. Powerful ribs divide the ceiling into bays which contain frescos of the Virgin Mary and her Old Testament prototypes. The stucco is dense and abundant: garlands of fruit and flowers, foliage, and very lavish figures; the lower zone has a larger-than-life Holy Kindred. Tastes had changed in the early 18C: the stucco had become lighter and more graceful, and massiveness and the strong contrast between the white decoration and darker furnishings was no longer considered beautiful. However, the church barely lasted a generation; Abbot Nivard Dierer finally found a way of 'modernizing' his church without incurring too much expenditure. A wood-carved gilded screen with arabesques was placed in front of the pilasters and gallery balustrades. This screen lightened the heavy early baroque design; the colouring was heightened by inserting oval-framed paintings: graceful flower still lifes, an unusual feature in a church. The high altar, pulpit, organ, and the altar painted by J.M. Rottmayr and depicting the mystic marriage of St. Catherine are also worth noticing.

Abbey buildings: *Marienkapelle* in the cloister, with the *Schlierbach Madonna,* a lovely work dating from *c.* 1320, which the

Schlierbach, Stift 1 Wirtschaftshof 2 Outer courtyard 3 Bernhardisaal (1st floor) 4 Abbey or gate tower 5 Prälatenhof 6 Church 7 Cloister with Marienkapelle 8 Library

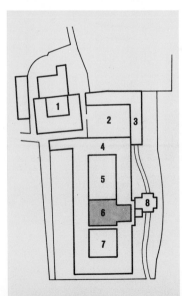

first nuns brought from their mother convent of Baindt near Ravensburg. *Grosser Festsaal (Bernhardisaal):* A room with rich stucco decorations and frescos. Middle fresco: Glorification of Art. On each of the long sides we find four tall windows with 'ox-eyes' above them. An original feature of the narrow sides is that they each have three blind 'ox-eyes' with trompe l'oeil views painted on them. There are portraits of Emperors in the window niches, and on the pillars are sumptuously framed paintings of historical scenes involving Saints of the blood royal. Marble fireplace and door frame. *Library:* Free-standing on three sides, with a noteworthy ground plan and decorations. The ground plan is a Greek cross, with a dome over the central area and tunnel vaults above the arms of the transept. The date is 1712, and J.M. Prunner is thought to be the architect. Frescos cover the ceiling, the surrounding gallery on Corinthian pillars is of especial charm, and the balustrade panels have delicate gilded wrought-iron. Fine rococo cupboards. The building had begun to deteriorate seriously, but was thoroughly restored with great technical skill and artistry.

Environs: Wartberg an der Krems (about 8 km. N.): *Pfarrkirche hl.Kilian:* A room with two bays and two aisles, it is a so-called Einsäulenraum (single-columned room), with narrower choir and a net vault. Fine S. door and gallery. Excellent altars and pulpit in the 'gnarled' style. In the choir there are eight panels, painted on both sides, from a winged altar: they depict the legend of St.Kilian and the Passion, and date from *c.* 1470. **Pettenbach** (some 12 km. to the W.): *Pfarrkirche St. Benedikt:* This church was mentioned in 777 and has since that time been part of the abbey of Kremsmünster. It is an attractive little late-15C hall church. The patterns in the net vaulting do not run along the aisles in the usual manner, but across

the individual bays, that is to say across the breadth of the church, thus accentuating the width of the building. Seated Virgin Mary dating from *c.* 1620–30.

Schlosshof an der March = Marchegg Bahnhof 2294
Lower Austria   p.278☐X 5

Schloss: Originally a fortress, it was altered in 1725–9 by order of Prince Eugen von Hildebrandt. He added two buildings to create a courtyard. Small pavilions with mansard roofs at the ends of the buildings. The balustrade and the fountain were removed from the courtyard in the 19C. In 1732, Hildebrandt completed the *'finest baroque garden layout'*. The Canalettos show the Schloss as it was before it was altered; in the background the river March and the Theben ruin. In 1755, the Empress purchased the Schloss from Viktoria of Savoy, the heiress of Prince Eugen, and had it raised and renovated. The *Kapelle,* perfect in its elegance, was completed in 1725: it is a square room with a ceiling fresco by C.Carlone and a Descent from the Cross by F.Solimena.

Schönbühel an der Donau 3392
Lower Austria   p.278☐S 4

Schloss: This was the property of Passau as early as the early 9C. It has often been altered: a copper etching by Georg M. Vischer dating from 1672 shows the medieval castle dating from 1414. Most of the present building dates from rebuilding in 1819, making use of the old walls; the chapel was not affected. The Schloss shares its wonderful site on the bank of the Danube with the *Pfarrkirche hl.Rosalia* and the attached *Servite monastery* dating from 1666. Behind the high altar we find a small gallery and a steep path down the rock to the Danube. There are rococo frescos by J.W. Bergl in the *Peregrinkapelle*.

Schöngrabern = Hollabrunn 2020
Lower Austria   p.278 ☐ U 3

Pfarrkirche Mariae Geburt: Founded in 1217 by Hadmar von Kuenring. It is a single-aisled late Romanesque building with two bays and rib vaulting. A W. tower was added in the 18C, and the W. choir was pulled down in the process. Only the base of a column and a capital with a leaf relief and human heads remained. Unique *sculptures in the apse:* similar figures, placed against a wall, are found in Lombardy, the South Tyrol and Regensburg (however, the figures of St.James in the N. portal are 100 years older). The pictures follow a definite pattern: the focal point is God the Father with the lily sceptre. At his right hand is Abel with the lamb, and behind Abel is Cain with his arm raised to murder. On the other side is a man with a sheaf (Abel?). At the foot of God the Father is the dragon devouring one man and holding another in its claws. In the left panel is the Temptation by the Serpent, while the right panel depicts Samson (David?) with the lion. The figures in the upper panels have never been convincingly interpreted (Hammer-Purgstall stated that they were Templars' symbols). In Tolstoy's 'War and Peace', Prince André and Prince Bagration discuss the position two weeks before the battle of Austerlitz on 2 December 1805.

Schrattenthal 2073
Lower Austria   p.278 ☐ U 3

This is an important town on the road from Krems to Znaim. After 1400, Schloss and town came into the possession of the Eyczings, who built a defensive wall and fortified the Schloss. In 1476 they founded an Augustinian priory of the Seven Sorrows of the Virgin Mary, which was dissolved in 1534. Torstenson had his

Schloss Schönbühel

headquarters in the Schloss in 1645. In 1822 and 1826, the poet Nikolaus Lenau was the guest of the steward of the Schloss.

Schloss: Fortress above the town. The oldest sections of this castle altered in the 17C are the *Schafstall* (sheep pen), a square room with an octagonal pillar and four rib vaults, and the Gothic *Wehrkapelle St. Martin,* built by Ulrich Eyczing in 1438. Below the high roof a wall passage runs over the arches in which the tracery windows of the nave are set into the castle.

Pfarrkirche St. Augustin: In 1450 an aisle was added to the 14C Marienkapelle. The church was redesigned in baroque style in 1783. The coat-of-arms tombstones of the Eyczings date from 1480–1563. There is a Gothic *font.*

Schwarzenau 3900
Lower Austria   p.278 □ S 3

The Strein family were the rulers of Schwarzenau from 1198–1636. In 1592 they converted a late-12C moated castle into one of the finest Renaissance palaces in Lower Austria. Franz von Polheim (d. 1761) had the interior decorated in baroque style by J.B. Allio. From 1818–84 it was owned by the Pereira-Arnstein banking family (Fanny Arnstein had the most famous 'Salon' in Vienna).

Schloss: The fine façade is flanked by two heavy corner towers, and in the middle is a small ridge turret with wooden cornice and clock tower. Inside the building some good stucco and linen wall-coverings dating from 1748. There is a small *Schlosskapelle* with stucco by Allio and four Apostle figures. The Schloss was badly damaged by the Russians after the war. There is a baroque wayside chapel on the way towards Windigsteig.

Schwaz 6130
Tirol   p.284 □ G 8

First mentioned in 930. The knights of Freundsberg built their ancestral castle here in 1150. There were already three churches here *c.* 1200: the Liebfrauenkirche, the Martinskirche and the Jakobskapelle on the Freundsberg. In 1284, Count Meinhard II of Görz-Tirol acquired the Inntal valley together with Schwaz, which from that time on was an integral part of the Tyrol. Ore was discovered shortly after 1400. The resultant economic success meant that art and culture flourished too. The area declined in the 16&17C, only to revive again in the 18C. Schwaz was looted and damaged by fires in 1809, during the war of independence; it was only from 1830 onwards that things began to improve again. Schwaz was granted a charter in 1899.

Stadtpfarrkirche Unserer Lieben Frauen Himmelfahrt (Franz-Josef-

Schwaz, Stadtpfarrkirche Unserer Lieben Frauen Himmelfahrt

Strasse): There was an earlier building here c. 1300. Hans Mitterhofer started on a new building c. 1460, and this was completed in 1478 by his son Gilg. The N. choir, the N. wall and three rows of pillars inside still survive from that hall church with nave and two aisles. At that time there was also a *tower* here (1469–77), and its lower storeys have survived. The church had to be expanded in 1490. The Munich architect Erasmus Grasser lengthened it by adding two bays in the W., and widened it towards the S. by the addition of a fourth aisle and a second choir (all the pilasters used in this alteration were of light grey dolomite). The church was consecrated in 1502. Jakob and Hans Singer, two architects from Schwaz, redesigned the building in baroque style in 1728. In 1905–11, the baroque decorations were removed and the old net vault replaced. The *bell tower* in the graveyard (S.) was also built at this period. The exterior was restored in 1954–9. The copper-covered roof of the hall, and the tower, 235 ft. in height, with its copper spire, are conspicuous features. Most impressive is the W. façade. This has two massive portals, two large windows above them, and a delicate gable which has 13 turrets and is divided into narrow panels by 13 pilaster strips. The carved doors by Sigmund Wirt, with the bronze lion-head rings, date from 1512. The Virgin Mary statue on the central pillar dates fom the 17C. Inside, the nave produces the impression of being an enormous hall, with three rows of massive round pillars and large tracery-work windows which light the four aisles and the two choirs equally (the aisles and choirs are all of equal height; there is no triumphal arch between choir and tower). The W. gallery (1518–20), with its rich red marble tracery balustrade, and the *Fürstenchörl* (1516–18; on the right of the right-hand choir), are both by Konrad Vogel from Frankfurt. Neo-Gothic high altar (1913) on the left of the N. choir, and the S. choir (Knappenchor) has a Virgin Mary statue

dating from c. 1510 on the altar table, and also late Gothic choir stalls (c. 1500, by Hanns Holtzmüller). The left side altar is by Simon Thaddäus Baldauf, with an altarpiece by J. Zanussi (1730), a wooden statue, and a Madonna and Child (c. 1410, the oldest item in the church). The right side altar still has three late Gothic statues (c. 1510) from the former Annenaltar. On the Kreuzaltar is a triumphal cross dating from c. 1503. The organ and confessional boxes are by Bartholomäus Alter (between 1730 and 1740). The pulpit dates from 1685, the pews from 1707–09. The guild poles are 17&18C, the font dates from 1470. Noteworthy 15C tombstones, and bronze epitaphs dating from 1531 and 1578. In 1505–08, Christof Reichartinger built the two-storey *sacristy* on to the choir. The Gothic *Lichtsäule* in the graveyard dates from 1518.

Totenkapelle (to the N. of the church in the graveyard): This double chapel was built by Christof Reichartinger in 1504–07. Fine stone portals and a charming arcade lead to the Veitskapelle (above; below is the Michaelskapelle). Below, 16C Crucifixion and the remains of a Mount of Olives group. Above, carved altar dating from 1510/11.

Franziskanerkirche and monastery: The church and monastery were built by C.Reichartinger in 1508 – 15 and redesigned in baroque style by J.Singer in 1735. Most of the original buildings still survive. The exterior is articulated by three-cornered pilaster strips, and large windows with sills. The tall roof has two ridge turrets. The inside of the church is the finest Gothic space in the Inntal, even though the Gothic ribs were removed from the nave and aisles in 1735&6 when the building was being redesigned in baroque style. The stucco, the Kreuzaltar (in the S.)

Schwaz, Stadtpfarrkirche

and the pulpit are by Hans and Cassian Singer. The furnishings include altar paintings by Franz S. Unterberger, 1740, stone crucifix (1521) by the Kreuzaltar in the S. aisle, late Gothic Virgin Mary group at the Schmerzensaltar dating from 1518, memorial stone (1599), choir stalls of 1618 by Michael Pirtaler and J. Wolf, and new church windows by Professor Fred Hochschwarzer.

Cloister: This was built by C.Reichartinger on the S. side of the church in 1509–12. The founder portraits and coats-of-arms on the corbels and keystones provide an interesting insight into cultural history. The cloister contains a *cycle of paintings* (mostly Passion scenes) dating from 1519–26 by Pater Wilhelm of Swabia,

Schwaz, Pfarrkirche U.L.F. Himmelfahrt: Church from 1460–78; **1** Bürgerchor **2** Knappenchor **3** Tower 1509-13 **4** Sacristy 1505-8 **5** Portals **6** Staircase **7** Fürstenchörl **8** W. gallery, 1518-20 **9** Church doors, 1512 **10** Annenaltar **11** Choir stalls, 1506 **12** High altar **13** Gothic Madonna, c. 1510, at the Apostelaltar **14** Kreuzaltar **15** Madonna and Child, c. 1430, at the Firmianaltar by S. Thaddäus Baldauf **16** Pulpit, 1685 **17** Font, 1470

who made some use of woodcuts and copper etchings (some by Dürer, Schongauer and Hans Schäufelein) as a model for this work. The heads of the characters, including Austrian and Turkish soldiers, are notable for their wild appearance. The vaults were painted *c.* 1600. The *Bonaventurakapelle* (1509) in the E. contains a crucifix with St.Mary Magdalene, *c.* 1520.

Burg Freundsberg (on a hill in the S. of the town): This ancestral seat of the knights of Freundsberg was mentioned in 1100, and a castle chapel was consecrated in 1177. Part of the keep is all that survives from this period. The castle was completed under Duke Sigmund in 1472 – 5. The *Schlosskapelle*, built in 1477, was altered in Renaissance style by Peter Thumb of Schwaz in 1634–7, and is well furnished. The altars and sculptures are by Peter Zwinger (1637). The pulpit and gallery date from *c.* 1630, and the painted symbols of the Apostles dating from *c.* 1750 are the work of Christof Anton Mayr. The interesting *museum of the town of Schwaz* is housed in the keep. The *Heiliggrabkapelle*

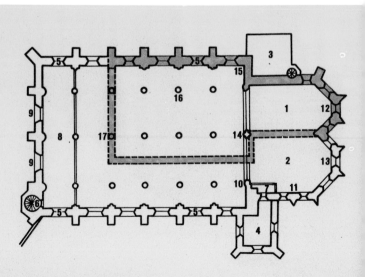

dating from 1688 stands beside the Schlosskapelle. Underneath the castle is the *Wasserkapelle* from *c.* 1750.

Also worth seeing: *Pfleggericht* (Ludwig-Penz-Strasse 13): This was purchased in 1484, expanded in 1513, and badly damaged in 1944. It was rebuilt, much altered, in 1962. *Orglerhaus* (Ludwig-Penz-Strasse 15), with a Gothic portal. *Fugger-wohnhaus* (Ludwig-Penz-Strasse 21), a typical Tyrolean aristocratic residence from the period around the 16C, with tower-like oriels at the corners. *Handelshaus* (Franz-Josef-Strasse 2): Built in 1500 by Hans and Jörg Stöckl, it is a sturdy building with oriels at the corners, and façade painting by C.A. Mayr dating from 1760. The *Palais Enzenberg* outside the parisch church was built in 1515 by Veit J. Tänzl, and was converted into a baroque aristocratic palace in 1700. Other churches include the *Spitalkirche zum Heiligen Geist* (on the bridge beyond the Inn, Innallee), which was built by Konrad Vogel in 1520–43, redesigned in baroque style on the inside in 1749, changed back to the Gothic

style in the 19C, and altered again in 1948. The *St.-Martins-Kirche* (E. end of the town) was built by Jenewein Angerer (?) in 1510–21 as a church of the Augustiner-Eremitinnen-Kloster, and redesigned in baroque style in 1764. Its frescos are by C.A. Mayr (1764).

Seckau 8732
Steiermark   p.282☐Q 8

Benedictine abbey: Former seat of a bishop and Augustinian priory. An Augustinian priory was founded in St. Marein in 1140 and, two years later, was moved to the secluded highlands of Seckau. A convent was added in 1150. The archbishop of Salzburg, who had authority over both the monastery and the convent, established a diocese here in 1218. The abbey was dissolved in 1782, and taken over by Benedictines from Beuron in 1883.

Basilika Mariae Himmelfahrt: Built in 1150–64. A groin vault was installed

Burg Freundsberg (Schwaz)

after a fire in 1259; this became the present late Gothic stellar vault in the late 15C. The interior, plain but monumental, is articulated by two rows of arches above powerful columns with heavy cushion capitals, and Saxon alternate order is still discernible. The only carvings here are to be found on an octagonal pillar. They include symbols of the Evangelists. The Beuron monks extended the building in the 19C by adding the transept and by moving the three apses and the towers on the W. front forwards. The best of the medieval furnishings is the early *Crucifixion* in the choir: Virgin Mary and St.John *c.* 1150, Christ *c.* 1220. Important fragments from the Romanesque and early Gothic church are the *portal lions* and the Virgin and Child (*c.* 1260) in the W. portico, and also the *frescos* (life of St.John the Baptist) which have been transferred to the S. wall of the transept and date from *c.* 1270. On the third pillar, there is also the fresco of the 'Madonna and Child' dating from *c.* 1260.

The *mausoleum* of Archduke Karl II in this church is an important early baroque monument. Italian influence was strengthened as a result of the Counter-Reformation. A. de Verda, an artist from Lugano, began the work in 1587, and S. Carlone completed it in the first decades of the 17C. The *chapel in the S. tower* has sections of Gothic triptychs; the *bishop's chapel* has since the 16C been the monks' crypt chapel (memorial stones and tombstone slabs) with the unconventional *altar of the Coronation of the Virgin Mary,* 1507. The *Sakramentskapelle* contains what is described as an 'original image': a 13C Venetian-Byzantine alabaster relief, and above it is an expressive 14C crucifix. There are 15C *stained-glass windows* in the NE.

Abbey buildings: The present buildings are dominated by the enormous early baroque façade by P.F. Carlone. Extensions

(chapel in the wings) were added in the 1st half of the 17C. In 1640, when Emperor Leopold I paid a visit here, the *Kaisersaal* with its festive stucco decorations was completed. Also: The spacious *Huldingssaal* (homage room) and the *Ursprungskapelle* (the former chapterhouse of the medieval building; Romanesque columns with foliate capitals). Extensive arcaded courtyard with Tuscan order of pilasters. The foundation walls of the *Romanesque ossuary* are in the former E. courtyard.

The *Markt* is the settlement which developed from the abbey in the 13C. It contains the 'Haus des Hofwirtes' (house of the court housekeeper; *c.* 1720) and the late Gothic chapel of St.Lucia, with valuable frescos.

Environs: St. Marein with its 15C Gothic *parish church.* Pilgrimage church of *Maria Schnee* on the 'Seckauer Hochalm'; built in 1660.

Seefeld im Tirol 6100
Tirol   p.286☐F 8

Pfarrkirche hl.Oswald: This church, mentioned in documents as early as 1320, was begun in 1432 under Duke Friedrich of the empty pocket and not completed until 1474 under Archduke Sigmund the rich. The church was large for the size of the village at that time, and was a popular pilgrimage church for centuries because it had a Sacred Host. The legend has it that in 1384, on the day of the Annunciation, a knight called Oswald Milser, who was an administrator at Burg Schlossberg near Seefeld, asked for the large sacred host at communion instead of the small Host. Hardly had the wafer touched his lips than the knight sank into the ground up to his knees, and blood dripped from the host,

Seckau, basilica

which was kept, and displayed in Seefeld until 1919. The church is dedicated to this miracle of the Host and also to St. Oswald. The dedication is displayed in delicate relief figures in the bipartite tympanum of the church's very beautifully articulated and decorated main portal, considered to be the late Gothic portal in best condition in the Tyrol. The interior, with nave and two aisles, has late Gothic articulated tunnel vaults; the ribs are richly decorated and have painted, carved keystones. The choir is lower than the nave and has a simpler net vault; it was probably the nave of the old church. The *frescos* in the choir support this theory. Those on the triumphal arch depict saints, while those on the left wall show the life of St. Oswald, Christ's Passion, and the story of Mary Magdalene. Some of the decorations on the *neo-Gothic high altar* are old figures from the 15&16C. The choir also contains a *picture* dating from 1502 in which Jörg Kölderer depicted the legend associated with the miracle of the host. The central figures on the *right side altar* date from 1515. The relief of the *Miracle of Pentecost*

on the wall is early 16C, as is the *Gothic font* which has a Renaissance wooden cover dating from 1608. The *pulpit* was built by Peter Dosser in 1525. From the side aisle the broad marble staircase with red-and-white steps leads to the *Heiligblutkapelle*, added by G. Luchese in 1574 for Archduke Ferdinand II. This chapel was redesigned in 1724, and its altar contains the 'Sacred Host'. The Last Supper painting by Giovanni Baptista Fontana, dating from 1580, is part of the original decorations of the chapel, which has a flat ceiling with painted stucco and a ceiling fresco by J. Anton Puellacher dating from 1772. Adjacent to the church in the W. is the *former Augustinian monastery* founded by Maximilian I in 1516 and completed in 1604. All that survives of this is a building arranged around a rectangular courtyard, with portals and baroque wall paintings, now an inn.

Seekapelle zum hl. Kreuz: Archduke Leopold V had this charming chapel built in 1682 to contain a miraculous early-16C crucifix which is still on the high altar. The

Seefeld, Kirchenportal St. Oswald

Seefeld, Gothic font

small rotunda with Renaissance portal and onion tower includes a dome fresco by Hans Schor dating from the 1st half of the 17C.

Environs: Leutasch, consisting of **Oberleutasch** with the *Pfarrkirche hl.Magdalena* (neoclassical, with baroque tower) and **Unterleutasch** with beautifully painted 18C houses. **Zirl** with the imposing 13C *ruins of Fragenstein* and the *Martinsberg,* at a narrow point on the road to Innsbruck; it has the remains of a *hunting lodge* belonging to Maximilian I, and a small *church* with nave dating from the 11C and fragments of 13&14C frescos. Finds from the 6C have been uncovered beneath the church.

Seebenstein 2824
Lower Austria   p.280☐U 7

The castle of Seebenstein, and the town, came into the hands of the lords of Königsberg in 1432. They retained these powers until they died out in 1653. Count Pergen had the *Neues Schloss* built in the town in 1732. David Steiger Am Stein acquired the old Schloss for the 'Wildensteiner Ritterschaft auf blauer Erde'. This was a harmless society founded by Steiger and subscribing to knightly ideals. The Emperor suspected it of connections with illegal secret societies, blue (blau) being the colour of the Freemasons, and disbanded it in 1823. The Schloss was sold to Count Liechtenstein, who commissioned the romantic Türkensturz ruins on a rock.

Castle: This stands on a conical hill and is overlooked by the Gothic *keep,* which is visible from great distances. Starting from the *tiltyard,* the visitor passes through three gates, crosses two drawbridges and reaches the castle outworks. The ruins of the oldest part of the castle are to be found beyond a rocky gorge. On the right-hand side is the long residence section; the gables have round turrets rising from the roof zone on either side. A flight of steps with a baldachin leads from the courtyard, overgrown with greenery, of the citadel into

Zirl (Seefeld), panorama with Fragenstein ruins

the inner rooms which are equipped as a *museum* (Madonna by Riemenschneider).

Pfarrkirche St.Andreas: The original building dates from 1290. From 1448 onwards, the church was used as a burial site for the Königsbergs (16 tombstones). The square hall, with nave and two aisles, has net vaults and dates from 1525. Neo-Gothic alteration in 1850; the interior of the same period contains some fine older items: a Madonna and Child dating from 1480 and six gilded reliefs, 1500.

Seitenstetten 3353

Lower Austria   p.276□Q 5

In 1109 or shortly before, Reginbert of Hagenau (on the river Inn) and his brother-in-law Udalschalk of Stille (in Upper Austria) established an Augustinian foundation by the present graveyard church of St.Veit. However, the founders dissolved it again, because the canons were not in accordance with the their ideals. Then, in 1112, Udalschalk founded the Benedictine abbey, which has continued uninterrupted to the present day, and endowed it with his large estate in Seitenstetten and his inherited property in Upper Austria. In 1114, the monks, led by Leopold, the prior whom Udalschalk had summoned from Göttweig, moved into the new monastery. The first church was consecrated two years later, and the new foundation was made over to the diocese of Passau. In about 1180 Archbishop Wichmann of Magdeburg, from the nearby district of Gleiss (on the Ybbs), presented the abbey with his inherited possessions in Ybbsitz. Passau granted the abbey the large parishes of Aschbach and Wolfsbach, from which its present 14 parishes developed.

Stiftskirche Hl.Maria: The Romanesque *Ritterkapelle*, known in the Middle

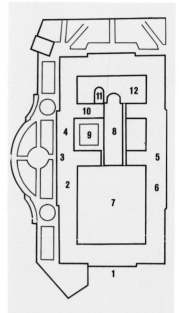

Seitenstetten, Stiftskirche **1** Entrance (with Festsaal above) **2** Main stairs **3** Marmorsaal **4** Prior's house with chapel **5** Library **6** Mineralienkabinett **7** Stiftshof **8** Stiftskirche **9** Cloister **10** Beichtkapelle **11** Ritterkapelle **12** Konventhof

Ages as Marienkapelle, was built shortly after the abbey's foundation, and was all that survived a fire at the monastery *c.* 1250. The present abbey church was built after this fire, and completed in about 1300. The early Gothic character of the building survives to the present day, despite the baroque ceiling stucco dating from 1677. The pictures on the ceiling were painted by Johann Ritsch of Säustenstein in 1702, and whitewashed over only a little later, but were then uncovered and completed in the most recent renovation in 1976. For practical reasons, Abbot Placidus Bernhard (1627–48) ordered a

Seitenstetten, Stiftsportal ▷

projecting choir gallery to be built. The present *Benediktuskapelle*, originally a chapel of St.Barbara, was added in the S. at the same period, its function being that of a burial site for the lords of Schloss Salaberg near Haag. The chapel's early baroque altar still survives. Abbot Benedikt Abelzhauser (1687 – 1717) endowed the present high baroque furnishings. The sculptures on the altars and pulpit are mostly by F.J. Feuchtmayr, while the high altarpiece of the Assumption is among the best achievements of Karl Reselfeldt.

Abbey: J.Munggenast commenced work on the present baroque abbey in 1718 by constructing the Konventtrakt in the E. After his death in 1741, work was continued in the W. by J.G. Hayberger. The building, the shell of which was completed in 1747, is rectangular (525 x 295 ft.). The old church is at the centre of it and is connected to it by transepts. The large ceiling paintings in the *Marmorsaal* (1735; Virtue and Asceticism on one side, and Art and Science on the other; the four qualities demanded for life in the abbey) were painted by P.Troger while the building was still under construction, he was also responsible for those in the *library* (1740 –41; scene from the Apocalypse: only the Lamb of God is able to open the Book with the Seven Seals, whereupon the 24 elders rise from their seats to worship the Lamb). In 1744, B.Altomonte painted the ceiling fresco in the *stairwell*. It depicts the triumph of St.Benedict, the father of the order. Next to the library is the *Mineralienkabinett* with attractive rococo cupboards (1766). The *Sommerrefektorium*, with 19 paintings by Kremser Schmidt, was completed at the same period. A second cycle of 12 paintings by Schmidt adorns the so-called *Maturasaal* (the Matura is the qualification acquired by succesful grammar school pupils). The large *Promulgationssaal* above the entrance

hall is also used by the grammar school, which has been public since 1814. Numerous paintings (Troger, D. Gran, M.J. Schmidt, Dutch and Italian artists including four paintings by Magnasco) were purchased in the 18C for the decoration of the large abbey building. Since 1819 they have been collected in a *picture gallery*.

Seltenheim = Wölfnitz 9061
Kärnten   p.282□P 11

Filialkirche hl.Andreas: This small Gothic rib-vaulted church with its fortified W. tower is set in a graveyard on a hill. Some of the design is still Romanesque. There are baroque altar decorations and Roman stones in the wall.

Schloss: This building, with its fine baroque *Dreifaltigkeitskapelle* (1668) was restored in 1848 after a long period of neglect; two storeys around an arcaded courtyard.

Serfaus 6534
Tirol   p.286□D 9

Some of the houses in this old village, such as the *Gatterhof,* are of interest for their painted decorations from the 2nd half of the 16C. The *Schalberhof* with some remains of a village castle dating from 1300 is worth looking at, also the *priests's house* which has a room which may have been the original church; it has a shallow wooden tunnel roof which has been much restored.

Alte Pfarrkirche zu Unserer Lieben Frau im Walde: This church dating from the Romanesque period was rebuilt in the Gothic era. The Late-14C exterior frescos

Serfaus, Gnadenbild, Alte Pfarrkirche ▷

are in poor condition. The *fresco fragments* inside are considerably more interesting, having been brought to light in restoration work in 1962. There are depictions of Christ, Saints' legends, Evangelists, and the Virgin Mary. The miraculous image of the Madonna Enthroned with Child is probably 12C. A relief of 'Christ with Apostles' is dated 1510, and the *font* is from 1415.

Neue Pfarrkirche Mariae Himmelfahrt: The new church was built near the old one in the late 15C, and was redesigned in baroque style throughout in *c.* 1760. The outside is Gothic and has buttresses, pointed-arched windows and W. portal, and a tower with tracery louvres and a curving gable; it is attached to the church. The interior is dominated by rococo stucco and ceiling paintings dating from 1761 by Philipp J. Greil (he also painted the altarpieces), the altars of 1797&8 and the pulpit of 1763. Underneath the gallery there is an early-16C relief of the Virgin Mary and on the lower gallery is a St. Anne with Virgin and Child dating from the 16C.

Environs: Fiss with beautiful houses (Nos. 4 and 39) and the *Pfarrkirche hl. Johann* with a Gothic tower, 18C Stations of the Cross, and altars with paintings by Jakob Laukas, 1719. **Tösens** with the 18C *Pfarrkirche hl. Laurentius* and the *Kirche zum hl. Georg,* a very fine Gothic church on the site of a Romanesque building. Flat coffered wooden ceiling in the nave, choir with net vaulting. Inside the church are good frescos dating from 1482, showing the Passion, Annunciation and various Saints. The original reliquary dating from 1250 is now in the Ferdinandeum in Innsbruck, copy in the Kirche zum hl. Georg. At the side there is a late Gothic triptych dating from *c.* 1500. The high altar by Martin Stemer dates from 1680.

Sierndorf 2011

Lower Austria   p.278 □ U/V 4

The lords of Zelking owned the Schloss and ruled the town from 1496 until 1604. Wilhelm von Zelking, who decorated the

Tösens (Serfaus), frescos in St. Georg

Schlosskirche, died in 1541. The famous Austrian family of Colloredo were the successors to the fief (their coat-of-arms is on the Schloss portal).

Schloss: A simple rectangular structure. The Festsaal has 18C frescos. The *Kapelle Mariae Geburt*, now the *Pfarrkirche* (built between 1511–15), is in the SE corner of the arcaded courtyard. This single-aisled church with net vault was altered in the Renaissance period. The two outstanding portrait busts (1516) of Wilhelm von Zelking and his wife Margarethe von Sandizell are in the window-like niches in the end wall of the choir. *High altar:* Triptych with stone central shrine (Annunciation). The life of the Virgin Mary (1518) to models by Dürer on the wooden panels.

Environs: See also Oberhautzenthal and Göllersdorf.

Silz 6424
Tirol   p.286□E 8

The old village has some noteworthy houses such as the *Steinerhof* with its stucco ceilings and fine wrought-iron banisters from the 1st half of the 18C. The *Pfarrkirche zu den hll.Peter und Paul,* dating originally from the 13C, was rebuilt in neo-Romanesque style in 1846&7. The *St.-Sebastians-Kirche* has a charming site in a meadow. Built in 1334, it has pointed-arched windows and net vaults in the choir, and also a sacristy cupboard dating from 1633. The domed octagonal Mount of Olives chapel dates from the 18C.

Söll 6306
Tirol   p.284□I 7

Pfarrkirche zu den hll.Petrus und

Paulus: This large, heavy building with its double-domed tower in the N. was erected by Franz Bock from Kufstein in 1764–8 on the site of an old church dating from 1361. The present church was restored in 1953. The fine ceiling paintings are by Christof Anton Mayr (1768), who was also responsible for the painting on the high altar (1770). The altar itself with its impressive statues is the work of J. Martin Lengauer. The four other altars, the pulpit and the confessionals are also in the rococo style.

Also worth seeing: *Gasthof Post,* a hotel with baroque façade paintings by Christof Anton Mayr and interesting interior decorations. The 17C *Stampfanger-Kapelle.*

Sonntagberg = Rosenau a. S. 3332
Lower Austria   p.276□Q 6

A hungry shepherd boy, waking from a deep sleep, found a loaf on a stone with heathen inscriptions. Abbot Benedikt of Seitenstetten ordered a chapel to be built over the stone in 1440. The chapel soon became a popular place of pilgrimage, especially after the 'Turkish miracle' of 1529, in which the horses of plundering Turks were brought to their knees on a mountain by a spring (called 'Türkenbrunnen'—Turkish fountain) and could go no further. In 1614, after suffering attacks from the Protestants for idolatory, the Abbot of Seitenstetten ordered a copper plaque to be set up showing the image of the Holy Trinity above the stone. The pilgrimage has since then been known as Sonntagberg. Prandtauer supervised the baroque reconstruction in 1705–18 and transferred the responsibility for the completion of the work to his nephew Munggenast. The church was consecrated by the Bishop of Passau in 1729. Up to 132,000

Sonntagberg, Wallfahrtskirche

this is the Holy Ghost. In the nave is a Last Judgement with St.Michael as the central figure. The last fresco by D.Gran dates from 1753 and is above the minstrels' choir: it depicts Jacob's Dream. *High altar:* This was designed by Michael Hefele from the Tyrol, with fine angel figures by J.Schletterer, a friend of G.R. Donner. In the transepts are altarpieces by Kremser Schmidt, showing the Baptism of Christ and the Assumption. The *pulpit* by Hefele has a bas-relief of Saul. At the two *side altars* in front of the crossing are two Roman Saints, St. Prospera and St. Felicitas. They were donated by Empress Maria Theresa in 1763. The *treasure chamber* contains interesting votive images including a panel from St.Pölten dating from 1757: 'May Father, Son and Holy Ghost preserve the town from Prussia's wrath as they preserved it in the Turkish war 73 years ago.' There is also the beautiful *Fiakerkreuz*, a gilded processional cross presented by the coachmen of Vienna in 1731.

pilgrims were coming here annually in the mid 18C.

Wallfahrtskirche: A slight variation on the Melk principle: two towers with tall domes, and between them is a concave façade with alabaster figures by Prandtauer's son-in-law P.Widerin above the portal and in the roof zone. The ground plan is cruciform. Inside there is a tunnel-vaulted nave with a dome over the crossing and lunettes. On each side are three chapels between ponderous pillars. The *decorations* are excellent: Antonio Tassi's architectural paintings are the splendid framework to the *vault frescos* by Gran (1738; the workings of the Holy Trinity). The Creation and Paradise are seen in the presbytery, and in the dome is the Glorification of the Trinity. The Nativity of Christ is in the transepts, and opposite

Spital am Pyhrn 4582
Upper Austria   p.276☐P 7

Former Kollegiatstift: This endowment owes its foundation to its site on the road over the Pyhrn pass. Connecting the N. and S., the route was of particular significance at the time of the Crusades. In 1190, during the Third Crusade, Bishop Otto of Bamberg built a hospice in order to provide shelter to the pilgrims in this rough mountainous territory. The hospice was called 'Hospital,' abbreviated to 'Spital'. The name was retained when, in 1418, the 'Spital' was converted into a Kollegiatstift (collegiate endowment) which continued until 1807. Benedictines from St.Blasien moved into the deserted

Spital am Pyhrn, Stiftskirche ▷

monastery because their own had been dissolved. However, the monks found the climate too inhospitable and they soon moved to St.Paul in Carinthia, taking their books and art treasures with them. A devastating fire caused great damage in 1847, but the sanctuary, with its unique frescos by B.Altomonte, miraculously survived the disaster.

Former Stiftskirche Mariä Himmelfahrt: The new building was consecrated in 1737, J.M. Prunner being the architect. It has an impressive twin-towered façade with a fine portal. Inside there is a single aisle, flanked on each side by three galleried chapels. The great fire destroyed the original painting; the result is that the rather sober nave contrasts all the more strikingly with the choir, which shines with brilliant colour. The entire sanctuary with its vaults is covered with frescos. Using a splendid trompe-l'oeil technique, the artist created the impression of a series of open arcades in which the Apostles are standing around the Virgin's empty coffin; the Mother of God, borne by angels, is seen floating upwards towards Heaven. This creation by B.Altomonte is an almost unsurpassable pinnacle of baroque fresco art. *Also worth seeing:* High altar in tempietto form by V.Königer from Graz, 1769. Pulpit richly decorated with figures; balanced by St.John of Nepomuk in glory, also the work of Königer. An excellent grille. The choir has rococo choir stalls, and oratories with gilded reliefs and lattice work. Some of the altarpieces are by B.Altomonte and M.J. Schmidt. *Sacristy and Schutzengelkapelle:* Both of these have frescos by Wolfgang A. Heindl and also contain some good tombstones.

St.Leonhard: Located about 1 km. to the S., this is a graveyard church today. The small, unusual church was built in the 15C on a crag on the mountain pass. The *Unterkirche* was originally a Mount Calvary and Mount of Olives chapel. There is a fresco of Heavenly Jerusalem bearing the date 1476. Two spiral staircases ascend the N. and S. towers to the *Oberkirche*. There is a fine net vault with splendid Gothic arabesques; the altars are baroque and rococo.

Spittal a.d. Drau, Schloss Salamanca

Spittal an der Drau 9800
Kärnten   p.282☐M 10

This town was of no cultural interest until the Salamancaschloss was built in the 16C. However, the town's foundation dates back to the Hohenstaufens (1191), when the counts of Ortenburg built a church and hospital at the intersection of the Drau valley and Salzburg trade routes.

Stadtpfarrkirche Maria Verkündigung: The present building is a successor to the original church which was probably built in the late 13C and was consecrated in 1307. This Gothic structure was enlarged in Renaissance style in 1584.

Several radical alterations were made after this, the most recent being in 1966. The groin-vaulted nave dates from the older structure. There are two late Gothic stone reliefs dating from 1420 in the modern choir, and in the chapel in the N. aisle there is a Pietà, also late Gothic (early-15C). Late Gothic and Renaissance tombstones are to be seen on the inner and outer W. wall, and also on the inside N. wall. One such slab, to the Ortenburg-Salamanca family, is outside on the W. wall and dates from 1530.

Schloss Salamanca (Porcia): Gabriel von Salamanca, Archduke Ferdinand's treasurer, was granted the feudal tenure of the county of Ortenburg in 1524, and in 1527 he began building an impressive and 'modern' residence. He died in 1539, but the buildings were mostly completed in his lifetime. The decorations and furnishings were altered and expanded in subsequent centuries, especially under the Princes Porcia (1662–1915), but the severe, noble architectural design based on plans and models for Italian and Spanish Renaissance palaces was largely retained. Four three-storeyed wings are are arranged around a courtyard and form a square, with the windows and portals facing the road in one unified façade. Thus the schloss is still in the tradition of town palaces built for defence—hence the NE and SW turrets. The Mannerist arrangement of the windows, and the baroque Porcia portal in the centre (decorated by K.Pittner in *c.* 1700), gave the façade rhythm, and balanced the splendid inner courtyard: three-storeyed arcades with steep staircases, the spatial concept still being Gothic. There are sculptured ornaments on the capitals and in the spandrels of the arches. The rooms also have Renaissance decoration (the coffered ceiling in the main hall dates from 1530), as well as late- and post-baroque additions. The *Schlossmuseum* on the 2nd floor has art and folklore exhibits. These

display the style and life of the lords who lived in Schloss Salamanca between 1550 and 1900. The *Rathaus* stands opposite to the N., and has fine Renaissance forms. The windows and portal date from *c.* 1540.

Spitz an der Donau 3620
Lower Austria   p.278 □ S 4

In 830, Ludwig the German confirmed Charlemagne's gift to the monastery of Niederaltaich of an area stretching from the Danube to the Jauerling mountains. From 1242 until the 15C, the feudal tenure of the monastery was in the hands of the Bavarian dukes, whose lordship was repeatedly challenged by the Austrian nobles. The Bavarians relinquished their hold to Emperor Maximilian I in 1504. The town was Protestant in the 16C: there is a 'Pastorenturm' (tower) in the graveyard. Severe damage was inflicted by Swedish, Imperial, and French troops who repeatedly looted the monastery. There was a Jewish community here until 1670.

Pfarrkirche St.Mauritius: A late Gothic church standing high up with a nave, two aisles, and a W. tower. Its lower storey is 100 years older than the rest. There are two lanterns between staggered buttresses, a Gothic turret containing a staircase, and a fluted doorway. In the floor there is a tombstone with a Cross from *c.* 1300. Inside the church, the raised choir dates from 1508 and is set to the N. of the axis. Net vault and rich traceried windows. On the side walls there are baroque figures beneath Gothic ragulé tabernacles. The high altar from Niederaltaich dates from 1630 and has a painting by Kremser Schmidt depicting the martyrdom of St.Maurice (1799). The nave of 1517 has an irregular net vault. In the tabernacle niches in the Gothic gallery, there are carved wooden figures of Christ and the twelve Apostles. These delicate works date from *c.* 1380. Archaic brackets with masks are seen by the window on the Gospel side, and opposite these is the baptistery of 1395, with a Danube school crucifix.

Also worth seeing: *Niederes Schloss:* Built in 1256 and altered in the 16&17C. Fine portals. The ruined *Hinterhaus:* This stands on a steep rock and has a Romanesque keep, Gothic outworks and Renaissance fortifications. The Altes Rathaus and the Bürgerspital (first mentioned in 1419, with an imperial salt chamber), with fine tracery on the portal.

Staatz = Kautendorf 2134
Lower Austria   p.278☐V 3

An outcrop of the Jura, almost 330 ft. in height, rises abruptly at the S. edge of the almost entirely flat Laa plain. From the 11&12C onwards it was the site of what was thought to be an impregnable castle. However, on 24 April 1645 the Swedes took it by a trick and partly destroyed it. Some makeshift fortifications were raised to counter the Turks, and subsequently fell into disrepair. Today only the keep and the main residence are identifiable.

Stadtschlaining 7461
Burgenland   p.280☐V 8

Burg Schlaining: Schlaining is one of the most powerful castles in the province. Emperor Frederick III presented it to the knight A.Baumkirchner in 1445, and it was greatly enlarged at that time. It later passed to the Batthyanys and into the hands of commoners. The castle was completely destroyed in World War 2, but was saved by Dr. U.Illig, the former Austrian Federal Minister. The visitor crosses a

Burg Schlaining (Stadtschlaining)

bridge flanked by a statue of the Virgin Mary and St. John of Nepomuk, passes through the outer gate and enters the large and picturesque courtyard. To the SW, a Gothic tower crowned by a baroque belfry overlooks the curtain walls which are 16 ft. thick. There is a self-portait in relief of A.Baumkirchner (1450) at the foot of the keep. It is 'neither a tombstone, nor a memorial, but a glorious monument' (Schmeller). The core of the complex consists of the buildings, including the massive keep, which are grouped around the sombre 'black courtyard'. The interior is well worth seeing: a Gothic chapel with baroque decorations, splendid stucco ceilings (such as the 'Engelsaal' from the 2nd half of the 17C), a rare collection of wrought-iron pieces, and cultural exhibits.

Katholische Pfarrkirche: Founded by

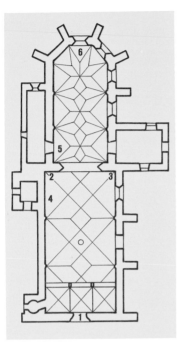

Stainz, St. Katharina

Stadtschlaining, kath. Pfarr-, former Klosterkirche 1 Entrance with Baumkirch coat-of-arms **2** Altar Mariä Verkündigung **3** Altar Hl. Drei Könige **4** Pulpit **5** Font **6** High altar

Baumkirchner, this fine Gothic church is distinguished by a splendid baroque pulpit and baroque altars. There is a Gothic font. Key obtainable from the Katholisches Pfarramt.

Evangelische Pfarrkirche: This, the oldest 'tolerance prayer-house' in the Burgenland, was built in 1782, immediately after the Edict of Tolerance issued by Joseph II. The spatial effect is magnificent, and the monumental pulpit altar is a peculiar feature which recurs in other Protestant churches in Franconia and elsewhere. The key to the church can be obtained from the Evangelisches Pfarramt.

Environs: Goberling (about 3 km. N.): *Evangelische Filialkirche:* A Romanesque structure with interesting secco paintings dating from the 1st half of the 14C in the apse. **Markt Neuhodis** (about 12 km. E.): 'Neues Kastell'; there is an *open-air museum* with works by Rudolf Kedl (modern sculptures) in the park with its rare old trees. **Rechnitz** (about 16 km. E.): Late-17C *Pfarrkirche* with a splendid high altar from 1680.

Stainz 8510
Steiermark   p.280 □ S 10

Former Augustiner-Chorherrnstift: This was founded by Luitpold von Wildon. From 1229 onwards, a priory with a church stood on the site of a fortified refuge with a chapel of St.Catherine. Alterations and enlargements were carried out after the Counter-Reformation (1st quarter of the 17C) under Prior Rosolenz. The building was secularized in 1785, and from 1840 onwards it was owned by Archduke Johann of Austria.

Dekanatskirche zur hl. Katharina/ former Stiftskirche: The plain exterior of the church is dominated by the two W. towers which, like the portal, are early Gothic (the domes are 18C). The choir was moved west under Prior Rosolenz; in *c.* 1680, pupils of Sciassia removed the arcades, converting it into a baroque pilastered church. Inside there is a single aisle, with a somewhat low tunnel vault which is richly stuccoed and has frescos by Mathias Echter. Between the piers there are side chapels with galleries above them. A narrow 'Porta coeli' (resulting from the two towers) opens into the bright choir, whose end wall is almost entirely filled by the two-storeyed high altar (1689). The altarpiece by H.A. Weissenkirchner depicts the martyrdom of St.Catherine. The adjacent altars and side altars are mainly rococo period and bear numerous statues, V. Königer being one of the artists (Kreuzaltar). The 'Marienaltar' (Mary Magdalene and Salome), the Skapulieraltar (with a Virgin Mary, the miraculous image of Stainz), and the pulpit are all of interest.

Stiftsgebäude/Schloss: The strikingly low W. wing has been used as the priest's house since 1785. The first courtyard and the stone staircase were rebuilt under Prior Rosolenz in 1620. The second court is three-storeyed and has arcades on two sides. It was formed by expanding the S. and NE wings in the 17&18C and by linking them to the W. wing. Note the former refectory (in the S. wing) with frescos by Echter, a staircase in the E. wing, and various good stuccoed ceilings dating from *c.* 1700.

There are some attractive *garden pavilions* (*c.* 1730) before the E. front.

Stallhofen = Obervellach 9821
Kärnten   p.282□M 10

Wallfahrtskirche Maria Tax: The choir of this late Gothic hall church was completed in 1476, while the net-vaulted nave, the work of L.Rieder, was finished in 1506. The baroque burial chapel of the Baron von Stampfer, built on to the N. of the nave, has fine frescos by J.J. Fromiller (1717). At its baroque altar there is also a late Gothic Madonna and Child (*c.* 1520). In the vaults of the nave are quatrefoils and paintings on the keystones (1506). The frescos in the choir date from 1476. The high altar dating of 1753 is impressively tall. Its statues and ornaments are rococo, as are the pulpit and side altars.

Environs: Unterfalkenstein: *Schloss Unterfalkenstein*, altered in historical style, is near the ruined Romanesque castle of *Oberfalkenstein* and the *Johanneskapelle*, which has been restored in baroque style.

Stams 6422
Tirol   p.286□E 8

Pfarrkirche zum hl. Johannes d.T.: The history of the pilgrimage chapel to St.John the Baptist dates back to the first millennium. The building which still stands today was erected on its site and consecrated in 1318. The fire of 1593 completely destroyed the roof of the church, and also damaged part of the tower, however, the Gothic louvres survived. The nave has retained much of its Gothic character despite being altered in 1755. The inside of the church, on the other hand, is now baroque throughout. The excellent sculptures at the altars are by

J.Reindl, while the ceiling paintings and other frescos are by F.A. Zoller. At the high altar there is the object of pilgrimage, the image of St.John the Baptist. This early-15C figure was somewhat altered in the baroque period.

Zisterzienserstift: The Cistercian abbey of Stams was founded in 1273 by Meinhard II, Count of Tyrol, and his wife Elisabeth of Bavaria, the widow of King Conrad IV Hohenstaufen and the mother of Conradin; the monks coming from the monastery of Kaisheim in Swabia. The medieval complex, consisting of church, abbey, domestic buildings, and walls, was completed in 1284. Structural alterations to the cloister and to the assembly building were begun in the early 15C. The cloister was vaulted, and the unglazed Romanesque round-arched windows were replaced by glass windows. A new dormitory was added to the monastery building, which in its present form is the result of extensive alterations and rebuilding carried out from 1440–1660. This extensive two-storeyed building is ar-ranged around a rectangular courtyard. There is good metal-work on the doors and fittings. Both storeys were richly painted in 1661–2 by a Carmelite monk who was staying at the abbey as a guest. These paintings have been successfully uncovered in the last few years. Seen from the W., the abbey did not present a uniform appearance until the 2nd half of the 17C. Several sections, especially the guests' quarters, were built at different periods and in different styles. These sections were then replaced by an extensive new building, begun under Abbot Edmund Zoz (1690–9). This large and impressive W. section was built to plans drawn up by the Innsbruck court architect J. Gumpp, the main purpose being to accommodate aristocratic and noble guests. After this, an elegant abbot's house was added in the then prevalent style. Apart from the rich decoration of the living apartments, other highlights are a splendid staircase and hall. The *Bernardisaal* is decorated with paintings by Franz Michael Hueber, assisted by the young Georg Zoller, depicting scenes from the life of St.Bernard. The

Stams, Zisterzienserstift

staircase has a ceiling fresco surrounded by a splendid stucco frame. A beautifully wrought metal banister sweeps gently upwards: the work of Bernhard Bachnetzer from the nearby village of Silz. Abbot Edmund began this extensive project in *c.* 1690, but it was not finally completed until the time of Abbot Augustin II Kastner (1714–38).

Klosterkirche Mariae Himmelfahrt: This monastery church dedicated to the Virgin Mary in 1284 was a Romanesque structure with a nave and two aisles. The low side aisles ran alongside the nave. The nave, with its flat painted wooden ceiling, ended in three E. apses, while the side aisles each finished in one apse. The three apses of the nave, and the large Romanesque window in the central one, are all that have survived of this old structure. Alterations were made in the 15&16C. However, the church was thoroughly rebuilt in the 18C, becoming a baroque structure with side chapels instead of aisles. The massive *high altar* (1613) by B.Steinle of Weilheim extends up to the top of the vault. It has been retained, owing to its beauty and rarity, and is still the high altar. Artists and craftsmen from near and far were employed to decorate the rest of the church. They included Johann Georg Wolker of Augsburg, who painted the frescos, still in fresh condition today, and the large altarpieces; F.X. Feuchtmayr, the famous stucco artist from Wessobrunn, and his colleague J.Vischer from Füssen; the Tyrolean sculptors Andrä Thamasch from See i. Paznaun, Andreas Kölle from Fendels, J.Reindl from Stams. The rose-pattern grille and the grilles of the gates in the church are by the metal-workers and smiths Bernhard Bachnetzer and Brother Michael Neurauter from Stams. The joinery and inlay on the choir stalls and confessionals are by Christoph Gumpp from Innsbruck and Brother Georg Zoller from Silz.

Starhemberg = Piesting 2753
Lower Austria   p.278□U 6

Ruined castle: A castle dating from 1140 owned by a Styrian margrave. Frederick the Valiant ordered the main residence to be rebuilt in 1241. He used the castle as a refuge, as he did Wiener Neustadt. After his death, the Babenberg archive and the family treasure passed to the Teutonic Order. After the castle had been in a number of different hands, it was inherited by the Taxis in the 16C, who retained it until 1817. Archduke Rainer, the Viceroy of Lombardy and the Veneto, purchased the castle in 1830. It was then inherited by the Salvator family and is still in its possession.

The ruins: There is an extensive curtain wall and a gate at one side. The Romanesque *tower chapel*, a 12C round building with an apse and a beehive vault, still survives. In the NW of the castle courtyard is the simple irregular *palas* with the 'Schatzgewölbe' (vault) and the 'Säulenhalle' (columned hall). The *Annenkapelle*, a double 14C chapel, is separate from the rest of the building.

Stein = Krems an der Donau
Lower Austria   p.278□T 4

Stein is at the end of the Wachau, where the narrow passage of the Danube opens out into the broad plain. An area of charming countryside, it has been settled since antiquity. In the 5C, the castle of Feletheus, the Rugii prince, stood on the Frauenberg, where an unplanned settlement developed around the Michaelskirche in the 8C. However, the focal point of the settlement soon moved further and further down the mountain towards the river. As a result of the trade in salt and wine on the Danube, a trading settlement began to flourish on the river bank and today forms the core of the town. There is a single long main street opening towards the river through small squares and picturesque alleyways. Stein was granted the status of a town in 1305 and subsequently grew continuously, despite invasions by the Hungarians, Swedes, Bavarians and French, before declining as a result of the building of the railway.

Pfarrkirche St.Nikolaus: This is a 15C church with a nave, two aisles, a long choir, and spirited late Gothic details on the lower part of the W. tower and on the traceried windows. It was altered both outside and inside in 1901, again in Gothic style. The altarpieces and the ceiling fresco by M.J. Schmidt are worth seeing, as are the tombstones dating from the transition between the Gothic and the Renaissance. The pilastered and richly stuccoed façade of the *Pfarrhof* opposite is the work of Johann Michael Flor. The Gothic *ossuary* (1462) is wedged between church and cliff. The upper part of it has been converted into living apartments.

Frauenbergkirche: This church, with its square tower visible from afar, supplanted the old Michaelskirche in the 2nd half of the 14C. It was deconsecrated in 1785 and has not been used for religious purposes since.

Former Minoritenkirche St. Ulrich: This is one of the earliest vaulted buildings of the German Mendicant orders. In *c.* 1300, a tall, well-lit choir, which is slightly off the central axis, was added to the nave of this pillared basilica, which has a nave and two aisles. The crypt, with its twin aisles beneath the E. end of the choir, is also a later addition. The *frescos* which were uncovered during the restoration of the choir date from the 2nd half of the 14C and include a Virgin Mary with founders; they were painted by an itinerant Italian artist. On the N. side of the choir there is the entrance to the Gothic *sacristy* with a small choir, and then through a Gothic door into the *chapterhouse,* a beautiful room which is supported by a single column. Today the church is used as an exhibition hall.

Stein a.d. Donau, St. Nikolaus

Burg Stein above the Drautal

Also worth seeing: The former *Hof of the Stift Göttweig* (Göttweigerhofgasse; mentioned in 1286) with its fine frescos in the chapel, oratory and portico from the 1st half of the 14C. The *Steiner Landstrasse* running parallel to the Danube, with old houses, alleyways, and squares that open down towards the river, with baroque statues and columns. The *Johann-Nepomuk monument* (1715) on the Rathausplatz. The *Kleiner* and *Grosser Passauer Hof* (Nos. 74, 76 Landstrasse; 13C; this is the tithe building of the bishop of Passau). The former imperial *Mauthaus* (toll-house dating from 1536, No. 84 Landstrasse), one of the most gorgeous and beautiful Renaissance buildings in Stein. Ludwig Köchel's birthplace (No. 8 Schürerplatz), a splendid baroque house; Köchel catalogued Mozart's works. No. 6, the house next door, is the *Gasthof zur Goldenen Sonne,* and it is adjoined by the Fischerturm, once used to defend the town. Finally, the *Pestsäule* (plague column) dating from the 1st half of the 18C stands in the Joh.-Michael-Ehmann-Platz.

Environs: On the road to Krems: the former *Kapuzinerkloster St.Katharina* in **Und.** Its church, a small, domed, centrally planned building begun in 1614, was rebuilt by Sciassia after a fire, and frescoed by D.Gran in 1756.

Stein im Drautal = Dellach im Drautal 9772

Kärnten   p.284□L 11

Castle: This Romanesque castle, first mentioned in 1190, stands on a tall rock above the Drautal. The *keep* (watch-tower) and *palas* are separate from one another. The vault in the upper ceiling of the *Romanesque double chapel* was added by B.Firtaler in 1505. The other vault, with its symbols of the church fathers, was designed by Simon von Taisten in 1505.

The symbols of the Evangelists in the apse are by the same artist. The late Gothic carved figures date from 1500 (St.Martin, St.Valentine and the Virgin). The altar decorations are baroque.

Steinach 6150

Tirol   p.286□F 9

Pfarrkirche zum hl. Erasmus: In 1763, F. de Paula Penz built a church here on the site of a chapel mentioned in *c.* 1300. The church burned down in 1853, and in 1863 J. Vonstadl replaced it with a new, neo-Romanesque church. The lower parts of the octagonal towers are from the baroque church, as is the bright choir with its splendid high altar by J.Perger from Sterzing —it is one of the finest baroque choirs in the Tyrol. Unfortunately, the side altars are not original, but like the high altar they are decorated with altarpieces by Martin Knoller, taken from the baroque church. In the *graveyard* are some fine tomb crosses from 1800.

Kirche zur hl. Ursula (in Mauern): It is said that a heathen temple originally stood on the highest hill above the town, on the site of the oldest burial place in the region. On it there is now a church whose exterior is still Romanesque, despite rebuilding in 1678, although the E. portal is clearly Renaissance. Inside, the sacristy door is Gothic; St.Anne with the Madonna and Child on the left side altar, 1515.

Sternberg = Velden am Wörther See 9220

Kärnten   p.282□O 11

Pfarr- und Wallfahrtskirche St.Georg: This originally Romanesque church with an E. tower stands high up the Sternberg and is on the site of a Celtic and Roman shrine. It was altered at various times up until the 19C. The flat ceilings were replaced by a groin vault in the choir in the 14C, and by a net vault in the nave in the 15C. A Renaissance portico was added in 1586, and two chapels, one in the N. and one in the S., were added during the baroque. Inside, there is a fine late Gothic figure of St.George (*c.* 1500) in the sacristy, as well as a baroque high altar (*c.* 1780) and charming side altars (18C). The cover of the octagonal font has late Gothic paintings (*c.* 1480).

Ruined castle: The old Romanesque count's seat, once owned by the Sternbergs, and then the Ortenburgs, was destroyed by imperial troops in the 15C during a war of succession.

Steyersberg = Warth 2831
Lower Austria   p.280☐U 7

Castle: The most powerful castle in the Bucklige Welt region. It was built by Styrian dukes in the late 12C to provide defence against Austria. In 1278 the lords of Steyersberg were retainers of the powerful Schenken von Hassbach family. The Stubenbergs held the castle for 200 years from 1386 onwards, and in 1600 it passed to the barons of Wurmbrandt. In 1622 they enlarged the castle into a grand schloss and in 1734, being highly honoured in the services of the Empress, they built the Schlosskapelle zur Kreuzerhöhung. Today the schloss is owned by the counts of Wurmbrandt. The entrance is to the S., through a gatehouse flanked by a tower with a tall hipped roof. A narrow barbican leads to a second gate behind which there is a triangular courtyard with the 'Wurmbrunnen' (well). The castle is arranged on terraces which follow the terrain, and steps lead up to the upper castle. The square *keep*

is in the SE corner. The living apartments are arcaded; the N. and W. wings are late Gothic and were altered in the 17C.

Steyr 4400
Upper Austria   p.276☐P 5

In the 10C, a massive castle, the 'Stirapurch', the seat of the counts of Traungau, stood on the wedge-shaped rock where the river Steyr flows into the Enns. The last of the Traungaus gained Styria the status of a dukedom and the panther of the 'Traungaus' still adorns the Styrian coat-of-arms today. In 1192, after the Styrian Otakars had died out, the Babenbergs inherited the territory which since that time has been part of Austria; however, the area traditionally held by the Otakars, which gave Styria its name, was separated from the rest of Styria in 1254 and became part of the duchy on the Enns. The processing and transport of iron ore from the Erzberg along the Danube provided the basis of the town's fortune. In the 19C, Josef Werndl (1831–89) gradually turned Steyr into the 'arms factory of Europe' by mass producing a breech-loading rifle (the 'Werndl rifle'). Steyr had the first electric street lighting in Europe. This was on the occasion of the electrical exhibition in 1894. Fortunately the splendid old centre of this iron-producing town has survived almost undamaged, despite the vast amount of industry and new building.

The town: The town developed on the old trade route on the left bank of the Enns. At one point this road broadens out to form the magnificent Stadtplatz. There are two particular features: the castle to the N., which stands on a dominant rocky crag at the confluence of Enns and Steyr, and in the S. the parish church, also in a dominating position. Suburbs developed at an early date: Ennsdorf on the right bank of the Enns, Steyrdorf on the left bank of the Steyr. The houses are mainly Gothic, with hip-ended gables facing the street; many of them were given courtyards during the Renaissance, while the façades were decorated in baroque and rococo style. *I. Town centre:* Many of the best buildings are to be found in the *Stadtplatz. Rathaus:* One of the few 18C reconstructions, built by J.G. Hayberger in 1765–78; a splendid rococo façade, surmounted by a slender tower. *32 Hauptplatz, Bummerlhaus:* This assumed its present form in 1497. It is one of the finest and best-preserved late Gothic houses and has three arcaded courtyards. Today it is a bank, and visits are possible. Information obtainable from: FV-Amt Rathaus, Tel.: (07252) 3229. *25 Stadtplatz:* An interesting example with an 18C façade that has retained the Gothic tracery. *12 Stadtplatz, Sternhaus.* A notable façade dating from 1768. *39 Stadtplatz:* A two-gabled structure with a fine Renaissance courtyard. At the S. end of the square is the *Marienkirche (former Dominikaner-Kirche):* An early baroque façade with two towers; the decorations are mainly rococo;

Jesuitenkirche and Spitalskirche

there is a rich curving gallery dating from the 2nd half of the 18C, with a delicate grille. Some other interesting houses are to be found in the *Enge Gasse* and in the *Grünmarkt. 26 Grünmarkt, Innerberger Stadel;* a former municipal storehouse with a stately façade dating from 1612 (see Stadtmuseum). At the end of the Grünmarkt is the *Neutor,* built as a defence against flooding after the flood of 1572. It has three eastward openings towards the river, and one southwards opening. *II. Steyrdorf,* an old suburb on the left bank of the Steyr. Two churches dominate the view from the bridge: the massive twin-towered façade of the *former Jesuit church* (now the Pfarrkirche St. Michael), and the deconsecrated *Spitalskirche* with a slender tower and delicate baroque crown. A two-aisled late Gothic hall still survives from the Bürgerspital. There are excellent houses in the Kirchengasse, Gleinkergasse, and Sierninger Strasse. The *Heilig-Geist-Apotheke,* a pharmacy, is at No. 16 Kirchengasse. The 'Dunklhof' is the finest Gothic arcaded courtyard. The *Lebzelter-Haus* is No. 1 Sierninger Strasse, and at *22 Sierniger Strasse* there is a 17C arcaded courtyard. Of the former fortifications, the *Schnallentor* in Gleinker Strasse still survives. It has a charming tower with rich sgraffito decoration.

Stadtpfarrkirche hl. Ägydius und hl. Koloman: This church, with its massive saddle roof and tower, stands on a high terrace to the S. and dominates the town. The plans for the present building were drawn up by H. Puchsbaum, the architect of the Dom of St. Stephan (the plans survive in the Akademie der bildenden Künste in Vienna). The choir is interestingly arranged. After Puchsbaum's death in 1454 there were various architects. In 1522, a disastrous fire devastated the church, which was almost complete, along with its decoration. Work on the building was not restarted until 1630 – 6. The baroque decorations were removed in the mid 19C and replaced by neo-Gothic ones. In 1876 there was another fire, which destroyed the tower; it was rebuilt to plans by F. von Schmidt. The *interior* was impaired by the lengthy interruption in the building of the church and by the Gothic alterations. The altars and pulpit are neo-Gothic. There is a splendid tabernacle by Puchsbaum, and a metal gate with six different swirling motifs, a masterpiece of metal-working. The choir tabernacle is also by Puchsbaum. There are some outstanding stained-glass windows on the S. wall, which probably originally came from the abbey of Klosterneuburg (the Risen Christ, St.Leopold, St.Agnes, early-14C). A Renaissance stained-glass window of the Virgin, 1523. The font, 1569, has relief panels in tin, and the cover has a carved acanthus pattern (early-17C). *N. portal:* A double portal with a portico; the statues date from *c.* 1410 and are attributed to an artist from Grosslobming. In the tympanum there are early-16C scenes from the life of the Virgin, with some later additions. Outside the N. portal there is a statue of the Virgin on a granite pedestal, 1692. *Margarethenkapelle:* Originally a graveyard chapel, this is a delicate structure by H.Puchsbaum dating from *c.* 1430. *Mesnerhaus with 'Brucknerstiege':* A Gothic house with a picturesque outdoor staircase; it was here that the composer Bruckner frequently visited his friend Bayer, who was the choirmaster.

Schloss: Situated in the N. of the town, between the Enns and Steyr, this was originally the old 'Stirapurch'. The oldest section is the sturdy *keep*, popularly known as the 'Römerturm'. Since 1666 it has been owned by the counts of Lamberg. After a fire in 1727 it was completely rebuilt to a design by Domenico d'Angeli, executed by J.M. Prunner. In the courtyard there is an imposing portico in the style of J.L. von Hildebrandt, and opposite this is the fine

façade of the Schlosskapelle. The Burg-grabenbrücke carries a long arcaded passage which ends in a rotunda opening towards the Schlosspark, which contains a charming pavilion.

Stadtmuseum: 'Innerberger Stadel' (26 Grünmarkt): Apart from its collections devoted to art, culture and to folklore, the museum also has exhibits relating to the iron industry: there is a complete scythe hammer from the period of Maria Theresa; old nail forge; the Petermandel knife collection with some 500 knives from every continent.

Steyrer Kripperl: This is the last mechanical Nativity theatre in the German-speaking area. Some of the figures date back to the 18C. Performances are held on Sundays, from early Advent to Candlemas. There is a mixture of religious and secular scenes. It is a most interesting curiosity both in terms of culture and folkore. Information on performances ob-

Steyr, Rathaus, 1769-78 by J.G. Hayberger, splendid rococo façade with slender tower

Steyr, Bummerlhaus

tainable from: FV-Amt, Rathaus, Tel: (07252) 3229.

Environs: Former Benediktinerstift Gleink (in the N. of the town): This was founded in 1125 by Arnhalm and Poppo von Gleink, and dissolved in 1784. The present plain buildings date from the 2nd half of the 17C. The church is not centrally situated. *Former Stiftskirche hl. Andreas:* Originally a Romanesque basilica with no transept, altered in the 15C and rebuilt in baroque style in the late 17C and early 18C. Some of the many frescos have been disfigured by being painted over. *Furnishings:* A massive high altar dating from 1664. In the choir there are two paintings by M.Altomonte in excellently carved frames. The organ, dating from 1732, is a splendid work by J.C. Egedacher. There are two Romanesque door-knockers (lions'

heads) on the W. portal. *Sacristy:* Richly carved cupboards and lavabo. *Marienkapelle* (beside the sacristy): This is a fine vaulted chapel with an elliptical ground plan. The ceiling fresco has trompe-l'oeil architecture. The dome is painted. There is a rich stuccoed altar.

Stockerau 2000
Lower Austria   p.278☐V 4

Thietmar von Merseburg reports in his chronicle that St.Koloman was murdered in Stockerau on 17 July 1012 while on a pilgrimage from Ireland to Jerusalem. According to the Melk Vita, he was hanged as a Bohemian spy, being ignorant of the language of the place. Two years later, Margrave Heinrich II ordered his relics to be transferred to Melk. He was the patron saint of Austria until 1663, when he was replaced by St.Leopold.

Worth seeing: The fine *Pfarrhof* with coat-of-arms on the portal. The *Rathaus* is the former Puchheimisches Schloss, and has a baroque façade. The *Pfarrkirche hl. Stephan* dating from 1725: the side altarpiece is by Führich, 1839. The father of Lenau, the German poet, was born in 1777 at Stockerau. After the early death of Lenau's father, Lenau's education was continued by his grandparents — his grandfather was Colonel Nimbsch von Strehlenau, commander of the Monturs-Ökonomie-Hauptkommission in Stockerau. *Stadtmuseum. Festival peformances.*

Strassburg 9341
Kärnten   p.282☐P 10

Pfarrkirche St.Nikolaus: Parts of the original Romanesque church (mentioned as a chapel in 1169) can still be made out in the walls. The building was rebuilt in late Gothic style in the 1st half of the 15C (net vaulting, buttresses in the choir, pointed windows). The side aisles were transformed into chapels in the baroque (1630–43). *Inside* the church, there is a late Gothic limestone Pietà dating from 1425 in the Maria-Elend-Kapelle in the SW. Of the *tombstones*, the red marble double tomb of the Bishops von Schallermann (d. 1453) and von Sonnenberg (d. 1469) on the N. wall of the choir is by of H.Eybenstock and is a masterpiece of its kind. Some other memorials are 17C. The baroque high altar, by V. Erhard (1747), has fine statues by B.Prandtstätter. The painting of St. Nicholas in the centre of the altar is by J.F. Fromiller of Klagenfurt.

Spitalskirche hl. Geist: (on the W. edge of the town). This small late Romanesque centrally planned building, mentioned in a document in 1337, has Gothic choirs attached. Inside there are wall paintings dating from 1330. The choir contains depictions of the Coronation of the Virgin Mary, the Descent of the Holy Ghost, the Holy Trinity, and figures of saints and founders. The altar furnishings (1720) are excellent and the style of the figures of St.Sebastian and St.Roch is influenced by the early baroque of Hönel and may even be from his workshop (*c.* 1640).

Former Bischofsburg: The powerful Prince Bishops of Gurk lived and ruled here from 1147, the year when this imposing fortress was begun, until 1787, when their seat moved to Klagenfurt. The two *keeps* and the Romanesque *Mauritiuskapelle* survive from the original building of Roman I. Over the centuries, the damage wreaked by wars, fires and earthquakes made alterations necessary. The castle essentially assumed its present form under Bishop Gerold (1326–33) and there was then a great fire in 1368. It was in

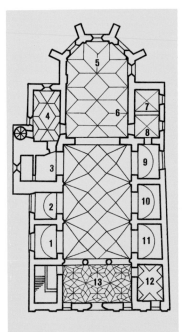

Strassburg, Stadtpfarrkirche **1** Sebastianikapelle **2** Katharinenkapelle **3** Rosenkranzkapelle **4** Double tomb of the bishops of Schallemann and Sonnenberg **5** High altar **6** Apse **7** Tomb of Prince Bishop Urban Sagstetter **8** Tomb of Prince Bishop and Cardinal Salm **9** Kreuzkapelle **10** Georg-Kapelle **11** Michael-Kapelle **12** Maria-Elend-Kapelle **13** Choir

1584, under Bishop Christoph Andreas (1573–1603), that J.A. Verda built the Stall- und Kastengebäude, with an arcaded passage leading to the main building. The three-storeyed S. wing dates from 1611, while the two-storeyed courtyard arcades by Johann Payr were constructed in 1682 –9. The two baroque portals by Gabriel Wittini and Johann Claus date from the same period. The schloss fell into disrepair from the mid 19C onwards, and restoration work has been in progress since 1956.

500 years of architectural history can be traced in this castle, which not only spans the Romanesque-Gothic, the Renaissance

and the baroque, but in so doing was transformed from a medieval fortified castle to a residential schloss (see the inner courtyard). The *Burgkapelle St.Mauritius* in the SE is a Romanesque double chapel which is referred to in a document dated 1228 and was rebuilt in baroque style in 1685. The altar and decorations are late 17C. The *Schlossmuseum* has exhibits relating to Carinthian culture. There is a *hunting museum.*

Also worth seeing: There are two fine Romanesque reliefs on the town wall, near the W. gate. They depict a lion and Bishop Walter von Disentis (*c.* 1200).

Strassen=Sillian 9920
Tirol   p.284☐I 10

Pfarrkirche hl. Jakob d. Ä.: A document dating from 1293 states that there was a chapel on a hill on which a castle is once said to have stood. The Gothic church, enlarged in the 19C, was built in 1455.

Stuben, frescos in Kirche z. U.L.F.

The interior, where there is a nave with a stellar vault, is mainly of interest for its beautiful frescos which extend all over the choir, and in particular over the vault of the sanctuary. Some of them were rediscovered in 1936 and subsequently uncovered. They date from the 15C and are regarded as a masterpiece by Leonhard von Brixen.

Pfarrkirche zur Hl. Dreifaltigkeit: This attractive centrally planned building appears very compact. It has a façade tower and a dome, and was begun and completed by Thomas Mayr in 1763. The fine frescos in the dome are by F.A. Zeiller, 1768, while the high altar by J.Mitterwurzer is from 1778.

Stuben=Pfunds 6542
Tirol   p.286☐D 10

Stuben, a part of the town of Pfunds, has many charming houses, including the 16 –18C court building with its painted coats-of-arms.

Kirche zu Unserer Lieben Frau: This late Gothic building was erected in 1470 and restored in 1913. Externally, its finest features are the powerful buttresses, the pointed arch of the portal and the pointed windows. The rectangular N. tower was restored in 1680. The nave has a massive net vault. In the choir, which is better lit, the vault is much more compact. The church's original frescos in the nave and in the vault of the choir are very good. Statues by Jörg Lederer dating from 1513 on the high altar (1689). The pulpit and the Crucifixion on the triumphal arch are from 1680.

Tamsweg 5580

The name first occurs as the estate of 'Tamswich' in 1160. The layout of the town is surprisingly regular because it was a new foundation, incorporating an earlier village. In 1480 it was sacked by imperial troops in the Hungarian War. Tamsweg

traded in salt and iron, and its increasing importance can be seen in some of the 16C houses which remain. Tamsweg has had its own court since 1790.

Dekanatspfarrkirche hl.Jakobus der Ältere: First mentioned 1246, rebuilt 1738–41 under Fidelis Hainzl. The tunnel-vaulted church with three bays and side chapels has a semicircular apse. The

Tamsweg, St. Leonhard

delicate, almost rococo, stucco in the interior is by J.Kajetan d'Androy of Graz. The massive high altar and the rococo side altars have figures by J.Pult and J.G.Mohr taken over from earlier altars. Altar pictures by G.Lederwasch.

Also worth seeing: Market-place with fine *houses,* and *Rathaus* (since 1895), built in the mid 16C by the Gressing family. The *Barbaraspitalkirche,* closed in 1961, is to house the *Lungauer Heimatmuseum* (local history).

Wallfahrtskirche St.Leonhard (in the foothills of the Schwarzenberg, SW of Tamsweg): The church was founded as the result of a pilgrimage started in 1421. The reason for the pilgrimage was the rediscovery in a tree of a small figure of St.Leonard which had three times disappeared near the site of the pilgrimage church, dedicated in 1433. It is the seat of a Brotherhood of St.Leonard and with ▷ Mariazell and ▷ St.Wolfgang the most important place of pilgrimage in Austria. The building took on the aspect of a *fortress church* when the curtain wall with fortified towers was built, presumably during the Hungarian War *c.* 1480 - 90. The chapels set between the step buttresses make the exterior of the church look rather like a basilica. A painted and now scarcely visible strip of tracery on the roof cornice corresponds with the tracery facing on the elegant tower with spire. Peter Harperger of Salzburg was responsible for the church, which has a nave with net vaulting and side chapels, and a slightly narrower choir with a polygonal apse. Harperger and the suffragan bishop are represented in the *fresco* on the N. choir wall dating from 1433. The partially visible set of *Apostle medallions* on the choir walls date from the same period. It is the furnishings above all which make this one of the finest examples of late medieval art in Austria. The sequence of *stained glass windows* dates from 1430 - 50. Archbishop Johann II (1431 - 1442) endowed the famous *gold window,* which has only blue and golden panes (the few red ones for reasons of heraldic necessity). The window with the *Apostles' mill* is of iconographic importance; it is a symbolic representation of the communication of the Word of God. Parts of the two altars dating from the 50s and early 60s have survived. The panels with the legend of St.Leonard and the church fathers, and also the statue of St.Leonard now on the pillar of the organ gallery came from the former *Leonhardsaltar* (presumably a fixed retable). The pairs of relief panels, the inner sides of the wings and the corresponding painted outer panels (Life of Mary) are from the *former Marien-altar* (high altar). The shrine figures have also survived: a Madonna and Child (N. wall of the nave) and St.Leonard and St.James the Greater (head renewed in the baroque) form the centrepiece of the high altar decorated by J.Gerold of Salzburg in 1660. In one of the S. chapels *choir stall* with three seats and lavishly carved ends. The furnishings attributed to Master Petrus Pescator, who worked *c.* 1445 - 50, are among the earliest inlaid woodwork N. of the Alps. On the outside of the S. door splendid bronze lion head holding the handle-ring, dating from *c.* 1440.

Environs: Ramingstein with the ruins of *Burg Finstergrün,* once a prince's castle, mentioned in the 12C. Nearby is the residential castle built in 1900&1 to a mock-13C design.

Tanzenberg = Maria Saal 9063
Kärnten   p.282□P 11

Former Schloss: The building performed an exclusively defensive function

St.Leonhard, Golden Window

until it came into the possession of the lords of Keutschach in 1515, when many of the representative features of a Renaissance palace were added (above all under Leonhard II). The fine Renaissance arcaded courtyard has buildings on all four sides. The lower two storeys are typically 16C, as are the portals and windows in the N. and S. The N. wing is older. The neo-Romanesque basilica in the NW is 19C, and stands on the site of the former great hall. The Schloss is now a seminary, and has lost much of its former character. In the *church* there is a notable late Gothic crucifix.

Bad Tatzmannsdorf 7431
Burgenland   p.280□V 8

This spa was mentioned in the 17C and became very fashionable in the 19C. The writers Grillparzer and Stifter were visitors here.

Freilichtmuseum: This open-air museum on the edge of the Kurpark was established in 1967 and is still being built up: farmhouses, barns, 'Kittinge', (typical Burgenland storehouses), wine cellars, stables, belfry, hand well, forge.

Environs: Mariasdorf. The church is a few kilometres N. of Bad Tatzmannsdorf on a terrace above the village. This fine Gothic building was unhappily 'restored' in the late 19C; the roof turret and the oriel with ogee arch and Mary statue on the W. façade are new. The original architect was Emmerich Steindl, a pupil of Friedrich Schmidt, the master builder of the Dom in Vienna. The tympanum of the W. portal gives the best impression of the older building; it has a rose tree over two coats-of-arms with a lion and a unicorn. Sanctuary extended. The interior gives a good impression of Steindl's work.

Telfes im Stubai 6165
Tirol   p.286□F 9

Pfarrkirche zum hl.Pankraz: The church of the parish mentioned *c.* 1000 was redesigned in the Gothic style in 1434 and completely rebuilt by Franz de Paula Penz in 1754&5. The handsome N. tower with large louvre and crown dates from 1626. Exterior trompe l'oeil painting imitates architectural detail. Over the W. portal is a fresco by A.Zoller of the patron saint of the church. A.Zoller's ceiling paintings (1757) are a fine feature of the interior. The fresco on the dome above the crossing is particularly expressive and a very fine example of trompe l'oeil. 17C Crucifixion on the high altar. The mid-18C font is unusual in its design.

Telfs 6410
Tirol   p.286□E 8

There are fine oriels, stone gates and façade paintings among the houses with broad, low gables (e.g. 22 Untermarktstrasse and 17 Einbergerstrasse). The impressive *Pfarrkirche zu den hl.Peter and Paul* is neo-Romanesque with Nazarene frescos. The *Franziskanerkloster* and *Franziskanerkirche* date from the early 18C. The high altar in the church is now neo-Romanesque and has a painting by Fr.Lukas Platzer *c.* 1710. The *St. Georgs-Kapelle* near Lehen is a building which is still essentially Gothic; it dates from the 14&17C and has pointed windows and portal. The high altar of 1720 shows St.Vitus in the cauldron. The pretty *Kirche Maria Himmelfahrt* on the Birkenberg dates from the 17C and has three rococo altars by Andreas Thamasch dating from 1693.

Environs: Pfaffenhofen with *Pfarrkirche zu Unserer Lieben Frau Himmelfahrt.*

The choir of the present church, which was built *c.* 1300, rebuilt 1414 and extended 1860–3, is on the site of an early Christian church (remains discovered 1961). The choir still has 15C rib vaulting and acanthus painting. Near Pfaffenhofen are the ruins of *Burg Hörtenberg,* mentioned in 1227, which was destroyed by an explosion. The keep with restored battlements and roof has survived, also the W. gatehouse and ruins of the curtain wall.

Thal-Assling 9911
Tirol   p.284 □ K 10

Kirche zum hl.Ulrich: This church was built in the 15C and altered in the 16&17C; it has late Gothic net vaulting in the nave, fine black and gold altars dating from 1687, a handsome pulpit of 1680 and choir stalls dating from 1686.

Kirche zum hl.Korbinian: This charming early-15C church stands on a lonely hill above the valley; it has survived in its original form. The striking exterior features are large tracery louvres, a fine spire, buttresses and a fresco of St. Christopher which is unfortunately not in good condition. Inside, net vaulting with 11 painted keystones, early 16C wall paintings over the sacristy door and on the N. side of the church a fresco cycle by Andre Peuerweg, a popular work dating from 1579&80. The three Gothic side altars are the artistic high point of the church: the *Passionsaltar* has a magnificently painted central panel full of movement and expression; it was created by the Master of St. Sigismund (Pustertal) *c.* 1430, the *Magdalenenaltar* of 1498 and the *Korbinianaltar* of 1480, both by F.Pacher. A very fine late Gothic crucifix and a late 15C *Madonna* are also worth seeing. The high altar dates from 1660.

Thal-Assling, Magdalenenaltar

Thaur 6065
Tirol   p.286 □ F8

Pfarrkirche Maria Himmelfahrt: The church mentioned in 1244 was altered *c.* 1497. The base and belfry of the massive tower, the exterior with single-aisled nave, buttresses and side door with pointed arch date from this period. The W. door is Renaissance. Interesting 14 – 18C gravestones. The interior was redesigned in the baroque style by J.M.Umhauser and restored in 1878. Late 15C Madonna and Child on the high altar in a baroque surround.

Kirche zum hl.Ulrich: The Afrahof, a farm attached to the Augsburg Hochstift, still has old vaulting; it is directly by the church, which was originally Romanesque.

In the apse late Gothic frescos dating from 1480, Gothic sacrament niche, Gothic grille and a triptych dating from the second half of the 16C. On the right side altar an early Gothic Man of Sorrows, on the left a Mater Dolorosa, first half of the 18C. In the nave carved statue of St. Ulrich, early 15C.

Also worth seeing: 17C *Kirche zum hl.Virgilius* with a fine tower; the beautifully sited little rotunda of the *Wallfahrtskirche St.Peter und Paul,* built in 1783; the 16C Loreto-Kapelle on the road to Hall and the *Thaur ruin,* originally 11C (all that now remains are fragments of Gothic alterations, a round tower and another tower dating from 1500).

Thörl-Maglern 9602
Kärnten   p.282□N 11

Pfarrkirche St. Andreas: This essentially late Gothic church dating from the last quarter of the 15C and the first quarter of the 16C has a massive W. tower, double-bay articulation, stellar vaulting in the nave and decorative rib vaulting in the choir. The carvings on the corbels which support the half-columns of the lower part of the wall are of interest: the demon masks (of the type usually found on Romanesque capitals) illustrate the historical fact that Christian art has its roots in paganism: the canopy of Heaven rises over the demons of the earth. The church is of great artistic importance because of its *wall paintings.* Thomas von Villach, the outstanding late Gothic Carinthian artist, created a series of paintings (*c.* 1470–80) on the wall and in the vaulting which make the world of the late Middle Ages spring to life. Figures of saints alternate with scenes from the Bible; modern composition speaks through medieval technique, and the whole work is informed with vitality of movement and

colourful narrative. Most admirable are the Christ legend and the vision of the Kingdom of Heaven (in the choir). The 'living Cross' made the death on the Cross intelligible to someone who could neither read nor write: Hell gapes, the synagogue is pierced with a spear (representing heresy) and other symbols of death and deliverance teem in a highly restricted space. Altar furnishing (17C) with 'gnarled' ornamentation; 2 late Gothic candlestick-angels.

Environs: Arnoldstein (to the NE in the Villach direction): On a hill are the *ruins* of an old Benedictine foundation, damaged in the Turkish War (1476) and by several fires. In the village late Gothic *Pfarrkirche St.Lambert* (interesting grave slabs) and the *Kreuzkapelle* (stone crucifix, 1517). Opposite the priest's house is a *Heimatmuseum* (local history).

Thürnthal = Fels am Wagram 3481
Lower Austria   p.278□T/U 4

Schloss: Renaissance Schloss altered in the baroque for Baron Enkevoirt. The unknown architect was clearly influenced by Fischer von Erlach. Rectangular building with four identical wings. Cellars in the castle moat. Over the tripartite doorway balcony with scrolls, Corinthian columns rising through the double storey of state rooms to the roof. Baroque chapel with fine oratories and stucco dating from 1720.

Tiffen = Feldkirchen 9560
Kärnten   p.282□O 11

Pfarrkirche St.Jakob der Ältere: Late Gothic hall with two aisles dating from the

Thörl-Maglern, Crucifixion fresco ▷

second half of the 15C surrounded by remains of Gothic fortifications (Carolingian capital in front of the W. portal). Numerous Roman stones in the masonry (2&3C BC). Inside in the nave vaulting late Gothic frescos of the Danube school with Crucifixion. Important frescos of St. Barbara and St. Helena by Thomas von Villach, 1472. The panel painting of the 'Tiffen Resurrection' dating from 1350 (possibly by Urban Görtschacher) is also late Gothic in style. Choir extended in the baroque style 1758, high altar of the same date. Baroque side altars 1708–20, rococo pulpit *c.* 1780.

Tratzberg = Jenbach 6200
Tirol   p.284 □ G 8

Schloss Tratzberg: Originally built to defend the border with Bavaria, the castle burned down completely in 1491. In 1499 the ruin came by barter to the ennobled Tänzl family, who commissioned a new building in 1500–15; it consisted of the present S., E., and part of the W. sections of the building; parts of the walls of the ruin were used. The rest of the W. wing and the N. wing were built around the rectangular courtyard in 1560–71 under the direction of the owner, Georg Ilsung. Tratzberg has had many owners over the years. The façade of the S. wing, which faces the valley, has three storeys with two side towers and a central tower; there is a wall with steps in front of it. The W. side has the Schloss portal (1060–71) with an arcade in front of it and a round tower in the NW corner. The inner courtyard has a late Gothic E. wing with pointed-arched arcades, a late Gothic S. wing and W. and N. wings with shallow pilaster articulation in the Renaissance style. Lavish façade frescos dating from 1600. On the N. wall columned portal of 1560–71. The main stairs are in the spiral staircase tower ('Maximiliansschnegg' = 'Maximilian's snail') in the SE corner, dating from 1500. Striking rooms in the Schloss are the *armoury* with octagonal column and a beamed roof (important weapon collection and hatchments), the *Fuggerstube* with panelling of 1510 and fine carved wooden door and

Schloss Tratzberg, Maximiliansstube

inlaid tables dating from 1515, and the *Fuggerkammer* with a Renaissance cupboard dating from 1510. The most interesting room of all is the *Habsburgersaal* with twisted central pillar in red marble, coffered ceiling and rib vaulting in the oriel. The 148 ancestral portraits of the family of Emperor Maximilian I were painted here in 1508, probably by Hans Maler of Schwaz; they were restored, unfortunately rather badly, in 1850. Legend has it that a criminal knight was fetched by the devil from the so-called *Teufelszimmer* (Teufel=devil); it has a Renaissance ceiling and marble pillar dating from 1560. A good collection of *paintings* is usually on show in this room (Friedrich, Pacher, Mabuse etc.). The *Schlosskapelle St. Katharina* in the NE corner (1508) has net vaulting and a red marble tabernacle with St.Catherine, early 16C. Interesting rooms on the second floor are the *Maximiliansstube* and the *Maximilianskammer* with late Gothic ceiling and fine Gothic furnishings, and the *Tänzlzimmer* with panelling, coffered ceiling, inlaid doors and early Renaissance furnishings.

Trautenfels 8951

Steiermark   p.282 ☐ O 7

Schloss: Known as 'Neuhaus' in the Middle Ages, when it was important in the defence of the valley. In the 13C it belonged to the Archbishop of Salzburg. It was extended by the counts of Trautmannsdorf, who owned it from 1664–1815; the three-storey Schloss is surrounded by massive bastions and a ditch. The side wings protrude in the S. façade; round tower in the NW corner. Lavish *interior furnishings* in the rooms, striking *Galeriesaal;* also *Schlosskapelle* and the Ennstal *Heimatmuseum* (local history).

Treffen bei Villach 9521

Kärnten   p.282 ☐ O 11

Pfarrkirche St.Maximilian: Choir, S. chapel and W. portal are late Gothic; the masonry of the massive choir tower is actually Romanesque. The building and fur-

Tratzberg, Maximilianskammer, Ritterliches Turnier by Hans Schäufelein, 16C

nishings have been altered and extended over the years; they are now predominantly neoclassical (1812). The large Crucifixion on the right wall of the nave is early 19C; the paintings by Joseph Anton Cusetti above the altars (*c.* 1785) are not pure baroque, but the ceiling paintings and the acanthus ornaments are high baroque, *c.* 1700. A late Gothic fresco (Mount of Olives, 1495) was revealed on the W. wall of the chapel in 1973.

Also worth seeing: The *Alttreffen ruin* is the former seat of the counts of Treffen, destroyed *c.* 1490. Baroque *Schloss* (1691), an austere three-storey building with dignified rooms.

Trins 6152
Tirol   p.286□F 9

Pfarrkirche zum hl.Georg: This church on a hill was built in the late 15C on the site of a church mentioned in 1359, altered presumably in the 16C and 1835, and largely restored to its original condition in

Tulln, ossuary

1941. On the E. tower with pointed-arched louvres and octagonal spire are remains of a large St.Christopher fresco dating from *c.* 1500, and a sundial of 1573. Above the main door is a basket-arched niche with a wooden St. George with two knights, dating from the early 16C. In the interior articulated tunnel vaulting, a pointed triumphal arch and a late Gothic carved Madonna, early 16C. The poet Rudolf Borchardt (d. 1945) is buried in the cemetery.

Schloss Schneeberg: The medieval Schloss burned down in 1771. In 1780 two former farm buildings were extended as a hunting lodge. Only walls in the W. and S. and two round towers now remain of the original large building.

Tulln 3430
Lower Austria   p.278□U 4

A Danube flotilla was stationed here in Roman times, in the so-called *Commagena;* in the early Middle Ages the first meeting between Kriemhild and Etzel (Attila) took place here (Nibelungenlied); in the 11C the Babenbergs built a residence here, and Rudolf I of Habsburg founded a Dominican monastery after the Battle of Marchfeld (1278) and his victory over King Ottokar II of Bohemia, the successor of the Babenbergs. In 1159 Tulln was granted a charter and *c.* 1200 the rectangular town wall with 4 gates was built.

Pfarrkirche St.Stephan: The Romanesque pillared basilica with nave and two aisles and two W. towers dates from the late 12C, with Gothic additions in the 15C and early 16C; the choir and towers were later redesigned in the baroque style. The heavy, simple portal in the W. façade is pure Romanesque. The door jambs are decorated in a most unusual way; on each side there are 6 half figures in round-arched niches, presumably the 12 Apostles; they are reminiscent of Roman tombstones and make the portal part of the 'Renaissance current' which started to flow in the 13C.

Ossuary/Dreikönigskapelle: The largest and finest in Austria; it combines late Romanesque and early Gothic in the most harmonious fashion. The slender half columns and steep pointed arches give the stocky building a sense of lightness and a soaring quality. Splendid lavishly ornamented portal.

Also worth seeing: The *church* (1732–9) of the *Minorite monastery* founded in the first half of the 13C; single-aisled church, impressive in the unity of its architecture and colours, with an underground baroque crypt and a hermitage decorated with shells, stones and bones. Many of the single-storey houses in the country town are worth seeing: *priest's house* (15C, much extended in the baroque); *16 Wiener Strasse* (handsome baroque façade and portal); *Babenbergerhof* (8 Hauptplatz, 16C, round corner tower and battlements); the row of houses opposite (*Nos. 21–5) with Gothic entrance; 1 Rudolfsgasse* (baroque façade dating from the first half of the 18C); *Mariensäule* (1695, in the Hauptplatz).

Tulln, St. Stephan, Romanesque portal

Villach 9500
Kärnten
p.282□O 11

Villach is now the second-largest town in Carinthia; its history goes back more than 2000 years. The oldest finds are the tumuli in the Napoleonwiese, which date from the Hallstatt period of the New Stone Age. In Roman times the settlements at the Drau bridge, of economic and strategic impor-

tance even in modern times, were called Santicum and Bilachinium (Villach). In the Carolingian period the town was important as the fulcrum between the patriarchate of Aquileia and the archbishopric of Salzburg. Under Heinrich II Villach came under the control of the bishops of Bamberg (1007) and remained under their direct rule until 1759, when Maria Theresa bought the town and the surrounding area for 1,000,000 guilders. In 1240

Villach, Khevenhüller tomb relief

Villach, St. Jakob, pulpit

Villach was named as a town and its walls were mentioned in 1233. Only fragments of the fortifications have survived. The town flourished in the 15&16C. Material and spiritual stimuli for artistic achievement were the early influence of Lutheran ideas of reform, the connection with humanism and the town's economic importance. Important figures include the painter and carver Thomas von Villach, Lukas and Heinrich Tausmann and Urban Görtschacher.

The fine late medieval town with its well organised and beautiful streets and squares was badly damaged in the Second World War and also suffered from alterations in the 20C. The Khevenhüller Renaissance house for example was destroyed in an air raid.

Hauptstadtpfarrkirche St.Jakob: It is assumed that this was not the first church on the site. The present building is largely Gothic. After earthquake damage in 1348 the choir (*c.* 1370) and then the nave (*c.* 1460) were rebuilt. In 1462 the Katharina von Görz chapel was added in the S., and the Leiniger chapel in the N. in 1482. The hall church with nave and two aisles has a massive tower (*c.* 1300) in the W. façade, connected to the nave by an archway.

In the *interior* the relationship of the vaulted bays and the 10 round pillars is pleasingly harmonious. The ornate ribs of the vaulting, the last word in Gothic decoration, were certainly not added until after the fire of 1524. The vaulting in the choir, the painting and the stucco are 17C baroque. The S. wall of the choir has a late 15C St.Christopher fresco. The stone gable relief next to it with Adoration and Virgin of Mercy date from *c.* 1400. The *tombs* in the church are of particular quality. The most important are: at the E. end of the S. aisle the red marble tomb of Balthasar von Weissbriach (d. 1484), an early work by H.Valkenauer of Salzburg. The strictly asymmetrical composition

shows the knight in full armour. The Görzkapelle in the S. contains the tomb of Siegmund von Dietrichstein (d. 1533), a work by Loy Hering of Eichstatt. The severe Renaissance surround is in stark contrast with the fluid Gothic movement of the figure. In the *Khevenhüllerkapelle* in the S. the two tomb reliefs show clearly the new

Villach, Haupstadtpfarrkirche 1 Choir **2** Khevenhüllerkapelle **3** Leiningerkapelle **4** W. fortified tower **5** S. wall of choir (fresco of St. Christopher) **6** Tombstone of Balthasar von Weisspriach **7** Dietrichsteinkapelle **8** Stone pulpit **9** High altar

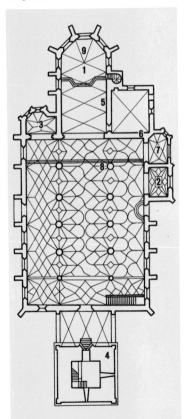

Renaissance view of shape and space. It was a triumph of the modern age to immortalise the dead in the life-like quality of the images. The two slabs date from the mid 16C. G.Seliger's interesting *stone pulpit* dates from the same period. Biblical texts are carved on each of the 8 sides of the base. The larger-than-life *crucifix* on the late baroque high altar dates from 1502; it is a late Gothic masterpiece in which Christ's suffering is depicted with expressive force.

Stadtpfarrkirche hl.Kreuz (St. Peter): This pure baroque building dates from 1726 and 1744; it is cruciform, with a central domed octagon, domical vaulting and a twin-towered façade with two-storey articulation. The church is a clear example of the baroque manipulation of space: all the pictorial and architectural energy is directed towards blurring the boundaries between the various sections of the church,

Villach, Stadtpfarrkirche Hl. Kreuz **1** Domed octagon **2** W. double-towered façade **3** High altar **4** Pulpit

relating sculptural and scenic design to the surrounding architecture and directing the eye to altars, pulpit and vaults. The altars are lavishly decorated (Crucifixion, Lamentation, Mount of Olives) and the pulpit (Evangelists, Moses, Virtues); all *c.* 1740.

Stadtpfarrkirche St. Martin: The church was probably mentioned in 979; the present church was completely rebuilt in 1962, when the tower collapsed. Extremely valuable furnishings: the baroque high altar (1670) has a late Gothic carved relief (Virgin of Mercy) by Master Heinrich (*c.* 1510). In the S. transept is a fine Pietà presumed to date from *c.* 1420. The motif of the Madonna with her dead son shows a style of worship new to the late Middle Ages. The moving subject, the format, usually small, and the frequently secluded position of these images suggest a personalisation of the faith. The fine mannerist paintings on the S. wall of the nave (1580) and the organ gallery (*c.* 1550) are both by A.Blumenthal.

Villach, Stadtpfarrkirche hl. Kreuz

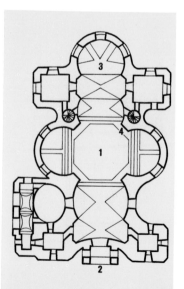

Museum (38 Widmanngasse): In the courtyard is a fragment of the former town wall with a reconstructed wall passage. In the building are numerous finds from the ancient and prehistoric periods, and also various exhibits on medieval and modern art, craft and customs (panel painting by Thomas Artula von Villach).

Also worth seeing: In the *Pfarrkirche St. Leonhard* are Gothic wall paintings (1400) and a late Gothic carved altar dating from 1500. It is worth walking round the *Old Town:* the number of fine houses which have survived 500 years of war, fire and earthquake (n.b. the portals, stairs and arcades) shows clearly how important the ordinary citizens were in the 16C (n.b. the Widmanngasse). No 18 in the central square contains the *Paracelsushof* (Villach was the home of the famous doctor and humanist). In the Klagenfurter Strasse is a fine *niche shrine* with late-14C Gothic pictures. *Schloss Mörtenegg:* the three-storey Renaissance building (1546) was the home of the powerful lords of Khevenhüller, who rose to the nobility because of their economic power.

Vils 6682
Tirol   p.286☐D 7

Vils seems rather rural today, but it was granted a charter by Emperor Ludwig the Bavarian. The Obere Tor (by the Schlössl) and the Untere Tor (by the Gasthaus zum Schwarzen Adler) have survived from the town fortifications. There is an old stone cross in the town square.

Pfarrkirche Maria Himmelfahrt: Built in 1723, presumably to plans by Johann Jakob Herkomer; 18C stucco and ceiling paintings. Only the coat-of-arms tablets in the choir are 16C.

Kirche zur hl.Anna: The tower still has Romanesque features; the three altars date from 1720.

Vilseck ruin: Only the massive rec-

Villach, Roman road in Napoleonwiese

Gampern (Vöcklabruck), 'Gamperner Hölle'

tangular keep on a rocky slope has survived of the 13C Burg.

Vöcklabruck 4840

Lower Austria   p.276☐N 5

In 1134 Wezelo of Schöndorf (first mentioned in 824, now part of Vöcklabruck) endowed a bridge, a church and a hospital of the brotherhood N. of the Vöckla. A settlement developed along the road S. of the Vöckla and was soon granted market rights; in the 14C it became the town of Vöcklabruck. Two fine gatehouse towers, the lower decorated with coats-of-arms dating from *c*. 1500, have survived. The Schöndorfer Kirche in the S. continued to be the town parish church even though it was outside the city walls. The priest's house was by the former hospice N. of the Vöckla, also outside the walls, 2 km. from the church, an unusual state of affairs in the Middle Ages. Josef II made the little Ulrichskapelle the parish church in 1785.

Mariä Himmelfahrt (Schöndorf): Parish church until 1785, now daughter church. The church makes an unforgettable impression: two completely different towers are set one behind the other. The reason for this unique situation was that new building started from the E. in 1450 and stopped when it reached the W. tower of the earlier building. The massive tower to the W. of this was intended for the new building. After building stopped a wooden belfry was added to the incomplete tower, and so the two different towers still stand next to each other. Splendid hall with two aisles, fine gallery with tracery. On the neo-

Vöcklabruck, Caspar von Perkheim

Vöcklabruck, Stadttor

Gothic high altar excellent statue of Mary *c.* 1440. Stained glass dating from the first half of the 15C behind the high altar. Tomb of Caspar von Perkheim *c.* 1520. 4 baroque figures of saints on the gallery.

St.-Ägidius-Kirche and priest's house: N. of the Vöckla bridge on the site of the 12C hospice, now a charming set of buildings by C.A.Carlone. Small cruciform domed basilica, fine baroque interior, ceiling frescos: Life of Mary and Sufferings of Christ. Priest's house: horseshoe-shaped, in the courtyard central projection with steps. *Heimathaus:* 19 Hinterstadt, in the former Benefiziatenhaus; fine local history collections and memorabilia of Bruckner.

Environs: Gampern (about 12 km. W.): *Pfarrkirche hl.Remigius.* First mentioned *c.* 800, present church begun 1480. Fine unified building, net vaulting with frescos, tabernacle. The finest feature of the church is the *triptych* 1497–1507. In the central shrine Madonna and Child, with the church's patron Remigius and St. Pantaleon, the doctor. Figures of saints in the five upper towers. On the inner panel: Life of Mary, bas-reliefs. Only 2 of the excellent predella pictures are in the church; there are two more in the Stiftsgalerie in Steinstetten, to the NE. Outer wings: Passion. On the back of the altar: Last Judgement with the famous 'Gampern Hell'. The Gampern altar, artist unknown, is one of the finest carved altars in Upper Austria, alongside those in St. Wolfgang, Kefermarkt and Hallstadt. The painting too is among the best of its period. **Schloss Neuwartenburg** (*c.* 3 km. W.): country house, fine group of Schloss and farm buildings, built 1730–2 by A.Martinelli. Not open to the public. **Zell am Pettenfirst** (11 km. N.): *Pfarrkirche Mariä Heimsuchung;* late Gothic hall, fine net and stellar vaulting, tabernacle; baroque interior by T.Schwanthaler. **Schloss Kammer bei Seewalchen** (11 km. S.): 16&17C. Picturesque site on an island; the *Rittersaal* can only be visited on the occasion of concerts or other functions.

Voitsberg 8570
Steiermark   p.282☐R 9

Leopold VI founded the town below the Burg Ober-'Voitesperch', built in 1170; he also built a Schloss in the valley.

Ruined Burg Obervoitsberg: Mentioned 1183, in ruins since 1760. The core of the building, the curtain wall and parts of the outer ward have survived.

Stadtpfarrkirche hl.Michael: The square E. tower and the originally flat-ceilinged nave are Romanesque; hall with nave and two aisles and octagonal pillars revaulted *c.* 1500.

St.-Josefs-Kirche: The church of the former Carmelite monastery was built 1690–1708; splendid high altar of 1711 with excellent sculptural decoration by Schokotnigg; founder's tomb in red marble.

Filialkirche hl.Blut (some way outside the town): 16C single-aisled late Gothic building with low net vaulting. Remains of a triptych of 1520; high altar 1777 with Crucifixion with figures.

Schloss Greisenegg: Perhaps on the site of Burg Untervoitsberg; rebuilt as a country house in the 19C.

Volders 6111
Tirol   p.284☐G 8

Pre-Roman foundations have been ex-

Schloss Friedberg (Volders)

cavated on the Himmelreich hill. A large pre-Roman burial ground has been found at the W. end of the village.

Pfarrkirche hl.Johannes d.T.: The 15C late Gothic church was enlarged in 1965 by Prof.Clemens Holzmeister and redesigned in the modern style.

Kirche zum hl.Karl Borromäus: The doctor Hippolytus Guarinioni built this church in 1620–54 according to his own ideas, which often had symbolic connotations. The rotunda is laid out in a strange fashion; a central domed area has three half domes and a rectangular outer bay grouped around it; the tower before the apse has the same plan; the whole building is a dilettante work which nevertheless shows the lively imagination of a talented amateur. Only fragments of the original stucco remain behind the side altars. The interior was redesigned in the rococo style in 1765&6; the stucco is by Georg Gigl and the ceiling frescos and high altar picture by Martin Knoller. On the left and right of the outer bay are the *Kapelle zur hl.Anna*

of 1710 with wrought-iron grille by Oswald Kayser (1682) and the *Kapelle zur Schmerzhaften Muttergottes* of 1693 with frescos by Kaspar Waldmann and another fine rococo grille. There is a simple monastery built in 1692 attached to the *Servite church.*

Kapelle hl.Franz Borgia: Small church built in 1677 in the Volderer Wald; baroque rotunda with late 17C stucco and altar of 1678.

Kapelle hl.Kosmas and Damian: Church built in 1660 near the Volderer Wildbad on an oval plan *c.* 1660, with a painted dome; it was clearly influenced by the Karlskirche.

Environs: Schloss Friedberg: Impressively sited Schloss on the hill above Volders; it has a striking 13C *keep* and NE section of the residential wing. In the late 15C and in 1847–54 the Schloss was altered and extended; it has been owned by the counts of Trapp since 1845. Interesting features are the picturesque courtyard with an old cistern and late Gothic galleries, the

Volders, Kirche zum hl. Karl Borromäus

Völkermarkt, Stadtpfarrkirche

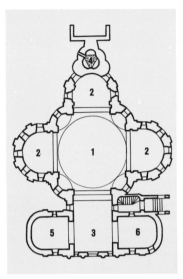

Volders, Kirche zum hl. Karl Borromäus 1
Domed area **2** half-domes **3** Entrance bay **4** Tower
5 Kapelle zur Schmerzhaften Muttergottes **6**
Kapelle zur hl. Anna

Schlosskapelle zum hl.Bartholomäus with late Gothic portal and fragments of frescos dating from 1440, and the Rittersaal with a fresco cycle dating from 1510.

Völkermarkt 9100

Kärnten   p.282☐Q 11

The wedge-shaped town goes back to a foundation of Count Engelbert von Sponheim (d. 1096). In the first half of the 13C the dukes of Sponheim built a bridge over the Drau and thus enabled the town to develop into one of the most important junctions in Carinthia. The 14C *Herzogsburg* lent added dignity to the town, granted its charter in 1254. Some of this Gothic castle still remains on the N. side of the fine Hauptplatz (new Rathaus). The town was fortified against the Turks in the

15C, and numerous houses in the Old Town have survived from this period. There was even trade between the Augsburg Fuggers and Venice in the 16C, the high summer of the Carinthian trading towns, and southern Renaissance design began to make its appearance.

Stadtpfarrkirche hl. Maria Magdalena: The church was built around the time of the charter, *c.* 1240. The late Romanesque W. building with its two towers altered in the Gothic period and splendid late Romanesque portal have survived; these features show how Romanesque art used antique elements. It is only in the tight articulation of the attached columns, bases and capitals and the palmettes on the arches that the magical symbolism of the entwining ornaments finds the geometrical basis which allowed later designs to develop. In the niches to the right and left are a *late Gothic Mount of Olives* (c. 1480) and a *baroque Crucifixion* dating from the 18C. There are remarkable works of art in the *interior* of the late Gothic hall with net vaulting. The *frescos* in the choir vaulting are late Gothic and date from 1460, according to the founder, prior Conrad. They represent symbols of the Evangelists. It is almost certain that the rest of the paintings in the S. chapel, the S. aisle and the N.chapel date from the same period. The fresco fragments in the vestibule are older (probably 14C). The *Pietà* in the S. side choir, a stone sculpture dating from the early 15C, the *late Gothic crucifix* on the cross altar (with baroque sections) and the Madonna statue (c. 1330) at the entrance to the chapel are worth seeing. The baroque interior of the church (figures of the saints, pulpit) is of high quality and dates from 1735 (altars) and 1769 (pulpit). Also 16&17C *heraldic tombs*.

Pfarrkirche St.Ruprecht (in the NW of the town): It may be that the 11&12C early Romanesque basilica had a Carolingian predecessor, possibly consecrated in 760. The lower section of the impressive choir tower is the oldest surviving part of the building. Fine pilaster-strip and blind-arch articulation. The rosette ornament in the tympanum is a Roman stone cut in a semicircle. In the single-aisled nave with articulated tunnel vaulting and sloping retaining walls (interior heavily restored in the 19C) there is fine baroque decoration on 3 altars and the pulpit, all dating from the first half of the 18C.

Also worth seeing: The late Gothic *Lichtsäule* in the W. outside St. Maria Magdalena dates from 1477. Its function was to keep a symbolic watch over the dead in the former cemetery. The *St. Michael ossuary* outside St.Ruprecht is a Romanesque rotunda with Gothic groin vaulting, mentioned in 1389.

Environs:Neudenstein (SW of Völkermarkt) has a *baroque parish church* with a fine late 17C high altar. The *Schloss* is essentially Gothic, reworked in the baroque, and has a lavishly decorated interior which is well worth seeing (14–18C).

Vorau 8250
Steiermark   p.280☐U 8

Augustiner-Chorherrnstift: Founded in 1163 by Ottokar III, Margrave of Steyr. Fire in 1237, rebuilt c. 1300. Fortified in the 15C with 4 towers, rampart and ditch. The building was redesigned as a unified whole from 1625 until the early 18C. It is still occupied by Augustinian canons.

Stiftspfarrkirche hl.Thomas: Only the lower section of the S. façade tower remains of the original church, completed c. 1300. The rest of the building is the result of baroque and Counter-Reformation taste for display: in 1660–2 D.Sciassia built the single-aisled pilastered church with tunnel vaulting and galleried chapels on both sides. The most striking feature of the interior is the impressive *high altar,* dating from 1704 and designed by M.Steinl, who was also responsible for the pulpit (1706) with lavish figure decoration: represented on the altar are the Assumption (carved Apostles with coffin, above them oil painting of the Assunta by the Venetian Antonio Bellucci). The statues of the 4 Church Fathers placed in front of the choir lead the eye of the visitor to the altar. The lavish frescos in the church were painted by Karl Ritsch, Josef Grafenstein, Joh.Kaspar Waginger and Karl Unterhuber. C.J.Hackhofer's frescos in the sacristy are also of interest (including 'Last Judgement' and 'Descent into Hell').

Stiftsgebäude: In the 17&18C stylistically uniform sections were added to the church: the *Klausur* (1625) in the

Stift Vorau

S.and the *Prälatur* in the N. (1688–1733).
In the Klausur *chapterhouse* and *refectory*
with paintings by C.J.Hackhofer. In the
Prälatur is the *library* with shallow tunnel
vaulting and lavish fresco and stucco
decoration. A double spiral staircase leads
to the *former manuscript room* (ceiling paintings by J.G.Mayr: 'Cardinal Virtues' and
'Immaculata' by H.A.Weissenkirchner),
which contains valuable manuscripts, in-
cludung the so-called 'Vorauer manuscript'
(*c.* 1190), the earliest collection of early
Middle High German poetry, and the
famous *Kaiserchronik.* Also worth seeing:
Fürstenzimmer with painted wall coverings, *refectory* and *Prälatenkapelle.*

Marktkirche hl.Ägydius: Consecrated
1202. The square choir is Romanesque,
the other choir dates back to an extension
after 1700. Ceiling frescos and altar panel

by C.J.Hackhofer (1708). The high altar
(with statue of Mary) is unusually placed
between the two choirs. The pulpit came
from the Stiftskirche. Hackhofer's tomb is
outside the church.

Also worth seeing: *Friedhofskirche St.
Johann* unter den Linden. 1306, Romanesque nave vaulted in the 17C. *Friedhofskirche des Marktes,* built 1445, altered
1711. Seven Passion pictures (18C) and
frescos by C.J.Hackhofer (niche chapels).

Environs: Festenburg: Castle in a
wooded area, first mentioned 1353. It
came into the possession of Vorau in 1616,
after changing hands on many occasions.
It was altered in the 18C by prior Leistl as
a sanctuary for the nuns of the area.
C.J.Hackhofer conceived a coherent baroque design which blended into a unified

Vorau, library

whole paintings, frescos and sculpture (by J.Fenest to Hackhofer's design); the theme is meditation on the Christian notions of suffering and redemption. Conceptual and artistic heights are reached in the *Pfarrkirche hl.Katharina,* a rectangular space devoted to the theme of the arrival of the martyr in heaven. Triumph and the fulfilment of faith are impressively combined here in the rejoicing hosts of angels in the frescos and the high altar panel. The other chapels and rooms leading to the church are no less impressive in their astonishing trompe l'oeil effects: the *Loretokapelle* and the *Krippenkapelle,* and also the highly dramatic representations of the various *Stations of the Cross;* the whole sequence is accompanied by the sufferings of St. Catherine and the secrets of the rosary. Large statues at the Schloss gate: beheading of St. Catherine and Christ the Saviour.

Also *Kernstockmuseum:* home of the poet and priest Ottokar Kernstock (1848–1928).

Vordernberg 8794
Steiermark   p.282 □ R 8

There have been 'Radwerke' to process the ore from the Erzberg since the 13C. A museum in Radwerk shows the oldest known steam-driven bellows.

Laurentiuskirche: Built in 1465, surrounded by a curtain wall. In the choir late Gothic tabernacle. Fragments of 15C frescos. On the outer walls two stone reliefs after Veit Stoss (1520).

Pfarrkirche Maria Himmelfahrt: Completed 1660, with crucifix from the Laurentiuskirche; 18C Mary altar.

W

Waidhofen an der Thaya 3830
Lower Austria   p.278□S2

Founded *c.* 1170 by the counts of Pernegg.
Burned in 1278 by the troops of King Ot-
tokar and completely destroyed by the
Bohemians 50 years later. By the end of the
Thirty Years War there were only 60

citizens living in the town. The numerous
underground refuge tunnels, many of them
on two levels with wells, date from the
16C. The town was almost burned to the
ground on five occasions, the last in 1873.

Pfarrkirche Mariae Himmelfahrt: a
baroque tower was built in 1713, and the
rest of the church was added to it: date of

*Waidhofen a.d. Thaya, Bürgerspitalkapelle, Madonna and Child and thirteen
Auxiliary Saints*

completion 1723. A broad building with straight apse and elaborate ceiling fresco. Large figures on the columned altar (1721): St.Leopold and St.Charles Borromeo. Fine choir stalls, baroque organ. In the Marienkapelle small rococo altar with Madonna dating from 1440.

Bürgerspitalkapelle: built in 1365 outside the town wall. In the Gothic choir rib vaulting and tracery windows. Striking E. tower. Side altar with late Gothic wooden relief: Auxiliary Saints and Madonna c. 1500.

Schloss: built in 1770 on the site of an earlier building; owned by the counts of Gudenus for 200 years. Fine old rooms with exquisite furnishings.

Waidhofen an der Ybbs 3340
Lower Austria   p.276□Q6

In 995 Emperor Otto presented land for timber-felling to the Freising Hochstift.

Waidhofen was part of Freising until the Reichsdeputationsabschluss of 1803. It was called Bayerisch Waidhofen until the last century and still has the moor of Freising in its coat-of-arms. In the early 13C Waidhofen was systematically fortified by Freising: the upper Stadtpfalz with the Burg is the older section, connected with the Lower Town by the 'Freisinger Berg' c. 1270. Some walls and towers and the Ybbstor have survived of the former fortifications. A Gau trade agreement brought Styrian iron by barter to Waidhofen and it was made into swords, knives and scythes (in 1500 there were 250 forges). There was division and decline at the time of the Reformation: Paul Rebhuhn, the son of a smith, studied in Wittenberg and became the friend of Melanchthon and Luther. In the Counter-Reformation 160 families emigrated. In 1532 the Turks were beaten off, and in memory of this the hands of the N. face of the town clock are permanently set at quarter to one. Economic decline in the 18&19C. In 1875 Baron Rothschild bought the ruined castle and had it rebuilt in the neo-Gothic style by Friedrich von

Waidhofen a.d. Ybbs

Schmidt. The town with its beautifully kept old houses is among the most charming in Austria.

Stadtpfarrkirche hll. Maria Magdalena and Lambert: late Gothic building, started in 1439 and completed in 1510. It is reached via the cemetery gate with fine curlicue wrought iron dating from 1691. The church has tracery windows between the buttresses and a 15C Mount of Olives by the entrance. In the vestibule is the tomb of Sigmund von Eyczing and his wife Walpurga von Säusenegg (1749). Broad, rather short hall with nave and two aisles with a niche-like polygonal choir. Eight slender pillars with flowers carved on the capitals support the vaulting. *High altar:* shrine altar of 1500. In the shrine a delicate Madonna with Christ Child, St.Barbara and St.Catherine. Bas-reliefs on both sides: lives of Elisabeth, Agatha, Catherine and Ursula. *Side altars:* gospel side: St.Mary Magdalene, opposite Pietà, both 1460. *Baroque organ* with three manuals. *Marienkapelle:* Madonna with scapular on the marble altar. *Cutlers' monstrance:* the knifemakers presented a monstrance to the church in 1512: gilded silver set with jewels, 40 inches high. The guardians of the shrine are St.Sigismund and St.Korbinian.

Also worth seeing: *Grabenkirche:* built by the Capuchins in 1644. Fine statue: Mary with Child, school of Hans Leinberger. *Spitalkirche:* church late Gothic, interior early baroque. Stone pulpit and glass *c.* 1470. A fine crib is stored for safety elsewhere. *Schloss:* fine site on the high bank of the Ybbs; older parts are the keep and neo-Gothic arcaded courtyard. *Stadtturm* raised to a height of over 160 ft. with furnished room for the tower watchman and the famous clock. *Old Town:* triangular layout of great unity, 2 large squares with houses from the Gothic to the baroque. *Graben:* (former town ditch)

charming edge of the old town with Biedermeier houses, chapels, monastery church with small houses of the Third Order and remains of a fortified tower.

Heimatmuseum: founded in 1905, and considered one of the most important town museums in Lower Austria. Exhibits on the history of the town, craft and folklore. *Privatsammlung Piaty:* a charming rural collection of old domestic implements, wax figures, verre églomisé etc.

Waidring 6384
Tirol   p.264 □ K7

Pfarrkirche St. Veit: first mentioned in 1381, rebuilt in 1505 in the late Gothic style and from 1757–60 in the rococo style by Kassian Singer, completed by A. Hueber after Singer's death. The massive church with decorative onion-domed towers and three side portals has a nave with three bays and three shallow domes, and a fourth shallow dome in the choir; the décor is exuberantly rococo. The four dome frescos were painted in 1761 by J.Perwanger and Matthias Mader. The baldachino altar with statues of the Apostles Peter and Paul is the work of J.Martin Lengauer. The stucco and the pulpit are by J.Gratl, 1958&9.

Waitschach=Hüttenberg 9375
Kärnten   p.282 □ Q10

Pfarr- und Wallfahrtskirche Unsere Liebe Frau: at a height of over 3,700 ft. and visible for miles stands a heavily fortified church begun under Bishop Leonhard von Keutschach in 1447 and completed *c.* 1500. There are still traces of a picture of Mary in the tympanum of the lavishly decorated W. portal, which has an ogee arch. The interior gives a pleasing impression of spaciousness. In the choir and somewhat narrower nave net vaulting, in the aisles rib vaulting. The keystones are decorated with figures and ornaments. The lavishly carved *tabernacle* (late Gothic, *c.* 1480) is a fine feature of the choir. The splendid *high altar* dates from 1670 and has one of the finest miraculous images in Carinthia in its three-tier central section with columns. It is a late Gothic *Madonna and Child* dating from *c.* 1440, and so probably came from an older church. The finest of the side altars is the so-called *Landschaftsaltar* (landscape altar, N. wall of the nave). It is dated 1626, and is in the mannerist or early baroque style. There is an Annunciation between the two columns of the central shrine.

Waldhausen im Strudengau 4391
Upper Austria   p.278□R4

Former Augustiner-Chorherrenstift: first founded in 1147 in Burg Säbnich above Sarmingstein. After the death of the founder Otto von Machland (▷ Baumgartenberg) the monastery was moved to the N: 'Silvia domus' = Waldhausen; new foundation completed in 1161. The monastery was dissolved in 1792, much of the building was then pulled down and used to build the 'Franzensburg' in Laxenburg.

Former Stiftskirche Mariä Himmelfahrt: one of the earliest baroque buildings, started by C.Canevale in 1650. Pilaster church with side chapels and galleries. Lavish stucco ceiling with 6 large and countless smaller frescos (almost 300 in all). Beautifully coherent baroque interior: colour scheme typical of the early baroque: altars, pulpit, choir stalls, confessionals and organ in black and gold, white stucco. Intricate lavabo *c.* 1680 in the sacristy. Church well restored.

Marktkirche hl.Johannes der Täufer: rebuilt 1608–12 using the earlier choir and tower. Although the church is only a generation older than the Stiftskirche, it is

Weissenkirchen i.d. Wachau with Pfarrkirche

a remarkable example of the 'Gothic hangover'. The architecture is Gothic, with Renaissance features in the detail, especially the S. portal and a tabernacle. The high altar, *c.* 1680, Schwanthaler school, the font with acanthus and fruit dating from *c.* 1700 and the pulpit, Swiss pine, *c.* 1612 are notable.

Wängle = Reutte 6600

Tirol   p.286 □ D8

Pfarrkirche hl.Martin: inconspicuous early 18C building. Articulated tunnel vaulting in the choir, otherwise the choir and tunnel-vaulted nave are splendid baroque, with 18C altars, pulpit, confessionals, organ and gallery. The trompe l'oeil ceiling paintings are by F.A.Zeiller and date from 1704. The Stations of the Cross paintings are by Johann Balthasar Riepp, 1735.

Weissenkirchen in der Wachau 3610

Lower Austria   p.278 □ S4

In 850 Ludwig the German granted possessions in the Wachau valley to the monastery of Niederaltaich; the gift consisted of the settlements of Wösendorf, Joching, St.Michael and Weissenkirchen. In 1531, on the orders of Emperor Ferdinand I, the town and church were fortified with ditches, ramparts and four towers, and armed with 44 cannons. The town suffered a disastrous fire in 1793.

Pfarrkirche Mariae Himmelfahrt: the church is set on an eminence and is reached by a covered bridge; its fortifications are almost intact. By the massive W. tower is a small Gothic tower dating from 1400 with a masonry roof. The W. en-

trance has a lavishly profiled main portal with tympanum. Chamfered S. portal 1450. Interior with delicate net vaulting, and irregular in appearance, clearly showing the phases of building: S.aisle 1300, nave 1439, chapels added 1460. *High altar:* Assumption with monumental figures. On the triumphal arch: Danube school Madonna of 1520. Baroque furnishings 1736. Rococo organ 1777.

Also worth seeing: *Teisenhoferhof* or *Schützenhof* in the market-place with *Wachaumuseum.* 16C fortress-like building with fine arcaded courtyard full of interesting nooks and crannies. Fine old houses with Renaissance loggias and 15C towers: salt store, Raffelsberger Hof (the former house of the ships' masters), Lehenritterhof with tower chapel, Manghof etc.

Weistrach 3351

Lower Austria   p.276 □ Q5

Pfarrkirche hl.Stephan: old foundation of the abbey of Admont. In 1151 a priest known as Gundelbertus in 'Wiztra' is mentioned. The late Gothic hall church has splendid net vaulting dating from 1520: the dynamic movement of the Danube style is finely expressed in the complexities and imaginative penetration of the narrow, shadowed ribs. The ribs end at the broad chancel arch in low cones with keystones. The nave was extended in 1868.

Weiten 3653

Lower Austria   p.278 □ S4

Large Jewish community in the Middle Ages (temple behind the church). Fortified in 1480 with a curtain wall and 4 gates, of which one has survived, by the church.

Pfarrkirche hl.Stephan: a first church was consecrated in 1050, and it is presumed that traces of this remain in the W. wall. Hall church with nave and two aisles and a free-standing tower. There are empty baldachinos intended to house figures on the choir buttresses—only on the N. wall is there a Man of Sorrows, dating from 1450. The vaulting was redesigned in the baroque style after a fire in 1727. Fine large tracery windows with stained glass (1380–1593) with saints, founders, coats-of-arms, an Annunciation (dove kissing Mary on the forehead). High Gothic choir with frescos on both walls and seating niches with colourful surrounds. High altar 1640 with gold tabernacle.

Weitra 3970

Lower Austria   p.278☐R3

A customs post mentioned in 1190 and known as Witrahe (possibly a corruption of Weidenstange=willow rod) became Altweitra. Hadmar II of Kuenring founded a fortified town built to a formal design on rocks sloping steeply to the Lainsitz before 1208. It was the centre of the 'districtus witrensis', directly dependent on the empire and principal base of the revolt of the Ministerialien against the last Babenberg Friedrich II. After it had been frequently attacked and had changed hands on many occasions, Emperor Rudolf II awarded the fief to his Oberkämmerer Wolf Rumpf von Wielross (1581). Wielross had the castle with its two towers pulled down and rebuilt by the imperial architect Pietro Ferabosco, who built the Stallburg in Vienna. Through Rumpf's widow, a Countess Arco, the title came to the princes of Fürstenberg, who still own it today. The town walls have partially survived. The Osttor on the road to Gmünd is 17C: a heavy tower with rounded battlements, rounded arches and painted coats-of-arms.

Pfarrkirche hll.Peter und Paul: Gothic nave on Romanesque foundations. Net vaulting 1439. In the two-bayed high choir, baroque high altar by J.Walser (1749). On the epistle side Gothic niches. Adjacent is

Weissenkirchen i.d. Wachau, Teisenhoferhof

the baroque *Kapelle zum Hl.Kreuz* with an unusual altar (a free-standing scrolled baldachino on gnarled oak trunks). Frescos of the Last Judgement in the left aisle, in the right Lenten veil fresco with Passion scene dating from 1450 and altar with a picture of Mary by Walter Schmidt, 1747.

Schloss: built 1590–1606. Renaisssance round-arched portal with stone urns and double refuge. Rectangular building with smooth longitudinal walls. Ferabosco's pillared arches on the narrow sides are more elegant than those in Vienna. Venetian chimneys and Renaissance fountains in the courtyard (1590–1606).

Also worth seeing: Altweitra: *Kirche hll.Peter und Paul,* pre-1197. Heavy granite building with Romanesque round-arched windows and remains of frescos in the choir (St.Erasmus). Single-aisled nave with square choir and semicircular apse. There is a contemporary fortified storey above the entire nave. *Castellihaus,* built in 1785 on remains of the former ossuary.

Weiz 8160

Steiermark   p.280☐T9

The oldest part of the settlement, made secure by Taborite fortification of the Thomaskirche, was on the W. bank of the Weizbach; in the 13C a rectangular marketplace was built. Charter granted 1932.

Taborkirche hl.Thomas von Canterbury: formerly a fortified church with Romanesque core. The E. choir tower was altered as a defensive tower. The Tabor, built *c.* 1689, was later used for residential purposes. *Interior:* nave with groin vaulting. The 13&14C frescos were restored in 1933. High altar picture by J.A. von Mölk (1771).

Dekanats- und Wallfahrtskirche Schmerzhafte Maria (on the Weizberg): the church was redesigned by the Graz architect J.Hueber in 1757. A relief by the approach shows the church in its original form. The main axis of the late baroque interior is the dominant central bay with elliptical dome; semicircular altar niches provide side openings. Walls articulated with columns and pilasters. *Frescos* by J.A. von Mölk; note the trompe l'oeil raising of the central dome. Furnishings: high altar by V.Königer with 15C Pietà. 6 side altar paintings by J.A. von Mölk.

Schloss Ratmansdorf: built 1555&6 by a family of this name. Three-storey central building with protruding corner towers; characteristic windows of the dell'Allio school. Now a local court.

Schloss Thannhausen: present building 16C. The three-storey Schloss buildings are grouped around a rectangular arcaded courtyard. In the E. section articulated windows in carved stone, derived from the dell'Allio school. In the 18C addition of a show staircase and new connecting corridors. Chapel 1606.

Wels 4600

Upper Austria   p.276☐O5

The town of Wels is on the site of an ancient settlement. Potted history: Neolithic finds; important Roman colonial town of Ovilava; first mention of the castle at the crossing of the Traun in 776, seat of the powerful counts of Wels-Lambach; Emperor Maximilian I died in the castle of Wels on January 12 1519. The town of Wels is now an agricultural and industrial centre. The Wels trade fairs have made the town internationally famous.

Town: the heart of the town is the long and

splendid *Stadtplatz*. Some of the façades are simple and some more elaborate, but almost none of them disturbs the overall balance of the picture. At the W. end is the *Ledererturm*, one of the old town gates, at the E. end is the parish church. *Rathaus:* palace-like building on the site of two houses, built in 1738 by J.M.Prunner. *No. 18:* Roman stone in the façade, round medallion with double portrait; *No. 24* house of Salome Alt, the consort of the Salzburg Archbishop Wolf Dietrich; corner oriel, tile-like façade painting, coats-of-arms; *No. 39: Weiss'sches Freihaus* (▷ Würting) 1589, façade with facetted ashlar; *No. 63:* Kremsmünsterer Hof, rococo façade, courtyard. Fine courtyards: *Nos. 34, 40, 46, 52 66.* Other buildings worth mentioning: *Kaiser-Joseph-Platz:* No. 12, former palace; No. 56: stucco façade with Madonna; *25 Schmidtgasse:* arcaded courtyard. Am Zwinger, at the opening of the Traungasse: *J. Nepomuk group:* niche with architectural painting, in it stone figure of the saint with angels. Accessible from the Zwinger *Sigmarkapelle* (=Barbarakapelle): the only part of the Minorite church which has not been secularised, now *war memorial chapel.* Single aisle, late-15C, wall frescos contemporary with the building.

Stadtpfarrkirche St. Johannes Ev.: essentially a Romanesque basilica with nave and two aisles; the W. portal of this building has survived; high Gothic choir, first half of the 14C; tower raised in 1718 and fine lantern added; outer W. door *c.* 1730 with plague saints; extremely important Gothic stained glass in the apse, second half of the 14C. Under the tower excellent *tombs* of the counts of Polheim, 16C (brought here from the secularised Minoritenkirche; usually open, but there are no lights: take a torch!).

Burg: Gothic building with two wings, room in which Maximilian I died; recent general restoration.

Stadtmuseum (17 Polheimerstrasse): prehistory to early Middle Ages; outstanding exhibits from the Roman period.

Environs: Schauersberg (*c.* 4 km. S.): *Wallfahrtskirche Mariä Himmelfahrt:* remarkable Gothic single-aisled church, late 15C, with rib vaulting. Gothic Madonna in carved baroque surround. **Thalheim bei Wels** (*c.* 3 km. S.): *Pfarrkirche St. Stephan;* late Gothic hall with nave higher than the aisles; pulpit 1662. In the priest's house, which dates from 1655, two fine baroque rooms. **Würting** (about 18 km. W.): impressive *moated Schloss;* the Wels merchant Christoph Weiss, husband of Felicitas von Altenau (daughter of the Salzburg Archbishop Wolf Dietrich and Salome Alt), commissioned this dignified building with princely furnishings. Fine stucco in the entrance. In two of the round towers coffered ceilings with excellent paintings on mythological

Wels, house of Salome Alt with oriel and painted façade

Wenns, Platzhaus

subjects; arcaded courtyard; *museum* with interesting geological and palaeontological exhibits.

Wenns 6473
Tirol   p.286☐D9

Pfarrkirche hl.Johannes Ev.: only the polygonal choir survived the fire of 1564; church first mentioned in 1233. In 1612 the nave was rebuilt, and in 1613 the tower with louvres and spire. The church was enlarged at the same time and much altered in the 18C. Franz Altmutter painted the ceiling of the old late Gothic hall in which the ribs had been removed and the pillars and pilasters altered in 1792. The pulpit has survived from the baroque and the crucifix (1500) from the Gothic.

Also worth seeing: *Johannes-Nepomuk-Kapelle* of 1734 with altar from the first half of the 18C and three fine statues by Andreas Kölle dating from 1735 (now a war memorial); *Platzhaus* with lavish 16C façade painting.

Environs: see also Karres, Imst and Tarrenz.

Werfen 5450
Salzburg   p.282☐M8

Mentioned in 1242 as a market. The long square lost much of its character in the fire of 1866. The most striking building on the E. side is the district court, birthplace of the poet Ferdinand Sauter, with Gothic tower. The W. row of houses includes the

Burg Hohenwerfen (Werfen)

Eisriesenwelt near Werfen

massive 'Brennhof', built in 1561–5 under Archbishop J.J. Kuen-Belasi; its street façade has the mock-Gothic tracery of the period.

Pfarrkirche hl.Jakob der Ältere: first mentioned 1332. The tower with baroque onion spire and louvres (closed in the early 19C) was part of an earlier building, presumably 14C; the church itself dates from 1652–62. It is an extraordinarily sober building for its period; very large, with a false flat ceiling and a presbytery formed by two extra buildings. The main altars date from the 17C. On the N. wall under the organ gallery fine tomb with a putto (1660) leaning on a death's head.

Kapuzinerkirche Mariahilf: built in 1736 as the church of an anti-Lutheran Capuchin mission; it is of the austere design favoured by the Order and decorated with pictures by the painter Jakob Zanussi.

Burg Hohenwerfen: built under Archbishop Gebhard at the time of the Investiture quarrel of 1077 as a temporary fortress, contemporary with Hohensalzberg and Petersberg ob Frriesach. These foundations were not made permanent until 1122, under Archbishop Konrad I, when they were extended. Hohenwerfen was strengthened after the Peasant Wars of 1525&6 under Archbishop Matthäus Lang, and the Burg developed to its present shape under Archbishop J.J.Kuen-Belasi from 1563 onwards. It was restored by Emperor Franz I in 1824 because of its 'picturesque antiquity', and recently after the fire of 1931. The heart of the Burg with a palas dating back to the Middle Ages (now a police college) and the dominant bell tower of 1563 with fine Renaissance bell by Christoph Löffler of Innsbruck (1565). Interesting little *Burgkapelle*, altered in 1563 incorporating parts of the medieval building. Below the chapel is the remarkable 'dark bridge', or Riemergang, leading to the Persen or Waller tower. Complex outer works and picturesque gatehouse.

Environs: Pfarrwerden: old parish of the N. Pongau, mentioned 1074, with *Pfarrkirche hl.Cyriak,* one of the most balanced Gothic churches in the region. The vaulted connecting passage to the priest's house makes the building look like a fortress. The church is a hall with higher nave and two aisles; the net vaulting dates from the late 15C. Remarkable neo-Gothic altar in the S. aisle; apse with good figures dating from *c.* 1520. The N. aisle ends in the chapel of the Auxiliary Saints with a small altar by the Laufen master Gordian Gugg (*c.* 1520), which has survived intact. **Eisriesenwelt** (kingdom of the ice-giant): important natural phenomenon with nearly 900 yards of entrance tunnel with ice; the entire cave system in the Tennengebirge is nearly 30 miles long; reached by private road and cable car (open May to September).

Wernberg = Föderlach 9241
Kärnten   p.282 □ O11

Schloss: first mentioned in 1227, at the time when Wernberg ceased to be governed by Bamberg and became a ducal possession. 2 people have had a decisive effect on the history of the castle: 1. Georg von Khevenhüller, one of the most interesting personalities in 16C Carinthia; he was a warrior and a scholar, and changed the building, then still a medieval fortress, into a modern Renaissance Schloss *c.* 1575; the 4 corner towers are a reminder of the original defensive function. 2. Virgilius Gleissenberger (1725 – 37), the lively Benedictine Abbot of Ossiach, who brought the building up to date in the representative baroque style (St-Katharinen-Kirche). *Exterior:* three three-storey buildings around a south-facing arcaded courtyard. There is a fine view from the terrace on the S. side. The main portal in the N. has a pictorial relief of the Khevenhüller family (1575). The E. portal was not decorated until the baroque, (1735), when the Schloss was occupied by the Benedictines. In the *interior* the most interesting feature is the *chapel* or *Katharinenkirche;* its stucco ornament and trompe l'oeil ceiling painting (*c.* 1730) mark the high point of baroque manipulation of interior space.

Environs: Damtschach (NE between Villach and Velden) with *parish church* and *Renaissance/baroque Schloss.* Two storeys built in 1511 by Augustin Khevenhüller and altered in the late 17C. Gardens 19C.

Weyer 3335
Upper Austria   p.276 □ Q6

Weyr and Steyr, both 'iron towns' on the navigable Enns, started with equal opportunities. It was the favour of the local princes which made Steyr develop so rapidly. Weyer remained a flourishing community to a certain extent, the 'little golden market of the Middle Ages'. In 1532 it suffered badly at the hands of the Turks; it was one of the most westerly points which they reached.

Pfarrkirche St. Johannes Ev.: mentioned in 1259 'ad piscinam' (=by the pool). On a little hill outside the town, 15C with 20C extensions. *Marktkirche St. Sebastian:* with its handsome baroque tower it is one of the finest buildings in the long market square. *Priest's house:* pretty façade dating from 1760, charming pavilion in the garden. *Schloss* with picturesque arcaded courtyard. 2 *market fountains, c.* 1600. Many remarkable *houses.*

Environs: Kastenreith: tavern on the left bank of the Enns, 2 km. to the W. Old 17C sailors' inn. On the exterior fresco of St. Nikolaus with catch of fish, 1699. Now a notable *Flössermuseum* (raftsmen's museum).

Wien/Vienna 1010–1230

Wien   p.278□V4/5

Contents:

I. Introduction: important points on the situation of the town, its development and history; Vienna and music; geography of the town.
II. Buildings: A I Bezirk; B II–IX Bezirk; C X–XXIII Bezirk.
III. Museums, collections and other important sights.
IV. Memorials.
V. Theatres and concert halls.

Sequence of information on buildings: 1. General: topography, notable groups of buldings, parks and gardens, monuments, houses. 2. Ecclesiastical buildings. 3. Secular buildings.

'Vienna—a town introduces itself.' This was the idea behind the plaques on about 200 artistic or historical monuments; they give the visitor essential information as concisely as possible. They are marked with small flags in the summer months, and are extremely useful to anyone who is getting to know the town.

I. INTRODUCTION

Vienna, the federal capital of Austria

(and a Land in the federation since 1924), is one of the finest and most interesting capitals in Europe. It is almost irresistibly attractive because of its role in history, its magnificent ecclesiastical and secular buildings, its outstanding art treasures and, above all, its significance for music lovers all over the world.

Situation of the town: Vienna is at a meeting-point of ancient *routes:* the 'amber road' from the Baltic to the Mediterranean, and the Danube, which has conveyed the peoples of Europe from time immemorial. It is also the point at which the air routes from Istanbul to Amsterdam and Rome to Leningrad intersect. The *Danube* formed the northern boundary of the Roman Empire; on the other side of the river were the 'barbarians'. In later centuries armies followed the river: the crusaders to the East, Huns, Avars, Magyars, Turks, Kuruz and the Red Army to the West. Vienna has been called *the bridgehead of the West* or the *bridge between East and West* according to period and point of view. The Rhinelander Metternich arrived at the formulation 'Asia begins in the Landstrasse' (the road leading out of the town to the E., in the III Bezirk). Vienna is a town among mountains—the western suburbs are on the slopes of the Vienna Woods, which are foothills of the Alps, and a city of the plains—the eastern suburbs are part of the Pannonian landscape. Vienna has two climates—cool and damp, an ocean climate, in the hills, dry and hot, continental, in the plain; it is a town of many faces and contrasts, a town on the edge and in the centre.

Development of the town and history: the starting point for the development of the town was a Roman camp established in the first century; its boundaries can still be traced, and two archaeological sites may be visited to see what is left of it (Hoher Markt and Am Hof). Marcus Aurelius died in 'Vindobona' in 180. At the end of the

Roman period Vienna was plunged into the 'Dark Ages', like the rest of Europe. Written sources mention 'Vindomina' *c.* 493, then there is a gap until 881, when there are reports of a Magyar battle at 'Wenia'. In spite of the sparsity of this information we can assume that there was always a settlement within the protecting walls of the citadel. A decisive moment in the history of Vienna was the year 976, when the Babenbergs were granted the fief of the Ostmark. Under this family Vienna became the capital of the Duchy, and by 1200 had grown to be one of the most important towns in the German-speaking world. This town, called 'civitas' from 1137, occupied what is now the I Bezirk. The walls which surrounded it until 1858 were essentially those built in the 13C. The Bohemian king *Przemysl Ottokar*, successor to the Babenbergs, encouraged the development of the town. The question of whether the Hofburg and the surviving westwork of the Stephansdom were started under the later Babenbergs or Ottokar remains unanswered. The victory of Rudolf von Habsburg over Ottokar (1278) and the granting of the territory of Austria to his sons in 1282 decided the fate of the town: Vienna was the residence of the *Habsburgs* until 1918; they wore the imperial crown of the Holy Roman empire from 1438–1806, with one short interruption. In the 16C, thanks to a skilful marriage policy, they succeeded in uniting the territory of the Wenzels and the crown of Stephen with Austria. Vienna, the city on the Danube, was no longer a border town, it became the natural centre of an empire which included the eastern Alps, the Carpathians and the Sudetenland. In 1806, German princes in alliance with Napoleon caused Emperor Franz II to abandon the crown of the Holy Roman Empire, but two years before he had taken the title of Emperor of Austria. Vienna remained the centre of a mighty state of many peoples at the heart of Europe. Under the royal and imperial

monarchy Czechs, Poles, Hungarians, Ruthenians, Serbs, Croats, Slovenes, Italians and Ladins came to Vienna, and the Viennese telephone directory still contains many names from the former crown territories. In 1910 the population rose above two million; the collapse of 1918 had the unnatural consequence that about a third of the population of the country, which had shrunk to the area around the Alps, lived in Vienna. It was raised to the status of a federal Land in 1924, sank to be the 'Gau capital' from 1938–45 and was divided into four under the occupying forces. After May 15 1955, the day of the signing of the State Treaty, Vienna began to flourish again and is now a major centre of art and culture and of the economic world. On the basis of both history and situation it is ideally suited to the role of conference town and seat of international organisations.

Vienna and music: music lovers associate Vienna with Viennese classicism. Why was it here and only here that music could emancipate itself from the Italian baroque—was it the rich diversity of the town, was it the joie de vivre and innate musicality of the Viennese, or was it the magic of the Vienna Woods? Nothing can explain why, in the second half of the 18C and the first half of the 19C, five men—Gluck, Haydn, Mozart, Beethoven and Schubert—raised music to undreamed of heights. Of the five only Schubert was born in Vienna. The others came from elsewhere, but could not tear themselves away. They lived, worked and died here. Their works, some of the most life-enhancing in the history of music, are bound once and for all to Vienna. Vienna continued to be fertile soil for musical talent afterwards. In the second half of the 19C it was again three 'foreigners', Bruckner, Brahms and Hugo Wolf who

Vienna, St. Stephan ▷

Pestsäule am Graben (faith and plague)

is divided into 23 Bezirke (districts): I Bezirk town centre, II–IX Bezirk the inner districts, X–XXIII Bezirk the outer districts. The venerable Stephansdom is at the heart of the town, surrounded by the 'inner city', which is bounded in the N. by the Danube canal, and in the E., S. and W. by the Ringstrasse, which replaced the former open field of fire outside the town walls (I Bezirk). Then come the old 'Vorstädte', Bezirke III–IX, which stretch to the Gürtel, the ring road on the site of the former outer fortifications. Outside the Gürtel are Bezirke X–XIX, essentially the old suburbs (Vororte). The exceptions to this clear arrangement are Bezirke II and XX, which are on the island between the Danube and the Danube canal. On the left bank of the river, which had no significance for the medieval town, are Bezirke XXI and XXII. Some outer areas were included in 1938, but excluded again in 1961, and only the southern district of Rodaun, XXIII, remained part of the town.

upheld the Viennese tradition. A unique genre, which could only come into being here because it springs from the nature of the people of Vienna, a singular mixture of joie de vivre and sentimentality, is the Viennese waltz. The Strauss dynasty, most closely associated with the Viennese waltz, but also responsible for the best of Viennese operetta, presented the Austrians with their 'national anthem', the Blue Danube Waltz. Institutions like the Vienna State Opera, the Vienna Philharmonic and the Vienna Boys' Choir ensure that the town is known throughout the world as a centre of musical excellence.

Geography of the town: area 415 square kilometres, population 1,614,841 (1973). Highest point: Hermannskögel 1778 ft.; Stephansplatz: 561 ft. above sea level. The layout of the town is easy to follow: Vienna

II. BUILDINGS:

A Bezirk I:

1. General: the I Bezirk is the old core of the town, once surrounded by walls and ramparts (see Basteien); the fortifications were removed as a result of a decree of 20.12.1857 by Franz-Joseph. A number of the important sights are in the inner city area. There are a surprising number of baroque façades on both palaces and ordinary houses.

Am Hof: first residence of the Babenbergs in 1158. Mariensäule, a bronze copy of the Mariensäule in Munich, built in 1677; its marble predecessor is in ▷ Schärding (Wernstein). *No. 12:* façade in the manner of L. von Hildebrandt. *7 Bäckerstrasse:* famous Renaissance courtyard. *Basteien* (remains of the ramparts): Dominikaner-

Donner-Brunnen

Johann Strauss monument in Stadtpark

Bastei with church and monastery; Coburg-Bastei: Palais Coburg with neoclassical columned façade; Augustiner-Bastei: Albrechtsrampe ▷Albertina; Mölker-Bastei: No. 8, memorial rooms for Beethoven and Stifter. 10 Schreyvogelgasse: *Dreimäderlhaus,* charming Biedermeier house, erroneously associated with Schubert. *Fleischmarkt 9:* Renaissance house with Madonna relief; No. 11: picturesque building with flying buttress; No. 15: façade of 1718, birthplace of Moritz von Schwind. *Franziskanerplatz:* fine square with Moses fountain; ▷Franziskanerkirche. *Freyung:* so called because the Schottenstift had rights of sanctuary there (Frey=free). No. 7, priory of the Schottenstift *c.* 1774, Austria fountain. ▷Schottenkirche; ▷Palais Kinsky.

Parks: *Burggarten:* laid out *c.* 1820 as a private garden for the Emperor (in contrast with the Volksgarten). Monuments to Franz I, Franz-Joseph and Mozart. *Rathauspark:* the green area around the Rathaus, monuments to Waldmüller and Johann Strauss the Elder with Lanner. *Stadtpark:* 'Kursalon' neo-baroque concert restaurant; famous Strauss monument with Danube nymphs; *'Grüne Galerie' (open-air exhibition of modern sculpture). Volksgarten:* first public park, laid out from 1819; Theseus-Tempel: Canova's Theseus sculpture is now in the Kunsthistorisches Museum; monuments to Grillparzer and Empress Elisabeth.

Graben: elegant shopping street following the line of the 'Graben' (ditch) which formed the S. boundary of the Roman camp. *Plague column:* designed by L.Burnacini and carved by P.Strudel and

J.B.Fischer von Erlach. *Leopold* and *Joseph*
fountains. *Griechengasse 7:* in the courtyard
is the only Gothic residential tower in
Vienna. *Hoher Markt:* centre of medieval
Vienna; fountain ('marriage fountain') by J.E.Fischer
von Erlach; 'Anker-Uhr': Jugendstil clock
with historical figures; all the figures appear at 12 noon; Roman ruins. *Dr.-Ignaz-
Seipel-Platz:* fine buildings, Jesuitenkirche
and Acadamy of Science. *Neuer Markt:
Donner fountain* by G.R.Donner: 'Pro-
videntia' with putti and river gods,
originals in the Österreichisches
Barockmuseum. *Schönlaterngasse:* No. 5
▷ Heiligenkreuzerhof-Kapelle; No. 6: 'Zur
schönen Laterne', No. 7: Basiliskenhaus,
named in 1212, with monster said to have
polluted the fountain; No. 9: ▷ 'Alte
Schmiede' in III.

Vienna, Dom St.Stephan **1** Riesentor **2** N. and
S. Heidenturm **3** Bischofstor **4** Adlerturm with
portico **5** Catacomb entrance, Kapistran pulpit **6**
Mesnerhaus, ascent to tower **7** Stephansturm
with portico **8** Singertor **9** Kreuzkapelle, tomb of
Prinz Eugen **10** Three Gothic canopied altars **11**
Pilgramscher Orgelfuss **12** Wiener Neustädter
Altar **13** High altar **14** Tombstone of Frederick III
15 Katharinenkapelle with font **16** Pulpit

2. Ecclesiastical buildings:

Stephansdom: episcopal cathedral 1469,
archi-episcopal 1723. *Building history:* in
the 12C the only churches in Vienna were
those of St.Peter and St.Ruprecht. Then
a new church was started, destined to out-
shine them and become the finest of all
Gothic cathedrals. 1. Nothing survives of
the first building, consecrated in 1147. 2.
A Romanesque building was consecrated
in 1263, W. façade with 'Heidentürme'
and 'Riesentor'. 3. 'Albertine' choir, hall
dating from 1304 – 40. 4. In 1359 the
foundation-stone of the 'Rudolfine' nave
was laid and the most important phase of
the building began. In 1433 the S. tower
('Steffel') was completed by Hand von
Prachatitz, and building continued under
H.Puchsbaum: nave, start of the N, tower
('Adlerturm'). In 1511 work on the tower
stopped, marking the end of the major
phase of building. In the mid 16C the N.
tower with its onion dome was completed.
In the 17&18C the interior was redesigned
in the baroque style, in the 19C parts of
the building were completed or restored.

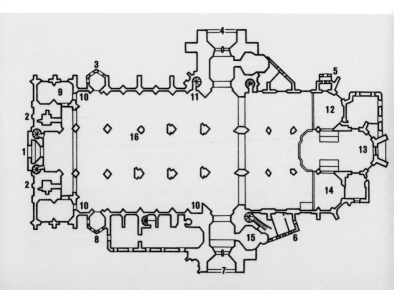

Extensive war damage in April 1945; in 1948 partial reconsecration (nave); in 1952 rebuilding of the interior was completed. *Exterior:* the emblem of Vienna is the Steffel, the 450 ft. S. tower. With its huge roof patterned with coloured tiles it dominates the town even in early pictures. The towers stand outside the walls of the nave. The Stephansturm rises unbroken, which makes it the ideal of the Gothic tower. (Visitors may climb the tower; fine views). The Adlerturm (197 ft.) contains the *Pummerin*, a bell weighing 21,383 kilos. (Lift). The roof covers the nave and both aisles (roof-tree of the nave roof 171 ft. high; the nave itself is 92 ft. high, thus the roof is higher than the nave). The gigantic medieval wooden construction was destroyed by fire, and has been replaced by steel supports, which are shown to visitors on conducted tours. Decorative pierced gables above the walls of the nave lighten the overpowering effect of the roof. W. façade: taken over from the late Romanesque church, extended to its present width by the addition of two Gothic chapels. *Riesentor,* portal with splendid carving; 'Heiden-türme', 217 ft. high; their effect is somewhat dimmed by the Gothic building. 2 *side portals* with excellent ornamentation (some of the statues in the Museum der Stadt Wien). Many fine tombs by the outer walls of the Dom.
Interior: 3 sections: light hall choir, 72 ft. high; transept with adjacent tower vestibules; nave 92 ft. high, aisles 72 ft. *Furnishings:* monumental baroque high altar with stoning of the patron saint of the church. *Pulpit* and *organ pedestal* by Master Pilgram, both masterpieces of medieval carving with self-portraits of the sculptor. The *baldachin statues* on the pillars, 70 figures in all, some of very high quality, are characteristic of the St.Stephen's masons' lodge. Tomb of Friedrich III by Nikolaus Gerhart of Leyden, with relief figure of the Emperor. *Wiener Neustädter Altar,* Mary altar, important carved altar of 1447. *Kreuzkapelle:* tomb of Prince Eugen, *Katharinenkapelle:* splendid keystone, font of 1481. 'Messenger Madonna' c. 1320. Three altars with pierced stone baldachins. *Catacombs:* subterranean passages and rooms, partly a burial

St.Stephan, pulpit

St.Stephan, Riesentor

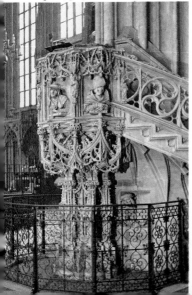

ground; founders' vault (Rudolf IV and Katharina von Luxemburg), urns containing entrails of the Habsburgs, new bishop's vault. Open to the public.

Augustinerkirche/former Hofpfarre St. Augustin (Augustinerstrasse 7): Augustinian monastery founded in 1327 by Friedrich the Fair. Gothic hall, interior 18C Gothic by J.F.von Hohenberg. Famous pyramid grave of Archduchess Maria Christine (A.Canova 1798–1805). *Georgskapelle:* hall with two aisles *c.*1341, *high tomb* of Leopold II by F.A.Zauner. In the *Herzgrüftl* silver urns containing the hearts of 54 Habsburgs.

Burgkapelle (Hofburg, Schweizerhof): built 1447–9. In 1498 the Hofmusikkapelle was founded by Maximilian I. Interior 'classical Gothic'; statues late 15C. Sunday masses by the Vienna Boys' Choir.

Deutschordenskirche/St. Elisabeth (Singerstrasse 7): Gothic with baroque alterations. Excellent triptych from

Mecheln dating from 1520. Shields of the Teutonic knights. Treasury.

Franziskanerkirche/St. Hieronymus (Franziskanerplatz 1): early 16C building. Interesting mixture of S. German Renaissance with Gothic features. Splendid trompe l'oeil high altar with Gothic Mary statue; outstanding organ by J.Wöckerl, dating from 1642.

Kapuzinerkirche mit Kapuzinergruft (1 Neuer Markt): in 1618 Empress Anna founded a Capuchin monastery intended as the burial place for herself and Emperor Matthias, and this later became the last resting place of the Habsburgs; 145 people, (including 12 Emperors and 16 Empresses) are buried here. Only the governess of Maria Theresa, Countess Fuchs, was not a member of the imperial household. Seven vaults and a chapel reflect architectural development from the early 17C to the most recent extensions in 1959–61. The Maria Theresa vault by Jadot is particularly splendid; it has frescos by J.I. Mildorfer and the fine double sar-

Vienna Boy's Choir

Zu den neun Chören der Engel

Michaelerkirche

Maria am Gestade

cophagus of the Empress and her consort by Balthasar Moll.

Maria am Gestade (Salvatorgasse): this church was built on Roman foundations and used to stand on the steep bank above the branch of the Danube. The present building dates from the 14C and early 15C, and is a Gothic masterpiece. Elegant pierced tower, domed apse *c.*1400. The W. façade, at the top of the steps called 'Am Gestade', makes a very powerful impression. Fine portals, some with baldachins. Outstanding 14C stained glass in the choir, mid-14C pillar statues.

Michaelerkirche (Michaelerplatz): former court parish church. Behind the neoclassical façade is a 13C pillared basilica with 14C transepts and choir; the tower was built in mock-Gothic style in 1598 after earthquake damage. *St.Michael statue* over the portal by L.Mattielli. The Gothic choir is of a most unusual design: a relief stucco of the fall of the angels covers altar and vaulting, proving that differing styles can achieve a harmonious effect. Design: J.B.d'Avrange, 1781. In the 'Michaeler Durchhaus', adjacent to the S., is a Mount of Olives relief dating from *c.*1500.

Minoritenkirche/Maria Schnee (Minoritenplatz): the present building is a 14C hall with nave and two aisles; some of the side windows are round, some are pointed, and all have lavish tracery. Excellent *main portal* by Frater Jacobus of Paris. The neo-Gothic features were introduced by Hohenberg in the 18C. Best-known work of art: mosaic copy of Leonardo da Vinci's *Last Supper*, early

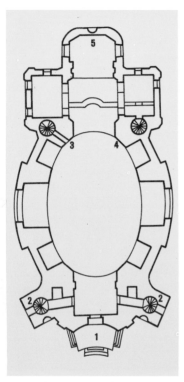

Vienna, St. Peter 1 Porch **2** Towers **3** Pulpit **4**
Joh.-Nepomuk-Altar **5** High altar

19C; the *Family Madonna* endowed by
Duke Albrecht II *c.* 1345 is an outstanding
stone statue.

Zu den neun Chören der Engel (Am
Hof): endowed by Duke Albrecht III in
1386 as a Carmelite church, later a Jesuit
church, now owned by the archdiocese.
From 1945–8 the church served as cathedral. The Gothic choir is visible from
the Schulhof. Splendid, palace-like *façade*
of 1662 with large balcony, attributed to
C.A.Carlone. Pope Pius VI gave a blessing
from this balcony in 1782, and it was from
here that, on 6.8.1806, a herald proclaimed

the abdication of Franz II, thus signalling
the end of the Holy Roman Empire, which
had existed since the coronation of
Charlemagne in the year 800. The famous
Albrechtsaltar, endowed in 1438 by King
Albrecht II for the Carmelite church, is
now in Klosterneuburg; it contains the
earliest known view of Vienna.

Peterskirche (Petersplatz): founded, according to legend, by Charlemagne. Many
theorists maintain that it dates back to a 4C
Christian church. The present building
dates from after 1703, and was begun by
Gabriele Montani and probably completed
by L. von Hildebrandt. Charming portal
by A.Altomonte (▷ Wilhering). The
diagonally-placed towers are an unusual
feature. Rotunda with a massive elliptical
dome, splendid wall articulation,
uniformly excellent furnishings. The
dome fresco is an important work of
J.M.Rottmayr, pulpit M.Steinl; the
Nepomuk altar has a dramatic sculpture
of the Fall of the Saint from the Moldau
bridge by L.Mattielli.

Schottenkirche (Freyung): Abtei- und
Pfarrkirche Unserer Lieben Frau bei den
Schotten. The Scottish abbey was endowed in 1155 by Duke Heinrich
Jasomirgott. In the Middle Ages Ireland
was known as 'Scotia maior', the 'Scots'
were in fact Irish Benedictines; the name
was kept when German monks moved in
in 1418. Fine Romanesque sections have
survived by the choir (guided tour). The
church was rebuilt in the first half of the
17C. Furnishings partly 19C. The *Scottish
Madonna* is the earliest statue of Our Lady
in Vienna, and is much revered. Fine *crypt*
with tombs (including Duke Heinrich with
his Byzantine wife and Rüdiger von
Starhemberg, the defender of Vienna in
1683). *Stift:* neoclassical building by
J.Kornhäusel; collection of paintings
(▷ III). University from 1310, now houses
a famous grammar school.

**Other interesting churches in the I
Bezirk:** *St. Anna* (Annagasse): building
17C, furnishings 18C. Festive-looking
church, frescos by D.Gran; 'St Anne with
the Virgin and Child', early 16C, attributed to Veit Stoss or the master of the
Mauer altar. *Dominikanerkirche/Maria
Rotonda* (Postgasse): rebuilt in the first half
of the 17C, W. façade in the Roman early
baroque style; E. façade with two towers
built to be seen from the 'Glacis'. Fine furnishings, stucco contemporary with the
building. *Protestant church A.B.*
(Dorotheergasse 18): built 1582&3 as a
monastery church, handed over to the Protestants in 1783 and thus the oldest Protestant church in Vienna (Patent of
Tolerance from Josef II in 1781). Façade
1786. Renaissance interior with later
alterations. *Heiligenkreuzerhofkapelle*
(Schönlaterngasse 5): large town church of
the abbey in the Vienna Woods; parts of
the building date from the 12&13C, present building 17&18C, the atmospheric
chapel also dates from this period. High
altar picture M.Altomonte, sculpture
G.Giuliani. *Jesuitenkirche/Univeritätskir-
che* (Dr.-Ignaz-Seipel-Platz): built in the
first half of the 17C, altered 1703-5 by Andrea Pozzo. Impressive twin-towered
façade. Trompe l'oeil ceiling paintings and
dome. Galleries on alternate straight and
twisted columns, Roman motif. *Melkerhof-
Kapelle* (Schottengasse 3): chapel in the
large town establishment of the Donaustift.
Interior renewed 1769 – 74; frescos by
J.W.Bergl, altar picture by J.M.Schmidt.
12C Romanesque crucifix from St.
Ruprecht. Access difficult. *Ruprechtskirche* (Ruprechtsplatz): founded *c.*740 according to tradition, thought to be the oldest
church even in the Middle Ages. Small
Romanesque church with massive W.
tower, presumably 11C, S. aisle added
*c.*1434. *Salvatorkapelle* (Salvatorgasse): Old
Catholic church, since restoration one of
the most interesting churches in the town.
S. aisle built in 1298 as a private chapel on

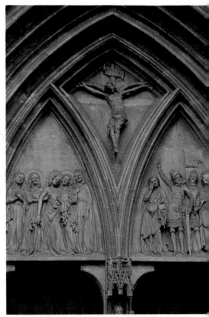

Minoritenkirche, portal

the first floor, later lowered to street level;
N. aisle and splendid Renaissance portal
added *c.* 1520. Mount of Olives fresco 14C.
Charming little baroque organ. *Stanislaus-
Kostka-Kapelle* (Kurnetgasse 2): St.
Stanisluas, who died in Rome, lived here
from 1564 – 7. Very attractive interior of
1742, wall cupboard doors with good
flower pieces. *Synagogue* (Seitenstät-
tengasse 2-4): built 1825 by J.Kornhäusel,
elliptical rotunda. Stylish furnishings.

3. Secular buildings:

Hofburg: If St. Stephan is the spiritual
centre of Vienna, then the Hofburg is the
secular centre. The expression 'Not for the
Hofburg' is used by the Viennese to ex-
press something that they would not dream
of doing. The Hofburg is a very large
group of buildings dating from the 13C on-

wards (18 sections, 54 staircases, 19 courtyards, about 2,600 rooms). It is the residence of the President of the Republic, and his standard flies from the Leopoldinische Trakt when he is in residence. The former imperial chambers are open to the public, and numerous museums and collections are accommodated here. The Vienna Boys' Choir sing at Sunday masses in the Burgkapelle. The Lippizaners are stabled in the mews, and their morning training and demonstrations take place in the 'Winterreitschule'. The larger rooms are equipped as a conference centre and are a worthy setting for international meetings. Numerous important public institutions are based here.

Building history: the Hofburg is in the SW corner of the Old Town, at the point where

the main road into the town from the W. meets Wiental-Mariahilfestrasse. There was a fortress at this important strategic point even under the later Babenbergs, presumably near the Michaelerkirche, but nothing of it has survived. The core of the present Hofburg is the *Schweizerhof,* a building with four wings started under King Ottokar and completed under Rudolf von Habsburg. The Burgkapelle was added 1447-9. Two Renaissance buildings, the Stallburg and the Amalienburg, followed in the 16C; they were at first separate from the rest of the Burg. The long, early baroque building known as the 'Leopoldinische Trakt' was built under Leopold I, and connected the Schweizerhof with the Amalienburg. The 'Reichskanzleitrakt' then made the connection in the E. (1729-35 by J.E.Fischer von Erlach), and completed the fine square 'In der Burg'. The Hofbibliothek (Österreichische Nationalbibliothek), one of the finest libraries in the world, is the work of the elder and younger Fischers von Erlach. The side wings were added by N.Pacassi in the 60s of the same century, giving the

Vienna, Hofburg 1 Michaelertrakt (entrance to Kaiserappartements) **2** Schweizerhof (Schatzkammer, Burgkapelle) **3** 'In der Burg' (Schweizertor) **4** Amalienburg **5** Stallburg **6** Josefsplatz **7** Nationalbibliothek **8** Augustinerkirche **9** Albertina **10** Burggarten **11** Neue Hofburg (museums) **12** Heldenplatz **13** Kongresszentrum **14** Leopoldinischer Trakt (Federal President) **15** Outer Burgtor (heroes' monument)

Michaelertor ▷

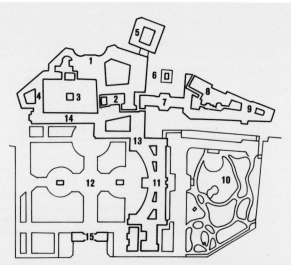

Josephsplatz its wonderful feeling of uniformity. The younger Fischer von Erlach was also responsible for the noble Festsaal of the *Reitschule* (Spanische Reitschule). He also prepared plans for the rebuilding of the Michaelertrakt, but they were never used. An existing theatre was enlarged *c.* 1760 and the fine façade on the Michaelerplatz added. In 1776 Joseph II named this building the 'National Theatre'; this was the moment at which the *Burgtheater* came into being. In the early 19C L.Moyer's 'Zeremoniensaal' was built; it is now the main hall of the conference centre. The removal of the fortifications in the Burg area, ordered by Napoleon, created more space; two gardens (▷ Burggarten and Volksgarten) and the *Äussere Burgtor*, built by P.Nobile as a monument to the Battle of Leipzig, and redesigned in 1934 as a memorial to heroes of Austria, replaced the old Bastei. At the time of the building of the Ringstrasse a new imperial castle was needed: the first design by G.Semper and K.Hasenauer envisaged a massive imperial forum; the main building was to be in front of the Leopoldinische Trakt. Two huge semicircular wings were to form the sides of the square, and the Burg was to be continued on the other side of the Ring by the two court museums. The court stables were planned to complement the new main wing. Only the present wing of the 'Neue Burg' was completed, however, and this means that there is an uninterrupted view over the lawns to the splendid buildings on the Ringstrasse. The *Heldenplatz* offers a view of a kind seldom found in the heart of a major city. The last phase of building was the *Michaelertrakt*. Not until the theatre moved into the 'Neue Burgtheater' on 14.10.1888 could J.E.Fischer von Erlach's amended plans be carried out. The mighty domed building between two concave wings with smaller domes (the S. built in 1729 by the younger Fischer of Erlach for the riding school), was completed by

Kirschner in 1893. The façade is enhanced by two splendid fountains, the 'Macht zu Lande' and the 'Macht zur See'.
Especially worth seeing: Schweizertor, named after the Swiss Guard (Schweizer Garde), magnificent gateway dating from *c.* 1552, painted coats-of-arms in the vaulting. Adjacent is a remnant of the castle moat. *Reichskanzleitrakt:* articulated with three lightly stressed projections, 'Deeds of Hercules' statue by L.Mattielli. *Amalienburg* (dower house of Amalie, wife of Joseph I): late-16C rusticated façade, roof turret with moon and sundials later. *Neue Burg:* main façade on the Heldenplatz, rear on the Burggarten; it houses many collections (see III). *Stallburg:* four wings with arcaded courtyard, later mews and gallery; it contains the oldest pharmacy in Austria, mentioned as the court pharmacy in 1542. *Österreichische Nationalbibliothek:* built to plans by J.B.Fischer von Erlach by his son. A massive pavilion literally leaps out of the wall; the high roof and the quadriga driven by Minerva emphasise its centrality. Above the lightly accented side projections are atlantes supporting globes. Statues by L.Mattielli. In the interior a sequence of libraries leads to an oval main hall, one of the finest library halls in the world. Architecture and décor harmonise incomparably. The ceiling fresco, a masterpiece by D.Gran, is an allegory of Karl VI, who built this academic temple after victories in war. Statues of emperors by Peter and Paul Strudel.
Monuments: the equestrian statues of *Prinz Eugen* and Duke Karl in the Heldenplatz are two of Vienna's best-known monuments; the latter is supported by the hind legs of the horse alone; almost every other equestrian statue uses the tail as a third support. Its creator, A.Fernkorn, was tormented by the idea that it might collapse, and he died a lunatic. *Emperor Josef II,* a fine late-18C equestrian statue by

Nationalbibliothek ▷

F.A.Zauner. *Franz I* of Austria, surrounded by personified virtues, by Canova pupil Marchesi.

Akademie der Wissenschaften (Dr.-Ignaz-Seipel-Platz): former Aula of the old university. Built by J.N.Jadot de Ville-Issy, an artist brought from Lorraine by Franz Stephan. A cubic building, piano nobile with colonnade, lavishly decorated attic storey. Two wall fountains. G.Gugliemi's splendid ceiling painting was destroyed by fire in in 1961; the fine copy is by P.Reckendorfer.

Altes Rathaus (Wipplingerstrasse 8): in 1316 Duke Friedrich the Fair gave this house, which he had confiscated from a rebellious citizen, to the town. It was the Town Hall until the new building was erected on the Ring. Fine façade 1699; in the courtyard famous 'Andromeda fountain' by G.R.Donner.

Burgtheater (Dr.-Karl-Lueger-Ring): by G.Semper and K.Hasenauer. Built as the home of the 'Hof- und Nationaltheater'

founded in 1776 by Josef II in the Michaelerplatz (▷ Hofburg). Auditorium in the central section, stage to the rear, massive staircases in the side wings. Largely destroyed in the war, reopened 15.10.1955 with Grillparzer's 'König Ottokars Glück und Ende'.

Finanzministerium (Himmelpfortgasse 8): former winter palace of Pfrinz Eugen by J.B.Fischer von Erlach. Lavishly decorated façade (typical of the artist's early period), splendid staircase, atlantes by G.Giuliani. A series of rooms (gold cabinet) have survived and been restored. The great military leader and patron of the arts died here on 21.4.1736.

Kunsthistorisches und Naturhistorisches Museum (Burgring 5): extremely splendid buildings each with a main dome surrounded by four smaller domes. The exterior is largely by G. Semper, the interior mainly by K.Hasenauer (see III). Between the museums and dominating the square is the *Maria Theresa monument* by Zumbusch

Hofburg, study of Franz Jos. I

Lipizzaner, Spanish Riding School

(the Empress surrounded by her generals and statesmen).

Landhaus (Herrengasse 13 and Minoritenplatz): the house contains fine late Gothic, Renaissance, baroque and Biedermeier rooms. This was the starting-point of the revolution of 1848, and the Republic was founded here on 21.10.1918.

Parlament (Dr.-Karl-Renner-Ring): built 1873–83 by Th.Hansen. The design for this parliament building was borrowed from Greece, the cradle of democracy. The centre is dominated by a portico, approached on either side by a large ramp. Large wings to the left and right contain the rooms. Lavish sculptural decoration: Greek thinkers, horse trainers, 8 quadrigas on the roofs. Magnificent Athene fountain by K.Kundmann.

Rathaus (Rathausplatz): built 1872–83 by F. von Schmidt. Towns began to be important in the late Middle Ages; thus the Gothic style was chosen for the Bürgerschaft building. It is striking that

the fine central tower is placed in front of the façade, in contrast with German Town Halls; the model is the Town Hall in Brussels. On the 321 ft. tower the 'Eiserner Rathausmann' keeps watch; the figure is over 11 ft. high; the standard measures nearly 20 ft. 8 statues of important Austrians on either side of the approach; they were once on a bridge over the river Wien.

Sezession (Friedrichstrasse 12): gallery for art exhibitions, built *c.* 1900 for modern artists by J.Olbrich. Stereometric building, dome with laurel branches in gilded iron; architecturally important as one of the earliest Jugendstil buildings. The monument in front of it shows Mark Antony in a chariot drawn by lions.

Staatsoper (Opernring 2): built 1861–9 by A. von Siccardsburg and E. van der Nüll in Renaissance style. One of the most impressive buildings on the Ring; the loggia with frescos by M.Schwind and the grandiose staircase survived the bombs. The character of the old auditorium was

Heldenplatz with Neue Hofburg

Parlament with Athene-Brunnen

Rathaus

fortunately respected in the rebuilding (reopened in 1955 with Beethoven's 'Fidelio').

Other buildings worth seeing: *Akademie der bildenden Künste* (Schillerplatz 3) by Th.Hansen (see III). *Albertina*, 1804 by L. von Montoyer, neoclassical (see III). *former Böhmische Hofkanzlei* (Wipplingerstrasse 7 and Judenplatz): built by J.B.Fischer von Erlach, extended by M.Gerl, splendid portals, statues by L.Mattielli. *Bundeskanzleramt* (Ballhausplatz 2): former Geheime Hofkanzlei, by J.L.Hildebrandt. This was the meeting-place of the 'Congress of Vienna'. Federal Chancellor Dollfuss was murdered here 25 July, 1934. *Palais Fürstenberg* (Grünangergasse 4): this stands out among the many fine baroque palaces because of

the unusual decoration on the portals: 2 greyhounds. *Palais Kinsky* (Freyung 4): J.L. von Hildebrandt. Characteristic shallow pilasters tapering as they descend, and delicate reliefs. The magnificent staircase makes brilliant use of a restricted space. Not open to the public. *Palais Liechtenstein* (Bankgass 2 and Minoritenplatz): architect D.Martinelli; fine staircase; not open to the public. Excellent portal with altlantes in the Minoritenplatz (artist disputed). *Palais Lobkowitz* (Lobkowitzplatz 2): J.B.Fischer von Erlach added the fine portal and attic storey to Tencala's late 17C palace in the early 18C. *Musikvereinsgebäude* (Dumbastrasse): by Th.Hansen. Magnificent concert hall with gilded caryatids; excellent acoustics. *Postsparkasse* (Georg-Coch-Platz 2): monumental Jugendstil building by Otto Wagner, 1904 – 6. *Savoysches Damenstift* (Johannesgasse 15): façade with fine Madonna by F.X.Messerschmidt; monumental fountain in the courtyard 'Widow of Sarepta' and lions. *Palais Schönborn-Bathyany* (Renngasse 4): J.B.Fischer von Erlach. Fischer enjoyed using vases for decoration; here they are set in oval niches. Sculptural decoration reminiscent of the Finanzministerium. *University* (Dr.-Karl-Lueger-Ring): in 1365 Rudolf, the founder of the Stephansdom, endowed the second German language university. The first was established by his father-in-law Karl IV in Prague. The new Renaissance-style building is by F.Ferstel, 1873–83.

B Bezirke II–IX:

1. General: Bezirke II – IX were the suburbs which grew up around the fortified town. The II Bezirk is on the left bank of the Danube canal, Bezirke III–IX are set around the 'inner town' in a clockwise direction, beginning in the NE and ending in the NW. Only the V Bezirk does not adjoin the I Bezirk; it was

Burgtheater

separated from the IV at a later date. The unfortified suburbs were largely destroyed by Turkish sieges in the 16&17C, and so there are no medieval buildings. In 1704 Prince Eugen, threatened by the Kuruz, built a massive rampart, which survived until 1898; the 'Gürtel' now occupies its site. After the defeat of the Turks the area was largely settled by the petite bourgeoisie and craftsmen, but there were also monasteries and the enormous garden palaces of the aristocracy; a number of these summer palaces still exist and are fine examples of baroque architecture.

Important houses: *baroque:* VII, Burggasse 13; VIII, Lange Gasse 34: 'Zur Heiligen Dreifaltigkeit' (see Museums, Alte Backstube); VII, Ulrichsplatz 2 and 4. *Jugendstil:* VI, linke Wienzeile 38 and 40, both by Otto Wagner.

Gardens: *Augarten* (II): originally the park of an imperial Schloss. Portal in the form of a triumphal arch. Josef II presented the park to the public in 1775. *Prater* (II): from the Latin 'pratum'=meadow. Former imperial hunting ground, opened to the public by Josef II in 1766. Known as the 'Wurstelprater' after the Kasperltheater (Punch and Judy shows) which used to perform here, among the other popular entertainments and eating-houses ('Wurstel' is a popular name for a Hanswurst, or clown figure.) The emblem of the Prater is the 220 ft. big wheel, built in 1897. Planetarium and Prater museum at the entrance on the Praterstern. The 4.5 km. Hauptallee leads to the 'Lusthaus', a charming coffe house dating from 1782. Sports grounds and exhibition area. Only a small section of the famous Prater meadows has survived in the 'Untern Prater'.

2. Ecclesiastical buildings:

Karlskirche, St. Karl Borromäus (IV, Karlsplatz): when Vienna was afflicted by the plague for the seventeenth time, in 1713, Karl VI swore to the plague saint Charles Borromeo that he would build a church, also intended as a dynastic monument to the House of Austria. J.B.Fischer of Erlach won a competition between the foremost architects of the period, and worked on the church from 1716 until his death in 1723; it was completed by his son Josef Emanuel in 1737.

The façade is a unique synthesis of different styles and concepts, and is intended to symbolise the greatness and significance of the ruler. It is known that the court antiquary Heraeus and the philosopher Leibniz contributed to the theoretical basis of the design. The church is a massive rotunda dominated by an oval dome and flanked by two columns; the design is based on the Temple of Solomon. The austere temple portico is reminiscent of the Temple of Jupiter in Rome, and the twin columns with relief spirals are like Trajan's columns (Karl VI, a new Solomon and a new Augustus!) Although the spiral reliefs on the two triumphal columns narrate the life of the patron saint, they do not have crosses at the top; their lanterns are set between imperial eagles, and there are Spanish crowns on their domes: the Habsburg Empire included the 'pillars of Hercules', Josef I and Karl VI fought for the throne of Spain. Beside the columns are 2 towers which look like town gates; their belfries are reminiscent of far Eastern pagodas. Finally the choice of the patron saint is part of the grand design; his characteristics are strength and constancy, and 'constantia et fortitudo' is the motto of Karl VI. The *interior* is dominated by the soaring dome, which was raised by the younger Fischer von Erlach and thus made steeper. Splendid *fresco* by J.M.Rottmayr: apotheosis of St. Charles Borromeo. The

Vienna, Karlskirche 1 Steps with figures of angels **2** Portico **3** Triumphal columns **4** Bell towers **5** Chapels with galleries **6** Mariä Himmelfahrt, S. Ricci **7** Sacristies, oratories above **8** Patron saint being received into Heaven, high altar **9** Hl. Elisabeth, Daniel Gran **10** Pulpit

◁ *Staatsoper, Stiegenhaus*

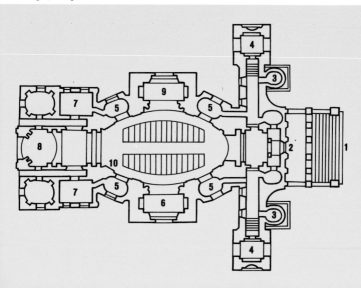

relief stucco on the high altar deals with the same subject; a design by the elder Fischer of Erlach. Fischer's beloved vases are also a feature of the church. Important church treasure.

Piaristenkirche 'Maria Treu' (VIII, Jodok-Fink-Platz): the church was begun in 1716 but not consecrated until 1771. The first design was by L. von Hildebrand, the idea of the shallow dome without lantern may have come from K.I.Dientzenhofer. Towers not completed until the mid 19C. The square, framed on three sides by church and monastery buildings and with a central Mariensäule is one of the most unified 18C architectural ensembles in Vienna. The ceiling frescos in the church are an outstanding early work by F.A.Maulbertsch; only 'Christ on the Cross' has survived of the artist's original 4 altar pictures. Approximately ten years later Maulbertsch painted the ceiling of the monastery refectory. The idyllic theme of 'Christ at the Well' is entirely suited to rococo treatment.

Votivkirche Zum göttlichen Heiland (IX, Rooseveltplatz): endowed as a thanksgiving for the survival of Emperor Franz Josef in the assassination attempt of 1853, built 1856–79 by H. von Ferstel in the French cathedral style. In the baptismal chapel is the tomb of Count Niklas Salm, defender of Vienna in 529, from the demolished Dorotheerkirche. Excellent Renaissance high tomb, attributed to Loy Hering.

Waisenhauskirche Mariä Geburt (III, Rennweg by No. 91): the twelve-year-old Mozart conducted his first festival mass at the consecration of this church 7.12.1768 in the presence of Maria Theresa. The present splendid organ was not complete at the time, however. Light, neoclassical single-aisled church in white and gold; good high altar picture, artist disputed,

possibly Maulbertsch. The two side altars contemporary with the building are notable; they could almost be Jugendstil. Two remarkable 'crib altars' in the nave.

Other notable churches: *Kirche der barmherzigen Brüder* (II, by Taborstrasse 16): endowed in 1614 as an infirmary, still a hospital today; church 17C. 'Baptism of Christ' by D.Gran, sculpture by L.Mattielli. Notable old pharmacy. *Gardekirche* (III, Rennweg 5a): rotunda with oval dome, excellent furnishings, built 1753–63 by N.Pacassi. *Mariahilf-Kirche* (VI, by Mariahilferstrasse 65): good baroque twin-towered façade; the miraculous image is a copy of the Mariahilf picture by L.Cranach in the Dom in Innsbruck. Haydn memorial in front of the church. *Salesianerinnen-Kirche Mariä Heimsuchung* (III, Rennweg 10): endowed in 1717 by Empress Amalia. A splendid portal leads to the main courtyard of the convent; the church has a massive dome, and on each side of the building are palace-like wings with colossal order pilasters; architect D.F. d'Allio. *Servitenkirche Mariä Verkündiging* (IX, by Servitenweg 9): built in the 17C in the Italian baroque style, twin-towered façade, oval dome with lavish heavy stucco by G.B.Barberino. Peregrini chapel of 1766 with frescos by J.A. von Mölk. 'Peregrini pilgrimage' from 27 April to 5 May, connected with 'Kirtag' (church anniversary) and the popular custom of the 'Peregrini-Kipferl' (croissant). Ottavio Piccolomini,the opponent of Wallenstein, is buried in the church (grave unmarked, at his own request).

3. Important secular buildings in the II–IX Bezirk:

Belvedere (III, Rennweg 6, Prinz-Eugen-Strasse 27): the summer seat of Prince Eugen is one of the most dazzling creations

Karlskirche ▷

of baroque architecture. The name comes from the building now called 'Oberes Belvedere', built as a 'belvedere', not intended for day-to-day living, but for feasts and celebrations. The strange thing is that this 'annexe' is far larger and more splendid than the main palace. J.L. von Hildebrandt was the architect of these wonderful buildings; from 1714–16 he built the 'Unteres Belvedere'; this is outwardly a plain country Schloss, its principal splendours are inside. The Marmorsaal, Marmorgalerie, Speigelsaal and Groteskensaal are all exquisitely decorated (painters: M.Altomonte, G.Fanti, J.Drentwett; stucco: G.Stanetti) and are an ideal setting for the exhibits of the baroque museum (see III). In the nearby Orangerie is an exhibition of medieval art (see III). A splendid baroque terraced garden with statues, fountains and

Vienna, **Belvedere 1–4** Unteres Belvedere (Austrian baroque museum): **1** Entrance pavilion **2** Marmorsaal **3** Groteskensaal **4** Marmorgalerie **5–7** Oberes Belvedere (Austrian 19&20C gallery): **5** Staircase **6** Marmorsaal (Staatsvertrag treaty) **7** Chapel **8** Orangerie (museum of medieval Austrian art)

cascades (designed by D.Girard) leads to the upper Schloss, the actual 'Belvedere'. The fascinating silhouette of the roof with its pavilions and domes is the most striking feature of the building when viewed from a distance, and gives the Schloss an air of unreality, especially when the light comes from the side or from behind. The masterly architectural design and the lavish decoration can only be discerned from closer quarters. A protruding central pavilion with a mansard roof not unlike a Turkish tent holds the building together: adjacent to the central projection are two wings, also with attic storeys with statues and canopied windows, then two lower gallery buildings, and at the end two octagonal corner towers with domes. The façade on the courtyard side makes a different impression: the 'Genoan' Hildebrandt knew how to make use of differing heights from the example of his native town. The Schloss is on a slope, and looks lower from the S.; the central pavilion recedes, and there is a splendid gabled entrance hall in front of the façade; to balance this the entire Schloss is

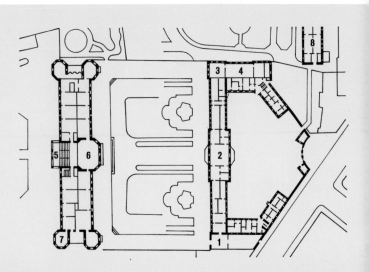

reflected in the calm water of the lake. If one enters from this side, one finds oneself on the landing of the stairs leading from the sala terrena to the first floor. Exuberant stucco surrounds the white ceilings and walls and the sala terrena and staircase; stucco: S.Bussi, statues: L.Mattielli. The 'Marmorsaal' is quieter and more reserved than the one in the lower Schloss; it was the scene of the signing of the State Treaty on 15.5.1955. For the picture gallery see III, Museums and Collections.

Other worthwhile secular buildings in the II – IX Bezirk: *Arsenal* (III, Arsenalstrasse): built as a fortress after the revolution of 1848, but to a Romantic, neo-Romanesque design. Military museum (see III). *Augarten-Palais* (II, Obere Augartenstrasse 1): late 17C, home of the Vienna Boys' Choir; one wing houses the porcelain factory of the same name. *Palais Liechtenstein* (IX, Fürstengasse 2): built 1698–1711 by D.Martinelli as a garden palace. Some of the splendid décor has survived, stucco by S.Bussi, statues by G.Giuliani, frescos by A.Pozzo among

others. Now building centre; open to the public. In the garden less well-known fountain by R.Donner: Venus and Cupid. *Palais Rasumofsky* (III, Rasumofskygasse 23; now Federal Geological Institute): built 1806&7 by L. von Montoyer for Prince Rasumofsky, the great patron of Beethoven. Colonnade on the street and garden façades; splendid main hall with coffered dome. *Palais Schönborn* (VIII, Laudongasse 17 – 19; now folklore museum): designed by J.L. von Hildebrandt, façade altered later. Exceptionally charming staircase (for museum see III). *Palais Schwarzenberg* (III, Rennweg 2): splendid garden palace, begun by J.L. von Hildebrandt, continued by J.B.Fischer von Erlach and completed by his son. In contrast with most of the other summer palaces the fine park and accompanying buildings on the courtyard and garden side have survived. The whole complex is a good example of a princely summer residence. The splendid rooms, e.g. Kuppelsaal, Marmorgalerie and chapel, were restored after bomb damage. The Palais is a hotel with restaurant, but is not otherwise

Oberes Belvedere

open to the public. *Theater in der Josefstadt* (VIII, Josefstädterstrasse 26): Beethoven conducted his 'Consecration of the House' overture when the house was rededicated in 1822. Charming Biedermeier auditorium and other rooms (Sträusselsäle) by J.Kornhäusel. *Theater an der Wien* (VI, Linke Wienzeile 6): important in the musical history of Vienna: premieres of 'Fidelio', the 'Eroica', the violin concerto and the 5th and 6th symphonies of Beethoven. Fine portal in the Millöckergasse with the theatre director and librettist of 'The Magic Flute' E.Schikaneder as Papageno. *Theresianum* (IV, Favoritenstrasse 15): former imperial summer residence 'Alte Favorita'. Maria Theresa founded an educational establishment for the daughters of noblewomen here in 1749. Now a famous state grammar school with boarding house. *Palais Trautson* (VII, Museumstrasse 7; now Ministry of Justice): designed by J.B.Fischer of Erlach; lavish façade with gabled central projection; decoration with figures on portal and above windows. Staircase with atlantes.

C Bezirke X – XXIII:

1. General: the 'Vorstädte' were settlements which developed outside the town walls because of lack of space inside; the 'Vororte' were village communities in the country and on the slopes of the Vienna Woods. It was not until the latter half of the 19C and the 20C that the elegant villa districts, called 'Cottage' came into being 'in the country' near the Vororte. The Vororte and Vorsädte grew together in the late 19C, when countless tenements were built between 'Cottage' and 'Gürtel'. The buildings covered up to 85 per cent of each plot; some of the kitchens looked on to the corridor in which the 'Bassena' (water supply) and the WC for the floor were located. The bombs scarcely affected this district and the building techniques were sound; so, sadly to say, there are still hun-

dreds of such flats in existence today. Faced with this problem of poor housing Vienna decided that the provision of good housing at moderate prices was a communal responsibility. The first of September 1923, on which the decision to build 25,000 'Volkswohnungen' was taken, can be considered the beginning of 'social housing'. Over 50 years the 'Gemeindebauten' developed from block-like monsters (e.g. Karl-Marx-Hof, Heiligenstädterstrasse, with a façade more than a kilometre long) to a less formal style of building with green open spaces.

Striking groups and individual buildings: *Breitenlee* (XXII): church, pasture and farm of the Schottenstift. *Grinzing* (XIX): church, Coblenzgasse, Himmelstrasse. *Heiligenstadt* (XIX): Pfarrplatz, Eroicagasse, Probusgasse. *Hietzing* (XIII): Biedermeier houses in Maxinggasse, Gloriettegasse, Trauttmannsdorfgasse. *Kahlenbergerdorf* (XIX): church, Bloschgasse, Heiligenstädterstrasse, Wigandstrasse. *Leopoldau* (XXI): church, Leopoldauerplatz, St. Leopold statue. *Mauer* (XXIII): Hauptstrasse 34, 44, 52, Hauptplatz. *Neustift am Walde* (XIX): Rathstrasse. *Nussdorf* (XIX): Greinergasse, Hackhofergasse, Armbrustergasse. *Salmannsdorf* (XIX): Dreimarksteingasse, Sulzweg. *Sievering* (XIX): church, Sieveringer Strasse, St.Nepomuk statue. *Stammersdorf* (XXI): church, priest's house, Mary column, 1 km. long Kellergasse.

Gardens: *Donaupark* (II): site of the International garden Exhibition of 1964, Donauturm 827 ft. high, near 'UNO-City'. *Lainzer Tiergarten* (XII and XXIII): former imperial hunting ground, surrounded by 24 km. of wall with 7 main and subsidiary gates; nature reserve 26 square kilometres in area with approximately 400 wild boars, 300 deer and stags, aurochs and moufflon. 'Hermesvilla', see under secular buildings. *Oberlaaer Park* (X): site of the

Theater an der Wien, Papagenotor

International Garden Exhibition of 1974; also Oberlaa spa, sulphur springs. *Pötzleinsdorfer Park* (XVIII): English park. Temple, statues, early-19C. *Schwarzenberg* (=Dornbacher) *Park* (XVII): nature park laid out by Field Marshal Count Lacy with sculpture; now partially reverted to woodland; deep in the wood is Lacy's grave in the form of an antique temple, late-18C. *Türkenschanzpark* (XVIII): with lookout tower; one of the most beautiful gardens in Vienna.

Monuments: *von Aspern lion* (XXII, Heldenplatz): in memory of the first victory over Napoleon by Archduke Karl in 1809, by A.Fernkorn. *Maximilian von Mexico* (XIII, Am Platz): in memory of Franz Josef's brother, shot by order of a court martial by Juarez in Queretaro in 1867. *Spinnerin am Kreuz* (X, Triester Strasse, by No. 52): mid-15C Gothic column by H.Puchsbaum; legend of the faithful wife who waited here, spinning, for the return of her husband from the Crusades.

2. Ecclesiastical buildings in the X–XXIII Bezirk:

Leopoldsberg-Kirche, St. Leopold (XIX, Leopoldsberg): the earliest church was the Georgskapelle of the Babenberg castle blown up in 1529 to prevent its being used as a refuge by the Turks. Present building 17&18C. Elegant rotunda with dome and twin-towered façade. Stone Pietà in the Soft Style. The matter of whether the mass before the great relief battle of 12.9.1683 was held here or on the Kahlenberg is still unsettled. Excellent view. Opposite the church wall rondel, remains of the castle fortifications, with an impressive monument to returning prisoners of war.

Mariabrunn (XIV, Hadersdorfer Hauptstrasse): parish and pilgrimage church on the left bank of the Wien. Built 1639–45 by D.Carlone, restored after damage in the Year of the Turks, 1683. Fine baroque altars, pulpit and organ. Splendid Gothic miraculous image on the high altar. Notable *baroque platform* dating from 1770 N. in the Wieskapelle. To the S. is the *Helenenkapelle*, a high chapel with gallery, impressive stucco and good confessionals. *Sacristy* also with excellent stucco and outstanding rococo cupboards with pictures.

Kirche am Steinhof, St.Leopold (XIV, Baumgartner Höhe 1): this church, an important work by Otto Wagner, is inside the large grounds of the Steinhof hospital. Cruciform building with a gold dome; the façades are clad in marble secured with copper nails, as in the Postsparkassenamt. Low bell towers with bronze statues of St.Leopold and St.Severin. Light interior with splendid use of space; remarkably uniform Jugendstil furnishings,

Other churches worth seeing: *Brigitta-Kapelle* (XX, Forsthausgasse): small octagonal rotunda with pyramid roof and lantern, mid-17C. *Heiligenstädter Kirche/hl.Jakob* (XIX, Pfarrplatz): Romanesque-Gothic building. Excavations revealed a Roman grave and font. It is still not clear whether this is the site of the grave of St.Severin. *Hietzinger Kirche/Mariä Geburt* (XIII, Am Platz): the Gothic church suffered in both Turkish sieges, and was restored in 1685. Fine high altar by M.Steindl, the image of Mary was much sought by pilgrims, particularly in the 18C. Josefsaltar by M.Rottmayr. *Kahlenbergkirche/St. Joseph* (XIX, Kahlenberg): built 1629 – 39 as a Camaldolese hermitage, now monastery of

Vienna, Schönbrunn 1 Ehrenhof **2** Hauptschloss **3** Schlosstheater **4** Wagenburg **5** Two Naiad fountains **6** Obelisk **7** Schöner Brunnen **8** Roman ruin **9** Neptune fountain **10** Gloriette **11** Menagerie with pavilion **12** Palmenhaus

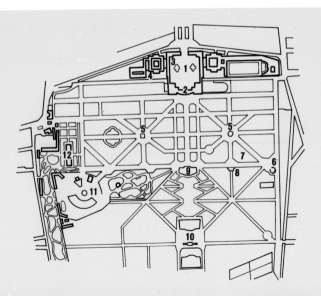

the Resurrection. Copy of the Black Madonna of Czenstochau. Sobieskikapelle with memorabilia of the relief battle of 1683 (▷ Leopoldskirche). *Kirche am Zentralfriedhof/St.Karl Borromäus/Karl Lueger Gedächtniskirche* (XI, Zentralfriedhof): magnificently decorative building influenced by Otto Wagner's Steinhofkirche, but without the originality of the latter.

3. Important secular buildings in the X–XXXIII Bezirk:

Schönbrunn (XIII, Schönbrunner Schlossstrasse): it is particularly fortunate that the palace of Schönbrunn and the park with its statues and buildings have survived in their original form to show what an imperial summer residence was like. The land was owned by the imperial family from 1559, and used for hunting. The present palace was built by the elder Fischer von Erlach 1696–1700, when it became clear that his earlier concept of a giant Schloss on what is now the 'Gloriette-Hügel' could not be realised. Under Maria Theresa, who was especially fond of Schönbrunn, N.Pacassi designed the interior and created the exquisite rococo rooms. Napoleon had his quarters here on two occasions, in 1805 and 1809; his only legitimate son, the Duke of Reichstadt, died of tuberculosis here, at the age of 21. Franz Josef was born in the E. wing on 19.8.1830, and died in the W. wing on 21.11.1916 after 68 years on the throne. 636 years of Habsburg rule came to an end on 11.11.1918 when Emperor Karl I signed the Document of Abdication in the 'Blauer Salon'; the Republic was declared on 12.11.1918. The palace is a long, massive building by the river Wien. The central section is decorated with flights of steps on the N. and S. façades. In the N. is a huge courtyard surounded by buildings. The park is in the S; its central axis is a large floral parterre concluding in the little hill on which the Gloriette stands.
Interior: particularly notable: Blaue Stiege (blue staircase); fresco by M.Rottmayr. Small and large galleries; frescos by G.Guglielmi. 'Millionenzimmer'; rosewood panelling with inlaid Indo-Persian miniatures in gilded rocaille

Schloss Schönbrunn with Naiad fountain

Schönbrunn, Vieux-laque-Salon

with trophies; splendid view of Schloss and park from the bridge. Roman ruin. Obelisk. 2 naiad fountains, Neptune fountain. More than 40 mythological figures. *Tiergarten:* built as a 'Menagerie' at the request of Franz Stephan of Lorraine; the centre was J.N.Janot's pavilion, in which the imperial couple used to take their breakfast and watch the animals. The oldest zoo in the world. The *Grosse Palmenhaus* was opened in 1882.

Other secular buildings worth seeing: *Hermes-Villa* (XXIII, Lainzer Tiergarten): villa built in 1882 by K.Hagenauer for Empress Elisabeth; rebuilt after serious bomb damage. Occasional exhibitions. *Schloss Hetzendorf:* (XII, Hetzendorferstrasse 79): late-17C, attributed to J.L. von Hildebrandt; altered from 1743 by N.Pacassi; splendid ballroom, decorated by D.Gran; Japanese salon. Now fashion school of the city of Vienna. Occasional exhibitions. *Schloss Laudon/Schloss Hadersdorf* (XIV, Mauerbachstrasse 43): romantic moated Schloss. Late medieval gatehouse, 2 round side towers, extended in 1775 for Field Marshal Gideon Laudon. Splendid frescos by J.W.Bergl, brought here from Schloss Donaudorf, which was submerged under 36 ft. of water when the Danube dam was built at Ybbs. Gideon Laudon's grave slightly raised, E. of the street, neoclassical sarcophagus with mourning warrior by F.Zauner. *Ältere Villa Wagner* (XIV, Hüttelbergstrasse 26) and *Jüngere Villa Wagner* (Hüttelbergstrasse 28): both villas built for himself by Otto Wagner; the older in 1885 in a 'free Renaissance' style, the more recent, 1912, is a modern reinforced concrete structure.

frames. 3 rooms with Far Eastern lacquer panelling. Blauer Salon; Chinese wallpaper. *Chapel:* altar picture by P.Troger, tabernacle by G.R.Donner, fresco D.Gran. *Bergl-Zimmer:* set of rooms in the Parterre with fantastic trompe l'oeil painting by J.Bergl. Only open in the summer. *Wagenburg:* former winter riding school, now houses a collection of imperial state coaches and sleighs. *Schlosstheater:* charming room dating from 1766&7 by Hohenberg; chamber operas performed in the summer.

Schlosspark: first design J.Trehet 1705, alterations by N.J.Jadot (menagerie), final layout by F. von Hohenberg; almost 2 square km. Buildings (by Hohenberg) and statues: 'Schöner Brunnen' (beautiful fountain), which gave the palace its name, pavilion above the spring with pretty spring nymph. *Gloriette:* open arcaded hall

III. MUSEUMS, COLLECTIONS AND OTHER SIGHTS:

Times of opening may be found in the

Heiligenstadt, Pfarrplatz, Eroica-Haus

Otto-Wagner-Haus in the Wienzeile

brochure 'Kulturstätten Wiens' (FV-Verband Wien, A-1095 Wien, Kinderspitalgasse 5); the publication appears annually.

1. Museums and collections, a selection: *Ägyptische Sammlung:* Egyptian collection, Kunsthistorisches Museum. *Akademie der bildenden Künste* (I, Schillerplatz 3): paintings, etchings. *Albertina/Graphische Sammlung* (I, Augustinerstrasse). *Antiken-Sammlung* (antiquities): Kunsthistorisches Museum and Neue Hofburg (I, Neue Burg, Heldenplatz). *Applied art:* see: Östereichisches Mueseum für Angewandte Kunst (I, Stubenring 5), Hoftafel und Silberkammer (tableware and silver, I, Hofburg, Michaelerplatz) and Kunsthistorisches Museum. *Baroque art:* Österreichisches Barockmuseum, Unteres

Belvedere (III, Rennweg 6a). *Carriages:* collection of historic state and standard coaches, Schloss Schönbrunn, Wagenburg (XIII, Schönbrunner Schlossstrasse). *Coins and banknotes:* Bundessammlung von Medaillen, Münzen und Geldzeichen: see Kunsthistorisches Museum. *Drawings:* see: Albertina, Akademie der bildenden Künste. *Folklore:* Österrreichisches Museum für Volkskunde (VIII, Laudongasse 15–19). Collection of religious folk art, former Ursulinenkloster (I, Johannesgasse 8, Alte Apotheke). *Furniture:* Bundessammlung alter Stilmöbel (VII, Mariahilferstrasse 88); Geymüller-Schlössel (XVIII, Khevenhüllerstrasse 2; early-19C interiors. *Heergeschichtliches Museum* (Army museum): III, Arsenal, Arsenalstrasse. *Historisches Museum der Stadt Wien* (history of Vienna): IV, Karlsplatz. *Kunsthistorisches Museum* (I,

Maria-Theresien-Platz), see under specific headings. *Medieval art:* Österreichisches Museum für Mittelalterliche Kunst, Orangerie of the Belvedere (III, Rennweg 6a). *Modern art:* Österreichische Galerie des 19&20C, Oberes Belvedere (III, Prinz-Eugen-Strasse 27); Neue Galerie in der Stallburg (I, Reitschulgasse 2, 19C). Museum des 20C (III, Schweizergarten. *Musical instruments:* Sammlung alter Musikinstrumente (I, Neue Burg, Heldenplatz). *Naturhistorisches Museum:* I, Maria-Theresien-Platz. *Niederösterreichisches Landesmuseum:* (Lower Austria; I, Maria-Theresienplatz). *Orientalische Sammlung:* see Kunsthistorisches Museum. *Painting:* see: Akademie, Kunsthistorisches Museum, Schottenstift and references under: Middle Ages, baroque and Modern Art. *Prähistorische Sammlung:* see Naturhistorisches Museum. *Religious art:* Erzbischöfliches Dom- und Diözesanmuseum (I, Stephansplatz 6); see Schatzkammer and folklore. *Roman ruins under the Hoher Markt:* I, Hoher Markt 3. *Schottenstift:* I, Freyung 6: picture gallery; Scottish master. *Technisches Museum:* XIV,

Mariahilferstrasse 212. *Treasuries:* Geistliche und Weltliche Schatzkammer (I, Hofburg, Schweizerhof); Schatzkammer des Deutschen Ordens (Teutonic Order, I, Singerstrasse 7. *Watches and clocks:* Uhrenmuseum der Stadt Wien (I, Schulhof 2). Geymüller-Schlössel (XVIII, Khevenhüllergasse 2 (first half of the 19C). *Weapon collection:* I, Neue Burg, Heldenplatz; see Heeresmuseum. *Zirkus-und Clownmuseum:* II, Karmelitergasse 9.

2. Various sights: *Ankeruhr:* I, Hoher Markt 10&11, clock with parade of figures daily at noon. *Alte Backstube:* VIII, Lange Gasse 34; old bakehouse; original 18&19C interior, restaurant. *Belvedere:* Oberes Belvedere (III, Prinz-Eugen-Strasse 27); Unteres Belvedere (III, Rennweg 6a); *Burgkapelle:* I, Hofburg, Schweizerhof. Guided tours; Sunday mass with Vienna Boys' Choir. *Burgtheater:* I, Dr.-Karl-Lueger-Ring 2; guided tours. *Hofburg:* I, Michaelerplatz, imperial appartments. *Kapuzinergruft:* I, Neuer Markt, imperial vault. *Liechtenstein, Gartenpalais:* IX, Fürstenstrasse 2, building trade fair. *Na-*

Breughel, Kunsthistorisches Museum

tionalbibliothek: I, Josefsplatz, state room. *Oper* (=Staaatoper): Opernring 2; guided tours. *Parlament:* I, Dr.-Karl-Lueger-Ring 3. *Rathaus,* Neues: I, Rathausplatz. *Schmiede,* Alte: I, Schönlatrnengasse 9, original smithy (restaurant). *Schönbrunn:* XIII, Schönbrunner Schlossstrasse, state rooms, Berglzimmer, Wagenburg, Gloriette with roof terrace, zoo, palm house. *Spanische Reitschule:* I, Reitschulgasse 1, Lippizaners; stable visits, morning training, demonstrations, *St. Stephan:* I, Stephansplatz, Dom, catacombs, ascent of towers, 'Pummerin': the great bell in the Adlerturm.

IV. MEMORIALS:

1. Memorial buildings and rooms: *Beethoven,* Ludwig van: I, Mölkereibastei 8; XIX, Probusgasse 6 (will); XIX Döblinger Hauptstrasse 92. *Freud,* Sigmund: IX, Bergstrasse 19. *Grillparzer,* Franz: living room in the Historisches Museum der Stadt Wien (IV, Karlsplatz); study in the Hofkammerarchiv (I, Johannesgasse 6).

Haydn, Josef: house in which he died (VI, Haydngasse 19). *Lehár,* Franz: 'Lehár-Schlössl' (also 'Schikaneder') (IX, Hackhofergasse 18. *Mozart,* Wolfgang Amadeus: 'Figaro-Haus' (I, Domgasse 5). *Schikaneder,* Emanuel: 'Schikaneder-Schlössl' (also 'Lehár') (XIX, Hackhofergasse 18). *Schubert,* Franz: birthplace (IX, Nussdorferstrasse 54; house in which he died (IV, Kettenbrückegasse 6. *Stifter,* Adalbert: I, Mölkereibastei 8.

Other memorials: Beethoven, Ludwig van: III, Ungargasse 5; VIII, Trautsongasse 2; XIX, Pfarrplatz 2; XIX, Kahlenberger Strasse 26; XIX Grinzinger Strasse 64; XXI, Jeneweingasse 17; XVIII, Schubert-Park, former Währingen cemetery, Währiner Strasse 123–5, first burial place; grave Zentralfriedhof, group 32 A-29. *Berg,* Alban: XIII, Trauttmansdorffgasse 27; Hietzinger Friedhof, XIII, Maxinggasse, group 39-24r. *Bruckner,* Anton: III, Oberes Belvedere, Kustodentrakt, Prinz-Eugen-Strasse 27, house in which he died. *Fischer von Erlach,* Johann Bernhard: I, Schultergasse 5. *Gluck,* Christoph

Treasury in Hofburg, Imperial crown

Willibald: IV, Wiener Hauptstrasse 32, house in which he died. Grave: XI, Zentralfriedhof, group 32 A-49. *Grillparzer, Franz:* grave: Hietzingr Friedhof, XIII, Maxinggasse, group 13, vault 107. *Haydn,* Josef: first grave: Haydnpark, former Hundsturmer Friedhof, Margarethengürtel between Herthergasse and Flurschützstrasse. *Hebbel,* Friedrich: XIX, Liechtensteinstrasse 13, grave: Protestant Friedhof Matzleinsdorf, X, Triester Strasse, corner Gudrunstrasse, grave 39. *Hofmannsthal,* Hugo von: III, Salesianergasse 12, birthplace; XXIII, Ketzergasse 471, house in which he died; grave: Kalksburger Friedhof, XXIII, Josef-Weber-Strasse. *Klimt, Gustav: grave: Hietzinger Friedhof, XIII, Maxinggasse, group V, 194-5. Mahler,* Gustav: grave: Grinzinger Friedhof, XIX, An den langen Lüssen 2, group 5, row 7. *Mozart,* Wolfgang Amadeus: Palais Collalto, I, Am Hof 13; Waisenhauskirche, III, Rennweg 91. Grave: St. Marxer Friedhof, III, Leberstrasse 6. *Raimund,* Ferdinand: VI, Mariahilferstrasse 45, birthplace. *Schubert,* Franz Lichtentaler Kirche, IX, Marktgasse 40; first grave: Schubert-Park, former Währinger Friedhof, XVIII, Währingerstrasse 123 – 5; grave: XI, Zentralfriedhof, group 32 A-28. *Schwind,* Moritz von: I, Fleischmarkt 15, birthplace. *Stifter,* Adalbert: Kornhäuselturm, I, Seitenstettenstrasse 2. *Strauss,* Johann the Elder: grave: XI, Zentralfriedhof, group 32 A-15. *Strauss,* Johann the Younger: XIII, Maxinggasse 18; XVIII, Dreimarksteingasse 13; grave: XI, Zentralfriedhof, group 32 A-27. *Strauss,* Richard: 'Strauss-Schlössl', III, Jacquingasse 8–10. *Wagner,* Otto: grave: Hietzinger Friedhof, XIII, Maxinggasse. *Wagner,* Richard: Hotel Imperial, I, Kärntner Ring 16; XIV, Hadikgasse 72. *Waldmüller,* Ferdinand: first grave: Waldmüller-Park, former Matzleinsdorfer Friedhof, X, Landgutgasse-Fernkrongasse. *Wolf,* Hugo: grave: XI, Zentralfriedhof, group 32, A-10

V. THEATRES AND CONCERT HALLS:

Straight theatres: *Akademietheater* (used

Flight into Egypt, with view of Vienna, Schottenstift

by the Burgtheater company): III, Lisztstrasse 1. *Burgtheater,* I, Dr.-Karl-Lueger-Ring 2. *Josefstadt,* Theater in der Josefstadt, VIII, Josefstädterstrasse 26. *Volkstheater,* VII, Neustiftgasse 1. *Theater der Jugend,* I, Hofburg, Batthyanystiege. *Renaissancetheater,* Neubaugasse 36.

Opera and operetta: *Schönbrunner Schlosstheater,* XIII, Schönbrunner Schlossstrasse (only open in the summer). *Staatsoper,* I, Opernring. *Volksoper,* IX, Währinger Strasse 78. *Wiener Kammeroper,* I, Fleischmarkt 24.

Performances in various genres: *Theater an der Wien,* VI, Linke Wienzeile 6.

Concert halls: *Konzerthaus,* III, Lothringerstrasse 20, home of the Vienna Symphony Orchestra. *Musikvereinsgebäude,* I, Dumbastrasse 3, home of the Vienna Philharmonic. *Wiener Stadthalle,* used for various purposes, XV, Vogelweidplatz 14. Occasional concerts in palaces in the summer; performances in courtyards and squares.

Wiener Neustadt 2700
Lower Austria   p.278□V6

The town was founded by the Babenbergs in 1194 (the charter of 1210 proved to be a forgery; charter 1277); it became important as a trading town. In the 13C fortifications were built: walls, towers (parts have survived in the S., N. and W. of the town), castle and churches. The Old Town has retained the feeling of coherent design which is the hallmark of the planning of the ancients. The town was an imperial residence under Emperor Frederick III (1440–93), a bishopric from 1469. It declined at the time of the Turkish invasions. Wiener

Neustadt became an important craft and industrial centre under Maria Theresa and Joseph II.

Stadtpfarrkirche Mariae Himmelfahrt: the church, essentially a late Romanesque basilica, is visible over long distances. Building probably started in the first half of the 13C. Poor ground conditions, earthquakes and also the response to changing architectural styles meant that the church was much altered inside and out until the 19C. The citizens rebuilt the late Romanesque E. section of the church in Gothic style *c.* 1400 (transept, choir and side apses). Under Emperor Frederick II the church was raised to the rank of cathedral in 1469, which meant more rebuilding. In 1449 galleries were built over the side choirs, in 1487 and 1491 chapels and sacristies were added. The two massive W. towers from the original church were pulled down in the 19C and rebuilt almost in the old style. In the museum are parts of the old W. portal, also historically reconstructed in the 19C, along with the small staircase tower. An important feature

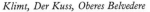

Klimt, Der Kuss, Oberes Belvedere

Wiener Neustadt, Stadtpfarrkirche, late Romanesque Brauttor

of the exterior of the church is the late-Romanesque *Brauttor* (bridal door *c.* 1230), on the S. side. It has an ornamented frame, columns and archivolts and blind arches at either side, and is placed neatly in a section of the building set forward of the main wall. The opposite portal on the N. side is not ornamented in the same way, but has demonic figures in the lintel. The outside of the aisles is decorated with pilaster strips and round arch friezes; the Gothic choir has splendid buttresses and tall pointed windows.

It is clear from the *interior* that the parish church (from 1785) was once a more important building. The articulation of walls and vaulting (responds, ribs, capitals, keystones) treads the middle ground between Romanesque moderation and Gothic power. The transitional style can also be seen in the difference between the nave,

and the choir and transepts. The latter have more vertical thrust, and the profiling is finer, more Gothic. The most important individual features are: a *Last Judgement picture* (*c.* 1300) was discovered in 1912 on the triumphal arch. The *panel paintings* of prophets in the nave are late Gothic. The excellent carved wooden *Apostle statues* on the pillars above the paintings date from only a little later (*c.* 1500, possibly by L.Luchsperger). The *high altar* with Domenico Cignaroli's Assumption painting (1769–75) is baroque. Of the *tombs*, that of Cardinal Melchior Khlesl in the choir on the right is of particular interest: the portrait has all the characteristics of Italian baroque, and may come from the studio of G.Lorenzo Bernini (1630).

Neukloster, Kirche Hl.Dreifaltigkeit:

Monument to Eleonore of Portugal

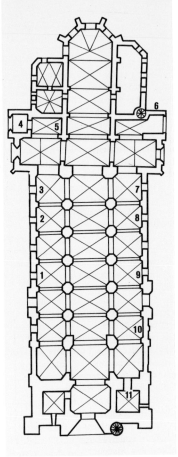

built in 1250 as a fortress and church by
the Ungarntor; Dominican monks lived
here until 1444, when it was taken over by
Cistercians. The outwardly plain hall
church with nave and two aisles dates
largely from the 15C, as can be seen from
the articulation. The light choir is older
(14C). The two chapels date from 1453.
The essentially baroque furnishings blend
well with the architecture: the high altar
(1698) has figures by Andreas Schellauf,
the altar panel is by A.Schoonjans, the
paintings on the Josefsaltar (F.Solimena),
the Robertaltar and the Annenaltar
(M.Altomonte) and on the Johann-
Nepomuk-Altar (P.Troger) are all notable
mid-18C work. The most valuable item is
the lid of the tomb of Eleonore of Portugal,
the consort of Frederick III, by Niklas
Gerhaert van Leyden (see Vienna, St.
Stephan), behind the high altar.

Wiener Neustadt, Dom 1 Leopoldsaltar **2**
Kreuzaltar **3** Dreikönigsaltar **4** Taufkapelle **5**
Gnadenkapelle **6** Seitenkapelle **7** Krippenaltar **8**
Andreasaltar **9** Allerheiligenaltar **10** Crucifix **11**
Turmkapelle 'Maria im Elend'

Kapuzinerkirche St.Jakob: the remains
of the former Minorite monastery in the
SW corner of the town (first mentioned
1267) were taken over by the Capuchins in
1623. The building, with late Gothic
vaulting and 15C buttresses, was

redesigned in the baroque style (vaulting, E. portal), and the altar moved. In the interior *Madonna and Child* and *St.Jakob*, 2 valuable sandstone statues, probably dating from *c.* 1340.

Former castle: this imposing fortress, which used to have 4 towers, three sections and a high W. wall with gate; it was intended to protect the town on the E. side, and must have been built to harmonise with the town (*c.* 1250). New buildings, extensions and alterations were necessitated by earthquakes and the more important representative role which the castle had to play in the reign of Frederick III (2nd half of the 15C) and his successors in the 16C. In 1751 Maria Theresa designated the building a *military academy,* a function which it started to perform again from 1958, when restoration of the castle after war damage was completed. The most important building is the *Georgskirche* (1449 –60) over the W. gateway. It has a temporal and a spiritual role, rather like the hall of a royal palace. The wall decoration on the E. façade (courtyard side) is of unique artistic importance; around the central window between the buttresses are *107 coats-of-arms* in stone (the idea for the wall probably came from the 'Österreichische Landeschronik' of the Viennese cleric Leopold Stainreuter, born *c.* 1340), 1453, a fine demonstration of imperial claims to power and government. In the lowest section is the statue of Emperor Frederick III. Above is a Madonna (copy) between 2 saints. The original of the Madonna is in the interior, a rectangular hall with nave, two aisles and groin and net vaulting. Fine 16C stained glass on the E. wall. Under the high altar, tomb of the famous Emperor Maximilian I, son of Frederick III. In the new building opposite the castle the Renaissance portal of the old *arsenal* has survived.

former fortress-monastery (mentioned *c.* 1250 as a Dominican abbey). Rebuilt 1450–75 by imperial architect P.Pusika. In ruins from 1834. Now exhibition rooms. *Former Karmeliterkirche* (Nordostecke), first mentioned in 1245; mannerist and baroque building. *Former Jesuitenkirche St.Leopold* (1737–43); the adjacent former Jesuit residence now houses the *Stadtmuseum* (fine collection). Baroque *Mariensäule* (1678) in the Hauptplatz. There are also many fine Gothic and Renaissance buildings in the town, despite much destruction.

Wilhering 4073
Upper Austria   p.276□P4

In 1146 the brothers Ulrich and Cholo von Wilhering founded an abbey on the narrow strip of river bank between the Danube and the Kürnbergerwald. Lavish endowment from the Schaunbergs encouraged the development of the abbey and led to the emergence of daughter foundations. The basilica and monastery buildings burned down in 1733. A large-scale plan for renewal was drawn up, in keeping with contemporary enthusiasm for building, but only the church was realised. Wilhering is a lively monastery community; there are 13 parishes in its care, it administers a large market garden and also runs a grammar school with boarding house.

Stiftskirche Mariä Himmelfahrt und Schutzengel: impressive W. façade with tower containing the *portal* taken over from the Romanesque building. Cruciform plan based on the earlier building. Architects were J.Haslinger of Linz and the imperial theatre architect Andreas Altomonte. The

Also worth seeing: *St.Peter an der Sperre:*

Wiener Neustadt, military academy ▷

important feature of this church is not the architecture, however, but the interior, one of the finest works of ecclesiastical rococo. All the arts work together to produce a unified whole which could hardly be bettered, despite the many magnificent churches in Austria and S. Germany. The superb frescos are the masterpiece of B.Altomonte (apotheosis of the Madonna in the Litany of the Loreto). Light is handled in a masterly fashion: it streams in through curved windows set high in the nave, enhancing the effect of paint and stucco. The stucco in the nave is by F.J.I.Holzinger, and work in the transepts and choir was shared by the Wessobrunn artists J.M.Feuchtmayr and J.G.Übelherr; the latter was also reponsible for the figures on altar, pulpit and organ. The beginning of the choir is marked on one side by N.Rummel's *choir organ,* one of Bruckner's favourite instruments, and on the other side by the imposing *pulpit,* with statues of David with his harp and St. Bernard. The splendid *choir stalls* are a no less masterly achievement by two lay brothers. The *high altar* is dedicated to the Assumption; the painting, like all the other altar panels, is the work of M.Altomonte. The main organ in the W. is divided in two and forms a splendid frame for the large window. On both sides of the entrance are 2 remarkable *high tombs* of the Schaunbergs from the old church: S. of the entrance early-14C; N. high Gothic with three-dimensional recumbent figure. *Grundmannkapelle:* in the NE of the transept family tomb of the counts Grundemann (▷ Waldenfels/Freistadt), ceiling fresco by B.Altomonte, of iconographic importance: the Christ Child bids farewell to Heaven.

Abbey buildings: cloister with late Romanesque elements. In the prelacy is a small but important *picture gallery* with sketches and designs by Austrian baroque painters.

Environs: Schloss Ottensheim (on the opposite side of the Danube, ferry): impressive building on a rock, keep with four corner turrets, round tower in the E.; some rebuilding in the 19C. **Pesenbach** (on the left bank of the Danube, about 10 km. W. of Ottensheim): *Filialkirche hl.Leonhard:* remarkable triptych dated 1495.

Wolfsberg 9400
Kärnten   p.282□R10

Wolfsberg, one of the most important towns in Carinthia, grew between the the old Bamberg castle, mentioned in 1178, and the Lavant (charter in 1331). In the late Middle Ages the settlement W. of the river was also fortified. Very little now remains of the once massive fortifications, but it must have been strong enough around 1480 to prevent the Turkish and Hungarian hordes from conquering the town. It was the plague and fire which were its downfall. The area in the E. between the river and the castle hill gives a good impression of what the town was once like. Here are the fine Gothic buildings of the *former Forstamt* (by the Reckturm, a relic of the old fortifications) and of the *Bauersches Haus* (Schlossstrasse 1). There are numerous Renaissance buildings in the *Hoher Platz,* the *Rindermarkt,* the *Getriedemarkt* and in *Johann-Offner-Strasse.*

Schloss/former castle: in the mid 19C the Romanesque-Gothic castle was hidden under mock-Gothic accretions. Architects Johann Julius Roman and August Schwendenwein follwed the taste of the times and altered all the façades in the Windsor style. The original building had already been redesigned once, in the

Wilhering, Stiftskirche ▷

Renaissance style in the 16C; the massive SW tower was completed in this way (1532). Extension for defensive purposes continued under the Italian del Murano until 1572. The bastion was extended in 1561, and the SW tower raised in 1565.

Stadtpfarrkirche St. Markus: this late Romanesque pillared basilica probably dates from the first half of the 13C; extensions and alterations followed in the Gothic period. The fine *Romanesque portal* in the W. dating from 1240 is one of the oldest parts of the church. The lucid balance between ornament and architecture (comparable with the portals in Gurk and Völkermarkt) shows a stylistic confidence drawn from the many ancient finds in Carinthia. The iron-mounted door itself is late Gothic (15C). *Interior:* the original spatial impression has been much altered by the furnishings of chapels and galleries. Most important features: *Romanesque figure relief* (Mark with lion, 13C) on the SE pillar of the nave. Here too the medieval artist's visual experience of Roman busts or tomb reliefs can be seen to have played a part in the design. Important *tombs* are the artistically outstanding epitaphs of Anton Himmelberger (1457) on the right choir entrance, of Heinrich von Gutenberg (1506) on the left choir entrance, of Christian von Schaumberg (1514) and of Hans von Himmelberg (1540). The *baroque altar furnishings* of 1776 include a large painting of St. Mark by M.J.Schmidt. The altar picture of St. Kunigunde by J.B. de Ruel (1667) in the NW chapel is also of interest.

Also worth seeing: *Kapelle St. Anna:* this little late Gothic building was first mentioned in 1497. The best feature of the interior is the excellent *late Gothic triptych* (c. 1470). In the baroque *Dreifaltigkeitskirche* are an important stone Pietà (c. 1410) and a carved Madonna dating from 1515. *Schloss Bayerhofen* has a Renaissance courtyard (1560).

Environs: St. Marein (Lavanttal, SW of Wolfsberg): impressive *Gothic hall church;* Roman stones in the walls, high quality baroque altar sculpture.

St. Markus, Romanesque relief

Y Z

Ybbs an der Donau 3370
Lower Austria   p.278☐R5

The huge dam bridge links Ybbs with Persenbeug. In the 8C the Hochstift of Salzburg founded a settlement on the cliff above the Danube and named it Ypusa; by the 11C the lords of Ebersburg had a castle, and they prospered through the iron trade from the 13–17C. The town was much damaged by flooding, and partially destroyed in the Thirty Years' War; major fires in 1716 and 1868 burned it down completely. The village contains a number of old houses, including the Passauer Kastenamt, which has early Gothic remains; some have 16C arcaded courtyards.

Pfarrkirche   hl.Lorenz/former Frauenkirche: hall church with a nave and two aisles, which dates from 1490 and

Ybbs a.d. Donau, tombstone

Ybbs a.d. Donau, organ front

has net vaulting and a choir with two bays and stellar vaulting of 1512, with an inscription on the chancel arch. The exterior features a Mount of Olives (1450) with clay figures in the tower niche, and some gravestones: Hans von Ybbs (1368) and Georg Schaubdacher (1480). Underneath the raised choir is a vaulted passage down to the Danube. The pulpit, the organ and the splendid and richly gilded high altar all date from 1730.

Ybbsitz 3341
Lower Austria   p.278☐R6

Archbishop Wichmann of Magdeburg gave his possessions on the Ybbs to the abbey of Seitenstetten in 1185; when Ybbsitz became a parish in 1292 it remained subject to Seitenstetten. It was burnt down by the Turks in 1532, but flourished through the iron trade in the 17C (there were 72 hammers working here in 1640). Economic decline in the 18&19C.

Pfarrkirche hl.Johannes der Täufer: the choir was consecrated in 1419, and the nave and two aisles were added 70 years later; the baroque tower dates from 1794. The S. vestibule has fine stellar vaulting, and the hall is supported by octagonal fluted pillars. The vaulting in the choir is a fine example of the Danube style, with its loops and pendant keystones; there are also branch designs on the baldachins and a Steyer style gallery starting in the W.choir. The N. choir chapel (high chapel) is over the Romanesque ossuary, now the sacristy. In 1498 the abbot of Seitenstetten, Kilian Heumacher, built a gallery chapel in honour of Archbishop Wichmann, including his image in glass and the abbey coat-of-arms. The marble high altar is from the charterhouse of Gaming and dates from 1750. There is also a late Gothic stone pulpit with a sounding board.

Zell am See 5700
Salzburg   p.284☐K8

Mentioned as 'Bisontio' in 743, and included c. 790 in the Notitia Arnonis, an index of the possessions of the Salzburg church compiled by Archbishop Arno. (A monk's cell (Zelle) gave the place its name.) A single-aisled Ottonian church was built around the middle of the 10C, and between 1121 and 1125 it was replaced by a pillared basilica with a nave and two aisles with attached Augustinian foundation. Zell am See is first mentioned as such in 1350, as a market with a Land court, but little of the original settlement has survived: the only interesting item is the so-called Vogtturm'.

Pfarrkirche hl.Hippolyt: the church of the Augustinian foundation became the parish church in 1217. An exemplary renovation project with excavation work, completed in 1975, has revealed a great deal about the development of the church: the Romanesque nave was vaulted c. 1230, but the vaulting collapsed after a fire c. 1770 and was replaced by a flat wooden ceiling in 1898. The vaulting of the aisle took from 1300 until the end of the 14C, and the huge fortified tower dates from the mid 15C. The crypt was blocked up in 1325, in the course of the redecoration of the chancel area and the rebuilding of the Gothic choir. The W. gallery with its elegant tracery balustrade was added c. 1514–1515. *Fresco fragments* which have come to light include a number of remarkable pieces from a range of periods: 13C Enthroned Madonna and Child in the apse of the N.aisle; St.Catharine receiving the Stigmata in the anteroom of the apse is late 14C; and the apostle fresco in the presbytery is early 16C. The Gothic redesign of the church in the 15C included decorative wall paintings (specimen in good condition in the first bay of the S.aisle). The highly impressive statues of St. George and St. Florian in the W.gallery wall date from around 1520 and are an exceptionally fine example of the Danube style in the Salzburg area.

Zell am Ziller 6280
Tirol   p.284☐H9

Pfarrkirche St. Veit: the church mentioned in 1304 was dismantled in the 18C; only the attractive tower, with dome, lantern and interior 15C frescos, dates from the Gothic period. In 1792–97 A.Hueber built a rotunda on to this tower, to a design by W.Hagenauer; it is surrounded by symmetrical spaces, alternately large and small. The two largest fuction as apse and vestibule, and the circular central area has a huge lantern dome, which F.A.Zeiller decorated in 1779 with one of the largest frescos of the late 18C, with almost 100 figures. Zeiller also worked on the altar pictures, and thus played a major part in creating the bright, festive, magnificent

but also solemn impression given by this church, in which Hueber's stucco pulpit, the lucidly articulated altar with columns, the pictures, statues and all the rest of the furnishings unite in a uniquely integrated design.

Also worth seeing: 18C *Wallfahrtskirche Maria Rast* in Hainzenberg.

Zistersdorf 2225
Lower Austria   p.278☐W3

Pfarrkirche zur Kreuzerhöhung/ former Franziskanerkirche: this was completed in 1640 (the tower was added in 1880); high interior in the simple Franciscan style; cruciform ground plan with tunnel vaulting. 18C Crucifixion on the high altar, two altars by Altamonte in the transept; Death of St.Joseph, St.Anne altar opposite. The Weinberg chapel houses a Madonna painting by Lukas Cranach (copy; the original is in the episcopal palace in Vienna).

Zell am See, St.Hippolyt

Wallfahrtskirche Maria Moos: this site, near a mineral spring, was originally that of a Romanesque church, whose choir was incorporated into the building we see today. The spring is in a room below the sacristy. The basilica has a nave with two narrow aisles and was completed in the 14C. It was altered in the 17C, with new vaulting and a tower over the choir. The furnishings are 18C, with a high altar by J.C.Schletterer and an altar panel by P.Troger, dating from 1753 (Assumption). There is a miraculous image on the gospel side, a 15C Mater Dolorosa.

Zweinitz 9343

Carinthia   p.282□P10

Pfarrkirche St.Egid: this Romanesque church was mentioned in 1169, and is unusual in having survived without alteration of its basic design or loss of the large number of valuable frescos in its interior. The only addition is 15C net vaulting in the choir. The exterior includes an interesting Romanesque W.portal, with imposts ornamented with guilloche and a male and a female head. The original relief decoration from the tympanum is mounted on the W. wall; it has been replaced by a late Gothic fresco depicting two angels with sudarium, c. 1430. The interior has a flat ceiling and frescos by a number of different artists from the 13–15C: the paintings in the apse are by Meister Heinrich c. 1400; the St.Leonard figure on the N. choir wall dates from c. 1430; the other fragment on the N. choir wall, a Madonna, is older, c. 1280; the saints' and founder's figures on the S. wall of the triumphal arch date from c. 1420. There is also a splendid late Gothic crucifix from around 1500 (S.wall). The baroque high altar dates from 1669, paintings by B.Seitlinger.

Also worth seeing: E. of the church is

Schloss Thurnhof (15&16C), which has a fine Renaissance portal.

Environs: Weitensfeld-Flattnitz (Oberes Gurktal): the Filialkirche *St. Johannes Ev.* is a Gothic rotunda dating from around 1330. The interior contains frescos, late Gothic carved wooden statues and a baroque high altar.

Zwettl Stadt 3910

Lower Austria   p.278□R/S3

This town was founded in the 12C by Hadmar von Kuenring at the confluence of the Zwettl and the Kamp as the centre of a royal fief. He built a castle on the hill and a church dedicated to St.John, mentioned as parish church in 1138 and connected to the castle by a passageway. Frederick II had the castle destroyed after a Ministerial conflict in 1230, but the church survived. Then, in 1483, during the reign of Friedrich III, a fortified Propstei was built on the site of the ruined castle, and in the 18C it was renovated in baroque style. Elements remaining from 1280 include six towers and the curtain wall, which is in good condition; the gates were pulled down 100 years ago. The small farming town (charter 1200) suffered severely in frequent Bohemian and Moravian raids, and also from plague and fire.

Pfarrkirche Mariae Himmelfahrt: the exterior walls and the arches on ashlar pillars have survived from the Romanesque basilica with a nave and two aisles. The nave was raised in 1490. Baroque galleries over the aisles, W. gallery with Gothic spiral staircase.

Propsteikirche hl.Johannes Ev.: brick wall on a Romanesque ashlar base; the doorway to the castle passage is visible on the W. side, next to it a nobles' gallery with several tiers. Baroque vaulting added in

1718; the choir and apse date from the 12C.

Also worth seeing: *Bürgerspitalskirche:* late Gothic (1448) with octagonal pillars and vault ribs added in the 17C. It has a baroque high altar. *Rathaus:* formerly the Kuenringen house, it became the Town Hall in 1483.

Stift Zwettl = Zwettl 3910
Lower Austria   p.278 □ S3

In Advent 1138, 13 monks were on their way to the first daughter foundation of Heiligenkreuz on the bank of the Kamp to accept a donation from Hadmar von Kuenring. According to the legend (see high altar) the Mother of God appeared to the abbot in a dream, and told him to look for a green oak in the wintry pine forest. He found one in a loop of the river between steep granite cliffs. The place became known as Svetla (=Claravallis=Clairvaux). The church was consecrated in 1159. As the stone was quarried on the far side of the river Kamp, an ashlar bridge was built, and this is still in use. Between 1180 and 1240, the cloisters and adjacent monastery buildings were erected. The radiating Gothic chapels around the Romanesque choir by Master Jans of Vienna were consecrated in 1348 under Abbot Grillo, and the high choir was completed 30 years later and consecrated in 1383. The end of the monastery was eventually brought about by a combination of fire, Hussites and the Reformation, and by 1651 there were only three monks resident there; the population was 90% Protestant. During the Counter-Reformation Abbot Ulrich began to rebuilt the monastery, and the ambitious Abbot Michael von Zaunagg commissioned M.Steinl to redesign the church in baroque style. His plans were realised by Munggenast, 1722-7. The monastery was badly damaged by Emperor Joseph's reforms and Napoleon's troops; it did not recover until the late 19C.

Stiftskirche Maria Himmelfahrt: splendid W.façade with a single tower, 300 ft. high and with three longitudinal axes, of which the central one is thrust forward, then curves back into the body of the tower. The façade is rich in detail: over the portal moulding are images of Hadmar and Rudolph von Kuenring, and above them Bernard of Clairvaux. On each side of the gable storey are St.Michael and St.Raffael as guardian angels, and in front of the lunettes and other windows are vases and statues of angels. Over the copper dome is a gilded statue of the Saviour (1727). The parapet of the belfry window forms the long side of the Gothic sarcophagus of Heinrich von Kuenring, 1286.
Interior: hall church with nave, two aisles, ambulatory and a W.choir extended in 1722. The hall is supported by multiple-rib pillars (an Austrian version of the basically French idea). The end of the central section of the choir is polygonal and the ambulatory has nine sides, resulting in a

Zweinitz, Türkenbrunnen

Stift Zwettl, W. portal

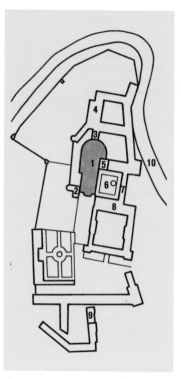

Zwettl, Stift 1 Stiftskirche **2** Heiliggrabkapelle **3** Sacristy **4** Library **5** Chapterhouse **6** Cloister with Brunnenhaus **7** Sommerrefektorium **8** Abbot's house **9** Spitalskirche **10** River Kamp

broken semicircle: 4 triangular tympanums smooth out the line. The choir is supported by 12 pentagonal pillars, whose height is equal to the width of the nave and aisles together. The closely-set tracery windows cast multiple shadows of the pillars, making a curious effect. The *high altar* was designed in 1731 by Munggenast, figures by J.M.Götz: it is a columned altar with an Assumption, and over the tabernacle is the oak of the legend, with the crucifix. The *altars of the radiating chapels* are also the work of renowned masters: Schletterer, Troger, Altomonte, and Schmidt of Krems. The second altar on the gospel side is a triptych; the shrine houses a Madonna with Child holding a blue grape, with St. Benedict and St.Bernhard on either side. The side panel paintings, scenes from the life of St. Bernard, are by J.Breu. The crowning was much altered in the 19C.

Monastery: all the administrative and residential rooms are set around the cloisters to the S. of the church. The *dormitory* is the oldest to survive in a German-speaking country. The broad ribs spring from an ashlar pillar. The *necessarium*, built over the mill-stream, is directly connected to the dormitory and is one of the oldest parts of the building. The *chapterhouse* is the oldest Cistercian chapterhouse anywhere. All the ribs spring from the elegant capital of a central column. *Cloister* (1180–1240): the apex of the vault runs in a zig-zag line. On the courtyard side arcades with rose windows and delicate columns with carved capitals. Hexagonal well house with baroque shell basin (1706). The *summer refectory* has five lunette pictures by P.Troger framed in lavish Wessobrunn stucco. *Library:* between the broad ribs are Hercules frescos by P.Troger (1774). The most interesting pieces in the rich *monastery treasury* are the *Zwettler Cross* of 1248, a huge silver processional cross with relics; the *founder's book*; the *bearskin of 1308* and a *Gothic ivory Madonna*. The library houses 420 manuscripts and 277 incunabula, including a 12C *psalter* with miniatures and initials and a 15C *book of hours* of extraordinary beauty.

Zwickenberg = Oberdrauburg 9781
Kärnten   p.284☐L10

Pfarrkirche St.Leonhard: this is an uncomplicated hall church with three bays, slightly narrower square choir and tower with spire to the N.; it is transitional from late Romanesque to early Gothic, which in

this region places it *c.* 1300. The earliest mention of St.Leonhard as a church was in 1334, and the murals on the S.exterior wall have been dated (by Ginhart) at around 1410. Two friezes of pictures, one above the other, recount the legend of St. Leonard, and next to it a Crucifixion *c.* 1460 and a St.Christopher from the same period. The fragments of the old St. Christopher fresco next to them probably date from the period of the church's foundation (around 1300). *Interior:* the nave has 15C stellar vaulting, and the choir rib vaulting dates from around 1300. There are painted symbols of the Evangelists and images of the saints on the keystones and in the vaulting. The date on the S.wall is 1438. The late Gothic *triptych* of around 1500 is of especial interest: although the absence of a predella or a crowning reduces the number of images, this is more than outweighed by the artistic depth of the sculpture and painting. In the shrine are carved figures of St.Leonard, St.Erhard and St.Laurence, and the reliefs include St.Dorothy, St.Margaret, St.Catharine and St.Barbara, and on the outside, painted

Stift Zwettl, cloister

with quite unusual excellence, are St. Christopher and St.Sebastian. The whole effect is markedly Tyrolean. There is also a fine carved *Madonna* in the nave; it is in the Soft Style and dates from around 1420.

Environs: Oberdrauburg (SW of Zwickenburg): the *Pfarrkirche St.Oswald*, fundamentally a 15C late Gothic building, was redesigned in post-baroque style in the 19C. The paintings in the vault are by C.Brandstätter the Elder, and date from 1809.

Zwischenwässern-
Pöckstein=Treibach 9330
Carinthia   p.282☐P10

Schloss Pöckstein: this early neoclassical building (1778–82 by J.G.Hagenauer) was among the first of its kind in Austria. It was commissioned by the prince bishop of Gurk, Joseph Count Auersperg, and was the residence of the lords of Gurk from 1783–1790. The four-storey building with hipped mansard roof and central onion tower with lantern has strictly ordered pilasters which strike a cool balance between windows and portals. The *interior* is an interesting combination of majestic baroque illusion (wall paintings, P.Troger's altar picture in the double chapel etc.) and neoclassical objectivity (wall coverings, mouldings and furnishings). Apart from Troger, the other artists involved were Franz Wagner, Martin Karl Kellner and Hagenauer of Vienna. N. of the Schloss is a large courtyard with a *garden temple* (1782).

Stift Zwettl, chapterhouse with central column

Glossary

Acanthus: Decorative element found especially on → Corinthian capitals; it developed from the stylized representation of a sharply serrated, thistle-like leaf.

Aedicule: Wall niche housing a bust or statue; usually with a → gable, → pillars or → columns.

Aisle: Longitudinal section of a church or other building, usually divided from other such sections by an → arcade.

Altar: Sacrificial table of Greeks and Romans. The Lord's table in the Christian faith. Catholic churches often have several side altars as well as the high altar.

Ambo: Stand or lectern by the choir screen in early Christian and medieval churches; predecessor of the → pulpit.

Ambulatory: A corridor created by continuing the side aisles around the choir; often used for processions.

Antependium: Covering for the front of the altar.

Apse: Large recess at end of the → choir, usually semicircular or polygonal. As a rule it contains the → altar.

Apsidiole: A small apsidal chapel.

Aquamanile: Pouring-vessel or bowl for ritual washing in the Catholic liturgy.

Aqueduct: Water pipe or channel across an arched bridge; frequently built as monumental structures by the Romans.

Arabesque: Stylized foliage used as a decorative motif.

Arcade: A series of arches borne by columns or pillars. When the arcade is attached to a wall (and is purely decorative), it is called a blind arcade.

Arch: A curved structure of support employed in spanning a space.

Architrave: Main stone member on top of the columns; lowest part of the → entablature.

Archivolt: The face of an arch in Romanesque and Gothic portals.

Ashlar: Hewn block of stone (as opposed to that straight from the quarry).

Atrium: In Roman houses a central hall with an opening in the roof. In Christian architecture, a forecourt usually surrounded by columns; also known as a → paradise.

Attic: A (usually richly decorated) storey above the main → entablature; intended to conceal the roof.

Aula: A hall for assemblies in schools or universities, or for festive purposes.

Auslucht: ('Utlucht' in Low German; an oriel on a solid base.

Baldacchino: Canopy above altars, tombs, statues, portals, etc.

Baluster: Short squat or shaped column.

Balustrade: Rail formed of → balusters.

Baptistery: Place of baptism; may be a separate building.

Baroque: Architectural style from *c.*1600 – *c.*1750. Distinguished by powerfully agitated, interlocking forms.

Bartizan: A small corner turret projecting from the top of a building.

Base: Foot of a column or pillar.

Basket arch: A flattened round arch.

Basilica: Greek hall of kings. In church architecture, a type of church with nave and two or more aisles, the roof of the nave being higher than the roofs above the aisles.

Bauhütte: → stonemasons' lodge.

Bay: Vertical division of a building between pillars, columns, windows, wall arches, etc.

Biedermeier: Art and culture from about 1815 to about 1850, particularly in German-speaking countries.

Blind arcade: → Arcade.

Blind tracery: → Tracery.

Bracket: A projection from the wall used as a support—for a bust, statue, arch, etc.

Calotte: Half dome with no drum.

Campanile: Bell tower; usually free standing.

Capital: Topmost part of a column. The shape of the capital determines the style or → order.

Cartouche: Decorative frame or panel imitating a scrolled piece of paper, usually with an inscription, coat of arms, etc.

Caryatid: A carved figure supporting the entablature.

Cella: Main room of ancient temple containing divine image.

Cenotaph: Monument to dead buried elsewhere.

Chapterhouse: Assembly room in which monks or nuns discuss the community's business.

Choir: That part of the church in which divine service is sung. Shorter and often narrower than the nave, it is usually raised and at the E. end. In the Middle Ages the choir was often separated from the rest of the church by a screen.

Ciborium: Canopy over high altar; usually in the form of a dome supported on columns.

Classicism: Revival of Greek and Roman architectural principles.

Clerestory: Upper part of the main

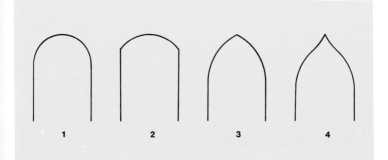

1.Round arch 2.Basket arch 3.Lancet arch 4.Ogee arch

walls of the nave, above the roofs of the aisles and pierced be windows.

Cloister: Four sided covered walk (often vaulted) and opening inwards by arcades.

Coffered ceiling: A ceiling divided into square or polygonal panels, which are painted or otherwise decorated.

Column: Support with circular cross-section, narrowing somewhat towards the top; the type of column is determined by the → order. → Pillar.

Compound pillar: Often found in Gothic buildings. A central shaft has attached or detached shafts or half-shafts clustered around it.

Conch: Semicircular recess with a half-dome.

Confessio: Chamber or recess for a relic near the altar.

Corinthian order: → Order with richly decorated→capitals; the base has two or more tiers and is similar to that of the → Ionic order.

Cornice: Projecting upper limit of a wall; topmost member of the→entablature of an → order.

Crocket: Gothic leaf-like decoration projecting from the sides of pinnacles, gables etc.

Crossing: The intersection of the nave and transept.

Crypt: Burial place, usually under the → choir. Churches were often built above an old crypt.

Curtain wall: Outer wall of castle.

Cyclops Wall: Ancient wall made of large rough bocks of stone of irregular shape.

Diptych: A painted hinged double (altar) panel.

Dolmen: Chamber tomb lined and roofed with megaliths.

Doric order: → Order in which the columns lack a base and bear flat, pad-shaped → capitals.

Dormer window: Window in sloping roof which projects and has its own gabled roof.

Drum: Substructure of a dome; as a rule either cylindrical or polygonal.

Dwarf Gallery: Romanesque feature; wall passage of small arches on the outside of a building.

English garden: An informal, landscaped park or garden, in contrast with the geometrical French style.

Entablature: Upper part of an→order; made up of → architrave, → frieze and → cornice.

Exedra: Apse, vaulted with a half dome; may have raised seats.

Façade: Main front of a building, often decoratively treated.

Facing: Panelling in front of structural components not intended to be visible.

Faience: Glazed pottery named after the Italian town of Faenza.

Fan vault: Looks like a highly decorated rib vault; Concave-sided cone-like sections meet or nearly meet at the apex of the vault.

Filigree work: Originally goldsmith's work in which gold and silver wire were ornamentally soldered on to a metal base. Also used in a more general sense for intricately perforated carvings and stucco.

Finial: Small decorative pinnacle.

Flying buttress: Very large Gothic windows made it necessary to buttress or strengthen the outer walls by half-arches and arches. This support transmitted the thrust of the vault to the buttress.

Foliate capital: Gothic capital in which the basic form is covered with delicate leaf ornaments.

Fosse: Artificially created ditch; often separated castles from the surrounding land with access by a drawbridge.

Fresco: Pigments dispersed in water are appplied without a bonding agent to the still-damp lime plaster. While the mortar dries, the pigments become adsorbed into the plaster.

Frieze: Decorative strips for the borders of a wall. The frieze can be two- or three-dimensional and can consist of figures or ornaments.

Gable: The triangular upper section of a wall. Normally at one end of a pitched roof but it may be purely decorative.

Gallery: Intermediate storey; in a church it is usually for singers and the organ. Arcaded walkway.

Gnarled style: (Knorpelstil) Transitional ornament between the Renaissance and baroque styles, with conch designs.

Gobelin: Pictorial tapestry made in the Gobelins factory in Paris.

Gothic: Period in European art and architecture stretching from the mid 12C to the 16C.

Grisaille: Painting in various shades of grey.

Groin vault: Vault in which two → barrel vaults intersect at right angles. The simple groin vault is to be distinguished from the rib vault, in which the intersecting edges are reinforced by ribs.

Half-timbering: Beams are used as supporting parts with an infill of loam or brick.

Hall church: In contrast to the→basilica, nave and aisles are of equal height; no → transept.

Hermitage: Pavilion in parks and gardens; originally the residence of a hermit.

Holy Sepulchre: Structure representing Christ's tomb as discovered by Constantine, who later encased it in a miniature temple.

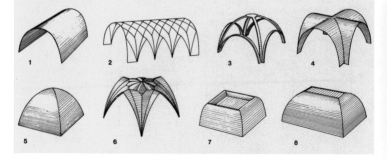

1. Barrel vault 2. Tunnel vault split into bays by transverse arches 3. Sail vault 4. Groin vault 5. Domical vault 6. Stellar vault 7. Coffered vault 8. Mirror vault

Intarsia: Inlaid work in wood, plaster, stone etc.

Ionic order: → Order in which the columns stand on a base of two or more tiers; the → capital has two lateral → volutes.

Jamb: Vertical part of arch, doorway or window.

Jugendstil: Named after the Munich periodical 'Jugend' ('Youth'); a style which resisted older design and sought for new means of artistic expression based on nature, mainly in the period from 1895 to about 1905.

Keep: Main tower of a castle; last refuge in time of siege.

Knorpelstil: → Gnarled style.

Lantern: Small windowed turret on top of roof or dome.

Loggia: Pillared gallery, open on one or more sides; often on an upper storey.

Lüftlmalerei: Painting on house walls, particularly in S. Germany and Austria.

Lunette: Semicircular panel above doors and windows, often with paintings or sculptures.

Mandorla: Almond shaped niche containing a figure of Christ enthroned.

Mannerism: Artistic style between → Renaissance and → baroque (c.1530–1630). Mannerism neglects natural and classical forms in favour of an intended artificiality of manner.

Mansard: An angled roof in which the lower slope is steeper than the upper. The area gained is also called a mansard and can be used to live in. (Named after the French architect F.Mansart.)

Mausoleum: A splendid tomb, usually in the form of a small house or temple. From the tomb of Mausolus at Halicarnassus.

Mensa: Flat surface of the altar.

Mezzanine: Intermediate storey.

Miniature: Small picture, hand illumination in old manuscripts.

Monks' choir: That section of the choir reserved for the monks, frequently closed off.

Monstrance: Ornamented receptacle in which the consecrated Host is shown (usually behind glass).

Mosaic: Decoration for wall, floor or vault, assembled from small coloured stones, pieces of glass or fragments of other materials.

Mullion: Vertical division of a window into two or more lights.

1.Doric capital 2.Cushion capital 3.Corinthian capital 4.Ionic capital 5.Crocket capital 6.Foliate capital

Narthex: Vestibule of basilica or church.

Nave: Central aisle of church, intended for the congregation; excludes choir and apse.

Neo-baroque: Reaction to the cool restraint of → classicism. Re-uses baroque forms; developed in the last part of the 19C as a historicizing, sumptuous style with exaggerated three-dimensional ornamentation and conspicuous colours.

Neo-Gothic: Historicizing 19C style, which was intended to revive Gothic structural forms and decorative elements.

Net vault: Vault in which the ribs cross one another repeatedly.

Nuns' choir: Gallery from which nuns attended divine service.

Obelisk: Free-standing pillar with square ground plan and pyramidal peak.

Olifant: Roland's horn, made of carved ivory and precious metal.

Onion dome: Bulbous dome with a point, common in Austria, S. Germany, Switzerland, Russia and E.Europe; not a true dome, i.e. without a vault.

Orangery: Part of baroque castles and parks originally intended to shelter orange trees and other southern plants in winter. However, orangeries often had halls for large court assemblies.

Oratory: Small private chapel.

Order: Classical architectural system prescribing decorations and proportions according to one of the accepted forms — → Corinthian, → Doric, → Ionic, etc. An order consists of a column, which usually has a base, shaft and capital, and the entablature, which itself consists of architrave, frieze and cornice.

Oriel: Projecting window on an upper floor; it is often a decorative feature.

Ossuary: House or vault in which bones are placed.

Ottonian: The period of Kings Otto I, Otto II and Otto III (936–1002); art and architecture were commissioned and financed by the Kings and church dignitaries.

Palas: The residence of a castle.

Pallium: A cloak worn by the Romans; in the Middle Ages, a coronation cloak for kings and emperors, later also for archbishops.

Pantheon: Temple dedicated to all gods; often modelled on that in Rome, which is a rotunda. Building in which distinguished people are buried or have memorials.

Paradise: → Atrium.

.**Pavilion:** Polygonal or round building in parks or pleasure grounds. The main structure of baroque castles is very often linked by corner pavilions to the galleries branching off from the castle.

Pedestal: Base of a column or the base for a statue.

Pendentive: The means by which a circular dome is supported on a square base; concave area or spandrel between two walls and base of a dome.

Peristyle: Continuous colonnade surrounding a temple or open court.

Pestsäule: → Plague column.

Pfalz: Residence of kings or emperors; in the Middles Ages they did not have a permanent seat, but moved from one place to another.

Pilaster: Pier projecting from a wall; conforms to one of the → orders.

Pilaster strip: Pilaster without base and capital; feature of Anglo-Saxon and early Romanesque buildings.

Pillar: Supporting member, like a → column but with a square or polygonal cross section; does not conform to any order.

Plague column: Medieval decorative column, placed as a memorial to periods in which a town or village has been ravaged by plague.

Plinth: Projecting lower part of wall or column.

Polyptych: An (altar) painting composed of several panels or wings.

Porch: Covered entrance to a building.

Portico: Porch supported by columns and often with a pediment; may be the centre-piece of facade.

Predella: Substructure of the altar. Paintings along lower edge of large altarpiece.

Pronaos: Area in front of ancient temple (also of churches); sides enclosed and columns in front.

Propylaeum: Entrance gateway, usually to temple precincts. The Propylaeum on the Acropolis in Athens, 437–432 BC, was the model for later buildings.

Pulpit: Raised place in church from which the sermon is preached. May be covered by a → baldacchino or → sounding board.

Putto: Figure of naked angelic child in → Renaissance, → baroque and → rococo art and architecture.

Pylon: Entrance gate of Egyptian temple; more generally used as isolated structure to mark a boundary.

Quadriga: Chariot drawn by four horses harnessed abreast.

Refectory: Dining hall of a monastery.

Relief: Carved or moulded work in which the design stands out. The different depths of relief are, in ascending order, rilievo stiacciato, bas-relief and high relief or alto-rilievo.

Reliquary: Receptacle in which a saint's relics are preserved.

Renaissance: Italian art and architecture from the early 15C to the mid 16C. It marks the end of the medieval conception of the world and the

beginning of a new view based on classical antiquity (Ital. rinascimento = rebirth).

Respond: Attached column carrying one end of an arch.

Retable: Shrine-like structure above and behind the altar.

Rib vault: → Groin vault.

Rocaille: Decorative ornaments adapted from the shell motif; chiefly late → Renaissance and → rococo.

Rococo: Style towards the end of the → baroque (1720–70); elegant, often dainty, tendency to oval forms.

Romanesque: Comprehensive name for architecture from 1000–c.1300. Buildings are distinguished by round arches, calm ornament and a heavy general appearance.

Rood screen: Screen between → choir and → nave, which bears a rood or crucifix.

Rose-window: A much divided round window with rich → tracery found especially in Gothic buildings; often above the portal.

Rotunda: Round building.

Rustication: Massive blocks of stone separated by deep joints.

Sanctuary: Area around the high altar in a church.

Sarcophagus: Stone coffin, usually richly decorated.

Scroll: Spiral-shaped ornament → .

Secularisation: The adoption of church or monastery buildings for secular use, particularly under Napoleon (1803).

Sedilia: Seats for clergy; usually in the wall of the S. side of the choir.

Sgraffito: Scratched-on decoration.

Soft Style: A phenomenon particular to late Gothic painting and sculpture in Germany, with flowing folds in garments and tender facial expressions.

Sounding board: → Pulpit.

Spandrel: The triangular space between the curve of an arch, the horizontal drawn from its apex, and the vertical drawn from the point of its springing; also the area between two arches in an arcade, and that part of a vault between two adjacent ribs.

Springer: The first stone in which the curve of an arch or vault begins.

Squinch: An arch or system of arches at the internal angles of towers to form the base of a round drum or dome above a square structure. → Pendentive.

Stela: Standing block.

Stonemasons' lodge: (Bauhütte) The workshop of craftsmen involved in the building of a cathedral.

Strapwork: Renaissance carved work modelled on fretwork or cut leather.

Stucco: Plasterwork, made of gypsum, lime, sand and water, which is easy to model. Used chiefly in the 17&18C for three-dimensional interior decoration.

Synagogue: Jewish place of worship.

Tabernacle: Receptacle for the consecrated host.

Tabor: Fortified camp or fortress against invasion by the Turks, particularly in Styria (Steiermark); also Tabor church.

Telamon: Support in the form of a male figure (male caryatid).

Terracotta: Fired, unglazed clay.

Thermal baths: Roman hot-water baths.

Tracery: Geometrically conceived decorative stonework, particularly used to decorate windows, screens, etc. If it embellishes a wall, it is known as blind tracery.

Transenna: Screen or lattice in open-work found in early Christian churches.

Transept: That part of a church at right angles to the nave; → basilica.

Triforium: Arcaded wall passage looking on to the nave; between the arcade and the clerestory.

Triptych: Tripartite altar painting.

Triumphal arch: Free-standing gateway based on a Roman original.

Truss frame: Frame of timbers joined together to span a gap and to support other timbers, as in a roof.

Tunnel vault: Simplest vault; continuous structure with semicircular or pointed cross section uninterrupted by cross vaults.

Tympanum: The often semicircular panel contained within the lintel of a doorway and the arch above it.

Volute: Spiral scroll on an Ionic capital; smaller volutes on Composite and Corinthian capitals.

Winged altar: Triptych or polyptych with hinged, usually richly carved or painted, wings.

Zwinger: The area between the inner and outer walls of medieval town fortifications, often where animals were kept. In the baroque period buildings for recreation were often placed on such sites.

Index of artists whose works are mentioned in this guide

List of towns and places of interest mentioned in the Environs sections. The entry in which they appear is indicated by the → symbol